THE **GLOBAL** SOLU

Print + Online

GLOBAL³ delivers all the key terms and core concepts for the **Global Business** course.

GLOBAL Online provides the complete narrative from the printed text with additional interactive media and the unique functionality of **StudyBits**—all available on nearly any device!

What is a StudyBit™? Created through a deep investigation of students' challenges and workflows, the StudyBit™ functionality of **GLOBAL Online** enables students of different generations and learning styles to study more effectively by allowing them to learn their way. Here's how they work:

StudyBit™

Collect What's Important
Create StudyBits as you highlight text, images or take notes!

Rate and Organize StudyBits
Rate your understanding and use the color-coding to quickly organize your study time and personalize your flashcards and quizzes.

WEAK
FAIR
STRONG
UNASSIGNED

Personalize Quizzes
Filter by your StudyBits to personalize quizzes or just take chapter quizzes off-the-shelf.

CORRECT
INCORRECT
CORRECT
CORRECT

Track/Monitor Progress
Use Concept Tracker to decide how you'll spend study time and study YOUR way!

85%

CENGAGE Learning

GLOBAL3
Mike W. Peng

Vice President, General Manager, 4LTR Press and the Student Experience: Neil Marquardt

Product Director, 4LTR Press: Steven E. Joos

Product Manager: Laura Redden

Content Developer: Daniel Celenza

Product Assistant: Lauren Dame

Marketing Manager: Emily Horowitz

Marketing Coordinator: Christopher Walz

Senior Content Project Manager: Kim Kusnerak

Manufacturing Planner: Ron Montgomery

Production Service: MPS Limited

Senior Art Director: Bethany Casey

Cover/Internal Design: Joe Devine/Red Hangar Design

Cover Image: iStockphoto.com/ymgerman

Intellectual Property

Analyst: Diane Garrity

Project Manager: Betsy Hathaway

Vice President, General Manager, Social Science & Qualitative Business: Erin Joyner

Product Director: Jason Fremder

Senior Product Manager: Mike Roche

WCN: 01-100-101

Library of Congress Control Number: 2015949188

ISBN: 978-1-305-62721-5

Cengage Learning
20 Channel Center Street
Boston, MA 02210
USA

Printed in the United States of America
Print Number: 02 Print Year: 2017

ABOUT THE AUTHOR

COURTESY OF MIKE PENG

Mike W. Peng is the Jindal Chair of Global Business Strategy at the Jindal School of Management, University of Texas at Dallas. He is also a National Science Foundation (NSF) CAREER Award winner and a Fellow of the Academy of International Business (AIB). At UT Dallas, he has been the number-one contributor to the list of 45 top journals tracked by *Financial Times*, which has consistently ranked UT Dallas as a top 20 school in research worldwide.

Professor Peng holds a bachelor's degree from Winona State University, Minnesota, and a PhD degree from the University of Washington, Seattle. He had previously served on the faculty at the Ohio State University, University of Hawaii, and Chinese University of Hong Kong. He has taught in five states in the United States (Hawaii, Ohio, Tennessee, Texas, and Washington), as well as in China, Hong Kong, and Vietnam. He has also held visiting or courtesy appointments in Australia, Britain, China, Denmark, Hong Kong, and the United States, and lectured around the world.

Professor Peng is one of the most-prolific and most-influential scholars in international business (IB). Both the United Nations and the World Bank have cited his work. During the decade 1996–2006, he was the top seven contributor to IB's number-one premier outlet: *Journal of International Business Studies*. In 2015, he received the *Journal of International Business Studies* Decade Award. A *Journal of Management* article found him to be among the top 65 most widely cited management scholars, and an *Academy of Management Perspectives* study reported that he is the fourth-most-influential management scholar among professors who obtained their PhD since 1991. Overall, Professor Peng has published more than 120 articles in leading journals, more than 30 pieces in non-refereed outlets, and five books. Since the launch of *GLOBAL*'s second edition, he has not only published in top IB journals, such as the *Academy of Management Journal, Journal of International Business Studies, Journal of World Business*, and *Strategic Management Journal*, but also in leading outlets in entrepreneurship (*Entrepreneurship Theory and Practice*), ethics (*Journal of Business Ethics*), and human resources (*International Journal of Human Resource Management*).

Used in more than 30 countries, Professor Peng's best-selling textbooks, *Global Business, Global Strategy*, and *GLOBAL*, are global market leaders that have been translated into Chinese, Portuguese, and Spanish. A European adaptation (with Klaus Meyer) and an Indian adaptation (with Deepak Srivastava) have been successfully launched.

Truly global in scope, Professor Peng's research has investigated firm strategies in Africa, Asia Pacific, Central and Eastern Europe, and North America. He is best known for his development of the institution-based view of strategy and his insights about the rise of emerging economies such as China in global business. With more than 18,000 Google citations and an H-index of 57, he is listed among *The World's Most Influential Scientific Minds* (compiled by Thomson Reuters based on citations covering 21 fields)—in the field of economics and business, he is one of the only 95 world-class scholars listed and the *only* IB textbook author listed.

Professor Peng is active in leadership positions. He has served on the editorial boards of the *AMJ, AMP, AMR, JIBS, JMS, JWB*, and *SMJ;* and guest-edited a special issue for the *JMS*. At AIB, he co-chaired the AIB/*JIBS* Frontiers Conference in San Diego (2006), guest-edited a *JIBS* special issue (2010), chaired the Emerging and Transition Economies track for the Nagoya conference (2011), and chaired the Richard Farmer Best Dissertation Award Committee for the Washington conference (2012). At the Strategic Management Society (SMS), he was elected to be the Global Strategy Interest Group Chair (2008). He also co-chaired the SMS Special Conferences in Shanghai (2007) and in Sydney (2014). He served one term as Editor-in-Chief of the *Asia Pacific Journal of Management*. He managed the successful bid to enter the Social Sciences Citation Index (SSCI), which reported *APJM*'s first citation impact to be 3.4 and rated it as the top 18 among 140 management journals (by citation impact factor) for 2010. In recognition of his significant contributions, *APJM* has named its best paper award the Mike Peng Best Paper Award. Currently, he is a Senior Editor at the *Journal of World Business*.

Professor Peng is also an active consultant, trainer, and keynote speaker. He has provided on-the-job training to more than 400 professors. He has consulted and been a keynote speaker for multinational enterprises (such as AstraZeneca, Berlitz, Nationwide, SAFRAN, and Texas Instruments), nonprofit organizations (such as World Affairs Council of Dallas-Fort Worth), educational and funding organizations (such as Canada Research Chair, Harvard Kennedy School of Government, and National Science Foundation), and national and international organizations (such as the UK Government Office for Science, US-China Business Council, US Navy, and The World Bank).

Professor Peng has received numerous honors, including an NSF CAREER Grant ($423,000), a US Small Business Administration Best Paper Award, a (lifetime) Distinguished Scholar Award from the Southwestern Academy of Management, a (lifetime) Scholarly Contribution Award from the International Association for Chinese Management Research (IACMR), and a Best Paper Award named after him. He has been quoted by *The Economist, Newsweek, Dallas Morning News, Smart Business Dallas, Atlanta Journal-Constitution, The Exporter Magazine, The World Journal, Business Times* (Singapore), CEO-CIO (Beijing), *Sing Tao Daily* (Vancouver), and *Brasil Econômico* (São Paulo), as well as on the Voice of America.

MIKE W. PENG

GLOBAL 3

BRIEF CONTENTS

ISTOCKPHOTO.COM/YMGERMAN

CONTENTS

Part 1
Laying Foundations

MEUNIERD/SHUTTERSTOCK.COM

Part 2 Acquiring Tools

8 Capitalizing on Global & Regional Integration 116

Part 3
Managing Around the World

9 Growing & Internationalizing the Entrepreneurial Firm 134

14 Competing in Marketing & Supply Chain Management 214

15 Managing Corporate Social Responsibility Globally 228

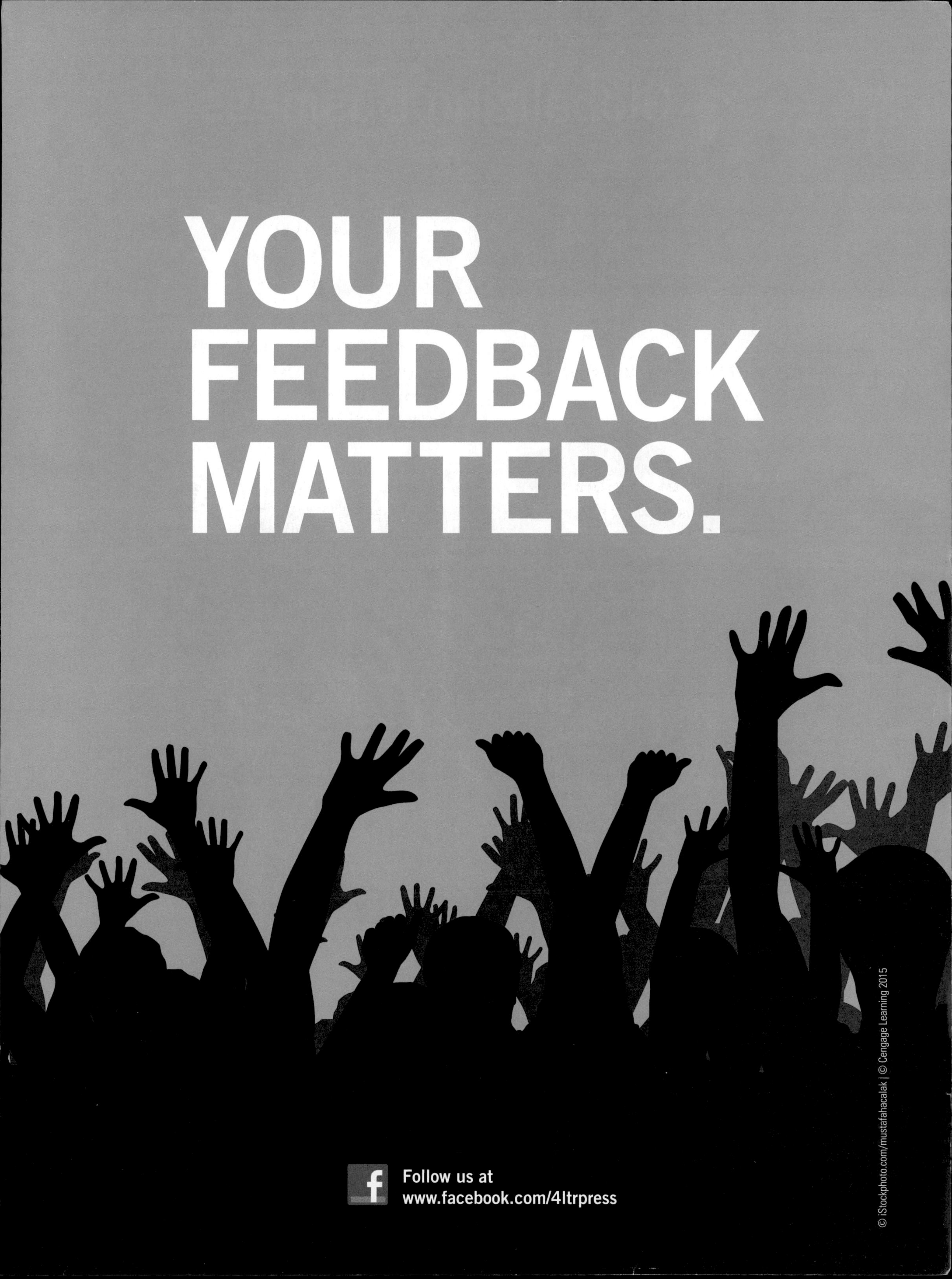
YOUR
FEEDBACK
MATTERS.
Follow us at
www.facebook.com/4ltrpress
© iStockphoto.com/mustafahacalak | © Cengage Learning 2015

PART 1

1 Globalizing Business

MEUNIERD/SHUTTERSTOCK.COM

LEARNING OBJECTIVES

After studying this chapter, you should be able to . . .

1-1 Explain the concepts of international business and global business.

1-2 Give three reasons why it is important to study global business.

1-3 Articulate the fundamental question that the study of global business seeks to answer and the two perspectives from which to answer it.

1-4 Identify three ways of understanding what globalization is.

1-5 Appreciate the size of the global economy and the strengths of multinationals.

After you finish this chapter, go to **PAGE 17** for **STUDY TOOLS**

ETHICAL DILEMMA/EMERGING MARKETS

Coca-Cola in Africa

Founded in 1892, Coca-Cola first entered Africa in 1929. While Africa had always been viewed as "backwater," it has recently emerged as a major growth market commanding strategic attention. Of the $27 billion that Coca-Cola would invest in emerging economies between 2010 and 2020, $12 billion would be used to beef up plants and distribution facilities in Africa. Why does Coca-Cola show such strong commitments to Africa? Both the push and pull effects are at work.

The push comes from the necessity to find new sources of growth for this mature firm, which has promised investors 7%–9% earnings growth. In 1998, its stock reached a high-water mark at $88. But it dropped to $37 in 2003. Since 2004, the share price rallied again, rising from $43 to a new peak of $90 in November 2014 (adjusted for a 2:1 share split in 2012). Can Coca-Cola's stock reach higher?

Its home markets are unlikely to help. Between 2006 and 2011, US sales declined for five consecutive years. Further, health advocates accused Coca-Cola of contributing to an epidemic of obesity in the United States and proposed to tax soft drinks to pay for health care. While Coca-Cola defeated the tax initiative, it is fair to say the room for growth at home is limited. In Europe and Japan, sales are similarly flat. Elsewhere, in China, strong local rivals have made it tough for Coca-Cola to break out. Its acquisition of a leading local fruit juice firm was blocked by the government, which did not seem to bless Coca-Cola's further growth. In India, Pepsi is so popular that "Pepsi" has become the Hindi shorthand for all bottled soft drinks (including Coke!). In Latin America, sales are encouraging but growth is limited. Mexicans on average are already guzzling 665 servings of Coca-Cola products every year, the highest in the world. There is only so much sugary water one can drink every day.

In contrast, Coca-Cola is pulled by Africa, where it has a commanding 29% market share versus Pepsi's 15%. With 65,000 employees and 160 plants, Coca-Cola is Africa's largest private sector employer. Yet, annual per capita consumption of Coca-Cola products is only 39 servings in Kenya. For the continent as a whole, disposable income is growing. In 2014, 100 million Africans earned at least $5,000 per person. While Africa indeed has some of the poorest countries in the world, 12 African countries (with a combined population of 100 million) have a GDP per capita that is greater than China's. Coca-Cola is hoping to capitalize on Africa's improved political stability and physical infrastructure. Countries not fighting civil wars make Coke's operations less disruptive, and new roads penetrating the jungle can obviously elevate sales.

Coca-Cola is already in all African countries. The challenge now, according to chairman and CEO Muhtar Kent, will be to deep dive into "every town, every village, every township." This will not be easy. War, poverty, and poor infrastructure make it extremely difficult to distribute and market products in hard-to-access regions. Undaunted, Coca-Cola is in a street-by-street campaign to increase awareness and consumption of its products. The crowds and the poor roads dictate that some of the deliveries have to be done manually on pushcarts or trolleys. Throughout the continent, Coca-Cola has set up 3,000 manual distribution centers. Taking a page from its playbook in Latin America, especially Mexico, Coca-Cola has aggressively courted small corner stores. Coca-Cola and its bottlers offer small corner store owners delivery, credit, and direct coaching—ranging from the tip not to ice down the Cokes until the midday rush to save electricity to helping on how to buy a house after vendors make enough money.

In Africa, US-style accusations of Coca-Cola's alleged contribution to the obesity problem are unlikely. After all, the primary concern in many communities is too few available calories of any kind. However, this does not mean that Coca-Cola faces no criticisms in Africa. It has to defend itself from critics who accuse it of depleting fresh water, encouraging expensive and environmentally harmful refrigeration, and hurting local competitors who hawk beverages. In response, Coca-Cola often points out the benefits it has brought. In addition to the 65,000 jobs it has directly created, one million local jobs are indirectly created by its vast system of distribution, which moves beverages from bottling plants deep into the slums and the bush a few crates at a time.

"Ultimately," the *Economist* opined, "doing business in Africa is a gamble on the future." Overall, CEO Kent is very optimistic about Africa. In his own words at a media interview:

> *Africa is the untold story, and could be the big story, of the next decade, like India and China were the past decade. The presence and the significance of our business in Africa is far greater than India and China even today. The relevance is much bigger. . . . In Africa, you've got an incredibly young population, a dynamic population. Huge disposable incomes. I mean, $1.6 trillion of GDP, which is bigger than Russia, bigger than India. It's a big economy, and so rich underground. And whether the next decade becomes the decade of Africa or not, in my opinion, will depend upon one single thing—and everything is right there to have it happen—that is better governance. And it is improving, there is no question.*

Sources: M. Blanding, *The Coke Machine* (New York: Avery, 2010); "Coke's last round," *Bloomberg Businessweek*, 1 November 2010: 54–61; "For India's consumers, Pepsi is the real thing," *Bloomberg Businessweek*, 20 September 2010: 26–27; "Can Coke surpass its record high of $88 a share?" *Bloomberg Businessweek*, 6 June 2011: 49–50; "Business in Africa," *Economist*, 9 September 2006: 60–62; "Index of happiness," *Economist*, 5 July 2008: 58; "A continent goes shopping," *Economist*, 18 August 2012: 57–58; D. Zoogah, M. W. Peng, and H. Woldu, "Institutions, resources, and organizational effectiveness in Africa," *Academy of Management Perspectives* 29 (2015): 7–31.

How do firms such as Coca-Cola compete around the globe? How can competitors such as PepsiCo, Nestlé, and local hawkers fight back? What determines the success and failure of these firms—and numerous others—around the world? This book will address these and other important questions on global business.

1-1 WHAT IS GLOBAL BUSINESS?

Traditionally, **international business (IB)** is defined as a business (firm) that engages in international (cross-border) economic activities. It can also refer to the action of doing business abroad. A previous generation of IB textbooks almost always takes the foreign entrant's perspective. Consequently, such books deal with issues such as how to enter foreign markets and how to select alliance partners. The most frequently discussed foreign entrant is the **multinational enterprise (MNE)**, defined as a firm that engages in **foreign direct investment (FDI)** by directly investing in, controlling, and managing value-added activities in other countries.[1] Of course, MNEs and their cross-border activities are important. But they cover only one side of IB—the foreign side. Students educated by these books often come away with the impression that the other side of IB—namely, domestic firms—does not exist. But domestic firms obviously do not just sit around in the face of foreign entrants such as MNEs. They actively compete and/or collaborate with foreign entrants.[2] In other words, focusing on the foreign entrant side captures only one side of the coin at best.

There are *two* key words in IB: international (I) and business (B). However, previous textbooks all focus on the international aspect (the foreign entrant) to the extent that the business part (which also includes domestic business) almost disappears. This is unfortunate because IB is fundamentally about B in addition to being I. To put it differently, the IB course in the undergraduate and MBA curricula at numerous business schools is probably the *only* course with the word "business" in the course title. All other courses you take are labeled management, marketing, finance, and so on, representing one functional area but not the overall picture of business. Does it matter? Of course! It means that your IB course is an *integrative* course that has the potential to provide you with an overall business perspective grounded in a global environment (as opposed to a relatively narrow functional view). Consequently, it makes sense that your textbook should give you both the I and B parts, not just the I part.

To cover both the I and B parts, **global business** is defined in this book as business around the globe—thus the title of this book: *GLOBAL*. For the B part, the activities include *both* international (cross-border) activities covered by traditional IB books and domestic (non-IB) business activities. Such deliberate blurring of the traditional boundaries separating international and domestic business is increasingly important today, because many previously national (domestic) markets are now globalized. For example, not long ago, competition among college business textbook publishers was primarily on a nation-by-nation basis. The Big Three—Cengage Learning (our publisher), Prentice Hall, and McGraw-Hill—primarily competed in the United States. A different set of publishers competed in other countries. As a result, textbooks studied by British students would be

International business (IB) (1) A business (firm) that engages in international (cross-border) economic activities or (2) the action of doing business abroad.

Multinational enterprise (MNE) A firm that engages in foreign direct investment and operates in multiple countries.

Foreign direct investment (FDI) Investment in, controlling, and managing value-added activities in other countries.

Global business Business around the globe.

ISTOCKPHOTO.COM/EVIRGEN

authored by British professors and published by British publishers, textbooks studied by Brazilian students would be authored by Brazilian professors and published by Brazilian publishers, and so on. Now Cengage Learning (under British and Canadian ownership), Pearson Prentice Hall (under British ownership), and McGraw-Hill (under US ownership) have significantly globalized their competition, thanks to rising demand for high-quality business textbooks in English. Around the globe, they compete against each other in many markets, publishing in multiple languages. For instance, *GLOBAL* and its sister books—*Global Business, Global Strategy*, and *International Business* (a European adaptation)—are published by different subsidiaries in Chinese, Spanish, and Portuguese in addition to English, reaching customers in over 30 countries. Despite such worldwide spread of competition, in each market—down to each school—textbook publishers have to compete locally. In other words, no professor teaches globally, and all students study locally. This means that *GLOBAL* has to win adoption for every class every semester. Overall, it becomes difficult to tell in this competition what is international and what is domestic. Thus, "global" is a better word to capture the essence of this competition.

GLOBAL also differs from other IB books because most focus on competition in developed economies. Here, by contrast, we devote extensive space to competitive battles waged throughout **emerging economies**, a term that has gradually replaced the term "developing countries" since the 1990s. Another commonly used term is **emerging markets** (see PengAtlas Map 1). How important are emerging economies? Collectively, they command 48% of world trade, attract 60% of FDI inflows, and generate 40% FDI outflows. Overall, emerging economies contribute approximately 50% of the global **gross domestic product (GDP)**.[3] In 1990, they accounted for less than a third of a much smaller world GDP. Note that this percentage is adjusted for **purchasing power parity (PPP)**, which is an adjustment to reflect the differences in cost of living.

Of many emerging economies, Brazil, Russia, India, and China—commonly referred to as **BRIC**—command more attention. With South Africa, BRIC becomes **BRICS**. As a group, BRICS countries have 40% of the world's population, covers a quarter of the world's land area, and contribute more than 25% of global GDP (on a PPP basis). In addition to BRICS, other interesting terms include BRICM (BRIC + Mexico), BRICET (BRIC + Eastern Europe and Turkey), and Next Eleven (N-11—consisting of Bangladesh, Egypt, Indonesia, Iran, Korea, Mexico, Nigeria, Pakistan, the Philippines, Turkey, and Vietnam).

ISTOCKPHOTO.COM/ HENRIK5000

Overall, the Great Transformation of the global economy is embodied by the tremendous shift in economic weight and engines of growth toward emerging economies in general and BRIC(S) in particular. Led by BRIC(S), emerging economies accomplished "the biggest economic transformation in modern economy," according to the *Economist*.[4] In China, per capita income doubled in about ten years, an achievement that took Britain 150 years and the United States 50 years as they industrialized. Throughout emerging economies, China is not alone. While groupings such as BRIC(S) and N-11 are always arbitrary, they serve a useful purpose—namely, highlighting their economic and demographic scale and trajectory that enable them to challenge developed economies in terms of weight and influence in the global economy.

Of course, the Great Transformation is not a linear story of endless and uniform high-speed growth. Most emerging economies have experienced some significant slow down recently.[5] It is possible that they may not be able to repeat their extraordinary growth sprint during the decade between 1998 (the Asian economic crisis) and 2008 (the global financial crisis). For example, in 2007, Brazil accomplished an annual economic growth of 6%, Russia 8%, India 10%, and China 14%. In 2017, they would be very lucky if they could achieve half of these enviable growth rates. However, it seems that emerging economies *as a group* are destined to grow both their absolute GDP and their percentage of world GDP relative to developed economies. The debate centers on how much and how fast (or how slow) such growth will be in the future.

The global economy can be viewed as a pyramid shown in Exhibit 1.1. The top consists of about one billion people with per capita annual income of $20,000 or higher. These are mostly people who live in the developed economies of the **Triad**, which consists of North America, Western

Emerging economy (emerging market) A developing country.

Gross domestic product (GDP) The sum of value added by resident firms, households, and governments operating in an economy.

Purchasing power parity (PPP) A conversion that determines the equivalent amount of goods and services different currencies can purchase. This conversion is usually used to capture the differences in cost of living in different countries.

BRIC An acronym for the emerging economies of Brazil, Russia, India, and China.

BRICS An acronym for the emerging economies of Brazil, Russia, India, China, and South Africa.

Triad Three regions of developed economies (North America, Western Europe, and Japan).

EXHIBIT 1.1 THE GLOBAL ECONOMIC PYRAMID

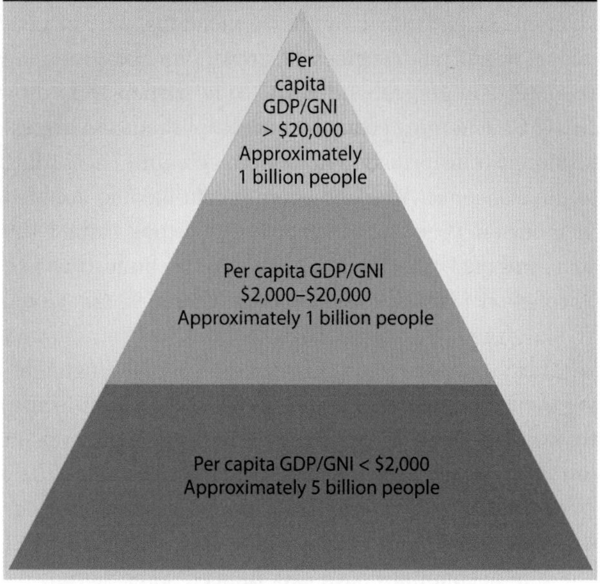

Source: C. K. Prahalad and S. Hart, "The fortune at the bottom of the pyramid," *Strategy+Business* 26 (2002): 54–67; S. Hart, Capitalism at the Crossroads (Philadelphia: Wharton School Publishing, 2005) 111.

Europe, and Japan. Another billion people making $2,000 to $20,000 a year form the second tier. The vast majority of humanity—about five billion people—make less than $2,000 a year and comprise the **base of the pyramid (BoP)**. Most MNEs (and most traditional IB books) focus on the top and second tiers and end up ignoring the BoP. An increasing number of such low-income countries have shown increasingly more economic opportunities as income levels have risen.[6] Today's students—and tomorrow's business leaders—will ignore these opportunities in BoP markets at their own peril. This book will help ensure that you will not ignore these opportunities.

1-2 WHY STUDY GLOBAL BUSINESS?

Global business (or IB) is one of the most exciting, challenging, and relevant subjects offered by business schools. There are at least three compelling reasons why you should study it—and study hard (Exhibit 1.2). First, you don't want to be a loser. Mastering global business knowledge helps advance your employability and career in an increasingly competitive global economy. An ignorant individual is unlikely to emerge as a winner in global competition.

Base of the pyramid (BoP) The vast majority of humanity, about five billion people, who make less than $2,000 a year.

Expatriate manager (expat) A manager who works outside his or her native country.

International premium A significant pay raise commanded by expatriates when working overseas.

Second, expertise in global business is often a prerequisite to join the top ranks of large firms, something many ambitious students aspire to. It is now increasingly difficult, if not impossible, to find top managers at large firms who do not possess significant global competence. Eventually you will need hands-on global experience, not merely knowledge acquired from this course. However, in order to set yourself apart as an ideal candidate to be selected for an executive position, you will need to demonstrate that you are interested in global business and have mastered such knowledge during your education. This is especially true if you are interested in gaining experience as an **expatriate manager** (or "expat" for short)—a manager who works abroad (see Chapter 13 for details).

Thanks to globalization, low-level jobs not only command lower salaries, but are also more vulnerable. On the other hand, top-level jobs, especially those held by expats, are both financially rewarding and relatively secure. Expats often command a significant **international premium** in compensation—a significant pay raise when working overseas. In US firms, their total compensation package is approximately $250,000 to $300,000 (including benefits; not all is take-home pay). For example, if a 2,000-employee ball bearing factory in Canton, Ohio, is shut down and the MNE sets up a similar factory in Canton (Guangzhou), China, only about 10 to 20 jobs would be saved. Yes, you guessed it: Those jobs would consist of a few top-level positions such as the CEO, CFO, factory director, and chief engineer who will be sent by the MNE as expats to China to start up operations there. The MNE often gives them many more perks in China than it did in Ohio. How about company-subsidized luxury housing plus maid services, free tuition for children in American or international schools, and all-expenses-paid vacations for the whole family to see

EXHIBIT 1.2 WHY STUDY GLOBAL BUSINESS?

- Advancing your employability and your career in the global economy
- Better preparation for possible expatriate assignments abroad
- Stronger competence in interacting with foreign suppliers, partners, and competitors and in working for foreign-owned employers in your own country

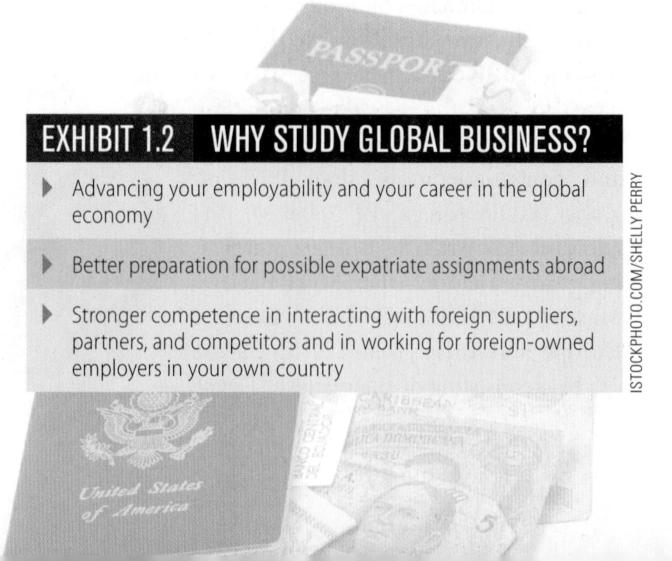

ISTOCKPHOTO.COM/SHELLY PERRY

their loved ones in Ohio? Moreover, these expats do not live in China forever. When they return to the United States after a tour of duty (usually two to three years), if their current employer does not provide attractive career opportunities, they are often hired away by competitor firms. This is because competitor firms are also interested in globalizing their business by tapping into the expertise and experience of these former expats. And, yes, competitor firms will have to pay them even more to hire away these internationally experienced managers. This indeed is a virtuous cycle.

This hypothetical example is designed to motivate you to study hard so that someday, you may become one of these sought-after, globe-trotting managers. But, even if you don't want to be an expat, we assume that you don't want to join the ranks of the unemployed due to factory closings and business failures (see Exhibit 1.3).

Lastly, even if you do not aspire to compete for the top job at a large firm or work overseas, and even if you work at a small firm or are self-employed, you may find yourself dealing with foreign-owned suppliers and buyers, competing with foreign-invested firms in your home market, and perhaps even selling and investing overseas. Alternatively, you may find yourself working for a foreign-owned firm, your domestic employer may be acquired by a foreign player, or your unit may be ordered to shut down for global consolidation. Any of these is a very likely scenario, because approximately 80 million people worldwide, including 18 million Chinese, six million Americans, and one million British, are employed by foreign-owned firms. In the private sector, Taiwan-based Foxconn is the largest employer in China, India-based Tata Group is the largest employer in the UK, IBM is the second largest employer in India, and Coca-Cola is the largest employer in Africa (see the Opening Case). Understanding how global business decisions are made may facilitate your own career in such firms. If there is a strategic rationale to downsize your unit, you would want to be prepared and start polishing your resume right away. In other words, it is your career that is at stake. Don't be the last to know! To avoid the fate humorously portrayed in Exhibit 1.3, a good place to start is to study hard and do well in your IB course. Of course, don't forget to put *this* course on your resume as a highlight of your education. (In Focus has additional advice on what language and what fields to study).

EXHIBIT 1.3 JOBS OUTSOURCED

Source: *Harvard Business Review*, April 2012: 34.

1-3 A UNIFIED FRAMEWORK

Global business is a vast subject area. It is one of the few courses that will make you appreciate why your university requires you to take a number of diverse courses in general education. We will draw on major social sciences such as economics, geography, history, psychology, political science, and sociology. We will also draw on a number of business disciplines such as finance, marketing, and strategy. The study of global business is thus very interdisciplinary.[7] It is easy to lose sight of the forest while scrutinizing various trees or even branches. The subject is not difficult, and most students find it to be fun. The number one student complaint is about the overwhelming amount of information. Truth be told: this is also *my* number one complaint as your author. You may have to read and learn this material, but I have to bring it all together in a way that makes sense and in a compact book that does not go on and on and on for 900 pages. To make your learning more focused, more manageable, and hopefully more fun, in this book we will develop a unified framework consisting of one fundamental question and two core perspectives (shown in Exhibit 1.4).

1-3a One Fundamental Question[8]

What is it that we do in global business? Why is it so important that practically all students in business schools around the world are either required or recommended

InFocus: Emerging Markets

What Language and What Fields Should I Study?

WOAISS/SHUTTERSTOCK.COM

On September 3, 2007, Markéta Straková of Tabor, the Czech Republic, wrote to *BusinessWeek* columnists Jack Welch and Suzy Welch:

> *I am thinking of studying Portuguese, but in your opinion, what language should I learn to succeed in the world of business? And what fields of study hold the most potential?*

Jack Welch was the former chairman and CEO of General Electric (GE), and Suzy Welch was the former editor of *Harvard Business Review*. They wrote back in the same issue of *BusinessWeek*:

> *You're on to something with Portuguese, since it will give you a leg up in several markets with good potential, such as Brazil and some emerging African nations. Spanish is also a good choice, as it will allow you to operate with more ease throughout Latin America, and, increasingly, the United States. But for our money—and if you can manage the much higher order of commitment—Chinese is the language to learn. China is already an economic powerhouse. It will only gain strength. Anyone who can do business there with the speed and intimacy that fluency affords will earn a real competitive edge.*
>
> *As for what to study—and if you want to be where the action is now and for the next couple of decades—consider the industries focused on alternative sources of energy. Or learn everything you can about the confluence of three fields: biotechnology, information technology, and nanotechnology. For the foreseeable future, the therapies, machines, devices, and other products and services that these fields bring to market will revolutionize society—and business.*
>
> *That said, when it comes to picking an education field and ultimately a career, absolutely nothing beats pursuing the path that truly fascinates your brain, engages your energy, and touches your soul. Whatever you do, do what turns your crank. Otherwise your job will always be just work, and how dreary is that?*

Source: J. Welch and S. Welch, "Ideas: The Welch way," *BusinessWeek*, 3 September 2007, 104.

EXHIBIT 1.4 A UNIFIED FRAMEWORK FOR GLOBAL BUSINESS

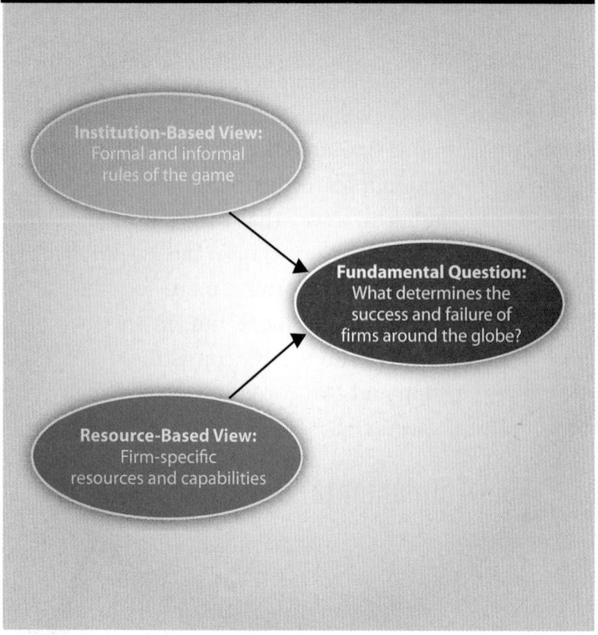

to take this course? While there are certainly a lot of questions to raise, a relentless interest in what determines the success and failure of firms around the globe serves to focus the energy of our field. Global business is fundamentally about not limiting yourself to your home country. It is about treating the global economy as your potential playground (or battlefield). Some firms may be successful domestically but fail miserably overseas. Other firms successfully translate their strengths from their home markets to other countries. If you were expected to lead your firm's efforts to enter a particular foreign market, wouldn't you want to find out what drives the success and failure of other firms in that market?

Overall, the focus on firm performance around the globe defines the field of global business (or IB) more than anything else. Numerous other questions all relate in one way or another to this most fundamental question. Therefore, all chapters in this book will be centered on this fundamental question: What determines the success and failure of firms around the globe?

1-3b First Core Perspective: An Institution-Based View[9]

An **institution-based view** suggests that the success and failure of firms are enabled and constrained by institutions. By **institutions**, we mean the rules of the game. Doing business around the globe requires intimate knowledge about both formal rules (such as laws) and informal rules (such as values) that govern competition in various countries as an **institutional framework**. Firms that do not do their homework and thus remain ignorant of the rules of the game in a certain country are not likely to emerge as winners.

Formal institutions include laws, regulations, and rules. For example, Hong Kong's laws are well known for treating all comers, whether from neighboring mainland China (whose firms are still technically regarded as "nondomestic") or far-away Chile, the same as they treat indigenous Hong Kong firms. Such equal treatment enhances the potential odds for foreign firms' success. It is thus not surprising that Hong Kong attracts a lot of outside firms. Other rules of the game discriminate against foreign firms and undermine their chances for success. India's recent attraction as a site for FDI was only possible after its regulations changed from confrontational to accommodating. Prior to 1991, India's rules severely discriminated against foreign firms. For example, in the 1970s, the Indian government demanded that Coca-Cola either hand over the recipe for its secret syrup, which it does not even share with the US government, or get out of India. Painfully, Coca-Cola chose to leave India. Its return to India since the 1990s speaks volumes about how much the rules of the game have changed in India.

Informal institutions include cultures, ethics, and norms. They also play an important part in shaping the success and failure of firms around the globe (see the Closing Case). For example, individualistic societies, particularly the English-speaking countries such as Australia, Britain, and the United States, tend to have a relatively higher level of entrepreneurship as reflected in the high number of business start-ups. Why? Because the act of founding a new firm is a widely accepted practice in individualistic societies. Conversely, collectivistic societies such as Japan often have a hard time fostering entrepreneurship. Most people there refuse to stick their neck out to found new businesses because it is contrary to the norm.

Overall, an institution-based view suggests that institutions shed a great deal of light on what drives firm performance around the globe. Next, we turn to our second core perspective.

1-3c Second Core Perspective: A Resource-Based View[10]

The institution-based view suggests that the success and failure of firms around the globe are largely determined by their environment. However, insightful as this perspective is, there is a major drawback. If we push this view to its logical extreme, then firm performance

Institution-based view A leading perspective in global business that suggests that firm performance is, at least in part, determined by the institutional frameworks governing firm behavior around the world.

Institution Formal and informal rules of the game.

Institutional framework Formal and informal institutions that govern individual and firm behavior.

ISTOCKPHOTO.COM/EKASH

around the globe would be *entirely* determined by environments. The validity of this extreme version is certainly questionable.

The **resource-based view** helps overcome this drawback. While the institution-based view primarily deals with the *external* environment, the resource-based view focuses on a firm's *internal* resources and capabilities. It starts with a simple observation: In a harsh, unattractive environment, most firms either suffer or exit. However, against all odds, a few superstars thrive in such an environment. For instance, despite the former Soviet Union's obvious hostility toward the United States during the Cold War, PepsiCo began successfully operating in the former Soviet Union in the 1970s (!). In another example, airlines often lose money. But a small number of players, such as Southwest in the United States, Ryanair in Ireland, Hainan in China, and IndiGo in India, have been raking in profits year after year. In the fiercely competitive fashion industry, Zara has been defying gravity. How can these firms succeed in such a challenging environment? What is special about them? A short answer is that PepsiCo, Southwest, Ryanair, Hainan, IndiGo, and Zara must have certain valuable and unique *firm-specific* resources and capabilities that are not shared by competitors in the same environment.

Doing business outside one's home country is challenging. Foreign firms have to overcome a **liability of foreignness**, which is the *inherent* disadvantage that foreign firms experience in host countries because of their nonnative status.[11] Just think about all the differences in regulations, languages, cultures, and norms. Think about the odds against Toyota and Honda when they tried to eat some of General Motors' and Ford's lunch in the American heartland. Against such significant odds, the primary weapons that foreign firms such as Toyota and Honda employ are *overwhelming* resources and capabilities that can offset their liability of foreignness. Today, many of us take it for granted that the best-selling car in the United States rotates between the Toyota Camry and the Honda Civic, that Coca-Cola is the best-selling soft drink in Mexico, and that Microsoft Word is the world's number one word-processing software. We really shouldn't. Why? Because it is *not* natural for these foreign firms to dominate nonnative markets. These firms must possess some very rare and powerful firm-specific resources and capabilities that drive these remarkable success stories. This is a key theme of the resource-based view, which focuses on how winning firms develop unique and enviable resources and capabilities and how competitor firms imitate and then innovate in an effort to outcompete the winning firms.

Resource-based view A leading perspective in global business that suggests that firm performance is, at least in part, determined by its internal resources and capabilities.

Liability of foreignness The inherent disadvantage that foreign firms experience in host countries because of their nonnative status.

Globalization The close integration of countries and peoples of the world.

1-3d A Consistent Theme

Given our focus on the fundamental question of what determines the success and failure of firms around the globe, we will develop a unified framework by organizing the material in *every* chapter according to the two core perspectives, namely, the institution-based and resource-based views (see the Closing Case).[12] With our unified framework—an innovation in IB textbooks—we will not only explore the global business "trees," but also see the global business "forest."

1-4 WHAT IS GLOBALIZATION?

Globalization, generally speaking, is the close integration of countries and peoples of the world. This abstract five-syllable word is now frequently heard and debated. Those who approve of globalization count its contributions to include greater economic growth, higher standards of living, increased technology sharing, and more extensive cultural integration. Critics argue that globalization undermines wages in rich countries, exploits workers in poor countries, gives MNEs too much power, destroys the environment, and promotes inequality. So what exactly is globalization? This section outlines three views on globalization, recommends the pendulum view, and introduces the idea of semiglobalization.

1-4a Three Views on Globalization

Depending on what sources you read, globalization could be one of the following:

- A new force sweeping through the world in recent times.
- A long-run historical evolution since the dawn of human history.
- A pendulum that swings from one extreme to another from time to time

An understanding of these views helps put the debate about globalization in perspective. First, opponents of globalization suggest that it is a new phenomenon beginning in the late 20th century, driven by recent technological innovations and a Western ideology focused on exploiting and dominating the world through MNEs. The arguments against globalization focus on an ideal world free of environmental stress, social injustice, and sweatshop labor, but present few clear alternatives to the present economic order. Advocates and anti-globalization protesters often argue that globalization needs to be slowed down, if not stopped.

ISTOCKPHOTO.COM/ROMAOSLO

A second view contends that globalization has always been part and parcel of human history. Historians debate whether globalization started 2,000 or 8,000 years ago. MNEs existed for more than two millennia, with their earliest traces discovered in Phoenician, Assyrian, and Roman times. International competition from low-cost countries is nothing new. In the first century A.D., the Roman emperor Tiberius was so concerned about the massive quantity of low-cost Chinese silk imports that he imposed the world's first known import quota of textiles. Today's most successful MNEs do not come close to wielding the historical clout of some earlier MNEs, such as the East India Company during colonial times (see the Closing Case). In a nutshell, globalization is nothing new and will always exist.

A third view suggests that globalization is the "closer integration of the countries and peoples of the world which has been brought about by the enormous reduction of the costs of transportation and communication and the breaking down of artificial barriers to the flows of goods, services, capital, knowledge, and (to a lesser extent) people across borders."[13] Globalization is neither recent nor one-directional. It is, more accurately, a process similar to the swing of a pendulum.

1-4b The Pendulum View on Globalization

The third, pendulum view probably makes the most sense, because it can help us understand the ups and downs of globalization. The current era of globalization originated in the aftermath of World War II, when major Western nations committed to global trade and investment. However, between the 1950s and the 1970s, this view was not widely shared. Communist countries, such as the former Soviet Union and China, sought to develop self-sufficiency. Many noncommunist developing countries such as Argentina, Brazil, India, and Mexico focused on fostering and protecting domestic industries. But refusing to participate in global trade and investment ended up breeding uncompetitive industries. In contrast,

ISTOCKPHOTO.COM/MIPAN

four developing economies in Asia—namely, Hong Kong, Singapore, South Korea, and Taiwan—earned their stripes as the "Four Tigers" by participating in the global economy. They became the *only* economies once recognized as less developed (low-income) by the World Bank to have subsequently achieved developed (high-income) status.

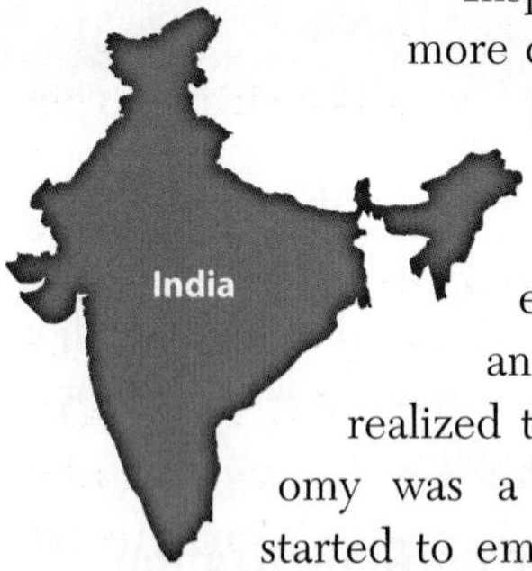

Inspired by the Four Tigers, more countries and regions—such as China in the late 1970s, Latin America in the mid 1980s, Central and Eastern Europe in the late 1980s, and India in the 1990s—realized that joining the world economy was a must. As these countries started to emerge as new players in the world economy, they became collectively known as "emerging economies." As a result, globalization rapidly accelerated.

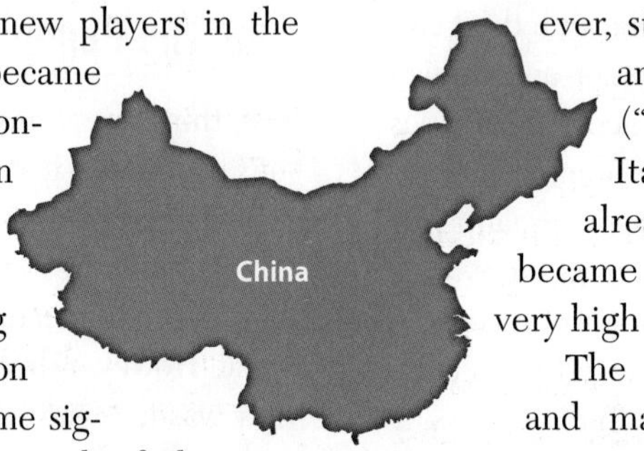

However, globalization, like a pendulum, is unable to keep going in one direction. Rapid globalization in the 1990s and the 2000s saw some significant backlash. First, the rapid growth of globalization led to the historically inaccurate view that globalization is new. Second, it created fear among many people in developed economies that they would lose jobs. Finally, some factions in emerging economies complained against the onslaught of MNEs, alleging that they destroy not only local companies, but also local cultures and values.

The December 1999 protests in Seattle and the September 2001 terrorist attacks in New York and Washington are undoubtedly some of the most visible and most extreme acts of anti-globalization forces at work. As a result, international travel was curtailed, and global trade and investment flows slowed in the early 2000s. Then in the mid 2000s, worldwide GDP, cross-border trade, and per capita GDP all soared to historically high levels. It was during that period "BRIC" became a buzzword.

Risk management Identification and assessment of risks and the preparation to minimize the impact of high-risk, unfortunate events.

Scenario planning A technique to prepare and plan for multiple scenarios (either high or low risk).

Unfortunately, the party suddenly ended in 2008. The 2008–2009 global economic crisis was unlike anything the world had seen since the Great Depression (1929–1933). The crisis showed, for better or worse, how interconnected the global economy has become. Deteriorating housing markets in the United States, fueled by unsustainable subprime lending practices, led to massive government bailouts of failed firms. The crisis quickly spread around the world, forcing numerous governments to bail out their own troubled banks. Global output, trade, and investment plummeted, while unemployment skyrocketed. The 2008–2009 crisis became known as the Great Recession. Many people blamed globalization for the Great Recession.

After unprecedented government intervention in developed economies, confidence was growing that the global economy had turned the corner.[14] However, starting in 2010, the Greek debt crisis and then the broader PIGS debt crisis ("PIGS" refers to Portugal, Ireland or Italy, Greece, and Spain) erupted. The already slow recovery in Europe thus became slower, and unemployment hovered at very high levels.

The Great Recession reminds all firms and managers of the importance of **risk management**—the identification and assessment of risks and the preparation to minimize the impact of high-risk, unfortunate events. As a technique to prepare and plan for multiple scenarios (either high risk or low risk), **scenario planning** is now extensively used around the world. The recovery has seen more protectionist measures, since the stimulus packages and job creation schemes of various governments often emphasize "buy national" (such as "buy American") and "hire locals." In short, the pendulum is swinging back.

Like the proverbial elephant, globalization is seen by everyone yet rarely comprehended. The sudden ferocity of the 2008–2009 crisis surprised everybody—ranging from central bankers to academic experts. Remember all of us felt sorry when we read the story of a bunch of blind men trying to figure out the shape and form of the elephant. We really shouldn't. Although we are not blind, our task is more challenging than the blind men who study a standing animal. Our beast—globalization—does not stand still and often rapidly

CHRUPKA/SHUTTERSTOCK.COM

moves, back and forth (!). Yet, we try to live with it, avoid being crushed by it, and even attempt to profit from it. Overall, relative to the other two views, the view of globalization as a pendulum is more balanced and more realistic. In other words, globalization has both rosy and dark sides, and it changes over time.

1-4c Semiglobalization

Despite the hype, globalization is not complete. Do we really live in a globalized world? Are selling and investing abroad just as easy as at home? Obviously not. Most measures of market integration, such as trade and FDI, have recently scaled new heights, but still fall far short of pointing to a single, globally integrated market. In other words, what we have may be labeled **semiglobalization**, which is more complex than extremes of total isolation and total globalization. Semiglobalization suggests that barriers to market integration at borders are high, but not high enough to insulate countries from each other completely.[15]

Semiglobalization calls for more than one way of strategizing around the globe. Total isolation on a nation-state basis would suggest localization—a strategy of treating each country as a unique market. An MNE marketing products to 100 countries will need to come up with 100 versions. This strategy is clearly too costly. Total globalization, on the other hand, would lead to standardization—a strategy of treating the entire world as one market. The MNE can just market one version of "world car" or "world drink." But the world obviously is not that simple. Between total isolation and total globalization, semiglobalization has no single right way of doing business around the globe, resulting in a wide variety of experimentations. Overall, (semi)globalization is neither to be opposed as a menace nor to be celebrated as a panacea; it is to be *engaged*.

1-5 A GLANCE AT THE GLOBAL ECONOMY

Twenty-first century business leaders face enormous challenges (see Debate). This book helps overcome some of these challenges. As a backdrop for the remainder of this book, this section offers a basic understanding of the global economy. The global economy in 2013 was an approximately $75 trillion economy (total global GDP calculated at official, nominal exchange rates—alternatively, $100 trillion on a PPP basis).[16] While there is no need to memorize a lot of statistics, it is useful to remember this $75 trillion (or $100 trillion) figure to put things in perspective.

One frequent observation in the globalization debate is the enormous size of multinationals. Take a look at the largest MNE within one sizeable country: Volkswagen's worldwide sales would represent 10% of German GDP, Samsung's sales 17% of South Korean GDP, and BP's sales 26% of British GDP.[17] Exhibit 1.5 shows the most recent top ten firms. The top three largest MNEs—measured by sales—happened to be headquartered in North America, Europe, and Asia. If the largest MNE, Walmart, were an independent country, it would be the 27th largest economy—its sales were smaller than Belgium's GDP but larger than Venezuela's. The sales of

Semiglobalization A perspective that suggests that barriers to market integration at borders are high but not high enough to completely insulate countries from each other.

EXHIBIT 1.5 TOP TEN LARGEST FIRMS IN THE WORLD (MEASURED BY SALES)

	Corporate name	Country	Revenues
1	Walmart Stores	United States	$476 billion
2	Royal Dutch Shell	Netherlands	$460 billion
3	Sinopec Group	China	$457 billion
4	China National Petroleum Corporation	China	$432 billion
5	Exxon Mobil	United States	$408 billion
6	BP	United Kingdom	$396 billion
7	State Grid	China	$333 billion
8	Volkswagen	Germany	$261 billion
9	Toyota Motor	Japan	$256 billion
10	Glencore	Switzerland	$233 billion

Source: Adapted from *Fortune*, "Global 500," 21 July 2014: F-1. Data refer to 2013.

Debate: Ethical Dilemma

The Globalization Debate and You

As a future business leader, you are not a detached reader. The globalization debate directly affects *your* future. Therefore, it is imperative that you participate in the globalization debate instead of letting other people make decisions on globalization that will significantly affect your career, your consumption, and your country. It is important to know your own biases when joining the debate.

By the very act of taking an IB course and reading this book, you probably already have some pro-globalization biases compared to non-business majors elsewhere on campus and the general public in your country. You are not alone. In the last several decades, most executives, policy makers, and scholars in both developed and emerging economies, who are generally held to be the elite in these societies, are biased toward acknowledging the benefits of globalization. Although it is long known that globalization carries both benefits and costs, many of the elite have failed to take into sufficient account the social, political, and environmental costs associated with globalization. However, just because the elite share certain perspectives on globalization does *not* mean that most other members of the society share the same views. To the extent that powerful economic and political institutions are largely controlled by the elite in almost every country, it is not surprising that some anti-globalization groups, feeling powerless, end up resorting to unconventional tactics such as mass protests to make their point.

Many of the opponents of globalization are **nongovernmental organizations (NGOs)** such as environmentalists, human rights activists, and consumer groups. Ignoring them will be a grave failure when doing business around the globe. Instead of viewing NGOs as opponents, many firms view them as partners. NGOs do raise a valid point when they insist that firms, especially MNEs, should have a broader concern for the various stakeholders affected by the MNEs' actions around the world (see Chapter 15 for details).

It is certainly interesting and perhaps alarming to note that as would-be business leaders who will shape the global economy in the future, current business school students already exhibit values and beliefs in favor of globalization similar to those held by executives, policy makers, and scholars, and different from those held by the general public. Shown in Exhibit 1.6, US business students have significantly more positive (almost one-sided) views toward globalization than the general public. While these data are based on US business students, my teaching and lectures around the globe suggest that most business students in the world—regardless of their nationality—seem to share such positive views on globalization. This is not surprising. Both self-selection to study business and socialization within the curriculum, in which free trade is widely regarded as positive, may lead to certain attitudes in favor of globalization. Consequently, business students tend to focus more on the economic gains of globalization and be less concerned with its darker sides.

Nongovernmental organization (NGO) An organization that is not affiliated with governments.

EXHIBIT 1.6 VIEWS ON GLOBALIZATION

Overall, do you think globalization is *good* for…	General public	Business students
…US consumers like you?	68%	96%
…US companies?	63%	77%
…the US economy?	64%	88%
…strengthening poor countries' economies?	75%	82%

Sources: A. Bernstein, "Backlash against globalization," *BusinessWeek*, 24 April 2000: 43; M. W. Peng and H. Shin, "How do future business leaders view globalization?," *Thunderbird International Business Review* 50, no. 3 (2008): 179. All dierences are statistically signi cant.

Current and would-be business leaders need to be aware of their own biases embodied in such one-sided views toward globalization. Since business schools aspire to train future business leaders by indoctrinating students with the dominant values managers hold, these results suggest that business schools may have largely succeeded in this mission. However, to the extent that current managers (and professors) have strategic blind spots, these findings are potentially alarming. They reveal that business students already share these blind spots. Despite possible self-selection in choosing to major in business, there is no denying that student values are shaped, at least in part, by the educational experience business schools provide. Knowing such limitations, business school professors and students need to work especially hard to break out of this mental straitjacket.

In order to combat the widespread tendency to have one-sided, rosy views, a significant portion of this book is devoted to the numerous debates that surround globalization. Debates are systematically introduced in *every* chapter to provoke more critical thinking and discussion. It is debates that drive practice and research forward. Therefore, it is imperative that you be exposed to cutting-edge debates and encouraged to form your own views. In addition, ethics is emphasized throughout the book. At least one Ethical Dilemma feature can be found in each chapter (in this chapter, see the Opening Case and the Closing Case in addition to this Debate box). Two whole chapters are devoted to ethics, norms, and cultures (Chapter 3) and corporate social responsibility (Chapter 15).

Sources: T. Friedman, *The World Is Flat* (New York: Farrar, Straus, and Giroux, 2005); M. W. Peng and E. Pleggenkuhle-Miles, "Current debates in global strategy," *International Journal of Management Reviews* 11 (2009): 51–68; M. W. Peng, S. Sun, and D. Blevins, "The social responsibility of international business scholars," *Multinational Business Review* 19 (2011): 106–119; R. Rajan, *Fautlines* (Princeton, NJ: Princeton University Press, 2010); D. Rodrik, *The Globalization Paradox* (New York: Norton, 2011).

the largest EU-based MNE, Royal Dutch Shell, were larger than the GDP of each of the following EU member countries: Austria, Denmark, Finland, Ireland, and Portugal. The sales of the largest Asia-based MNE, Sinopec, were larger than the GDP of each of the following Asian economies: Hong Kong, Malaysia, Phillippines, Singapore, and Thailand. Today, over 82,000 MNEs manage at least 810,000 subsidiaries overseas.[18] Total annual sales for the largest 500 MNEs exceed $31 trillion (about one third of global output).[19]

Exhibit 1.7 documents the change in the makeup of the 500 largest MNEs. While MNEs from the Triad (North America, Europe, and Japan) dominate the list, their share has been shrinking—thanks to the Great Transformation (discussed earlier). Among MNEs from emerging economies, those from BRIC contribute 118 firms to the *Fortune* Global 500 list. In particular, MNEs from China have come on strong.[20] With 52 *Fortune* Global 500 company headquarters, Beijing now has the heaviest concentration of such headquarters. In comparison, Tokyo has 41 *Fortune* Global 500 headquarters (the world's second heaviest concentration) and New York 20 (third heaviest concentration). Clearly, global rivals cannot afford to ignore emerging multinationals such as those based in Beijing, and students studying this book need to pay attention to these emerging multinationals.

ISTOCKPHOTO.COM/ZONECREATIVE

EXHIBIT 1.7 RECENT CHANGES IN THE *FORTUNE* GLOBAL 500

	2005	2010	2014
Developed economies			
United States	170	133	128
European Union	165	149	128
Japan	70	68	57
Switzerland	12	15	13
Canada	14	11	10
Australia	8	8	8
Emerging economies			
China	20	61	95
India	6	8	8
Brazil	4	7	7
Russia	5	7	8
BRIC	35	83	118

Sources: Compiled from various *Fortune* issues. The most recent *Fortune* Global 500 list (for 2014) was published in *Fortune*, 21 July 2014.

1-6 ORGANIZATION OF THE BOOK

This book has three parts. Part 1 is *foundations*. Following this chapter, Chapters 2, 3, and 4 deal with the two leading perspectives: institution-based and resource-based views. Part 2 covers *tools*, focusing on trade (Chapter 5), foreign investment (Chapter 6), foreign exchange (Chapter 7), and global and regional integration (Chapter 8). Part 3 focuses on *managing* around the world. We start with the internationalization of small, entrepreneurial firms (Chapter 9), followed by ways to enter foreign markets (Chapter 10), to make alliances and acquisitions work (Chapter 11), to strategize, structure, and learn (Chapter 12), to manage human resources (Chapter 13), to deal with marketing and supply chain management (Chapter 14), and finally to manage corporate social responsibility (Chapter 15).

ETHICAL DILEMMA/EMERGING MARKETS

The Rebirth of the East India Company

Before picking up this book, the majority of readers are likely to have already heard of the East India Company. Yes, we are talking about *the* East India Company, the colonial trading company that created British India, founded Hong Kong and Singapore, and introduced tea, coffee, and chocolate to Britain and large parts of the world. Wait a minute—as you scratch your head over your rusty memory from history books—wasn't the company dead? Yes, it was dead—or, technically, dissolved or nationalized in 1874 by the British government. But, no, it was not dead.

After a hiatus of over 130 years, the East India Company was reborn and relaunched in 2005 by a visionary and entrepreneurial Indian businessman Sanjiv Mehta. With permissions granted by the UK Treasury for an undisclosed sum of money, Mumbai-born Mehta became the sole owner, chairman, and CEO of the *new* East India Company with the rights to use the name and original trademarks. His goals were to unlock and strengthen the potential value of the world's first global brand. In 2010, with much fanfare the East India Company launched its first luxury fine foods store in the prestigious Mayfair district of London. In 2014, the East India Company set up a new boutique inside London's most prestigious department store Harrods—a format called "store in store." The initial products included premium coffees and teas, artisan sweet and savory biscuits, an exquisite range of chocolates, and gourmet salts and sugars. While the old company obviously never had a website, the new one proudly announced on its website:

> *We see our role as bringing together the best the world has to offer; to create unique goods that help people to explore and experience what's out there. Products that help people see their world in a different and better light. Products that have the power to amaze and astonish.... The East India Company made a wide range of elusive, exclusive, and exotic ingredients familiar, affordable, and available to the world; ingredients which today form part of our daily and national cuisines. Today we continue to develop and market unique and innovative products that breathe life into the history of the Company. We trade foods crafted by artisans and specialists from around the world, with carefully sourced ingredients, unique recipes, and distinguished provenances.*

Just like the old East India Company, the new company is a "born global" enterprise, which immediately declared its intention to expand globally upon its launch. By 2014 it had expanded throughout Europe (Austria, Finland, France, Germany, the Netherlands, Norway, and Spain), Asia Pacific (Australia, China, Hong Kong, Japan, Malaysia, and South Korea), and the Middle East (Kuwait and Qatar). Its online store can deliver anywhere worldwide. Overall, in the first five years since 2005, the East India Company spent $15 million to develop its new business. In 2011, the Mahindra Group, one of India's most respected business houses, acquired a minority stake in the East India Company. After receiving capital injection from Mahindra, the East India Company announced that it would invest $100 million in the next five years to grow the iconic brand.

LEON NEAL/GETTY IMAGES

What made the (old) East India Company such a household name? Obviously the products it traded had to deliver value to be appreciated by customers around the world. At its peak, it employed a third of the British labor force, controlled half of the world's trade, issued its own coins, managed an army of 200,000, and ruled 90 million Indians. Its organizational capabilities must have been awesome. Equally important was its political abilities to leverage and control the rules of the game around the world, ranging from managing politicians back home in the UK to manipulating political intrigues in India. Granted a royal charter by Queen Elizabeth I in 1600, the old East India Company certainly benefitted from formal backing of the state. Informally, the brand still resonates with the two and a half billion people in the British Commonwealth, especially Indians. Mehta was tremendously moved by the over 14,000 e-mails from Indians all over the world wishing him well when he announced the acquisition. In his own words: "I have not created the brand, history has created it. I am just the curator of it."

Blending continuity and change, the saga of the East India Company continues. Mehta said he believed the East India Company was the Google of its time. But one reporter suggested that "Google is in fact the East India Company of its modern era. Let's see if Google is still around and having the same impact in 400 years' time."

Case Discussion Questions

1. From an institution-based view and a resource-based view, explain what was behind the success and (ultimate) failure of the old East India Company?
2. Visit a (new) East India Company store in (or near) your city or visit its online store. Do you like it? Why?
3. From a resource-based view, explain what is special about the new East India Company?
4. From an institution-based view, predict the likely success or failure of the new East India Company.
5. ***ON ETHICS***: Critics argue that the old East India Company was a vanguard of colonialism and was associated with all the dark shades associated with colonialism. As a spokesperson for the new East India Company, how do you react to such criticisms to defend and promote the new venture?

Sources: "The empire strikes back," *Arabian Business*, 4 October 2014: www.arabianbusiness.com; East India Company, "EIC today," "History," "Press," 2015: www.theeastindiacompany.com; East India Company, "History of fine foods," 2014: www.eicfinefoods.com; "The company that ruled the waves," *Economist*, 17 December 2011: www.economist.com; "Hidden germs," *Economist*, 12 April 2014: www.economist.com.

STUDY TOOLS 1

LOCATED AT THE BACK OF YOUR BOOK:

- ☐ Rip out and study the Chapter Review Card at the end of the book

LOG IN TO WWW.CENGAGEBRAIN.COM TO:

- ☐ Review key term flashcards
- ☐ Complete a practice quiz to test your knowledge of key concepts
- ☐ Take and complete the chapter crossword puzzle
- ☐ Complete interactive content, watch chapter videos, and take a graded quiz
- ☐ Track your knowledge of key concepts in Global Business
- ☐ Read and discuss additional case study content

2 Understanding Politics, Laws, & Economics

LEARNING OBJECTIVES

After studying this chapter, you should be able to. . .

- 2-1 Identify two types of institutions.
- 2-2 Explain how institutions reduce uncertainty.
- 2-3 Identify the two core propositions underpinning an institution-based view of global business.
- 2-4 List the differences between democracy and totalitarianism.
- 2-5 List the differences among civil law, common law, and theocratic law.
- 2-6 Articulate the importance of property rights and intellectual property rights.
- 2-7 List the differences among market economy, command economy, and mixed economy.
- 2-8 Explain why it is important to understand the different institutions when doing business abroad.

After you finish this chapter, go to **PAGE 33** for **STUDY TOOLS**

ETHICAL DILEMMA/EMERGING MARKETS

The Future of Cuba

Cuba is the only practitioner of communism in the Western hemisphere. Five decades of communism have delivered some accomplishments. Life expectancy (at 79 years) is on par with that of the United States, and Cuba has more doctors per 100,000 persons than Britain and France. Social benefits cover everyone from cradle to grave, providing free world-class health care and education in addition to free pensions and funerals. However, people are poor and income is low. The average monthly wage is only $19. Food is often in shortage, forcing the government to ration supply. Cuba's 11 million people enjoy only 600,000 cars, with an average age of 15 years. Half of them belong to the state. Many 1950s vintage cars are still workhorses in the streets.

Raúl Castro, the younger brother of the 88-year-old leader Fidel Castro, took over as Cuba's president in 2008 and as first secretary of the Communist Party in 2011. (For compositional simplicity, this case will refer to each Castro brothers by his first name.) Raúl has been busy, transferring a substantial chunk of the state-owned enterprises (SOEs) to private hands, freeing political prisoners, and signing the UN Convention on Human Rights, something that Fidel had refused to do. While change seems to be in the air, there are limits—after all, Raúl is also a Castro. Neither "reform" nor "transition" is allowed to be mentioned. These words immediately bring back the painful memory of the collapse of the Soviet Union, which overnight withdrew subsidies and traumatized Cuba's leaders. Instead, the changes are labeled "updating," in which "nonstate actors" and "cooperatives" will be tolerated. "But," noted the *Economist*, "whatever the language, this means an emerging private sector."

Thanks to the Soviet collapse, the Cuban economy shrank by a painful 35% between 1989 and 1993. In desperation, Fidel declared a national emergency, opened Cuba for foreign direct investment (FDI) and mass tourism, and legalized small family businesses and the use of the dollar. He also found a new benefactor, Venezuelan president Hugo Chávez, who (prior to his death in 2013) provided Cuba with cheap oil. In exchange, Fidel sent 20,000 doctors and professionals to work in Venezuela. Thus, the regime's widely predicted demise did not materialize. After surviving the emergency, Fidel went back to the old ways. Many family businesses and foreign ventures were shut down, and the dollar ceased to be legal tender in 2004.

This time, Raúl has proclaimed that changes are here to stay. While Fidel has a massive ego and is famously ideological, Raúl is more modest and more pragmatic. Raúl seems to realize that Cuban communism lives on borrowed time. The economy is terribly unproductive. Cuba has a legendary agricultural past—think of its world-famous cigars and sugar. However, state ownership of farms has been disastrous. Output per head of sugar in 2012 has dropped to an eighth of its level in 1958. State farms control 75% of arable land, but 45% of this lies idle. Raúl has allowed private farmers and co-ops to lease idle state land. Yet, private farmers have a hard time scraping a living off the land. This is not because the land is not fertile; it is. It is because of the grip of Acopio, the state-owned monopoly supplier of seeds, fertilizer, and equipment as well as the monopoly purchaser of farm produce. There is hardly a market to motivate farmers to try harder.

In manufacturing and services, SOEs are also notorious for shoddy quality and low pay. But there is one advantage in working for SOEs: plenty of opportunities to pilfer (steal) supplies from the workplace. Employees' justification goes like this: The SOE belongs to the state, which belongs to the people—that is, us. Since our wages are so low, we should feel free to take home the stuff that, after all, belongs to us anyway (!). Experimenting on a limited scale, Raúl has allowed private entrepreneurs to own and operate small shops such as barber shops, beauty parlors, and restaurants, as well as private taxis. Although by global standards, these entrepreneurial opportunities are extremely limited, they nevertheless have attracted well-educated (but starving) professionals, such as teachers, doctors, and accountants. For example, a doctor who used to make $23 per month can now take home $40 in an improvised craft shop.

Slowly but surely, outside influence has arrived. While US firms cannot do business in Cuba, multinationals from Brazil, Canada, China, and Spain have no such institution-based barriers. In 2013, 2.7 million tourists (a record) flocked to Cuba. While the US embargo is still technically in effect, from Miami, eight flights—technically labeled "charter" (not regularly scheduled) flights—go to Havana every day. In 2014, the parliament approved the Foreign Investment Law, which for the first time allows Cubans living abroad to invest in Cuba (unless, according to the foreign minister, they are part of the "Miami terrorist mafia"—otherwise known as the Cuban American community in Miami). Such investors are exempt from profit taxes for eight years, after which, instead of paying tax at the normal 30%, a 15% rate will apply. *Havana Reporter* calls this new law "game changing."

Although still healthy, Raúl is already 84. Given the inescapable "biological factor" (a Cuban euphemism referring to the eventual death of the Castro brothers), the days of the Castros running the show in Cuba are clearly numbered. In December 2014, President Barack Obama announced plans to gradually lift sanctions. Both Obama and Raúl—separately in Washington and Havana—declared interests to restore commercial and diplomatic relations. How does the future hold for Cuba?

Sources: "Revolution in retreat," *Economist*, 24 March 2012: 3–4; "Edging toward capitalism," *Economist*, 24 March 2012, 7–9; "The deal's off," *Economist*, 24 March 2012, 5–7; "The Miami mirror," *Economist*, 24 March 2012, 10–11; "Cuba's economy," *Economist*, 20 July 2013, 33–34; "The new normal," *Economist*, 3 January 2015, 11–12; "Growing interest in Cuban investment opportunities," *Havana Reporter*, 6 May 2014, 14; J. Sweig and M. Bustamante, "Cuba after communism," *Foreign Affairs*, July (2013), 101–114.

What are the benefits and costs of private ownership? What are the pros and cons of state ownership? What are the political ideologies behind such ownership arrangements? Why are the stakes so high? As the Opening Case illustrates, these decisions are affected by institutions, popularly known as the "rules of the game" (first introduced in Chapter 1). As economic players, individuals and firms play by these rules. However, institutions are not static and they may change, as evidenced by the ongoing reforms in Cuba. Such **institutional transitions** are "fundamental and comprehensive changes introduced to the formal and informal rules of the game that affect firms as players."[1]

Overall, the success and failure of firms around the globe are to a large extent determined by firms' ability to understand and take advantage of the different rules of the game. In other words, how firms play the game and win (or lose), at least in part, depends on how the rules are made, enforced, and changed. This calls for firms to constantly monitor, decode, and adapt to the changing rules of the game in order to survive and prosper. As a result, such an institution-based view has emerged as a leading perspective on global business.[2] This chapter first introduces the institution-based view. Then, we focus on *formal* institutions (such as political, legal, and economic systems). *Informal* institutions (such as cultures, ethics, and norms) will be discussed in Chapter 3.

2-1 UNDERSTANDING INSTITUTIONS

Building on the "rules of the game" metaphor, Douglass North, a Nobel laureate in economics, more formally defines institutions as "the humanly devised constraints that structure human interaction."[3] An institutional framework is made up of both the formal and informal institutions governing individual and firm behavior. Richard Scott, a leading sociologist, identifies three pillars that support these institutions: regulatory, normative, and cognitive.[4]

Institutional transition Fundamental and comprehensive changes introduced to the formal and informal rules of the game that affect organizations as players.

Regulatory pillar The coercive power of governments exercised through laws, regulations, and rules.

Normative pillar The mechanisms through which norms influence individual and firm behavior.

Cognitive pillar The internalized, taken-for-granted values and beliefs that guide individual and firm behavior.

Shown in Exhibit 2.1, formal institutions include laws, regulations, and rules. Their primary supportive pillar, the **regulatory pillar**, is the coercive power of governments. For example, out of patriotic duty, many individuals may pay taxes. However, many other individuals pay taxes out of fear—if they did not pay and got caught, they would go to jail. In other words, it is the coercive power of governments' tax laws that forms the regulatory pillar to compel many individuals to pay taxes.

EXHIBIT 2.1 DIMENSIONS OF INSTITUTIONS

Degree of formality	Examples	Supportive pillars
Formal institutions	Laws Regulations Rules	Regulatory (coercive)
Informal institutions	Norms Cultures Ethics	Normative Cognitive

ISTOCKPHOTO.COM/XYNO

On the other hand, informal institutions include norms, cultures, and ethics. Informal institutions are supported by two pillars: normative and cognitive. The **normative pillar** refers to how the values, beliefs, and actions—collectively known as norms—of other relevant players influence the behavior of focal individuals and firms. For example, a recent norm among Western firms is the rush to invest in China and India. This norm has prompted many Western firms to imitate each other without a clear understanding of how to make such moves work. Cautious managers who resist such herding are often confronted by board members and investors with the question "Why are we not in China and India?" In other words, "Why don't we follow the norm?"

The **cognitive pillar** is the second support for informal institutions. It refers to the internalized (or taken-for-granted) values and beliefs that guide individual and firm behavior. For example, whistleblowers reported Enron's wrongdoing out of a belief in what is right and wrong. While most employees may not feel comfortable with organizational wrongdoing, the social norm in any

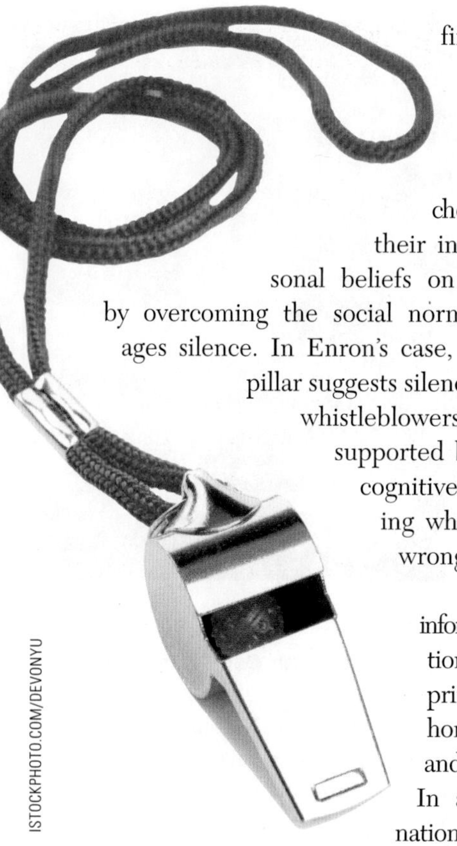

ISTOCKPHOTO.COM/DEVONYU

firm is to shut up and not to rock the boat. Essentially, whistleblowers choose to follow their internalized personal beliefs on what is right by overcoming the social norm that encourages silence. In Enron's case, the normative pillar suggests silence, whereas the whistleblowers' actions are supported by their strong cognitive pillar regarding what is right and wrong.

Formal and informal institutional forces stem primarily from home countries and host countries. In addition, international and regional organizations such as the World Trade Organization (WTO), the International Monetary Fund (IMF), and the European Union (EU) may also influence firm conduct in terms of do's and don'ts. See Chapters 7 and 8 for more details.

2-2 WHAT DO INSTITUTIONS DO?

While institutions do many things, their key role is to *reduce uncertainty*. Specifically, institutions influence the decision-making process of both individuals and firms by signaling what conduct is legitimate and acceptable and what is not. Basically, institutions constrain the range of acceptable actions. Why is it so important to reduce uncertainty? Because uncertainty can be potentially devastating. Political uncertainty such as an uprising may render long-range planning obsolete. Political deadlocks in Washington have made the US government "less stable, less effective, and less predictable," which led Standard & Poor's—a private but influential rating agency—to downgrade its AAA credit rating to AA+.[5] In Focus illustrates some pitfalls of such a lack of predictability. Economic uncertainty such as failure to carry out transactions as spelled out in contracts may result in economic losses. See the Closing Case for the ongoing political and economic uncertainty in Russia and Ukraine.

Uncertainty surrounding economic transactions can lead to **transaction costs**, which are the costs associated with economic transactions or, more broadly, the costs of doing business. Nobel laureate Oliver Williamson makes the comparison to frictions in mechanical systems: "Do the gears mesh, are the parts lubricated, is there needless slippage or other loss of energy?" He goes on to suggest that transaction costs can be regarded as "the economic counterpart of frictions: Do the parties to exchange operate harmoniously, or are there frequent misunderstandings and conflicts?"[6]

An important source of transaction costs is **opportunism**, defined as the act of seeking self-interest with guile. Examples include misleading, cheating, and confusing other parties in transactions that will increase transaction costs. Attempting to reduce such transaction costs, institutional frameworks increase certainty by spelling out the rules of the game so that violations (such as failures to fulfill contracts) can be mitigated with relative ease (such as through formal courts and arbitration).

Without stable institutional frameworks, transaction costs may become prohibitively high, and certain transactions simply would not take place. For example, in the absence of credible institutional frameworks that protect investors, domestic investors may choose to put their money abroad. Although Africa is starving for capital, rich people in Africa put a striking 39% of their assets outside of Africa.[7]

Institutions are not static. Institutional transitions in some emerging economies are so pervasive that these countries are simply called transition economies (a *subset* of emerging economies). Examples include those countries that are moving from central planning to market competition, such as China, Cuba (see the Opening Case), Poland, and Russia. Institutional transitions in these countries as well as other emerging economies such as Brazil, India, and South Africa create both huge challenges and tremendous opportunities for domestic and international firms.

Having outlined the definitions of various institutions and their supportive pillars as well as the key role of institutions in uncertainty reduction, next we will introduce the first core perspective on global business: an institution-based view.

Transaction cost Cost associated with economic transactions or, more broadly, the cost of doing business.

Opportunism The act of seeking self-interest with guile.

InFocus: Ethical Dilemma

Regulating America

AP IMAGES/PABLO MARTINEZ MONSIVAIS

As formal institutions, regulations are supposed to reduce uncertainty. However, the recent proliferation of regulations in the United States seems to enhance uncertainty. The Dodd-Frank law of 2010 has become Exhibit A in this debate. Its aim is noble: to prevent another financial crisis by improving transparency and forbidding banks from taking on excessive risk. But at 848 pages, it is simply too complex. Hardly anyone in America has read Dodd-Frank. Voracious Chinese officials, who pay close attention to regulatory developments elsewhere, half jokingly shared with an *Economist* correspondent that nobody outside Beijing has the stomach to read Dodd-Frank in full. The *Economist* correspondent protested because at least one *Economist* colleague in New York, in order to work on one report, read all the 848 pages of verbiage.

It is not just the mammoth length, but also the uncertainty embedded in Dodd-Frank that makes it very scary to the business community. Of the 400 specific rules it mandates, only 93 have been finalized and the rest is yet to be filled in. So US financial services firms must cope with a law that is "partly unintelligible and partly unknowable." When uncertainty is gradually removed, the true nature of the beast becomes striking. For example, sections 404 and 406 of Dodd-Frank only consume a couple of pages. In October 2011, regulators finally transformed these few pages into a form that hedge funds and other financial services firms must fill out: that form itself goes on and on and on to 192 pages (!). It would cost each firm $100,000–$150,000 the first time it fills the form out, and $40,000 every year after.

Given the princely sum that hedge funds make, perhaps they should just cough up the costs and get the form filled out. But the larger point is whether the benefits outweigh the costs of such complicated rule making. In comparison, the 1864 law that set up America's banking system went to 29 pages. The Federal Reserve Act of 1913 was only 32 pages. The Glass-Steagall law, which was a response to the earlier Wall Street crash of 1929, ran to only 37 pages. Dodd-Frank is 23 times longer than Glass-Steagall.

ISTOCKPHOTO.COM/HENRIK5000

Although extreme in its length, Dodd-Frank is part of a wider trend of increasingly complicated rule making and ever increasing costs of compliance. The Sarbanes-Oxley (SOX) law, enacted a decade ago to prevent Enron-style frauds, successfully made it so hard to list shares on US stock exchanges that US firms increasingly list elsewhere or go private, whereas foreign firms shy away from US listings. The upshot? US share of global initial public offerings (IPOs) dropped from 67% in 2002 (when SOX passed) to 16% in 2011. BB&T, a regional bank, disclosed the following in its annual filing to the SEC: "Additional regulations resulting from Dodd-Frank may materially adversely affect BB&T's business, financial condition, or results of operations." Given that banks and numerous other firms have to lay off employees to stay afloat, one has to wonder how many jobs have been (or will be) destroyed by these new regulations. Not surprisingly, the *Economist* has nicknamed Dodd-Frank "Dodd-Frankenstein."

Sources: "Over-regulated America," *Economist*, 18 February 2012, 9; "Too big not to fail," *Economist*, 18 February 2012, 22–24.

2-3 AN INSTITUTION-BASED VIEW OF GLOBAL BUSINESS

Shown in Exhibit 2.2, an institution-based view of global business focuses on the dynamic interaction between institutions and firms, and considers firm behavior as the outcome of such an interaction. Specifically, firm behavior is often a reflection of the formal and informal constraints of a particular institutional framework. In short, institutions matter.

How do institutions matter? The institution-based view suggests two core propositions (see Exhibit 2.3). First, managers and firms *rationally* pursue their interests and make choices within institutional constraints. In Brazil, government tax revenues at all levels reach 35% of GDP, much higher than Mexico's 18% and China's 16%. Not surprisingly, the gray market in Brazil accounts for a much higher percentage of the economy than in Mexico and China.[8] Likewise, in the United States, the government's proposal to tax the overseas earnings of US-based multinationals, which

EXHIBIT 2.2 INSTITUTIONS, FIRMS, AND FIRM BEHAVIORS

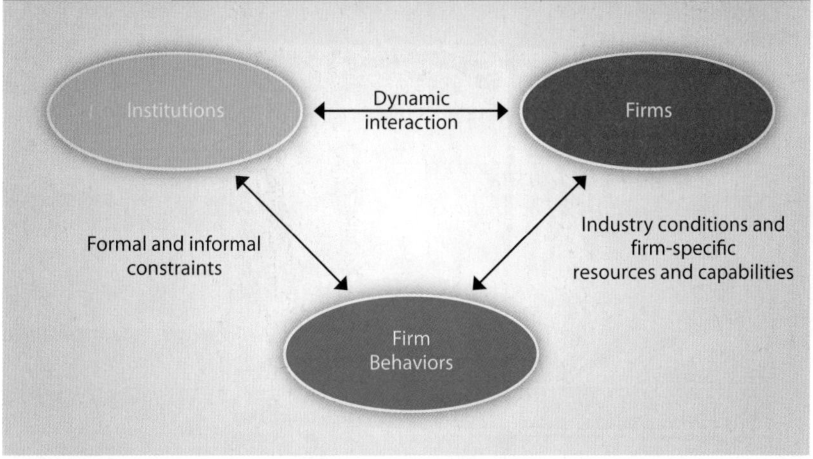

are currently exempt from US taxes, met fierce resistance from the business community. Having already paid overseas taxes, US-based multinationals naturally resented having to pay $190 billion extra US taxes, when their global competitors pay lower taxes. "Doesn't the Obama administration recognize that most big US companies are multinationals that happen to be headquartered in the United States?" asked Duncan Niederauer, CEO of NYSE Euronext in a *BusinessWeek* interview.[9] One case in point is Seagate Technology, a formerly Silicon Valley-based disk-drive maker that incorporated in the Cayman Islands a few years ago.[10] Avoidance of such a financial hit was one of the reasons behind Seagate's move, and more US-based multinationals are likely to follow Seagate.[11] Both Brazilian firms' migration to the gray market and US firms' interest in migrating overseas are rational responses when they pursue their interests within formal institutional constraints in these countries.

Second, while formal and informal institutions combine to govern firm behavior, informal constraints play a *larger* role in reducing uncertainty and providing constancy for managers and firms in situations where formal constraints are unclear or fail. For example, when the former Soviet Union collapsed and with it the formal regime, the growth of many entrepreneurial firms was facilitated by informal constraints based on personal relationships and connections (called *blat* in Russian) among managers and officials.

Many observers have the impression that relying on informal connections is relevant only to firms in emerging economies and that firms in developed economies pursue only market-based strategies. This is far from the truth. Even in developed economies, formal rules make up only a small (though important) part of institutional constraints, and informal constraints are pervasive. Just as firms compete in product markets, firms also fiercely compete in the political marketplace characterized by informal relationships.[12] Basically, if a firm cannot be a market leader, it may still beat the competition on other grounds—namely, the nonmarket, political environment. In September 2008, a rapidly failing Merrill Lynch was able to sell itself to Bank of America for $50 billion. Supported by US government officials, this mega deal was arranged over 48 hours (shorter than the time most people take to buy a car) and the negotiations took place *inside* the Federal Reserve building in New York. In contrast, Lehman Brothers failed to secure government support and had to file for bankruptcy. Overall, the skillful use of a country's institutional frameworks to acquire advantage is at the heart of the institution-based view.

While there are numerous formal and informal institutions, in this chapter we focus on *formal* institutions. (Informal institutions will be covered in Chapter 3.) Chief among formal institutions are political systems, legal systems, and economic systems. We introduce each in turn.

EXHIBIT 2.3 TWO CORE PROPOSITIONS OF THE INSTITUTION-BASED VIEW

1. Managers and firms *rationally* pursue their interests and make choices within the formal and informal constraints in a given institutional framework.
2. While formal and informal institutions combine to govern firm behavior, in situations where formal constraints are unclear or fail, informal constraints will play a *larger* role in reducing uncertainty and providing constancy to managers and firms.

ISTOCKPHOTO.COM/BLACKRED

2-4 POLITICAL SYSTEMS

A **political system** refers to the rules of the game on how a country is governed politically. At the broadest level, there are two primary political systems: democracy and totalitarianism. This section first outlines these two

Political system The rules of the game on how a country is governed politically.

systems and then discusses their ramifications for political risk.

ATTILA JANDI/SHUTTERSTOCK.COM

2-4a Democracy

Democracy is a political system in which citizens elect representatives to govern the country on their behalf. Usually, the political party with the majority of votes wins and forms a government. Democracy was pioneered by the Athenians in ancient Greece. In today's world, Great Britain has the longest experience of running a democracy (by history), and India has the largest democracy (by population).

A fundamental aspect of democracy that is relevant to global business is an individual's right to freedom of expression and organization. For example, starting up a firm is an act of economic expression, essentially telling the rest of the world: "I want to be my own boss! And I want to make some money!" In most modern democracies, the right to organize economically has been extended not only to domestic individuals and firms, but also to *foreign* individuals and firms that come to do business. While those of us fortunate enough to have been brought up in a democracy take the right to establish a firm for granted, we should be reminded that this may not necessarily be the case under other political systems. Before the 1980s, if someone dared to formally establish a private firm in the former Soviet Union, he or she would have been arrested and *shot* by the authorities.

2-4b Totalitarianism

On the opposite end of the political spectrum from democracy is **totalitarianism** (also known as **dictatorship**), which is defined as a political system in which one person or party exercises absolute political control over the population. There are four major types of totalitarianism:

- *Communist totalitarianism* centers on a communist party. This system was embraced throughout Central and Eastern Europe and the former Soviet Union until the late 1980s. It is still practiced in China, Cuba (see the Opening Case), Laos, North Korea, and Vietnam.
- *Right-wing totalitarianism* is characterized by its intense hatred of communism. One party, typically backed by the military, restricts political freedom because its members believe that such freedom would lead to communism. In the decades following World War II, Argentina, Brazil, Chile, South Africa, South Korea, and Taiwan practiced right-wing totalitarianism. Most of these countries have recently become democracies.
- *Theocratic totalitarianism* refers to the monopolization of political power in the hands of one religious party or group. Iran and Saudi Arabia are leading examples.
- *Tribal totalitarianism* refers to one tribe or ethnic group (which may or may not be the majority of the population) monopolizing political power and oppressing other tribes or ethnic groups. Rwanda's bloodbath in the 1990s was due to some of the most brutal practices of tribal totalitarianism.

Democracy A political system in which citizens elect representatives to govern the country on their behalf.

Totalitarianism (dictatorship) A political system in which one person or party exercises absolute political control over the population.

2-4c Political Risk

While the degree of hostility toward business varies among different types of totalitarianism (some can be more pro-business than others), totalitarianism in general is not as good for business as democracy. Totalitarian countries often experience wars, riots, protests, chaos, and breakdowns. As a result, these countries often suffer from a high level of **political risk**, which is a risk associated with political changes that may negatively impact domestic and foreign firms. The most extreme political risk may lead to nationalization (expropriation) of foreign assets. This happened in many totalitarian countries from the 1950s through the 1970s. It has not become a thing of the past. Recently, Argentina expropriated the assets of YPF—the subsidiary of a major Spanish oil firm Repsol. Zimbabwe demanded that foreign mining companies cede 51% of their equity without compensation.[13] It is hardly surprising that foreign firms are sick and tired and would rather go to "greener pastures" elsewhere.

Firms operating in democracies also confront political risk, but such risk is qualitatively different than that in totalitarian countries. For example, Scotland's potential independence from the rest of the UK creates some political risk.[14] Although firms highly exposed to Scotland experience some drop in their stock price, there is no general collapse of stock price in the UK or flight of capital out of the country.[15] Investors are confident that should Scotland become independent, the British democracy is mature enough to manage the breakup process in a relatively nondisruptive way.

Obviously, when two countries are at each other's throats, we can forget about doing business between them. No two democracies have reportedly gone to war with each other. In this regard, the recent advance of democracy and retreat of totalitarianism is highly beneficial for global business. It is not a coincidence that globalization took off in the 1990s, a period during which both communist and right-wing totalitarianism significantly lost its power and democracy expanded around the world (see Chapter 1).

Is democracy conducive to economic growth? While champions of democracy shout "Yes!" the fastest-growing major economy in the last three decades, China, remains totalitarian. The growth rate of India, the world's largest democracy, in the same period is only about half of China's. In another example, Russia grew faster under Putin's more authoritarian rule during the 2000s compared with the 1990s, when Russia was presumably more democratic under Yeltsin (see the Closing Case). On the other hand, no one can seriously argue the case for totalitarianism in order to facilitate economic development. In an influential 2012 paper concerned about the decline of US competitiveness and the rise of Chinese competitiveness, strategy guru Michael Porter nevertheless wrote that "We do not want to copy China, whose speed comes partly from a political system unacceptable to Americans."[16] The few examples of "benign" totalitarian regimes that delivered strong economic growth, such as South Korea and Taiwan, have become democracies in the last three decades. Overall, there is no doubt that democracy has spread around the world (from 69 countries in the 1980s to 120 in the 2000s). However, whether democracy necessarily leads to strong economic development is still subject to debate.[17]

2-5 LEGAL SYSTEMS

A **legal system** refers to the rules of the game on how a country's laws are enacted and enforced. By specifying the do's and don'ts, a legal system reduces transaction costs by minimizing uncertainty and combating opportunism. This section first introduces three different legal traditions and then discusses crucial issues associated with property rights and intellectual property.

2-5a Civil Law, Common Law, and Theocratic Law

Laws in different countries typically are not enacted from scratch but are often transplanted—voluntarily or otherwise—from three legal traditions (or legal families): civil law, common law, and theocratic law. Each is introduced here.

Civil law was derived from Roman law and strengthened by Napoleon's France. It is "the oldest, the most influential, and the most widely distributed around the world."[18] It uses comprehensive statutes and codes as a primary means to form legal judgments. Over 80 countries practice civil law. **Common law**, which is English in origin, is shaped by precedents and traditions from previous judicial decisions. Common law has spread to all English-speaking countries, most of which were at one time British colonies.

Political risk Risk associated with political changes that may negatively impact domestic and foreign firms.

Legal system The rules of the game on how a country's laws are enacted and enforced.

Civil law A legal tradition that uses comprehensive statutes and codes as a primary means to form legal judgments.

Common law A legal tradition that is shaped by precedents from previous judicial decisions.

Relative to civil law, common law has more flexibility because judges have to resolve specific disputes based on their *interpretation* of the law, and such interpretation may give new meaning to the law, which will in turn shape future cases. Civil law has less flexibility because judges have the power only to *apply* the law. Thus civil law is less confrontational because comprehensive statutes and codes serve to guide judges. Common law, on the other hand, is more confrontational because plaintiffs and defendants, through their lawyers, must argue and help judges to favorably interpret the law largely based on precedents. This confrontation is great material for movies. You may have seen common law in action in Hollywood movies such as *A Few Good Men, Devil's Advocate,* and *Legally Blond*. In contrast, you probably have rarely seen a civil law court in action in movies—you have not missed much because civil law lacks the drama and its proceedings tend to be boring.

The third legal family is **theocratic law**, a legal system based on religious teachings. Examples include Jewish and Islamic laws. Although Jewish law is followed by some elements of the Israeli population, it is *not* formally embraced by the Israeli government. Islamic law is the only surviving example of a theocratic legal system that is formally practiced by some governments, including those in Iran and Saudi Arabia. Despite the popular characterization of Islam as anti-business, it is important to note that Mohammed was a merchant trader and that the tenets of Islam are pro-business in general. However, the holy book of Islam, the Koran, does advise against *certain* business practices. In Saudi Arabia, McDonald's operates "ladies only" restaurants in order to comply with the Koran's ban on direct, face-to-face contact between unrelated men and women (who often wear a veil) in public. Moreover, banks in Saudi Arabia have to maintain two retail branches: one for male customers staffed by men and another for female customers staffed by women. This requirement obviously increases property, overhead, and personnel costs. To reduce costs, some foreign banks such as HSBC staff their back office operations with both male and female employees who work side by side.

Overall, legal systems form the first regulatory pillar that supports institutions. They directly impose do's and don'ts on businesses around the globe. Of a legal system's numerous components, two of these, property rights and intellectual property, are discussed next.

2-6 PROPERTY RIGHTS AND INTELLECTUAL PROPERTY RIGHTS

2-6a Property Rights

One fundamental economic function that a legal system serves is to protect **property rights**, which are the legal rights to use an economic property (resource) and to derive income and benefits from it. Examples of property include homes, offices, and factories.

What difference do property rights supported by a functioning legal system make? A lot. Why did developed economies become developed? (Remember, for example, the United States was a "developing" or "emerging" economy 100 years ago.) While there are many answers, a leading answer, most forcefully put forward by Hernando de Soto, a Peruvian economist, focuses on the protection of property rights.[19] In developed economies, every parcel of land, every building, and every trademark is represented in a property document that entitles the owner to derive income and benefits from it. That property document is also important when violators are prosecuted through legal means.

When a legal system is stable and predictable, tangible property also makes other, less tangible economic activities possible. For example, property can be used as collateral for credit. The single most important source of funds for new start-ups in the United States is the mortgage of entrepreneurs' houses. But this cannot be done without documented right to the property. If you live in a house but cannot produce a title document specifying that you are the legal owner of the house (which is a very common situation throughout the developing world, especially in shantytowns), no bank in the world will allow you to use your house as collateral for credit. To start up a new firm, you end up borrowing funds from family members,

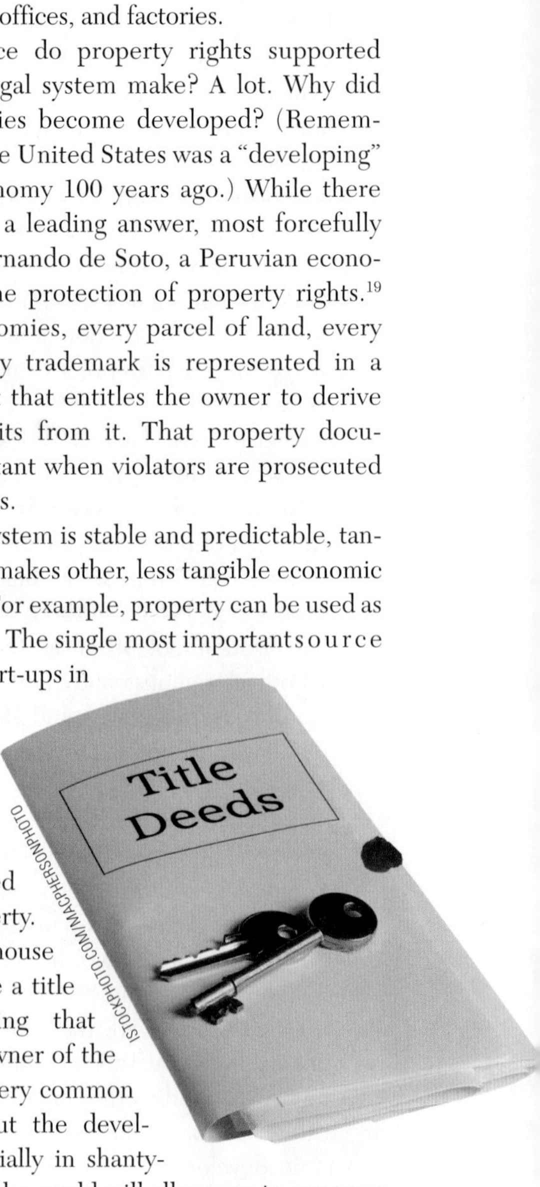

ISTOCKPHOTO.COM/MACPHERSONPHOTO

Theocratic law A legal system based on religious teachings.

Property right Legal right to use an economic property (resource) and to derive income and benefits from it.

friends, and other acquaintances through *informal* means. But funds through informal means are almost certainly more limited than funds that could have been provided formally by banks. Insecure property rights are why, in general, the average firm size in the developing world is smaller than that in the developed world. Insecure property rights also result in using technologies that employ little fixed capital ("cash and carry" is the best) and do not entail long-term investment (such as research and development [R&D]). These characteristics of firms in developing economies do not bode well in global competition where leading firms reap benefits from economies of scale, capital-intensive technologies, and sustained investment in R&D. What the developing world lacks and desperately needs is formal protection of property rights in order to facilitate economic growth.

2-6b Intellectual Property Rights

While the term "property" traditionally refers to *tangible* pieces of property such as land, **intellectual property (IP)** specifically refers to *intangible* property that is the result of intellectual activity (such as the content of books, videos, and websites). **Intellectual property rights (IPR)** are legal rights associated with the ownership of intellectual property. IPR primarily include rights associated with patents, copyrights, and trademarks.

- **Patents** are legal rights awarded by government authorities to inventors of new products or processes. The inventors are given exclusive (monopoly) rights for a period of time to derive income from such inventions through activities such as manufacturing, licensing, or selling.
- **Copyrights** are the exclusive legal rights of authors and publishers to publish and disseminate their work. For example, the book you are reading now is protected by copyright.
- **Trademarks** are the exclusive legal rights of firms to use specific names, brands, and designs to differentiate their products from others.

ISTOCKPHOTO.COM/DELIORMANLI

IPR need to be asserted and enforced through a *formal* system designed to provide an incentive for people and firms to innovate.[20] To be effective, the system must also punish violators. But the intangible nature of IPR makes enforcement difficult. **Piracy**, or unauthorized use of IPR, is widespread around the world. Acts of piracy range from unauthorized sharing of music files to deliberate counterfeiting of branded products.

Overall, an institution-based view suggests that the key to understanding IPR violation is realizing that violators are not amoral monsters but ordinary people and firms. When filling out a survey on "What is your dream career?" no high school graduate anywhere in the world will answer "Counterfeiting." Nevertheless, thousands of individuals and firms *voluntarily* choose to be involved in this business worldwide. Why? Because IPR protection is weak in many countries. In other words, given an institutional environment of weak IPR protection, violators have made a rational decision by investing in the skills in and knowledge of counterfeiting (see Proposition 1 in Exhibit 2.3). For example, counterfeiters in China will be criminally prosecuted only if their profits exceed approximately $10,000. No counterfeiters are dumb enough to keep records to show that they make that much money. If caught, they can usually get away by paying a small fine. Stronger IPR protection may significantly reduce the incentive to be involved in piracy and counterfeiting. However, IP reforms to criminalize *all* counterfeiting activities regardless of the amount of profits, which have been discussed in China, may significantly reduce counterfeiters' incentive.

2-7 ECONOMIC SYSTEMS

2-7a Market, Command, and Mixed Economies

An **economic system** refers to the rules of the game on how a country is governed economically. A pure **market economy** is characterized by the "invisible hand" of market forces first noted in 1776 by Adam Smith in *The Wealth of Nations*. The government takes a *laissez faire* (hands-off)

Intellectual property (IP) Intangible property that results from intellectual activity (such as the content of books, videos, and websites).

Intellectual property right (IPR) Legal right associated with the ownership of intellectual property.

Patent Exclusive legal right of inventors to derive income from their inventions through activities such as manufacturing, licensing, or selling.

Copyright Exclusive legal right of authors and publishers to publish and disseminate their work.

Trademark Exclusive legal right of firms to use specific names, brands, and designs to differentiate their products from others.

Piracy The unauthorized use of intellectual property rights.

Economic system The rules of the game on how a country is governed economically.

Market economy An economy that is characterized by the "invisible hand" of market forces.

approach. Theoretically, all factors of production should thus be privately owned. The government performs only functions the private sector cannot perform, such as providing roads and defense.

A pure **command economy** is defined by a government taking, in the words of Vladimir Lenin, the "commanding heights" in the economy. Theoretically, all factors of production should be state owned and state controlled, and all supply, demand, and pricing are planned by the government. During the heydays of communism, the former Soviet Union and China approached such an ideal.

A **mixed economy**, by definition, has elements of both a market economy and a command economy. It boils down to the relative distribution of market forces versus command forces. In practice, no country has ever completely embraced Adam Smith's ideal *laissez faire* approach. Question: Which economy has the highest degree of economic freedom (the lowest degree of government intervention in the economy)? Hint: Given extensive government intervention (such as bailouts) since 2008, it is obviously *not* the United States. Answer: A series of surveys report that it is Hong Kong (the post-1997 handover to Chinese sovereignty does not make a difference). The crucial point here is that there is still some noticeable government intervention in the economy, even in Hong Kong. During the aftermath of the 1997 economic crisis when the share price of all Hong Kong firms took a nose dive, the Hong Kong government took a highly controversial course of action. It used government funds to purchase 10% of the shares of all the blue chip firms listed in the Hang Seng index. This action slowed down the sliding of share prices and stabilized the economy, but it turned all the blue chip firms into state-owned enterprises (SOEs)—at least 10% owned by the state. In 2008, US and European governments did something similar, nationalizing a large chunk of their failing banks and financial services firms via bailouts and turning them into SOEs (see the Debate).

Command economy An economy in which theoretically all factors of production are state-owned and state-controlled, and all supply, demand, and pricing are planned by the government.

Mixed economy An economy that has elements of both a market economy and a command economy.

Likewise, no country has ever had a complete command economy, not even in the Eastern Bloc during the Cold War. Poland never nationalized its agriculture. Hungarians were known to have second (and private!) jobs, while all of them theoretically worked only for the state. Black markets hawking agricultural produce and small merchandise existed in practically all former communist countries. While the former Soviet Union and Central and Eastern European countries have recently thrown away communism, ongoing practitioners of communism such as China and Vietnam have embraced

Debate: Ethical Dilemma/Emerging Markets

Private Ownership Versus State Ownership

Private ownership is good. State (or public) ownership is bad. Although crude, these two statements fairly accurately summarize the intellectual and political reasoning behind three decades of privatization around the world since the early 1980s. As providers of capital, private owners are otherwise known as capitalists, and their central role in the economic system gives birth to the term "capitalism." State ownership emphasizes the social and public nature of economic ownership, and leads to the coinage of the term "socialism." Both forms of ownership have their pros and cons. The debate is which form of ownership is better—whether the pros outweigh the cons.

The debate on private versus state ownership underpins much of the global economic evolution since the early 20th century. It was the failure of capitalism, most disastrously embodied in the Great Depression (1929–1933), that made the Soviet-style socialism centered on state ownership shine. Numerous elites in developing countries and a nontrivial number of scholars in developed economies noticed this. As a result, in postwar decades, state ownership was on the march, and private ownership was in decline. State ownership was not only extensive throughout the former Eastern bloc (the former Soviet Union, Central and Eastern Europe, China, Vietnam, and Cuba), but was also widely embraced throughout developed economies in Western Europe.

However, state-owned enterprises (SOEs) typically suffered from a lack of accountability and a lack of concern for economic efficiency. SOEs were known to feature relatively equal pay between the executives and the rank and file. Since extra work did not translate into extra pay, employees had little incentive to improve their work. Given the generally low pay and the non-demanding work environment, former Soviet SOE employees summed it well: "They pretend to pay us, and we pretend to work."

Britain's prime minister Margaret Thatcher privatized a majority of British SOEs in the 1980s. Very soon, SOEs throughout Central and Eastern Europe followed suit. After the Soviet Union collapsed, the new Russian government unleashed some of the most aggressive privatization schemes in the 1990s. Eventually, the privatization movement became global, reaching Brazil, India, China, Vietnam, and many other countries. In no small part, such a global movement was championed by the **Washington Consensus**, spearheaded by the US government and two Washington-based international organizations: the International Monetary Fund (IMF) and the World Bank. A core value of the Washington Consensus is the unquestioned belief in the superiority of private ownership over state ownership. The widespread privatization movement suggested that the Washington Consensus clearly won the day—or it seemed.

Unfortunately, the pendulum suddenly swung back in 2008. During the Great Recession (2008–2009), major governments in developed economies, led by the US government, bailed out numerous failing private firms using public funds, effectively turning them into SOEs. As a result, the arguments in favor of private ownership and "free market" capitalism collapsed. Since SOEs had such a dreadful reputation (essentially a "dirty word"), the US government has refused to acknowledge that it has SOEs. Instead, it admits that the United States has government-sponsored enterprises (GSEs). GSEs include the General Motors (GM), whose new nickname is "Government Motors," and Citigroup, which has become "Citigovernment."

Critics argue that despite noble goals to rescue the economy, protect jobs, and fight recession, government bailouts serve to heighten **moral hazard**—recklessness when people and organizations (including firms and governments) do not have to face the full consequences of their actions. In other words, capitalism without the risk of failure becomes socialism. It is long known that executives in SOEs face a "soft budget constraint" in that they can always dip into state coffers to cover their losses. When executives in private firms who make risky decisions to "bet the farm" find out when these decisions turn sour, their firms do not go under—thanks to generous bailouts—they are likely to embrace more risk in the future. In other words, bailouts foster the kind of thinking among executives regarding state coffers and taxpayer dollars: "Heads I win, tails you lose." Per Proposition 1 (Exhibit 2.3), these executives are being perfectly rational: Taking on risks, if successful, will enrich their private firms, their owners (shareholders), and themselves; if unsuccessful, Uncle Sam will come to the rescue.

Far from being swept to the dustbin of history, SOEs as an organizational form have shown some amazing longevity. Today, SOEs represent approximately 10% of the global GDP. Even in developed (OECD member) countries, they command 5% of the GDP. From the ashes of the Washington Consensus emerged a **Beijing Consensus**, which centers on state ownership and government intervention. Anchored by SOEs, China over the past 30 years has grown its GDP by 9.5% a year and its international trade volume by 18% a year. SOEs represent 80% of China's stock market capitalization. But China is not alone. In Russia the figure is 62%, in Brazil 38%, and in Norway 37%. In 2014, SOEs occupied four spots among the top ten largest firms worldwide (measured by sales)—China's SINOPEC (#3), CNPC (#4), and State Grid (#7) as well as Germany's Volkswagen (#8). SOEs also represented six of the top ten most *profitable* firms globally (measured by amount of profits)—Fannie Mae (#2) and Freddie Mac (#3) of the United States, ICBC of China (#4), Gazprom of Russia (#5), China Construction Bank (#7) and Agriculture Bank of China (#10).

Sources: P. Bernstein, "The moral hazard economy," *Harvard Business Review* July (2009), 101–102; G. Bruton, M. W. Peng, D. Ahlstrom, C. Stan, and K. Xu, "State-owned enterprises around the world as hybrid organizations," *Academy of Management Perspectives* 29 (2015): 92–114; "Global 500," *Fortune*, 21 July 2014; S. Harrington, "Moral hazard and the meltdown," *Wall Street Journal*, 23 May 2009; M. W. Peng, *Business Strategies in Transition Economies* (Thousand Oaks, CA: Sage, 2000); M. W. Peng, G. Bruton, and C. Stan, "Theories of the (state-owned) firm," working paper, University of Texas at Dallas (2014); "The rise of state capitalism," *Economist*, 21 January 2012, 11.

Washington Consensus A view centered on the unquestioned belief in the superiority of private ownership over state ownership in economic policy making, which is often spearheaded by the US government and the two Washington-based international organizations: the International Monetary Fund and the World Bank.

Moral hazard Recklessness when people and organizations (including firms and governments) do not have to face the full consequences of their actions.

Beijing Consensus A view that questions Washington Consensus' belief in the superiority of private ownership over state ownership, which is often associated with the position held by the Chinese government.

DNY59/GETTY IMAGES

market reforms. Cuba has a lot of foreign-invested hotels (see the Opening Case). Even North Korea is now interested in attracting foreign investment.

Overall, the economic system of most countries is a mixed economy. In practice, when we say a country has a market economy, it is really a shorthand version for a country that organizes its economy *mostly* (but not completely) by market forces and that still has certain elements of a command economy. China, France, Russia, Sweden, and the United States all claim to have a market economy now, but the meaning is different in each country. In other words, "free markets" are not totally free. It boils down to a matter of degree. It seems prudent to drop the "F" word ("free") from the term "free market economy." Instead, it makes sense to acknowledge the variety of capitalism, with each version of "market economy" differing in some ways.[21]

EVERETT HISTORICAL/SHUTTERSTOCK.COM

Adam Smith

2-7b What Drives Economic Development?

Regardless of the economic system used, developing the economy is one of the aims for most governments. The differences in economic development around the globe are striking (see PengAtlas Map 4). The highest and lowest per capita income countries in the world are Norway ($76,450) and Burundi ($110). Why are some countries such as Norway so developed (rich), while others such as Burundi are so underdeveloped (poor)? More generally, what drives economic development in different countries? Scholars and policy makers have been debating this important question since Adam Smith. Various debate points boil down to three explanations: (1) culture, (2) geography, and (3) institutions.

The culture side argues that rich countries tend to have a smarter and harder working population driven by a stronger motivation for success, such as the Protestant work ethic identified by Max Weber over a century ago. Still, it is difficult to imagine that Norwegians are, on average, over *700 times* smarter and harder working than Burundians. This line of thinking, bordering on racism, is no longer acceptable in the 21st century.

The geography school of thought suggests that rich countries tend to be well endowed with natural resources. But one can easily point out that some poor countries also possess rich natural resources, while some rich countries are very poor in natural resources. The Democratic Republic of the Congo (formerly Zaire) is rich in diamonds, oil and natural gas, water, timber, and minerals, while Denmark and Japan lack significant natural resources. In addition, some countries are believed to be cursed by their poor geographic location, which may be landlocked (such as Malawi) and/or located near the hot equator zone and infested with tropical diseases (such as Burundi). This argument is not convincing either, because some landlocked countries (such as Switzerland) are phenomenally well developed and some countries near the equator (such as Singapore) have accomplished enviable growth. Clearly, geography is important, but it is not destiny.

A third side of the debate argues that institutions are "the basic determinants of the performance of an economy."[22] Because institutions provide the incentive structure of a society, formal political, legal, and economic systems have a significant impact on economic development by affecting the incentives and the costs of doing business.[23] In short, rich countries are rich because they have developed better market-supporting institutional frameworks. Consider these points:

- The presence of formal, market-supporting institutions encourages individuals to specialize and firms to grow in size. This is the "division of labor" thesis first advanced by Adam Smith (see Chapter 5). Specialization is economically advantageous because firms are able to grow to capture the gains from transactions with distant trading partners. For example, as China's market institutions progress, many Chinese firms have grown substantially. In 2014, 91 Chinese firms were among the *Fortune* Global 500 largest firms in the world (measured by sales). There were none in 1984.
- A lack of strong, formal, market-supporting institutions forces individuals to trade on an informal basis with a small neighboring group. The term "cash and carry" says it all (!). This forces firms to remain small and local in nature, as are most firms in Africa. Over 40% of Africa's economy is reportedly informal, the highest proportion in the world.[24]

ISTOCKPHOTO.COM/HENRIK5000

- Formal, market-supporting institutions that protect property rights fuel more innovation, entrepreneurship, and thus economic growth. While spontaneous innovation has existed throughout history, why has its pace accelerated significantly since the Industrial Revolution starting in the 1700s? A big factor was the Statute of Monopolies enacted in Great Britain in 1624, which was the world's first patent law to formally protect the IPR of inventors and make innovation financially lucrative.[25] This law has been imitated around the world. Its impact is still felt today, as we now expect continuous innovation to be the norm—think of the doubling of computing power every couple of years. This would not have happened had there not been a system of IPR protection that protects and rewards innovation.

These arguments, of course, are the backbone of the institution-based view of global business, which has clearly won this debate.

2-8 MANAGEMENT SAVVY

Focusing on *formal* institutions, this chapter has sketched the contours of an institution-based view of global business. How does the institution-based view help us answer our fundamental question of utmost concern to managers around the globe: What determines the success and failure of firms around the globe? In a nutshell, this chapter suggests that firm performance is determined, at least in part, by the institutional frameworks governing firm behavior. It is the growth of the firm that, in the aggregate, leads to the growth of the economy. Not surprisingly, most developed economies are supported by strong, effective, and market-supporting formal institutions, and most underdeveloped economies are pulled back by weak, ineffective, and market-depressing formal institutions. In other words, when markets work smoothly in developed economies, formal market-supporting institutions are almost invisible and taken for granted. However, when markets work poorly, the absence of strong formal institutions may become conspicuous.

For managers doing business around the globe, this chapter suggests two broad implications for action (see Exhibit 2.4). First, managerial choices are made rationally within the constraints of a given institutional framework. Therefore, managers aiming to enter a new country need to do their homework by having a thorough understanding of the formal institutions affecting their business. The rules for doing business in a democratic market economy are certainly different from the rules in a totalitarian command economy. In short, "When in Rome, do as the Romans do." While this is a good start, managers also need to understand *why* "Romans" do things in a certain way by studying the formal institutions governing "Roman" behavior.

EXHIBIT 2.4 IMPLICATIONS FOR ACTION

- When entering a new country, do your homework and have a thorough understanding of the formal institutions governing firm behavior.
- When doing business in countries with a strong propensity for informal relational exchanges, insisting on formalizing the contract right away may backfire.

Second, while this chapter has focused on the role of formal institutions, managers should follow the advice of the second proposition of the institution-based view: In situations where formal constraints are unclear or fail, informal constraints such as relationship norms will play a *larger* role in reducing uncertainty. If, for example, you are doing business in a country with a strong propensity for informal, relational exchanges, it may not be a good idea to insist on formalizing the contract right away; such a plan could backfire. Because such countries often have relatively weak legal systems, personal relationship building is often used to substitute for the lack of strong legal protection. Attitudes such as "business first, relationship afterwards" (have a drink *after* the negotiation) may clash with the norm that puts things the other way around (lavish entertainment first, talk about business later). We often hear that, because of their culture, the Chinese prefer to cultivate personal relationships (*guanxi*) first. This is *not* entirely true. Investing in personal relationships up front may simply be the initial cost one has to pay if interested in eventually doing business together, given the absence of a strong and credible legal and regulatory regime in China. In other words, the value on personal relationships has as much to do with the absence of institutional constraints as it does with cultural norms. In fact, personal relationships are key to business in a broad range of countries from Argentina to Zimbabwe, each with *different* cultural traditions. So the interest in cultivating what the Chinese call *guanxi*, the Russians call *blat* or *sistema*, or the Vietnamese call *guan he* is not likely to be driven by culture alone, but more likely by these countries' common lack of formal market-supporting institutions.

ETHICAL DILEMMA/EMERGING MARKETS
The Peril and Promise of Russia

Russia is not the Soviet Union. But what is it? Despite the extraordinary transitions moving from a centrally planned economy to a market economy and from a totalitarian regime to a democracy, most of the news we read (in the West) on Russia is negative. Corruption is widespread (Russia ranks 146th out of 180 countries, according to Transparency International). In 2004, Russia was downgraded from "Partly Free" to "Not Free"—on a 1–3 scale of "Free," "Partly Free," and "Not Free"—by Freedom House, a leading nongovernmental organization (NGO) promoting democracy. In 2012, Vladmir Putin's was reelected as president (after he served as president for two terms between 2000 and 2008 and as prime minister between 2008 and 2012). The election was largely symbolic as all viable candidates were not allowed to run against him. In 2014, Russia first successfully staged the Winter Olympics in Sochi. Then Russia quickly showed its aggressive side, swallowing Crimea and destabilizing Ukraine. Even before the geopolitical events in 2014, some commentators bearish on Russia had suggested kicking Russia out of the BRIC group given its alleged lack of dynamism, and to focus more business attention on China, India, and Brazil. After Russia became deeply involved in the mess of Ukrainian politics, the United States, the European Union, Norway, Australia, Canada, and Japan imposed a series of sanctions to "punish" and "isolate" Russia.

ANTON GVOZDIKOV/SHUTTERSTOCK.COM

Is Russia really that bad? The answer is: of course not! Russia is simply being Russia. While Russia's GDP is smaller than China's and Brazil's, it is larger than India's. Russia's per capita GDP, approximately $16,000 (at purchasing power parity), is one-third higher than Brazil's, three times China's, and five times India's. Russia has the second largest automobile market in Europe (behind Germany), and it has more college graduates (as a percentage of population) than any other country. Simply put, Russia is too big and too rich to ignore. None of the high-tech giants (such as Cisco, HP, and Intel) and industrial and consumer goods firms (such as Carrefour, Danone, IKEA, Nestlé, PepsiCo, and Unilever) has announced plans to quit Russia. Russia's economic growth may not be as fast as China's or India's, but it will certainly be higher than US or EU growth. Russia exports more than 30% of its GDP, in contrast to 26% for China, 25% for India, and 13% for Brazil.

Because Russia is so large and complex, how to "read" Russia has remained a constant debate. The debate centers on political, economic, and legal dimensions. Politically, Russia has indeed become less democratic. Certain segments of the population (especially the better educated) are disappointed by the return of Putin. But a more relevant question is: Is Russia better off under Putin's more authoritarian rule since 2000, compared with Boris Yeltsin's more democratic (and more chaotic) rule in the 1990s? Russia under Putin between 2000 and 2008 grew 7% annually, whereas Russia under Yeltsin during the 1990s experienced a catastrophic economic decline.

Economically, the Russian economy indeed has great room for development. It is overly dependent on oil and gas exports, contributing 70% of its $515 billion exports. In the World Economic Forum's *Global Competitiveness Report*, Russia ranks only 51st in innovation (out of 133 countries), behind China (26th) and India (30th). Dmitry Medvedev, who served as president between 2008 and 2012 (while Putin was prime minister), published an article in 2009 titled "Russia Forward!" He asked a provocative question: "Should we drag a primitive economy based on raw materials and endemic corruption into the future?"

Legally, establishing the rule of law that respects private property is important. In a society whereby nobody had any significant private property until recently, how a small number of individuals became superrich oligarchs (tycoons) almost overnight is intriguing. By the 2000s, the top ten families or groups owned 60% of Russia's total market capitalization. The government thus faced a dilemma: Redistributing wealth by confiscating assets from the oligarchs creates more uncertainty, whereas respecting and protecting the property rights of the oligarchs results in more resentment among the population. Thus far, the government has largely sided with the oligarchs, as long as the oligarchs play by Putin's rules:

(1) mind your own business—do not get involved in politics, and (2) pay taxes.

Internationally, the sanctions were designed to target Putin's inner circles first. They soon spilled over to the financial, energy, and defense industries. In retaliation, Russia banned agricultural imports from any country that imposed sanctions. As a result, $6.5 billion worth of EU agricultural products that normally would go to Russia ended up being dumped in the EU. Since Russia accounted for one-third of EU's fruit and vegetable exports and one-quarter of EU's beef exports, the Russian ban caused prices for Dutch beef, Finnish dairy products, Latvian cabbage, and Spanish peaches to *collapse*. Dealing with the more abundant and cheaper food, the German agriculture minister urged Germans to eat fruits at least five times a day. While governments butt heads, European farmers could not sustain their losses. In August 2014, European taxpayers ended up coughing up $200 million of new subsidies to farmers. Firms withdrawing from Russia due to its peril obviously cannot benefit from its promise, and can only salivate over those firms that can tap into the promise of Russia. Since Russians had to eat, Chinese farmers happily started to fill the market vacated by EU farmers. Likewise, as European demand for Russian gas declined, in 2014 China's CNPC signed an unprecedented $300 billion deal with Gazprom, unlocking the vast promise of Russia's underground wealth.

Case Discussion Questions

1. How would you characterize Russia's political system?
2. Does Russia have a market economy? Why or why not?
3. ***ON ETHICS:*** If you are the owner of a US or EU firm that currently exports to Russia with good profits, would you like to lose your Russia business (and profits) for Ukraine (which currently is not an export market of yours)?

Sources: "Putin's paradox," *Bloomberg Businessweek*, 1 September 2014, 12–13; "This apple was once headed to Russia, not anymore," *Bloomberg Businessweek*, 15 September 2014, 13–15; "Moscow doesn't believe in tears," *Economist*, 10 March 2012, 62–63; "Moscow spring," *Economist*, 11 February 2012, 12; "The long game," *Economist*, 6 September 2014, 15; S. Michailova, S. Puffer, and D. McCarthy, "Russia: As solid as a BRIC?" *Critical Perspectives on International Business* 9 (2013): 5–18; www.freedomhouse.org.

STUDY TOOLS 2

LOCATED AT THE BACK OF YOUR BOOK:

- ☐ Rip out and study the Chapter Review Card at the end of the book

LOG IN TO WWW.CENGAGEBRAIN.COM TO:

- ☐ Review key term flashcards
- ☐ Complete a practice quiz to test your knowledge of key concepts
- ☐ Take and complete the chapter crossword puzzle
- ☐ Complete interactive content, watch chapter videos, and take a graded quiz
- ☐ Track your knowledge of key concepts in Global Business
- ☐ Read and discuss additional case study content

3 Emphasizing Cultures, Ethics, & Norms

RAWPIXEL/SHUTTERSTOCK.COM

LEARNING OBJECTIVES

After studying this chapter, you should be able to . . .

3-1 Explain where informal institutions come from.

3-2 Define culture and articulate its two main manifestations.

3-3 Articulate three ways to understand cultural differences.

3-4 Explain why understanding cultural differences is crucial for global business.

3-5 Explain why ethics is important.

3-6 Identify ways to combat corruption.

3-7 Identify norms associated with strategic responses when firms deal with ethical challenges.

3-8 Explain how you can acquire cross-cultural literacy.

After you finish this chapter, go to **PAGE 49** for **STUDY TOOLS**

ETHICAL DILEMMA

Cut Salaries or Cut Jobs

As a Japanese expatriate in charge of US operations of Yamakawa Corporation, you scratch your head confronting a difficult decision: Do you cut salaries across the board or cut jobs when dealing with a horrific economic downturn with major losses? Headquarters in Osaka has advised that earnings at home are bad, and that you cannot expect headquarters to bail out your operations. Unfortunately, US government bailouts are only good for US-owned firms and are thus irrelevant for your unit, which is 100% owned by the Japanese parent company.

As a person brought up in a collectivistic culture, you instinctively feel compelled to suggest across-the-board pay cuts for all 1,000 employees in the United States. Personally, as the highest-paid US-based employee, you are willing to take the *highest* percentage of a pay cut (you are thinking of 25%). If implemented, this plan would call for other executives, who are mostly Americans, to take a 20% to 25% pay cut, mid-level managers and professionals a 15% to 20% pay cut, and all the rank-and-file employees a 10% to 15% pay cut. Indeed, in your previous experience at Yamakawa in Japan, you did this with positive results among all affected Japanese employees. This time, most executive colleagues in Japan are doing the same. However, since you are now managing US operations, headquarters in Osaka (being more globally minded and sensitive) does not want to impose any uniform solutions around the world and asks you to make the call.

As a conscientious executive, you have studied all the books—in both Japanese and English—that you can get your hands on for this tough decision. While you understand that US executives routinely undertake reduction in force (RIF), which is a euphemism for mass layoffs, you have also noticed that in the recent recession, even "bona fide" US firms, such as AMD, FedEx, HP, and *The New York Times*, have all trimmed the base pay for all employees. If there is a time to change the norm moving toward more across-the-board pay cuts in an effort to preserve jobs and avoid RIF, this time may be it, according to some US executives quoted in the media.

At the same time, you have also read that some experts note that across-the-board pay cuts are *anathema* to a performance culture enshrined in the United States. "The last thing you want is for your A players—or people in key strategic positions delivering the most value—to leave because you have mismanaged your compensation system," said Mark Huselid, a Rutgers University professor and a leading expert on human resource management, in a media interview. You have also read in a *Harvard Business Review* survey that during the Great Recession of 2008–2009, 20% of high-potential players in US firms voluntarily jumped ship, in search of greener pastures elsewhere. Naturally, you are worried that should you decide to implement the across-the-board pay cuts you have envisioned, you may end up losing a lot of American star performers and end up with a bunch of mediocre players who cannot go elsewhere—and you may be stuck with the mediocre folks for a long time, even after the economy recovers. After spending two days reading all the materials you have gathered, you still do not have a clear picture. Instead, you have a big headache. You scratch your head again. How would you proceed?

Sources: This case is fictitious. It was inspired by M. Brannen, "Global talent management and learning for the future: Pressing concerns for Japanese multinationals," *AIB Insights* 8 (2008): 8–12; "Cutting salaries instead of jobs," *BusinessWeek*, 8 June 2009, 46–48; "Pay cuts made palatable," *BusinessWeek*, 4 May 2009, 67; N. Carter and C. Silva, "High potentials in the downturn: Sharing the pain?" *Harvard Business Review* (September 2009): 25.

Why does the Japanese executive in the Opening Case, who was brought up in a collectivistic culture, feel uncomfortable about mass layoffs? Why do US executives who have grown up in an individualistic culture routinely undertake mass layoffs when their firms run into difficulties? What is the right (ethical) thing to do? What action would you recommend to this Japanese executive? More fundamentally, how do informal institutions govern individual behavior and firm behavior in different countries?

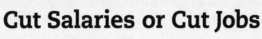

This chapter continues our coverage on the institution-based view, which began with formal institutions in Chapter 2. Here we focus on informal institutions represented by cultures, ethics, and norms. As informal institutions, cultures, ethics, and norms play an important part in shaping the success and failure of firms around the globe. Remember that the institution-based view suggests two propositions. First, managers and firms rationally pursue their interests within a given institutional framework. Second, in situations where formal institutions are unclear or fail, informal institutions play a larger role in reducing uncertainty. The first proposition deals with both formal and informal institutions. The second proposition hinges on the informal institutions we are about to discuss. As the Opening Case shows, informal institutions are about more than just how to wine and dine properly. Informal institutions on the do's and don'ts can make or break operations, which is why they deserve a great deal of our attention.

3-1 WHERE DO INFORMAL INSTITUTIONS COME FROM?

Recall that any institutional framework consists of both formal and informal institutions. While formal institutions such as politics, laws, and economics (see Chapter 2) are important, they only make up a small (although important) part of the rules of the game that govern individual and firm behavior. As pervasive features of every economy, informal institutions can be found almost *everywhere*.

Where do informal institutions come from? They come from socially transmitted information and are a part of the heritage that we call cultures, ethics, and norms. Those within a society tend to perceive their own culture, ethics, and norms as "natural, rational, and morally right."[1] This self-centered mentality is known as **ethnocentrism**. For example, many Americans believe in "American exceptionalism," a view that holds the United States to be exceptionally well endowed to lead the world. The Chinese call China *zhong guo*, which literally means "the country in the middle" or "middle kingdom."

Recall from Chapter 2 that informal institutions are underpinned by the normative and cognitive pillars, while formal institutions are supported by the regulatory pillar. While the regulatory pillar clearly specifies the do's and don'ts, informal institutions, by definition, are more elusive. Yet, they are no less important. Thus it is imperative that we pay attention to three different informal institutions: culture, ethics, and norms.

3-2 CULTURE

Out of many informal institutions, culture is probably the most frequently discussed. Before we can discuss its two major components—language and religion—first we must define culture.

3-2a Definition of Culture

Although hundreds of definitions of culture have appeared, we will use the definition proposed by the world's foremost cross-cultural expert, Geert Hofstede, a Dutch professor. He defines **culture** as "the collective programming of the mind which distinguishes the members of one group or category of people from another."[2] Before proceeding, it is important to make two points to minimize confusion. First, although it is customary to talk about the American culture, no strict one-to-one correspondence between cultures and nation-states exists. Many subcultures exist within multiethnic countries such as Australia, Belgium, Brazil, Britain, Canada, China, India, Indonesia, Russia, South Africa, Switzerland, and the United States. Second, culture has many layers, such as regional, ethnic, and religious. Even firms may have a specific organizational culture (such as the IKEA culture). Acknowledging the validity of these two points, we will, however, follow Hofstede by using the term "culture" to discuss *national* culture unless otherwise noted. While this is a matter of expediency, it is also

ISTOCKPHOTO.COM/IOFOTO

Ethnocentrism A self-centered mentality held by a group of people who perceive their own culture, ethics, and norms as natural, rational, and morally right.

Culture The collective programming of the mind which distinguishes the members of one group or category of people from another.

a reflection of the institutional realities of the world with about 200 nation-states.[3]

Culture is made up of numerous elements. Although culture is too complex to dissect in the space we have here, we will highlight two major components of culture that impact global business: language and religion.

3-2b Language

Approximately 6,000 languages are spoken in the world. Chinese is the largest language in terms of the number of native speakers (20% of the world population). English is a distant second (8% of the world population), followed closely by Spanish (6%) and Hindi (5%). Yet, the dominance of English as a global business language, or ***lingua franca***, is unmistakable.[4] This is driven by two factors. First, English-speaking countries contribute the largest share (approximately one-third) of global output. Such economic dominance not only drives trade and investment ties between English-speaking countries and the rest of the world, but also generates a constant stream of products and services marketed in English. Think about the ubiquitous Hollywood movies, *Economist* magazine, and Google's search engine. In the online world, the dominance of English is more extraordinary: one in three log on in English.

HELGA ESTEB/SHUTTERSTOCK.COM

Second, recent globalization has called for the use of one common language. For firms headquartered in English-speaking countries as well as Scandinavia and the Netherlands (where English is widely taught and spoken), using English to manage operations around the globe poses little difficulty. However, settling on a global language for the entire firm is problematic for firms headquartered in Latin countries (such as France) or Asian countries (such as South Korea), in which English is not widely spoken. Yet, even in these firms, it is still difficult to insist on a language other than English as the global corporate *lingua franca*. Around the world, nonnative speakers of English who can master English increasingly command a premium in jobs and compensation, and this fuels a rising interest in English. Think, for example, of the Taiwanese-born Hollywood director Ang Lee, Hong Kong-born kung-fu master Jackie Chan, Colombian-born pop star Shakira, and Austrian-born actor and politician Arnold Schwarzenegger.

On the other hand, the dominance of English may also lead to a disadvantage. Although native speakers of English have a great deal of advantage in global business, an expatriate manager who does not know the local language misses a lot of cultural subtleties and can only interact with locals fluent in English. Weak (or no) ability in foreign languages makes it difficult or even impossible to detect translation errors, which may result in embarrassments. For example, Rolls-Royce's Silver Mist was translated into German as "Silver Excrement." Coors Beer translated its slogan, "Turn it loose!" into Spanish as "Drink Coors and get diarrhea!" Electrolux advertised its powerful vacuum machines in the United States with a slogan: "Nothing sucks like an Electrolux!" To avoid such embarrassments, you will be better off if you can pick up at least one foreign language during your university studies.

3-2c Religion

ISTOCKPHOTO.COM/HENRIK5000

Religion is another major manifestation of culture. Approximately 85% of the world's population report having some religious belief. PengAtlas Map 5 shows the geographical distribution of different religious heritages. The four leading religions are Christianity (approximately 1.7 billion adherents), Islam (1 billion), Hinduism (750 million), and Buddhism

Lingua franca A global business language.

EXHIBIT 3.1 HIGH-CONTEXT VERSUS LOW-CONTEXT CULTURES

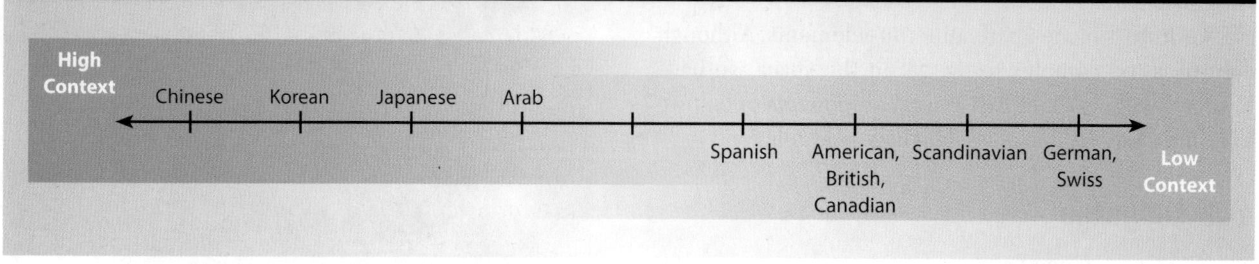

(350 million). Of course, not everybody claiming to be an adherent actively practices a religion. For instance, some Christians may go to church only *once* every year—at Christmas.

Because religious differences have led to numerous challenges, knowledge about religions is crucial even for *non*-religious managers. For example, in Christian countries, the Christmas season represents the peak in shopping and consumption. Half of toy sales for a given year in the United States occur during the month before Christmas. Since American kids consume half of the world's toys and virtually all toys are made outside the United States (mostly in Asia), this means 25% of the world's toy output is sold in one country in a month, thus creating enormous production, distribution, and coordination challenges. For toy makers and stores, missing the boat from Asia, whose transit time is at least two weeks, can literally devastate an entire holiday season and probably the entire year.

3-3 CLASSIFYING CULTURAL DIFFERENCES

Before reading this chapter, every reader already knows that cultures are different. There is no controversy in stating that the Indian culture is different from the Russian culture. But, how are the Indian and Russian cultures *systematically* different? This section outlines three ways to understand cultural differences: (1) the context approach, (2) the cluster approach, and (3) the dimension approach.

Context The background against which interaction takes place.

Low-context culture A culture in which communication is usually taken at face value without much reliance on unspoken conditions or assumptions.

High-context culture A culture in which communication relies heavily on the underlying unspoken conditions or assumptions, which are as important as the words used.

3-3a The Context Approach

Of the three main approaches to cultural difference, the context approach is the most straightforward. It focuses on a single dimension: context.[5] **Context** is the background against which interaction takes place. Exhibit 3.1 outlines a spectrum of countries along the dimension of low versus high context. In **low-context cultures** such as North American and Western European countries, communication is usually taken at face value without much reliance on unspoken conditions or assumptions, which are features of context. In other words, "no" means "no." In **high-context cultures** such as Arab and Asian countries, communication relies heavily on unspoken conditions or assumptions, which are as important as the words used. "No" does not necessarily mean "no," and you must rely much more on the context in order to understand just what "no" means.

Why is context important? Failure to understand the differences in interaction styles may lead to misunderstandings. For example, in Japan, a high-context culture, negotiators prefer not to flatly say "no" to a business request. They will say something like "We will study it" or "We will get back to you later." Their negotiation partners are supposed to understand the context of these unenthusiastic responses and interpret them as essentially "no," even though the word "no" is never explicitly said. By contrast, lawyers in the United States, a low-context culture, are included in negotiations to essentially help remove the context—a contract should be as straightforward as possible, and there should be no room for parties to read between the lines. But negotiators from high-context cultures such as China often prefer *not* to involve lawyers until the very last phase of contract drafting. In high-context cultures, initial rounds of negotiations are supposed to create the context for mutual trust and friendship. For individuals brought up in high-context cultures, decoding the context and acting accordingly becomes second nature. Straightforward communication and confrontation, typical in low-context cultures, often baffle them.

3-3b The Cluster Approach

The cluster approach groups countries that share similar cultures together as one **cluster**. Exhibit 3.2 shows three influential sets of clusters. This table is the first time these three major systems of cultural clusters are compiled side by side. Viewing them together can allow us to see their similarities and differences. The first is the Ronen and Shenkar clusters, proposed by management professors Simcha Ronen and Oded Shenkar.[6] In alphabetical order, these clusters are (1) Anglo, (2) Arabic, (3) Eastern Europe, (4) Far East, (5) Germanic, (6) Latin America, (7) Latin Europe, (8) Near East, (9) Nordic, and (10) sub-Saharan Africa. Brazil, India, Israel, and Japan are classified as independents.

The second set of clusters is called the GLOBE clusters, named after the Global Leadership and Organizational Behavior Effectiveness project led by management professor Robert House.[7] The GLOBE project identifies ten clusters and covers 62 countries. Seven clusters use identical labels as the Ronen and Shenkar clusters: (1) Anglo, (2) Eastern Europe, (3) Germanic Europe, (4) Latin America, (5) Latin Europe, (6) Nordic Europe, and (7) sub-Saharan Africa. In addition, GLOBE has the clusters of (8) Confucian Asia, (9) Middle East, and (10) Southern Asia.

The third set of clusters is the Huntington civilizations, popularized by political scientist Samuel Huntington. A **civilization** is "the highest cultural grouping of people and the broadest level of cultural identity people have."[8] Huntington divides the world into eight civilizations: (1) African, (2) Confucian (Sinic), (3) Hindu, (4) Islamic, (5) Japanese, (6) Latin American, (7) Slavic-Orthodox, and (8) Western. While this classification shares a number of similarities with the Ronen and Shenkar and GLOBE clusters, Huntington's Western civilization is a very broad cluster that is subdivided into Anglo, Germanic, Latin Europe, and Nordic clusters by Ronen and Shenkar and by GLOBE. In addition to such an

Cluster A group of countries that have similar cultures.

Civilization The highest cultural grouping of people and the broadest level of cultural identity people have.

EXHIBIT 3.2 CULTURAL CLUSTERS[1]

Ronen and Shenkar clusters	GLOBE clusters	Huntington civilizations
Anglo	Anglo	Western (1)[2]
Arab	Middle East	Islamic
Eastern Europe	Eastern Europe	Slavic-Orthodox
Far East	Confucian Asia	Confucian (Sinic)
Germanic	Germanic Europe	Western (2)
Latin America	Latin America	Latin American
Latin Europe	Latin Europe	Western (3)
Near East	Southern Asia	Hindu
Nordic	Nordic Europe	Western (4)
Sub-Saharan Africa	Sub-Saharan Africa	African
Independents: Brazil, India, Israel, Japan		Japanese

Notes:

1. This table is the *first* time these three major systems of cultural clusters have been compiled side by side. Viewing them together can allow us to see their similarities. However, there are also differences. Across the three systems (columns), even though clusters sometimes share the same labels, there are still differences. For example, Ronen and Shenkar's Latin America cluster does not include Brazil (which is regarded as an "independent"), whereas GLOBE and Huntington's Latin America includes Brazil.
2. For the Western civilization, Huntington does not use such labels as Western 1, 2, 3, and 4 as in the table. They are added by the present author to establish some rough correspondence with the respective Ronen and Shenkar and GLOBE clusters.

Sources: Based on (1) S. Huntington, *The Clash of Civilizations and the Remaking of World Order* (New York: Simon & Schuster, 1996); (2) R. House, P. Hanges, M. Javidan, P. Dorfman, and V. Gupta (eds.), *Culture, Leadership, and Organizations: The GLOBE Study of 62 Societies* (Thousand Oaks, CA: Sage, 2004); (3) S. Ronen and O. Shenkar, "Clustering countries on attitudinal dimension," *Academy of Management Review* 10 (1985): 435–454; (4) S. Ronen and O. Shenkar, "Mapping world cultures," *Journal of International Business Studies*, 44 (2013): 867–897.

uncontroversial classification scheme, Huntington has advanced a highly controversial idea that Western civilization will clash with Islamic and Confucian civilizations in the years to come.

For our purposes, we do not need to debate the validity of Huntington's provocative thesis of the "clash of civilizations." We will leave that debate to your political science or international relations classes. However, we do need to appreciate the underlying idea that people and firms are more comfortable doing business with other countries within the same cluster/civilization. Having a common language, history, and religion reduces the liability of foreignness when operating in another country but within the same cluster/civilization (see Chapter 1). For example, Hollywood movies are more likely to succeed in English-speaking countries. Most foreign investors in China are from Hong Kong and Taiwan—they are not very "foreign." Brazilian firms enjoy doing business in Africa's Angola and Mozambique, which are also Portuguese-speaking countries.

Power distance The extent to which less powerful members within a culture expect and accept that power is distributed unequally.

3-3c The Dimension Approach

While both the context and cluster approaches are interesting, the dimension approach is more influential. The reasons for such influence are probably twofold. First, insightful as the context approach is, it represents only one dimension. What about other dimensions? Second, the cluster approach has relatively little to offer regarding differences of countries *within* one cluster. For example, what are the differences between Argentina and Chile, both of which belong to the same Latin America cluster according to Ronen and Shenkar and GLOBE? By focusing on multiple dimensions of cultural differences both within and across clusters, the dimension approach aims to overcome these limitations. While there are several competing frameworks, the work of Hofstede and his colleagues is by far the most influential and thus our focus here.

Shown in Exhibit 3.3, Hofstede and his colleagues have proposed five dimensions. **Power distance** is

EXHIBIT 3.3 HOFSTEDE DIMENSIONS OF CULTURE

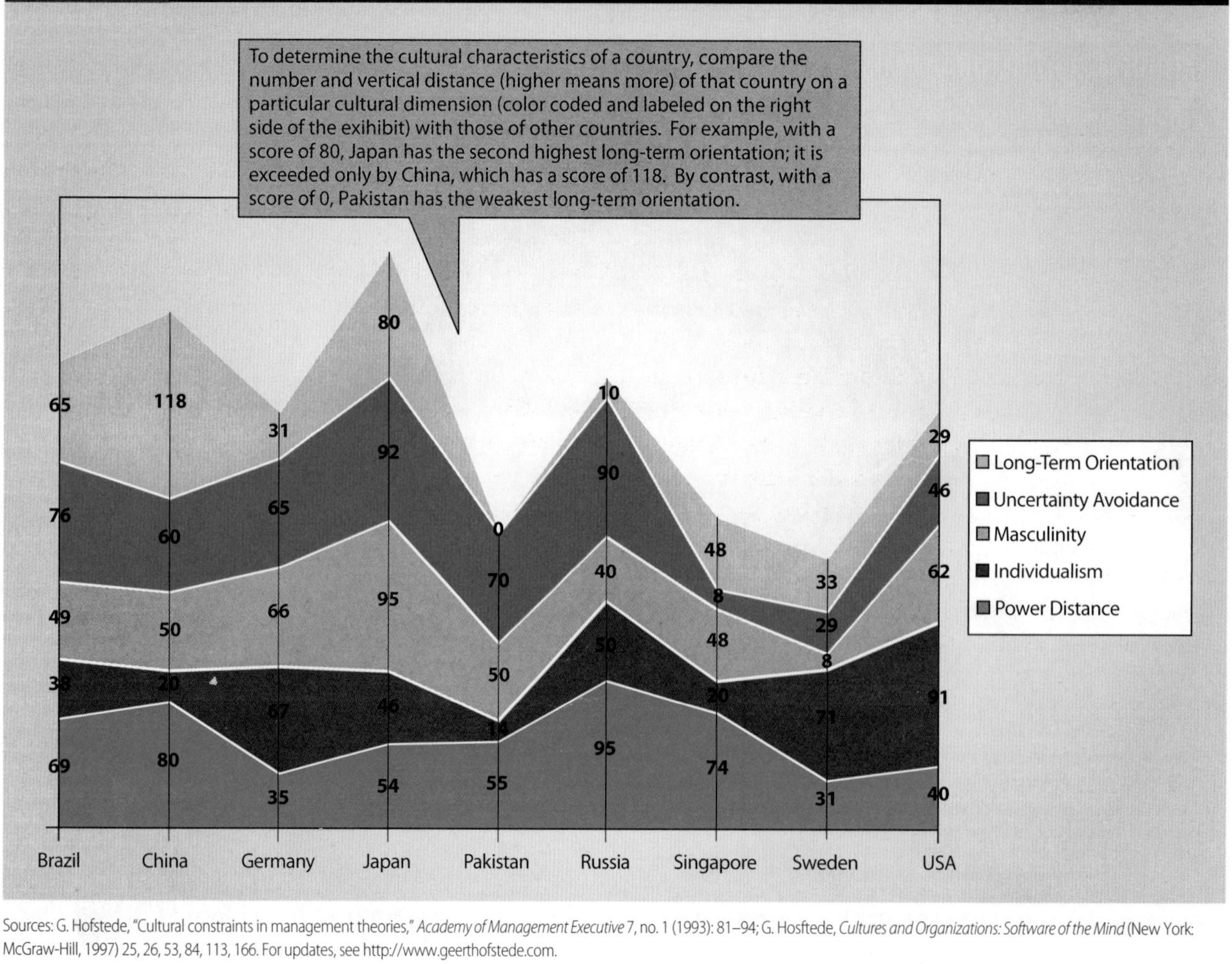
To determine the cultural characteristics of a country, compare the number and vertical distance (higher means more) of that country on a particular cultural dimension (color coded and labeled on the right side of the exihibit) with those of other countries. For example, with a score of 80, Japan has the second highest long-term orientation; it is exceeded only by China, which has a score of 118. By contrast, with a score of 0, Pakistan has the weakest long-term orientation.
65 76 49 38 69
118 60 50 20 80
31 65 66 67 35
80 92 95 46 54
0 70 50 14 55
10 90 40 50 95
48 8 48 20 74
33 29 8 71 31
29 46 62 91 40
Long-Term Orientation
Uncertainty Avoidance
Masculinity
Individualism
Power Distance
Brazil
China
Germany
Japan
Pakistan
Russia
Singapore
Sweden
USA

Sources: G. Hofstede, "Cultural constraints in management theories," *Academy of Management Executive* 7, no. 1 (1993): 81–94; G. Hosftede, *Cultures and Organizations: Software of the Mind* (New York: McGraw-Hill, 1997) 25, 26, 53, 84, 113, 166. For updates, see http://www.geerthofstede.com.

the extent to which less powerful members within a country expect and accept that power is distributed unequally. In high power distance Brazil, the richest 10% of the population pockets approximately 50% of the national income, and everybody accepts this as "the way it is." In low power distance Sweden, the richest 10% only obtains 22% of the national income. Major differences occur even within the same cluster. For example, in the United States, subordinates often address their bosses on a first name basis, a reflection of a relatively low power distance. While your boss, whom you call Mary or Joe, still has the power to fire you, the distance appears to be shorter than if you have to address this person as Mrs. Y or Dr. Z. In low power distance American universities, all faculty members, including the lowest-ranked assistant professors, are commonly addressed as "Professor A." In high power distance British universities, only full professors are allowed to be called "Professor B" (everybody else is called "Dr. C" or "Ms. D" if D does not have a PhD). German universities are perhaps most extreme: Full professors with PhDs need to be honored as "Prof. Dr. X." Your author would be "Prof. Dr. Peng" if I were to teach at a German university.

ORESTIS PANAGIOTOU/EPA /LANDOV

Individualism refers to the idea that an individual's identity is fundamentally his or her own, whereas **collectivism** refers to the idea that an individual's identity is fundamentally tied to the identity of his or her collective group, be it a family, village, or company. In individualistic societies, led by the United States, ties between individuals are relatively loose and individual achievement and freedom are highly valued. In collectivist societies such as many countries in Africa, Asia, and Latin America, ties between individuals are relatively close and collective accomplishments are often sought after. In Chinese restaurants, most dishes are served "family style" to be shared by all the people around the table. In American restaurants, most dishes are served "individual style" to be only enjoyed by particular persons who order them. Shown in our Opening Case, in Japan when facing an economic downturn, the norm is to impose across-the-board pay cuts. In the United States, expect mass layoffs so that people who keep their jobs will not suffer from pay cuts.

The **masculinity** versus **femininity** dimension refers to sex role differentiation. In every traditional society, men tend to have occupations that reward assertiveness, such as politics, military, and management. Women, on the other hand, usually work in caring professions such as teaching and nursing in addition to being homemakers. High masculinity societies (led by Japan) continue to maintain a sharp role differentiation along gender lines. In low masculinity societies (led by Sweden), women are increasingly likely to become politicians, scientists, and executives, and men frequently assume the role of nurses, teachers, and *househusbands*.

Uncertainty avoidance refers to the extent to which members in a culture accept or avoid ambiguous situations and uncertainty. Members of high uncertainty avoidance cultures (led by Greece) place a premium on job security and retirement benefits. They also tend to resist change, which often

Individualism The idea that the identity of an individual is fundamentally his or her own.

Collectivism The idea that an individual's identity is fundamentally tied to the identity of his or her collective group.

Masculinity A relatively strong form of societal-level sex-role differentiation whereby men tend to have occupations that reward assertiveness and women tend to work in caring professions.

Femininity A relatively weak form of societal-level sex-role differentiation whereby more women occupy positions that reward assertiveness and more men work in caring professions.

Uncertainty avoidance The extent to which members of a culture accept or avoid ambiguous situations and uncertainty.

In Focus: Criticizing Hofstede's Framework

Despite the influence of Hofstede's framework, it has attracted a number of criticisms outlined next:

- Cultural boundaries are not the same as national boundaries.
- Although Hofstede was careful to remove some of his own cultural biases, "the Dutch software" of his mind, as he acknowledged, "will remain evident to the careful reader." Being more familiar with Western cultures, Hofstede might inevitably be more familiar with dimensions relevant to Westerners. Thus, crucial dimensions relevant to Easterners (Asians) could be missed.
- Hofstede's research was based on surveys of more than 116,000 IBM employees working at 72 national subsidiaries from 1967 to 1973. This had both pros and cons. On the positive side, it took place not only in the same industry, but also in the same company. Otherwise, it would have been difficult to determine whether findings were due to differences in national cultures or industry or organizational cultures. However, because of such a single firm/single industry design, it was possible that Hofstede's findings captured what was unique to that industry or to IBM. Given anti-American sentiments in some countries, some individuals might refuse to work for an American employer. Thus, it was difficult to ascertain whether employees working for IBM were true representatives of their respective national cultures.
- Because the original data are now over 40 years old, critics contend that Hofstede's framework would simply fail to capture aspects of recent cultural change.

Hofstede responded to all four criticisms. First, he acknowledged that his focus on national culture was a matter of expediency with all its trappings. Second, since the 1980s, Hofstede and colleagues relied on a questionnaire derived from cultural dimensions most relevant to the Chinese, and then translated it from Chinese to multiple languages. That was how he uncovered the fifth dimension, long-term orientation (originally labeled "Confucian dynamism"). In response to the third and fourth criticisms, Hofstede pointed out a large number of more recent studies conducted by other scholars, using a variety of countries, industries, and firms. Most results were supportive of his findings. Overall, while Hofstede's work is not perfect, on balance, its values seem to outweigh its drawbacks.

COURTESY OF GEERT HOFSTEDE

Sources: T. Fang, "Asian management research needs more self-confidence," *Asia Pacific Journal of Management* 27 (2010): 155–170; G. Hofstede, "What did GLOBE really measure?" *Journal of International Business Studies* 37 (2006): 882–896; G. Hofstede, "Asian management in the 21st century," *Asia Pacific Journal of Management* 24 (2007): 411–420; M. Javidan, R. House, P. Dorfman, P. Hanges, and M. Luque, "Conceptualizing and measuring cultures and their consequences," *Journal of International Business Studies* 37 (2006): 897–914; B. Kirkman, K. Lowe, and C. Gibson, "A quarter century of *Culture's Consequences*," *Journal of International Business Studies* 37 (2006): 285–320; R. Maseland and A. van Hoorn, "Explaining the negative correlation between values and practices," *Journal of International Business Studies* 40 (2009): 527–532; B. McSweeney, "Hofstede's model of national cultural differences and their consequences," *Human Relations* 55 (2002): 89–118; L. Tang and P. Keveos, "A framework to update Hofstede's cultural value indices," *Journal of International Business Studies* 39 (2008): 1045–1063; R. Tung and A. Verbeke, "Beyond Hofstede and GLOBE," *Journal of International Business Studies* 41 (2010): 1259–1274.

creates uncertainty. Low uncertainty avoidance cultures (led by Singapore) are characterized by a greater willingness to take risks and less resistance to change.

Long-term orientation emphasizes perseverance and savings for future betterment. China, which has the world's longest continuous written history of approximately 4,000 years and the highest contemporary savings rate, leads the pack. On the other hand, members of short-term orientation societies (led by Pakistan) prefer quick results and instant gratification.

Long-term orientation A perspective that emphasizes perseverance and savings for future betterment.

Overall, Hofstede's dimensions are interesting and informative. It is also important to note that Hofstede's dimensions are not perfect and have attracted some criticisms (see In Focus). However, it is fair to suggest that these dimensions represent a *starting point* for us as we try to figure out the role of culture in global business.

3-4 CULTURE AND GLOBAL BUSINESS

A great deal of global business activity is consistent with the context, cluster, and dimension approaches to cultural differences. For instance, the average length of contracts is longer in low-context countries (such as Germany) than in high-context countries (such as Vietnam), where a lot of agreements are unspoken and not necessarily put in a legal contract.

Also, as pointed out by the cluster approach, firms are a lot more serious in preparation when doing business with countries in other clusters compared to how they deal with fellow countries within the same cluster. Countless new books in English have recently been published on "how to do business in China." Two decades ago, gurus wrote about "how to do business in Japan." However, has anyone ever seen a book in English on "how to do business in Canada?"

Hofstede's dimension approach can be illustrated by numerous real-world examples. For instance, managers in high power distance countries such as France and Italy have a greater tendency for centralized authority. Although widely practiced in low power distance Western countries, asking for feedback and participation from subordinates—known as empowerment—is often regarded as a sign of weak leadership and low integrity in high power distance countries such as Egypt, Russia, and Turkey.

Individualism and collectivism also affect business activities. Individualist US firms may often try to differentiate themselves, whereas collectivist Japanese firms tend to follow each other. Because entrepreneurs stick their necks out by founding new firms, individualistic societies tend to foster a relatively higher level of entrepreneurship.

Likewise, masculinity and femininity affect managerial behavior. The stereotypical manager in high masculinity societies is "assertive, decisive, and aggressive," and the word "aggressive" carries positive connotations. In contrast, high femininity societies generally consider "aggressive" a negative term, and managers are "less visible, intuitive rather than decisive, and accustomed to seeking consensus."[9]

Managers in low uncertainty avoidance countries such as Britain rely more on experience and training, whereas managers in high uncertainty avoidance countries such as China rely more on rules. In addition, cultures with a long-term orientation are likely to nurture firms with long horizons. In comparison, Western firms often focus on relatively short-term profits (often on a *quarterly* basis).

Overall, there is strong evidence for the importance of culture. Sensitivity to cultural differences does not guarantee success but can at least avoid blunders. For instance, a Chinese manufacturer exported to the West a premium brand of battery called White Elephant without knowing the meaning of this phrase in Western culture. In another example, when a French manager (a man) was transferred to a US subsidiary and met his American secretary (a woman) for the first time, he greeted her with an effusive cheek-to-cheek kiss, a harmless "Hello" in France. However, the secretary later filed a complaint for sexual harassment. More seriously, Mitsubishi Motors encountered major problems when operating in the United States. While Japan leads the world in masculinity, the company's US facilities had more female participation in the labor force, typical of a country with a relatively higher level of femininity. Yet, its US division reportedly tolerated sexual discrimination and sexual harassment behaviors. Mitsubishi ended up paying $34 million to settle these charges.

3-5 ETHICS

Cross-cultural differences can be interesting. But they can also be unethical, all depending on the institutional frameworks in which firms are embedded (see the Opening Case). This is discussed next.

3-5a Definition and Impact of Ethics

Ethics refers to the principles, standards, and norms of conduct that govern individual and firm behavior. Ethics is not only an important part of informal institutions, but is also deeply reflected in formal laws and regulations. To the extent that laws reflect a society's minimum standards of conduct, there is a substantial overlap between what is ethical and legal as well as between what is unethical and illegal. However, in some cases, what is legal may be unethical. For example, mass layoffs are legal, but are widely viewed as unethical in many countries (see the Opening Case).

Recent scandals have pushed ethics to the forefront of global business discussions. Numerous firms have introduced a **code of conduct**—a

Ethics The principles, standards, and norms of conduct that govern individual and firm behavior.

Code of conduct A set of guidelines for making ethical decisions.

AP IMAGES/LEFTERIS PITARAKIS

set of guidelines for making ethical decisions. But firms' ethical motivations are still subject to debate. Three views have emerged:

- A *negative view* suggests that firms may simply jump onto the ethics bandwagon under social pressure to *appear* more legitimate without necessarily becoming better.
- A *positive view* maintains that some (although not all) firms may be self-motivated to do it right regardless of social pressure.
- An *instrumental view* believes that good ethics may simply be a useful instrument to help make money.

Perhaps the best way to appreciate the value of ethics is to examine what happens after some crisis. As a reservoir of goodwill, the value of an ethical reputation is *magnified* during a time of crisis. After the 2008 terrorist attacks on the Taj Mahal Palace Hotel in Mumbai, India, that killed 31 people (including 20 guests), the hotel received only praise. Why? The surviving guests were overwhelmed by employees' dedication to duty and their desire to protect guests in the face of terrorist attacks. Eleven employees laid down their lives while helping between 1,200 and 1,500 guests safely escape. Paradoxically, catastrophes may allow more ethical firms such as the Taj, which is renowned for its integrity and customer service, to shine.[10] The upshot seems to be that ethics pays.

Ethical relativism A perspective that suggests that all ethical standards are relative.

Ethical imperialism The absolute belief that "there is only one set of Ethics (with a capital E), and we have it."

3-5b Managing Ethics Overseas

Managing ethics overseas is challenging because what is ethical in one country may be unethical elsewhere. There are two schools of thought.[11] First, **ethical relativism** follows the cliché, "When in Rome, do as the Romans do." If Muslim countries discriminate against women, so what? Likewise, if industry rivals in Mexico can fix prices, who cares? Isn't that what "Romans" do in "Rome"? Second, **ethical imperialism** refers to the absolute belief that "There is only one set of Ethics (with a capital E), and we have it." Americans are especially renowned for believing that their ethical values should be applied universally. For example, since sexual discrimination and price fixing are wrong in the United States, they must be wrong everywhere. In practice, however, neither of these schools of thought is realistic. At the extreme, ethical relativism would have to accept any local practice, whereas ethical imperialism may cause resentment and backlash among locals.

Three middle-of-the-road guiding principles have been proposed by Thomas Donaldson, a business ethicist. These are shown in Exhibit 3.4. First, respect for human dignity and basic rights—such as concern for health, safety, and the need for education rather than working at a young age—should determine the absolute, minimal ethical thresholds for *all* operations around the world.

Second, firms should respect local traditions. If a firm bans giving gifts, it can forget about doing business in China and Japan. While hiring employees' children and relatives instead of more qualified applicants is illegal in the United States under equal opportunity laws, it is routine practice for Indian companies and is expected to strengthen employee loyalty. What should US companies setting up subsidiaries in India do? Donaldson advises that such nepotism is not necessarily wrong, at least not in India.

EXHIBIT 3.4 MANAGING ETHICS OVERSEAS: THREE APPROACHES

- Respect for human dignity and basic rights
- Respect for local traditions
- Respect for institutional context

Sources: T. Donaldson, "Values in tension: Ethics away from home," *Harvard Business Review* (September-October 1996): 4–11; J. Weiss, *Business Ethics*, 4th ed. (Cincinnati: South-Western Thomson, 2006).

EXHIBIT 3.5 TEXAS INSTRUMENTS (TI) GUIDELINES ON GIFTS IN CHINA

- These China-Specific Guidelines are based on TI's Global Standard Guidelines, taking into consideration China's local business climates, legal requirements, customs, and cultures as appropriate. Employees of TI entities in China ("TIers") should comply with both these China-Specific Guidelines and Global Standard Guidelines. In any event of conflict, the stricter standard will apply.
- Acceptable gifts include calendars, coffee cups, appointment books, notepads, small pocket calculators, and ball point pens.
- Gifts with excessive value refer to those that are worth more than RMB 200 yuan (approximately $32), and need approval from Asia Finance Director.
- If you are not sure when you can accept or offer any gift, the following two Quick Tests are recommended:
    a. "Reciprocity" Test. Ask this question: Based on your knowledge of TI's policy and culture, would TI under similar circumstances allow you to provide a TI business partner a gift of an equivalent nature? If the answer is no, then politely refuse the offer.
    b. "Raise Eyebrow" or "Embarrassments" Test. Ask these questions: Would you "raise eyebrows" or feel uncomfortable in giving or receiving the gift in the presence of others in a work area? Would you feel comfortable in openly displaying the gift you are offering or receiving? Would you feel embarrassed if it were seen by other TI business partners or by your colleagues/supervisor?
- No cash or cash equivalent gift cards may be given. Gift cards that are redeemable only for a specific item (and not cash) with a fixed RMB value, such as a Moon Cake card,* are permitted as long as the gift is otherwise consistent with these Guidelines.

* Moon Cake is a special dessert for the Mid-Autumn Festival, which is a major holiday for family reunion in September.

Source: Adapted from Texas Instruments, *Comprehensive Guidelines on Gifts, Entertainment, and Travel in China* (2014).

Finally, respect for institutional context calls for a careful understanding of local institutions. Codes of conduct banning bribery are not very useful unless accompanied by guidelines for the scale and scope of appropriate gift giving/receiving (see Exhibit 3.5). Citigroup allows employees to accept noncash gifts whose nominal value is less than $100. The *Economist* allows its journalists to accept any gift that can be consumed in a single day; a bottle of wine is acceptable, but a case of wine is not.[12] Overall, these three principles, although far from perfect, can help managers make decisions about which they may feel relatively comfortable.

3-6 ETHICS AND CORRUPTION

Ethics helps to combat **corruption**, often defined as the abuse of public power for private benefits usually in the form of bribery, in cash or in kind.[13] Competition should be based on products and services, but corruption distorts that basis, causing misallocation of resources and slowing economic development. Corruption discourages foreign direct investment (FDI). If the level of corruption in Singapore (very low) were to increase to the level in Mexico (in the middle range), it reportedly would have the same negative impact on FDI inflows as raising the tax rate by 50%.[14]

In the global fight against corruption, the Foreign Corrupt Practices Act (FCPA) was enacted by the US Congress in 1977. It bans bribery of foreign officials. Many US firms complain that the act has unfairly restricted them. They also point out that overseas bribery expenses were often tax deductible (!) in many EU countries such as Austria, France, and Germany until the late 1990s. Even with the FCPA, however, there is no evidence that US firms are inherently more ethical than others. The FCPA itself was triggered in the 1970s by investigations of many corrupt US firms. Even the FCPA makes exceptions for small grease payments to get through customs abroad. Most alarmingly, a World Bank study reported that despite over three decades of FCPA enforcement, US firms "exhibit systematically *higher* levels of corruption" than other firms in the Organization for Economic Co-operation and Development (OECD).[15]

Overall, the FCPA can be regarded as an institutional weapon in the global fight against corruption. Recall that every institution has three supportive pillars: regulatory, normative, and cognitive (Exhibit 2.1). Despite the FCPA's formal *regulatory* teeth, for a long time it had neither a *normative* pillar nor a *cognitive* pillar. Until recently, the norm among other OECD firms was to pay bribes first and get tax deductions later, a clear sign of ethical relativism. Only in 1997 did the OECD Convention on Combating Bribery of Foreign Public Officials commit all 30 member countries (essentially all developed economies) to criminalize bribery. The regulation went into force in 1999. A more ambitious campaign is the UN Convention against Corruption, signed by 106 countries in 2003 and came into force in 2005. If every country criminalizes bribery and every firm resists corruption,

Corruption The abuse of public power for private benefits, usually in the form of bribery.

their combined power will eradicate it.[16] But this will not happen unless FCPA-type legislation is institutionalized and *enforced* in every country.

3-7 NORMS AND ETHICAL CHALLENGES

As an important informal institution, **norms** are the prevailing practices of relevant players—the proverbial "everybody else"—that affect the focal individuals and firms. How firms strategically respond to ethical challenges is often driven, at least in part, by norms. Shown in Exhibit 3.6, four broad strategic responses are (1) reactive strategy, (2) defensive strategy, (3) accommodative strategy, and (4) proactive strategy.

A **reactive strategy** is passive. Firms do not feel compelled to act when problems arise, and denial is usually the first line of defense. In the absence of formal regulation, the need to take action is neither internalized through cognitive beliefs, nor embodied in any practicable norm. For example, as early as in 2005, General Motors (GM) had been aware that the ignition switch of some of its cars could accidentally shut off the engine. Yet, it refused to take any actions and proceeded to produce and sell the cars for a decade. Sure enough, accidents happened and people were killed and injured due to the faulty switches. Only when victims' families sued and Congressional pressures increased did GM belatedly recall millions of cars in 2014.

A **defensive strategy** focuses on regulatory compliance. In the early 1990s, media and activist groups charged Nike with running sweatshops, although there was no existing regulation prohibiting sweatshops. Nike's initial response was "We don't make shoes," because Nike did not directly own and manage the factories. Its contractors in Indonesia and Vietnam were in charge. This response, however, failed to convey any ethical responsibility. Only when several senators began to suggest legislative solutions—regulations with which Nike would need to comply—did Nike become more serious.

Norm The prevailing practices of relevant players that affect the focal individuals and firms.

Reactive strategy A response to an ethical challenge that often involves denial and belated action to correct problems.

Defensive strategy A response to an ethical challenge that focuses on regulatory compliance.

Accommodative strategy A response to an ethical challenge that involves accepting responsibility.

EXHIBIT 3.6 STRATEGIC RESPONSES TO ETHICAL CHALLENGES

Strategic responses	Strategic behaviors	Examples in the text
Reactive	Deny responsibility; do less than required	GM (the 2000s)
Defensive	Admit responsibility but fight it; do the least that is required	Nike (the 1990s)
Accommodative	Accept responsibility; do all that is required	Toyota (the 2010s), Ford (the 2000s)
Proactive	Anticipate responsibility; do more than is required	BMW (the 1990s)

An **accommodative strategy** features emerging organizational norms to accept responsibility and a set of increasingly internalized cognitive beliefs and values toward making certain changes. In other words, higher levels of ethical and moral responsibility, beyond simply the minimum of what is legally required, are accepted. During 2009 and 2010, Toyota initially was reluctant to recall 12 million vehicles, some of which had a tendency to suffer from unintended acceleration. In 2011, Toyota again recalled 1.7 million vehicles for fuel leaks. This time, Toyota became more accommodative, aggressively carrying out recalls before they turned into a bigger mess.

Companies can change their strategic response. In 2000, when Ford Explorer vehicles equipped with Firestone tires had a large number of fatal rollover accidents, Ford evidently took the painful lesson from its Pinto fire fiasco in the 1970s. In the 1970s Ford marketed the Pinto car, being aware of a design flaw that could make the car susceptible to exploding in rear-end collisions. Similar to GM's recent scandal, Ford had not recalled the Pinto until Congressional, consumer, and media pressures heated up. In 2000, Ford aggressively initiated a speedy recall, launched a media campaign featuring its CEO, and discontinued the 100-year-old relationship with Firestone. While critics argued that Ford's accommodative strategy simply attempted to place the blame squarely on Firestone, the institution-based view (especially Proposition 1 in Chapter 2) suggests that such highly rational actions are to be expected. Even if Ford's public relations campaign was only window dressing designed to make the company look good to the public, it publicized a set of ethical criteria against which Ford

Debate: Ethical Dilemma/Emerging Markets

Are Cultures Converging or Diverging?

Every culture evolves and changes. But what is the *direction* of change? This question is at the center of a great debate. In this age of globalization, one side of the debate argues that there is a great deal of convergence, especially toward more modern, Western values such as individualism and consumerism. As evidence, convergence gurus point out the worldwide interest in Western products, such as iPhones, Kindle, Levi's jeans, McDonald's, and MTV, especially among the youth.

Another side of the debate suggests that Westernization in consumption does not necessarily mean Westernization in values. In a most extreme example, on the night of September 10, 2001, the "9/11" terrorists drank American soft drinks, ate American pizzas, and enjoyed American movies—and then went on to kill thousands of Americans the next day. In another example, the increasing popularity of Asian foods (such as tofu and sushi) and games (such as Pokemon and Bakugan) in the West does not necessarily mean that Westerners are converging toward Asian values. In short, the world may continue to be characterized by cultural divergence.

A middle-of-the-road group makes two points. First, the end of the Cold War, the rise of the Internet, and the ascendance of English as the language of business all offer evidence of some cultural convergence, at least on the surface and among the youth. For example, younger Chinese, Japanese, and Russian managers are typically more individualistic and less collectivistic than the average citizen of their respective countries. Second,

VYTAUTAS KIELAITIS/SHUTTERSTOCK.COM

deep down, cultural divergence may continue to be the norm. So perhaps a better term is "crossvergence," which acknowledges the validity of both sides of the debate. This idea suggests that when marketing products and services to younger customers around the world, a more global approach featuring uniform content and image may work, whereas local adaptation may be a must when dealing with older, more tradition-bound consumers.

Sources: National Commission on Terrorist Attacks on the United States, *The 9/11 Report* (New York: St. Martin's, 2004) 364; M. Chen and D. Miller, "West meets East," *Academy of Management Perspectives* (November 2010): 17–24; H. Lin and S. Hou, "Managerial lessons from the East," *Academy of Management Perspectives* (November 2010): 6–16.

could be judged and opened doors for more scrutiny by concerned stakeholders. It is probably fair to say that Ford was a better corporate citizen in 2000 than it was in 1975.

Finally, firms that take a **proactive strategy** anticipate institutional changes and do more than is required. In 1990, the German government proposed a "take-back" policy, requiring automakers to design cars whose components can be taken back by the same manufacturers for recycling. With this policy in mind, BMW anticipated its emerging responsibility. It not only designed easier-to-disassemble cars, but also enlisted the few high-quality dismantler firms as part of an exclusive recycling infrastructure. Further, BMW actively participated in public discussions and succeeded in establishing its approach as the German national standard for automobile disassembly. Other automakers were thus required to follow BMW's lead. However, other automakers had to fight over smaller, lower-quality dismantlers or develop in-house dismantling infrastructures from scratch. Through such a proactive strategy, BMW set a new industry standard for environmentally friendly norms.

3-8 MANAGEMENT SAVVY

The institution-based view emphasizes the importance of informal institutions—cultures, ethics, and norms—as the soil in which business around the globe either thrives or stagnates. How does this perspective answer our fundamental question: What determines the success and failure of firms around the globe? The institution-based view argues that firm performance is determined, at least in part, by the informal cultures, ethics, and norms governing firm behavior.

This emphasis on informal institutions suggests two broad implications for savvy managers around the globe. First, managers should enhance their **cultural intelligence**, defined as an individual's ability to understand and adjust to new cultures. Acquisition of cultural intelligence

Proactive strategy A strategy that anticipates ethical challenges and addresses them before they happen.

Cultural intelligence An individual's ability to understand and adjust to new cultures.

EXHIBIT 3.7 IMPLICATIONS FOR ACTION
▶ Be prepared.
▶ Slow down.
▶ Establish trust.
▶ Understand the importance of language.
▶ Respect cultural differences.
▶ Understand that no culture is inherently superior in all aspects.

passes through three phases: (1) awareness, (2) knowledge, and (3) skills. *Awareness* refers to the recognition of both the pros and cons of your own cultural mental software and the appreciation of people from other cultures. *Knowledge* refers to the ability to identify the symbols, rituals, and taboos in other cultures. Knowledge is also known as cross-cultural literacy. While you may not share (or may disagree) with their values, you will at least have a road map of the informal institutions governing their behavior. Finally, *skills* are good practices based on awareness and knowledge of other cultures (see Exhibit 3.7).

While skills can be taught in a classroom, the most effective way to learn them is total immersion in a foreign culture. Even for gifted individuals, learning a new language and culture well enough to function at a managerial level will take at least several months of full-time studies. Most employers do not give their expatriates that much time to learn before sending them abroad. Most expatriates are thus inadequately prepared, and the costs for firms, individuals, and families are tremendous (see Chapter 13). This means that you, a student studying this book, are advised to invest in your own career by picking up at least one foreign language, spending one semester (or year) abroad, and reaching out to make some international friends who are taking classes with you (and perhaps even sitting next to you). Such an investment will make you stand out among the crowd and propel your future career to new heights.

Savvy managers should also be aware of the prevailing norms and their transitions globally. The norms around the globe in the 21st century are more culturally sensitive and more ethically demanding than, say, in the 1970s (see the Closing Case). This is not to suggest that every local norm needs to be followed. Failing to understand the changing norms or adapting to them in an insensitive and unethical way may lead to unsatisfactory or disastrous results. The best managers expect norms to shift over time and constantly decipher changes in the informal rules of the game in order to take advantage of new opportunities. How BMW managers proactively shape the automobile recycling norms in Germany serves as a case in point. Firms that fail to realize the passing of old norms and adapt accordingly are likely to fall behind or even go out of business.

ETHICAL DILEMMA/EMERGING MARKETS

Chiquita Is the Top Banana When It Comes to Social Responsibility

Founded in 1870, Chiquita is a leading international producer, marketer, and distributor of bananas, other tropical fruits such as pineapples and avocadoes, as well as salads. Headquartered in Cincinnati, Ohio, Chiquita employs more than 21,000 people on six continents. Chiquita's early history (when it was named the United Fruit Company) was better known as an aggressive and exploitative multinational that treated some of the Central American countries in which it operated as "banana republics." However, Chiquita's recent efforts to be a socially responsible firm have truly made it stand out among industry peers. Chiquita is committed to conducting business ethically—not only in compliance

SIMON DAWSON/BLOOMBERG VIA GETTY IMAGES

with the letter and spirit of the law, but also leading the industry in areas that it feels are the right thing to do.

In Chiquita's core product markets, it views its mission as "to help the world's consumers broaden mindsets about nutrition and bring healthy, nutritious, and convenient foods that taste good and improve people's lives." Joining the army to fight obesity, Chiquita in 2011 became a strategic partner with the US Department of Agriculture (USDA) to promote the new MyPlate dietary guidelines. A large part of Chiquita's corporate social responsibility (CSR) efforts involves how it treats employees and stakeholders around the world. More than a decade ago, Chiquita adopted the Social Accountability 8000 (SA8000) labor rights standard developed by Social Accountability International (SAI). SA8000 prohibits the use of child labor and forced labor, monitors health and safety measures, and promotes appropriate working hours and fair compensation. One crucial component of SA8000 is to reach a global agreement with local and international food workers' unions. On the environmental dimension, Chiquita has been working with Rainforest Alliance since 1992. By 2000, 100% of the plantations owned by Chiquita were certified by Rainforest Alliance as engaging in sustainable farming practices. In 2011, in response to the demands made by a green group called ForestEthics, Chiquita agreed not to buy fuel made from Canadian tar sands. Extracting oil from tar sands is energy intensive and dirty. Environmentalists worked vigorously to block a pipeline, Keystone, which would carry such oil from Canada to the United States.

However, not all is rosy for Chiquita's CSR efforts. Its agreement not to buy fuel made from Canadian tar sands provoked a pro-business lobby in Canada called EthicalOil.org to launch a boycott of Chiquita, with mounting losses (although Chiquita would not quantify such losses). Its work with SA8000 and Rainforest Alliance adds to its cost—think about all the expenses involved in the hiring of so many people to engage in certification, auditing, and compliance. Neither Dole nor Del Monte, its two main rivals, bothers to follow Chiquita to sign a global union agreement, leaving Chiquita to be the high-cost (and less price-competitive) producer. What has Chiquita received in return for all its good work? Big retailers increasingly dump Chiquita and place orders with Dole, Del Monte, and other smaller plantations whose environmental practices may not be as sustainable and whose labor practices may not be as worker friendly as Chiquita. Driven by one of its core values, integrity (the other three are respect, opportunity, and responsibility), Chiquita in 2003 became the only American company to voluntarily admit to the US Department of Justice that it had paid protection money to Colombian paramilitary militia that surrounded its plantations. The payoff for such honesty was a series of American and Colombian lawsuits against it.

Chiquita's conspicuous lack of reward for its good deeds is frustrating. Even the head of the international foodworkers' union was sympathetic, saying, "It's not sustainable for any company in a competitive sector to make progress and gain no recognition for it."

Case Discussion Questions

1. ***ON ETHICS***: Why has Chiquita chosen to be proactive along a number of CSR dimensions?
2. ***ON ETHICS***: Why has Chiquita not been successful in changing industry norms?
3. ***ON ETHICS***: As Chiquita's CEO, what are you going to recommend to the board?
4. ***ON ETHICS***: As Dole's or Del Monte's CEO, what are you going to do in response to Chiquita's moves?

Sources: "Going bananas," *Economist*, 31 March 2012, 74; www.chiquita.com.

STUDY TOOLS 3

LOCATED AT THE BACK OF YOUR BOOK:

☐ Rip out and study the Chapter Review Card at the end of the book

LOG IN TO WWW.CENGAGEBRAIN.COM TO:

☐ Review key term flashcards

☐ Complete a practice quiz to test your knowledge of key concepts

☐ Take and complete the chapter crossword puzzle

☐ Complete interactive content, watch chapter videos, and take a graded quiz

☐ Track your knowledge of key concepts in Global Business

☐ Read and discuss additional case study content

4 Leveraging Resources & Capabilities

EMILIANO LASALVIA/LATINCONTENT STRINGER/GETTY IMAGES

LEARNING OBJECTIVES

After studying this chapter, you should be able to . . .

4-1 Define resources and capabilities.

4-2 Explain how value is created from a firm's resources and capabilities.

4-3 Articulate the difference between keeping an activity in-house and outsourcing it.

4-4 Explain how to use a VRIO framework to understand a firm's resources and capabilities.

4-5 Identify three things you need to do (and one thing you should avoid) as part of a successful career and business strategy.

After you finish this chapter, go to **PAGE 62** for **STUDY TOOLS**

EMERGING MARKETS

Natura Makes Brazil Look Beautiful

Many people in the world agree that Brazil is beautiful. Likewise, Brazilians are widely known to be beautiful. However, beauty has to be maintained. Brazilian women's spending on beauty products is legendary. Although Brazil has the fifth largest population (with 200 million people) and the seventh largest economy in the world, it has become the second largest market for beauty products—only behind the United States. Beauty products spending per woman in Brazil matches that in Britain, which has a much higher income. While Brazil is obviously the attractive B in BRIC, beauty products are among Brazil's most attractive consumer markets, with multinationals such as Avon, Estée Lauder, L'Oreal, P&G, Shiseido, and Unilever salivating over a share of the growing spoils. Emerging as the leading foreign player, Avon now sells more cosmetics in Brazil than in the United States. Yet, the queen of Brazil's highly attractive and competitive market is its home-grown Natura. It is everywhere in Brazil. Its cosmetics, perfume, and hygiene products are in 60% of all households, and it leads the market with a 14% share in terms of sales (total of $3 billion). Founded in 1969 and listed on the São Paulo Stock Exchange since 2004, Natura is already the world's 20th most valuable cosmetics brand. But since 90% of its sales are in Brazil and almost 100% of its sales are in Latin America, few people outside the region have heard about it.

What is Natura's recipe for dominating such a large and diverse market? Its recipe has at least two ingredients. First, by definition, Natura is green. About 70% of its products are plant-based and approximately 10% come from the Amazon region, where it purchases from village cooperatives and indigenous tribes. Natura is also among the first cosmetics firms in the world to pay attention to the specific hair-care needs of black women, which tend to be ignored by mainstream firms.

Second, Natura relies on a small army of 1.2 million direct sales ladies, who work like the legendary Avon Ladies and since 2006 have been beating the Avon Ladies—Natura's number one foreign rival in the country. With $3 billion sales, Natura's total number of employees is only 6,200. In comparison, Avon worldwide has $10 billion sales but has 37,000 employees (and 6.4 million Avon Ladies). Thanks to Brazil's sky-high labor costs and tax rates, Natura has deliberately kept its employee base small in order to save cost. Since 1974, its marketing has been relying on direct sales, leveraging hard-working women who go the extra mile to deliver products (sometimes literally penetrating into the jungles of the Amazon). Direct sales thus give Natura a cost advantage relative to its number one domestic rival, O Boticário, which relies on a traditional retail format. An additional beauty of direct sales is that Natura's sales force is directly in touch with end users, whose needs, wants, and aspirations can be conveyed back to corporate headquarters for new product development.

Facing the onslaught of multinational cosmetics giants, Natura has realized that the best defense is offense. In 2005, Natura opened its first boutique in Paris, announcing its arrival in the cosmetics capital of the world. While progress has been slow overseas (in part thanks to the hot growth back home, which dominates executive attention and capital allocation), Natura is indeed committed to making a big push globally. While around the world Brazil is famous for commodity exports such as coffee and soy beans and for one high-tech firm (Embraer, which is renowned for its regional jets), no Brazilian consumer products have made a big splash overseas. Can Natura leverage Brazil's positive country-of-origin effect of being beautiful? In addition to soccer and beaches, most people associate Brazil with the rainforest and biodiversity, which seems to be an obvious advantage for a firm that calls itself Natura using a heavy dose of ingredients from the Amazon. So stay tuned . . .

Sources: J. Chelekis and S. Mudambi, "MNCs and micro-entrepreneurship in emerging economies: The case of Avon in the Amazon," *Journal of International Management* 16 (2010): 412–424; J. Chelekis and S. Mudambi, "Direct selling at the base of the pyramid," in M. W. Peng, *Global Business*, 3rd ed. (Cincinnati: Cengage Learning, 2014) 28–30; "Consumer goods: Looks good," *Economist*, 28 September 2013 (special report), 14–15.

Why is Natura able to outcompete its much larger and more visible global rivals in Brazil? What is so special about Natura? The answer is that there must be certain resources and capabilities specific to Natura that are not shared by competitors. This insight has been developed into a resource-based view, which has emerged as one of the two core perspectives on global business.[1]

One leading tool in global business is **SWOT analysis**. A SWOT analysis identifies a firm's strengths (S), weaknesses (W), opportunities (O), and threats (T). The institution-based view of global business we discussed in Chapters 2 and 3 deals with the

SWOT analysis An analytical tool for determining a firm's strengths (S), weaknesses (W), opportunities (O), and threats (T).

external opportunities and threats, enabled and constrained by formal and informal rules of the game. The resource-based view, on the other hand, concentrates on a firm's *internal* strengths and weaknesses. In this chapter, we first define resources and capabilities. Then we discuss the value chain analysis concentrating on the decision to keep an activity in-house or outsource it. We then focus on a VRIO framework centered on value (V), rarity (R), imitability (I), and organization (O).

PETR VACLAVEK/SHUTTERSTOCK.COM

4-1 UNDERSTANDING RESOURCES AND CAPABILITIES

A basic proposition of the resource-based view is that a firm consists of a bundle of productive resources and capabilities. **Resources** are defined as "the tangible and intangible assets a firm uses to choose and implement its strategies."[2] There is some debate regarding the definition of capabilities. Some scholars define them as a firm's capacity to dynamically deploy resources, suggesting a potentially crucial distinction between resources and capabilities and resulting in a "dynamic capabilities" view.[3]

While scholars may debate the fine distinctions between resources and capabilities, these distinctions are likely to "become badly blurred" in practice.[4] For example, is Natura's ability to successfully identify what women in Brazil want a resource or capability? How about its ability to motivate its direct sales force that is modeled after Avon Ladies and that is able to beat Avon Ladies? For current and would-be managers, the key is to understand how these attributes help improve firm performance, not to figure out whether they should be labeled as resources or capabilities. Therefore, in this book, we will use the terms "resources" and "capabilities" *interchangeably* and often in *parallel*. In other words, **capabilities** are defined here the same as resources.

All firms, even the smallest ones, possess a variety of resources and capabilities. How do we meaningfully classify such diversity? One useful way is to separate the resources and capabilities into two categories: tangible and intangible (Exhibit 4.1). **Tangible resources and capabilities** are assets that are observable and quantifiable. They can be broadly organized in four categories: financial, physical, technological, and organizational resources and capabilities.

By definition, **intangible resources and capabilities** are harder to observe and more difficult (or even impossible) to quantify (see Exhibit 4.1). Yet, it is widely acknowledged that they must be there, because no firm is likely to generate competitive advantage by relying on tangible resources and capabilities alone. Examples of intangible assets include human, innovation, and reputational resources and capabilities. Note that all resources and capabilities discussed here are merely *examples* (see In Focus). They do not represent an exhaustive list. Firms will forge ahead to discover and leverage new resources and capabilities.

Resource (capability) The tangible and intangible assets a firm uses to choose and implement its strategies.

Tangible resource and capability Assets that are observable and easily quantified.

Intangible resource and capability Assets that are hard to observe and difficult (if not impossible) to quantify.

EXHIBIT 4.1 EXAMPLES OF RESOURCES AND CAPABILITIES

Intangible	Tangible
Human	Financial
Innovation	Physical
Reputational	Technological

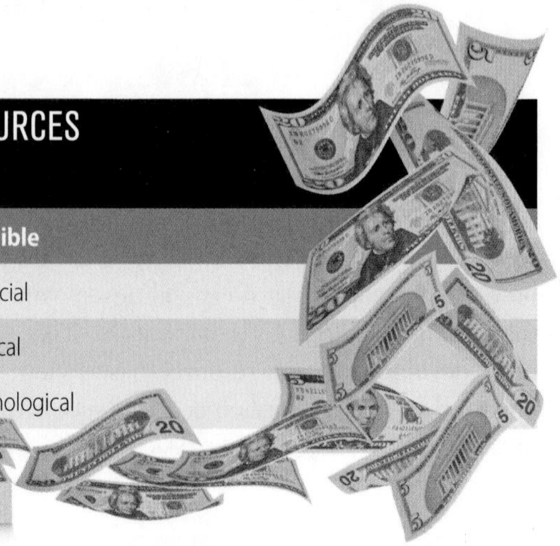
ISTOCKPHOTO.COM/CLAUDIO BALDINI

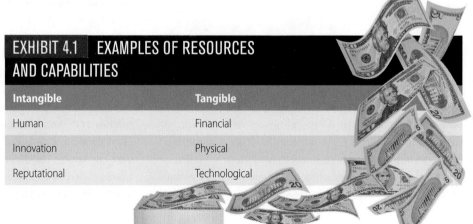

InFocus: Nordic Multinationals

DARIOS/SHUTTERSTOCK.COM

Nordic countries have small populations (six million in Denmark, nine million in Sweden, five million in Finland, and five million in Norway). But they are big in breeding globally competitive multinationals. Denmark boasts world leaders in beer (Carlsberg), fur (Kopenhagen Fur), medical insulin (Novo Nordisk), shipping (Maersk), toys (LEGO), and wind turbines (Vestas). Tiny Denmark is also an agricultural superpower, which is home to 30 million pigs—five pigs for every Dane. Leading global players include Arla, Danish Crown, Rose Poultry, and DuPont Danisco (a household name with over 100 years of history, Danisco was acquired by DuPont in 2011).

Sweden is a world leader in fighter jets (SAAB), mining equipment and machine tools (Sandvik and Atlas Copco), retail (IKEA and H&M), telecom equipment (Ericsson), and trucks (Scania). Finland leads the world in elevators and escalators (Kone), games (Ravio, the creator of Angry Birds), and telecom (Nokia, whose mobile phones had been a sensation until pushed aside by Apple's iPhones more recently). Norway has world-class competitors in oil services (Statoil) and fishing (Aker BioMarine and Havfisk—formerly Aker Seafoods).

Nordic multinationals also often collaborate and sometimes merge with each other. TeliaSonera is the result of the merger between Telia of Sweden and Sonera of Finland in 2002. TeliaSonera is the fifth largest telecom operator in Europe, and is the world's first operator of 4G networks. If you climb on top of Mount Everest and want to call down to brag about your views, it will be TeliaSonera that connects you from such a remote corner to the rest of the world.

The small size of the domestic markets has propelled Nordic firms to go international at a relatively young age. Some are founded to be born globals. Beyond this urge, three common characteristics make Nordic multinationals stand out among global peers. The first is their commitment to relentless innovation. Second, they foster a consensus-based approach to management, which promotes trust and cooperation. Finally, they share a passion for replacing labor with machines. In some advanced farms, robots can now automatically milk cows—with no human intervention. In one Swedish farm your author has visited, two owners—with the aid of milking robots—can manage 70 productive milk cows.

Sources: The author's interviews in Mora, Sweden; "Global niche players," *Economist*, 2 February 2013 (special report: The Nordic countries), 8–10; "Adventures in the skin trade," *Economist*, 3 May 2014, 62; "Bringing home the bacon," *Economist*, 4 January 2014, 52; C. Mutlu, "TeliaSonera: A Nordic investor in Eurasia," in M. W. Peng, *Global Strategy*, 3rd ed. (Cincinnati: Cengage Learning, 2014) 404–408.

4-2 4-3 RESOURCES, CAPABILITIES, AND THE VALUE CHAIN

If a firm is a bundle of resources and capabilities, how do they come together to add value? A value chain analysis allows us to answer this question. Shown in Panel A of Exhibit 4.2, most goods and services are produced through a chain of vertical activities (from upstream to downstream) that add value—in short, a **value chain**. The value chain typically consists of two areas: primary activities and support activities.

Each activity requires a number of resources and capabilities. Value chain analysis forces managers to think about firm resources and capabilities at a very micro, activity-based level. Given that no firm is likely to be good at all primary and support activities, the key is to examine whether the firm has resources and capabilities to perform a *particular* activity in a manner superior to competitors—a process known as **benchmarking** in SWOT analysis. If managers find that their firm's particular activity is unsatisfactory, a decision model (shown in Exhibit 4.3) can remedy the situation.

Value chain A series of activities used in the production of goods and services that make a product or service more valuable.

Benchmarking Examining whether a firm has the resources and capabilities to perform a particular activity in a manner superior to competitors.

EXHIBIT 4.2 THE VALUE CHAIN

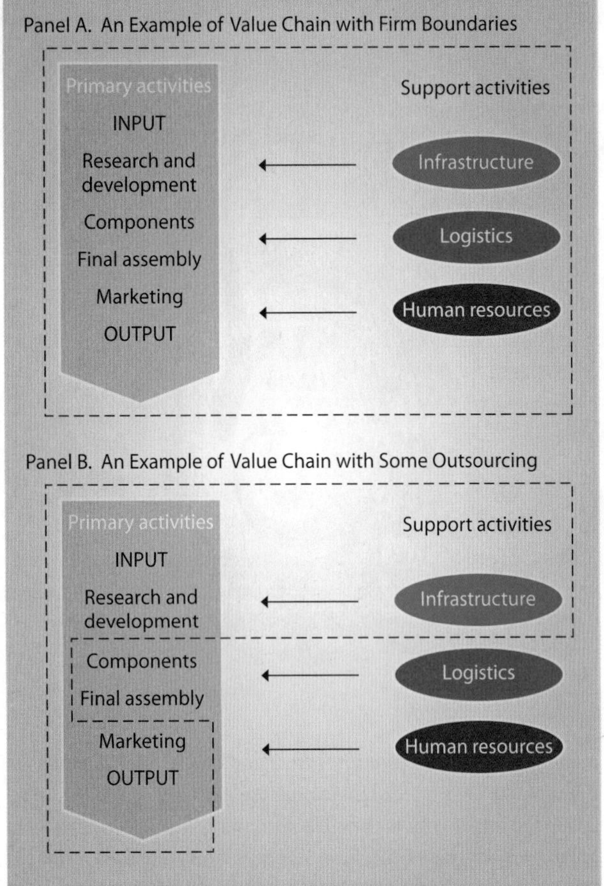

Note: Dashed lines represent firm boundaries.

In the first stage, managers ask, "Do we really need to perform this activity in-house?" Exhibit 4.4 introduces a framework to take a hard look at this question, the answer to which boils down to (1) whether an activity is industry-specific or common across industries, and (2) whether this activity is proprietary (firm-specific) or not. The answer is "No," when the activity is found in Cell 2 in Exhibit 4.4 with a great deal of commonality across industries and little need for keeping it proprietary—known in the recent jargon as a high degree of **commoditization**. The answer may also be "No" if the activity is in Cell 1 in Exhibit 4.4, which is industry-specific but also with a high level of commoditization. Then, the firm may want to outsource this activity, sell the unit involved, or lease the unit's services to other firms (see Exhibit 4.3). This is because operating multiple stages of uncompetitive activities in the value chain may be prohibitively costly.

Think about steel, definitely a crucial component for automobiles. But the question for automakers is: "Do we need to make steel by ourselves?" The requirements for steel are common across end-user industries—that is, the steel for automakers is essentially the same for construction, defense, and other steel-consuming end users (ignoring minor technical differences for the sake of our discussion). For automakers, while it is imperative to keep the automaking activity (especially engine and final assembly) proprietary (Cell 3 in Exhibit 4.3), there is no need to keep steelmaking in-house. Therefore, although many automakers, such as Ford and GM, historically were involved in steelmaking, none of them does it now. In other words, steelmaking is outsourced and steel is commoditized.

Outsourcing is defined as turning over an activity to an outside supplier that will perform it on behalf of the focal firm. For example, many consumer products companies (such as Nike and Apple), which possess strong capabilities in upstream activities (such as design) and downstream activities (such as marketing), have outsourced manufacturing to suppliers in low-cost countries. A total of 70% of the value of Boeing's new 787 Dreamliner is provided by outside suppliers. This compares with 51% for existing Boeing aircraft.[5] Recently, not only is manufacturing often outsourced but a number of service activities, such as IT, HR, and logistics, are also outsourced. The driving force is that many firms, which used to view certain activities as a very special part of their industries (such as airline reservations and bank

EXHIBIT 4.3 A TWO-STAGE DECISION MODEL IN VALUE CHAIN ANALYSIS

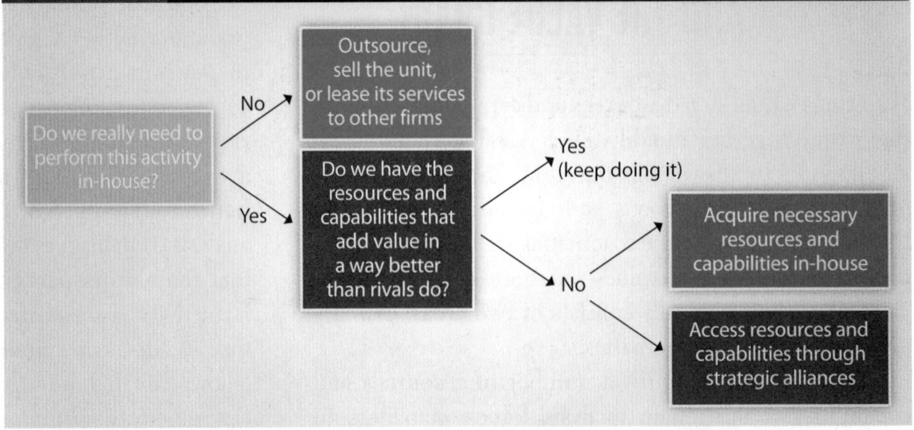

Commoditization A process of market competition through which unique products that command high prices and high margins gradually lose their ability to do so, thus becoming commodities.

Outsourcing Turning over an activity to an outside supplier that will perform it on behalf of the focal firm.

EXHIBIT 4.4 IN-HOUSE VERSUS OUTSOURCE

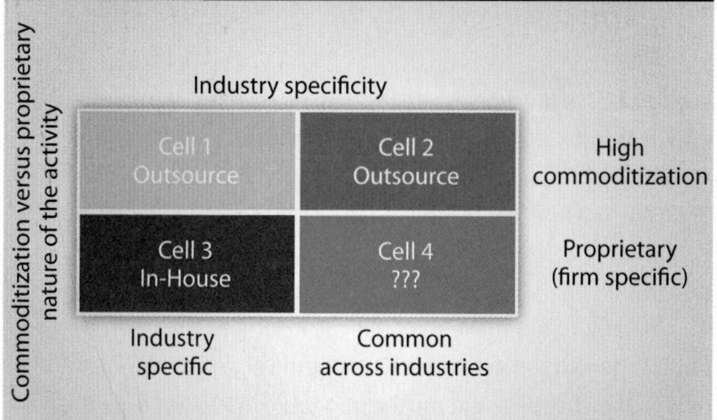

Note: At present, there are no clear guidelines for Cell 4, where firms either choose to perform activities in-house or outsource.

EXHIBIT 4.5 LOCATION, LOCATION, LOCATION

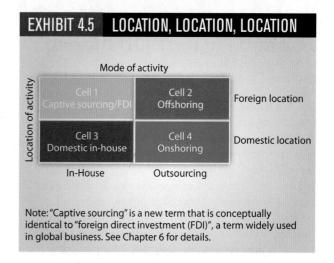

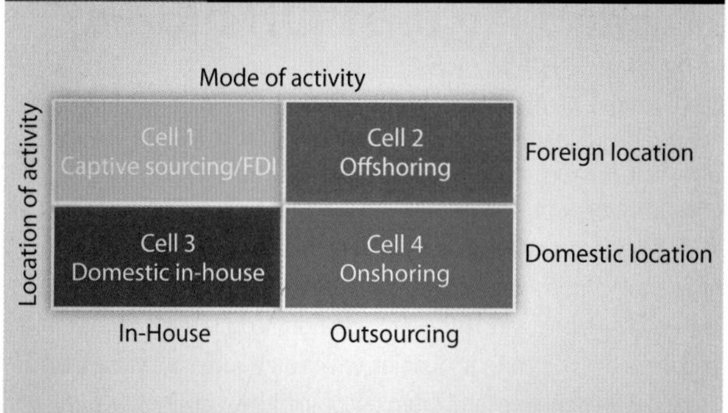

Note: "Captive sourcing" is a new term that is conceptually identical to "foreign direct investment (FDI)", a term widely used in global business. See Chapter 6 for details.

call centers), now believe that these activities have relatively generic attributes that can be shared across industries. Of course, this changing mentality is fueled by the rise of service providers, such as IBM and Infosys in IT, Manpower in HR, Foxconn in contract manufacturing, and DHL in logistics. These specialist firms argue that such activities can be broken off from the various client firms (just as steelmaking was broken off from automakers decades ago) and leveraged to serve multiple clients with greater economies of scale. Such outsourcing enables client firms to become "leaner and meaner" organizations, which can better focus on their core activities (see Exhibit 4.2, Panel B).

If the answer to the question "Do we really need to perform this activity in-house?" is "Yes" (Cell 3 in Exhibit 4.4), but the firm's current resources and capabilities are not up to the task, then there are two choices (see Exhibit 4.3). First, the firm may want to acquire and develop capabilities in-house so that it can perform this particular activity better. Second, if a firm does not have enough skills to develop these capabilities in-house, it may want to access them through alliances.

Conspicuously lacking in both Exhibits 4.3 and 4.4 is the *geographic* dimension—domestic versus foreign locations. Because the two terms "outsourcing" and "offshoring" have emerged rather recently, there is a great deal of confusion, especially among some journalists, who often casually equate them. So, to minimize confusion, we go from two terms to four terms in Exhibit 4.5, based on locations and modes (in-house versus outsource):

- **Offshoring**—international/foreign outsourcing.
- **Onshoring**—domestic outsourcing.
- **Captive sourcing**—setting up subsidiaries to perform in-house work in foreign locations.
- Domestic in-house activity.

Outsourcing—especially offshoring—has no shortage of controversies (see Debate). Despite this set of new labels, we need to be aware that "captive sourcing" is conceptually identical to foreign direct investment (FDI), which is nothing new in the world of global business (see Chapters 1 and 6). We also need to be aware that "offshoring" and "onshoring" are simply international and domestic variants of outsourcing, respectively. While offshoring low-cost IT work to India, the Philippines, and other emerging economies has been widely practiced, interestingly, eastern Germany; northern France; and the Appalachian, Great Plains, and southern regions of the United States have emerged as new hotbeds for onshoring. In job-starved regions such as Michigan, high-quality IT workers may accept wages 35% lower than at headquarters in Silicon Valley.

One interesting lesson we can take away from Exhibit 4.5 is that even for a single firm, value-adding activities may be geographically dispersed around the world, taking advantage of the best locations and modes to perform certain activities. For instance, a Dell laptop may be designed in the United States (domestic in-house activity), its components may be produced in Taiwan (offshoring) as well as the United States (onshoring), and its final assembly may be done in China (captive sourcing/FDI). When customers call for help, the call center may be in India, Ireland, Jamaica, or the Philippines, manned by an outside service provider—Dell may have outsourced the service activities through offshoring.

Offshoring Outsourcing to an international or foreign firm.

Onshoring Outsourcing to a domestic firm.

Captive sourcing Setting up subsidiaries abroad so that the work done is in-house but the location is foreign. Also known as foreign direct investment.

Debate: *Emerging Markets/Ethical Dilemma*

For and Against Offshoring

Offshoring—or, more specifically, international outsourcing—has emerged as a leading corporate movement in the 21st century. However, it is debatable whether such offshoring proves to be a long-term benefit or hindrance to Western firms and economies.

Proponents argue that offshoring creates enormous value for firms and economies. Western firms are able to tap into low-cost yet high-quality labor, translating into significant cost savings. Firms can also focus on their core capabilities, which may add more value than dealing with non-core (and often uncompetitive) activities. In turn, offshoring service providers, such as Infosys, TCS, and Wipro, develop *their* core competencies in information technology (IT), especially **business process outsourcing (BPO)**. A McKinsey study that focused on offshoring between the United States and India reported that for every dollar spent by US firms in India, US firms save 58 cents (see Exhibit 4.6). Overall, $1.46 of new wealth is created, of which the US economy captures $1.13 through cost savings and increased exports to India. India captures the other 33 cents through profits, wages, and additional taxes. While acknowledging that some US employees may lose their jobs, proponents suggest that on balance, offshoring is a win-win solution for both US and Indian firms and economies.

Critics make three points on strategic, economic, and political grounds. Strategically, if "even core functions like engineering, R&D, manufacturing, and marketing can—and often should—be moved outside," what is left of the firm? US firms have gone down this path before—in manufacturing—with disastrous results. In the 1960s, Radio Corporation of America (RCA) invented the color TV and then outsourced its production to Japan, a low-cost country at that time. Fast forward to the 2000s and the United States no longer has any US-owned color TV producers. Critics argue that offshoring nurtures rivals. Why are Indian IT/BPO firms now emerging as strong rivals? It is in part because they built up their capabilities doing work for EDS and IBM in the 1990s, particularly by working to help the IT industry prevent the "millennium bug" (or Y2K) problem.

Business process outsourcing (BPO) The outsourcing of business processes such as loan origination, credit card processing, and call center operations.

Economically, critics question whether developed economies, on the whole, actually gain more. While shareholders and corporate highflyers embrace offshoring, it increasingly results in job losses in high-end areas such as design, R&D, and IT/BPO. While white-collar individuals who lose jobs will naturally hate it, the net impact on developed economies may still be negative.

Finally, critics make the political argument that many large firms in developed economies are unethical and are interested only in the cheapest and most exploitable labor. Not only is work commoditized, but people are also degraded as tradable commodities that can be jettisoned. As a result, large firms that outsource work to emerging economies are often accused of destroying jobs at home, ignoring corporate social responsibility, violating customer privacy (for example, by sending medical records, tax returns, and credit card numbers to be processed overseas), and in some cases undermining national security. Not surprisingly, the debate often becomes emotional and explosive when such accusations are made.

For firms in developed economies where this debate primarily takes place, the choice is not really offshoring versus nonoffshoring, but where to draw the line on offshoring. There is relatively little debate in emerging economies because they clearly stand to gain from offshoring. Taking a page from the Indian playbook, the Philippines, with numerous English-speaking professionals, is trying to eat some of India's lunch. Northeast China, where Japanese is widely taught, is positioning itself as an ideal location for call centers for Japan. Central and Eastern Europe gravitates toward serving Western Europe. Central and South American countries want to grab call center contracts for the large Hispanic market in the United States.

Sources: D. Farrell, "Offshoring," *Journal of Management Studies* 42 (2005): 675–683; M. Gottfredson, R. Puryear, and S. Phillips, "Strategic sourcing," *Harvard Business Review* (February 2005): 132; P. Jensen, M. Larsen, and T. Pedersen, "The organizational design of offshoring," *Journal of International Management* 19 (2013): 315-323; S. Mudambi and S. Tallman, "Make, buy, or ally?" *Journal of Management Studies* 47 (2010): 1434–1456; D. Mukherjee, A. Gaur, and A. Dutta, "Creating value through offshore outsourcing," *Journal of International Management* 19 (2013): 377-389; C. Weigelt and M. Sarkar, "Performance implications of outsourcing for technological innovations," *Strategic Management Journal* 33 (2012): 189–216.

EXHIBIT 4.6 BENEFIT OF $1 US SPENDING ON OFFSHORING TO INDIA

Benefit to the United States	$	Benefit to India	$
Savings accruing to US investors/customers	0.58	Labor	0.10
Exports of US goods/services to providers in India	0.05	Profits retained in India	0.10
Profit transfer by US-owned operations in India back to the United States	0.04	Suppliers	0.09
Net direct benefit retained in the United States	0.67	Central government taxes	0.03
Value from US labor re-employed	0.46	State government taxes	0.01
Net benefit to the United States	1.13	*Net benefit to India*	0.33

Source: D. Farrell, "Offshoring: Value creation through economic change," *Journal of Management Studies* (2005) 42: 675–683.

Of course, decisions on offshoring are not one-off. More recently as the cost of manufacturing in China rises because of rising labor cost and unreliable quality, some Western firms have brought some of the work back to their home countries—a process known as **reshoring**.

Overall, a value chain analysis engages managers to ascertain a firm's strengths and weaknesses on an activity-by-activity basis, *relative to rivals*, in a SWOT analysis. The recent proliferation of new labels is intimidating, causing some gurus to claim that "21st century offshoring really is different."[6] In reality, it is not. Under the skin of the new vocabulary, we still see the time-honored SWOT analysis at work. The next section introduces a VRIO framework on how to do this.

4-4 FROM SWOT TO VRIO

Recent progress in the resource-based view has gone beyond the traditional SWOT analysis. The new work focuses on the value (V), rarity (R), imitability (I), and organizational (O) aspects of resources and capabilities, leading to a **VRIO framework**. Summarized in Exhibit 4.7, addressing these four important questions has a number of ramifications for competitive advantage.

4-4a The Question of Value

Do firm resources and capabilities add value? The preceding value chain analysis suggests that this is the most fundamental question to start with. Only value-adding resources can lead to competitive advantage, whereas non-value-adding capabilities may lead to competitive *disadvantage*. With changes in the competitive landscape, previous value-adding resources and capabilities may become obsolete. The evolution of IBM is a case in point. IBM historically excelled in making hardware, including tabulating machines in the 1930s, mainframes in the 1960s, and PCs in the 1980s. However, as competition for hardware heated up, IBM's capabilities in hardware not only added little value, but also increasingly stood in the way for it to move into new areas. Since the 1990s, IBM has been focused more on lucrative software and services, where it has developed new value-adding capabilities, aiming to become an on-demand computing *service* provider for corporations. As part of this new strategy, IBM purchased PricewaterhouseCoopers, a leading technology consulting firm, and sold its PC division to Lenovo.

"WHATEVER BUSINESS YOU'RE IN, IT'S GOING TO COMMODITIZE OVER TIME, SO YOU HAVE TO KEEP MOVING IT TO A HIGHER VALUE AND CHANGE."[8]

The relationship between valuable resources and capabilities and firm performance is straightforward. Instead of becoming strengths, non-value-adding resources and capabilities, such as IBM's historical expertise in hardware, may become weaknesses. If firms are unable to get rid of non-value-adding assets, they are likely to suffer from below-average performance.[7] In the worst case, they may become extinct, a fate IBM narrowly skirted during the early 1990s. According to IBM's CEO Ginni Rometty, "Whatever business you're in, it's going to commoditize over time, so you have to keep moving it to a higher value and change."

Reshoring Moving formerly offshored activities back to the home country of the focal firm.

VRIO framework The resource-based framework that focuses on the value (V), rarity (R), imitability (I), and organizational (O) aspects of resources and capabilities.

EXHIBIT 4.7 THE VRIO FRAMEWORK AND FIRM PERFORMANCE

Is a resource or capability . . .

Valuable?	Rare?	Costly to imitate?	Exploited by organization?		Competitive implications	Firm performance
No	—	—	No	→	Competitive disadvantage	Below average
Yes	No	—	Yes	→	Competitive parity	Average
Yes	Yes	No	Yes	→	Temporary competitive advantage	Above average
Yes	Yes	Yes	Yes	→	Sustained competitive advantage	Persistently above average

Sources: J. Barney, *Gaining and Sustaining Competitive Advantage*, 2nd ed. (Upper Saddle River, NJ: Prentice Hall, 2002) 173; R. Hoskisson, M. Hitt, and R. D. Ireland, *Competing for Advantage* (Cincinnati: Cengage Learning, 2004) 118.

4-4b The Question of Rarity

Simply possessing valuable resources and capabilities may not be enough. The next question asks: How rare are valuable resources and capabilities? At best, valuable but common resources and capabilities will lead to competitive parity but not an advantage. Consider the identical aircraft made by Boeing and Airbus used by numerous airlines. They are certainly valuable, yet it is difficult to derive competitive advantage from these aircraft alone. Airlines have to work hard on how to use these same aircraft *differently*.

Only valuable and rare resources and capabilities have the potential to provide some temporary competitive advantage. Overall, the question of rarity is a reminder of the cliché: If everyone has it, you can't make money from it. For example, the quality of the American Big Three automakers is now comparable with that of the best Asian and European rivals. However, even in their home country, the Big Three's quality improvements have not translated into stronger sales. Embarrassingly, in 2009 both GM and Chrysler, despite the decent quality of their cars, had to declare bankruptcy and be bailed out by the US government (and also by the Canadian government). The point is simple: Flawless high quality is now expected among car buyers, is no longer rare, and thus provides little advantage.

4-4c The Question of Imitability

Valuable and rare resources and capabilities can be a source of competitive advantage only if competitors have a difficult time imitating them. While it is relatively easy to imitate a firm's *tangible* resources (such as plants), it is a lot more challenging and often impossible to imitate *intangible* capabilities (such as tacit knowledge, superior motivation, and managerial talents).

Imitation is difficult. Why? In two words: **causal ambiguity**, which refers to the difficulty of identifying the causal determinants of successful firm performance. What exactly has caused Burberry to be such an enduring and continuously relevant luxury goods company (see the Closing Case)? Burberry has no shortage of competitors and imitators. Its performance has not always been enviable. Yet, in the past 160 years Burberry has always been able to turn around by finding new paths to growth (sometimes by returning to roots, as evidenced by its most recent turnaround).

A natural question is: How does Burberry do it? Usually a number of resources and capabilities will be nominated, such as a commitment to customer relationships, a willingness to change, a strong leadership team, and a multinational presence. While all of these are plausible, what *exactly* is it? This truly is a million dollar question, because knowing the answer to this question is not only intriguing to scholars and students, it can also be hugely profitable for Burberry's rivals. Unfortunately, outsiders usually have a hard time understanding what a firm does inside its boundaries. We can try, as many rivals have, to identify Burberry's recipe for success by drawing up a long list of possible reasons, labeled as "resources and capabilities" in our classroom discussion. But in the end, as outsiders we are not sure.

Causal ambiguity The difficulty of identifying the actual cause of a firm's successful performance.

What is even more fascinating for scholars and students and more frustrating for rivals is that often managers of a focal firm such as Apple do not know exactly what contributes to its success. When interviewed, they can usually generate a long list of what they do well, such as a strong organizational culture, a relentless drive, and many other attributes. To make matters worse, different managers of the same firm may have a different list. When probed as to which resource or capability is "it," they usually suggest that it is all of the above in *combination*. After Apple made a record-breaking $18 billion profit in the fourth quarter of 2014 (never before had so much money been made by a single firm in three months), its CEO Tim Cook told the media that it was "hard to comprehend."[9] This is probably one of the most interesting and paradoxical aspects of the resource-based view: If insiders have a hard time figuring out what unambiguously contributes to their firm's performance, it is not surprising that outsiders' efforts in understanding and imitating these capabilities are usually flawed and often fail.

Overall, valuable and rare but imitable resources and capabilities may give firms some temporary competitive advantage, leading to above-average performance for some period of time. However, such advantage is not likely to be sustainable. Shown by the example of Apple and Burberry, only valuable, rare, and *hard-to-imitate* resources and capabilities may potentially lead to sustained competitive advantage.

4-4d The Question of Organization

Even valuable, rare, and hard-to-imitate resources and capabilities may not give a firm a sustained competitive advantage if it is not properly organized.[10] Although movie stars represent some of the most valuable, rare, and hard-to-imitate (as well as highest paid) resources, *most* movies flop. More generally, the question of organization asks: How can a firm (such as a movie studio) be organized to develop and leverage the full potential of its resources and capabilities?

Numerous components within a firm are relevant to the question of organization. In a movie studio, these components include talents in "smelling" good ideas, photography crews, musicians, singers, makeup artists, animation specialists, and managers on the business side. These components are often called **complementary assets**,[11] because by themselves they are difficult to generate box office hits. For the favorite movie you saw most recently, do you still remember the names of its photographers and makeup artists? Of course not—you probably only remember the names of the stars. However, stars alone cannot generate hit movies. It is the *combination* of star resources and complementary assets that create hit movies. "It may be that not just a few resources and capabilities enable a firm to gain a competitive advantage but that literally thousands of these organizational attributes, bundled together, generate such advantage."[12]

Known as the ability to use one's two hands equally well, **ambidexterity** in the management literature describes capabilities to simultaneously deal with paradoxes. For example, in emerging economies, ambidexterity to manage both market forces and government forces simultaneously—as a bundle of complementary resources—is key to navigate the competitive waters.[13] In other words, to attain competitive advantage, market-based and nonmarket-based (political) capabilities need to complement each other. This is not only important for foreign firms, but also crucial for domestic firms. Case in point: The Tata Nano, the much-hyped, cheapest car that presumably would allow many Indians to become first-time car owners and create thousands of jobs, could not be made in its originally planned factory in the Indian state of West Bengal. Thousands of farmers who lost their land used to build the Nano factory protested. Political pressures forced Tata to abandon the plan and start another factory in another state, Gujarat, at a great cost. The fact that such an influential and otherwise respected firm can mess up its political relations *domestically* underscores the importance of ambidexterity as capabilities to manage both market-based and nonmarket-based relationships. Otherwise, strong market performers, such as Tata in India, may nevertheless hit a wall when messing up government relations.

ISTOCKPHOTO.COM/HANA76

XTRAVAGANT/FOTOLIA LLC

Another idea is **social complexity**, which refers to the socially complex ways of organizing typical of many firms. Many multinationals consist of thousands of people scattered in many different countries. How they overcome cultural differences and are organized as one corporate entity and achieve corporate goals is profoundly complex. Oftentimes, it is their invisible relationships that add value.[14] Such organizationally embedded capabilities are thus very difficult for rivals to imitate. This emphasis on social complexity refutes what is half-jokingly called the "LEGO" view of the firm, in which a firm can be assembled (and dissembled) from modules of technology and people (a la LEGO toy blocks). By treating employees as identical and replaceable blocks, the "LEGO" view fails to realize that social capital associated with complex relationships and knowledge permeating many firms can be a source of competitive advantage.

Overall, only valuable, rare, and hard-to-imitate capabilities that are organizationally embedded and exploited can lead to sustained competitive advantage and persistently above-average performance. Because capabilities cannot be evaluated in isolation, the VRIO framework presents four interconnected and increasingly difficult hurdles (Exhibit 4.7). In other words, these four V, R, I, and O aspects come together as one "package."

Complementary asset The combination of numerous resources and assets that enable a firm to gain a competitive advantage.

Ambidexterity Ability to use one's both hands equally well. In management jargon, this term has been used to describe capabilities to simultaneously deal with paradoxes (such as exploration versus exploitation).

Social complexity The socially intricate and interdependent ways that firms are typically organized.

4-5 MANAGEMENT SAVVY

How does the resource-based view answer the big question in global business: What determines the success and failure of firms around the globe? The answer is straightforward. Fundamentally, some firms outperform others because winners possess some valuable, rare, hard-to-imitate, and organizationally embedded resources and capabilities that competitors do not have. This view is especially insightful when we see firms such as Natura (Opening Case) and Burberry (Closing Case) persistently succeed while others struggle in difficult industries.

Shown in Exhibit 4.8, the resource-based view suggests four implications for action. First, the proposition that firms "compete on resources and capabilities" is not novel. The subtlety comes when managers attempt, via the VRIO framework, to distinguish resources and capabilities that are valuable, rare, hard-to-imitate, and organizationally embedded from those that do not share these attributes. In other words, the VRIO framework can greatly aid the time-honored SWOT analysis, especially the S (strengths) and W (weaknesses) parts. Managers, who cannot pay attention to everything, must have some sense of what *really* matters. Managers commonly fail to assess how their resources and capabilities compare with those of their rivals. As a result, most firms end up having a mixed bag of both good and mediocre capabilities. Using the VRIO framework, a value chain analysis helps managers make decisions on what capabilities to focus on in-house and what to outsource. Increasingly, what really matters is not tangible resources that are relatively easy to imitate, but intangible capabilities that are harder for rivals to wrap their arms around. Therefore, managers need to identify, develop, and leverage valuable, rare, hard-to-imitate, and organizationally embedded resources and capabilities, which are often intangible. It is thus not surprising that capabilities not meeting these criteria are increasingly outsourced.

EXHIBIT 4.8 IMPLICATIONS FOR ACTION

- Managers need to build firm strengths based on the VRIO framework.
- Relentless imitation or benchmarking, while important, is not likely to be a successful strategy.
- Managers need to build up resources and capabilities for future competition.
- Students need to make themselves into "untouchables" whose jobs cannot be easily outsourced.

Second, relentless imitation or benchmarking, while important, is not likely to be successful in the long run. By the time Elvis Presley died in 1977, there were a little over 100 Elvis impersonators. After his death, the number skyrocketed.[15] But obviously none of these imitators achieved any fame remotely close to the star status attained by the King of Rock 'n' Roll. Imitators have a tendency to mimic the most visible, the most obvious, and, consequently, the *least* important practices of winning firms. At best, follower firms that meticulously replicate every resource possessed by winning firms at best can hope to attain competitive parity. Firms endowed with sufficient resources to imitate others may be better off developing their own unique capabilities. The best-performing firms such as world-class Nordic multinationals (e.g., Ericsson, H&M, LEGO, Vestas—featured in In Focus) often create new ways of adding value.

Third, even a sustainable competitive advantage will not last forever, particularly in today's global competition. All a firm can hope for is a competitive advantage that can be sustained for as long as possible. Over time, all advantages may erode. As noted earlier, each of IBM's product-related advantages associated with tabulating machines, mainframes, and PCs was sustained for a period of time. But, eventually, these advantages disappeared. Even IBM's newer focus on software and servers is challenged by cloud computing heavyweights such as Amazon.[16] Therefore, the lesson for all firms, including current market leaders, is to develop strategic *foresight*—over-the-horizon radar is a good metaphor. Such strategic foresight enables firms to anticipate future needs and move early to identify, develop, and leverage resources and capabilities for future competition.

Finally, here is a very personal and relevant implication for action. As a student who is probably studying this book in a developed (read: high-wage and thus high-cost!) country such as the United States, you may be wondering: What do I get out of this? How do I cope with the frightening future of global competition? There are two lessons you can draw. First, the whole debate on offshoring, a part of the larger debate on globalization, is very relevant and directly affects your future as a manager, a consumer, and a citizen (see Chapter 1). So don't be a couch potato. Be active, get involved, and be prepared because it is not only their debate, it is *yours* as well. Second, be very serious about the VRIO framework of the resource-based view. While the resource-based view has been developed to advise firms, there is no reason you cannot develop that into a resource-based view of the *individual*. In other words, you can use the VRIO framework to develop yourself into an "untouchable"—a person whose job cannot be outsourced, as defined by Thomas Friedman in *The World Is Flat* (2005). An untouchable individual's job cannot be outsourced because he or she possesses valuable, rare, and hard-to-imitate capabilities that are indispensable to an employer. This won't be easy. But you really don't want to be mediocre. A generation ago, American parents told their kids: Eat your food—kids in China and India are starving. Now, Friedman would advise you: Study this book and leverage your education—students in China and India are starving for your job.[17]

Enhancing Value, Rarity, and Inimitability at Burberry

Asked to name an iconic British luxury brand, most people would probably nominate Burberry. Founded in 1856, Burberry grew to become a leading global fashion house with $5.2 billion revenue in 2012. Most famous for its trench coats worn by soldiers in the trenches during World War I, Burberry became such a part of British culture that it earned a royal warrant as an official supplier to the royal family.

THINGLASS/SHUTTERSTOCK.COM

However, by the mid 2000s, Burberry lost its focus. It had 23 licensees in a variety of products and locations around the world, each doing something different ranging from dog cover-ups and leashes to kilts. In luxury, ubiquity by definition is the killer of exclusivity. Among numerous Burberry products, outerwear exemplified by the "boring old trench coat" only represented 20% of its global revenue. While luxury sales were growing globally, Burberry seemed to be losing out, with a lackluster growth rate of only 2% per year by 2006. Each of Burberry's two leading global rivals (LVMH and Gucci) had more than ten times of Burberry's revenue and much higher growth. How could Burberry, which became a "David," grow against such "Goliaths"?

In 2006, with the arrival of new CEO Angela Ahrendts, significant soul searching took place at Burberry. Focusing on value, rarity, and inimitability of Burberry's resources and capabilities, the firm realized that its greatest assets lied in its *Britishness*, more specifically its trench coat roots—hence the highest value it could deliver. Further, such a focus on Britain's positive country-of-origin image would be rare in a world largely populated by French and Italian luxury brands. It would also be difficult (or sometimes impossible) to imitate if this heritage were emphasized and strengthened.

With this powerful insight, Burberry adopted a new strategy centered on the iconic trench coat—its first social media platform was named www.artofthetrench.com. Before the transformation, Burberry sold just a few styles of trench coats and almost all were beige with the signature check lining. Now with centralized and consistent design (a significant intangible capability), it sells more than 300 products in a wide variety of styles and colors related to trench coats. By 2012, 60% of its revenue came from apparel, and outerwear made up more than half of that. Many of its stylish trench coats are priced over $1,000. Further, instead of outsourcing, Burberry has concentrated its trench coat production at the Castleford factory in the north of England, adding more than 1,000 jobs in the UK (of a global labor force of 9,000). In summary, a Burberry trench coat designed and manufactured in the UK is valuable, rare, and impossible to imitate by rivals.

The upshot? Burberry has been rewarded handsomely by the market. In five years (2007–2012), its revenue and operating income doubled. In 2011, Interbrand named it the fourth fastest-growing global brand (behind Apple, Google, and Amazon) and the fastest-growing luxury brand. So impressed was Apple that in 2013 it poached Ahrendts, who quit Burberry and became Apple's senior vice president in charge of retail and online operations.

Case Discussion Questions

1. Why did Burberry choose to focus on the value, rarity, and inimitability of its core products centered on outwear, as opposed to the proliferation of unrelated products?
2. Why was Burberry able to turn around?
3. Burberry is 160 years old in 2016. Find another firm in any industry and any country that has also survived over 150 years (or at least 100 years). What are the "secrets" behind its longevity?
4. ***ON ETHICS***: Some argue that there is no future in made-in-UK textile products. Others suggest iconic UK firms have a special responsibility to create jobs by manufacturing products in the UK. What is your view on this debate?

Sources: A. Ahrendts, "Burberry's CEO on turning an aging British icon into a global luxury brand," *Harvard Business Review* (January 2013): 39–42; "Burberry share price plummets after CEO Angela Ahrents quits fashion house to take key role at Apple," *Daily Mail*, 13 October 2013, www.dailymail.co.uk; M. W. Peng, "High fashion fights recession," in M. W. Peng, *Global Strategy*, 3rd ed. (Cincinnati: Cengage Learning, 2014) 57–59; M. W. Peng and K. Meyer, 2013, "Winning the future markets for UK manufacturing output," *Future of Manufacturing Project Evidence Paper* 25 (London: UK Government Office for Science, 2013); www.artofthetrench.com; www.burberry.com.

STUDY TOOLS 4

LOCATED AT THE BACK OF YOUR BOOK:

- ☐ Rip out and study the Chapter Review Card at the end of the book

LOG IN TO WWW.CENGAGEBRAIN.COM TO:

- ☐ Review key term flashcards
- ☐ Complete a practice quiz to test your knowledge of key concepts
- ☐ Take and complete the chapter crossword puzzle
- ☐ Complete interactive content, watch chapter videos, and take a graded quiz
- ☐ Track your knowledge of key concepts in Global Business
- ☐ Read and discuss additional case study content

PART 2

5 Trading Internationally

LEARNING OBJECTIVES

After studying this chapter, you should be able to . . .

5-1 Use the resource-based and institution-based views to explain why nations trade.

5-2 Identify and define the classical and modern theories of international trade.

5-3 Explain the importance of political realities governing international trade.

5-4 Identify factors that should be considered when your firm participates in international trade.

After you finish this chapter, go to **PAGE 83** for **STUDY TOOLS**

EMERGING MARKETS

Is China the Largest Trading Nation in the World?

International trade has two directions: export and import. It has two components: merchandise (goods) and services. Worldwide the ratio between merchandise and service trade is generally 4:1. Is China now the world's largest trading nation?

The ubiquitous made-in-China products around the world are the most visible evidence of the rise of China as a trading nation. Since 2011, China has dethroned Germany to become the world's champion merchandise exporter. Why does the rest of the world buy so many made-in-China products? Without getting into details, we can safely say—from a resource-based view—that Chinese exports win markets because they deliver value, are rare, and possess hard-to-imitate attributes. Such products range from low-tech shoes and toys to high-tech smartphones (made by Lenovo and Xiaomi) and telecom equipment (made by Huawei and ZTE). With 33% of GDP coming from manufacturing (the world's highest), China's manufacturing capabilities have not only propelled its export growth, but also underpinned its rise as the world's second largest economy.

From an institution-based view, China's accession to the World Trade Organization (WTO) in 2001 has certainly contributed to its rise as a trading nation. In addition, it has free trade agreements (FTAs) with the Association of Southeast Asian Nations (ASEAN—ten member countries), Chile, Costa Rica, New Zealand, Pakistan, Peru, and Singapore. China is also negotiating FTAs with Australia, Iceland, Japan, Norway, and South Korea as well as two regional bodies, the (Persian) Gulf Cooperation Council (GCC) and Southern Africa Customs Union (SACU).

While China's merchandise exports often attract attention, less visible but equally important is China's voracious appetite for merchandise imports. At about the same time China became a champion merchandise exporter, China displaced Germany as the second largest merchandise importer—only behind the United States. The majority of Chinese imports consists of raw materials (such as Australian coal, Chilean copper, and Russian oil) and industrial supplies (such as Toshiba electronic components and Texas Instruments semiconductors). A curious feature of Chinese exports is that most of them are produced by non-Chinese firms operating in China. These firms source a lot of components from around the world to be assembled in China. Meticulous research on "designed in California, assembled in China" Apple iPhones and iPads finds that 60%–70% of their value comes from imports from economies such as Germany, Japan, South Korea, Taiwan, and the United States. The real value added in China is only about 10%—the rest is captured by Apple. Given that iPhones and iPads are made in China by Taiwan-based Foxconn, which repatriates some of its earnings to shareholders in Taiwan, the real value added that stays in China due to all that hard work to assemble and export iPhones is significantly less than 10%. While iPhones and iPads may be extreme cases, overall China only adds 67% of the value of its exports. In comparison, the United States adds 89% of the value to its exports (see the Closing Case).

China does enjoy the world's second largest merchandise trade surplus ($259 billion)—behind Germany's slightly larger merchandise surplus ($264 billion). At the same time, China suffers from the world's biggest deficit in service trade ($124 billion). As an active trader of services, China is fifth in service exports (behind the United States, Britain, Germany, and France) and second in service imports (behind the United States). Its leading contributor to service trade deficit is tourists. As the largest group of international tourists, one out of every ten international tourists is now Chinese (see Chapter 14 Closing Case). As a group they spend more and focus more on shopping. In 2013 they spent $129 billion, followed by American tourists who spent $86 billion. The average Chinese tourist indulges himself/herself with $1,130 tax-free purchases vis-à-vis $494 by the average Russian tourist.

With $4.2 trillion in merchandise trade, China is the world's largest merchandise trader. However, adding all the merchandise exports and imports as well as service exports and imports, China, whose total trade volume is $4.7 trillion, is *not* the largest trading nation. It is the second largest trading nation. With a total trade volume of $5 trillion, the United States is the world's trade champion. In percentage terms, a substantially higher percentage (53%) of Chinese GDP is traded vis-à-vis a lower 30% of US GDP that is traded. In the next decade as the overall size of the Chinese economy becomes larger than the US economy, it is likely that China will dethrone the United States to become the largest trading nation by absolute volume. While examining the total volume of trade is interesting, on a per capita basis, China only ranks 99th in the world given its huge population of 1.34 billion.

Sources: "Taiwan's protests point to a deeper crisis," *Bloomberg Businessweek*, 17 April 2014, 17–18; "A number of great import," *Economist*, 15 February 2014, 40; "Coming to a beach near you," *Economist*, 19 April 2014, 53–54; "Picking the world champion of trade," *Economist*, 18 January 2014, 72–73; "Trading places," *Economist*, 5 April 2014, 49; M. W. Peng and K. Meyer, "Winning the future markets for UK manufacturing output," *Future of Manufacturing Project Evidence Paper* 25 (London: UK Government Office for Science, 2013); World Trade Organization, *World Trade Report 2014* (Geneva: WTO, 2014).

Why are Chinese merchandise exports so competitive in the world? Why does China's service trade suffer from a huge deficit? More generally, how does international trade contribute to a nation's economic growth and prosperity? International trade is the oldest and still the most important building block of international business. It has never failed to generate debates. Debates on international trade tend to be very ferocious, because so much is at stake. We begin by addressing a crucial question: Why do nations trade? Then we outline how the two core perspectives introduced in earlier chapters—namely, resource-based and institution-based views—can help answer this question. The remainder of the chapter deals with the theories and realities of international trade. As before, implications for action follow.

5-1 WHY DO NATIONS TRADE?

Internationally, trade means **export** (sell abroad) and **import** (buy from abroad). Discussed in the Opening Case, international trade consists of both merchandise trade and service trade. **Merchandise trade** is the buying and selling of tangible products, while **service trade** is the buying and selling of intangible services.

International trade is far more complex than domestic trade. So why do nations go through the trouble of trading internationally? Without getting into details, we can safely say that there must be economic gains from trade. More importantly, such gains must be shared by *both* sides. Otherwise, there would be no willing exporters and importers. In other words, international trade is a *win-win* deal. Exhibit 5.1 shows that world trade growth (averaging over 5% between 1993 and 2013) generally outpaces GDP growth (averaging nearly 3% during the same period). However, in 2012 and 2013, world trade grew at roughly the same rate as world GDP growth.

Why are there gains from trade?[1] How do nations benefit from such gains? The remainder of this chapter will answer these questions. Before proceeding, it is important to realize that it is misleading to say that *nations* trade.[2] A more accurate expression would be: *Firms* from different nations trade.[3] Unless different governments directly buy and sell from each other (such as arms sales), the majority of trade is conducted by firms that pay little attention to country-level ramifications. For example, Walmart imports large quantities of goods into the United States and does not export much. Walmart thus directly contributes to the US trade deficit. Because **trade deficit** occurs when a nation imports more than it exports, the US government does not like it. But in most countries, governments cannot tell firms such as Walmart what to do (and not to do) unless they engage in illegal activities. Likewise, when we discuss US-China trade, we are really referring to thousands of US firms buying from and selling to China, which also has thousands of firms buying from and selling to the United States. Unlike the United States, China has a **trade surplus**, which occurs when a nation exports more than it imports. The aggregation of such importing and exporting by firms on both sides leads to the country-level **balance of trade**—namely, whether a country has a trade surplus or deficit. Overall, we need to be aware that when we ask "Why do nations trade?" we are really asking "Why do *firms* from different nations trade?"

Having acknowledged the limitations of the expression "nations trade," we will still use it. Why? Because it is commonly used and serves as a short-hand version of the more accurate but more cumbersome expression "firms from different nations trade." This clarification does enable us to use the two *firm-level* perspectives introduced earlier—resource-based and institution-based views—to shed light on why nations trade.

Recall from Chapter 4 that valuable, rare, inimitable, and organizationally derived (VRIO) products determine a firm's competitive advantage. Applying this insight, we can suggest that valuable, rare, and inimitable products generated by organizationally strong firms in one nation such as China and the United States can lead to the competitive advantage of their exports (see the Opening Case and the Closing Case).[4] Further, recall from Chapters 2 and 3 that numerous politically and culturally derived rules of the game, known as institutions, constrain individual and firm behavior. Institutions can either limit or facilitate trade. For example, although American movies dominate the world market, Canada,

ISTOCKPHOTO.COM/HENRIK5000

Export To sell abroad.

Import To buy from abroad.

Merchandise trade Tangible products being bought and sold.

Service trade Intangible services being bought and sold.

Trade deficit An economic condition in which a nation imports more than it exports.

Trade surplus An economic condition in which a nation exports more than it imports.

Balance of trade The country-level trade surplus or deficit.

EXHIBIT 5.1 GROWTH IN WORLD TRADE GENERALLY OUTPACES GROWTH IN WORLD GDP (ANNUAL % CHANGE)

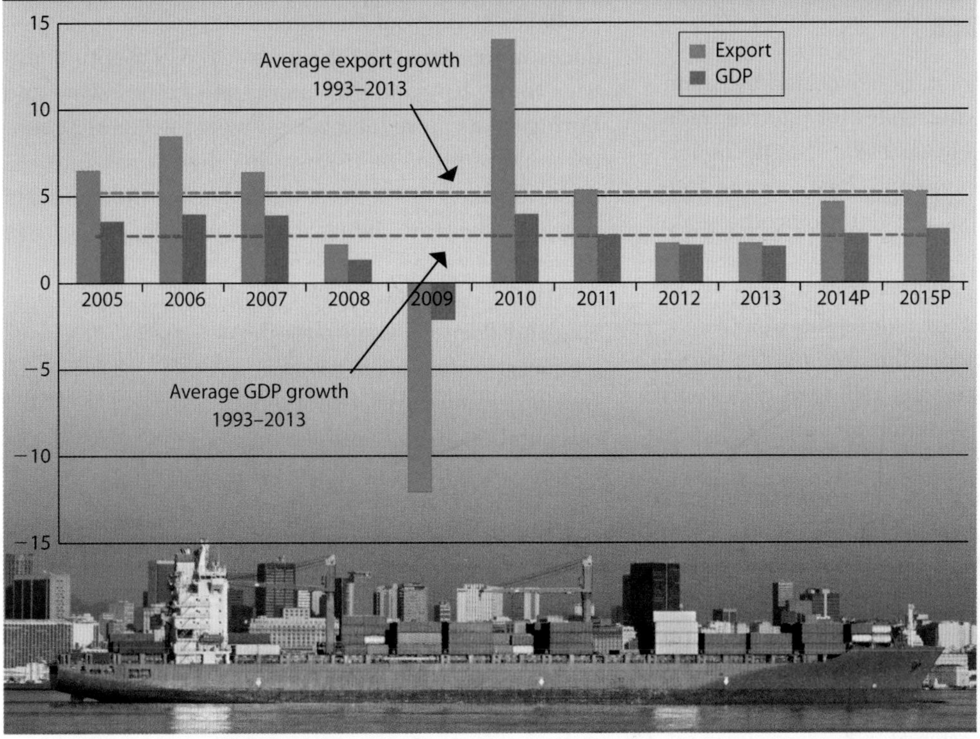

Source: World Trade Organization, "Modest trade growth anticipated for 2014 and 2015 following two year slump," press release, 14 April 2014, Geneva: WTO (www.wto.org). The figure refers to merchandise (goods) exports.

France, and South Korea use regulations to limit the market share of American movies in order to protect their domestic movie industries. On the other hand, we also see the rise of rules that facilitate trade, such as those promoted by the World Trade Organization (WTO) (see Chapter 8).

Overall, why are there economic gains from international trade? According to the resource-based view, it is because some firms in one nation generate exports that are valuable, unique, and hard to imitate that firms from other nations find it beneficial to import.[5] How do nations benefit from such gains? According to the institution-based view, different rules governing trade are designed to determine how such gains are shared (or not shared). The remainder of this chapter expands on these two perspectives.

5-2 THEORIES OF INTERNATIONAL TRADE

Theories of international trade provide one of the oldest, richest, and most influential bodies of economic literature. Although the publication of Adam Smith's *The Wealth of Nations* in 1776 is usually considered the foundation of modern economics, theories of international trade predate Adam Smith. In fact, Adam Smith wrote *The Wealth of Nations* to challenge an earlier theory: mercantilism. This section introduces six major theories of international trade: (1) mercantilism, (2) absolute advantage, (3) comparative advantage, (4) product life cycle, (5) strategic trade, and (6) national competitive advantage of industries. The first three are often regarded as classical trade theories, and the last three are viewed as modern trade theories.

5-2a Mercantilism

Widely practiced during the 17th and 18th centuries, the theory of **mercantilism** viewed international trade as a zero-sum game. It suggested that the wealth of the world (measured in gold and silver at that time) was fixed, so a nation that exported more than it imported would enjoy the net inflows of gold and silver and become richer. On the other hand, a nation experiencing a trade deficit would see its gold and silver flowing out and, consequently, would become poorer. The upshot? Self-sufficiency would be best.

Although mercantilism is the oldest theory in international trade, it is not an extinct dinosaur. Very much alive, mercantilism is the direct intellectual ancestor of modern-day **protectionism**, which is the idea that governments should actively protect domestic industries from imports and vigorously promote exports. Even

Mercantilism A theory that holds that the wealth of the world (measured in gold and silver) is fixed and that a nation that exports more than it imports will enjoy the net inflows of gold and silver and become richer.

Protectionism The idea that governments should actively protect domestic industries from imports and vigorously promote exports.

today, many modern governments may still be mercantilist at heart.

5-2b Absolute Advantage

The theory of absolute advantage, advocated by Adam Smith in 1776, opened the floodgates for the free trade movement that is still going on today. Smith argued that in the aggregate, the "invisible hand" of the free market, not government, should determine the scale and scope of economic activities. By trying to be self-sufficient and to (inefficiently) produce a wide range of goods, mercantilist policies *reduce* the wealth of a nation in the long run. The idea that free market forces should determine the buying and selling of goods and services with little or no government intervention is called **free trade**.

Specifically, Smith proposed a **theory of absolute advantage**: With free trade, a nation gains by specializing in economic activities in which it has an absolute advantage. What is absolute advantage? A nation that is more efficient than anyone else in the production of any good or service is said to have an **absolute advantage** in the production of that good or service. For instance, Smith argued that Portugal enjoyed an absolute advantage over England in producing grapes and wines because Portugal had better soil, water, and weather. Likewise, England had an absolute advantage over Portugal in raising sheep and producing wool. It cost England more to grow grapes: An acre of land that could raise high-quality sheep and produce fine wool would only produce an inferior grape and a lower quality wine.

international trade is a *win-win* game

Everyone has heard of port wine, one of Portugal's most famous exports, but who has heard of any world-famous English wine? Smith recommended that England specialize in sheep and wool, that Portugal specialize in grapes and wines, and that they trade with each other. Here are two of Smith's greatest insights. First, by specializing in the production of goods for which each has an absolute advantage, both can produce more. Second, both can benefit more by trading. By specializing, England produces more wool than it can use, and Portugal produces more wine than it can drink. When both countries trade, England gets more (and better) wine and Portugal gets more (and better) wool than either country could produce on its own. In other words, international trade is not a zero-sum game as mercantilism suggests. Instead, international trade is a *win-win* game.

Free trade The idea that free market forces should determine the buying and selling of goods and services with little or no government intervention.

Theory of absolute advantage A theory that suggests that under free trade, each nation gains by specializing in economic activities in which it is the most efficient producer.

Absolute advantage The economic advantage one nation enjoys because it can produce a good or service more efficiently than anyone else.

How can this be? Smith's England-Portugal example offers a general sense, but let us use a specific example with hypothetical numbers (see Exhibits 5.2 and 5.3). For the sake of simplicity, assume that there are only two nations in the world: China and the United States. They perform only two economic activities: growing wheat and making aircraft. Production of wheat or aircraft, naturally, requires resources such as labor, land, and technology. Assume that both countries are equally endowed with 800 units of resources. Between the two activities, the United States has an absolute advantage in the production of aircraft: It takes 20 resources to produce an aircraft (for which China needs 40 resources), and the total US capacity is 40 aircraft if it does not produce wheat (point D in Exhibit 5.2). China has an absolute advantage in the production of wheat: It takes 20 resources to produce 1,000 tons of wheat (for which the United States needs 80 resources), and the total Chinese capacity is 40,000 tons of wheat if it does not make aircraft (point A). It is important to note that the United States can grow wheat and China can make aircraft, albeit inefficiently. Both nations need wheat and aircraft. Without trade, each nation would have to produce *both* by spending half of their resources on each—China at point B (20,000 tons of wheat and 10 aircraft) and the United States at point C (5,000 tons of wheat and 20 aircraft). Interestingly, if they stay at points A and D, respectively, and trade one-quarter of their output with each other (that is, 10,000 tons of Chinese wheat with 10 American aircraft), these two countries, and by implication the global economy, both produce more and consume more (see Exhibit 5.3). In

EXHIBIT 5.2 ABSOLUTE ADVANTAGE

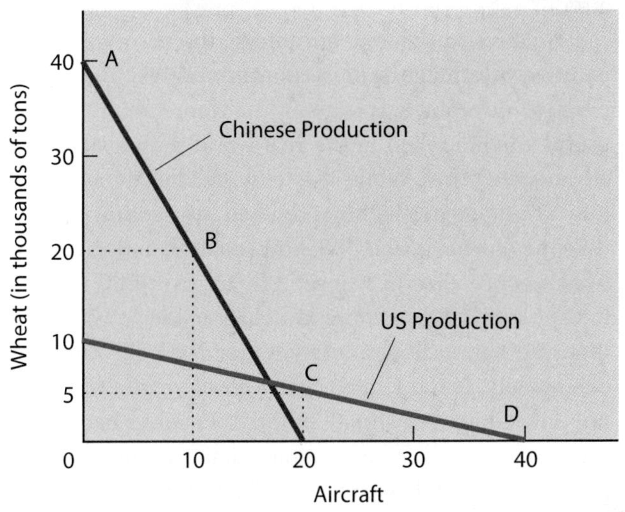

other words, the numbers show that there are *net* gains from trade based on absolute advantage.

5-2c Comparative Advantage

According to Adam Smith, each nation should look for absolute advantage. However, what can nations do when they do *not* possess absolute advantage? Continuing our two-country example of China and the United States, what if China is absolutely inefficient than the United States in the production of *both* wheat and aircraft (which is the real case today)? What should they do? Obviously, the theory of absolute advantage runs into a dead end.

British economist David Ricardo responded to Smith in 1817 by developing a **theory of comparative advantage**. This theory suggests that even though the United States has an absolute advantage in both wheat and aircraft over China, as long as China is not equally less efficient in the production of both goods, China can still choose to specialize in the production of one good (such as wheat) in which it has comparative advantage. **Comparative advantage** is defined as the relative (not absolute) advantage in one economic activity that one nation enjoys in comparison with other nations. Exhibits 5.4 and 5.5 show that China's comparative advantage lies in its *relatively less inefficient* production of wheat. If China devotes all resources to wheat, it can produce 10,000 tons, which is four-fifths of the 12,500 tons that the United States can produce. However, at a maximum, China can produce only 20 aircraft, which is

ISTOCKPHOTO.COM/SHARPLY_DONE

merely half of the 40 aircraft that the United States can make. By letting China specialize in the production of wheat and

Theory of comparative advantage A theory that suggests that a nation gains by specializing in production of one good in which it has comparative advantage.

Comparative advantage The relative (not absolute) advantage in one economic activity that one nation enjoys in comparison with other nations.

EXHIBIT 5.3 ABSOLUTE ADVANTAGE

Total units of resources = 800 for each country		Wheat	Aircraft
1. Resources required to produce 1,000 tons of wheat and one aircraft	China US	20 resources 80 resources	40 resources 20 resources
2. Production and consumption with no specialization and without trade (each country devotes *half* of its resources to each activity)	China (point B) US (point C) *Total production*	20,000 tons 5,000 tons *25,000 tons*	10 aircraft 20 aircraft *30 aircraft*
3. Production with specialization (China specializes in wheat and produces no aircraft, and the United States specializes in aircraft and produces no wheat)	China (point A) US (point D) *Total production*	40,000 tons 0 *40,000 tons*	0 40 aircraft *40 aircraft*
4. Consumption after each country trades one fourth of its output while producing at points A and D, respectively (scenario 3 above)	China US *Total consumption*	30,000 tons 10,000 tons *40,000 tons*	10 aircraft 30 aircraft *40 aircraft*
5. *Gains* from trade: Increase in consumption as a result of specialization and trade (scenario 4 versus scenario 2 above)	China US	+10,000 tons +5,000 tons	0 +10 aircraft

EXHIBIT 5.4 COMPARATIVE ADVANTAGE

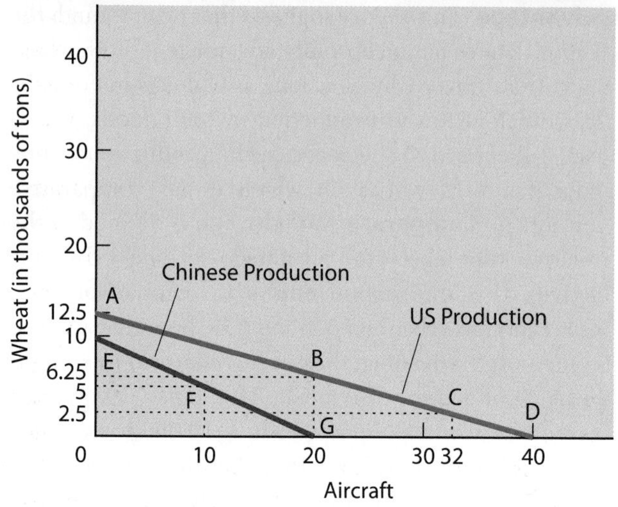

importing some wheat from China, the United States is able to leverage its strengths by devoting its resources to aircraft. For example, if the United States devotes four-fifths of its resources to aircraft and one-fifth to wheat (point C in Exhibit 5.4), if China concentrates 100% of its resources on wheat (point E), and if the two trade with each other, then both countries produce and consume more than what they would produce and consume if they inefficiently devoted half of their resources to each activity (see Exhibit 5.5).

Again, the numbers show that there are *net* gains from trade—this time from comparative advantage. One crucial concept here is **opportunity cost**, which refers to the cost of pursuing one activity at the expense of another activity, given the alternatives. For the United States, the opportunity cost of concentrating on wheat at point A in Exhibit 5.4 is tremendous relative to producing aircraft at point D, because it is only 25% more productive in wheat than China but is 100% more productive in aircraft.

Relative to absolute advantage, the theory of comparative advantage seems counterintuitive. But comparative advantage is actually far more realistic and useful when applied in the real world than is absolute advantage. Why? While it is easy to identify an absolute advantage in a highly simplified, two-country world (like the one in Exhibit 5.2), how can each nation decide what to specialize in when there are over 200 nations in the world? It is simply too challenging to ascertain that one nation is absolutely better than all others in one activity. Is the United States *absolutely* better than not only China but also all other 200 nations in aircraft production? European nations that produce Airbus planes obviously beg to differ. The theory of comparative advantage suggests that even without an absolute advantage, the United States can still specialize profitably in aircraft as long as it is relatively more efficient than others. This insight has greatly lowered the threshold for specialization because absolute advantage is no longer required.

Where do absolute and comparative advantages come from? In a word: productivity. Smith looked at *absolute* productivity differences, and Ricardo emphasized *relative* productivity differences. In this sense, absolute advantage is really a special case of comparative advantage. But what leads to such productivity differences? In the early 20th century, Swedish economists Eli Heckscher and Bertil Ohlin argued that

EXHIBIT 5.5 COMPARATIVE ADVANTAGE

Total units of resources = 800 for each country		Wheat	Aircraft
1. Resources required to produce 1,000 tons of wheat and one aircraft	China US	80 resources 64 resources	40 resources 20 resources
2. Production and consumption with no specialization and without trade (each country devotes *half* of its resources to each activity)	China (point F) US (point B) *Total production*	5,000 tons 6,250 tons *11,250 tons*	10 aircraft 20 aircraft *30 aircraft*
3. Production with specialization (China devotes all resources to wheat, and the United States devotes one fifth of its resources to wheat and four fifths of its resources to aircraft)	China (point E) US (point C) *Total production*	10,000 tons 2,500 tons *12,500 tons*	0 32 aircraft *32 aircraft*
4. Consumption after China trades 4,000 tons of wheat for 11 US aircraft while producing at points E and C, respectively (scenario 3 above)	China US *Total consumption*	6,000 tons 6,500 tons *12,500 tons*	11 aircraft 21 aircraft *32 aircraft*
5. *Gains* from trade: Increase in consumption as a result of specialization and trade (scenario 4 versus scenario 2 above)	China US	+1,000 tons +250 tons	+1 aircraft +1 aircraft

Opportunity cost The cost of pursuing one activity at the expense of another activity.

"Federal budget 2018 aims to increase workforce participation of women" Andy Blatchford, Global News, February 21, 2018

SUMMARY:

With new Federal Budget, the Liberal government would like to boost Canada's potential economic growth by increasing the workforce participation of women. To archive that, budgetary table includes narrowing the pay equity gap, ensuring more gender equality in boardroom, easing access to capital for female entrepreneurs and opening up more funding opportunities for female scientific researchers. However, Finance Minister Bill Morneau's briefing note estimated that if everything remains, the potential growth will "remain low" over the next 15 years at 1.7 per cent by closing labour market participation gap between men and women which would raise average of 0.25 percentage point per year.

ANALYSIS/OPINION:

Historically, the increasing potential economic growth is based on many factors, such as technology innovation, labour force participation and etc. In the past, economy in Asia was grown slowly ~~except Japan~~, but recently most of countries in Asia are growing rapidly. The big changed in their economy is the workforce labour from women because the Asian women before had to stay at home and took care the children and housework due to their culture. However, overall, the labour force participation from women is still low compared to men because of their children which is a huge obstacle. Comparing between their low income earning and high expenditure for child care without subsidies, they will choose staying at home and taking care their children with subsidies. Moreover, the world is continuing closing the inequality between women and men so with the federal budget focusing on encouragin[illegible] to enter labour workforce, the gap inequality could be smaller in future

RELEVANCE:

On our text, economic growth is [illegible]

With more women [illegible]

absolute and comparative advantages stem from different **factor endowments**—namely, the extent to which different countries possess various factors of production such as labor, land, and technology. This **factor endowment theory** (or **Heckscher–Ohlin theory**) proposed that nations will develop comparative advantages based on their *locally abundant* factors, such as plentiful labor supply in China and innovative commercialization of basic research in the United States.

5-2d Product Life Cycle

The three classical theories—mercantilism, absolute advantage, and comparative advantage—all paint a *static* picture: If England has an absolute or comparative advantage in textiles, which it does mostly because of its factor endowments such as favorable weather and soil, it should keep making textiles. But factor endowments and trade patterns change over time, so the assumption that trade is static does not always hold in the real world. Adam Smith's England, over 200 years ago, was a major exporter of textiles, but today England's textile industry is rather insignificant. So what happened? While one may argue that the weather in England has changed and the soil has become less fertile for sheep (and wool), it is difficult to believe that weather and soil have changed so much in 200 years, which is a relatively short period for long-run climatic changes. Now consider another example that has nothing to do with weather or soil change. Since the 1980s, the United States has changed from being a net exporter to a net importer of personal computers (PCs), while Malaysia has gone from being a net importer to a net exporter. Why have patterns of trade in PCs changed over time? Classical theories would have a hard time answering this intriguing question.

In 1966, American economist Raymond Vernon developed the **product life cycle theory**, which is the first *dynamic* theory to account for changes in the patterns of trade over time. Vernon divided the world into three categories: lead innovation nation (which, according to him, is typically the United States), other developed nations, and developing nations. Further, every product has three life cycle stages: new, maturing, and standardized. Shown in Exhibit 5.6, the first stage involves production of a new product (such as TV) that commands a price premium. Such production will concentrate in the United States, which exports to other developed nations. In the second, maturing stage, demand and ability to produce grow in other developed nations such as Australia and Italy, so it becomes worthwhile to produce there. In the third stage, the previously new product is standardized (or commoditized). Thus, much production will now move to low-cost developing nations that export to developed nations. In other words, comparative advantage may change over time.

While this theory was first proposed in the 1960s, some later events such as the migration of the PC production have supported its prediction. However, this theory has been criticized on two accounts. First, it assumes that the United States will always be the lead innovation nation for new products. This may be increasingly invalid. For example, the fanciest mobile (cell) phones are now routinely pioneered in Asia and Europe. Second, this theory assumes a stage-by-stage migration of production, taking at least several years, if not decades. In reality, however, an increasing number of firms now launch new products such as iPods *simultaneously* around the globe.

5-2e Strategic Trade

Except for mercantilism, none of the theories discussed above say anything about the role of governments. Since the days of Adam Smith, government intervention is usually regarded by economists as destroying value because, they contend, it distorts free trade. But government intervention is extensive and is not going away. Can government intervention actually add value? Since the 1970s, a new theory, strategic trade theory, has been developed to address this question.

Strategic trade theory suggests that strategic intervention by governments in certain industries can enhance their odds for international success. What are these industries? They tend to be highly capital-intensive industries with high barriers to entry, where domestic firms may have little chance of entering and competing without government assistance. These industries also

Factor endowment The extent to which different countries possess various factors of production such as labor, land, and technology.

Factor endowment theory (Heckscher–Ohlin theory) A theory that suggests that nations will develop comparative advantages based on their locally abundant factors.

Product life cycle theory A theory that suggests that patterns of trade change over time as production shifts and as the product moves from new to maturing to standardized stages.

Strategic trade theory A theory that suggests that strategic intervention by governments in certain industries can enhance their odds for international success.

EXHIBIT 5.6 THEORY OF PRODUCT LIFE CYCLES

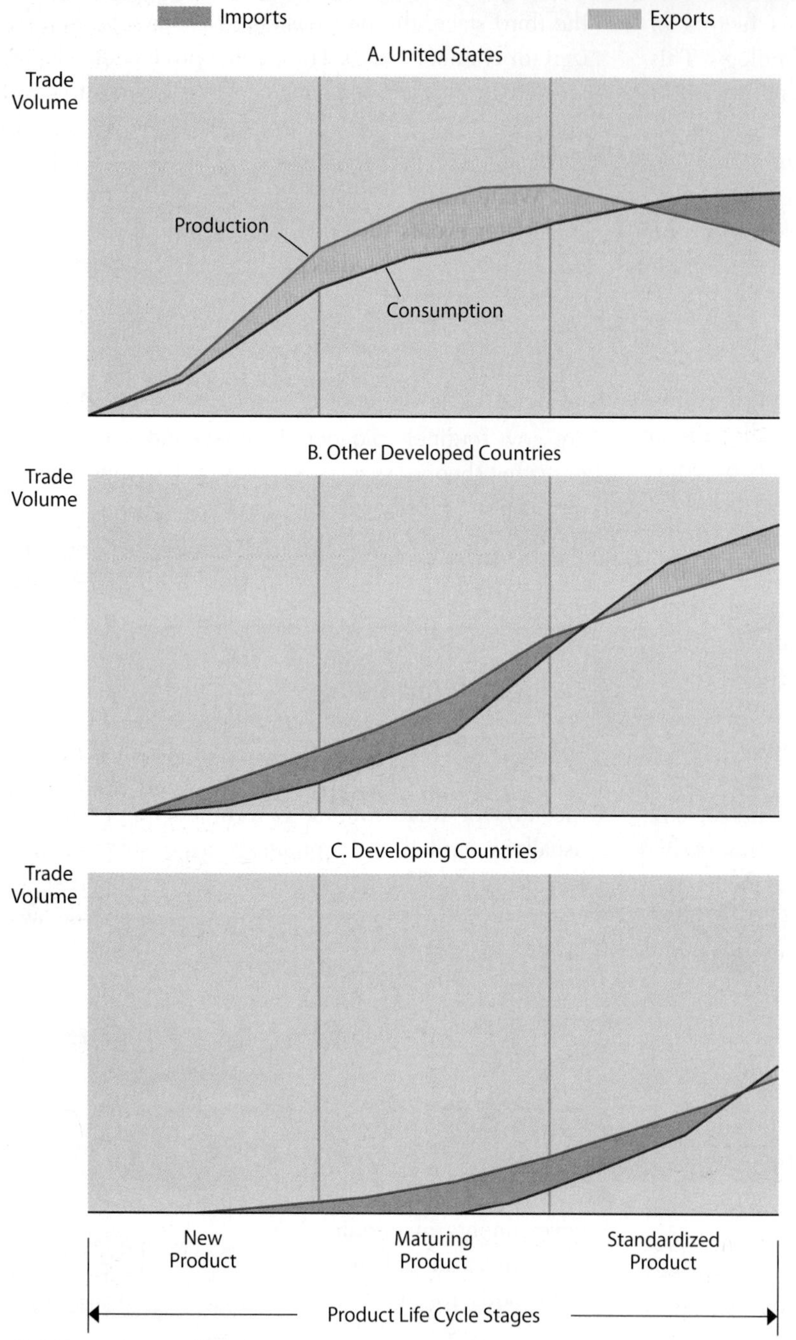

feature substantial **first-mover advantages**—namely, advantages that first entrants enjoy and do not share with late entrants. A leading example is the commercial aircraft industry. Founded in 1915 and strengthened by large military orders during World War II, Boeing has long dominated this industry. In the jumbo jet segment, Boeing's first-mover advantages associated with its 400-seat 747, first launched in the late 1960s, are still significant today. Alarmed by such US dominance, British, French, German, and Spanish governments realized in the late 1960s that if they did not intervene, individual European aerospace firms might be driven out of business by US rivals. So these European governments agreed to launch and subsidize Airbus. In four decades, Airbus has risen from scratch to splitting the global market 50-50 with Boeing.

How do European governments help Airbus? Let us use the superjumbo aircraft, which is larger than the Boeing 747, as an example. Both Airbus and Boeing are interested in entering this market. However, the demand in the next 20 years is only about 400 to 500 aircraft and a firm needs to sell at least 300 just to break even, which means that only one firm can be supported profitably. Shown in Exhibit 5.7 (Panel A), the outcome will be disastrous if both enter because each will lose $5 billion (Cell 1). If one enters and the other does not, the entrant will make $20 billion (Cells 2 and 3). It is also possible that both will choose not to enter (Cell 4). If a number of European governments promise Airbus a subsidiary of, say, $10 billion if it enters, then the picture changes to Panel B. Regardless of what Boeing does, Airbus finds it lucrative to enter. In Cell 1, if Boeing enters, it will lose $5 billion as before, whereas Airbus will make $5 billion ($10 billion subsidy minus $5 billion loss). So Boeing has no incentive to enter. Therefore, the more likely outcome is Cell 2, where Airbus enters and enjoys a profit of $30 billion. Therefore, the subsidy has given Airbus a *strategic* advantage, and the policy to assist Airbus is known as a **strategic trade policy**. This has indeed been the case, as the 550-seat A380 entered service in 2007 and became a formidable competitor for the Boeing 747.

First-mover advantage Advantage that first entrants enjoy and do not share with late entrants.

Strategic trade policy Economic policy that provides companies a strategic advantage through government subsidies.

EXHIBIT 5.7 ENTERING THE VERY LARGE, SUPER-JUMBO MARKET?

Panel A. Without Government Subsidy (Outcome = Airbus, Boeing)

Airbus \ Boeing	Enter	Don't Enter
Enter	Cell 1 –$5 billion, –$5 billion	Cell 2 $20 billion, 0
Don't Enter	Cell 3 0, $20 billion	Cell 4 0, 0

Panel B. With $10 Billion Subsidy From European Governments (Outcome = Airbus, Boeing)

Airbus \ Boeing	Enter	Don't Enter
Enter	Cell 1 $5 billion, –$5 billion	Cell 2 $30 billion, 0
Don't Enter	Cell 3 0, $20 billion	Cell 4 0, 0

Strategic trade theorists do not advocate a mercantilist policy to promote all industries. They propose to help only a few strategically important industries, such as those centered on clean energy like electric cars and batteries.[6] Still, this theory has been criticized on two accounts. First, many scholars and policy makers are uncomfortable with government intervention. What if governments are not sophisticated and objective enough to do this job? Second, many industries claim that they are strategically important. For example, after 9/11, American farmers successfully argued that agriculture is a strategic industry because the food supply needs to be guarded against terrorists and extracted more subsidies. Overall, where to draw the line between strategic and nonstrategic industries is tricky.

DEGTYARYOV ANDREY LEONIDOVICH/SHUTTERSTOCK.COM

5-2f National Competitive Advantage of Industries

The most recent theory is known as the **theory of national competitive advantage of industries**. This is popularly known as the **diamond theory** because its principal architect, Harvard strategy professor Michael Porter, presents it in a diamond-shaped diagram, as shown in Exhibit 5.8.[7] This theory focuses on why certain *industries* (but not others) within a nation are competitive internationally. For example, while Japanese electronics and automobile industries are global winners, Japanese service industries are notoriously inefficient. Porter is interested in finding out why.

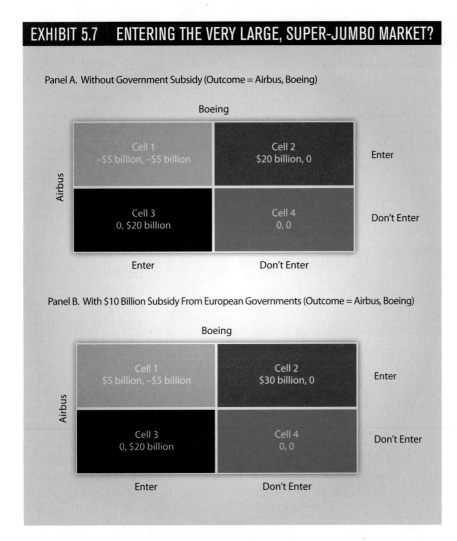

Porter argues that the competitive advantage of certain industries in different nations depends on four aspects, which form a diamond. First, he starts with factor endowments, which refer to the natural and human resources noted by the Heckscher–Ohlin theory. Some countries (such as Saudi Arabia) are rich in natural resources but short on population, while others (such as Singapore) have a well-educated population but few natural resources. Not surprisingly, Saudi Arabia exports oil, and Singapore exports semiconductors (which need

Theory of national competitive advantage of industries (or diamond theory) A theory that suggests that the competitive advantage of certain industries in different nations depends on four aspects that form a "diamond" shape when diagrammed.

EXHIBIT 5.8 NATIONAL COMPETITIVE ADVANTAGE OF INDUSTRIES: THE PORTER DIAMOND

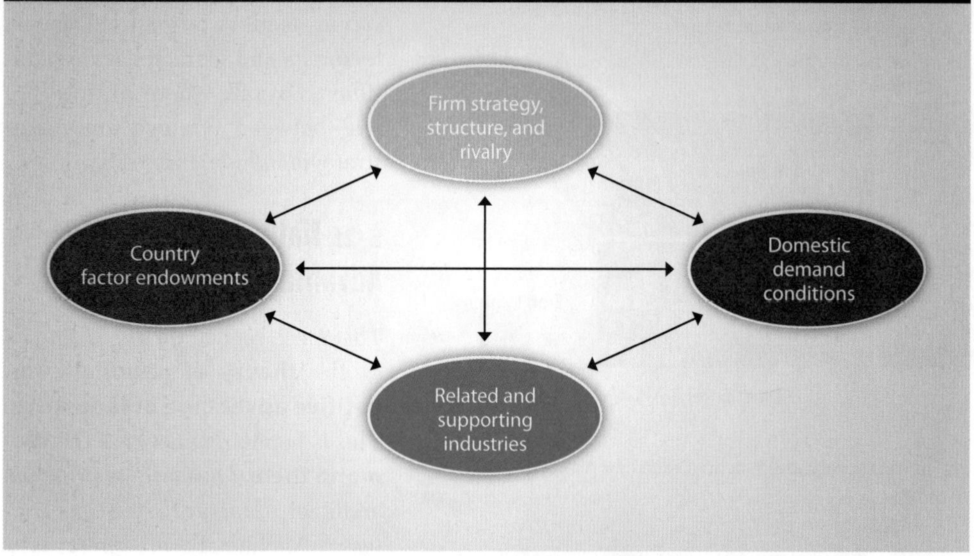

Source: M. Porter, "The competitive advantage of nations," *Harvard Business Review* (March-April 1990): 77.

abundant skilled labor). While building on these insights from previous theories, Porter argues that factor endowments are not enough.

Second, tough domestic demand propels firms to scale new heights. Why are American movies so competitive worldwide? One reason may be the level of extraordinary demand in the US market for exciting movies. Endeavoring to satisfy domestic demand, US movie studios unleash *High School Musical 3* after *High School Musical* and *High School Musical 2*, and *The Hunger Games: Mockingjay* after *The Hunger Games* and *The Hunger Games: Catching Fire*, each time packing in more excitement. Most movies—in fact, most products—are created to satisfy domestic demand first. Thus, the ability to satisfy a tough domestic crowd may make it possible to successfully deal with less demanding overseas customers.

Third, domestic firm strategy, structure, and rivalry in one industry play a huge role in its international success or failure. One reason the Japanese electronics industry is so competitive globally is because its *domestic* rivalry is probably the most intense in the world. If the 20 or so models of digital cameras or camcorders available in a typical American electronics store frustrate you, you will be even more frustrated when shopping for these items in Japan because the average store there carries about 200 models (!). Most firms producing such a bewildering range of models do not make money. However, the few top firms such as Canon that win the tough competition domestically may have a relatively easier time when venturing abroad because overseas competition is less demanding.

Finally, related and supporting industries provide the foundation upon which key industries can excel. In the absence of strong related and supporting industries such as engines, avionics, and materials, an aerospace industry cannot become globally competitive. Each of these related and supporting industries requires years (and often decades) of hard work and investment. For instance, inspired by the Airbus experience, the Chinese, Korean, and Japanese governments poured money into their own aerospace industries. Eventually, they all realized that Europe's long history and excellence in a series of critically related and supporting industries made it possible for Airbus to succeed. A lack of such industries made it unrealistic for the Chinese, Korean, and Japanese aerospace industries to succeed in making commercial aircraft.

Overall, Porter argues that the dynamic interaction of these four aspects explains what is behind the competitive advantage of leading industries in different nations. This theory is the first *multilevel* theory to realistically connect firms, industries, and nations, whereas previous theories work on only one or two levels. However, it has not been comprehensively tested. Some critics argue that the diamond places too much emphasis on domestic conditions. The recent rise of India's IT industry suggests that its international success is not entirely driven by domestic demand, which is relatively tiny compared with overseas demand—it is overseas demand that matters a lot more in this case.

5-2g Evaluating Theories of International Trade

In case you are tired after studying the six theories, you have to appreciate that we have just gone through over 300 years of research, debates, and policy changes around the world in about eight pages (!). As a student, that is not a small accomplishment. Exhibit 5.9 enables you to see the "forest." Keep the following four points in mind as you look at the forest.

EXHIBIT 5.9 THEORIES OF INTERNATIONAL TRADE: A SUMMARY

Classical theories	Main points	Strengths and influences	Weaknesses and debates
Mercantilism	▶ International trade is a zero-sum game; trade deficits are dangerous ▶ Governments should protect domestic industries and promote exports	▶ Forerunner of modern-day protectionism	▶ Inefficient allocation of resources ▶ Reduces the wealth of the nation in the long run
Absolute advantage	▶ Nations should specialize in economic activities in which they have an absolute advantage and trade with others ▶ By specializing and trading, each nation produces more and consumes more ▶ The wealth of all trading nations and the world increases	▶ Birth of modern economics ▶ Forerunner of the free trade movement ▶ Defeats mercantilism, at least intellectually	▶ When one nation is absolutely inferior to another, the theory is unable to provide any advice ▶ When there are many nations, it may be difficult to find an absolute advantage
Comparative advantage	▶ Nations should specialize in economic activities in which they have a comparative advantage and trade with others ▶ Even if one nation is absolutely inferior to another, the two nations can still gainfully trade ▶ Factor endowments underpin comparative advantage	▶ More realistic guidance to nations (and their firms) interested in trade but having no absolute advantage ▶ Explains patterns of trade based on factor endowments	▶ Relatively static, assuming that comparative advantage and factor endowments do not change over time
Modern theories			
Product life cycle	▶ Comparative advantage first resides in the lead innovation nation, which exports to other nations ▶ Production migrates to other advanced nations and then developing nations in different product life cycle stages	▶ First theory to incorporate dynamic changes in patterns of trade ▶ More realistic with trade in industrial products in the 20th century	▶ The United States may not always be the lead innovation nation ▶ Many new products are now launched simultaneously around the world
Strategic trade	▶ Strategic intervention by governments may help domestic firms reap first-mover advantages in certain industries ▶ First-mover firms, aided by governments, may have better odds at winning internationally	▶ More realistic and positively incorporates the role of governments in trade ▶ Provides direct policy advice	▶ Ideological resistance from many free trade scholars and policy makers ▶ Invites all kinds of industries to claim they are strategic
National competitive advantage of industries	▶ Competitive advantage of different industries in a nation depends on the four interacting aspects of a diamond ▶ The four aspects are (1) factor endowments; (2) domestic demand; (3) firm strategy, structure, and rivalry; and (4) related and supporting industries	▶ Most recent, most complex, and most realistic among various theories ▶ As a multilevel theory, it directly connects firms, industries, and nations	▶ Has not been comprehensively tested ▶ Overseas (not only domestic) demand may stimulate the competitiveness of certain industries

- The classical pro-free trade theories seem like common sense today, but they were *revolutionary* in the late 1700s and the early 1800s when the world was dominated by mercantilistic thinking.
- All theories simplify to make their point. Classical theories rely on highly simplistic assumptions of a model consisting of only two nations and two goods.
- The theories also assume perfect **resource mobility**—the assumption that a resource used in producing for one industry can be shifted and put to use in another industry (for example, one resource removed from wheat production can be moved to make aircraft). In reality, not all resources can be moved. Farm hands, for example, will have a hard time assembling modern aircraft.

Resource mobility The assumption that a resource used in producing a product in one industry can be shifted and put to use in another industry.

Debate: Ethical Dilemma

Trade Deficit Versus Trade Surplus

Smith and Ricardo would probably turn in their graves if they heard that one of today's hottest trade debates still echoes the old debate between mercantilists and free traders more than 200 years ago. Nowhere is the debate more ferocious than in the United States, which runs the world's largest trade deficit (combining the US deficit in merchandise trade with its surplus in service trade). In 2006, it reached a record-breaking $760 billion (6% of GDP). Thanks to reduced US (import) consumption due to the Great Recession and beefed-up export efforts (see the Closing Case), the US trade deficit was "only" $519 billion (3% of GDP) in 2013. Should this level of trade deficit be of concern?

Armed with classical theories, free traders argue that this is not a grave concern. They argue that the United States and its trading partners mutually benefit by developing a deeper division of labor based on comparative advantage. Former Secretary of the Treasury Paul O'Neill went so far as to say that trade deficit was "an antiquated theoretical construct." Paul Krugman, the 2008 Nobel laureate in economics, argued:

> *International trade is not about competition, it is about mutually beneficial exchange. . . . Imports, not exports, are the purpose of trade. That is, what a country gains from trade is the ability to import things it wants. Exports are not an objective in and of themselves: the need to export is a burden that a country must bear because its import suppliers are crass enough to demand payment.*

AP IMAGES/REMY DE LA MAUVINIERE

Critics strongly disagree. They argue that international trade is about competition—about markets, jobs, and incomes. Highlighting the importance of exports, Boeing CEO Jim McNerney said: "Every time a Boeing 777 lands in China, it lands with about four million parts reflecting the workmanship of some 11,000 small, medium, and large suppliers." Trade deficit has always been blamed on a particular country with which the United States runs the largest deficit, such as Japan in the 1980s. Because the US trade deficit with China reached $318 billion in 2013 (two-thirds of the total deficit), the recent trade deficit debate is otherwise known as the China trade debate. In addition to China, it is important to note that the United States runs trade deficits with all of its major trading partners—Canada, the EU, Japan, and Mexico—and is in trade disputes with them most of the time.

Sources: J. Bhagwati and A. Panagariya, "Trading opinions about free trade," *BusinessWeek*, 27 December 2004, 20; "America's trade deficit," *BusinessWeek*, 3 October 2005, 31; "Why free trade matters to companies like Caterpillar," *Fortune*, 26 July 2010, 40; P. Krugman, "What do undergrads need to know about trade?" *American Economic Review* 83 (1993): 24; M. W. Peng, "Canada and the United States fight over pigs," in M. W. Peng, *Global Business*, 3rd ed. (Cincinnati: Cengage Learning, 2014) 270–271.

- Classical theories assume no foreign exchange issues and zero transportation costs.

So is free trade still as beneficial as Smith and Ricardo suggested in the real world of many countries, numerous goods, imperfect resource mobility, fluctuating exchange rates, high transportation costs, and product life cycle changes? The answer is still *Yes!* Worldwide data support the *basic* arguments for free trade.[8] (See the Debate feature for disagreements.)

Instead of relying on simple factor analysis, modern theories rely on more realistic product life cycles, first-mover advantages, and the diamond to explain and predict patterns of trade. Overall, classical and modern theories have significantly contributed to today's ever deepening trade links around the world. Yet, the victory of pro-free trade theories is not complete. The political realities, outlined next, indicate that mercantilism is still alive and well.

5-3 REALITIES OF INTERNATIONAL TRADE

Although most theories support free trade, plenty of trade barriers exist. While some trade barriers are being dismantled (see In Focus), many will remain. Let us

In Focus: Ethical Dilemma

Canada Diversifies Its Trade

Canada has the 11th largest economy (measured by nominal GDP) or the 14th largest (measured by PPP) in the world. The bilateral trading relationship between Canada and the United States is the world's largest, with approximately $600 billion in volume. The two-way traffic that crosses the Ambassador Bridge between Windsor, Ontario, and Detroit, Michigan, alone equals all US trade with Japan. Approximately three-fourths of Canadian exports go to the United States, which also provides half of Canadian imports. While enjoying a $32 billion surplus in trading with the United States, Canadians have been frustrated by the occasional disputes, such as salmon runs, magazine content, softwood lumber, and food labeling.

While disputes are resolved in bilateral negotiations or through NAFTA or WTO forums, Canadians have also sought to diversify their trading relationship away from too much reliance on the United States. They have focused on two areas. The first is to cultivate trade ties with major Asian economies, such as China and Japan. As Canada's second largest trading partner, China now absorbs 5% of Canadian exports and contributes 10% of Canadian imports. The second area is to negotiate more free trade agreements (FTAs) beyond NAFTA. Canada has FTAs with Chile, Colombia, Costa Rica, Israel, Jordan, and Panama. While Canada is negotiating with a number of other countries, one of the major breakthroughs is the Comprehensive Economic and Trade Agreement (CETA) with the European Union (EU) announced in 2013. As a bloc, the EU is the largest economy in the world. CETA would not only eliminate 99% of tariffs on both sides, but would also open competition for large government contracts in Canada to European firms and contracts in the EU to Canadian firms. CETA is likely to boost the Canada-EU bilateral trade by 23%, thus reducing Canada's reliance on the United States whose share has decreased but still remained dominant.

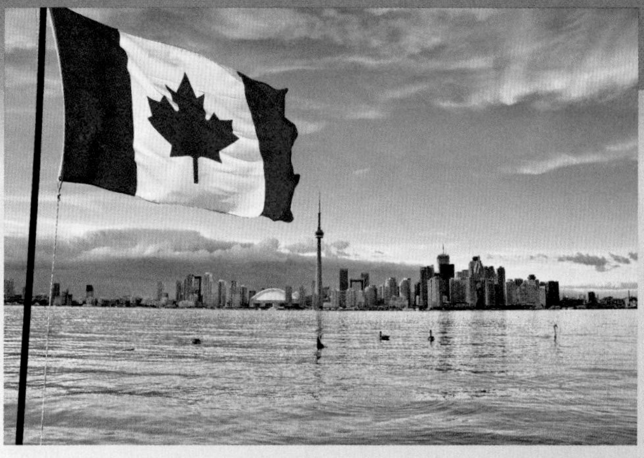
SURANGASL/SHUTTERSTOCK.COM

Sources: "Canada and the United States," *Economist*, 19 December 2011, 41; "Canada doesn't get any sexier than this," *Economist*, 26 October 2013, 18; "The Canada-EU trade deal," *Economist*, 26 October 2013, 44; "Canada turns to WTO over US label law," *Globe and Mail*, 8 October 2009, B7.

examine why this is the case. To do so, we will first discuss the two broad types of trade barriers: tariff barriers and non-tariff barriers.

5-3a Tariff Barriers

A **tariff barrier** is a means of discouraging imports by placing a tariff (tax) on imported goods. As a major tariff barrier, an **import tariff** is a tax imposed on a good brought in from another country. Exhibit 5.10 uses rice tariffs in Japan to show *unambiguously* that net losses, known as **deadweight costs**, occur when import tariffs are imposed.

- Panel A: In the absence of international trade, the domestic price is P_1 and domestic rice farmers produce Q_1, determined by the intersection of domestic supply and demand curves.
- Panel B: Because Japanese rice price P_1 is higher than world price P_2, foreign farmers export to Japan. Japanese farmers reduce output to Q_2. Japanese consumers enjoy more rice at Q_3 at a much lower price P_2.
- Panel C: The government imposes an import tariff, effectively raising the price from P_2 to P_3. Japanese farmers increase production from Q_2 to Q_4, and consumers pay more at P_3 and consume less by reducing consumption from Q_3 to Q_5. Imports fall from Q_2Q_3 in Panel B to Q_4Q_5 in Panel C.

Classical theorists such as Smith and Ricardo would have advised Japan to enjoy the gains from trade in Panel B. But political realities land Japan in Panel C, which, by limiting trade, introduces total inefficiency

Tariff barrier A means of discouraging imports by placing a tariff (tax) on imported goods.

Import tariff A tax imposed on imports.

Deadweight cost Net losses that occur in an economy as the result of tariffs.

EXHIBIT 5.10 TARIFF ON RICE IMPORTS IN JAPAN

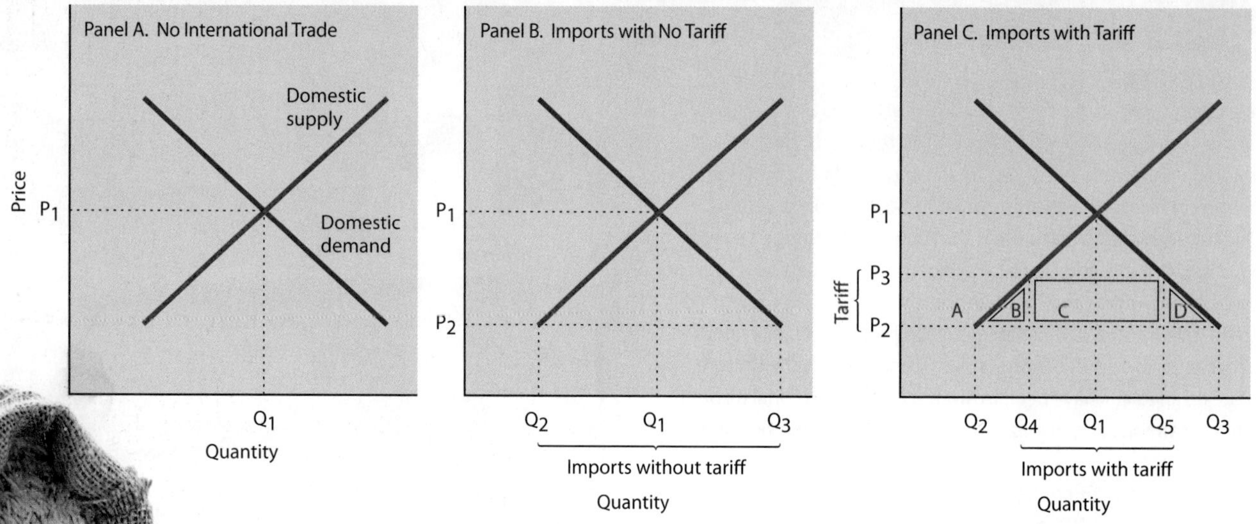

P_1: Japanese domestic price without imports. P_2: World price (and Japanese domestic price with no tariff). P_3: Japanese domestic price with import tariff.

ISTOCKPHOTO.COM/ELENATHEWISE

represented by the area consisting of A, B, C, and D. However, Japanese rice farmers gain the area of A, and the government pockets tariff revenues in the area of C. Therefore:

$$\begin{aligned}\text{Net losses} &= \text{Total inefficiency} - \text{Net gain}\\ \text{(deadweight)} &= \text{Area (A + B + C + D)} - \text{Area (A + C)}\\ &= \text{Area (B + D)}\end{aligned}$$

The net losses (areas B and D) represent unambiguous economic inefficiency to the nation as a whole. Japan is not alone in this regard. In 2010, an Apple iPad that retailed for \$600 in the United States costs \$1,000 in Brazil, after adding a 60% import tariff.[9] In 2009, the United States slapped a 35% import tariff on tires made in China. Brazilian iPad lovers and American tire buyers have to pay more, and some may be unable to afford the products. While not being able to lay your arms around an iPad will have no tangible damage, some economically struggling US drivers who should have replaced their worn-out tires may be forced to delay replacing their tires—and some may be *killed* should they be involved in accidents before they are able to afford the now more expensive tires.[10]

Nontariff barrier (NTB) A means of discouraging imports using means other than taxes on imported goods.

Subsidy A government payment to domestic firms.

Import quota A restriction on the quantity of goods brought into a country.

Given the well-known net losses, why are tariffs imposed? The answer boils down to the political realities. Although everybody in a country suffers because of higher prices, it is very costly to politically organize individuals and firms that are geographically scattered to advance the case for free trade. On the other hand, certain special interest groups tend to be geographically concentrated and skillfully organized to advance their interest. Although farmers represent less than 5% of the Japanese population, they represent disproportionate votes in the Diet (Japanese parliament). Why? Diet districts were drawn up in the aftermath of World War II when most Japanese lived in rural areas. Although the majority of the population now lives in urban areas, such districts were never re-zoned. Thus when the powerful farm lobby speaks, the Japanese government listens. The upshot? A whopping 777% tariff on imported rice.[11]

5-3b Nontariff Barriers

Today, tariff barriers are often criticized around the world, and nontariff barriers are now increasingly the weapon of choice in trade wars. A **nontariff barrier (NTB)** discourages imports using means other than tariffs on imported goods. NTBs include subsidies, import quotas, export restraints, local content requirements, administrative policies, and antidumping duties.

Subsidies are government payments to domestic firms. Much like their Japanese counterparts, European farmers are masters of extracting subsidies even though they constitute only 2% of the EU population. The Common Agricultural Policy (CAP) costs European taxpayers \$47 billion a year, eating up 40% of the EU budget.

Import quotas are restrictions on the quantity of goods that can be brought into a country. Import quotas are worse than tariffs because foreign goods can still be imported if tariffs are paid. Quotas are thus the most straightforward denial of absolute or comparative advantage. For example, between 2003 and 2009, Australia annually exported 770,000 head of live cattle to Indonesia, to the delight of Indonesian beef lovers. However, since 2009, import permits suddenly became harder to obtain. A quota of only 500,000 head of imported cattle was set for 2011.[12] For Indonesia, a densely populated island nation, importing beef from a sparsely populated cattle country next door would tap into Australia's comparative advantage and would be win-win for both countries. But with the shrinking quota, Aussie cattle exporters are devastated, and Indonesian beef lovers have to put up with skyrocketing prices—and some of them may have to quit eating beef at all.

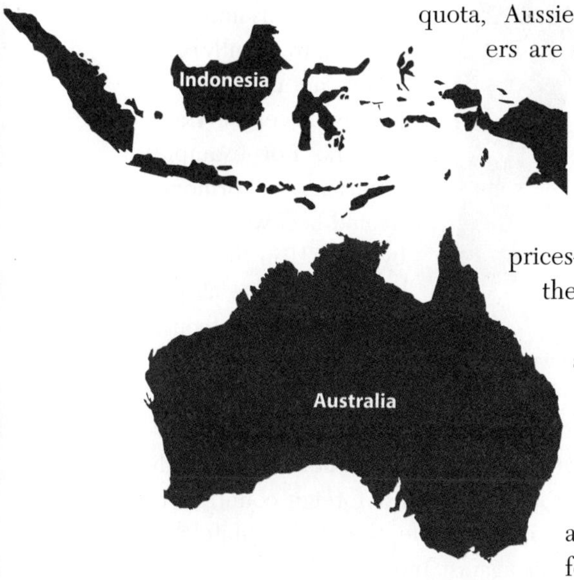

Because import quotas are protectionist pure and simple, they force countries to shoulder certain political costs in today's largely pro-free trade environment. In response, **voluntary export restraints (VERs)** have been developed to show that, on the surface, exporting countries *voluntarily* agree to restrict their exports. In essence, though, VERs are export quotas. One of the most (in)famous examples is the set of VERs that the Japanese government agreed to in the early 1980s to restrict US-bound automobile exports. The VERs, of course, were a euphemism because the Japanese did not really volunteer to restrict their exports. Only when faced with concrete protectionist threats did the Japanese reluctantly agree.

Another NTB is **local content requirements**, which are rules stipulating that a certain proportion of the value of the goods made in one country must originate from that country. The Japanese automobile VERs are again a case in point. Starting in the 1980s, because of VERs, Japanese automakers switched to producing cars in the United States through foreign direct investment (FDI). Initially, such factories were "screwdriver plants," because a majority of components were imported from Japan and only the screwdrivers were needed to tighten the bolts. To deal with this issue, many countries impose local content requirements, mandating that a domestically produced product will still be treated as an "import" subject to tariffs and NTBs unless a certain fraction of its value (such as the 51% specified by the Buy America Act) is produced locally.

Administrative policies are bureaucratic rules that make it harder to import foreign goods. India recently banned Chinese toys, citing safety concerns. Argentina has recently ordered importers of foreign cars to find export buyers of Argentine wines; otherwise, port authorities would not release imported cars. Foreign print publications, including time-sensitive newspapers and magazines, are held at the Buenos Aires airport unless subscribers go there to pay an additional fee.

Finally, the arsenal of trade weapons also includes **antidumping duties** levied on imports that have been "dumped," or sold below cost in order to unfairly drive domestic firms out of business. See the Debate feature in Chapter 10 for some specific examples.

5-3c Economic Arguments Against Free Trade

Overall, trade barriers reduce or eliminate international trade. While certain domestic industries and firms benefit, the entire country—or at least a majority of its consumers—tends to suffer. Given these well-known negative aspects, why do people make arguments against free trade? This section outlines economic arguments against free trade, and the next section deals with political arguments. Two prominent economic arguments against free trade are (1) the need to protect domestic industries and (2) the need to shield infant industries.

The oldest and most frequently used economic argument against free trade is the urge to protect domestic industries, firms,

Voluntary export restraint (VER) An international agreement that shows that an exporting country voluntarily agrees to restrict its exports.

Local content requirement A rule that stipulates that a certain proportion of the value of a good must originate from the domestic market.

Administrative policy A bureaucratic rule that makes it harder to import foreign goods.

Antidumping duty A cost levied on imports that have been "dumped," or sold below cost, to unfairly drive domestic firms out of business.

and jobs from allegedly "unfair" foreign competition—in short, protectionism. Calls for protection are not limited to commodity producers. Highly talented individuals, such as American mathematicians and Japanese sumo wrestlers, have also called for protection. Foreign math PhDs grab 40% of US math jobs, and recent US math PhDs face a jobless rate of 12%. Many American math PhDs have thus called for protection of their jobs. Similarly, Japanese sumo wrestlers insist that foreign sumo wrestlers should not be allowed to throw their weight around in Japan.

J. HENNING BUCHHOLZ/SHUTTERSTOCK.COM

The second argument is the infant industry argument. Young domestic firms need government protection. Otherwise, they stand no chance of surviving and will be crushed by mature foreign rivals. It is thus imperative that governments level the playing field by assisting infant industries. While this argument is sometimes legitimate, governments and firms have a tendency to abuse it. Some protected infant industries may never grow up—why bother? When Airbus was a true infant in the 1960s, it undoubtedly deserved some subsidies. By the 2000s, Airbus had become a giant that could take on Boeing. (In some years, Airbus has outsold Boeing.) However, Airbus continues to ask for subsidies, which European governments continue to provide.

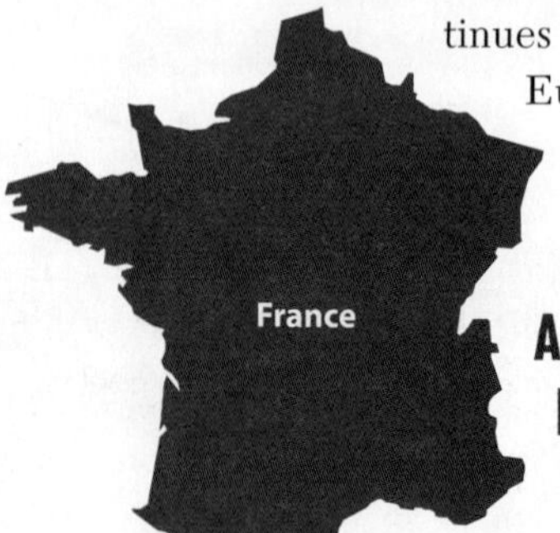

5-3d Political Arguments Against Free Trade

Political arguments against free trade are based on advancing a nation's political, social, and environmental agenda regardless of possible economic gains from trade. These arguments include national security, consumer protection, foreign policy, and environmental and social responsibility.

Trade embargo Politically motivated trade sanctions against foreign countries to signal displeasure.

First, national security concerns are often invoked to protect defense-related industries. France has always insisted on maintaining an independent defense industry to produce nuclear weapons, aircraft carriers, and combat jets. While the French can purchase such weapons at much lower costs from the United States, which is eager to sell them, the French answer has usually been "No, thanks!"

Second, consumer protection has frequently been used as an argument for nations to erect trade barriers. For example, American hormone-treated beef was banned by the EU in the 1990s because of the alleged health risks. Even though the United States won a WTO battle on this, the EU still has refused to remove the ban.

Third, trade intervention is often used to meet foreign policy objectives. **Trade embargoes** are politically motivated trade sanctions against foreign countries to signal displeasure. For example, the United States has enforced embargoes against Iran, Sudan, and Syria. In 2009, DHL paid a record fine of $9.4 million for sending illegal shipments to these countries. According to a US Treasury Department statement, DHL "may have conferred a significant economic advantage to these sanctioned countries that potentially created extraordinarily adverse harm." What are such dangerous shipments? Condoms, Tiffany jewelry, and radar detectors for cars, according to the same Treasury Department statement.[13]

Finally, environmental and social responsibility can be used as political arguments to initiate trade intervention against certain countries. In a "shrimp-turtle" case, the United States banned shrimp imports from India, Malaysia, Pakistan, and Thailand. Although the shrimp were not harvested from US waters, they were caught using a technique that also accidentally trapped and killed sea turtles, an endangered species protected by the United States. India, Malaysia, Pakistan, and Thailand were upset and brought the case to the WTO, alleging that the United States invoked an environmental law as a trade barrier.

5-4 MANAGEMENT SAVVY

How does this chapter answer the big question in global business, adapted for the context of international trade: What determines the success and failure of firms' exports around the globe? The two core perspectives lead to two answers. Fundamentally, the various economic theories underpin the resource-based view, suggesting that successful exports are valuable, unique, and hard-to-imitate products generated by certain firms from a nation. However, the political realities stress the explanatory and predictive power of the institution-based view: As rules of the game, laws and regulations promoted by various special interest groups can protect certain domestic industries, firms, and individuals; erect trade barriers; and make the nation as a whole worse off.

Listed in Exhibit 5.11, three implications for action emerge. First, location, location, location! In international trade, a savvy manager's first job is to leverage the comparative advantage of world-class locations. Shown in the Opening Case, one crucial reason behind China's rise as the world's top merchandise exporting nation is that many non-Chinese managers at non-Chinese firms have discovered China's comparative advantage as a low-cost production location. As a result, they set up factories and export from China—*two-thirds* of the value added of Chinese exports is generated by such foreign-invested firms.

Second, comparative advantage is not fixed. Managers need to constantly monitor and nurture the current comparative advantage of a location and take advantage of new promising locations. Managers who fail to realize when a location no longer has a comparative advantage are likely to fall behind. For example, numerous German managers have moved production out of Germany, citing the country's reduced comparative advantage in basic manufacturing. However, they still concentrate top-notch, high-end manufacturing in Germany, leveraging its excellence in engineering.

Third, managers need to be politically savvy if they appreciate the gains from trade. While managers at many uncompetitive firms have long mastered the game of using politicians to gain protection, managers at competitive firms tend to shy away from politics. But they often fail to realize that free trade is *not* free—it requires constant efforts to demonstrate and advance the gains from such trade. For example, the US-China Business Council, a pro-free trade (in particular, pro-China trade) group consisting of 250 large US corporations, has frequently spoken out in defense of trade with China.[14]

EXHIBIT 5.11 IMPLICATIONS FOR ACTION

- Discover and leverage comparative advantage of world-class locations.
- Monitor and nurture the current comparative advantage of certain locations, and take advantage of new locations.
- Be politically active to demonstrate, safeguard, and advance the gains from international trade.

Why Are US Exports So Competitive?

Since the launch of the first edition of *GLOBAL*, the rise of China as the leading exporter has been widely reported (see the Opening Case). Yet, what has been little reported by the media is that the United States also rocketed ahead of Germany and is now the world's second largest exporter.* Never mind all that talk about the "decline" of US competitiveness (!). An important part of your university education is to foster a critical thinking mindset by relying on data and forming evidence-based judgments, as opposed to being excessively influenced by media fads. Shown in Exhibit 5.12, the data suggest a story that is different from that typically portrayed by the media.

* This case only deals with *merchandise* (*goods*) exports. In service exports, the United States is even more competitive—it is the world champion.

MIROUNGA/SHUTTERSTOCK.COM

In 2013, the United States exported a record $1.58 trillion, with an enviable 8.4% annual increase. Of China's $2.21 trillion exports, only about two-thirds of the value added was contributed by China. The United States contributed approximately 89% of the value added of its exports. Do your math: The value added of US exports ($1.41 trillion) was almost the same as the value added of Chinese exports ($1.48 trillion). In addition, the United States again outsold the long-time

EXHIBIT 5.12 TOP FIVE MERCHANDISE (GOODS) EXPORTING NATIONS

	2006	2008	2011	2013
1	Germany	Germany	China	China
2	United States	China	United States	United States
3	China	United States	Germany	Germany
4	Japan	Japan	Japan	Japan
5	France	Netherlands	Netherlands	Netherlands

Sources: The first three columns are adapted from M. W. Peng, *Global Business*, 1st, 2nd, and 3rd eds. (Cincinnati: Cengage Learning, 2009, 2011, 2014). 2013 data are from the World Trade Organization, 2014, *World Trade Report 2014*, Geneva: WTO.

export champion Germany (which exported $1.45 trillion) and the formidable export powerhouse Japan (which exported $715 billion). Don't forget: The United States accomplished such enviable export success during the very difficult aftermath of the Great Recession, in which every nation was eager to export its way out of recession. What were the top US export categories? Refined petroleum products, civilian aircraft, semiconductors, passenger cars, and telecom equipment. The top five export states were Texas (which exported one-sixth of the nation's total exports), California, Illinois, Louisiana, and New York. The US Department of Commerce proudly noted that "fueling our economic recovery, exports are a bright spot in the US economy."

Why are US exports so competitive? What is unique about US exports? What has been driving their recent rise in a bleak global economic environment? On top of the Great Recession, one can add more recent catastrophes such as the Japanese earthquake, the Thai floods, the euro zone crisis, the Middle East turmoil, the Russian sanctions, and the Ebola crisis. To make a long story short, first, US exports have to deliver *value*. Consider civilian aircraft. One crucial reason that the new Boeing 787 Dreamliner became the hottest-selling airliner prior to its launch is its ability to reduce fuel consumption by 15%—music to the ears of airline executives who suffer from high oil prices. Second, US exports also have to be *rare* and *hard to imitate*. There is no shortage of global rivals tearing apart US products and trying to reverse engineer them. European, Russian, and Chinese aerospace firms are doing this at this moment by trying to out-Boeing Boeing. While Airbus has been quite successful, neither Russian nor Chinese civilian aircraft makers have much presence in export markets. Finally, US exporters have to *organize* themselves in a more productive and efficient manner relative to their global rivals. It is hard enough to design and manufacture world-class aircraft, but it is no less challenging to operate service, training, and maintenance networks for airlines that cannot afford any equipment breakdown for a long period—on a worldwide basis and for 20 to 30 years after the initial sale.

While the products themselves have to be strong and competitive, Uncle Sam has also helped. At least ten federal agencies offer export assistance: the Departments of Commerce, State, Treasury, Energy, and Agriculture as well as the Office of US Trade Representative (USTR), Export-Import Bank (Ex-Im Bank), US Agency for International Development (USAID), Overseas Private Investment Corporation (OPIC), and Small Business Administration (SBA). Since only approximately 1% of all US firms export and 58% of them export to just one country, clearly more assistance will be helpful if more firms are interested in joining the export game.

Going beyond routine export assistance, new initiatives focus on negotiating free trade agreements (FTAs) with trading partners. As of this writing, the United States has 12 FTAs in force with 18 countries: Australia, Bahrain, Chile, DR-CAFTA (Dominican Republic-Central America FTA, which covers Costa Rica, Dominican Republic, El Salvador, Guatemala, Honduras, and Nicaragua), Israel, Jordan, Morocco, NAFTA (which covers Canada and Mexico), Oman, Peru, Singapore, and South Korea. In addition, two FTAs with Panama and Colombia were negotiated, but they are still pending Congressional approval. FTAs typically reduce trade barriers to US exports and create a more stable and transparent trading environment. In the first FTA with an East Asian country, the South Korea–US FTA (also known as KORUS), South Korea agreed to phase out a 40% tariff on US beef imports, and the United States agreed to waive a 2.5% tariff on Korean auto imports.

In addition to FTAs, the US government often negotiates with other foreign governments for better market access and terms of trade for US exporters. The push to get the Chinese to let the yuan appreciate, so that the dollar can be cheaper and US exports can be more competitive, is a case in point. Despite an allegedly "artificially" low yuan and a government eager to promote China's own exports, China rose from being the ninth largest US export market in 2001 to the third largest in 2011 (behind Canada and Mexico). During that period, US exports to China jumped over 400%, while US exports to the rest of the world only grew 55%. Given the still huge US trade deficit (of which the US–China trade deficit is the largest component), clearly there is more room to push US exports.

In addition to formal institutions, informal norms and values, both at home and abroad, play a role behind US exports. At home, all the talk about the virtue and necessity of energy conservation and going green evidently has slowly become a part of the American cultural norm. One piece of evidence is that US oil consumption has declined since 2006. This helps explain why refined petroleum products (such as gasoline, diesel, and jet fuel) recently shot ahead of civilian aircraft to become the number one export category. This is partly because much of the refining capacity the

United States added in the past decade is now geared toward exports. While gurus write about the decline of US influence, the informal norms of consuming and appreciating US products seem to proliferate overseas. In Paris metro (underground) stations, almost every other poster seems to be about a Hollywood blockbuster. In Accra, the middle class flock into Ghana's first KFC and lick their fingers greased by grown-in-USA chicken. If you are studying *this* book outside the United States, then you are a US export customer, too. Enjoy!

Case Discussion Questions

1. ***ON ETHICS***: Prior to taking this class and studying this case, have you often heard or read about the decline of US export competitiveness? What are the social and ethical implications of such excessive (one-sided) negative reporting? Does this case change your mind? Why?
2. From a resource-based view, why are US exports so competitive?
3. From an institution-based view, why are US exports so competitive?

Sources: This case draws on a long line of my own research on US export strategy, starting with my PhD dissertation and more recently with an interview with the *Dallas Morning News* on Texas export competitiveness—cited below. "Yum's big game of chicken," *Bloomberg Businessweek*, 29 March 2012, 64–69; "The real way a trade deal gets done," *Bloomberg Businessweek*, 24 October 2011, 30–32; "Texas exports spike higher on energy goods," *Dallas Morning News*, 23 February 2012; "Go sell," *Economist*, 13 March 2010, 32; "Picking the world champion of trade," *Economist*, 18 January 2014, 72–73; M. W. Peng, 1998, *Behind the Success and Failure of US Export Intermediaries* (Westport, CT: Quorum, 1998); US Commercial Service, 2015, www.export.gov.

STUDY TOOLS 5

LOCATED AT THE BACK OF YOUR BOOK:

- ☐ Rip out and study the Chapter Review Card at the end of the book

LOG IN TO WWW.CENGAGEBRAIN.COM TO:

- ☐ Review key term flashcards
- ☐ Complete a practice quiz to test your knowledge of key concepts
- ☐ Take and complete the chapter crossword puzzle
- ☐ Complete interactive content, watch chapter videos, and take a graded quiz
- ☐ Track your knowledge of key concepts in Global Business
- ☐ Read and discuss additional case study content

6 Investing Abroad Directly

ISTOCKPHOTO.COM/MORDOLFF

LEARNING OBJECTIVES

After studying this chapter, you should be able to . . .

- **6-1** Identify and define the key terms associated with foreign direct investment (FDI).
- **6-2** Use the resource-based and institution-based views to answer why FDI takes place.
- **6-3** Explain how FDI results in ownership advantages.
- **6-4** Identify the ways your firm can acquire and neutralize location advantages.
- **6-5** List the benefits of internalization.
- **6-6** Identify different political views on FDI and understand its benefits and costs to host and home countries.
- **6-7** List three things you need to do as your firm considers FDI.

After you finish this chapter, go to **PAGE 99** for **STUDY TOOLS**

The Pros and Cons of Foreign Direct Investment in Britain

Britain is no stranger to foreign direct investment (FDI). Historically, the development of many countries such as Australia, Canada, India, and the United States benefited from FDI outflows from Britain. But now the news about FDI in Britain tends to focus on FDI inflows. Iconic brands and companies seem to slip out of British hands repeatedly. Recently, Cadbury was taken over by Kraft. The Rover Group was bought by BMW. But BMW failed to turn it around (except doing well with the smaller MINI division). The Land Rover part of the Rover Group was then sold to Ford, which more recently sold it to India's Tata. The Rover brand itself was sold to China's Nanjing Auto. Thanks to large inflows of FDI, a foreign firm is now Britain's largest private-sector employer: Tata UK has more than 50,000 employees—slightly ahead of BAE Systems (formerly known as British Aerospace). In addition to these high-profile cases, the extent of FDI's penetration into the British economy is indeed striking. The *Economist* noted the following examples:

> *Consider an imaginary Englishman's day. He wakes up in his cottage near Dover, ready to commute to London. Chomping a bowl of Weetabix, a British breakfast cereal resembling (tasty) cardboard, he makes a cup of tea. His private water comes from Veolia, and his electricity from EDF (both French firms). Thumps at the gate tell him another arm of Veolia is emptying his bins. He takes the new high-speed train to London: it is part-owned by the French firm Keolis, while the tracks belong to Canadian pension funds. At St. Pancras station, a choice of double-decker buses awaits. In the last couple of years, one of the big London bus companies was bought by Netherlands Railways. A second went to Deutsch Bahn, the German railway company. In March 2011, a third was taken over by RATP, the Paris public-transport authority (its previous owner was also French). . . . As for Weetabix, a French billionaire is interested in buying the firm. Yet, Britain still feels British.*

For three decades, the consensus seems to be that Britain gains more by welcoming FDI, which is a vote of confidence in the country's business climate. Although patriotism runs deep, the specific link between sovereignty and corporate ownership does not seem very strong in Britain. But increasingly, many people in Britain are not so sure that the benefits of FDI outweigh the costs. The most basic anxiety is that foreign ownership may lead to factory closures and job losses. More strategically, as head offices close, Britain risks becoming a "branch factory" economy. When the going gets tough, foreign multinationals are more likely to preserve factories and jobs in their home countries and put British jobs on the chopping board. Debates on how to fend off foreigners (and foreign firms) to defend British ownership rage. Advocates of more protectionist policies point to Germany, whose officials complain about a swarm of (largely American) "locusts" devouring its *Mittelstand*, the private companies behind Germany's export prowess. Such British advocates also cheer France's decision to designate Danone a firm in a "strategic industry" that would qualify for government protection should foreign rivals come sniffing.

Defenders of more open policies on FDI inflows make four points. First, if foreigners think they can do a better job in managing British operations, "good luck to them," according to the *Economist*. "The Spanish firm Ferrovial can hardly do a worse job of running London's Heathrow airport than did BAA, the British firm it took over." Second, being bought by foreign multinationals tends to boost productivity. Four out of five MINIs made in Oxford are now exported, and one in six BMWs sold is a made-in-Britain MINI. This contrasts sharply with the sorry state of Rover and MINI cars when under British ownership. Third, head offices and their jobs often stay. After GE bought Amersham, a British nuclear medicine systems firm, it moved GE Medical's head office from Milwaukee, Wisconsin, to Buckinghamshire. Finally, considering that British firms actively invest abroad, protectionist policies at home will certainly invite retaliation abroad. While debates rage, it is clear that blocking FDI inflows would undermine Britain's long-standing support for open markets, which would reduce its attractiveness as a place to do business.

Sources: "Small island for sale," *Economist*, 27 March 2010, 75–77; "A very British paradox," *Economist*, 18 June 2011; "Tata for now," *Economist*, 10 September 2011, 61–62; "Britain: Looking for a future," *Economist*, 9 November 2013 (special report); M. W. Peng and K. Meyer, "Winning the future markets for UK manufacturing output," *Future of Manufacturing Project: Evidence Paper 25* (London: UK Government Office for Science, 2013); N. Savithri, "Indian FDI in Britain," in M. W. Peng, *Global Business*, 4th ed. (Cincinnati: Cengage Learning, 2017).

Why are many foreign firms interested in undertaking foreign direct investment (FDI) in Britain? What are the benefits to these firms and to the British economy? What are the drawbacks? Recall from Chapter 1 that FDI is defined as putting money into activities that control and manage value-added activities in other countries. Also recall from Chapter 1 that firms that engage in FDI are known as multinational enterprises (MNEs). In 2014, while most developed economies slowly recovered from the Great Recession of 2008–2009, emerging economies as a group attracted approximately 60% of the FDI inflows. Firms from emerging economies such as those from India discussed in the Opening Case generated approximately 40% of the FDI outflows worldwide.[1]

This chapter starts by first defining key terms related to FDI. Then we address a crucial question: Why do firms engage in FDI? We outline how the core perspectives introduced earlier—namely, resource-based and institution-based views—can help answer this question.[2] We then look at a debate over whether countries should welcome certain FDI. Finally, we outline factors a firm should address as it considers engaging in FDI.

6-1 UNDERSTANDING THE FDI VOCABULARY

Part of FDI's complexity is associated with its vocabulary. This section will try to reduce the complexity by setting the terms straight.

6-1a The Key Word Is *Direct*

International investment happens primarily in two ways: FDI and **foreign portfolio investment (FPI)**. FPI refers to holding securities, such as stocks and bonds, of companies in countries outside one's own but does not entail the active management of foreign assets. Essentially, FPI is foreign *indirect* investment. In contrast, the key word in FDI is *direct*—namely, the direct, hands-on management of foreign assets. Some of you reading this book may have some FPI—that is, you own some foreign stocks and bonds. However, as a student taking this course, it is by definition impossible that you are also engaging in FDI at the same time, because that requires you to be a manager who is getting your feet wet by actively managing foreign operations rather than just learning about them.

For statistical purposes, the United Nations defines FDI as an equity stake of 10% or more in a foreign-based enterprise. A lower percentage invested in a foreign firm is considered FPI. Without a sufficiently large equity, it is difficult to exercise **management control rights**—namely, the rights to appoint key managers and establish control mechanisms. Many firms invest abroad for the explicit purpose of managing foreign operations, and they need a large equity (sometimes up to 100%) to be able to do that.

ISTOCKPHOTO.COM/JOSHBLAKE

Foreign portfolio investment (FPI) Holding securities, such as stocks and bonds, of firms in other countries but without a controlling interest.

Management control right The right to appoint key managers and establish control mechanisms.

Horizontal FDI A type of FDI in which a firm produces the same products or offers the same services in a host country as at home.

Vertical FDI A type of FDI in which a firm moves upstream or downstream in different value chain stages in a host country.

Upstream vertical FDI A type of vertical FDI in which a firm engages in an upstream stage of the value chain.

Downstream vertical FDI A type of vertical FDI in which a firm engages in a downstream stage of the value chain.

FDI flow The amount of FDI moving in a given period (usually a year) in a certain direction.

FDI inflow FDI moving into a country in a year.

FDI outflow FDI moving out of a country in a year.

6-1b Horizontal and Vertical FDI

FDI can be horizontal or vertical. Recall the value chain from Chapter 4, whereby firms perform value-adding activities stage by stage in a vertical fashion, from upstream to downstream. When a firm takes the same activity at the same value-chain stage from its home country and *duplicates* it in a host country through FDI, we call this horizontal FDI (see Exhibit 6.1). For example, BMW assembles cars in Germany. Through horizontal FDI, it does the same thing in host countries such as Britain (see the Opening Case). Overall, **horizontal FDI** refers to producing the same products or offering the same services in a host country as firms do at home.

If a firm moves upstream or downstream in different value chain stages in a host country through FDI, we label this **vertical FDI** (see Exhibit 6.2). For example, if BMW (hypothetically) only assembled cars and did not manufacture components in Germany but entered into components manufacturing through FDI in Russia (an earlier activity in the value chain), this would be **upstream vertical FDI**. Likewise, if BMW did not engage in car distribution in Germany but invested in car dealerships in Egypt (a later activity in the value chain), it would be **downstream vertical FDI**.

6-1c FDI Flow and Stock

Other words often associated with FDI are "flow" and "stock." **FDI flow** is the amount of FDI moving in a given period (usually a year) in a certain direction. **FDI inflow** usually refers to FDI moving into a country in a year, and **FDI outflow** typically refers to FDI moving out of a country in a year. PengAtlas Map 8

ISTOCKPHOTO.COM/HENRIK5000

EXHIBIT 6.1 HORIZONTAL FDI

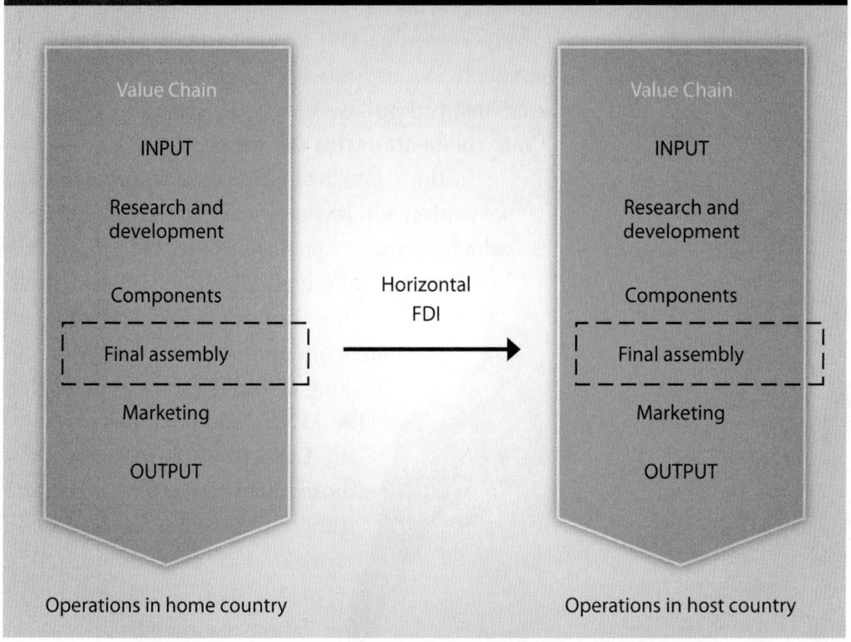

EXHIBIT 6.2 VERTICAL FDI

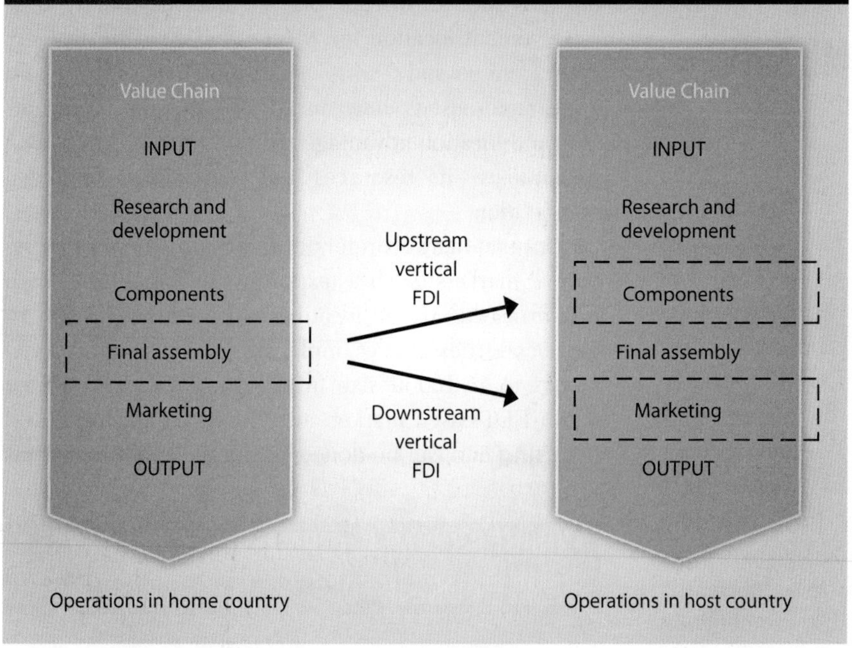

illustrates the top ten economies for FDI inflows and outflows. **FDI stock** is the total accumulation of inward FDI in a country or outward FDI from a country. Hypothetically, between two countries A and B, if firms from A undertake $10 billion of FDI in B in Year 1 and another $10 billion in Year 2, then we can say that in each of these two years, B receives annual FDI *inflows* of $10 billion and, correspondingly, A generates annual FDI *outflows* of $10 billion. If we assume that firms from no other countries undertake FDI in country B and prior to Year 1 no FDI was possible, then the total *stock* of FDI in B by the end of Year 2 is $20 billion. Essentially, flow is a snapshot of a given point in time, and stock represents the cumulative volume.

6-1d MNE Versus Non-MNE

An MNE, by definition, is a firm that engages in FDI when doing business abroad.[3] An MNE is sometimes called a multinational corporation (MNC) or a transnational corporation (TNC). To avoid confusion, we will stick with the term "MNE" throughout the book. Note that non-MNE firms can also do business abroad by exporting and importing, licensing and franchising, outsourcing, or engaging in FPI. What sets MNEs apart from non-MNEs is FDI. An exporter has to undertake FDI in order to become an MNE. In other words, BMW would not be an MNE if it manufactured all of its cars in Germany and exported them around the world. BMW became an MNE only when it started to directly invest abroad.

Although some people argue that MNEs are a new organizational form that emerged after World War II, it is simply not the case. MNEs have existed for at least 2,000 years, with some of the earliest examples found in the Phoenician, Assyrian, and Roman times. In 1903 when Ford Motor Company was founded, it exported its sixth car. Ford almost immediately engaged in FDI by having

FDI stock The total accumulation of inbound FDI in a country or outbound FDI from a country across a given period of time (usually several years).

a factory in Canada that produced its first output in 1904. It is true that MNEs have experienced significant growth since World War II. In 1970, there were approximately 7,000 MNEs worldwide. By 2010, over 82,000 MNEs managed approximately 810,000 foreign affiliates.[4] Clearly, there is a proliferation of MNEs lately.

ISTOCKPHOTO.COM/OJO_IMAGES

6-2 WHY DO FIRMS BECOME MNEs BY ENGAGING IN FDI?

Having set the terms straight, we need to address a fundamental question: Why do so many firms—ranging from those in the ancient world to today's BMW, Samsung, and Walmart—become MNEs by engaging in FDI? Without getting into details, we can safely say that there must be economic gains from FDI. More importantly, given the tremendous complexities associated with FDI, such gains must significantly outweigh the costs. What are the sources of such gains? The answer, as suggested by British scholar John Dunning and illustrated in Exhibit 6.3, boils down to firms' quest for ownership (O) advantages, location (L) advantages, and internalization (I) advantages—collectively known as **OLI advantages**.[5] The two core perspectives introduced earlier—resource-based and institution-based views—enable us to probe into the heart of this question.

In the context of FDI, **ownership** refers to possession and leveraging by an MNE of certain valuable, rare, hard-to-imitate, and organizationally embedded (VRIO) assets overseas. Owning the proprietary technology and the management know-how that goes into making a BMW helps ensure that the MNE can beat rivals abroad.

Location advantages are those enjoyed by firms because they do business in a certain place. Features unique to a place, such as its natural or labor resources or its location near particular markets, provide certain advantages to firms doing business there. For example, Vietnam has emerged as a convenient location for MNEs that want to diversify away from coastal China with rising labor costs.[6] From a resource-based view, an MNE's pursuit of ownership and location advantages can be regarded as flexing its muscles—its resources and capabilities—in global competition.

Internalization refers to the replacement of cross-border markets (such as exporting and importing) with one firm (the MNE) locating and operating in two or more countries. For example, BMW could sell its technology to an Indonesian firm for a fee. This would be a non-FDI-based market entry mode technically called **licensing** and can be done with intellectual property as

OLI advantages The advantages of ownership (O), location (L), and internalization (I) that come from engaging in FDI.

Ownership Possessing and leveraging of certain valuable, rare, hard-to-imitate, and organizationally embedded (VRIO) assets overseas in the context of FDI.

Location Advantages enjoyed by a firm that derive from the places in which it operates.

Internalization The replacement of cross-border markets (such as exporting and importing) with one firm (the MNE) located in two or more countries.

Licensing Buying and selling technology and intellectual property rights.

EXHIBIT 6.3 AN OLI FRAMEWORK FOR WHY FIRMS ENGAGE IN FDI

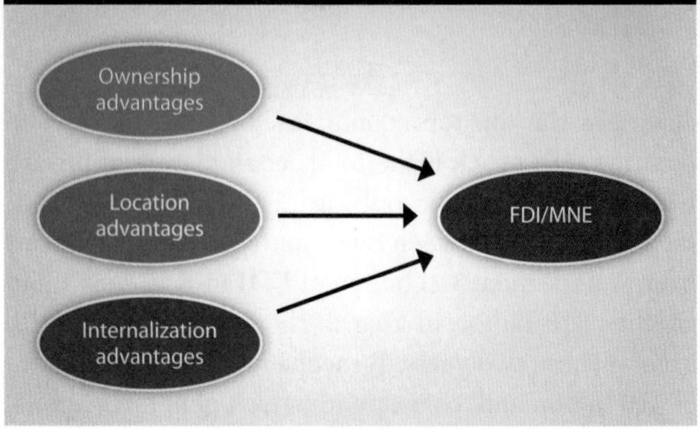

well as technology. Instead, BMW chooses to assemble cars in Indonesia via FDI. In other words, external market transactions (in this case, buying and selling of technology through licensing) are replaced by internalization. From an institution-based view, internalization is a response to the imperfect rules governing international transactions, known as **market imperfections** (or **market failure**). Evidently, Indonesian regulations governing the protection of intellectual property such as BMW's proprietary technology do not give BMW sufficient confidence that those rights will be protected. Therefore, internalization is a must.

Overall, firms become MNEs because FDI provides OLI advantages that they otherwise would not obtain. The next three sections explain why this is the case.

6-3 OWNERSHIP ADVANTAGES

All investments, including both FDI and FPI, entail ownership of assets. So what is unique about FDI? This section highlights the benefits of direct ownership and compares FDI to licensing when considering market entries abroad.

6-3a The Benefits of Direct Ownership

Remember that *direct* is the key word in foreign direct investment. FDI requires a significant equity ownership position. The benefits of direct ownership lie in the *combination* of equity ownership rights and management control rights. Specifically, the ownership rights provide the much-needed management control rights. In contrast, FPI represents essentially insignificant ownership rights and no management control rights. To compete successfully, firms need to deploy overwhelming resources and capabilities to overcome their liabilities of foreignness (see Chapters 1 and 4). FDI provides one of the best ways to facilitate such extension of firm-specific resources and capabilities abroad.

6-3b FDI Versus Licensing

Basic choices when entering foreign markets include exporting, licensing, and FDI. Successful exporting may provoke protectionist responses from host countries, thus forcing firms to choose between licensing and FDI. Between licensing and FDI, which is better? Exhibit 6.4 shows three reasons that may compel firms to prefer FDI to licensing.

EXHIBIT 6.4 WHY FIRMS PREFER FDI TO LICENSING

- FDI reduces dissemination risks.
- FDI provides tight control over foreign operations.
- FDI facilitates the transfer of tacit knowledge through "learning by doing."

First, FDI affords a high degree of direct management control that reduces the risk of firm-specific resources and capabilities being appropriated. One of the leading risks abroad is **dissemination risk**, defined as the possibility of unauthorized diffusion of firm-specific know-how. If a foreign company grants a license to a local firm to manufacture or market a product, the licensee (or an employee of the licensee) may disseminate the know-how by using it against the wishes of the foreign company. For example, Pizza Hut found out that its long-time licensee in Thailand disseminated its know-how and established a direct competitor, simply called The Pizza Company, which controlled 70% of the market in Thailand.[7] While owning and managing proprietary assets through FDI does not completely shield firms from dissemination risks (after all, their employees can quit and join competitors), FDI is better because licensing does not provide management control at all. Understandably, FDI is extensively used in knowledge-intensive, high-tech industries such as automobiles, electronics, chemicals, and IT.

Second, FDI provides more direct and tighter control over foreign operations. Even when licensees (and their employees) harbor no opportunistic intention to steal secrets, they may not always follow the wishes of the foreign firm that provides the know-how. Without FDI, the foreign firm cannot control its licensee. For example, Starbucks entered South Korea by licensing its format to ESCO. Although ESCO soon opened ten stores, Starbucks felt that ESCO was not aggressive enough in growing the chain.

ISTOCKPHOTO.COM/KATE_SEPT2004

Market imperfection (market failure) The imperfect rules governing international market transactions.

Dissemination risk The possibility of unauthorized diffusion of firm-specific know-how.

But there was little Starbucks could do. Eventually, Starbucks switched from licensing to FDI, which allowed it to directly promote the more aggressive growth of the chain in South Korea.

Finally, certain knowledge (or know-how) calls for FDI as opposed to licensing. Even if there is no opportunism on the part of licensees and if they follow the wishes of the foreign firm, certain know-how may simply be too difficult to transfer to licensees without FDI. There are two basic categories of knowledge: explicit and tacit. Explicit knowledge is codifiable—specifically, it can be written down and transferred without losing much of its richness. Tacit knowledge, on the other hand, is noncodifiable and its acquisition and transfer requires hands-on practice. For example, a driving manual represents a body of explicit knowledge. However, mastering the manual without any road practice does not make you a good driver. Tacit knowledge is more important and harder to transfer and learn—it can only be acquired by doing (in this case, practice driving under the supervision of an experienced driver). Likewise, operating a Walmart store involves a great deal of knowledge, some explicit (often captured in an operational manual) and some tacit. As such, simply giving foreign licensees—via a licensing agreement—a copy of the Walmart operational manual will not be enough. Foreign employees will need to learn directly from experienced Walmart personnel by actually doing the job.

From a resource-based standpoint, it is Walmart's tacit knowledge that gives it competitive advantage (see Chapter 4). Walmart owns such crucial tacit knowledge, and has no incentive to give that knowledge away to licensees without having some management control over how that knowledge is used. Therefore, properly transferring and controlling tacit knowledge calls for FDI. Overall, ownership advantages enable the firm, now becoming an MNE, to more effectively extend, transfer, and leverage firm-specific capabilities abroad.

6-4 LOCATION ADVANTAGES

Given the well-known liability of foreignness, foreign locations must offer compelling advantages to make it worthwhile to undertake FDI. We may regard the continuous expansion of international business (IB), such as FDI, as an unending saga in search of location advantages.[8] This section highlights the sources of location advantages and outlines ways to acquire and neutralize those advantages.

Agglomeration The clustering of economic activities in certain locations.

6-4a Location, Location, Location

Certain locations possess geographical features that are difficult to match by others. For example, although Austria politically and culturally belongs to the West, the country is geographically located in the heart of Central and Eastern Europe (CEE). In fact, Austria's capital Vienna is actually *east* of Prague, the Czech Republic, and Ljubljana, Slovenia. Therefore, Vienna attracts significant FDI from MNEs to set up regional headquarters for CEE. Due to its proximity to the United States, Mexico attracts numerous automakers to set up production there. Thanks to such FDI, 64% of Mexico's vehicle production is exported to the United States.

Beyond natural geographical advantages, location advantages also arise from the clustering of economic activities in certain locations, referred to as **agglomeration** (see In Focus). For instance, the Netherlands grows and exports two-thirds of the worldwide exports of cut flowers. Slovakia produces more cars per capita than any other country in the world, thanks to the quest for agglomeration benefits by global automakers. Dallas attracts all of the world's major telecom equipment makers and many telecom service providers, making it the Telecom Corridor. Overall, agglomeration advantages stem from:

- Knowledge spillover, or the diffusion of knowledge from one firm to others among closely located firms that attempt to hire individuals from competitors.
- Industry demand that creates a skilled labor force whose members may work for different firms without moving out of the region.
- Industry demand that facilitates a pool of specialized suppliers and buyers also located in the region.

6-4b Acquiring and Neutralizing Location Advantages

Note that from a resource-based view, location advantages do *not* entirely overlap with country-level advantages such as the factor endowments discussed in Chapter 5. Location advantages refer to the advantages that one firm obtains when operating in

In Focus:

Agglomeration of Wind Turbine Producers in Denmark

On a clear day, passengers with window seats on planes taking off and landing at Copenhagen airport can clearly see dozens of huge wind turbines offshore in Oresund (the strait that separates Denmark and Sweden). Chances are that these wind turbines are also developed and made in Denmark. Thanks to visionary government policies that offer generous subsidies, Denmark is a first mover and now a world leader in the wind turbine industry. At present, *one-third* of Danish energy consumption comes from wind. No other country comes close. Denmark's goal is to become the first country in the world to meet 50% of energy needs with wind power by 2020 and 100% by 2050. Underpinning these achievements and ambitions is a cluster of wind turbine manufacturers and suppliers in one part of Denmark—Jutland, the peninsula in western Denmark that is attached to the European mainland (Copenhagen is located in the easternmost part of the country on the island of Zealand).

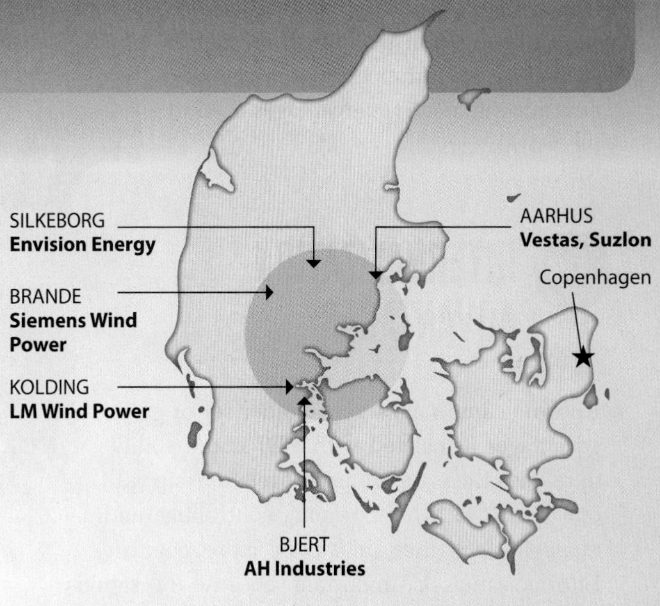

Source: "A wind energy hub," *Focus Denmark*, summer--autumn 2014: 24. © Danish Ministry of Foreign Affairs.

Based in Aarhus (Denmark's second largest city), Vestas is the world leader in terms of installed turbines (60 GW), accounting for nearly one-fifth of the total capacity of all the installed turbines in the world. Founded in 1979, Vestas employs 15,000 people, including 4,000 in Denmark. About 80 kilometers west of Aarhus, in the small town of Brande, Siemens Wind Power is headquartered there. Founded in 2004 following the acquisition of Bonus Energy, which was established in 1979, Siemens Wind Power (a division of Siemens) is another giant in this industry. It has 23 GW-installed turbines and 11,000 employees worldwide (of which 5,500 are in Denmark). In addition, major Danish-owned suppliers LM Wind Power and AH Industries are also nearby. Attracted by the greatest agglomeration of know-how in this specialized but rapidly expanding industry, a number of international wind turbine manufacturers, such as India's Suzlon and China's Envision Energy, have also undertaken foreign direct investment (FDI) in this region of Denmark. With an investment of $400 million, Japan's Mitsubishi Heavy Industries (MHI) has recently established a 50-50 joint venture with Vestas named MHI Vestas Offshore Wind that focuses on the huge 8.0 MW turbines. Anders Rebsdorf, director of Envision Energy (Denmark) located in Silkeborg, a town almost equidistant between the global headquarters of the two giants Vestas and Siemens Wind Power, articulated the firm's location choice:

> *Our choice of Denmark is directly related to the country's strong cluster of know-how in the area of turbine design. It is also important that there are manufacturers of turbine components and experts in turbine service. The entire value chain is represented to a degree that is not found anywhere else. . . . If we are to earn the right to join the battle for international orders, then we must be visible where the competition is fierce.*

Sources: "A wind energy hub," *Focus Denmark*, summer–autumn 2014, 24; "Titans of wind energy arm for battle," *Focus Denmark*, summer–autumn 2014, 18–23; Vestas, "MHI Vestas Offshore Wind now operational," announcement, 1 April 2014; "Vestas, Mitsubishi form offshore joint venture," *Wall Street Journal*, 27 September 2013, online.wsj.com.

a location due to its *firm-specific* capabilities. In 1982, General Motors (GM) ran its Fremont, California, plant into the ground and had to close it. Reopening the same plant in 1984, Toyota initiated its first FDI project in the United States in a joint venture (JV) with GM. Since then, Toyota (together with GM) has leveraged this plant's location advantages by producing award-winning cars that American customers particularly like—the Toyota Corolla and Tacoma. The point is: It is Toyota's unique capabilities, applied to the California location, that literally have saved the plant from its demise. The California location in itself does not provide location advantages *per se*, as shown by GM's inability to make it work prior to 1982.

Firms do not operate in a vacuum. When one firm enters a foreign country through FDI, its rivals are likely to increase FDI in that host country either to acquire location advantages themselves or to at least neutralize the first mover's location advantages. These actions to imitate and follow competitors are especially likely in oligopolies—industries (such as aerospace and semiconductors) populated by a small number of players. The automobile industry is a typical oligopolistic industry. Volkswagen was the first foreign entrant in China, starting production in 1985 and enjoying a market share of 60% in the 1990s. Now, every self-respecting global automaker has entered China trying to eat some of Volkswagen's lunch. Overall, competitive rivalry and imitation, especially in oligopolistic industries, underscores the importance of acquiring and neutralizing location advantages around the world.

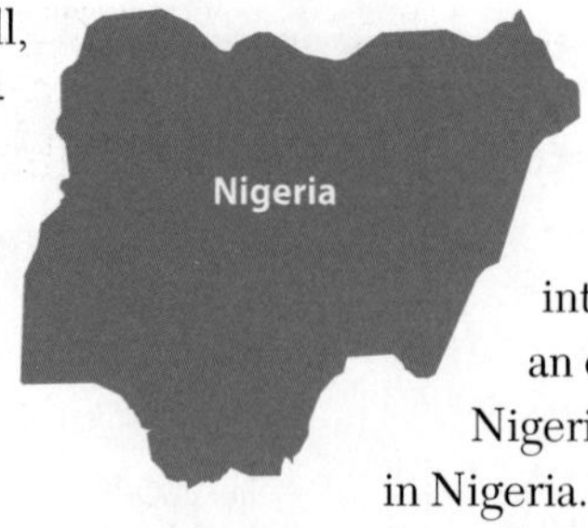

6-5 INTERNATIONALIZATION ADVANTAGES

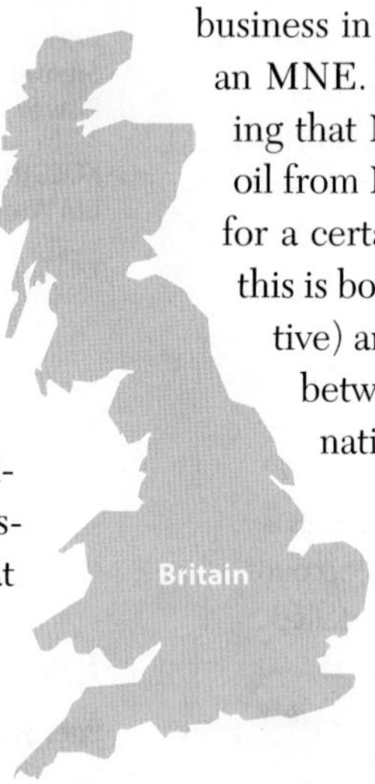

Known as internalization, another set of great advantages associated with FDI is the ability to replace the external market relationship with one firm (the MNE) owning, controlling, and managing activities in two or more countries. Internalization is important because of significant imperfections in international market transactions. The institution-based view suggests that markets are governed by rules, regulations, and norms that are designed to reduce uncertainties. Uncertainties introduce transaction costs—costs associated with doing business (see Chapter 2). This section outlines the necessity of combating market failure and describes the benefits brought by internalization.

6-5a Market Failure

International transaction costs tend to be higher than domestic transaction costs. Because laws and regulations are typically enforced on a nation-state basis, enforcement can be an issue on the international level. Suppose two parties from different countries are doing business. If the party from country A behaves opportunistically, the other party from country B will have a hard time enforcing the contract. Suing the other party in a foreign country is not only costly but also uncertain. In the worst case, such imperfections are so grave that markets fail to function, and many firms simply choose not to do business abroad to avoid being burned. High transaction costs can therefore result in market failure in cases where the market imperfections actually prohibit transactions altogether. However, recall from Chapter 5 that there are gains from trade. Not doing business together prevents firms from reaping such gains. In response, MNEs emerge to overcome and combat such market failure through FDI.

6-5b Overcoming Market Failure Through FDI

How do MNEs combat market failure through internalization? Let us use an example involving an oil importer, BP in Britain, and an oil exporter, Nigerian National Petroleum Corporation (NNPC) in Nigeria. For the sake of our discussion, assume that BP does all of its business in Britain and NNPC does all of its business in Nigeria—in other words, neither of them is an MNE. BP and NNPC negotiate a contract specifying that NNPC will export a certain amount of crude oil from Nigeria to BP's oil refinery facilities in Britain for a certain amount of money. Shown in Exhibit 6.5, this is both an export contract (from NNPC's perspective) and an import contract (from BP's standpoint) between two firms. In other words, it is an international market transaction.

An international market transaction between an importer and an exporter like BP and NNPC may suffer from high transaction costs. What is especially costly is the potential opportunism on both sides. For example, NNPC may demand a higher than agreed upon price, citing a variety of reasons such as inflation, natural disasters, or simply rising oil prices after the deal is signed. BP then has to either pay more than the agreed-upon price or refuse to pay and suffer from the huge costs of keeping expensive refinery facilities idle. In other words, NNPC's opportunistic behavior can cause a lot of losses for BP.

Opportunistic behavior can go both ways in a market transaction. In this particular example, BP can also be

EXHIBIT 6.5 AN INTERNATIONAL MARKET TRANSACTION

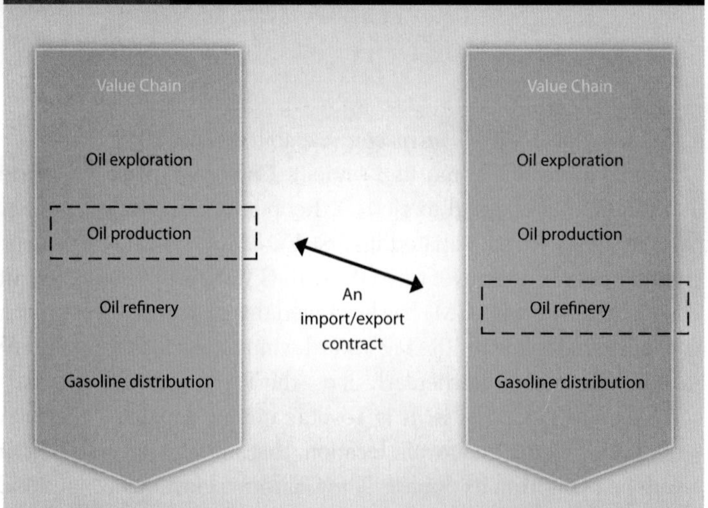

opportunistic. It may refuse to accept a shipment after its arrival from Nigeria citing unsatisfactory quality, but the real reason may be BP's inability to sell refined oil downstream because gasoline demand is going down. People in Britain are driving less due to the recession—the jobless do not need to commute to work that much. NNPC is thus forced to find a new buyer for a huge tanker load of crude oil on a last-minute, "fire sale" basis with a deep discount, losing a lot of money.

Overall, once one side in a market (export/import) transaction behaves opportunistically, the other side will not be happy and will threaten or initiate law suits. Because the legal and regulatory frameworks governing such international transactions are generally not as effective as those governing domestic transactions, the injured party will generally be frustrated while the opportunistic party can often get away with it. All of these are examples of transaction costs that increase international market inefficiencies and imperfections, ultimately resulting in market failure.

In response, FDI combats such market failure through internalization, which involves replacing the external market with in-house links. The MNE reduces cross-border transaction costs and increases efficiencies by replacing an external market relationship with a single organization spanning both countries.[9] In our example, there are two possibilities for internalization: BP could undertake *upstream* vertical FDI by owning oil production assets in Nigeria, or NNPC could undertake *downstream* vertical FDI by owning oil refinery assets in Great Britain (see Exhibit 6.6). FDI essentially transforms the international trade between two independent firms in two countries to **intrafirm trade** between two subsidiaries in two countries controlled by the same MNE. By coordinating cross-border activities better, the MNE can thus achieve internalization advantages relative to non-MNEs.

Overall, the motivations for FDI are complex. Based on resource-based and institution-based views, we can see FDI as a reflection of both a firm's motivation to extend its firm-specific capabilities abroad and its responses to overcome market imperfections and failures.

EXHIBIT 6.6 COMBATING MARKET FAILURE THROUGH FDI: ONE COMPANY (MNE) IN TWO COUNTRIES

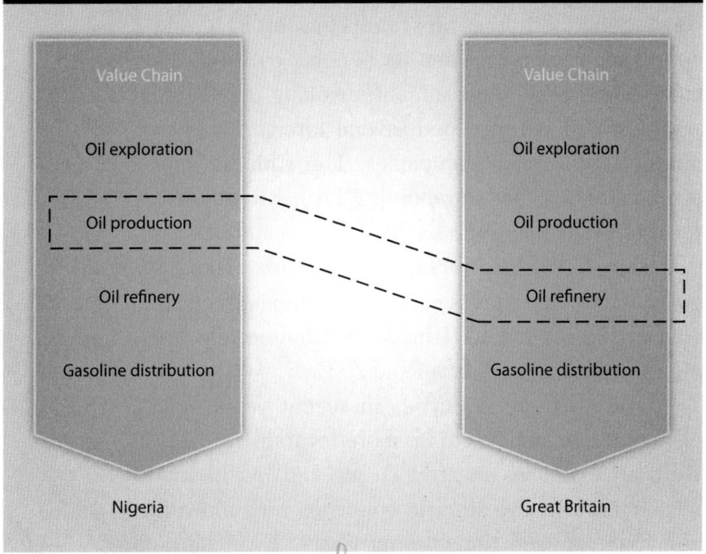

6-6 REALITIES OF FDI

The realities of FDI are intertwined with politics. This section starts with three political views on FDI and follows with a discussion of pros and cons of FDI for home and host countries.

Venzuela

6-6a Political Views on FDI

There are three primary political views on FDI. First, the **radical view on FDI** is hostile to FDI. Tracing its roots to Marxism, the radical view treats FDI as an instrument of imperialism and a vehicle for exploiting domestic resources, industries, and people by foreign capitalists and firms. Governments embracing the radical view often nationalize MNE assets or simply ban (or discourage) inbound MNEs. Between the 1950s and the early 1980s, the radical view was influential throughout Africa, Asia, Eastern Europe, and Latin America.

On the other hand, the **free market view on FDI** suggests that FDI, unrestricted by government intervention, will enable countries to tap into their absolute or comparative advantages by specializing in the production of certain goods and services. Similar to the win-win logic for international trade as articulated by Adam Smith and David Ricardo (see Chapter 5), free market–based FDI should lead to a win-win situation for both home and host countries. Since the 1980s, a series of countries such as Brazil, China, Hungary, India, Ireland, and Russia have adopted more FDI-friendly policies.

Intrafirm trade International trade between two subsidiaries in two countries controlled by the same MNE.

Radical view on FDI A political view that sees FDI as an instrument of imperialism and a vehicle for foreign exploitation.

Free market view on FDI A political view that holds that FDI, unrestricted by government intervention, will enable countries to tap into their absolute or comparative advantages by specializing in the production of certain goods and services.

However, a totally free market view does not really exist in practice. Most countries embrace the **pragmatic nationalism view on FDI**, considering both the pros and cons of FDI and approving FDI only when its benefits outweigh its costs. The French government, invoking "economic patriotism," has torpedoed several foreign takeover attempts of French companies. The Chinese government insists that automobile FDI has to take the form of JVs with MNEs so that Chinese automakers can learn from their foreign counterparts. The US government has expressed alleged "national security concerns" over the FDI made by Chinese telecom equipment makers Huawei and ZTE.

Overall, more countries in recent years have changed their policies to be more favorable to FDI. Restrictive policies toward FDI succeed only in driving out foreign investors to countries with more favorable policies (see the Closing Case). Even hard-core countries such as Cuba and North Korea that had a radical view on FDI are now experimenting with some FDI. However, there is some creeping increase of restrictions in the form of policies discouraging inbound FDI in some countries. For example, France and Russia have recently issued decrees reinforcing control for FDI in the interest of public security or national defense.

6-6b Benefits and Costs of FDI to Host Countries

Underpinning pragmatic nationalism is the need to assess the various benefits and costs of FDI to host (recipient) countries and home (source) countries. In a nutshell, Exhibit 6.7 outlines these considerations. This section focuses on *host* countries, and the next section deals with *home* countries.

EXHIBIT 6.7 EFFECTS OF FDI ON HOME AND HOST COUNTRIES

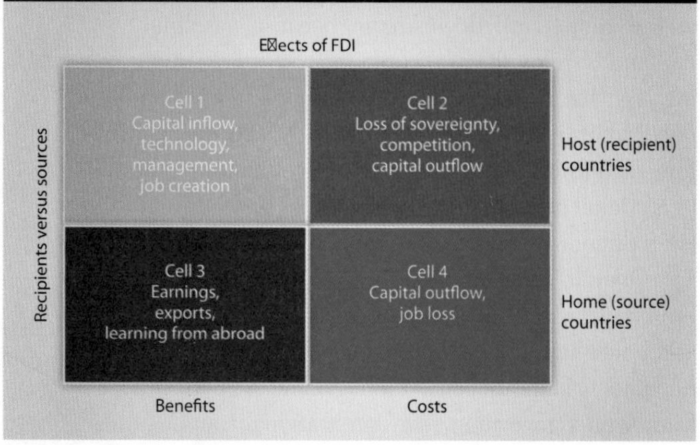

Cell 1 in Exhibit 6.7 shows four primary benefits to host countries. First, *capital inflow* can help improve a host country's balance of payments. The balance of payments measures a country's payments to and receipts from other countries. Chinese firms undertake FDI by acquiring US-based assets. By bringing more capital into the United States, such FDI helps improve the US balance of payments. (See Chapter 7 for more details.)

Second, *technology*, especially more advanced technology from abroad, can create **technology spillovers** that benefit domestic firms and industries. Technology spillover is the domestic diffusion of foreign technical knowledge and processes.[10] After observing such technology, local rivals may recognize its feasibility and strive to imitate it. This is known as the **demonstration effect**, sometimes also called the **contagion** (or **imitation**) **effect**. It underscores the important role that MNEs play in stimulating competition in host countries.

Third, *advanced management know-how* may be highly valued. In many developing countries, it is often difficult for the development of management know-how to reach a world-class level in the absence of FDI.

Finally, FDI creates a total of 80 million jobs, which represent approximately 4% of the global workforce.[11] FDI creates jobs both directly and indirectly. Direct benefits arise when MNEs employ individuals locally. In Ireland, more than 50% of manufacturing employees work for MNEs.[12] In the UK, the largest private sector employer is an MNE: India's Tata has over 50,000 employees in the UK working for a variety of businesses such as Jaguar, Land Rover, Tata Steel (formerly Corus), Tata Tea (formerly Tetley), and Tata Consultancy Services (see the Opening Case). Indirect benefits include jobs created when local suppliers increase hiring and when MNE employees spend money locally, which also results in more jobs.

Cell 2 in Exhibit 6.7 outlines three primary costs of FDI to host countries: loss of sovereignty, adverse effects on competition, and capital outflow. The first concern is the loss of some (but not all) economic sovereignty associated with FDI. Because of FDI, decisions to produce and market products and services in a host country are being made by foreigners. Even if locals

Pragmatic nationalism view on FDI A political view that approves FDI only when its benefits outweigh its costs.

Technology spillover The domestic diffusion of foreign technical knowledge and processes.

Demonstration effect (contagion or imitation effect) The effect that occurs when local rivals recognize the feasibility of foreign technology and imitate it.

serve as heads of MNE subsidiaries, they represent the interest of foreign firms. Will foreigners and foreign firms make decisions that are in the best interest of host countries (see the Opening Case)? This is truly a million dollar question. According to the radical view, the answer is "No!" because foreigners and foreign firms are likely to maximize their own profits by exploiting people and resources in host countries. Such deep suspicion of MNEs leads to policies that discourage or even ban FDI. On the other hand, countries embracing free market and pragmatic nationalism views agree that despite some acknowledged differences between foreign and host country interests, the interests of MNEs and host countries overlap sufficiently. Host countries are thus willing to live with some loss of sovereignty.

A second concern is associated with the negative effects on local competition. While we have just discussed the positive effects of MNEs on local competition, it is possible that MNEs may drive some domestic firms out of business. Having driven domestic firms out of business, in theory, MNEs may be able to monopolize local markets. While this is a relatively minor concern in developed economies, it is a legitimate concern for less developed economies where MNEs are generally so much larger and financially stronger when compared with local firms. For example, as Coca-Cola and PepsiCo extended their "cola wars" from the United States to countries around the world, they have almost "accidentally" wiped out much of the world's indigenous beverages companies, which are—or were—much smaller.

A third concern is associated with capital outflow. When MNEs make profits in host countries and repatriate (send back) such earnings to headquarters in home countries, host countries experience a net outflow in the capital account in their balance of payments. As a result, some countries have restricted the ability of MNEs to repatriate funds.

6-6c Benefits and Costs of FDI to Home Countries

As exporters of capital, technology, management, and, in some cases, jobs, home (source) countries often reap benefits and endure costs associated with FDI that are *opposite* to those experienced by host countries. Cell 3 of Exhibit 6.7 shows three benefits to home countries:

- Repatriated earnings from profits from FDI.
- Increased exports of components and services to host countries.
- Learning via FDI from operations abroad.

Cell 4 in Exhibit 6.7 shows that the costs of FDI to home countries primarily center on capital outflow and job loss. First, since host countries enjoy capital inflow because of FDI, home countries naturally suffer from some capital outflow. Less confident home country governments often impose capital controls to prevent or reduce FDI from flowing abroad.

The second concern is now more prominent: job loss. Many MNEs simultaneously invest abroad by adding employment overseas and curtail domestic production by laying off employees. It is not surprising that restrictions on FDI outflows have been increasingly vocal, called for by politicians, union members, journalists, and activists in many developed economies.

In some parts of the developing world, tension over foreign ownership can turn into political action. Given the recent worldwide trend toward more FDI-friendly policies, many people thought optimistically that nationalization and expropriation against MNE assets were a thing of the past. During 2006, however, the optimists had a rude awakening. In 2006, Venezuelan president Hugo Chavez ordered Chevron, ENI, Royal Dutch Shell, Total, and other oil and gas MNEs to convert their operations in the country into forced JVs with the state-owned Venezuelan firm PDVSA, and PDVSA would hold at least 60% of the equity. When France's Total and Italy's ENI rejected the terms, the Venezuelan government promptly seized their fields. Also in 2006, Bolivia seized control of the MNEs' oil fields. Soon after, Ecuador expropriated the oil fields run by America's Occidental Petroleum. More recently, in 2012 Argentina nationalized YPF, which was owned by Spain's Repsol (see the Closing Case).

It is important to note that the anti-MNE actions in Latin America were not sudden impulsive policy changes. The politicians leading these actions were all democratically elected. These actions were the result of lengthy political debates concerning FDI in the region, and such takeovers were mostly popular among the public. Until the 1970s, the treatment and dealings with MNEs

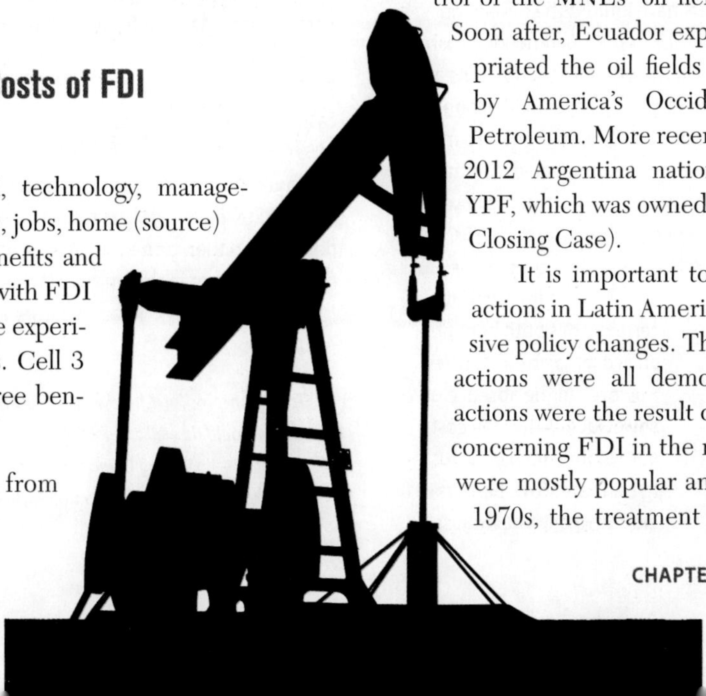

ISTOCKPHOTO.COM/GRAFISSIMO

among Latin American governments was largely harsh and confrontational. Only in the 1990s when these countries became democratic did they open their oil industry to inbound FDI. So the 180-degree policy reversal is both surprising (considering how recently these governments welcomed MNEs) and not surprising (considering historical dealings with MNEs in the region). Some argue that the recent actions represent the swing of a pendulum (see Chapter 1 on the pendulum of globalization).

Debate: Ethical Dilemma/Emerging Markets

Welcoming Versus Restricting Sovereign Wealth Fund Investments

A **sovereign wealth fund (SWF)** is a state-owned investment fund composed of financial assets such as stocks, bonds, real estate, or other financial instruments funded by foreign exchange assets. Although the term "SWF" was only coined in 2005 by Andrew Rozanov, a senior manager at State Street Global Advisors, outside the United States investment funds that we now call SWFs were first created in 1953 by Kuwait. Both the United States and Canada have had their own SWFs—at least at the state and provincial level, such as the Alaska Permanent Fund and Alberta Heritage Fund. In the United States, the Texas Permanent School Fund was established in 1854.

WITHGOD/SHUTTERSTOCK.COM

In the recent global financial crisis, SWFs came to the rescue. For example, in 2007, the Abu Dhabi Investment Authority injected $7.5 billion (4.9% of equity) into Citigroup. In 2008, China Investment Corporation (CIC) invested $5 billion for a 10% equity stake in Morgan Stanley.

Such large-scale investments have ignited the debate on SWFs. On the one hand, SWFs have brought much-needed cash to rescue desperate Western firms. On the other hand, concerns are raised by host countries, which are typically developed economies. One primary concern is national security in that SWFs may be politically (as opposed to commercially) motivated. Another concern is SWFs' inadequate transparency. Governments in several developed economies, in fear of the "threats" from SWFs, have been erecting anti-SWF measures to defend their companies.

Foreign investment certainly has both benefits and costs to host countries. However, in the absence of any evidence that the costs outweigh benefits, the rush to erect anti-SWF barriers is indicative of protectionist (or, some may argue, even racist) sentiments. For executives at hard-pressed Western firms, it would not seem sensible to ask for government bailouts on the one hand, and to reject cash from SWFs on the other hand. Most SWF investment is essentially free cash with few strings attached. For example, CIC, which now holds 10% of Morgan Stanley equity, did not demand a board seat or a management role. For Western policy makers, it makes little sense to spend taxpayers' dollars to bail out failed firms, run huge budget deficits, and then turn away SWFs. Commenting on inbound Chinese investment in the United States (including SWF investment), then Secretary of the Treasury Henry Paulson argued in *Foreign Affairs*:

> *These concerns [on Chinese investment] are misplaced . . . the United States would do well to encourage such investment from anywhere in the world—including China—because it represents a vote of confidence in the US economy and it promotes growth, jobs, and productivity in the United States.*

Sovereign wealth fund A state-owned investment fund composed of financial assets such as stocks, bonds, real estate, or other financial instruments funded by foreign exchange assets.

Lastly, thanks to the financial crisis in 2008–2009, recent SWF investment in developed economies suffered major losses. Such a "double whammy"—both the political backlash and the economic losses—has severely discouraged SWFs. Some SWFs, especially those from the Gulf, are increasingly investing in their domestic public services (health care, education, and infrastructure). As a result, the competition for funds puts a premium on maintaining a welcoming climate. As part of the efforts to foster such a welcoming climate in times of great political and economic anxiety, the US-China Strategic and Economic Dialogue (S&ED) in July 2009 confirmed:

> *The United States confirms that the Committee on Foreign Investment in the United States (CFIUS) process ensures the consistent and fair treatment of all foreign investment without prejudice to the place of origin. The United States welcomes sovereign wealth fund investment, including that from China.*

In September 2008, major SWFs of the world at a summit in Santiago, Chile, agreed to a voluntary code of conduct known as the Santiago Principles. These principles are designed to alleviate some of the concerns for host countries of SWF investment and to enhance the transparency of such investment. These principles represent an important milestone of SWFs' evolution. Since then SWF assets have grown faster than the assets of any other institutional investor group, including private equity and hedge funds. Today more than 70 major SWFs manage approximately $6.4 trillion in assets. In the EU, between 15% and 25% of listed firms have SWF shareholders. Norway's Government Pension Fund Global, the world's largest SWF, owns an average of 2.5% of every European listed firm and 1% of all the equities in the world.

Sources: D. Drezner, "Sovereign wealth funds and the (in)security of global finance," *Journal of International Affairs* 62 (2008): 115–130; "More money than Thor," *Economist*, 14 September 2013, 73; V. Fotak and W. Megginson, "Are SWFs welcome now?" *Columbia FDI Perspectives*, No. 9, 21 July 2009, www.vcc.columbia.edu; H. Paulson, "The right way to engage China," *Foreign Affairs*, September/October 2008, www.foreignaffairs.org; A. Rozanov, "Who holds the wealth of nations?" *Central Banking Journal*, May 2005; Sovereign Wealth Fund Institute, "About sovereign wealth fund," 2014, www.swfinstitute.org; United Nations, *World Investment Report 2014* (New York and Geneva: UN) 19–20; US Department of the Treasury, *The First US-China Strategic and Economic Dialogue Economic Track Joint Fact Sheet*, 28 July 2009, Washington.

6-7 MANAGEMENT SAVVY

The big question in global business, adapted to the context of FDI, is: What determines the success and failure of FDI around the globe? The answer boils down to two components. First, from a resource-based view, some firms are good at FDI because they leverage ownership, location, and internalization advantages in a way that is valuable, unique, and hard to imitate by rival firms. Second, from an institution-based view, the political realities either enable or constrain FDI from reaching its full economic potential. Therefore, the success and failure of FDI also significantly depend on institutions governing FDI as "rules of the game."

Shown in Exhibit 6.8, three implications for action emerge. First, you should carefully assess whether FDI is justified in light of other possibilities such as outsourcing and licensing. This exercise needs to be conducted on an activity-by-activity basis as part of the value chain analysis (see Chapter 4). If ownership and internalization advantages are not deemed critical, then FDI is not recommended.

Second, once a decision to undertake FDI is made, you should pay attention to the old adage, "location, location, location!" The quest for location advantages has to fit with the firm's strategic goals. For example, if a firm is searching for innovation hot spots, then low-cost locations that do not generate sufficient innovations will not be attractive (see Chapters 10 and 12). High-cost locations such as Denmark would be ideal for wind turbine makers in search of cutting-edge innovations (see In Focus).

EXHIBIT 6.8 IMPLICATIONS FOR ACTION

- Carefully assess whether FDI is justified in light of other foreign entry modes such as outsourcing and licensing.
- Pay careful attention to the location advantages in combination with the firm's strategic goals.
- Be aware of the institutional constraints and enablers governing FDI, and enhance legitimacy in host countries.

Finally, given the political realities around the world, be aware of the institutional constraints. Savvy MNE managers should not take FDI-friendly policies for granted. Setbacks are likely. The global economic slowdown has made many developed economies less attractive to invest, and the credit crunch means that firms are less able to invest abroad. Attitudes toward certain forms of FDI (such as sovereign wealth funds discussed in the Debate feature) are changing, which may lead to FDI policies to become more protectionist. In the long run, the interests of MNEs in host countries can be best safeguarded if MNEs accommodate, rather than neglect or dominate, the interests of host countries (see the Closing Case). In practical terms, contributions to local employment, job training, education, and pollution control will tangibly demonstrate MNEs' commitment to host countries.[13]

ETHICAL DILEMMA/EMERGING MARKETS
Cry for Me, Argentina

Argentina's relationship with foreign investors in its energy industry has historically been rocky. The government in 1955 canceled international oil contracts signed by a previous president, Perón, in 1952. The next president signed new contracts in 1958, which were nullified in 1963 by a different president. Foreign oil companies were then invited to return in 1966, expelled in 1973, and again encouraged to enter after 1976. Not surprisingly, many foreign investors shied away from this country.

Since the 1990s, the pro-market reform policies centered on trade liberalization, deregulation, and privatization brought more stability. More foreign investors showed up. In 1993, YPF, the formerly state-owned oil giant, was privatized. In 1999, Spain's Repsol bought 57% of the shares of YPF and became its controlling shareholder. Although Argentina suffered from the government's default on its $155 billion public debt (a world record at that time) in 2002 and the country struggled to recover since then, Repsol's operations had been relatively smooth—until recently.

In 2012, Argentina again was engulfed in a major crisis. Given the severe trade deficit, the government, under President Cristina Fernández de Kirchner, unleashed a series of radical measures to curb imports. Importers of foreign cars were required to find export buyers of Argentine wines; otherwise, port authorities would not release their cars. Foreign print publications, including magazines and newspapers, were held at the Buenos Aires airport unless subscribers went there to pay a highly unpopular additional tax—an import tariff.

In addition to making the life of Argentine firms and citizens harder, Fernández also targeted foreign direct investors. Specifically, Repsol was singled out as a high-profile target for nationalization (or expropriation). Repsol's alleged wrongdoing was that it failed to boost oil and natural gas production needed to keep up with rising local demand. In 2003, when Néstor Kirchner, Fernández's late husband and predecessor, took office, Argentina was a net energy exporter. Ten years later, Argentina imported 15% more than its energy production, resulting in more than $10 billion of cash outflows. The government argued that the largest producer, YPF, which contributed 45% of the country's energy production, was responsible for this mess. In Fernández's own words in her announcement:

> *If YPF's policy continues—draining fields dry, no exploration, and practically no investment—the country will end up having no viable future, not because of a lack of resources but because of business policies. . . . Our goal is for YPF to be aligned with the interests of the country. When corporate interests are not aligned with national interests, when companies are concerned only with profits, that's when economies fail, which is what happened globally in 2008 and what happened to Argentina in 2002.*

ROB WILSON / SHUTTERSTOCK.COM

In the words of a Congressional leader, who participated in the debate on the YPF renationalization bill submitted by the president:

> *All oil companies that operate in Argentina, Repsol and the rest, have to work in the public interest, which in this case means energy self sufficiency for Argentina. . . . Repsol invested little in Argentina. But it was YPF and Argentine oil that financed Repsol's growth around the world.*

Fernández framed the YPF renationalization as central to fulfill her campaign pledges to tighten the interventionist policies in order to rescue the economy. YPF was an iconic symbol of national pride, and the cash-strapped government would love to have its revenues, estimated at $1.3 billion a year. Fernández's measures were popular with ordinary Argentines. Many of them blamed free market reforms such as privatization of the 1990s to be a cause of the economic devastation of the 2000s. Not surprisingly, the YPF renationalization bill passed Congress by a landslide. In May 2012, Fernández signed the measure into law and formally (re)nationalized—for the time being *without compensation*—Repsol's assets, which according to Repsol would be valued at more than $9.3 billion.

Outraged, both Repsol and the Spanish government protested, but there was little they could do. Argentina had little FDI in Spain, while Spanish FDI in Argentina's highly regulated banking, telecommunications, and utilities industries could suffer if tensions were to escalate between the two countries. In retaliation, Spain quickly moved to limit imports of biofuels from Argentina, which annually exported $1 billion to Spain. Spain also threatened to initiate complaints to the World Trade Organization, called for EU-wide boycotts of Argentine products, and took the case to the World Bank's International Center for Settlement of Investment Disputes (ICSID). In response, Fernández said:

This president is not going to respond to any threats . . . because I represent the Argentine people. I'm the head of the state, not a thug.

Argentina might indeed be defiant, because it already had a very bad record at ICSID, whereby one-quarter of all ICSID cases had been brought against Argentina (thanks to its 2002 default). While renationalizing YPF brought more revenues and helped the president gain more popularity, according to the *Economist*, "it is a disaster for Argentina." Although in 2014 Argentina eventually agreed to pay Repsol $5 billion in bond that will mature between 2017 and 2033 (this was hardly generous as Repsol demanded $10 billion in cash), in the long run such expropriation has grave ramifications far beyond the oil industry and beyond foreign investors from Spain (Argentina's largest foreign investor). In fairness, Fernández also nationalized the country's private pension funds and (re)nationalized the flagship airline, Aerolineas Argentinas. So, she did not just target foreign investors such as Repsol. Nevertheless, foreign investors entertaining large-scale entries in the rapidly growing Latin American region are likely to be lured more strongly by Brazil, Chile, and Mexico, as opposed to risking their capital in a country known to be a global rule-breaker.

Case Discussion Questions

1. What are the costs and benefits of FDI inflows for a host country such as Argentina?
2. Will foreign firms such as Repsol make decisions in the best interest of Argentina?
3. ***ON ETHICS***: As a Spanish manager at YPF, how would you cooperate with the Argentine government to expropriate YPF? If you were an Argentine manager at YPF, would your action be different?
4. ***ON ETHICS***: If you were a member of Argentina's Congress, would you vote to support Fernández's renationalization bill for YPF? Defend your vote.
5. ***ON ETHICS***: If you were a member of the arbitration panel assembled by ICSID (which would require you to come from a neutral country—neither from Argentina nor Spain), how much compensation would you think Argentina's government should pay Repsol?

Sources: "Argentina goes rogue again," *Bloomberg Businessweek*, 23 April 2012, 16–17; "Cristina scrapes the barrel," *Economist*, 21 April 2012, 16; "Fill 'er up," *Economist*, 21 April 2012, 49–50; "Swallowed pride," *Economist*, 30 November 2013, 36; M. Guillen, *The Limits of Convergence* (Princeton, NJ: Princeton University Press, 2001) 135; Repsol, "Argentina and Repsol reach a compensation agreement over the expropriation of YPF," press release, 25 February 2014, www.repsol.com; Reuters, 2012, "Argentina moves to seize control of Repsol's YPF," 17 April 2012, www.reuters.com; Reuters, "Argentina nationalizes oil company YPF," 4 May 2012, www.reuters.com; Reuters, "Spain has few ways to pressure Argentina over YPF," 18 April 2012, www.reuters.com; United Nations, *World Investment Report* 2014 (New York and Geneva: UN, 2014) 102.

STUDY TOOLS 6

LOCATED AT THE BACK OF YOUR BOOK:

- ☐ Rip out and study the Chapter Review Card at the end of the book

LOG IN TO WWW.CENGAGEBRAIN.COM TO:

- ☐ Review key term flashcards
- ☐ Complete a practice quiz to test your knowledge of key concepts
- ☐ Take and complete the chapter crossword puzzle
- ☐ Complete interactive content, watch chapter videos, and take a graded quiz
- ☐ Track your knowledge of key concepts in Global Business
- ☐ Read and discuss additional case study content

7 Dealing with Foreign Exchange

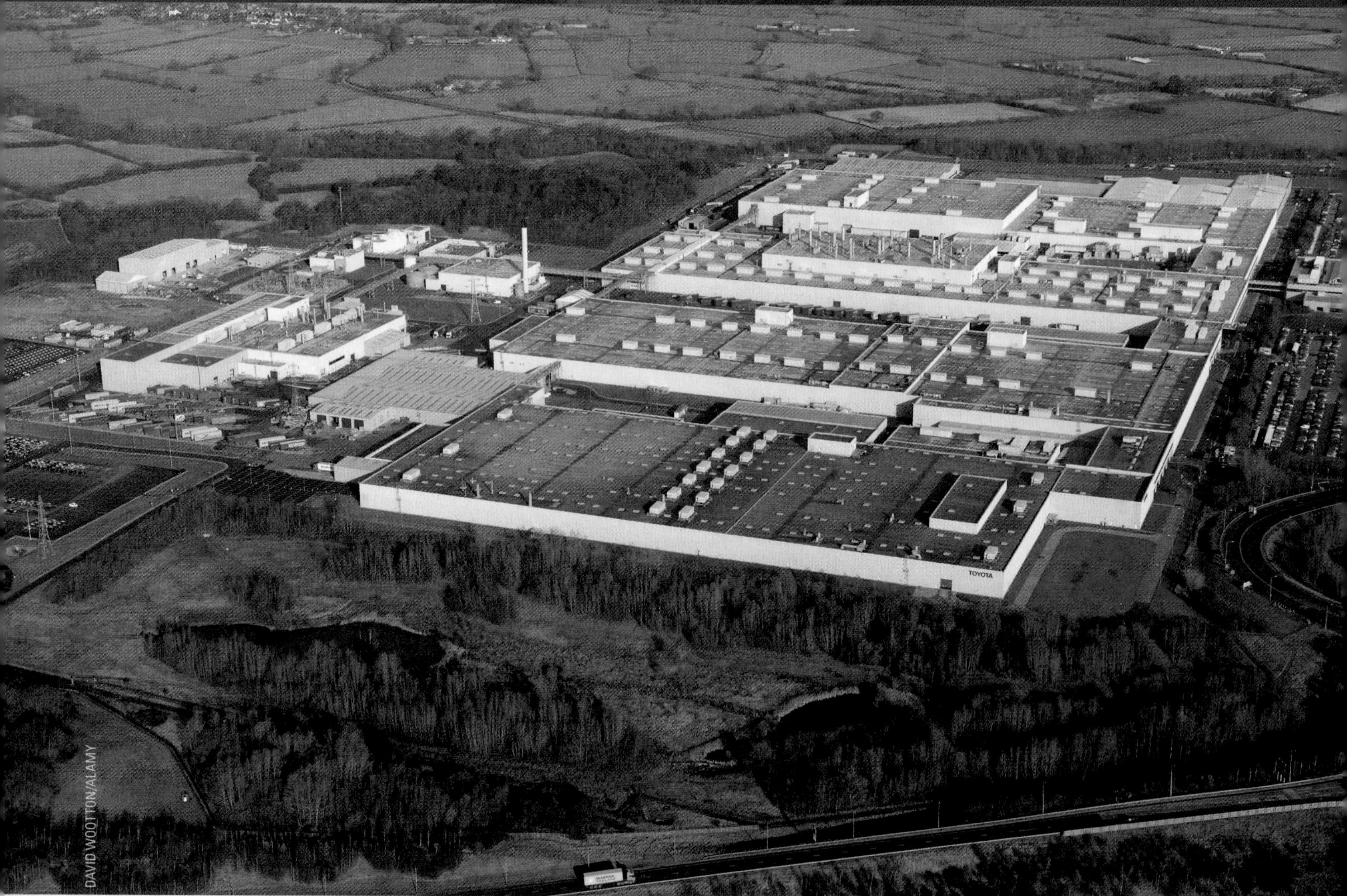
DAVID WOOTTON/ALAMY

LEARNING OBJECTIVES

After studying this chapter, you should be able to . . .

- **7-1** List the factors that determine foreign exchange rates.
- **7-2** Articulate and explain the steps in the evolution of the international monetary system.
- **7-3** Identify strategic responses firms can take to deal with foreign exchange movements.
- **7-4** Identify three things you need to know about currency when doing business internationally.

After you finish this chapter, go to **PAGE 115** for **STUDY TOOLS**

Toyota's Yen Advantage

Thanks to an obsessive emphasis on quality, Toyota Motor grew from a tiny spinoff of a Japanese loom manufacturer in the 1930s into the world's largest automaker. Chief Executive Officer Akio Toyoda has nothing more virtuous than Japan's weakening currency for a recent assist in his quest for even greater market-share dominance. The yen has fallen 16% against the dollar since October 31, 2012. That gives Toyota and other Japanese carmakers a financial gain on every car, which they can use to cut prices, boost advertising, or improve their vehicles in ways not open to US rivals.

Morgan Stanley estimates the currency boost to operating profits at about $1,500 per car, while Detroit carmakers put the figure closer to $5,700. "We're concerned about what the long-term ramifications are," says Joe Hinrichs, Ford Motor's Americas chief. Sergio Marchionne, CEO of Chrysler Group and Fiat, also frets about the impact. "We didn't need this, to put it bluntly," he told Bloomberg TV on March 5, 2013. "It's going to make life tougher."

Toyota in February 2013 raised its profit forecast by 10% for the fiscal year ending March 31, 2013, to 860 billion yen ($9 billion), a five-year high. That would more than double the previous year's profit and signal a convincing comeback from the global recalls and 2011 Japanese earthquake that shook Toyota's standing as a leader in earnings, sales, and quality.

Detroit automakers are watchful for a replay of the 1990s and 2000s, when a weak yen allowed Japanese automakers to offer American buyers cars loaded with extra features at prices US companies could not match. It took government-backed bankruptcies at General Motors (GM) and Chrysler in 2009 and a wrenching restructuring at Ford to get their costs in line with Toyota's. Those gains are being eroded by the currency shift, says Morgan Stanley auto analyst Adam Jonas. "This is, without a doubt, the biggest change affecting the global auto industry," Jonas says. "The dollar versus the weak yen will make the Japanese automakers richer, and they can use those profits to target more aggressive growth. Ford and GM are in their bull's-eye. This is a real threat."

Toyota enjoys a special edge because it exports more than two million vehicles from Japan annually, according to a recent analysis by Deutsche Bank. About 27% of the models Toyota sells in the United States are imported, compared with 10% of those sold by Honda Motor, Deutsche Bank says. "We see Toyota as having the most to gain from a weaker yen with improved profits on exports," write Deutsche Bank analysts Jochen Gehrke and Kurt Sanger. They see Toyota's net profit margin topping 6% next year, up from 1.5% in the year ended March 31, 2012.

Just as Toyota was cautious of not trumpeting its toppling of GM from the global No. 1 automaker title in 2012—a sensitive issue in the United States—it has been similarly restrained about any benefits from the weak yen. Toyota spokesman Steve Curtis says the automaker is working to build more models in North America, which would reduce the impact of currency swings. "We do our best to reduce currency fluctuations by localizing production," Curtis says. "Whether it's a greenfield plant that came online a year and a half ago in Mississippi or the expansion of our component plants or the expansion of capacity for Highlander [built in Princeton, Indiana], across the operations in North America, that's the way we've approached this."

Yet even Toyota's North American production benefits from a weak yen, according to Deutsche Bank. Citing data from the National Highway Traffic Safety Administration, Deutsche Bank says 15%–35% of the parts in Toyota's North American–built models actually come from Japan, providing another advantage US makers do not have.

Morgan Stanley's Jonas says Toyota typically does not discount as deeply as Detroit automakers, so rather than waging a price war, Toyota may use its yen-effect benefits elsewhere. The carmaker is replacing 60% of its lineup by 2014 and now can afford to appoint those models with more lavish interiors and high-tech features that would be costly for US carmakers to match, Jonas says. The result: "We could see the Japanese gaining a couple points of [market] share in the US," he says.

Source: "Toyota's awesome yen advantage," *Bloomberg Businessweek*, 25 March 2013, 21–22. © Bloomberg L.P.

Why is the value of currencies so important in the global automobile industry? What determines foreign exchange rates? How do foreign exchange rates affect trade and investment undertaken by firms such as Toyota as well as Chrysler, Fiat, Ford, GM, and Honda? Finally, how can firms respond strategically? This chapter addresses these crucial questions. At the heart of our discussion lie the two core perspectives introduced earlier: the institution-based and resource-based views. Essentially, the institution-based view suggests that domestic and international institutions (such as the International Monetary Fund [IMF]) influence foreign exchange rates and affect capital movements. In turn, the resource-based view sheds light on how firms can profit from favorable foreign exchange movements by developing their own firm-specific resources and capabilities.

We start with a basic question: What determines foreign exchange rates? Then, we track the evolution of the international monetary system culminating in the IMF, and continue with firms' strategic responses.

7-1 WHAT DETERMINES FOREIGN EXCHANGE RATES?

A **foreign exchange rate** is the price of one currency, such as the dollar ($), in terms of another, such as the euro (€). Exhibit 7.1 provides some examples. An **appreciation** is an increase in the value of the currency, and a **depreciation** is a loss in the value of the currency. This section addresses a key question: What determines foreign exchange rates?

7-1a Basic Supply and Demand

The concept of an exchange rate as the price of a commodity—in this case, a country's currency—helps us understand its determinants. Basic economic theory suggests that a commodity's price is fundamentally determined by its supply and demand. Strong demand will lead to price hikes, and oversupply will result in price drops. Of course, here we are dealing with a most unusual commodity—money—but the basic principles still apply. When the United States sells products to China, US exporters often demand that they be paid in US dollars because the Chinese yuan is useless (or, using the technical term, nonconvertible) in the United States. Chinese importers of US products must somehow generate US dollars in order to pay for US imports. The easiest way to generate US dollars is to *export* to the United States, whose buyers pay in US dollars. In this example, the dollar is the common transaction currency involving both US imports and US exports. As a result, the demand for dollars is much stronger than the demand for yuan (while holding the supply constant). A wide variety of users, such as Chinese exporters, Colombian drug dealers, and Swiss bankers, prefer to hold and transact in US dollars, thus fueling the demand for dollars. Such a strong demand explains why the US dollar is the most sought after currency in the postwar decades. At present, about 60% of the world's foreign exchange holdings are in US dollars, followed by 25% in euros, 4% in yens, and 3% in pounds.

Foreign exchange rate The price of one currency in terms of another.

Appreciation An increase in the value of the currency.

Depreciation A loss in the value of the currency.

The next question is: What determines the supply and demand of foreign exchange? Because foreign exchange involves such a unique commodity, its markets are influenced by not only economic but also political and psychological factors. Exhibit 7.2 sketches the five underlying building blocks, which are discussed next.

7-1b Relative Price Differences and Purchasing Power Parity

Some countries (such as Switzerland—see the Closing Case) have famously expensive prices, and others (such as the Philippines) are known to have cheap prices. How do these price differences affect exchange rates? An answer is provided by the theory of purchasing

EXHIBIT 7.1 EXAMPLES OF KEY CURRENCY EXCHANGE RATES

	US dollar (US$)	Euro (€)	UK pound (£)	Swiss franc (SFr)	Mexican peso (Mex$)	Japanese yen (¥)	Canadian dollar (C$)
Canadian dollar (C$)	1.10	1.41	1.79	1.16	0.08	0.010	—
Japanese yen (¥)	109.05	139.90	177.61	115.89	8.25	—	99.49
Mexican peso (Mex$)	13.21	16.95	21.52	14.04	—	0.121	12.05
Swiss franc (SFr)	0.94	1.21	1.53	—	0.07	0.009	0.859
UK pound (£)	0.61	0.79	—	0.65	0.05	0.006	0.56
Euro (€)	0.78	—	1.27	0.83	0.06	0.007	0.71
US dollar (US$)	—	1.28	1.63	1.06	0.08	0.009	0.91

Source: Adapted from "Key currency cross rates," *Wall Street Journal*, 19 September 2014 (online.wsj.com). Reading *vertically*, the first column means US$1 ⊠ C$1.10 ⊠ ¥109.05 ⊠ Mex$13.21 ⊠ SFr0.94 ⊠ £0.61 ⊠ €0.78. Reading *horizontally*, the last row means €1 ⊠ US$1.28; £1 ⊠ US$1.63; SFr1 ⊠ US$1.06; Mex$1 ⊠ US$0.08; ¥1 ⊠ US$0.009; C$1 ⊠ US$0.91. The official code for Mexican peso is MXN. The official code for Swiss franc is CHF.

EXHIBIT 7.2 WHAT DETERMINES FOREIGN EXCHANGE RATES?

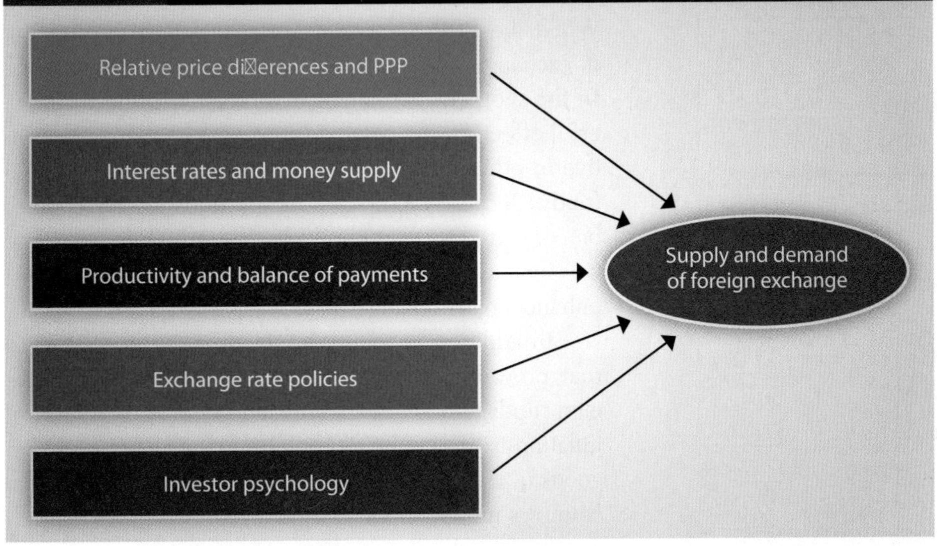

power parity (PPP). Recall from Chapter 1 that PPP is a conversion that determines the equivalent amount of goods and services different currencies can purchase. This conversion is usually used to capture the differences in cost of living between countries. PPP is essentially the "law of one price." The theory suggests that in the absence of trade barriers (such as tariffs), the price for identical products sold in different countries must be the same. Otherwise, traders may buy low and sell high, eventually driving different prices for identical products to the same level around the world. The PPP theory argues that in the long run, exchange rates should move toward levels that would equalize the prices of an identical basket of goods in any two countries.

One of the most influential (and the most fun-filled) applications of the PPP theory is the Big Mac index, popularized by the *Economist* magazine. The *Economist* compares the cost of a McDonald's Big Mac hamburger in about 120 countries. According to the PPP theory, a Big Mac should cost the same anywhere around the world. In reality, it does not. Exhibit 7.3 shows that in 2014, a Big Mac cost \$4.8 in the United States and 16.76 yuan in China, which was \$2.73 according to the nominal exchange rate of 6.14 yuan to the dollar. If the Big Mac indeed cost the same, the de facto exchange rate based on the Big Mac index became 3.49 yuan to the dollar (that is, 16.76 yuan/\$4.8). According to this calculation, the yuan was 43% "undervalued" against the dollar ([6.14 – 3.49]/6.14). But the yuan, which several years ago used to be the most undervalued currency, was only the 12th most undervalued currency in the Big Mac universe. The Ukrainian hryvnia and the Indian rupee were the most undervalued currencies. In other words, the Big Mac in Ukraine and the chicken-based Maharaja Mac in India (where the beef-based Big Mac is not available) had the best "value" in the world, based on official exchange rates. They only cost \$1.63 and \$1.75, respectively.[1]

Overall, four observations emerge:

- The Big Mac index confirms that prices in some European countries are very expensive. A Big Mac in Norway was the most expensive in the world, costing \$7.76.
- Excluding the special case of Ukraine (which was engulfed in a conflict), a Big Mac in South Africa and Indonesia and a Maharaja Mac in India are cheap in dollar terms. This makes sense because a Big Mac is a product with both traded and non-traded inputs. To simplify our discussion, let us assume that the costs for traded inputs (such as flour for the bun) are the same, it is obvious that

ERIKO SUGITA/REUTERS/LANDOV

EXHIBIT 7.3 THE BIG MAC INDEX

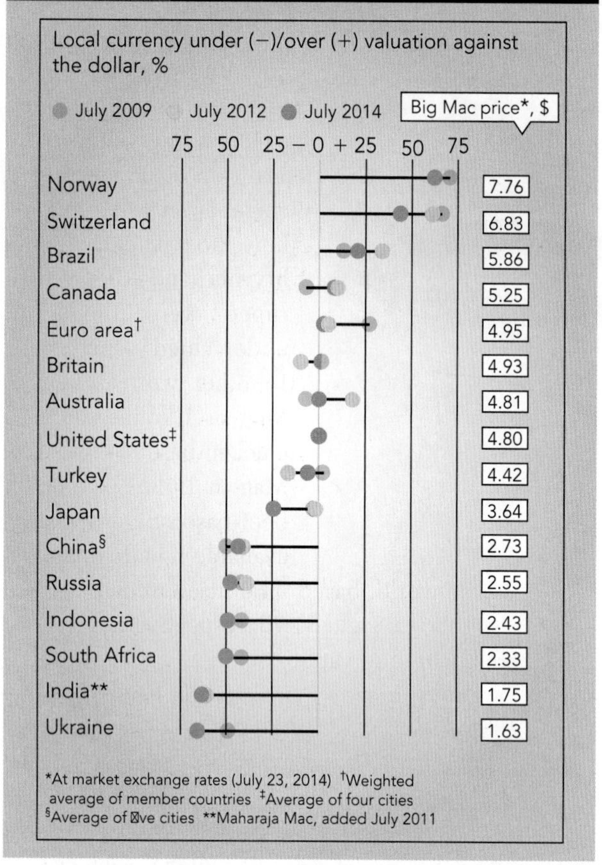

Local currency under (−)/over (+) valuation against the dollar, %

● July 2009 ● July 2012 ● July 2014 Big Mac price*, $

Norway	7.76
Switzerland	6.83
Brazil	5.86
Canada	5.25
Euro area†	4.95
Britain	4.93
Australia	4.81
United States‡	4.80
Turkey	4.42
Japan	3.64
China§	2.73
Russia	2.55
Indonesia	2.43
South Africa	2.33
India**	1.75
Ukraine	1.63

*At market exchange rates (July 23, 2014) †Weighted average of member countries ‡Average of four cities §Average of five cities **Maharaja Mac, added July 2011

nontraded inputs (such as labor and real estate) are cheaper in emerging economies.

▶ The Big Mac is not a traded product. No large number of American hamburger lovers would travel to South Africa simply to get the best deal on the Big Mac, and then somehow take with them large quantities of the made-in-South-Africa Big Mac (perhaps in portable freezers). If they did that, the Big Mac price in South Africa would be driven up and the price in the United States would be pushed down—remember supply and demand?

▶ After having a laugh, we shouldn't read too much into this index. PPP signals where exchange rates may move in the *long run*. But it does not suggest that the yuan should appreciate by 43% or the Norweigian kroner should depreciate by 62% next year. According to the *Economist*, anyone interested in the PPP theory "would be unwise to exclude the Big Mac index from their diet, but Super Size servings (of this index) would equally be a mistake."[2]

7-1c Interest Rates and Money Supply

While the PPP theory suggests the long-run direction of exchange rate movement, what about the short run? In the short run, variations in interest rates have a powerful effect. If one country's interest rates are high relative to other countries, that country will attract foreign funds. Because inflows of foreign funds usually need to be converted to the home currency, a high interest rate will increase the demand for the home currency, thus enhancing its exchange value.

In addition, a country's rate of inflation relative to that prevailing abroad affects its ability to attract foreign funds and hence its exchange rate. A high level of inflation is essentially too much money chasing too few goods in an economy. Technically, it is an expansion of a country's money supply. When a government faces budgetary shortfalls, it may choose to print more currency—known as "quantitative easing" as a recent euphemism. More currency tends to stimulate inflation. Inflation, in turn, would cause the currency to depreciate. Why does this chain of events happen? As the supply of a given currency (such as the Mexican peso) increases while the demand stays the same, the per unit value of that currency (such as one peso) goes down. Therefore, the exchange rate is highly sensitive to changes in monetary policy. It responds swiftly to changes in money supply. To avoid losses from holding assets in a depreciated currency, investors sell them for assets denominated in other currencies. Such massive sell-offs may worsen the depreciation. This happened in Britain during the 2008–2009 crisis. Reacting to the Bank of England's loose monetary policy to print more money in order to combat the recession, numerous investors sold off assets held in pound sterling, forcing it to depreciate relative to the euro.

7-1d Productivity and Balance of Payments

A rise in a country's productivity relative to other countries will improve its competitive position in international trade. This is the basic proposition of the theories of absolute and comparative advantage discussed in Chapter 5. In turn, more FDI will be attracted to the country, fueling demand for its home currency. One recent example is China. Most of the China-bound FDI inflows in dollars, euros, and pounds have to be converted to the local currency, boosting the demand for the yuan and hence its value.

Recall from Chapter 5 that changes in productivity will change a country's balance of trade. A country highly productive in manufacturing may generate

EXHIBIT 7.4 THE SIMPLIFIED US BALANCE OF PAYMENTS (BILLION DOLLARS)

I. Current Account		
1. Exports of goods (merchandise)	1,592	
2. Imports of goods (merchandise)	−2,294	
3. Balance on goods (merchandise trade—lines 1 + 2)		**−702**
4. Exports of services	682	
5. Imports of services	−456	
6. Balance on services (service trade—lines 4 + 5)		**226**
7. Balance on goods and services (trade deficit/surplus—lines 3 + 6)		**−476**
8. Income receipts on US-owned assets abroad	767	
9. Income payments on foreign-owned assets in the US	−558	
10. Government grants and private remittances	−137	
11. Balance on current account (current account deficit/surplus—lines 7 + 8 + 9 + 10)		**−405**
II. Financial Account		
12. US-owned private assets abroad (increase/financial outflow = − [negative sign])	−586	
13. Foreign-owned private assets in the US	959	
14. Balance on financial account (lines 12 + 13)		**373**
15. Overall balance of payments (Official reserve transactions balance—lines 11 + 14)		**−32**

Source: This is a simplified table adapted from US Department of Commerce, Bureau of Economic Analysis, 2014, *US International Transactions: Fourth Quarter and Year 2013*, Table 2, Washington: BEA (www.bea.gov [accessed 21 September 2014]). This table refers to 2013. The official table has 109 lines. Numbers may not add due to rounding.

a merchandise trade surplus, whereas a country less productive in manufacturing may end up with a merchandise trade deficit. These have ramifications for the **balance of payments (BOP)**, which is officially known as a country's international transaction statement and includes merchandise trade, service trade, and capital movement. Exhibit 7.4 shows that the United States had a merchandise trade deficit of $702 billion and a service trade surplus of $226 billion in 2013. In addition to merchandise and service trade, we add receipts on US assets abroad (such as repatriated earning from US multinational enterprises [MNEs] in Ireland and dividends paid by Japanese firms to American shareholders), subtract payments on US-based foreign assets (such as repatriated earnings from Canadian MNEs in the United States to Canada and dividends paid by US firms to Dutch shareholders), and government grants and private remittances (such as US foreign aid thrown at Iraq and the money that Mexican farm hands in America sent home). After doing all of the math, we can see that the United States ran a $405 billion current account deficit. Technically, the current account balance consists of exports minus imports of merchandise and services, plus income on a country's assets abroad minus payments on foreign assets in the focal country, plus unilateral government transfers and private remittances.

A current account deficit has to be financed by financial account—consisting of purchases and sales of assets. This is because a country needs to balance its accounts in much the same way as a family deals with its finances. Any deficit in a family budget has to be financed by drawing from savings or by borrowing.[3] In a similar fashion, the overall US deficit of $32 billion was financed by drawing from savings and borrowing (for example, selling US government securities such as Treasury bonds to foreign central banks such as the People's Bank of China).

To make a long story short, a country experiencing a current account surplus will see its currency appreciate. Conversely, a country experiencing a current account deficit will see its currency depreciate. This will not happen overnight, but will take place over a span of years and decades. The current movement between the yuan (appreciating) and the dollar (depreciating) is but one example. In the 1950s and 1960s, the rise of the dollar was accompanied by a sizable US surplus on merchandise trade. By the 1970s and 1980s, the surplus gradually turned into a deficit. By the 1990s and 2000s, the US current account deficit increased, forcing the dollar to depreciate relative to other currencies such as the yuan, the euro, and the Canadian dollar. Broadly speaking, the value of a country's currency is an embodiment of its economic strengths as reflected in its productivity and BOP positions.

7-1e Exchange Rate Policies

There are two major exchange rate policies: floating rate and fixed rate. The **floating** (or **flexible**) **exchange rate policy** is the willingness of a government to let demand and supply conditions determine exchange rates. Governments adopting

Balance of payments (BOP) A country's international transaction statement, which includes merchandise trade, service trade, and capital movement.

Floating (flexible) exchange rate policy A government policy to let demand and supply conditions determine exchange rates.

ISTOCKPHOTO.COM/R.R

this policy tend to believe in the free market and allow it to determine exchange rates, usually on a daily basis via the foreign exchange market. However, few countries adopt a **clean** (or **free**) **float**, which would be a pure market solution. Most countries practice a **dirty** (or **managed**) **float**, with selective government interventions. Of the major currencies, the US, Canadian, and Australian dollars, the yen, and the pound have been under managed float since the 1970s (after the collapse of the Bretton Woods system, which we will discuss in the next section). Since the late 1990s, Brazil, China, Hungary, Mexico, Poland, South Korea, and numerous other countries have also joined the managed float regime. Despite complaints from the US government, China currently does *not* fix its currency. Since 2005, China has been allowing the yuan to float—from 8.3 yuan to the dollar in 2005 to 6.14 yuan to the dollar in 2014 (a 26% appreciation).

The severity of intervention is a matter of degree. Heavier intervention moves the country closer to a fixed exchange rate policy, and less intervention enables a country to approach the free float ideal. A main objective for intervention is to prevent erratic fluctuations that may trigger macroeconomic turbulence. Some countries do not adhere to any particular rates. Others choose **target exchange rates**, which are specified upper and lower bounds within which the exchange rate is allowed to fluctuate. These are also known as **crawling bands**. A country that uses target exchange rates—an approach called "snake in a tube"—will intervene only when the snake (the exchange rate) crawls out of the tube (the upper or lower bounds). Technically, the yuan is now allowed to float, but only within a limited tube (up to 0.5% fluctuation per day).

The second major exchange rate policy is the **fixed exchange rate policy**. A country adopting a fixed rate policy fixes the exchange rate of its domestic currency relative to other currencies. A specific version of fixed rate policy involves pegging the domestic currency, which means to set the exchange rate of the domestic currency in terms of another currency (the peg). Many developing countries, for example, peg their currencies to the US dollar. There are two benefits to a peg policy. First, a peg stabilizes the import and export prices. Second, many countries with high inflation have pegged their currencies to the dollar in order to restrain domestic inflation because the United States has relatively low inflation.

Clean (free) float A pure market solution to determine exchange rates.

Dirty (managed) float Using selective government intervention to determine exchange rates.

Target exchange rate (crawling band) Specified upper or lower bounds within which an exchange rate is allowed to fluctuate.

Fixed exchange rate policy A government policy to set the exchange rate of a currency relative to other currencies.

7-1f Investor Psychology

While theories on price differences (PPP), interest rates and money supply, balance of payments, and exchange rate policies predict long-run movements of exchange rates, they often fall short of predicting short-run movements. What then determines short-run movements? They are largely driven by investor psychology, some of which is fickle and thus very hard to predict. Professor Richard Lyons at the University of California, Berkeley, is an expert on exchange rate theories. He was baffled when he observed currency trading firsthand:

As I sat there, my friend traded furiously all day long, racking up over $1 billion in trades each day. This was a world where the standard trade was $10 million, and a $1 million trade was a "skinny one." Despite my belief that exchange rates depend on macroeconomics, only rarely was news of this type his primary concern. Most of the time he was reading tea leaves that were, at least to me, not so clear. . . . It was clear my understanding was incomplete when he looked over, in the midst of his fury, and asked me: "What should I do?" I laughed. Nervously.[4]

TALAJ/GETTY IMAGES

Investors—currency traders (such as the one Lyons observed), foreign portfolio investors, and average citizens—may move in the same direction at the same time, like a herd, resulting in a **bandwagon effect**. The bandwagon effect seemed to be at play in August 2014, when the Argentinean peso plunged against key currencies such as the US dollar, the euro, and the pound sterling. Essentially, a large number of individuals and firms exchanged the peso for the key foreign currencies in order to minimize their exposure to Argentina's sovereign default (its second since 2001)—a phenomenon known as **capital flight**. This would push down the demand for, and thus the value of, the domestic currency. Then, more individuals and companies joined the "herd," further depressing the exchange rate and worsening an economic crisis.

ISTOCKPHOTO.COM/DIMOS

Overall, economics, politics, and psychology are all at play. The stakes are high, yet consensus is rare regarding the determinants of foreign exchange rates. As a result, predicting the direction of currency movements remains an art or, at best, a highly imprecise science.

7-2 EVOLUTION OF THE INTERNATIONAL MONETARY SYSTEM

Having outlined the basic determinants of exchange rates, let us examine the history of the international monetary system, divided into three eras: the gold standard, the Bretton Woods system, and the post–Bretton Woods system.

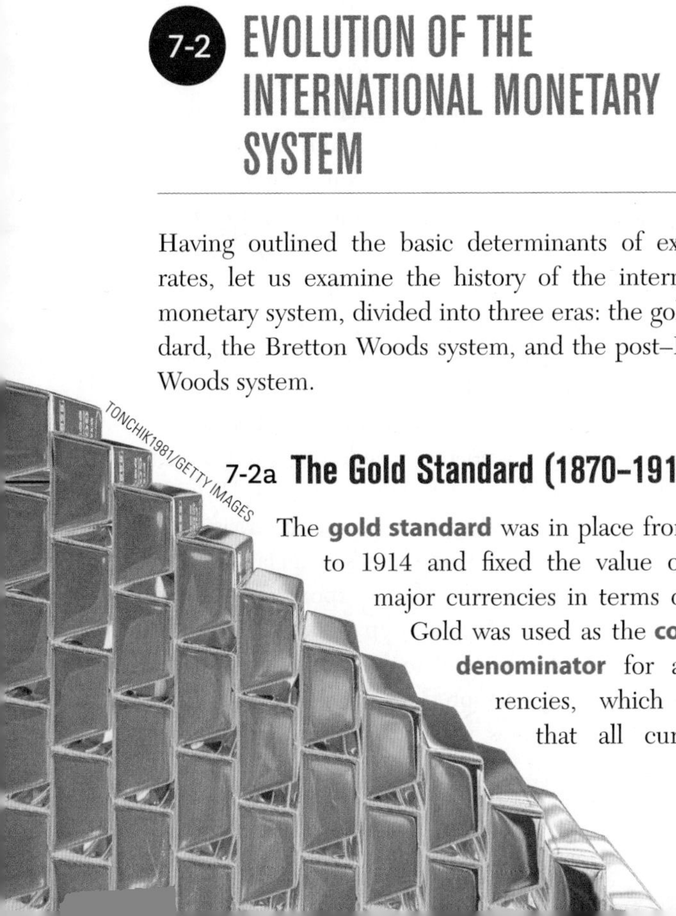
TONCHIK1981/GETTY IMAGES

7-2a The Gold Standard (1870–1914)

The **gold standard** was in place from 1870 to 1914 and fixed the value of most major currencies in terms of gold. Gold was used as the **common denominator** for all currencies, which means that all currencies were pegged at a fixed rate to gold. The gold standard was essentially a global peg system with little volatility and a great deal of predictability and stability. To be able to redeem its currency in gold at a fixed price, every central bank needed to maintain gold reserves. The system provided powerful incentives for countries to run current account surpluses, resulting in net inflows of gold.

7-2b The Bretton Woods System (1944–1973)

The gold standard was abandoned in 1914 when several World War I (WW I) combatant countries printed excessive amounts of currency to finance their war efforts. After WW I, especially during the Great Depression (1929–1933), countries engaged in competitive devaluations in an effort to boost exports at the expense of trading partners. But no country could win such a race to the bottom, and the gold standard had to be jettisoned.

Toward the end of World War II (WW II), at an allied conference in Bretton Woods, New Hampshire, a new system, known simply as the **Bretton Woods system**, was agreed upon by 44 countries. The system was centered on the US dollar as the new common denominator. All currencies were pegged at a fixed rate to the dollar. Only the dollar was convertible to gold at $35 per ounce. Other currencies were not required to be gold convertible.

The Bretton Woods system propelled the dollar to the commanding heights of the global economy. This system reflected the higher US productivity level and the large trade surplus the United States had with the rest of the world in the first two postwar decades. At the end of WW II, the US economy contributed approximately 70% of the global GDP and was the export engine and growth engine of the world.

Bandwagon effect The effect of investors moving in the same direction at the same time, like a herd.

Capital flight A phenomenon in which a large number of individuals and companies exchange domestic currencies for a foreign currency.

Gold standard A system in which the value of most major currencies was maintained by fixing their prices in terms of gold.

Common denominator A currency or commodity to which the value of all currencies are pegged.

Bretton Woods system A system in which all currencies were pegged at a fixed rate to the US dollar.

7-2c The Post-Bretton Woods System (1973–Present)

By the late 1960s and early 1970s, a combination of rising productivity elsewhere and US inflationary policies led to the demise of Bretton Woods. First, in the 1960s, President Lyndon Johnson increased government spending in order to finance both the Vietnam War and Great Society welfare programs. He did this not by additional taxation but by increasing money supply. These actions led to rising inflation levels and strong pressures for the dollar to depreciate. Second, the United States ran its first post-1945 trade deficit in 1971 as (West) Germany and other countries caught up to the United States in productivity and increased their exports. This pushed the (West) German mark to appreciate and the dollar to depreciate, a situation very similar to the yen–dollar relationship in the 1980s and the yuan–dollar relationship in the 2000s.

As currency traders bought more German marks, Germany's central bank, the Bundesbank, had to buy billions of dollars to maintain the dollar/mark exchange rate fixed by Bretton Woods. Being stuck with massive amounts of the dollar that were worth less now, Germany unilaterally allowed its currency to float in 1971.

The Bretton Woods system also became a pain in the neck for the United States because the exchange rate of the dollar was not allowed to unilaterally change. Per Bretton Woods agreements, the US Treasury was obligated to dispense one ounce of gold for every $35 brought to it by a foreign central bank such as the Bundesbank. Consequently, the United States was hemorrhaging gold into the coffers of foreign central banks. In order to stop the flow of gold out of the Treasury, President Richard Nixon unilaterally announced in 1971 that the dollar was no longer convertible into gold. After tense negotiations, the major countries collectively agreed in 1973 to allow their currencies to float, thus ending the Bretton Woods system. In retrospect, the Bretton Woods system had been built on two conditions. First, the US inflation rate had to be low. Second, the United States could not run a trade deficit. When both of these conditions were violated, the system's demise was inevitable.

Post–Bretton Woods system A system of flexible exchange rate regimes with no official common denominator.

International Monetary Fund (IMF) An international organization that was established to promote international monetary cooperation, exchange stability, and orderly exchange arrangements.

Quota The weight a member country carries within the IMF, which determines the amount of its financial contribution (technically known as its "subscription"), its capacity to borrow from the IMF, and its voting power.

As a result, today we live with a **post–Bretton Woods system**, which has no official common denominator and is characterized by the diversity of exchange rate systems discussed earlier (various floating systems and fixed rates). Diversity and flexibility are its strengths. Its drawbacks are turbulence and uncertainty. Although the US dollar has not been the official common denominator since the early 1970s, the dollar has retained a significant amount of soft power as a key currency. In November 2008 and then in April 2009, in the midst of the worst financial crisis in recent times, leaders of the Group of 20 (G-20) held two summits: first in Washington, DC, and then in London. Both summits called for an overhaul of the world's financial structure. These summits were labeled by the media as an effort to construct "Bretton Woods II."[5] The dust has yet to settle on the outcome of these efforts.

7-2d The International Monetary Fund

While the Bretton Woods system is no longer with us, one of its most enduring legacies is the **International Monetary Fund (IMF)**, founded in 1944 as a Bretton Woods institution. (The World Bank is the other Bretton Woods institution.) The IMF's mandate is to promote international monetary cooperation, exchange stability, and orderly exchange arrangements.

Lending is a core responsibility of the IMF, which provides loans to countries experiencing balance of payments problems. The IMF can be viewed as a lender of last resort to help member countries out of financial difficulty. Where does the IMF get its funds? The answer boils down to the same principle as how insurance companies obtain their funds to pay out insurance claims. Similar to insurance companies collecting premiums from subscribers to accumulate the funds necessary to cover claims, the IMF collects funds from member countries. Each member country is assigned a **quota** that determines its financial contribution to the IMF (technically known as its "subscription"), its capacity to borrow from the IMF, and its voting power. The quota is broadly based on a country's relative size in the global economy.

By definition, the IMF makes loans, not grants. IMF loans usually have to be repaid in one to five years. Although payments have been extended in some cases, no member country has defaulted. An ideal IMF loan scenario would be a balance of payments crisis that threatens to severely disrupt a country's financial stability, such as when it imports more than it exports and cannot pay for imports. The IMF could step in and inject funds in the short term to help stabilize the financial system.

While an IMF loan provides short-term financial resources, it also comes with strings attached. Those strings are long-term policy reforms that recipient countries must undertake as conditions of receiving the loan. These conditions usually entail belt tightening and push governments to undertake painful reforms that they otherwise probably would not have undertaken. For example, when the IMF (together with the EU) provided a loan to Greece in 2010, the Greek government agreed to cut pensions and wages for public sector employees by 15% to 20% in order to pay for government debt.[6] Since the 1990s, the IMF has helped Mexico (1994), Russia (1996 and 1998), Asia (Indonesia, South Korea, and Thailand, 1997), Turkey (2001), Brazil (2002), Iceland (2008), Ukraine (2008), Hungary (2008), Greece (2010), and several others.

While the IMF has noble goals, its actions are not without criticisms that call for reforms. A new alternative international organization, which is simply called the New Development Bank (NDB), has recently been set up by the BRICS countries (see Debate).

STEPHEN JAFFE/HANDOUT/GETTY IMAGES

IMF Managing Director Christine Lagarde speaks during the IMF-World Bank Group annual meeting in October 2014, in Washington, DC.

Debate: Ethical Dilemma/Emerging Markets

International Monetary Fund Versus New Development Bank

The complexity of the IMF's actions means that it cannot please everyone. Debates about the IMF rage throughout the world. First, critics argue that the IMF's lending may *facilitate* moral hazard, which means recklessness when people and organizations (including governments) do not have to face the full consequences of their actions. Moral hazard is inherent in all insurance arrangements, including the IMF. Basically, knowing that the IMF would come to the rescue, certain governments may behave more recklessly. For example, between 1958 and 2001, Turkey was rescued by 18 IMF loans.

A second criticism centers on the IMF's lack of accountability. Although the IMF can dictate terms over a host country that is being rescued and receiving loans, none of the IMF officials is democratically elected and most of them do not have deep knowledge of the host country. Consequently, they sometimes make disastrous decisions. For example, in 1997–1998, the IMF forced the Indonesian government to drastically cut back on food subsidies for the poor. Riots exploded the next day. Hundreds of people were killed and property damaged. Then, the IMF reversed its position by restoring food subsidies. However, in some quarters, the bitterness was all the greater. A lot of protesters argued: If food subsidies could have been continued, why were they taken away in the first place?

A third and perhaps most challenging criticism is that the IMF's "one-size-fits-all" strategy—otherwise known as the "bitter medicine"—may be inappropriate. Since the 1930s, in order to maintain more employment, most Western governments have abandoned the idea to balance the budget. Deficit spending has been used as a major policy weapon to pull a country out of an economic crisis. Yet, the IMF often demands governments in more vulnerable developing countries, in the midst of a major crisis, to balance their budgets by slashing spending (such as cutting food subsidies). These actions often make the crisis far worse than it needs to be. After the IMF came to "rescue" countries affected by the 1997 Asian financial crisis, the unemployment rate was up threefold in Thailand, fourfold in South Korea, and tenfold in Indonesia.

However, the momentum of the criticisms, the severity of the global crisis, and the desire to better serve the international community have facilitated a series of IMF reforms since 2009. Some of these reforms represent a total (180 degrees) change from its previous directions, resulting in an "IMF 2.0" dubbed by *Time*. For example, the IMF now starts to promote more fiscal spending in order to stimulate the economy and to ease money supply and reduce interest rates, given the primary concern for the global economy now is deflation and recession, but not inflation. Obviously, the IMF's change of heart is affected by the tremendous stimulus packages unleashed by developed economies since 2008, which result in skyrocketing budget deficits. If the developed economies can (hopefully) use greater fiscal spending and budget deficits to pull themselves out a crisis, the IMF simply cannot lecture developing economies that receive its loans to balance their budgets in the middle of a crisis. Further, given the stigma of receiving IMF loans and listening and then implementing IMF lectures, many countries avoid the IMF until they run out of options. In response, in April 2009, the IMF unleashed a new Flexible Credit

Line (FCL), which would be particularly useful for crisis *prevention* by providing the flexibility to draw on it at any time, with no strings attached—a radical contrast to its earlier requirement. Mexico, Colombia, and Poland have used the FCL so far.

Further, the IMF 2.0 has become three times bigger—leaders in the G20 Summit in London in 2009 agreed to enhance the IMF's funding from $250 billion to $750 billion. Of the $500 billion new funding (technically Special Drawing Rights [SDRs]), the United States, the EU, and Japan each was expected to contribute $100 billion. China signed up for $40 billion. Request for injection of substantial funding from emerging economies resulted in the calls for better representation of these countries. However, enhancing voting rights for emerging economies would lead to reduced shares for developed economies. As a result, progress is slow. Even with the new changes, Brazil, with 1.72% of the votes (up from the previous 1.38%), still carries less weight than Belgium (1.86%, down from the previous 2.09%). Despite having the world's second largest economy, China has failed to be admitted as one of the top five IMF shareholders—with 3.81% of the votes, it has become the sixth largest, behind the United States (16.75%), Japan (6.23%), Germany (5.81%), France (4.29%), and the UK (4.29%). Overall, Western countries, which have been overrepresented at the IMF, have refused to make room at the table for emerging economies.

In July 2014 at the sixth BRICS summit in Fortaleza, Brazil, BRICS countries—consisting of Brazil, Russia, India, China, and South Africa—launched a New Development Bank (NDB) as an alternative to the IMF. To be headquartered in Shanghai, the NDB, previously known as the BRICS Development Bank, represents a significant block of countries that have 2.8 billion people (40% of the world's population), cover a quarter of the world's land area, and account for more than 25% of global GDP. Unlike the IMF, which assigns votes to member countries differently, the NDB assigns each of the five participating countries one vote (each country contributing $10 billion initial paid-in capital for a total of $50 billion). While the NDB will focus on infrastructure and sustainable development projects, BRICS have also set up a $100 billion Contingency Reserve Arrangement (CRA), with China contributing $41 billion, Brazil, Russia, and India each $18 billion, and South Africa $5 billion. Designed to provide protection against global liquidity pressures, the CRA is a precautionary instrument in response to actual or potential short-term balance of payments problems.

NELSON ALMEIDA/AFP/GETTY IMAGES

The NDB and the CRA have been set up due to BRICS' frustration with the IMF, which together they only wield about 11% of the votes (after recent IMF reforms). Further, they are set up in response to the IMF's enforcement of conditions on countries seeking emergency loans. The founding statement signed by BRICS leaders has stated: "International governance structures designed within a different power configuration show increasingly evident signs of losing legitimacy and effectiveness." In a couple of decades and with expanding membership, the NDB and the CRA may indeed become a rival of the IMF. However, in the short run, how to coordinate the divergent interests—and paper over disagreements—among BRICS remains to be seen.

Sources: R. Desai and J. Vreeland, "What the new bank of BRICS is all about," *Washington Post*, 17 July 2014, www.washingtonpost.com; "New fund, old fundamentals," *Economist*, 2 May 2009, 78; "Beyond Bretton Woods 2," *Economist*, 6 November 2010, 85–87; "The 70-year itch," *Economist*, 5 July 2014, 12; R. Fuller, 2014, "Refusing to share: How the West created BRICS New Development Bank," www.rt.com; A. Ghosh, M. Chamon, C. Crowe, J. Kim, and J. Ostry, "Coping with the crisis: Policy options for emerging market countries," IMF staff position paper (Washington: IMF, 2009); C. Lagarde, "I try to spark new ideas," *Harvard Business Review* (November 2013): 111–114; R. Rajan, "The future of the IMF and the World Bank," *American Economic Review* 98 (2008): 110–115; J. Stiglitz, *Globalization and Its Discontents* (New York: Norton, 2002); "International Monetary Fund 2.0," *Time*, 20 April 2009.

7-3 STRATEGIC RESPONSES

From an institution-based view, knowledge about foreign exchange rates and the international monetary system (including the role of the IMF) helps paint a broad picture of the rules of the game that govern financial transactions around the world. Armed with this knowledge, savvy managers need to develop firm-specific resources and capabilities so they can rise to the challenge, or at least avoid having their firms crushed by unfavorable currency movements (see the Opening and Closing Cases). This section outlines the strategic responses of two types of firms: financial and non-financial companies.

Foreign exchange market The market where individuals, firms, governments, and banks buy and sell currencies of other countries.

7-3a Strategies for Financial Companies

One of the leading strategic goals for financial companies is to profit from the foreign exchange market. The **foreign exchange market** is where individuals, firms, governments, and banks buy and sell currencies of other countries. Unlike a stock exchange, the foreign exchange market has no central, physical location. This market is truly global and transparent. Buyers and sellers are geographically dispersed but constantly linked, and quoted prices change as often as 20 times a *minute*.[7] Each week, the market opens first in Sydney, then Tokyo, Hong Kong, and Singapore.

Gradually, Frankfurt, Zurich, Paris, London, New York, Chicago, and San Francisco wake up and come online.

Operating on a 24/7 basis, the foreign exchange market is the largest and most active market in the world. On average, the worldwide volume is approximately $5.3 trillion per *day*.[8] To put this mind-boggling number in perspective, the amount of one single *day* of foreign exchange transactions is more than three times the amount of entire worldwide FDI inflows in one *year* and more than one-third of worldwide merchandise exports in one *year*. Specifically, the foreign exchange market has two functions: (1) to service the needs of trade and investment and (2) to trade in its own commodity—namely, foreign exchange.

There are three primary types of foreign exchange transactions: spot transactions, forward transactions, and swaps. **Spot transactions** are the classic single-shot exchange of one currency for another. For example, Australian tourists visiting Italy go to a bank to exchange their Australian dollars for euros, essentially buying euros with Australian dollars.

Forward transactions allow participants to buy and sell currencies now for future delivery, typically in 30, 90, or 180 days after the date of the transaction. The primary benefit of forward transactions is to protect traders and investors from being exposed to the unfavorable fluctuations of the spot rate, an act known as **currency hedging**. Currency hedging is essentially a way to minimize the foreign exchange risk inherent in all nonspot transactions, which include most trade and FDI deals.[9] Traders and investors expecting to make or receive payments in a foreign currency in the future are concerned that they may be forced to make either a greater payment or receive less in terms of the domestic currency should the spot rate change. For example, if the forward rate of the euro (€/US$) is exactly the same as the spot rate, the euro is flat. If the forward rate of the euro per dollar is *higher* than the spot rate, the euro has a **forward discount**. If the forward rate of the euro per dollar is *lower* than the spot rate, the euro then has a **forward premium**.

Let's apply this to a hypothetical example. Assume that today's exchange rate of €/US$ is 1, that a US firm expects to be paid €1 million six months later, and that the euro is at a 180-day forward discount of 1.1 (or €1/US$1.1). The US firm could take out a forward contract now, and at the end of six months the euro earnings would be converted into $909,091 (€1 million/1.1). Does such a currency hedging move make sense? Maybe. The move makes sense if the firm knows in advance that the future spot rate will be higher. So in six months if the spot rate is 1.25, then the forward contract provides the US firm with $909,091 instead of $800,000 (€1 million/1.25). The difference is $109,091 (or 14% of $800,000). However, the move would backfire if after six months the spot rate were actually below 1.1. If the spot rate remained at 1, the firm could have earned $1 million *without* the forward contract, instead of only $909,091 with the contract. This simple example suggests a powerful observation: Currency hedging *requires* firms to have expectations or forecasts of future spot rates relative to forward rates.

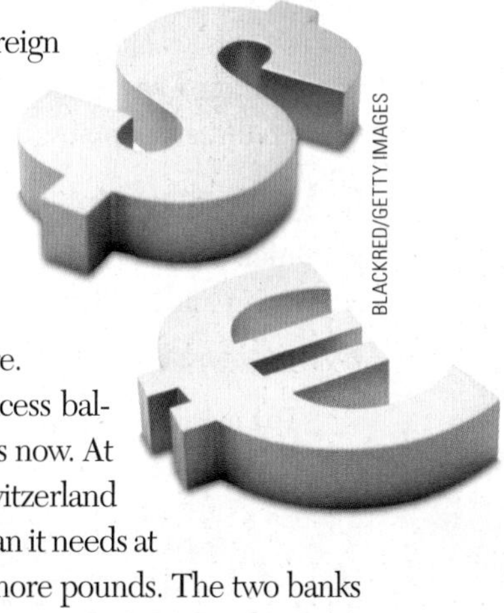

BLACKRED/GETTY IMAGES

Another major type of foreign exchange transactions is a swap. A **currency swap** is the conversion of one currency into another at Time 1, with an agreement to revert it back to the original currency at a specified Time 2 in the future. Deutsche Bank may have an excess balance of pounds but needs dollars now. At the same time, Union Bank of Switzerland (UBS) may have more dollars than it needs at the moment and is looking for more pounds. The two banks can negotiate a swap agreement in which Deutsche Bank agrees to exchange pounds for dollars with UBS today and dollars for pounds at a specific point in the future.

The primary participants of the foreign exchange market are large international banks such as Deutsche Bank, UBS, and Citigroup, which trade among themselves. How do these banks make money by trading money? They make money by capturing the difference between their **offer rate** (the price to sell) and **bid rate** (the price to buy)—the bid rate is *always* lower than the offer rate. In other words, banks buy low and sell high. The difference between the offer rate and the bid rate is technically called the **spread**. For example, Citigroup may quote offer and bid rates for the Swiss franc at $1.0877 and $1.0874, respectively, and the spread is $0.0003. That is, Citigroup is willing to sell 1 million francs for $1,087,700 and buy 1 million francs for $1,087,400. If Citigroup

Spot transaction The classic single-shot exchange of one currency for another.

Forward transaction A foreign exchange transaction in which participants buy and sell currencies now for future delivery.

Currency hedging A transaction that protects traders and investors from exposure to the fluctuations of the spot rate.

Forward discount A condition under which the forward rate of one currency relative to another currency is higher than the spot rate.

Forward premium A condition under which the forward rate of one currency relative to another currency is lower than the spot rate.

Currency swap A foreign exchange transaction between two firms in which one currency is converted into another at Time 1, with an agreement to revert it back to the original currency at a specified Time 2 in the future.

Offer rate The price at which a bank is willing to sell a currency.

Bid rate The price at which a bank is willing to buy a currency.

Spread The difference between the offer price and the bid price.

can simultaneously buy and sell 1 million francs, it can make $300 (the spread of $0.0003 × 1 million francs). Given the instantaneous and transparent nature of the electronically linked foreign exchange market around the globe (one new quote in London can reach New York before you finish reading this *sentence*), the opportunities can come and go very quickly. The globally integrated nature of this market leads to three outcomes:

- A razor-thin spread.
- Quick (often literally split-second) decisions on buying and selling.
- Ever-increasing volume in order to make more profits.

To envision the quick decisions, remember the observation by Lyons mentioned earlier. To get a sense of the ever-increasing volume, recall the daily volume of over $5 trillion. In the example above, $300 is obviously "small peanuts" for Citigroup. Do a little math: How much trading in Swiss francs does Citigroup have to do in order to make $1 million in profits for itself?

Currency risk The potential for loss associated with fluctuations in the foreign exchange market.

7-3b Strategies for Nonfinancial Companies

How do nonfinancial companies cope with the potential losses they may incur due to fluctuations in the foreign exchange market, broadly known as **currency risks**? There are three primary strategies: (1) invoicing in their own currencies, (2) currency hedging (as discussed above), and (3) strategic hedging. The most basic way is to invoice customers in your own currency. By invoicing in dollars, many US firms have enjoyed such protection from unfavorable foreign exchange movements. As the euro becomes a more powerful currency, firms based in countries that use the euro now increasingly demand that they be paid in euros. In Focus illustrates how some Chinese exporters insist on getting paid in yuan from African importers.

In Focus: *Emerging Markets*

Chinese Exporters Cope with Currency Fluctuation in Africa

In 2000, trade between China and Africa was only $10 billion. In 2010, the volume rocketed ahead to reach $127 billion. While China has become Africa's number-one trading partner, the downside of such intense trading is the complications of having to deal with currency fluctuation. The vast majority of the trade deals between China and Africa are conducted in US dollars, which have fluctuated substantially. Since the dollar is likely to depreciate and the yuan is likely to correspondingly appreciate further, Chinese exporters with costs in yuan and payments in dollars stand to lose. While currency hedging using forward contracts is an obvious coping strategy, many small exporters cannot afford the expenses. In addition, currency hedging is not risk-free. Wrong bets may end up burning firms big time.

NARVIKK/GETTY IMAGES

To better cope with currency fluctuation, one straightforward mechanism for Chinese exporters is to insist on payment in yuan. The question is: Why would African importers agree to pay in yuan? Two compelling reasons emerge. First, Chinese exporters can save approximately 7% to 10% of their costs if they are paid in yuan. If they can share some of these gains with their African trading partners with lower prices, the new deal to use yuan as the common transaction currency becomes a win-win solution for both sides. Second, an increasing number of Chinese firms have engaged in foreign direct investment (FDI) in Africa. Their subsidiaries in Africa would be comfortable to use yuan to buy supplies, components, and manufactured products from home.

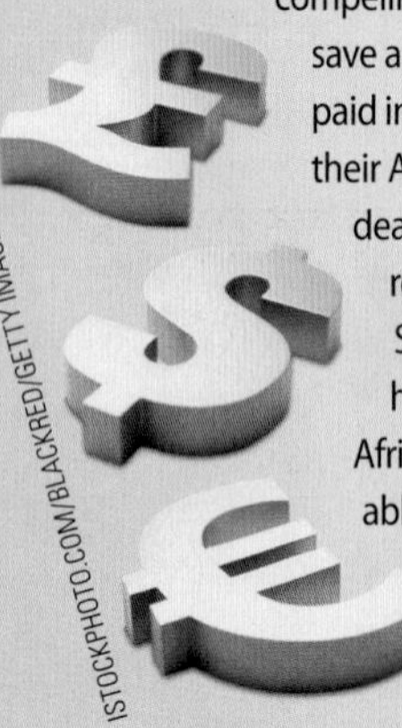
ISTOCKPHOTO.COM/BLACKRED/GETTY IMAGES; BLACKRED

Johannesburg, South Africa–based Standard Bank, which is the largest bank in Africa, has estimated that by 2015, 40% of the China-Africa trade (worth $100 billion) would be settled in yuan. This would significantly eliminate the headache of currency fluctuation for Chinese exporters. By 2014, approximately 18% of China's foreign trade was already being settled in yuan. Little by little, China's currency is gaining ground in Africa and elsewhere. However, adding all international payments together, the yuan in 2014 only ranked 14th in the world, behind Russia's ruble and Thailand's baht, according to SWIFT, a company that specializes in transfer of funds between banks. Therefore, the rise of the "redback" as a major currency for international trade in Africa and beyond still has a long way to go.

Sources: G. Allard, "Chinese OFDI in Africa," in I. Alon, M. Fetscherin, and P. Gugler (eds.), *Chinese International Investments* (New York: Palgrave, 2012) 279–299; "Renminbi is popular in Africa," *21st Century Business Insights*, 16 September 2011, 26; "Yuan for the money," *Economist*, 9 February 2013, 14–15; "The red and the green," *Economist*, 26 April 2014, 44; Standard Bank, 2015, www.standardbank.com.

Currency hedging is risky because, as discussed in the previous section, in trying to predict currency movements your bets could be all wrong. **Strategic hedging** means spreading out activities in a number of countries in different currency zones in order to offset any currency losses in one region through gains in other regions. Therefore, strategic hedging can be considered as currency diversification (see the Opening Case). It reduces exposure to unfavorable foreign exchange movements. Strategic hedging is conceptually different from currency hedging. Currency hedging focuses on using forward contracts and swaps to contain currency risks, a financial management activity that can be performed by in-house financial specialists or outside experts (such as currency traders). Strategic hedging refers to dispersing operations geographically—through sourcing or FDI—in multiple currency zones. By definition, this is more strategic because it involves managers from many functional areas such as production, marketing, and sourcing in addition to those from finance.

Overall, the importance of foreign exchange management for firms of all stripes interested in doing business abroad cannot be over-stressed. Firms whose performance is otherwise stellar can be devastated by unfavorable currency movements. For example, the Swiss franc appreciated 25% against the euro between 2010 and 2012. Swiss manufacturers thus had a hard time competing with relatively cheap imports (see the Closing Case). On the other hand, thanks to crises in countries such as Greece, Ireland, and Portugal, the euro depreciated sharply against the dollar during the same period. Euro-zone exporters such as Daimler-Benz (maker of Mercedes cars) and EADS (manufacturer of Airbus jets) could not be happier.[10]

From a resource-based view, it seems imperative that firms develop resources and capabilities that can combat currency risks in addition to striving for excellence in areas such as operations and marketing.[11] Developing such expertise is no small accomplishment, because, as noted earlier, predicting currency movements remains an art or at least a highly imprecise science. These challenges mean that firms able to profit from (or at least avoid being crushed by) unfavorable currency movements will possess valuable, rare, and hard-to-imitate capabilities that are the envy of rivals.

7-4 MANAGEMENT SAVVY

The big question in global business, adapted to the context of foreign exchange movements, is: What determines the success and failure of currency management around the globe? The answer boils down to two components. First, from an institution-based standpoint, the changing rules of the game—economic, political, and psychological—enable or constrain firms. For example, Swiss exporters' frustration with the appreciation of the Swiss franc relative to the euro stems from the centuries-old policy of Switzerland to maintain its political and economic independence. While all of Switzerland's neighbors have joined the EU and adopted the euro, Switzerland will not (see the Closing Case). Second, from a resource-based perspective, how firms develop valuable, unique, and hard-to-imitate capabilities in currency management may make or break them.

Shown in Exhibit 7.5, three implications for action emerge. First, foreign exchange literacy must be fostered. Savvy managers need to pay attention not only to the broad, long-run movements informed by PPP, productivity changes, and BOP, but also to the fickle short-run fluctuations triggered by interest rate changes and investor mood swings.

Second, risk analysis of any country must include its currency risks. Previous chapters have advised managers to pay attention to political, regulatory, and cultural risks of various countries. Here, a crucial currency risk dimension is added. An otherwise attractive country may suffer from devaluation of its currency. For example, prior to 2008, foreign and domestic banks in emerging European countries such as Hungary, Latvia, and Poland let numerous home buyers take out mortgage loans denominated in the euro, while a majority of these customers' assets and incomes were in local currencies. Unfortunately, local currencies in these countries were severely devaluated in the 2008–2009 crisis, making many home buyers unable to come up with the higher mortgage payments. Domestic and foreign banks in the region suffered from severe losses.

Finally, a country's high currency risks do not necessarily suggest that the country needs to be avoided totally. Instead, it calls for a prudent currency risk management strategy via invoicing in one's own currency, currency hedging, or strategic hedging. Not every firm has the power to invoice in its own currency. Smaller,

Strategic hedging Spreading out activities in a number of countries in different currency zones to offset any currency losses in one region through gains in other regions.

EXHIBIT 7.5 IMPLICATIONS FOR ACTION

- Fostering foreign exchange literacy is a must.
- Risk analysis of any country must include an analysis of its currency risks.
- A currency risk management strategy is necessary—via invoicing in one's own currency, currency hedging, or strategic hedging.

internationally inexperienced firms may outsource currency hedging to specialists such as currency traders. Strategic hedging may be unrealistic for smaller, inexperienced firms. On the other hand, many larger, internationally experienced firms (such as 3M) choose not to touch currency hedging, citing its unpredictability. Instead, they focus on strategic hedging. Although no one has found a fixed formula, firms without a well thought-out currency management strategy will be caught off guard when currency movements take a nasty turn.

ETHICAL DILEMMA

The Swiss Franc: A Currency from Where?

Situated in the middle of Europe, Switzerland enjoys splendid isolation politically. Unlike many non-EU member countries eager to join the EU, Switzerland does not bother to apply. Economically, the Swiss economy is closely integrated with its European neighbors—60% of its exports go to EU members. While the hoopla associated with the successful launch of the euro over a decade ago has been replaced by the recent pessimism associated with the euro mess, Switzerland can proudly point to its Swiss franc (SFr or CHF) as a rock-solid currency.

ILBUSCA/E+/GETTY IMAGES

Known as a "haven currency," the Swiss franc strengthens when US stock prices crash; when bond prices in Greece, Italy, and Spain rise; and when the euro takes a beating. On one of the most stressful days in recent history, September 11, 2001, the Swiss franc rose by a remarkable 3% within two *hours* after the first plane crashing into World Trade Center.

But here is a catch: To Swiss exporters, service providers catering to international tourists, and employees whose pay is cut or whose jobs are lost, the Swiss franc is not a "currency from haven"—it is actually a "currency from hell." Between 2010 and 2012, the Swiss franc appreciated 25% against the euro. "If you have loads of euro sales and lots of Swiss franc costs, you're getting killed," noted an expert. "It is a nightmare for everybody," said another expert, "We have to adapt." Mopac, a maker of food packaging materials, cut wages by 10% for its 260 employees in 2011, thanks to unfavorable foreign exchange movements. The firm adjusted wages every three months, depending on the exchange rate. The union protested, by arguing that "exchange rate fluctuations are a risk that should be taken on by the company's owner." The owner responded by pointing out that "If we hadn't cut wages, we would have had to move our production to the euro zone"—and most jobs at Mopac would be lost.

Prior to the recent spike, Swiss prices had already been hair-raisingly expensive. Now they became worse. A Big Mac in 2014 cost $6.83—the second most expensive in the world behind Norway (see Exhibit 7.3). The Swiss economics ministry commissioned a study that compared a standard Alpine skiing holiday in a medium-class hotel in the Swiss Alps versus in the Austrian Alps—Austria turned out to be one-third more price-competitive than Switzerland. For example, a regular room in a three-star hotel in Zermatt, where guests can view the spectacular, 4,478-meter (14,692-foot) Matterhorn peak from their balconies, costs $350 a night. While Switzerland still attracts a large number of visitors, an untold number have opted for vacations in Austria, France, and Italy, which also offer beautiful Alpine mountain scenery, excellent skiing, and other enticing tourist attractions.

When visitors do come, they spend less in Switzerland. A saleswoman at the famous Zett Meyer watch store on Zurich's Bahnhofstrasse sensed this when shoppers from abroad pulled out their phones. "Some customers come in with prices saved on their cell phones to compare them with ours," she said. For a TAG Heuer watch that cost $12,930, "even when we give them 10% off, it's still cheaper in their home country." In another example, Chinese tourists often look for Chinese restaurants, both for the more reasonable prices and for the more familiar dishes rather than the more "exotic" Swiss diet heavy with cheese and cream—two ingredients that the Chinese never use in their cuisine. Stepping out of Geneva's train station, a group of them found a Chinese restaurant, Le Mandarin. However, they were shocked to find that the cheapest dish—a bowl of Beijing street noodles (not even fancy Singapore or Shanghai noodles)—cost $32. But Beijing street noodles nevertheless became the most popular dish served by Le Mandarin, according to the staff. It is not uncommon to see a table of very rich Chinese tourists (anyone from China who can afford a holiday in Switzerland has to be very rich) devouring Beijing street noodles, which is something they probably do not do either in China or elsewhere around the world. They would only do that in Switzerland.

In September 2012, the Swiss National Bank (SNB) confronted unwelcome appreciation of the Swiss franc by intervening to cap its value at SFr1.20 to the euro. In its own words, these were efforts to counter the "massive overvaluation" of the Swiss franc, which became "a threat to the economy." The SNB was "prepared to buy foreign currency in unlimited quantities." In response to the announcement the Swiss franc fell against the euro, to 1.22 francs from 1.12 francs and lost 9% against the US dollar within one day.

For a country of its size (a population of seven million), Switzerland has an unusual number of large multinational manufacturers, such as ABB, Nestlé, Novartis, Roche, and Swatch. These firms all engage in strategic hedging by producing and sourcing in different currency zones around the world, so they are better able to cope with the Swiss franc spike. But 60% of Switzerland's employment is in small and medium-sized manufacturers, retailers, hotels, restaurants, and tour operators. To them, strategic hedging is not realistic, and most of them also do not bother to engage in currency hedging or simple currency diversification—most of them refuse to accept euros. With Swiss francs in hand, they are stuck between a rock and a hard currency.

Case Discussion Questions

1. Why is the Swiss franc a "haven currency" according to many international investors?
2. Why have the unfavorable foreign exchange movements made the Swiss franc a "currency from hell," according to a lot of Swiss firms, managers, and employees?
3. If you were a CEO of a medium-sized manufacturer in Switzerland, what are the options you may consider in response to the spike of the Swiss franc?
4. As a tourist looking to have a vacation in Europe, you are very interested in Switzerland, but you are concerned about the high prices. What other European countries would you consider?

Sources: The author's interviews in Bern, Geneva, and Zurich, Switzerland; "The Swiss can barely afford their currency," *Bloomberg Businessweek*, 6 June 2011, 20–21; "A special case: A survey of Switzerland," *Economist*, 14 February 2004; "Too strong for comfort," *Economist*, 3 September 2011, 76; "The weak shall inherit the earth," *Economist*, 16 October 2012, 25–26

STUDY TOOLS 7

LOCATED AT THE BACK OF YOUR BOOK:

- ☐ Rip out and study the Chapter Review Card at the end of the book

LOG IN TO WWW.CENGAGEBRAIN.COM TO:

- ☐ Review key term flashcards
- ☐ Complete a practice quiz to test your knowledge of key concepts
- ☐ Take and complete the chapter crossword puzzle
- ☐ Complete interactive content, watch chapter videos, and take a graded quiz
- ☐ Track your knowledge of key concepts in Global Business
- ☐ Read and discuss additional case study content

8 Capitalizing on Global & Regional Integration

BIKERIDERLONDON/SHUTTERSTOCK.COM

LEARNING OBJECTIVES

After studying this chapter, you should be able to . . .

8-1 Make the case for global economic integration.

8-2 Explain the evolution of the GATT and the WTO, including current challenges.

8-3 Make the case for regional economic integration.

8-4 List the accomplishments, benefits, and costs of the European Union.

8-5 Identify the five organizations that promote regional trade in the Americas and describe their benefits and costs.

8-6 Identify the four organizations that promote regional trade in the Asia Pacific and describe their benefits and costs.

8-7 Articulate how regional trade should influence your thinking about global business.

After you finish this chapter, go to **PAGE 132** for **STUDY TOOLS**

Launching the Learjet 85: A NAFTA Collaboration

The North American Free Trade Agreement (NAFTA) celebrated its 20th anniversary in 2014. Born in 1994, NAFTA was designed to make rules more market-friendly to facilitate more trade and investment among its three member countries. In response, smart companies have taken advantage of the changed rules of the game to build expanded supply chains across NAFTA in an effort to enhance their global competitiveness.

While the maiden flight of the Learjet 85 in April 2014 was a coincidence, how Canada's Bombardier took advantage of NAFTA and tapped into the comparative advantage of the three member countries is a shining new example of how high NAFTA can soar. In 1990, Montreal-based Bombardier acquired Wichita, Kansas-based Learjet. Although in the aerospace industry Bombardier is the world's third largest player, it is dwarfed by the two giants Boeing and Airbus. In the business aviation market, Bombardier competes intensely with Beech Hawker, Cessna, and Gulfstream from the United States, Dassault Falcon from France, and Embraer from Brazil. Boeing and Airbus have also elbowed their way into this market for smaller airplanes by dressing up the smallest of their large jets (such as Boeing 737 and A320) as business jets. Honda has jumped in with HondaJet. Although business aviation seems glamorous, its customers are the most demanding ones in the world. Evidenced by the fate of European rivals such as de Havilland, Fokker, and Short Brothers, crash landings (bankruptcies) are frequent. Firms need strong muscle to survive the brutal skies.

In 2007, Bombardier launched an innovative new eight-seat model, the Learjet 85. In 2010, it opened a $250 million, Learjet 85 aircraft component manufacturing facility in Querétaro, Mexico, which was inaugurated by President Felipe Calderón. The state-of-the-art factory makes the cockpit, fuselage, and tail sections of the Learjet 85. Instead of oily smells and the noisy sound of hammering, the factory is amazingly quiet. Technicians wear facial masks to work in a dust-free room. Instead of metal, the airplane uses carbon fiber, which is cut by laser. The carbon fiber is then baked in a giant oven to make a seamless combined section for the cockpit and the fuselage.

Except some parts of the wing made by another Bombardier unit in Belfast, Northern Ireland, UK, the Learjet 85 represents the fruit of NAFTA collaboration. The engine is designed by Pratt & Whitney in the United States and is made in Canada. Made-in-Mexico airframes are shipped to Wichita, Kansas, where Learjet's headquarters is located, for final assembly and testing prior to being delivered to customers. In short, the Learjet 85 is a high-flying example of a successful NAFTA endeavor. Such trilateral collaboration would not have taken place in the absence of NAFTA.

When the $250 million investment in Mexico was first announced, Bombardier employees in Montreal and Wichita, where the Learjet would have been made had NAFTA not been around, complained. However, given the bankruptcies of a number of old European rivals and the emergence of new entrants from China, Japan, Russia, and South Korea, Canadian and American employees came to appreciate that if outsourcing some manufacturing to Mexico reduces cost and helps ensure Bombardier's future, it would also help safeguard their jobs in the long run.

Sources: "Deeper, better, NAFTA," *Economist*, 4 January 2014, 8; "Ready to take off again?" *Economist*, 4 January 2014, 23–25; "Three countries or one continent?" *Economist*, 4 October 2014, 44.

Why did Bombardier deliberately tap into the three member countries in the **North American Free Trade Agreement (NAFTA)**, instead of concentrating its work in one country? In addition to NAFTA, why did it also manufacture some parts of the new Learjet 85 in Europe? In two words, the answer is: economic integration—both regionally and globally. **Regional economic integration** refers to efforts to reduce trade and investment barriers within one region, such as NAFTA. **Global economic integration**, in turn, refers to efforts to reduce trade and investment barriers around the globe.

This chapter is fundamentally about how the two core perspectives in global business interact. Specifically, how do changes in the rules of the game for global and regional economic integration, as emphasized by the institution-based view, lead firms to better develop and leverage their capabilities, as highlighted by the resource-based view? In other words, how do firms around the world such as Bombardier capitalize on global and regional economic integration? We start with a

North American Free Trade Agreement (NAFTA) A free trade agreement among Canada, Mexico, and the United States.

Regional economic integration Efforts to reduce trade and investment barriers within one region.

Global economic integration Efforts to reduce trade and investment barriers around the globe.

description of global economic integration. Then, we introduce regional economic integration around the world. Finally, we offer some practical tips for managers.

8-1 INTEGRATING THE GLOBAL ECONOMY

Current frameworks of regional and global economic integration date back to the end of World War II (WWII). The world community was mindful of the mercantilist trade policies in the 1930s, which worsened the Great Depression and eventually led to WWII. Two new developments after the war were initiated to prevent a repeat of these circumstances. Globally, the **General Agreement on Tariffs and Trade (GATT)** was created in 1948 as a multilateral agreement governing the international trade of goods (merchandise). In Europe, regional integration started in 1951. The agreement and ensuing integration proved so successful that they are now considerably expanded. GATT became the **World Trade Organization (WTO)**, which was established in 1995 as the global multilateral trading system and the organization that supports it. Economic integration in Europe led to the **European Union (EU)**.

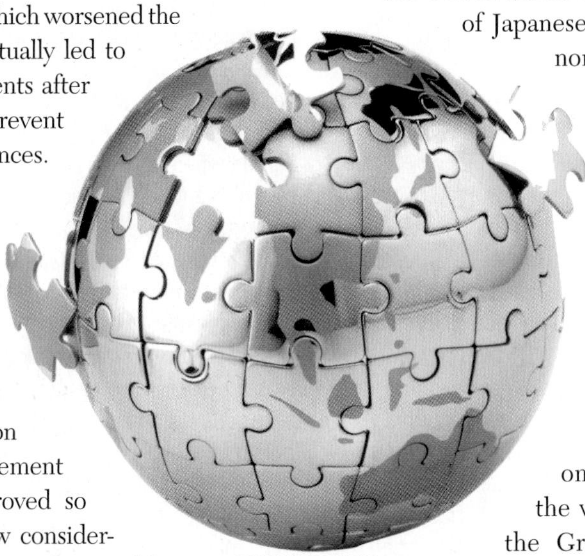

ISTOCKPHOTO.COM/R.R.

8-1a Political Benefits for Global Economic Integration

Recall from Chapters 5 and 6 that, theoretically, economic gains occur when firms from different countries can freely trade and invest. But these insights were not accepted by most governments until the end of WWII. In the late 1920s and the early 1930s, virtually all governments tried to protect domestic industries by imposing protectionist policies through tariffs and quotas. Collectively, these beggar-thy-neighbor policies triggered retaliation that further restricted trade. Trade wars eventually turned into WWII.

General Agreement on Tariffs and Trade (GATT) A multilateral agreement governing the international trade of goods (merchandise).

World Trade Organization (WTO) The official title of the multilateral trading system and the organization underpinning this system since 1995.

European Union (EU) The official title of European economic integration since 1993.

The postwar urge for global economic integration grew out of the painful lessons of the 1920s and the 1930s. While emphasizing economic benefits, global economic integration is *political* in nature. Its fundamental goal is to promote peace (see Exhibit 8.1). Simply put, people who buy and sell from each other are usually reluctant to fight or kill each other. For example, Japan decided to attack Pearl Harbor in 1941 only *after* the United States cut off oil sales to Japan in protest of Japanese aggression in China. Global economic integration also seeks to build confidence. The mercantilist trade policies in the 1930s were triggered by a lack of confidence. So confidence building is key to avoiding the tragedies of the 1930s. Governments, if they are confident that other countries will not raise trade barriers, will not be tempted to do the same.

Recently, as the global economy endeavors to recover from the worst economic crisis (now called the Great Recession) since the Great Depression, there is a grave danger of rising protectionism around the globe. Hopefully, leaders of the 21st century will be smarter and wiser than leaders of the 1920s and the 1930s. While protectionism may lead to short-term gains at the expense of trading partners, the world as a whole "has been there, done that"—with disastrous outcomes and tremendous wartime losses.

EXHIBIT 8.1 BENEFITS OF GLOBAL ECONOMIC INTEGRATION

Political benefits
Promotes peace by promoting trade and investment
Builds confidence in a multilateral trading system
Economic benefits
Disputes are handled constructively
Rules make life easier and discrimination impossible for all participating countries
Free trade and investment raise incomes and stimulate economic growth

8-1b Economic Benefits for Global Economic Integration

There are at least three compelling economic reasons for global economic integration. The first is to handle disputes constructively. The WTO's dispute resolution mechanisms (discussed later in this chapter) are designed to help countries do just this. Although there is an escalation in the number of disputes brought to the WTO, such an increase, according to the WTO, "does not reflect increasing tension in the world. Rather, it reflects the closer economic ties throughout the world, the WTO's expanding membership, and the fact that countries have faith in the system to solve their differences."[1] In other words, it is much better to bring disputes to the WTO than to declare war on each other.

A second benefit is that global economic integration makes life easier for all participants. Officially, the GATT/WTO system is called a **multilateral trading system** because it involves all participating countries (the key word being *multilateral*) and not just two countries (*bilateral*). A crucial principle in the multilateral trading system is **non-discrimination**. Specifically, a country cannot make distinctions in trade among its trading partners. Every time a country lowers a trade barrier, it has to do the same for *all* WTO member countries, except when giving preference to regional partners (an exception we will discuss later). Such non-discrimination makes things easier for all members.

Finally, global economic integration raises incomes, generates jobs, and stimulates economic growth. The WTO estimates that cutting global trade barriers by a third may raise worldwide income by approximately $600 billion. That's equivalent to adding an economy the size of Canada to the world. Benefits are not limited to countries as a whole. Individuals also benefit because more and better jobs are created. In the United States, 12 million people owe their jobs to exports. In China, 18 million people work for foreign-invested firms, which have the highest level of profits and pay among all China-based firms.

Of course, global economic integration has its problems. Critics may not be happy with the environmental impact and with the distribution of the benefits from more trade and investment among the haves and have-nots in the world. However, when weighing all of the pros and cons, most governments and people agree that global economic integration generates enormous benefits, ranging from preserving peace to generating jobs.

8-2 ORGANIZING WORLD TRADE

8-2a General Agreement on Tariffs and Trade: 1948–1994

Created in 1948, the GATT (unlike the WTO) was technically an agreement but *not* an organization. Its major contribution was to reduce the level of tariffs by sponsoring rounds of multilateral negotiations. As a result, the average tariff in developed economies dropped from 40% in 1948 to 3% in 2005. Between 1950 and 1995, when the GATT was phased out to become the WTO, world GDP grew about fivefold, but world merchandise exports grew about 100 times (!). During the GATT era, trade growth consistently outpaced GDP growth.

Despite the GATT's phenomenal success in bringing down tariff barriers, by the 1980s three concerns had surfaced that made it clear that reforms would be necessary. First, because of the GATT's declared focus on merchandise trade, neither trade in services nor intellectual property (IP) protection was covered. Both of these areas were becoming more important. Second, the many loopholes in merchandise trade needed reforming. The most (in)famous loophole was the Multifiber Arrangement (MFA) designed to *limit* free trade in textiles, a direct violation of the letter and spirit of the GATT. Finally, although the GATT had been successful in reducing tariffs, the global recessions in the 1970s and the 1980s led many governments to invoke nontariff barriers (NTBs) such as subsidies and local content requirements (see Chapter 5). Unlike tariff barriers, which were relatively easy to verify and challenge, NTBs were more subtle but pervasive, thus triggering a growing number of trade disputes. The GATT, however, lacked effective dispute resolution mechanisms. Therefore, at the end of the Uruguay Round in 1994, participating countries agreed to upgrade the GATT and launch the WTO.

8-2b World Trade Organization: 1995–Present

Established on January 1, 1995, the WTO is the GATT's successor. This transformation turned the GATT from a provisional treaty serviced by an *ad hoc* secretariat to a full-fledged international organization headquartered in Geneva, Switzerland. Significantly

Multilateral trading system The global system that governs international trade among countries—otherwise known as the GATT/WTO system.

Non-discrimination A principle that a country cannot discriminate among its trading partners.

broader in scope than the GATT, the WTO has several new features:

- An agreement governing the international trade of services, the **General Agreement on Trade in Services (GATS)**.
- An agreement governing IP rights, the **Trade-Related Aspects of Intellectual Property Rights (TRIPS)**.
- Trade dispute settlement mechanisms, which allow for the WTO to adjudicate trade disputes among countries in a more effective and less time-consuming way.
- Trade policy reviews, which enable the WTO and other member countries to peer review a country's trade policy.

ISTOCKPHOTO.COM CARMEN MARTÍNEZ BANÚS

8-2c Trade Dispute Settlement

One of the main objectives for establishing the WTO was to strengthen trade dispute settlement mechanisms. The old GATT mechanisms experienced long delays, blocking by accused countries, and inadequate enforcement. The WTO addresses all three of these problems. First, it sets time limits for a panel, consisting of three neutral countries as peers, to reach a judgment. Second, it removes the power of the accused countries to block any unfavorable decision. WTO decisions will be final. Third, in terms of enforcement, although the WTO has earned the nickname of "the world's supreme court in trade," it does *not* have real enforcement capability. The WTO simply recommends that the losing country change its laws or practices and authorizes the winning country to use tariff retaliation to compel the offending country to comply with the WTO rulings.

Understandably, enforcement by the WTO is controversial because the losing country experiences some loss of sovereignty. Fundamentally, a WTO ruling is a *recommendation* but not an order. No higher-level entity can order a sovereign government to do something against its wishes. In other words, the offending country retains full sovereignty in its decision whether or not to implement a WTO recommendation. Because the WTO has no real power to enforce its rulings, a country that has lost a dispute case can choose from one of two options: change its laws or practices to be in compliance or defy the ruling by doing nothing and suffer trade retaliation by the winning country known as "punitive duties." Most of the WTO's trade dispute rulings, however, are resolved without resorting to trade retaliation. This suggests that—per Proposition 1 in the institution-based view (see Chapter 2)—most member countries have reached a *rational* decision that after losing a case, being in (often painful) compliance with a WTO decision has more benefits than "rocking the boat."

8-2d The Doha Round—"The Doha Development Agenda"

The **Doha Round** was the only round of trade negotiations sponsored by the WTO. In 1999, a WTO meeting in Seattle intended to start a new round of trade talks was not only devastated by 30,000 protesters, but was also derailed by significant differences between developed and developing countries. Undeterred by the backlash, member countries went ahead to launch a new round in Doha, Qatar, in November 2001.

The Doha Round was significant for two reasons. First, it was launched in the aftermath of the 9/11 attacks. Members had a strong resolve to make free trade work around the globe in order to defeat the terrorist agenda to divide and terrorize the world. Second, this was the first round in the history of GATT/WTO to specifically aim at promoting economic development in developing countries. Consequently, the official title of the Doha Round was the "Doha Development Agenda." Doha was ambitious: it would (1) reduce agricultural subsidies in developed countries to facilitate exports from developing countries; (2) slash tariffs, especially in industries that developing countries might benefit (such as textiles); (3) free up trade in services; and (4) strengthen IP protection. In the Doha Round, *not* all meetings were held in Doha. Subsequent meetings took place in locations such as Bali, Indonesia; Cancun, Mexico; Geneva, Switzerland; and Hong Kong, China.

Unfortunately, numerous countries failed to deliver on promises made in Doha. The "hot potato" turned out to

General Agreement on Trade in Services (GATS) A WTO agreement governing the international trade of services.

Trade-Related Aspects of Intellectual Property Rights (TRIPS) A WTO agreement governing intellectual property rights.

Doha Round A round of WTO negotiations to reduce agricultural subsidies, slash tariffs, and strengthen intellectual property protection that started in Doha, Qatar, in 2001. Officially known as the "Doha Development Agenda," it was suspended in 2006 due to disagreements.

be agriculture. Australia, Argentina, and most developing countries demanded that Japan, the EU, and the United States reduce farm subsidies. Japan rejected any proposal to cut rice tariffs. The EU refused to significantly reduce farm subsidies. The United States actually *increased* farm subsidies. On the other hand, many developing countries, led by India, refused to tighten IP protection, citing their needs for cheap generic drugs to combat diseases such as HIV/AIDS. Overall, developing countries refused to offer concessions in IP and service trade in part because of the failure of Japan, the EU, and the United States to reduce farm subsidies.

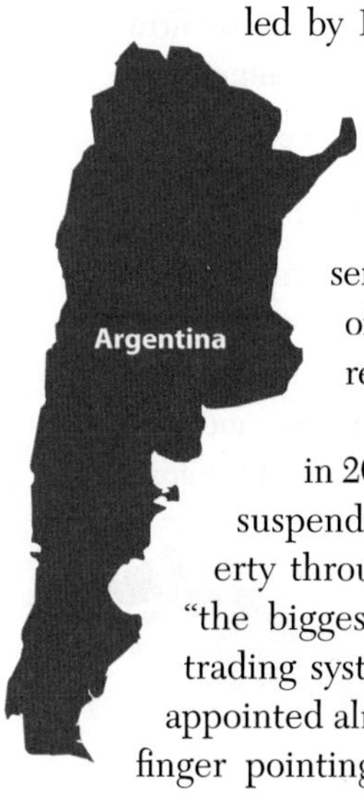

Eventually, at the Geneva meeting in 2006, the Doha Round was thus officially suspended. Hopes of lifting millions out of poverty through free trade were derailed. Labeled "the biggest threat to the postwar (multilateral) trading system" by the *Economist*,[2] the fiasco disappointed almost every country involved. Naturally, finger pointing started immediately. To be fair, no country was totally responsible for the collapse of the Doha Round, and all members collectively were culpable. The sheer complexity of reaching an agreement on "everything" among 153 member countries (in 2006) was simply mind boggling.

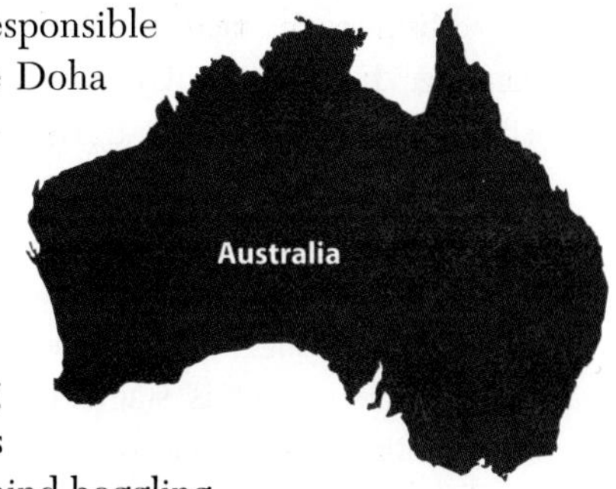

What happens next? Officially, Doha was "suspended" but not "terminated" or "dead." Members repeatedly tried again but failed again. Most recently in 2013 in Bali, Indonesia, 159 members finally struck a trade facilitation agreement (TFA)—a pledge to cut red tape at customs posts in all countries. Although the TFA was far narrower and less ambitious than the sweeping deal envisioned when Doha was first launched, it was viewed as Doha's first big win. Unfortunately in 2014, the TFA collapsed. This was because India withdrew its support. The "hot potato" again turned out to be food subsidies (see Debate).

Debate: *Emerging Markets/Ethical Dilemma*

Food Versus Trade

In December 2013 in Bali, Indonesia, 159 members of the WTO struck a trade facilitation agreement (TFA)—a pledge to cut red tape at customs posts around the world. This would be the only tangible achievement of the Doha Round, which was launched in 2001. Limited in scope, the deal would simplify customs red tape rather than tackling the far thornier problem of agricultural subsidies and intellectual property. Still, it would add up to $400 billion a year to a struggling global economy.

Unfortunately, in July 2014, the TFA collapsed. This was because India withdrew its support. The "hot potato" again turned out to be food subsidies. India, like many developing countries, strengthened "food security" policies (a euphemism for agricultural subsidies) in response to recent swings in food prices. Such subsidies would soon grow large enough to violate WTO rules, which dictate that no developing country could subsidize more than 10% of the total value of harvests to farmers. Already spending $19 billion (1% of GDP) on such subsidiaries, India is likely to exceed the 10% limit in the near future. When that happens, India could be subject to a WTO challenge. While the Bali deal was signed by a previous government, the new Narendra Modi administration, elected into power in early 2014, insisted that it would not sacrifice food security on the altar of global trade. Even the WTO's efforts to let India have four extra years (until 2017) of immunity from challenge were not viewed to be good enough. In other words, India would not trade food for trade.

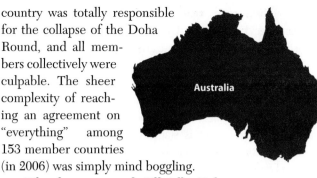

OLGA MILTSOVA/SHUTTERSTOCK.COM

India is hardly the only protectionist country when it comes to agricultural subsidies. According to the *Economist*, "the rich countries are the worst culprits." Japanese rice and sugar tariffs are, respectively, 778% and 328%. The EU dishes out 40% of its budget to farmers. But, by giving up the gains from more smooth trade, India is also hurting itself. Its massive food subsidies lead to huge stockpiles of unwanted, rotting produce and fan corruption. In the end, with Doha dead (technically "suspended") and Bali (a subset of Doha) scuttled, the WTO had no concrete deal to show when it celebrated its 20th anniversary in 2015.

Sources: "The Indian problem," *Economist*, 23 November 2013, 17; "Unaccustomed victory," *Economist*, 14 December 2013, 78; "Bailing out from Bali," *Economist*, 9 August 2014, 58–59; "No more grand bargains," *Economist*, 9 August 2014, 10.

Multilateral trade negotiations are notoriously challenging.[3] In 1990, the Uruguay Round of the GATT was similarly suspended, only to rise again in 1994 with a far-reaching agreement that launched the WTO. Whether history will repeat itself remains to be seen. On the other hand, although global deals may be hard to do, regional deals are moving "at twice the speed and with half the fuss."[4] The upshot is stagnation of multilateralism and acceleration of regionalism—a topic to which we turn next.

8-3 INTEGRATING REGIONAL ECONOMIES

There is now a proliferation of regional trade deals. All WTO members but one, Mongolia, are involved in some regional trade arrangement. This section first introduces the benefits for regional economic integration and discusses its major types.

8-3a The Pros and Cons of Regional Economic Integration

Similar to global economic integration, the benefits of regional economic integration center on both political and economic dimensions (see Exhibit 8.1). Politically, regional economic integration promotes peace by fostering closer economic ties and building confidence. Only in the last seven decades did the Europeans break away from their centuries-old habit of war and violence among themselves. A leading cause of this dramatic behavioral change is economic integration. In addition, regional integration enhances the collective political weight of a region, which has also helped fuel postwar European integration, particularly when dealing with superpowers such as the United States.

Economically, the three benefits associated with regional economic integration are similar to those associated with global economic integration (see Exhibit 8.1). First, disputes are handled constructively. Second, consistent rules make life easier and discrimination impossible for participating countries within one region. Third, free trade and investment raise incomes and stimulate economic growth.[5]

Free trade area (FTA) A group of countries that remove trade barriers among themselves.

Customs union One step beyond a free trade area, a customs union imposes common external policies on non-participating countries.

Common market Combining everything a customs union has, a common market additionally permits the free movement of goods and people.

Economic union Having all the features of a common market, members also coordinate and harmonize economic policies (in areas such as monetary, fiscal, and taxation) to blend their economies into a single economic entity.

However, not everything is rosy in regional integration. A case can be made *against* it. Politically, regional integration is centered on preferential treatments for firms within a region, leading to discrimination against firms outside a region and thus undermining global integration. Of course, in practice, global deals such as Doha are so challenging to accomplish that regional deals emerge as realistic alternatives. Economically, regional integration may result in some loss of sovereignty. For example, the 18 EU members adopting the euro can no longer implement independent monetary policies (see the Closing Case).

The simultaneous existence of both pros and cons means that some countries are cautious about joining regional economic integration. Norway and Switzerland chose not to join the EU. Even when countries are part of a regional deal, they sometimes choose not to participate in some areas. For example, three EU members—Britain, Denmark, and Sweden—refused to adopt the euro. Overall, different levels of enthusiasm call for different types of regional economic integration, which are outlined next.

8-3b Types of Regional Economic Integration

Exhibit 8.2 shows five main types of regional economic integration. A **free trade area (FTA)** is a group of countries that remove trade barriers among themselves. One of the newest examples is the Eurasian Union consisting of Belarus, Kazakhstan, and Russia, which was created in 2014. In an FTA, each member still maintains different external policies regarding nonmembers. For example, three NAFTA members have each pursued *different* FTA agreements with the EU.

A **customs union** is one step beyond an FTA. In addition to all the arrangements of an FTA, a customs union imposes common external policies on nonparticipants. Two examples are Andean Community and Mercosur in South America.

A **common market** has everything a customs union has, but also permits the free movement of goods and people. Today's EU used to be a common market. An **economic union** has all the features of a common

EXHIBIT 8.2 TYPES OF REGIONAL ECONOMIC INTEGRATION

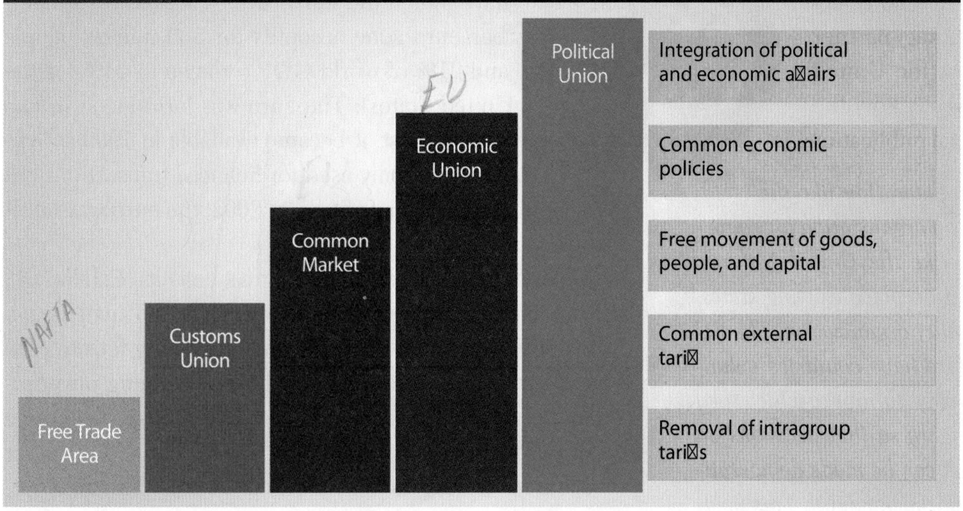

market, but members also coordinate and harmonize economic policies (monetary, fiscal, and taxation) in order to blend their economies into a single economic entity. Today's EU is an economic union. One possible dimension of an economic union is to establish a **monetary union**, which has been accomplished by 18 EU members through the adoption of the euro (see the next section).

A **political union** is the integration of political and economic affairs of a region. The United States and the former Soviet Union are two examples. The EU at present is not a political union. Overall, each of these five major types is an intensification of the level of regional economic integration from the one before. Next, we look at concrete examples of these arrangements.

8-4 REGIONAL ECONOMIC INTEGRATION IN EUROPE

At present, the most ambitious economic integration takes place in Europe. This section (1) outlines its origin and evolution, (2) introduces its current structure, and (3) discusses its challenges.

8-4a Origin and Evolution

Although European economic integration is now noted for its economic benefits, its origin was political in nature. In an effort to stop the vicious cycle of hatred and violence, Belgium, France, (West) Germany, Italy, Luxembourg, and the Netherlands in 1951 signed the European Coal and Steel Community (ECSC) Treaty, which was the first step toward what is now the EU. There was a good reason for the six founding members and the two industries to be involved. France and Germany were the main combatants in both WWI and WWII (and major previous European wars), each having lost millions of soldiers and civilians. Reflecting the public mood, statesmen in both countries realized that such killing needed to stop. Italy always had the misfortune of being dragged along and devastated whenever France and Germany went to war. The three small countries known as Benelux (Belgium, the Netherlands, and Luxembourg) had the unfortunate geographic location of being sandwiched between France and Germany, and were usually wiped out when France and Germany slugged it out. Naturally, Italy and Benelux would be happy to do anything to stop France and Germany from fighting again. Also, the industry focus on coal and steel was not an accident. These industries traditionally supplied the raw materials for war. Integrating them might help prevent future hostilities from breaking out.

In 1957, six member countries of ECSC signed the Treaty of Rome, which launched the European Economic Community (EEC)—later known as the European Community (EC). Starting as an FTA, the EEC/EC progressed to become a customs union and eventually a common market. In 1991, 12 member countries signed the Treaty on European Union in Maastricht, the Netherlands (in short, the "Maastricht Treaty") to complete the single market and establish an economic union. The title the "European Union" (EU) was officially adopted in 1993 when the Maastricht Treaty went into effect. Recently, the Lisbon Treaty, signed in 2007 and enacted in 2009, amended the Maastricht Treaty that served as a constitutional basis for the EU.

8-4b The EU Today

Headquartered in Brussels, Belgium, today's EU (see PengAtlas Map 9) has 28 member countries, 500 million citizens, and $18 trillion GDP. Contributing about 26% of the world's GDP, the

Monetary union A group of countries that use a common currency.

Political union The integration of political and economic affairs of a region.

ISTOCKPHOTO.COM/HENRIK5000

EU is the world's largest economy, the largest exporter and importer of goods and services, and the largest trading partner with major economies such as the United States, China, and India. Here is how the EU describes itself in an official publication:

The European Union is not a federation like the United States. Nor is it simply an organization for cooperation between governments, like the United Nations. Neither is it a state intended to replace existing states, but it is much more than any other organization. The EU is, in fact, unique. Never before have countries voluntarily agreed to set up common institutions to which they delegate some of their sovereignty so that decisions on specific matters of joint interest can be made democratically at a higher, in this case European, level. This pooling of sovereignty is called "European integration."[6]

The EU today is an economic union. Internal trade barriers have been mostly removed. In aviation, the EU now has a single market, which means all European carriers compete on equal terms across the EU (including domestic routes in a foreign country). US airlines are not allowed to fly between pairs of cities within Germany. However, non-German, EU airlines (such as Ireland's Ryanair) can fly between any pair of cities within Germany. On the ground, it used to take Spanish truck drivers 24 hours to cross the border into France due to paperwork and checks. Since 1992, passport and customs control within most (but not all) member countries of the EU has been disbanded, and checkpoints at border crossings are no longer manned. The area covered by EU countries became known as the **Schengen** passport-free travel zone, named after Schengen, Luxembourg, where the agreement was signed in 1985. Now, Spanish trucks can move from Spain to France non-stop, similar to how American trucks go from Texas to Oklahoma. At present, 22 of the 28 EU member countries are in the Schengen zone. Six other members are not yet in: Britain and Ireland chose to opt out, and four new members—Bulgaria, Cyprus, Romania, and Slovenia—have yet to meet requirements. (Interestingly, three non-EU member countries—Iceland, Norway, and Switzerland—are also in the Schengen area.)

Schengen A passport-free travel zone within the EU.

Euro The currency currently used in 18 EU countries.

Euro zone The 18 EU countries that currently use the euro as the official currency.

As an economic union, one of the EU's proudest accomplishments—but also one of its most significant headaches—is the introduction of a common currency, the **euro**, initially in 12 of the EU 15 countries. Since then, six more countries have joined the **euro zone**. Today, the 18-member euro zone accounts for 330 million people and 21% of world GDP (relative to 24% for the United States). The euro was introduced in two phases. First, it became available in 1999 as "virtual money" only used for financial transactions but not in circulation. Second, in 2002, the euro was introduced as banknotes and coins.

Adopting the euro has three great benefits (Exhibit 8.3). First, it reduces currency conversion costs. Travelers and businesses no longer need to pay processing fees to convert currencies for tourist activities or hedging purposes (see Chapter 7). Second, direct and transparent price comparison is now possible, thus channeling more resources toward more competitive firms. Third, adopting the euro imposes strong macroeconomic discipline. Prior to adopting the euro, different governments independently determined exchange rates. Italy, for example, sharply devalued its lira in the 1990s. While Italian exports became cheaper and more competitive, other EU members (especially France) were furious. But Italy can no longer devalue its currency, although it has been engulfed in an economic crisis. Also, when confronting recessions, governments often printed more currency and increased spending. Such actions cause inflation, which may spill over to neighboring countries. By adopting the euro, euro zone countries agreed to abolish monetary policy (such as manipulating exchange rates and printing more currency) as a tool to solve macroeconomic problems. These efforts in theory would provide macroeconomic stability. Overall, the euro has boosted intra-EU trade by about 10%. Commanding a quarter of global foreign currency reserves, the euro has quickly established itself as the only credible rival to the dollar.

However, there are also significant costs involved. The first, noted above, is the loss of ability to implement independent monetary policy. Since 2008, economic life

ISTOCKPHOTO.COM/ABABSOLUTUM

EXHIBIT 8.3 BENEFITS AND COSTS OF ADOPTING THE EURO

Benefits	Costs
Reduces currency conversion costs	Unable to implement independent monetary policy
Facilitates direct price comparison	Limits the flexibility in fiscal policy (in areas such as deficit spending)
Imposes monetary disciplines on governments	

ISTOCKPHOTO.COM/ZORAN KOLUNDZIJA

in many EU countries without the option of devaluation is tough. The possibility of leaving the euro zone has surfaced in public discussion in some countries. The second cost is the lack of flexibility in implementing fiscal policy in areas such as deficit spending. When a country runs into fiscal difficulties, it may be faced with inflation, high interest rates, and a run on its currency. When a number of countries share a common currency, the risks are spread. But some countries can become "free riders," because they may not need to fix their own fiscal problems—other, more responsible members will have to shoulder the burden (see the Closing Case).

8-4c The EU's Challenges

Politically, the EU and its predecessors—the ECSC, the EEC, and the EC—have delivered more than 70 years of peace and prosperity and have turned some Cold War enemies into members. Although some people complain about the EU's huge expenses and bureaucratic meetings, they need to be reminded that one day spent on meetings is one day member countries are not shooting at one another. Given that most European countries, until WWII, had been involved in wars as their primary conflict resolution mechanism, negotiating to resolve differences via EU platforms is not only cheaper but also far more peaceful. For this extraordinary accomplishment, the EU—in the middle of a major economic crisis—received the Nobel *Peace* Prize in 2012.

Economically, the EU has launched a single currency and has built a single market in which people, goods, services, and capital can move freely—known as the "four freedoms of movement"—within the core Schengen area (although not throughout the entire EU). While the accomplishments are enviable in the eyes of other regional organizations, the EU has been engulfed in a midlife crisis.[7] Significant challenges lie ahead, especially in terms of (1) internal divisions and (2) enlargement concerns.

Internally, there is a significant debate on whether the EU should be an economic and political union, or just an economic union. One school of thought, led by France, argues that an economic union should inevitably evolve toward a political union, through which Europe speaks as "one voice." Its proponents frequently invoke the famous term enshrined in the 1957 Treaty of Rome, "ever closer union."[8] Another school of thought, led by Britain, views the EU as primarily an economic union, which should focus on free trade, pure and simple.

The 2010–2012 bailouts to rescue Greece (and Ireland, Portugal, and Spain) have intensified this debate. While Germany reluctantly agreed to lead bailout efforts, Germany demanded that the EU-wide "economic governance" be strengthened, and that insolvent countries have to lose some of their economic sovereignty by having their budgets approved (or vetoed) by the EU. While this is viewed as a step toward closer political union, Gemany does not share France's political motivation for an "ever closer union." In fact the German media has called for Germany to withdraw from the euro zone in order to avoid the burden of paying for other countries' problems. However, abandoning the euro is not realistic for Germany. Germany ends up being a "reluctant hegemon" (see the Closing Case).

Britain, on the other hand, has seen its influence reduced. In 2011, Britain vetoed a new treaty supported by 26 EU members to enhance the "economic governance" for the euro zone. All EU treaties had to be signed off by *all* members—in this case, for a treaty on the euro zone governance, even members that did not use the euro (such as Britain) had to sign off. Thus, Britain's veto torpedoed the whole treaty, causing an uproar throughout the EU. Other EU members were forced to seek a separate pact to enforce greater fiscal discipline, which could be done despite the British veto. In 2013, British Prime Minister David Cameron announced that he would put the UK membership in the EU for a referendum by 2017. While his "bulldog spirit" won praise from Britain's Eurosceptics crowd, he was "gambling with his country's future."[9] Other EU leaders were infuriated, because Cameron was reigniting old debates settled through compromise a long time—in the 1970s, Britain's decision to join the EEC was itself the result of a referendum. As a real winner, France can now secure "a long-cherished French ambition: an agreement on holding frequent summits of EU leaders from an inner core of countries, excluding Britain."[10] Britain then finds it has little influence or leverage in further deliberations within the EU.

There are also significant concerns associated with enlargement. The EU's largest expansion took place in 2004, with ten new members. Eight of them—the Czech Republic, Estonia, Hungary, Latvia, Lithuania, Poland, Slovakia, and Slovenia—were former eastern bloc Central and Eastern Europe (CEE) countries. Three of these—Estonia, Latvia, and Lithuania—had previously been part of the Soviet Union. Such expansion was a political triumph, but it was also an economic burden. The ten new members constituted 20% of the overall population but contributed only 9% to GDP and had an average GDP per capita that was 46% of the average for the (pre-2004) EU 15. In 2007, Bulgaria and Romania joined and brought the average down further. In 2013, Croatia joined. With low growth and high unemployment throughout the EU and severe economic crisis in the so-called PIGS (Portugal, Ireland/Italy, Greece, and Spain) countries, many EU citizens are tired of taking on additional burdens to absorb new members. Many EU 15 countries have restricted immigration from these new members.

Another major debate regarding enlargement is Turkey, whose average income is even lower. In addition, its large Muslim population is also a concern for a predominantly Christian EU. If Turkey were to join, its population of 73 million would make it the second most populous EU country behind only Germany, whose population is 83 million now (but is declining). The weight of EU countries in voting is based (mostly) on population. Given the current demographic trends (high birth rates in Turkey and low birth rates in Germany and other EU countries), if Turkey were to join the EU, by 2020 it would become the most populous and thus the most powerful member by commanding most significant voting power. Turkey's combination of low incomes, high birthrates, and Muslim majority visibly concern current member countries, especially given the history of Christian–Muslim tension in Europe.

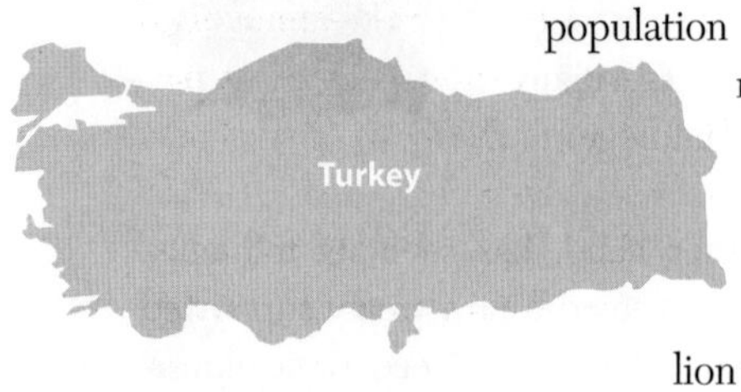

Since 2008, the EU's challenges were magnified. A total of eight members were engulfed in embarrassing financial crises that had to be bailed out by other members (and the International Monetary Fund [IMF]): Hungary (2008), Lativia (2008), Romania (2009), Greece (2010, 2011, 2012), Ireland (2010), Portugal (2011), Cyprus (2011), and Spain (2012). Not surprisingly, Germany and other relatively well off EU countries, in the middle of their own Great Recession, were reluctant to foot the bill to bail out other countries. While each crisis was painful in its own ways, the Greek crisis was particularly gut-wrenching, resulting in calls for Greece to exit or to be expelled (a "Grexit" scenario) (see the Closing Case). In addition, in 2014, with Russia's intervention in Ukraine, the EU felt compelled to join the US-led sanctions on Russia, inflicting economic wounds on itself by abandoning hard-to-win markets in Russia (see Chapter 2 Closing Case).

Overall, we can view the EU enlargement as a miniature version of globalization, and the "enlargement fatigue" as part of the recent backlash against globalization. Given the accomplishments and challenges, what does the future of the EU hold? One possible scenario is that there will be an "EU à la carte," where different members pick and choose certain mechanisms to join and other mechanisms to opt out of. Seeking consensus among 28 members during negotiations may be simply impractical. If every country's representative were to spend ten minutes on opening remarks, *nearly five hours* would be gone before discussions even begin. The translation and interpretation among the 23 official languages now cost the EU €1.1 billion ($1.4 billion) per year.[11] Since not every country needs to take part in everything, ad hoc groupings of member countries with similar interests are increasingly common, and discussions are more efficient.

8-5 REGIONAL ECONOMIC INTEGRATION IN THE AMERICAS

8-5a North America: North American Free Trade Agreement (NAFTA)

NAFTA is an FTA among Canada, Mexico, and the United States. Launched in 1994, NAFTA has no shortage of hyperbole and controversy. Because of the very different levels of economic development, NAFTA was labeled "one of the most radical free trade experiments in history."[12] Politically, the Mexican government was interested in cementing market liberalization reforms by demonstrating its commitment to free trade. Economically, Mexico was interested in securing preferential treatment for 80% of its exports. Consequently, by the stroke of a pen, Mexico declared itself a *North* American country. Many Americans, on the other hand, thought it was not the best time to open the borders, as the US unemployment rate was 7% at that time. Texas billionaire H. Ross Perot, a presidential candidate in 1992, described NAFTA's potential destruction of thousands of US jobs as a "giant sucking sound."

As NAFTA celebrated its 20th anniversary in 2014, NAFTA's supporters largely won the argument. In two decades, trilateral merchandise trade grew from $289 billion in 1993 to $1.1 trillion—a nearly fourfold increase. Approximately $1.8 billion in goods and services cross the border every day—$1.2 million every *minute*.[13] US trade with Canada tripled and US trade with Mexico increased by 506%—while US trade with the rest of the world grew 279%. In two decades, Mexico's GDP per capita almost tripled to $10,650 (ranked 64th in the world, based on nominal GDP)—over 40% higher than China's $7,000. While many Americans and Canadians think of Mexicans as "poor" and "infested with crimes"—thanks to the negative (and typically one-sided) media—Mexico is the second largest importer of US goods (next only to Canada), imports more US goods than China, and absorbs more US exports than Britain, France, and Germany combined.[14] Running the 14th largest economy in the world with a number of advanced manufacturing industries such as automobile, pharmaceuticals, and aerospace (see the Opening Case), Mexico, according to the *Economist*, has been "NAFTA's biggest beneficiary."[15]

What about jobs? In brief, job destruction on a large scale never materialized. *Maquiladora* (export assembly) factories blossomed under NAFTA, with jobs peaking at 1.3 million in 2000. Yet, no "giant sucking sound" was heard. Approximately 300,000 US jobs were lost due to NAFTA, but about 100,000 jobs were added. The net loss was small, since the US economy generated 20 million new jobs during the first decade of NAFTA. A hard count on jobs misses another subtle, but important, benefit. NAFTA has allowed US firms to *preserve* more US jobs, because 40% of the value of US imports from Mexico and 25% from Canada is actually made in USA—in comparison, only 10% of the value of US imports from China is made in USA. Without NAFTA, entire industries might be lost rather than just the labor-intensive portions.

As NAFTA celebrated its 20th anniversary, not all was rosy. Opponents of globalization in both Canada and the United States no longer focus on the negative impact of competition from Mexico but rather on China and India. Despite the impressive gains in their country, many Mexicans feel betrayed by NAFTA. Thanks to Chinese competition, many US, Canadian, European, and Japanese multinationals have shifted some of their factory work to China, which has now replaced Mexico as the second largest exporter to the United States (after Canada).[16] About 1,000 *maquiladora* factories have closed down since 2000. But rising wages in China and high fuel costs have recently led some multinationals to relocate back to Mexico.

ISTOCKPHOTO.COM/HENRIK5000

8-5b South America: Andean Community, Mercosur, USAN/UNASUR, and CAFTA

Despite NAFTA's imperfections, it is much more effective than the two customs unions in South America: **Andean Community** and **Mercosur**. Members of Andean Community (launched in 1969) and Mercusor (launched in 1991) are mostly countries on the *western* (Pacific-facing) and *eastern* (Atlantic-facing) sides of the Andean mountains, respectively (see PengAtlas Map 10). There is much mutual suspicion and rivalry between both organizations as well as within each of them. Mercosur is relatively more protectionist and suspicious of the United States, whereas Andean Community is more pro-free trade.

Neither regional initiative has been effective, in part because only about 5% and 20% of members' trade is within the Andean Community and Mercosur, respectively. Their largest trading partner, the United States, lies outside the region. An FTA with the United States, not among themselves, would generate the most significant benefits. For this reason, Chile, Colombia, Panama, and Peru signed bilateral FTAs with the United States, and reaped the benefits of higher economic growth than other countries.[17]

In 2008, Andean Community and Mercusur countries agreed to form the **Union of South American Nations** (**USAN**, more commonly known by its Spanish acronym, **UNASUR**, which refers to *Unión de Naciones Suramericanas*). Inspired by the EU, USAN/UNASUR announced its intention to eventually adopt a common currency, parliament, and passport. However, progress has been slow.

One regional accomplishment is the **United States–Dominican Republic–Central America Free Trade Agreement (CAFTA)**, which took effect in 2005.

ISTOCKPHOTO.COM/NIKADA

Andean Community A customs union in South America that was launched in 1969.

Mercosur A customs union in South America that was launched in 1991.

Union of South American Nations (USAN/UNASUR) A regional integration mechanism integrating two existing customs unions (Andean Community and Mercosur) in South America.

United States–Dominican Republic–Central America Free Trade Agreement (CAFTA) A free trade agreement between the United States and five Central American countries and the Dominican Republic.

Modeled after NAFTA, CAFTA is between "a whale and six minnows" (five Central American countries—Costa Rica, El Salvador, Guatemala, Honduras, and Nicaragua—plus the Dominican Republic). Although small, the six CAFTA countries collectively represent the second largest US export market in Latin America (behind only Mexico). Globally, CAFTA is the tenth largest US export market, importing more US goods than Russia, India, and Indonesia *combined*.[18]

8-6 REGIONAL ECONOMIC INTEGRATION IN THE ASIA PACIFIC

This section introduces regional integration efforts between Australia and New Zealand, in Southeast Asia, and throughout Asia and the Pacific. Their scale and scope differ from one another tremendously.

8-6a Australia–New Zealand Closer Economic Relations Trade Agreement (ANZCERTA or CER)

The **Australia–New Zealand Closer Economic Relations Trade Agreement (ANZCERTA or CER)**, launched in 1983, turned the historic rivalry between Australia and New Zealand into a partnership. As an FTA, the CER removed tariffs and NTBs. For example, both countries agreed not to charge exporters from the other country for dumping. Citizens from both countries also could freely work and reside in the other country. Thanks to the relatively high level of geographic proximity and cultural homogeneity, CER has been very successful.

Australia–New Zealand Closer Economic Relations Trade Agreement (ANZCERTA or CER) A free trade agreement between Australia and New Zealand.

Association of Southeast Asian Nations (ASEAN) The organization underpinning regional economic integration in Southeast Asia.

Asia-Pacific Economic Cooperation (APEC) The official title for regional economic integration involving 21 member economies around the Pacific.

8-6b Association of Southeast Asian Nations (ASEAN)

Founded in 1967, the **Association of Southeast Asian Nations (ASEAN)** was inspired by the EU's success. In 1992, the ASEAN Free Trade Area (AFTA) was set up. ASEAN suffers from a similar problem that Latin American countries face: ASEAN's main trading partners—the United States, the EU, Japan, and China—are outside the region. Intra-ASEAN trade usually accounts for less than a quarter of total trade. The benefits of AFTA, thus, may be limited.

In response, ASEAN in 2002 signed an ASEAN–China Free Trade Agreement (ACFTA), which was launched in 2010. Given the increasingly strong competition in terms of Chinese exports and China-bound FDI that could have come to ASEAN, ACFTA hopes to turn such rivalry into a partnership. ACFTA is estimated to boost ASEAN's exports to China by 48% and China's exports to ASEAN by 55%, thus raising ASEAN's GDP by 0.9% and China's by 0.3%. Similar FTAs are being negotiated with Japan and South Korea.

8-6c Asia-Pacific Economic Cooperation (APEC) and Trans-Pacific Partnership (TPP)

While ASEAN was deepening its integration, Australia was afraid that it might be left out and suggested in 1989 that ASEAN and CER countries form the **Asia-Pacific Economic Cooperation (APEC)**. Given the lack of a global heavyweight in both ASEAN and CER, Japan was invited. While the Japanese happily agreed to join, ASEAN and CER countries also feared that Japan might dominate the group and create a de facto "yen bloc." During WWII, Japan invaded most countries in the region, bombed Darwin and attacked Sydney harbor in Australia (see the movie *Australia*). Bitter memories of Japanese wartime atrocities seemed to die hard. At that time, China was far less significant economically than it is now, and thus could hardly counterbalance Japan.

Then the United States requested to join APEC, citing its long West Coast that would qualify it as a Pacific country. Economically, the United States did not want to be left out of the most dynamically growing region in the world. Politically, the United States was interested in containing Japanese influence in any Asian regional deals. While the United States could certainly serve as a counterweight for Japan, the US membership would also change the character of APEC, which had been centered on ASEAN and CER. To make its APEC membership less odd, the United States brought on board two of its NAFTA partners, Canada and Mexico. Canada and Mexico were equally interested in the economic benefits, but probably cared less about the US political motives. Once the floodgates for membership were open, Chile, Peru, and Russia all eventually got in, emphasizing their long Pacific coastlines.

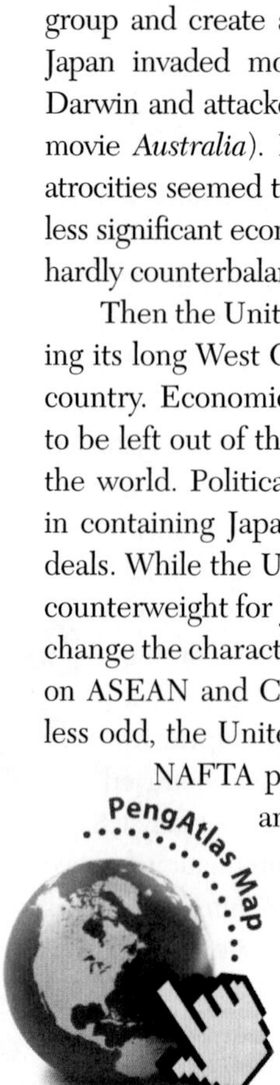

ISTOCKPHOTO.COM/HENRIK5000

Today, APEC's 21 member economies (shown in PengAtlas Map 11) span four continents, are home to 2.6 billion people, contribute 46% of world trade, and command 54% of world GDP, making it the largest regional integration grouping by geographic area and by GDP. While it is nice to include "everyone," APEC may be too big. Essentially as a talking shop, APEC (nicknamed "a perfect excuse to chat") provides a forum for members to make commitments that are largely rhetorical. In part because APEC is too big and too difficult to get anything meaningful done, a new and smaller **Trans-Pacific Partnership (TPP)** has been developing (see In Focus).

Trans-Pacific Partnership (TPP) A multilateral free trade agreement being negotiated by 12 Asia Pacific countries.

In Focus: *Ethical Dilemma*

Does the TPP Have a Future?

AP IMAGES/KIMIMASA MAYAMA

Launched in 2005 by four small member countries of APEC (Brunei, Chile, New Zealand, and Singapore), the Trans-Pacific Partnership (TPP) is a multilateral free trade agreement (FTA). A number of additional countries (all APEC members)—Australia, Canada, Malaysia, Mexico, Peru, Japan, the United States, and Vietnam—are negotiating to join the TPP. Although smaller and less complex than APEC (and certainly simpler than the WTO), the TPP talks have run into a similar bunch of problems: (1) agriculture, (2) intellectual property (IP), (3) investor-state dispute settlement (ISDS), and (4) domestic politics.

As ever, the United States and Japan fight over agricultural subsidies, especially in beef and pork—a small problem in the larger scheme of things. In the United States, less than 1% of GDP comes from beef and pork production. In Japan, a country with 46 million households, only 100,000 households are involved in the beef and pork sectors. But in October 2014, the bilateral talks collapsed. The Japanese trade minister stormed out of a working lunch, leaving only his sandwiches on the table. Ironically, on many larger issues, both countries agree with each other.

In IP, the United States has sought the TPP to agree with tighter IP protection that would go *beyond* TRIPS. This makes sense from a US standpoint. In 2010, 40% of worldwide payments made to IP rights holders—nearly $100 billion—went to Americans and American firms. These sums matched the profits from the export of aircraft, grain, and business services, the three leading US export sectors. Unfortunately, other countries are not so interested. Weaker IP protection enables faster diffusion of innovation (such as generic drugs) to less developed countries—a US practice for about 100 years in the nineteenth century when the United States was a developing country itself.

Designed to deter governments from expropriating foreign assets, ISDS allows foreign firms to launch arbitration to sue governments that allegedly deny their rights under an FTA. For example, Philip Morris sued the Australian government for its requirements for nasty pictures of lung cancer victims on cigarette packages. Lone Pine, a US firm, sued the Canadian province of Quebec for its ban on fracking. Taking the painful lesson, Australia opposes having ISDS in the TPP. In comparison, the WTO only allows national governments, not private firms, to launch such cases.

Domestic politics is messy in every country. Lacking "fast track authority" (also known as "trade promotion authority") since 2007, Presidents George W. Bush and Barack Obama cannot negotiate FTAs and then ask Congress to vote "go or no go" without the ability to amend any negotiated deals. Congressional intervention can thus be meticulous. For example, in July 2014, 140 members of the House of Representatives—107 Republicans and 33 Democrats—signed a letter demanding that Japan drop all farm tariffs; otherwise, forget about the TPP. Other countries understandably do not take US negotiators very seriously, since regardless of how the deal is reached, Congress is likely to tear it apart.

In an effort to aim for a "grand bargain," the TPP runs the risk of becoming another Doha, with endless negotiations that never reach agreement. Even if the TPP can be concluded, since all members are APEC members, what is the relationship between APEC and TPP remains to be seen. Finally, by deliberately excluding China (the second largest economy in APEC and in the world), how meaningful the TPP will become is also a huge question mark. In October 2014, at the APEC summit meeting in Beijing with Obama in attendance, Chinese President Xi Jingping openly called for the establishment of a Free Trade Area of the Asia-Pacific (FTAAP) consisting of all 21 members of APEC. Stay tuned . . .

Sources: "Trading winds," *Economist*, 19 May 2012, 50; "Stalemate," *Economist*, 4 October 2014, 47; "Bridge over troubled water," *Economist*, 15 November 2014, 15; "The Pacific age," *Economist*, 15 November 2014 (special report); B. Gordon, "Trading up in Asia," *Foreign Affairs*, July 2012, 17–22; R. Katz, 2014, "The Trans-Pacific Partnership: Lessons from negotiations," *NBR Analysis Brief*, September, Seattle: National Bureau of Asian Research; M. W. Peng, D. Ahlstrom, S. Carraher, and W. Shi, How history can inform the debate over intellectual property, working paper, Jindal School of Management, University of Texas at Dallas, 2015; US Trade Representative, "Trans-Pacific Partnership," 2014, www.ustr.gov.

8-7 MANAGEMENT SAVVY

Of the two major perspectives on global business (institution-based and resource-based views), this chapter has focused on the institution-based view. In order to address the question "What determines success and failure around the globe?" the entire chapter has been devoted to an introduction of the rules of the game as institutions governing global and regional economic integration. How does this knowledge help managers? Managers need to combine the insights from the institution-based view with those from the resource-based view to come up with strategies and solutions on how their firms can capitalize on the opportunities presented by global and regional economic integration. Listed in Exhibit 8.4, two broad implications for action emerge.

First, given the slowdown of multilateralism and the acceleration of regionalism, managers are advised to focus their attention more at regional than global levels.[19] To a large extent, they are already doing that. The largest multinational enterprises may have a presence all over the world, but their center of gravity (measured by revenues) is often still their home region (such as within the EU or NAFTA). Thus, they are not really global. Regional strategies make sense because most countries within a region share some cultural, economic, and geographic similarities that can lower the liability of foreignness when moving within the region, as opposed to moving from one region to another. From a resource-based standpoint, most firms are better prepared to compete at a regional rather than a global level.[20] Despite the hoopla associated with global strategies, managers, in short, need to think local and downplay—while not necessarily abandoning—global.

Second, managers also need to understand the rules of the game and their transitions at both global and regional levels. While trade negotiations involve a lot of politics that many managers could hardly care less about, managers who ignore these rules and their transitions do so at their own peril. When the MFA was phased out in 2005, numerous managers at textile firms, who had become comfortable under the MFA's protection, decried the new level of competition and complained about their lack of preparation. In fact, they had 30 *years* to prepare for such an eventuality. When the MFA was signed in 1974, it was agreed that it would be phased out by 2005. The typical attitude that "we don't care about (trade) politics" can lead to a failure in due diligence. The best managers expect their firm strategies to shift over time, constantly work to decipher the changes in the big picture, and are willing to take advantage of the new opportunities brought by global and regional trade deals.

EXHIBIT 8.4 IMPLICATIONS FOR ACTION

- Think regional, downplay global.
- Understand the rules of the game and their transitions at both global and regional levels.

ETHICAL DILEMMA

The German Question in the European Union

Since the German unification in 1871, the German Question has never ceased to provoke debate in Germany and beyond. The question is about the proper role of Germany, which may be too big for Europe but too small for the world—as former US Secretary of State Henry Kissinger famously put it. With the fourth largest economy in the world and the largest in Europe, today's Germany accounts for one-fifth of all EU GDP, generates a quarter of all EU exports, and possesses an enviably balanced budget. In 2013, Germany was the third largest merchandise exporter with $1.45 trillion exported (behind China and the United States) and enjoyed a record-breaking surplus ($270 billion—the highest ever in world history by any country). Strong, united, and rich, Germany is the beacon of hope

AR PICTURES/SHUTTERSTOCK.COM

for EU member countries such as Greece and Cyprus infested with unsustainable debt loads. Mean, bossy, and selfish, Germany also provokes a ton of resentment from the very countries that it has rescued. Prime Minister Angela Merkel has been portrayed as a Nazi with Hitler-style moustache in street protests and the press in Greece, Cyprus, and elsewhere. Of course, if Germany chooses not to bail out certain member countries in trouble, it would have been resented even more.

Labeled a "reluctant hegemon" by the *Economist*, Germany is reluctant to play an active leadership role. But without German leadership, practically nothing gets done in the EU. This dilemma stems from two sources. First, in terms of "do's and don'ts," German history is full of lessons of "don'ts." Even the German word for leader, *Führer*, brings up terrible memories of Nazism. Being aware of the year 2014 being the 100th anniversary of the outbreak of WWI and the 25th anniversary of the fall of the Berlin Wall, many Germans prefer their country to be a larger Switzerland: economically thriving, politically modest, and geopolitically enjoying splendid isolation.

Second, Germans, who themselves have suffered from the Great Recession since 2008, do not feel compelled to bail out others. Germany itself "bit the bullet" in the early 2000s by holding wage levels down. Since German labor costs only rose by 5% in one decade (2004–2014), the country was able to largely resist offshoring and to enhance its export competitiveness. Southern Europeans, according to Germans, got everything wrong.

Exhibit A: Greece. What led to its mess? Consumer demand increase and government spending binge fueled by the 2002 adoption of the euro and the 2004 Olympics. Excessive borrowing, budget deficits (15% of GDP), and crushing national debt (€300 billion—115% of GDP) with unserviceable payments. Widespread corruption and tax evasion. The shadow (informal) economy was estimated to be between 20% and 30% of GDP. In 2010, the Greek government had to ask for help from the EU and the IMF. "The best way to think of it is to think of Greece as a teenager," noted one expert, who continued:

> *Many Greeks view the state with a combination of a sense of entitlement, mistrust, and dislike similar to that of teenagers vis-à-vis their parents. They expect to be funded without contributing; they often act irresponsibly without care about consequences and expect to be bailed out by the state—but that only increases their sense of dependency, which only increases their feeling of dislike for the state. And, of course, they refuse to grow up. But, like every teenager, they will.*

While these comments describe the relationship between Greek citizens and the state, they also provide a great deal of insight into the relationship between Greece and the EU—in particular, Germany. But the metaphor can only go so far. At the end of the day, Germany is not Greece's parent. Although both countries belong to the "euro family," Germans are naturally furious as to why they have to foot the largest bill to bail out the profligate Greeks.

In 2010, Germany led the EU (and the IMF) rescue efforts by putting together for Greece the biggest bailout package in EU history: a €110 billion bailout loan. But in 2011, Greece came back being more broke. A larger €173 billion package was put together in 2012. Every time, the harsh medicine associated with the rescue dictated that the Greek government unleash sweeping reforms to put its financial house in order. Public sector pensions and wages were cut and value added and excise taxes raised. Unemployment rose from 8% in 2008 to a record high of 25% in 2014, while youth unemployment rose from 22% to 48%. Such shock therapy generated widespread misery and protests. There were only so many austerity measures that a frustrated and largely unemployed public (especially the youth) could take. The same drama of the Greek government begging for help, of EU governments debating what to do (with all eyes fixed on Merkel), and of the Greek public protesting in the streets unfolded again and again.

While Greece was an extreme example, it was not the only EU member requesting bailouts. Bailouts had to be dished out to Hungary (2008), Latvia (2008), Romania (2009), Ireland (2010), Portugal (2011), Cyprus (2011), and Spain (2012). The lion's share of the bailout funds would always come from Germany.

The tragedy was not only Greece's or Germany's, but also the EU's. It severely tested the logic of the euro, whose member countries are not only unequal economically, but also different in their spending and saving habits. Dumping the euro by individual countries was no longer unthinkable, but was increasingly discussed, especially since 2012. Leaving the euro zone—known as "Grexit"—would allow Greece to depreciate its own currency, which would enhance its export competitiveness. Dumping the euro would also relieve Germany's responsibility to honor an almost open-ended commitment to troubled countries. But here is the catch: A revived Deutsche mark would certainly appreciate and undermine export competitiveness. In the end, a reluctant Germany—and a reluctant EU—had little alternative.

In addition to individual bailouts, the EU in 2012 set up a €750 billion euro zone stabilization fund (including €250 billion from the IMF), which is called European Stability Mechanism (ESM). Germany, which pledged €220 billion, demanded stronger fiscal discipline in the name of better "economic governance" from all members, and threatened sanctions (such as being fined and losing voting rights) if certain members failed to apply a "debt brake." But Germany refused to let the EU to assume all sovereign debts. "Solidarity," which in EU-speak means "German cash," plays a role, but primarily as a means of buying time and encouraging reforms—not a means to encourage moral hazard. But by imposing reforms centered on spending cuts, debt reduction, and balancing budgets, Greek GDP shrank 30% since 2010 and growth was excruciatingly slow. Critics argued that such measures would prolong the recession. In 2014, the entire euro zone suffered from *deflation* where prices fell and growth became more challenging.

In 2015, a frustrated Greek public elected a new prime minister. His campaign platform was to break away from the previous governments' promises to the EU to embrace austerity. In other words, the new Greek government would challenge the EU—read "Germany"—by demanding that a large chunk of its debts be forgiven; that its citizens, especially the youth and the pensioners, be able to live in less misery; and that German (and other EU) taxpayers' euros be evaporated. Otherwise, the danger of a "Grexit" would be more likely than that in 2012. Emboldened by Greece, anti-austerity backlash in other PIGS countries is likely to challenge Germany- (and EU-) imposed austerity measures.

A physicist by training, Merkel is good at using data to make her point. She is fond of saying "7, 25, and 50." These numbers mean that the EU has 7% of the world's population, generates 25% of GDP, but consumes 50% of social spending. Clearly by spending beyond its means, the legendary European welfare state, according to Merkel, cannot sustain itself in the long run. In other words, unless the EU shapes up (and becomes like Germany), the Greek tragedy (and other tragedies) will have a bitter ending. Overall, how the German Question is answered will to a large part depend on what role Germany chooses to play in European drama such as the Greek tragedy.

Case Discussion Questions

1. Why is Germany a "reluctant hegemon" in the EU?
2. Why does Germany have to be assertive in the EU?
3. What are the benefits and costs of using a common currency for Germany, Greece, and the EU?
4. ***ON ETHICS***: While Greece needs help, the German economy has also suffered a major recession itself. As an advisor, how would you advise the chancellor: to bail out or to kick out Greece? As a German taxpayer, are you willing to pay higher taxes to help Greece?

Sources: "A more perfect union?" *Bloomberg Businessweek*, 6 December 2010, 11–12; "It's time to give Greece a break," *Bloomberg Businessweek*, 2 February 2015, 12; "Bite the bullet," *Economist*, 15 January 2011, 77–78; "Time for Plan B," *Economist*, 15 January 2011, 10; "Currency disunion," *Economist*, 7 April 2012, 65; "Tempted, Angela?" *Economist*, 11 August 2012, 9; "Don't make us *Führer*," *Economist*, 13 April 2013, 53–54; "Europe's reluctant hegemon," *Economist*, 15 June 2013, special report; "Back to reality," *Economist*, 25 October 2014, 73–74; "That sinking feeling," *Economist*, 30 August 2014, 10; "The world's biggest economic problem," *Economist*, 25 October 2014, 15; "Three illusions," *Economist*, 27 September 2014, 50; "Twenty-five years on," *Economist*, 8 November 2014, 54–55; "Go ahead, Angela, make my day," *Economist*, 31 January 2015, 9.

STUDY TOOLS 8

LOCATED AT THE BACK OF YOUR BOOK:

☐ Rip out and study the Chapter Review Card at the end of the book

LOG IN TO WWW.CENGAGEBRAIN.COM TO:

☐ Review key term flashcards

☐ Complete a practice quiz to test your knowledge of key concepts

☐ Take and complete the chapter crossword puzzle

☐ Complete interactive content, watch chapter videos, and take a graded quiz

☐ Track your knowledge of key concepts in Global Business

☐ Read and discuss additional case study content

PART 3

9 Growing & Internationalizing the Entrepreneurial Firm

JONATHAN ALCORN/REUTERS

LEARNING OBJECTIVES

After studying this chapter, you should be able to . . .

- 9-1 Define entrepreneurship, entrepreneurs, and entrepreneurial firms.
- 9-2 Identify the institutions and resources that affect entrepreneurship.
- 9-3 Highlight three characteristics of a growing entrepreneurial firm.
- 9-4 Describe how international strategies for entering foreign markets are different from those for staying in domestic markets.
- 9-5 Articulate what you should do to strengthen your entrepreneurial ability on an international level.

After you finish this chapter, go to **PAGE 147** for **STUDY TOOLS**

Sriracha Spices Up American Food

Named after a seaside city in eastern Thailand, Sriracha is a generic name for a hot sauce made from a paste of chili peppers (jalapeños), garlic, vinegar, sugar, and salt. As a dipping sauce, Sriracha has been used in Thai and Vietnamese cuisine for ages. However, in the United States, most people would associate Sriracha with the specific brand produced by Huy Fong Foods, based in Irwindale (a suburb of Los Angeles), California. It is indeed Huy Fong's Sriracha Hot Chili Sauce—often affectionately called the "rooster sauce" due to the prominent logo of the rooster on its squeeze bottle—that has popularized this once niche food and spiced up mainstream American taste buds. So what exactly is Sriracha? What does it do? Huy Fong's website has provided an official answer:

> *Sriracha is made from sun ripen chilies which are ground into a smooth paste along with garlic and packaged in a convenient squeeze bottle. It is excellent in soups, sauces, pastas, pizzas, hot dogs, hamburgers, chow mein, or anything else to give it a delicious, spicy taste.*

Founded in 1980 by a Vietnamese-Chinese immigrant David Tran, the firm was named after the freighter, *Huy Fong*, that carried him to the land of opportunity. Tran was born and raised in Vietnam. Already an entrepreneur back in Vietnam, he had a small business making a similar hot sauce there in the 1970s. But the Vietnam War made growth impossible. After the war, the Vietnamese government gave ethnic Chinese businessmen like Tran a hard time. In 1979, he left Vietnam. As a serial entrepreneur, Tran looked for opportunities in his new country. He quickly discovered that (in his view) there was no decent spicy food in the United States. Having identified this gap, he endeavored to fill it by making hot sauce again. By 1983, he came up with the winning recipe that has not changed much since.

Distinguished by a green cap and a clear plastic squeeze bottle, Huy Fong's Sriracha was first sold to Asian supermarkets and restaurants. While popular in the Asian community, Sriracha remained a niche product hardly noticed by mainstream America. Over time, the burgeoning Asian population in the United States made crossover into the mainstream possible. Sriracha created quite a sensation. In 2003, Walmart started selling it in its stores in Los Angeles and Houston. Eventually, Walmart would carry it in its more than 3,000 stores across the nation. Various restaurants, such as Applebee's, P. F. Chang's, Subway, and White Castle, introduced Sriracha-flavored dishes and dipping sauces. Potato chip king Lay's unleashed a sriracha-flavored potato chip. In 2010, *Bob Appétit*—an influential foodie magazine—named it Ingredient of the Year. In 2011, its first mainstream, kitchen bible, *The Sriracha Cookbook*, was published by Randy Clemens. In 2012, *Cook's Illustrated* claimed Sriracha to be the best-tasting hot sauce, ahead of rivals such as Tobasco, Colula Hot Sauce, and Frank's Red Hot. While focusing on the United States, Sriracha has been exported to many countries around the world.

Sriracha's success has not only inspired a number of imitators and counterfeiters (!), but has also caught the attention of McIlhenny Co., the maker of the standard-bearer of American hot sauce, Tobasco, for the past 160 years. McIlhenny Co. used to dismiss Sriracha as "a West Coast thing." But now Paul McIlhenny, its sixth-generation CEO, can pick up a bottle of rooster sauce at his local Walmart in rural Louisiana. In response, a Tobasco-version of Sriracha will be unleashed soon. Given such strong incumbents and a crowded field, what is Sriracha's secret? Again, Huy Fong's website has provided an official answer: "The secret? Continued high quality ingredients at low prices and great taste makes it a success in today's trend toward spicy foods."

Sources: "Burning sensation: How Sriracha hot sauce won the American kitchen," *Bloomberg Businessweek*, 21 February 2013, 67–69; www.huyfong.com; www.tobasco.com.

How do entrepreneurial firms such as Huy Fong grow? How do they enter international markets? What are the challenges and constraints they face? This chapter deals with these important questions. This is different from many international business (IB) textbooks that typically only cover large firms. To the extent that *every* large firm today started small and that some (although not all) of today's **small and medium-sized enterprises (SMEs)** may become tomorrow's multinational enterprises (MNEs), current and would-be managers will not gain a complete picture of the global business landscape if they only focus on large firms. SMEs are firms with fewer than 500 employees in the United States and with fewer than 250 employees in the European Union (other countries may have different definitions). Most students will join SMEs for employment. Some will also start up SMEs, thus further necessitating our attention on these numerous "Davids" (such as Huy Fong) instead of on the smaller number of "Goliaths."

Small and medium-sized enterprise (SME) A firm with fewer than 500 employees in the United States or with fewer than 250 employees in the European Union.

This chapter will first define entrepreneurship. Next, we will outline how our two leading perspectives—institution-based and resource-based views—shed light on entrepreneurship. Then, we will introduce the characteristics of a growing entrepreneurial firm and multiple ways to internationalize. In addition, you will encounter a debate about a growing entrepreneurial phenomenon: bankruptcy. Do's and don'ts follow.

LISE GAGNE/GETTY IMAGES

9-1 ENTREPRENEURSHIP AND ENTREPRENEURIAL FIRMS

Although entrepreneurship is often associated with smaller and younger firms, no rule bans larger and older firms from being entrepreneurial. So what exactly is entrepreneurship? Recent research suggests that firm size and age are *not* defining characteristics of entrepreneurship. Instead, **entrepreneurship** is defined as "the identification and exploitation of previously unexplored opportunities."[1] Specifically, it is concerned with "the sources of opportunities; the processes of discovery, evaluation, and exploitation of opportunities; and the set of individuals who discover, evaluate, and exploit them."[2] French in origin, the word "entrepreneurs" traditionally means intermediaries connecting others.[3] Today, **entrepreneurs** are founders and owners of new businesses or managers of existing firms, and **international entrepreneurship** is defined as "a combination of innovative, proactive, and risk-seeking behavior that crosses national borders and is intended to create wealth in organizations."[4]

Entrepreneurship The identification and exploitation of previously unexplored opportunities.

Entrepreneur Founders and owners of new businesses or managers of existing firms who identify and exploit new opportunities.

International entrepreneurship A combination of innovative, proactive, and risk-seeking behavior that crosses national borders and is intended to create wealth in organizations.

Although SMEs are not the exclusive domain of entrepreneurship, many people often associate entrepreneurship with SMEs because, on average, SMEs tend to be more entrepreneurial than large firms. To minimize confusion, the remainder of this chapter will follow that convention, although it is not totally accurate. That is, while we acknowledge that managers at large firms can be entrepreneurial, we will limit the use of the term "entrepreneurs" to owners, founders, and managers of SMEs. Further, we will use the term "entrepreneurial firms" when referring to SMEs. We will refer to non-SMEs (which are firms with more than 500 employees in the United States or firms with more than 250 employees in the European Union) as "large firms."

SMEs are important. Worldwide, they account for over 95% of the number of firms, create approximately 50% of total value added, and generate 60% to 90% of employment, depending on the country. Many entrepreneurs will try, and many SMEs will fail. Only a small number of entrepreneurs and SMEs will succeed.

9-2 INSTITUTIONS, RESOURCES, AND ENTREPRENEURSHIP

Shown in Exhibit 9.1, both the institution-based view and the resource-based view shed light on entrepreneurship. In this section, we will look at how institutions constrain or facilitate entrepreneurs and how firm-specific (and in many cases entrepreneur-specific) resources and capabilities determine their success and failure.

9-2a Institutions and Entrepreneurship

First introduced in Chapters 2 and 3, both formal and informal institutional constraints, as rules of the game, affect entrepreneurship.[5] The Opening Case illustrates how Vietnam's entrepreneur-hostile institutional framework drove away David Tran, and how the US entrepreneur-friendly institutional framework has offered rich soil on which his entrepreneurial firm Huy Fong Foods blossoms.

EXHIBIT 9.1 INSTITUTIONS, RESOURCES, AND ENTREPRENEURSHIP

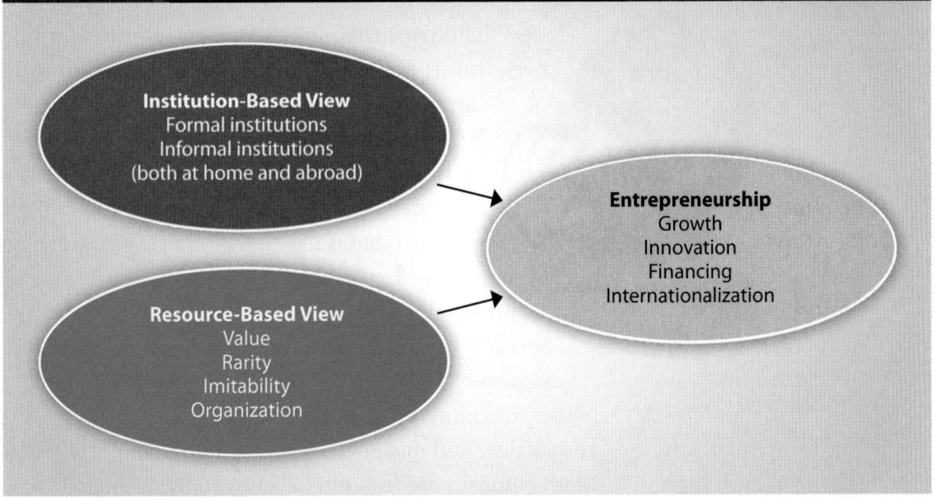

Although entrepreneurship is thriving around the globe in general, its development is unequal.[6] Whether entrepreneurship is facilitated or retarded significantly depends on formal institutions governing how entrepreneurs start up new firms.[7] A World Bank survey, *Doing Business*, reports some striking differences in government regulations concerning how easy it is to start up new entrepreneurial firms in terms of registration, licensing, and incorporation (Exhibit 9.2). Using the relatively straightforward (or even "mundane") task of connecting electricity to a newly built commercial building, the World Bank finds that in general, governments in developed economies impose fewer procedures (an average of 4.6 procedures for OECD high-income countries) and a lower total cost (free in Japan and 5.1% of per capita GDP in Germany). On the other hand, entrepreneurs have to put up with harsher hurdles in poor countries. As a class of its own, Burundi imposes a total cost of 430 times of its per capita GDP for entrepreneurs to obtain electricity. Sierra Leone leads the world in requiring entrepreneurs to spend 441 days to obtain electricity.

EXHIBIT 9.2 AVERAGE RANKING ON THE EASE OF DOING BUSINESS

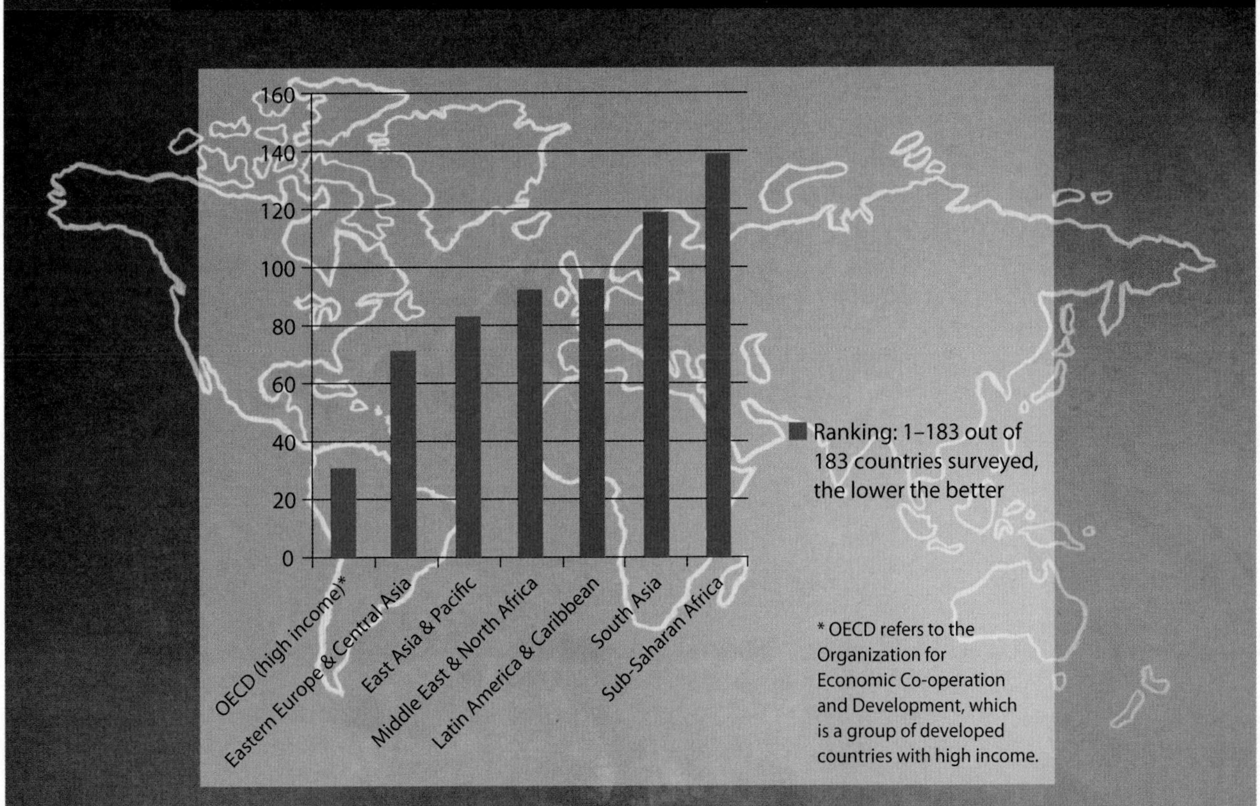

Source: Data extracted from the World Bank, 2010, *Doing Business* 2010 (database at www.doingbusiness.org).

VIKRAMRAGHUVANSHI/GETTY IMAGES

Overall, it is not surprising that the more entrepreneur-friendly these formal institutional requirements are, the more flourishing entrepreneurship is, and the more developed the economies become—and vice versa (see PengAtlas Map 12). As a result, more developing economies are now reforming their formal institutions in order to become more entrepreneur-friendly (see Peng Atlas Map 13).

ISTOCKPHOTO.COM/HENRIK5000

In addition to formal institutions, informal institutions such as cultural values and norms also affect entrepreneurship. For example, because entrepreneurs necessarily take more risk, individualistic and low uncertainty-avoidance societies tend to foster relatively more entrepreneurs, whereas collectivistic and high uncertainty-avoidance societies may result in relatively fewer entrepreneurs. For example, among developed economies, Japan has the lowest rate of start-ups, one-third of America's rate and half of Europe's.[8] In another example, Russians make heavy use of social networks online, averaging 9.8 hours per month—more than double the world average. While spending that much time online makes sense during the long and cold Russian winter, another important reason is the long-held Russian tradition of relying more on informal information networks for daily life. These informal norms help nurture social network entrepreneurs such as Russia's Vkontakte and attract foreign entrants such as Facebook.[9] Overall, the institution-based view suggests that both formal and informal institutions matter.[10] Later sections in this chapter will discuss how they matter.

9-2b Resources and Entrepreneurship

In addition to being subject to institutional constraints, entrepreneurial firms have a unique set of resources and capabilities.[11] A start-up primarily has entrepreneurial vision, drive, and leadership, which compensate for its shortage of tangible resources such as financial capital and formal organizational structure. The resource-based view, discussed in Chapter 4, sheds considerable light on entrepreneurship with a focus on its value (V), rarity (R), imitability (I), and organizational (O) aspects (see Exhibit 9.1). Like any other firm, an entrepreneurial firm must take the VRIO framework into account as it considers how to leverage its resources.

First, entrepreneurial resources must create *value*. For example, by offering cheap fares, convenient schedules, and Wi-Fi and power port on every seat, Megabus offers superb value to travelers for medium-haul trips that are too far for a leisurely drive but too close to justify the expenses and the increasing hassle to fly. On routes between New York and Boston and between Dallas and Austin, Megabus is rapidly changing the way Americans—especially the young—travel, so much so that it may help kill plans for the new high-speed rail that after all may not offer that much value.[12]

Second, resources must be *rare*. As the cliché goes, "If everybody has it, you can't make money from it." The best-performing entrepreneurs tend to have the rarest knowledge and insights about business opportunities. Math geniuses are few and far between, but the ability to turn a passion for math into profit is truly rare. Google's two founders are such rare geniuses.

Third, resources must be *inimitable*. For example, in the ocean of e-commerce firms, the ability to do the "dirtiest job on the Internet" as an online moderator is very hard to imitate. After being exposed to, and then cleaning up, the most nasty and most undesirable racism and bigotry on a daily basis, sometimes online moderators "feel you need to spend two hours in the shower just because it is so disgusting."[13] But then that is why firms such as eModeration and ICUC Moderation can charge a lot of money to clean up comments and tweets for established organizations.

Fourth, entrepreneurial resources must be *organizationally* embedded.[14] For example, as long as there have been wars, there have been mercenaries ready to fight on behalf of the highest bidder. But only in modern times have private military companies (PMCs) become a global industry. Entrepreneurial PMCs thrive on their organizational capabilities to provide military and security services in dangerous environments, particularly in places like Iraq and Afghanistan where individuals shy away and even national militaries withdraw.

9-3 GROWING THE ENTREPRENEURIAL FIRM

This section discusses three major characteristics associated with a growing entrepreneurial firm: (1) growth, (2) innovation, and (3) financing. A fourth characteristic, internationalization, will be highlighted in the next section.

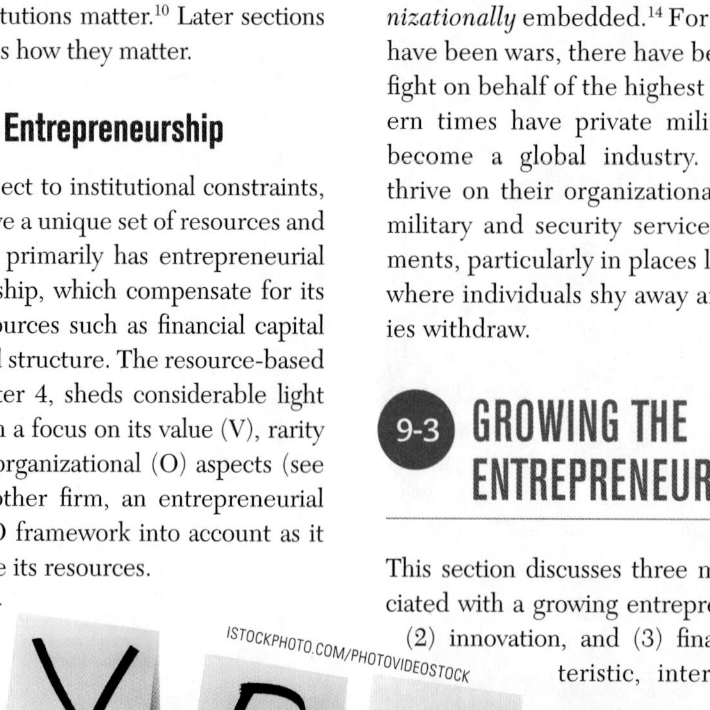

ISTOCKPHOTO.COM/PHOTOVIDEOSTOCK

InFocus: Emerging Markets

Israel: The Start-Up Nation

ARIEL JEROZOLIMSKI/BLOOMBERG/GETTY IMAGES

The young must shout if they want to be heard. In a stone hanger in the old port of Jaffa, 30 entrepreneurs have five minutes each to present their start-up companies to a panel of digital luminaries and an audience that includes potential investors. Not everyone in the room is ready to shut up and listen, so the hopefuls must battle against the din. Feng-GUI explains how, by simulating human vision, it can tell advertisers and designers which areas of a web page are most likely to grab people's attention. CopyV promises to send large files quickly and securely. With Fooducate, "a dietician in your pocket," on your smartphone, you can scan bar codes in the supermarket and find out what's really going into your trolley.

Israel's legions of young technology firms clamor for attention and money. Rapid-pitch events like this one, at DLD Tel Aviv, a two-day conference in November 2012, are common. More than 300 firms applied for a slot at DLD; 100 turned up; the lucky 30 were chosen by raffle. Yossi Vardi, a technology entrepreneur who has invested in 75 start-ups since 1996, says that he receives between three and eight approaches every day.

Dan Senor and Saul Singer called Israel the Start-Up Nation in a book of that name in 2009. The label has stuck because it fits. Everybody and his brother-in-law seems to be starting a company—with old schoolmates or army colleagues, in a spare room or the parental home. Starting a business is easier than ever, thanks to advances in information technology. Budding designers of smartphone apps can rent space when they need it on a remote server rather than buying huge amounts of computing power. "The Internet has democratized the right to innovate," says Mr. Vardi.

Israelis innovate because they have to. The land is arid, so they excel at water and agricultural technology. They have little oil, so they furrow their brows to find alternatives. They are surrounded by enemies, so their military technology is superb and creates lucrative spin-offs, especially in communications. The relationships forged during military service foster frenetic networking in civilian life. A flood of immigrants in the 1990s gave national brainpower a mighty boost. The results are the envy of almost everyone outside Silicon Valley.

Source: Excerpted from "What next for the start-up nation?" *Economist*, 21 January 2013, 69–70. © The Economist.

9-3a **Growth**

For many entrepreneurs such as David Tran in the Opening Case and Jack Ma in the Closing Case, the excitement associated with growing new firms such as Huy Fong and Alibaba is the very thing that attracts them in the first place. Recall from the resource-based view that a firm can be conceptualized as a bundle of resources and capabilities. The growth of an entrepreneurial firm can thus be viewed as an attempt to more fully use currently underutilized resources and capabilities. An entrepreneurial firm can leverage its (intangible) vision and drive in order to grow, even though it may be short on (tangible) resources such as financial capital.

9-3b **Innovation**

Innovation is at the heart of entrepreneurship. Evidence shows a positive relationship between a high degree of innovation and superior profitability. Innovation allows for a more sustainable basis for competitive advantage. Innovation can range from low-tech ones such as Huy Fong's humble Sriracha hot sauce (see the Opening Case) to high-tech ones such as Aliababa's Taobao that can handle millions of online transactions daily (see the Closing Case). Israeli SMEs, for example, are known for their innovation capabilities (see In Focus). Examples include firewalls (Checkpoint) and ICQ instant messaging software (Mirabilis).

Entrepreneurial firms are uniquely ready for innovation. Owners, managers, and employees at entrepreneurial firms tend to be more innovative and risk taking than those at large firms. In fact, many SMEs are founded by former employees of large firms who were frustrated by their inability to translate innovative ideas into realities at the large firms. Intel, for example, was founded by three former employees of Fairchild Semiconductor. Innovators at large firms also have limited ability to personally profit from their

EXHIBIT 9.3 VENTURE CAPITAL INVESTMENT AS A PERCENTAGE OF GDP

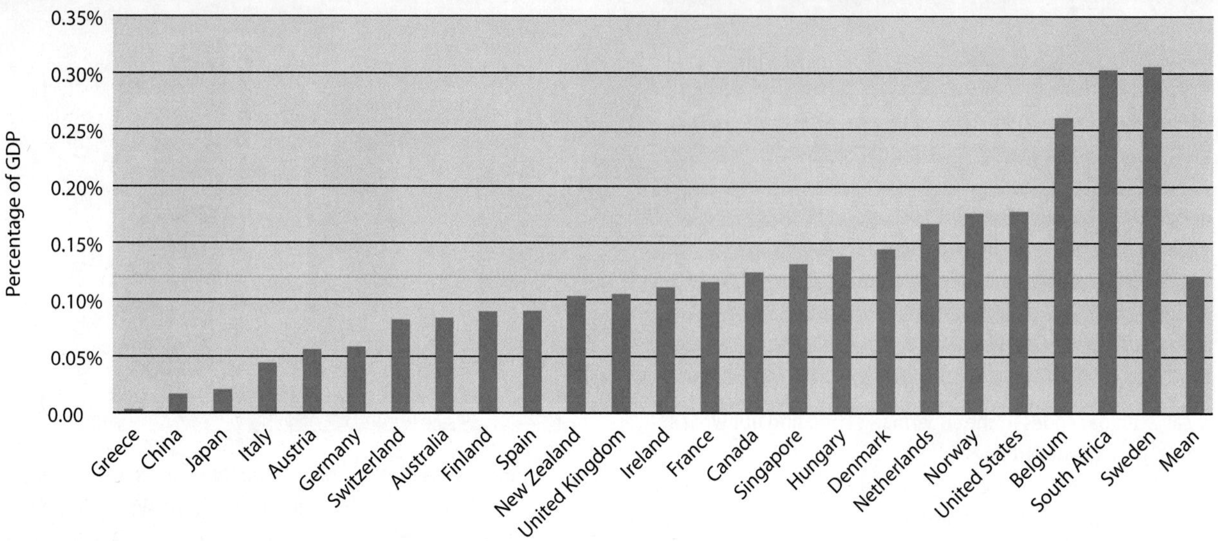

Source: Adapted from M. Minniti, W. Bygrave, and E. Autio, *Global Entrepreneurship Monitor 2006 Executive Report* (Wellesley, MA: Babson College/GEM, 2006) 49.

innovations because property rights usually belong to their employers. In contrast, innovators at entrepreneurial firms are better able to reap the financial gains associated with innovation, thus fueling their motivation to charge ahead.

9-3c Financing

All start-ups need capital. What are the sources of capital? Three of the "4F" sources of entrepreneurial financing are founders, family, and friends. What is the other "F" source? The answer is . . . *fools* (!). While this is a joke, it strikes a chord in the entrepreneurial world. Given the well-known failure risks of start-ups (a *majority* of them will fail—see the Debate), why would anybody other than a fool be willing to invest in a start-up? In reality, most outside strategic investors, who can be wealthy individual investors (often called angels), venture capitalists, banks, foreign entrants, or government agencies, are not fools. They often demand some assurance (such as collateral), examine business plans, and require a strong management team.

Microfinance Lending small sums ($50–$300) used to start small businesses with the intention of ultimately lifting the entrepreneurs out of poverty.

Around the world, the extent to which entrepreneurs draw on resources from outside investors (such as venture capitalists) rather than family and friends varies. Exhibit 9.3 shows that Sweden, South Africa, Belgium, and the United States lead the world in venture capital (VC) investment as a percentage of GDP. In contrast, Greece and China have the lowest level of VC investment. Exhibit 9.4 illustrates a different picture: informal investment (mostly by family and friends) as a percentage of GDP. In this case, China leads the world with the highest level of informal investment as a percentage of GDP. In comparison, Brazil and Hungary, on the other hand, have the lowest level of informal investment. While there is a lot of noise in such worldwide data, the case of China (second lowest in VC investment and highest in informal investment) is easy to explain: China's lack of formal market-supporting institutions, such as venture capitalists and credit-reporting agencies, requires a high level of informal investment for Chinese entrepreneurs and new ventures, particularly during a time of entrepreneurial boom.[15]

A highly innovative solution, called microfinance, has emerged in response to the lack of financing for entrepreneurial opportunities in many developing countries. **Microfinance** involves lending small sums ($50–$300) used to start small businesses with the intention of ultimately lifting the entrepreneurs out of poverty. Starting in Bangladesh in the 1970s by Muhammad Yunus, microfinance has now become a global movement. Yunus himself won a Nobel Peace Prize in 2006.

EXHIBIT 9.4 INFORMAL INVESTMENT AS A PERCENTAGE OF GDP

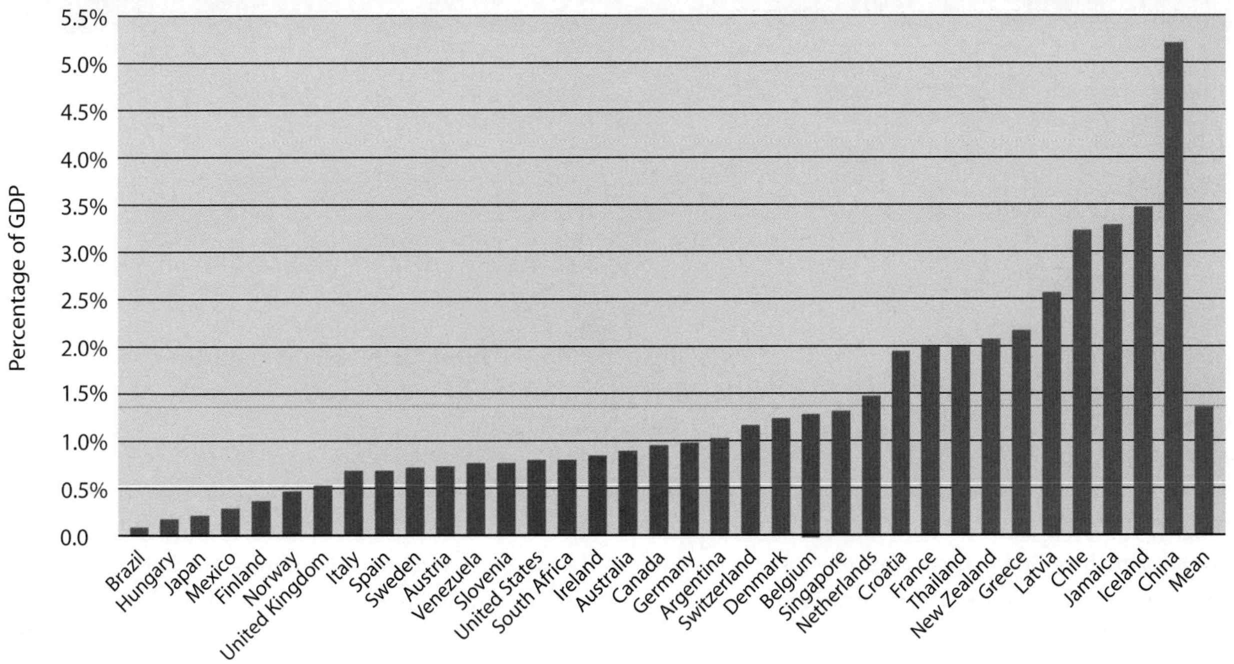

Source: Adapted from M. Minniti, W. Bygrave, and E. Autio, *Global Entrepreneurship Monitor 2006 Executive Report* (Wellesley, MA: Babson College/GEM, 2006) 53.

9-4 INTERNATIONALIZING THE ENTREPRENEURIAL FIRM

There is a myth that only large MNEs do business abroad and that SMEs mostly operate domestically. This myth, based on historical stereotypes, is being increasingly challenged as more SMEs go international.[16] Further, some start-ups attempt to do business abroad from inception. These are often called **born global firms** (or **international new ventures**). This section examines how entrepreneurial firms internationalize.

9-4a Transaction Costs and Entrepreneurial Opportunities

Compared with domestic transaction costs (the costs of doing business), international transaction costs are qualitatively higher. Some costs are high due to numerous innocent differences in formal institutions and informal norms (see Chapters 2 and 3). Other costs, however, may be due to a high level of potential opportunism that is hard to detect and remedy. For example, when a small business in Texas with $5 million annual revenues receives an unsolicited order of $1 million from an unknown buyer in Alaska, most likely the Texas firm will fill the order and allow the Alaska buyer to pay within 30 or 60 days after receiving the goods—a typical practice among domestic transactions in the United States. But what if this order comes from an unknown buyer (importer in this case) in Azerbaijan? If the Texas firm ships the goods but foreign payment does not arrive on time (after 30, 60, or even more days), it is difficult to assess whether firms in Azerbaijan simply do not have the norm of punctual payment or that particular importer is being deliberately opportunistic. If the latter is indeed the case, suing the importer in a court in Azerbaijan where Azeri is the official language may be so costly that it is not an option for a small US exporter.

Maybe the Azerbaijani importer is an honest and capable firm with every intention and ability to pay. But because the Texas firm may not be able to ascertain, prior to the transaction, that the Azerbaijani side will pay upon receiving the goods, the Texas firm may simply say "No, thanks!" Conceptually, this is an example of transaction costs being too high that many firms may choose

Born global firm (International new venture) A start-up company that attempts to do business abroad from inception.

EXHIBIT 9.5 INTERNATIONALIZATION STRATEGIES FOR ENTREPRENEURIAL FIRMS

Entering foreign markets	Staying in domestic markets
▶ Direct exports	▶ Indirect exports (through export intermediaries)
▶ Franchising/licensing	▶ Supplier of foreign firms
▶ Foreign direct investment (strategic alliances, greenfield wholly owned subsidiaries, and/or foreign acquisitions)	▶ Franchisee or licensee of foreign brands
	▶ Alliance partner of foreign direct investors
	▶ Harvest and exit (through sell-off to and acquisition by foreign entrants)

not to pursue international opportunities. Therefore, entrepreneurial opportunities exist to lower transaction costs and bring distant groups of people, firms, and countries together. Exhibit 9.5 shows that while entrepreneurial firms can internationalize by entering foreign markets, they can also add an international dimension without actually going abroad. Next, we discuss how an SME can undertake some of these strategies.

9-4b International Strategies for Entering Foreign Markets

SMEs have three broad modes for entering foreign markets: (1) direct exports, (2) licensing/franchising, and (3) foreign direct investment (FDI) (see Chapters 6 and 10 for more details). First, **direct exports** involve the sale of products made by entrepreneurial firms in their home country to customers in other countries. This strategy is attractive because entrepreneurial firms are able to reach foreign customers directly. However, a major drawback is that SMEs may not have enough resources to turn overseas opportunities into profits. Many SMEs reach foreign customers through **sporadic (passive) exporting**, meaning sales prompted by unsolicited inquiries. To actively and systematically pursue export customers would be a different ball game.

Export transactions are complicated. One particular concern is how to overcome the lack of trust between exporters and importers when receiving an order from unknown importers abroad. For example, while the US exporter in Exhibit 9.6 does not trust the Chinese importer, banks on both sides can facilitate this transaction by a **letter of credit (L/C)**, which is a financial contract stating that the importer's bank (Bank of China in this case) will pay a specific sum of money to the exporter upon delivery of the merchandise. It has several steps.

- The US exporter may question the unknown Chinese importer's assurance that it will promptly pay for the merchandise. An L/C from the highly reputable

EXHIBIT 9.6 AN EXPORT/IMPORT TRANSACTION

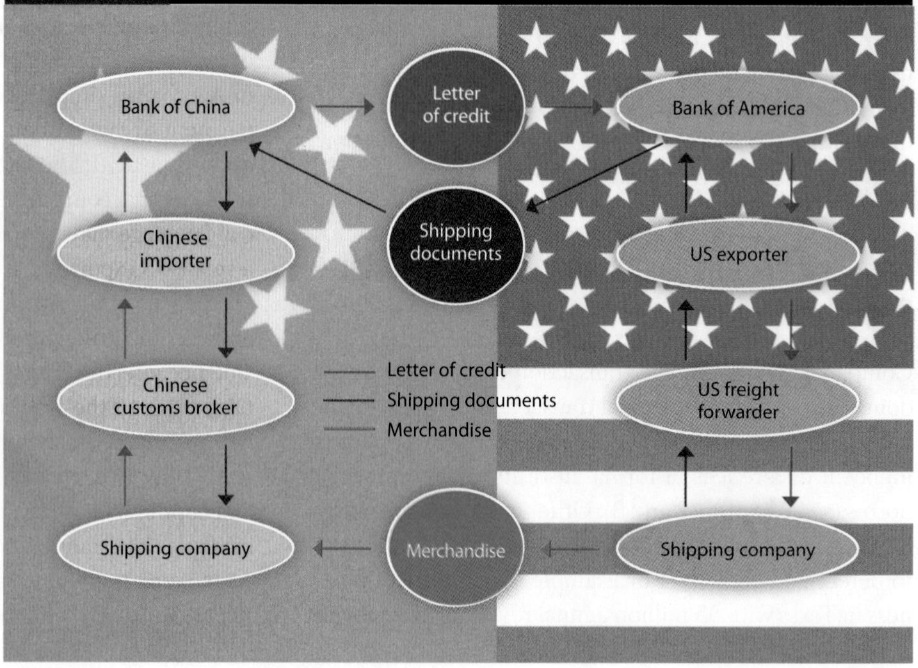

© ISTOCKPHOTO.COM/BEST-PHOTO / © ISTOCKPHOTO.COM/CLAUDIO DIVIZIA

Direct export The sale of products made by firms in their home country to customers in other countries.

Sporadic (passive) exporting The sale of products prompted by unsolicited inquiries from abroad.

Letter of credit (L/C) A financial contract that states that the importer's bank will pay a specific sum of money to the exporter upon delivery of the merchandise.

Bank of China will assure the US exporter that the importer has good creditworthiness and sufficient funds for the transaction. If the US exporter is not sure whether Bank of China is a credible bank, it can consult its own bank, Bank of America, which will confirm that an L/C from Bank of China is as good as gold.

- With the assurance through an L/C, the US exporter can release the merchandise, which goes through a US freight forwarder, then a shipping company, and then a Chinese customs broker. Finally, the goods will reach the Chinese importer.
- Once the US exporter has shipped the goods, it will present to Bank of America the L/C from Bank of China and shipping documents. On behalf of the US exporter, Bank of America will then collect payment from Bank of China, which, in turn, will collect payment from the Chinese importer.

In short, instead of having unknown exporters and importers deal with each other, transactions are facilitated by banks on both sides that have known each other quite well because of numerous such dealings. In other words, the L/C reduces transaction costs by lowering the transaction risks.

A second way to enter international markets is licensing and/or franchising. Usually used in *manufacturing* industries, **licensing** refers to Firm A's agreement to give Firm B the rights to use A's proprietary technology (such as a patent) or trademark (such as a corporate logo) for a royalty fee paid to A by B. Assume (hypothetically) that a US exporter cannot keep up with demand in Turkey. It may consider granting a Turkish firm the license to use its technology and trademark for a fee.

Franchising is essentially the same, except it is typically used in *service* industries such as fast food. A great advantage is that SME licensors and franchisors can expand abroad while risking relatively little of their own capital. Foreign firms interested in becoming licensees or franchisees have to put their own capital up front. For example, a McDonald's franchise now costs the franchisee approximately one million dollars. But licensors and franchisors also take a risk because they may suffer a loss of control over how their technology and brand names are used. If McDonald's (hypothetical) licensee in Finland produces sub-standard products that damage the brand and refuses to improve quality, McDonald's has two difficult choices: (1) sue its licensee in an unfamiliar Finnish court or (2) discontinue the relationship. Either choice is complicated and costly.

A third entry mode is FDI. FDI may involve strategic alliances with foreign partners (such as joint ventures), foreign acquisitions, and/or greenfield wholly owned subsidiaries. FDI has several distinct advantages. By planting some roots abroad, a firm becomes more committed to serving foreign markets. It is physically and psychologically closer to foreign customers. Relative to licensing and franchising, a firm is better able to control how its proprietary technology and brand name are used. However, FDI has a major drawback: its cost and complexity. It requires both a non-trivial sum of capital and a significant managerial commitment. Many SMEs are unable to engage in FDI.

In general, the level of complexity and resources required increases as a firm moves from direct exports to licensing/franchising and finally to FDI. Traditionally, it is thought that most firms will have to go through these different stages and that SMEs (perhaps with few exceptions) are unable to undertake FDI. Known as the **stage model**, this idea posits that SMEs that do eventually internationalize will do so through a slow, stage-by-stage process.

However, enough counter-examples of *rapidly* internationalizing entrepreneurial firms, known as born globals, exist to challenge stage models. Consider Logitech, now a global leader in computer peripherals. It was established by entrepreneurs from Switzerland and the United States, where the firm set up dual headquarters. Research and development (R&D) and manufacturing were initially split between these two countries and then quickly spread to Ireland and Taiwan through FDI. Its first commercial contract was with a Japanese company.

Given that most SMEs still fit the stereotype of slow (or no) internationalization but some entrepreneurial SMEs seem to be born global, a key question is: What leads to rapid internationalization? The key differentiator between rapidly and slowly (or no) internationalizing SMEs seems to be the international experience of the entrepreneurs. If entrepreneurs have solid previous experience abroad (such as David Tran's earlier experience in Vietnam as portrayed in the Opening Case), then doing business in a different country is not so intimidating. Otherwise,

Licensing Firm A's agreement to give Firm B the rights to use A's proprietary technology (such as a patent) or trademark (such as a corporate logo) for a royalty fee paid to A by B. This is typically done in manufacturing industries.

Franchising Firm A's agreement to give Firm B the rights to use A's proprietary assets for a royalty fee paid to A by B. This is typically done in service industries.

Stage model Model of internationalization that involves a slow step-by-step (stage-by-stage) process a firm must go through to internationalize its business.

the apprehension associated with the unfamiliar foreign business world may take over, and entrepreneurs will simply want to avoid trouble overseas.

While many entrepreneurial firms have aggressively gone abroad, it is probably true that a majority of SMEs will be unable to do so. They already have enough headaches struggling with the domestic market. However, as discussed next, some SMEs can still internationalize by staying at home.

9-4c International Strategies for Staying in Domestic Markets

Exhibit 9.5 also shows a number of strategies for entrepreneurial SMEs to internationalize without leaving their home country. The five main strategies are (1) export indirectly, (2) become suppliers for foreign firms, (3) become licensees or franchisees of foreign brands, (4) become alliance partners of foreign direct investors, or (5) harvest and exit through sell-offs.

First, whereas direct exports may be lucrative, many SMEs simply do not have the resources to handle such work. But they can still reach overseas customers through **indirect exports**, which involve exporting through domestic-based export intermediaries. **Export intermediaries** perform an important middleman function by linking domestic sellers and overseas buyers who otherwise would not have been connected. Being entrepreneurs themselves, export intermediaries facilitate the internationalization of many SMEs.[17]

Indirect export A way for SMEs to reach overseas customers by exporting through domestic-based export intermediaries.

Export intermediary A firm that acts as a middleman by linking domestic sellers and foreign buyers that otherwise would not have been connected.

A second strategy is to become a supplier for a foreign firm that enters a domestic market. For example, when Subway came to Northern Ireland, it secured a contract for chilled part-bake bread with a domestic bakery. This relationship was so successful that the firm now supplies Subway franchisees throughout Europe. SME suppliers thus may be able to internationalize by piggybacking on the larger foreign entrants.

Third, an entrepreneurial firm may consider becoming licensee or franchisee of a foreign brand. Foreign licensors and franchisors provide training and technology transfer—for a fee of course. Consequently, an SME can learn a great deal about how to operate at world-class standards. Further, licensees and franchisees do not have to be permanently under the control of licensors and franchisors. If enough learning has been accomplished, it is possible to discontinue the relationship and to reap greater entrepreneurial profits. In Thailand, Minor Group, which had held the Pizza Hut franchise for 20 years, broke away from the relationship. Its new venture, The Pizza Company, has become the market leader in Thailand.

A fourth strategy is to become an alliance partner of a foreign direct investor. Facing an onslaught of aggressive MNEs, many entrepreneurial firms may not be able to successfully defend their market positions. Then it makes great sense to follow the old adage, "If you can't beat them, join them!" While dancing with the giants is tricky, it is better than being crushed by them. (See Chapter 11 for examples of how smaller, domestic firms become alliance partners with MNEs.)

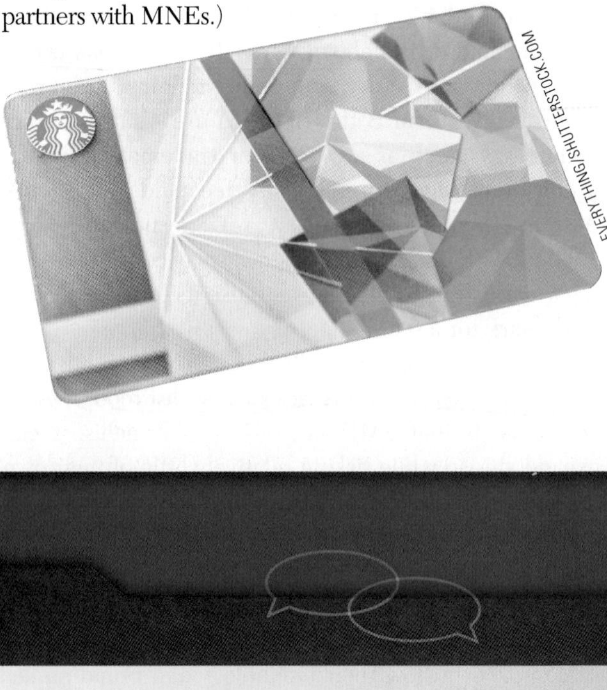

EVERYTHING/SHUTTERSTOCK.COM

Debate: Ethical Dilemma

Boom in Busts: Good or Bad?

Corporate bankruptcies* have climbed new heights since the Great Recession of 2008–2009. Firms ranging from mighty ones such as Lehman Brothers to tiny entrepreneurial outfits have dropped out left and right around the world. Since bankruptcies do not sound too good or inspiring, is there anything that we—the government, financial institutions, consumers, taxpayers, or the society at large—can do to prevent widespread bankruptcies?

360B/SHUTTERSTOCK.COM

Efforts trying to rescue failing firms from bankruptcies stem from an "anti-failure" bias widely shared among entrepreneurs, scholars, journalists, and government officials. Although a majority of entrepreneurial firms fail, this "anti-failure" bias leads to a strong interest in entrepreneurial success (remember how many times Google, Facebook, and Alibaba were written up by the press or your textbook author?). Yet scant attention has been devoted to the vast majority of entrepreneurial firms that end up in failure and bankruptcy. However, one perspective suggests that bankruptcies, which are undoubtedly painful to individual entrepreneurs and employees, may be *good* for the society. Consequently, bankruptcy laws need to be reformed to become more entrepreneur-friendly by making it easier for entrepreneurs to declare bankruptcy and to move on. Consequently, financial, human, and physical resources stuck with failed firms can be redeployed in a socially optimal way.

A leading debate is how to treat failed entrepreneurs who file for bankruptcy. Do we let them walk away from debt or punish them? Historically, entrepreneur-friendliness and bankruptcy laws are like an "oxymoron," because bankruptcy laws are usually harsh and even cruel. The very term "bankruptcy" is derived from a harsh practice: In medieval Italy, if bankrupt entrepreneurs did not pay their debt, debtors would destroy the trading bench (booth) of the bankrupt—the Italian word for broken bench, *banca rotta*, has evolved into the English word "bankruptcy." The pound of flesh demanded by the creditor in Shakespeare's *The Merchant of Venice* is only a slight exaggeration. The world's first bankruptcy law, passed in England in 1542, considered a bankrupt individual a criminal and penalties ranged from incarceration to death sentence.

However, recently, many governments have realized that entrepreneur-friendly bankruptcy laws can not only lower exit barriers, but also lower entry barriers for entrepreneurs. Although we are confident that many start-ups will end up in bankruptcy, up front it is impossible to predict which ones will go under. Therefore, from an institution-based standpoint, if entrepreneurship is to be encouraged, there is a need to ease the pain associated with bankruptcy by means such as allowing entrepreneurs to walk away from debt, a legal right that bankrupt US entrepreneurs appreciate. In contrast, until the recent bankruptcy law reforms, bankrupt German entrepreneurs might remain liable for unpaid debt for up to 30 years. Further, German and Japanese managers of bankrupt firms can also be liable for criminal penalties, and numerous bankrupt Japanese entrepreneurs have committed suicide. Not surprisingly, many failed entrepreneurs in Germany and Japan try to avoid business exit despite escalating losses, while societal and individual resources cannot be channeled to more productive uses. Therefore, as rules of the "end game," harsh bankruptcy laws become grave exit barriers. They can also create significant entry barriers, as fewer would-be entrepreneurs may decide to launch their ventures.

At a societal level, if many would-be entrepreneurs, in fear of failure, abandon their ideas, there will not be a thriving entrepreneurial sector. Given the risks and uncertainties, it is not surprising that many entrepreneurs do not make it the first time. However, if they are given two, three, or more chances, some of them will succeed. For example, approximately 50% of US entrepreneurs who filed bankruptcy resumed a new venture in four years. This high level of entrepreneurialism is, in part, driven by the relatively entrepreneur-friendly bankruptcy laws (such as the provision of Chapter 11 bankruptcy reorganization, instead of straight liquidation). On the other hand, a society that severely punishes failed entrepreneurs (such as forcing financially insolvent firms to liquidate instead of offering a US Chapter 11-style reorganization option) is not likely to foster widespread entrepreneurship. Failed entrepreneurs have nevertheless accumulated a great deal of experience and lessons on how to avoid their mistakes. If they drop out of the entrepreneurial game (or, in the worst case, kill themselves), their wisdom will be permanently lost. Overall, worldwide evidence from 29 countries—involving both developed and emerging economies from five continents—has identified a strong linkage between entrepreneur-friendly bankruptcy laws and new firm entries.

Institutionally, there is an urgent need to remove some of our anti-failure bias and design entrepreneur-friendly bankruptcy policies so that failed entrepreneurs are given more chances. At a societal level, entrepreneurial failures may be beneficial, since it is through a large number of entrepreneurial experimentations—although many will fail—that winning solutions will emerge and that economies will develop. In short, the boom in busts is not necessarily bad.

* The term "bankruptcies" in this case refers to *corporate* bankruptcies, and does not deal with *personal* bankruptcies.

Sources: S. Lee, M. W. Peng, and J. Barney, "Bankruptcy law and entrepreneurship development," *Academy of Management Review* 32 (2007): 257–272; S. Lee, Yamakawa, and M. W. Peng, "How does bankruptcy law affect entrepreneurship development?" SBA Best Research Papers Collection (Washington, DC: US Small Business Administration, 2007), www.sba.gov/advo/research/ rs326tot.pdf; S. Lee, Y. Yamakawa, M. W. Peng, and J. Barney, "How do bankruptcy laws affect entrepreneurship development around the world?" *Journal of Business Venturing* 26 (2011): 505–520; M. W. Peng, Y. Yamakawa, and S. Lee, "Bankruptcy laws and entrepreneur-friendliness," *Entrepreneur Theory and Practice* 34 (2010): 517–530; Y. Yamakawa, M. W. Peng, and D. Deeds, "Rising from the ashes: Cognitive determinants of venture growth after entrepreneurial failure," *Entrepreneurship Theory and Practice* 39 (2015): 209–236.

Finally, as a harvest and exit strategy, entrepreneurs may sell an equity stake or the entire firm to foreign entrants. An American couple, originally from Seattle, built a Starbucks-like coffee chain in Britain called Seattle Coffee. When Starbucks entered Britain, the couple sold the chain of 60 stores to Starbucks for a hefty $84 million. In light of the high failure rates of start-ups (see the Debate), being acquired by foreign entrants may help preserve the business in the long run.

9-5 MANAGEMENT SAVVY

What determines the success and failure of entrepreneurial firms around the globe? The answer boils down to two components. First, the institution-based view argues that institutional frameworks explain a great deal about what is behind the differences in entrepreneurial and economic development around the world. Second, the resource-based view posits that it is largely intangible resources such as vision, drive, and willingness to take risk that fuels entrepreneurship around the globe. Overall, the performance of entrepreneurial firms depends on how they take advantage of formal and informal institutional resources and leverage their capabilities at home, abroad, or both.

Two clear implications for action emerge (Exhibit 9.7). First, institutions that help entrepreneurship development—both formal and informal—are important. As a result, savvy entrepreneurs have a vested interest in pushing for more entrepreneur-friendly formal institutions in various countries, such as rules governing how to set up new firms and how to reduce the pain for failed entrepreneurs and their firms (see the Debate). Entrepreneurs also need to cultivate strong informal norms granting legitimacy to entrepreneurs. Talking to high school and college students, taking on internships, and providing seed money as angels for new ventures are some of the actions that entrepreneurs can undertake.

Second, when internationalizing, entrepreneurs are advised to be bold. Thanks to globalization, the costs of doing business abroad have fallen recently. But being bold does not mean being reckless. One specific managerial insight from this chapter is that it is possible to internationalize without actually venturing abroad. When the entrepreneurial firm is not ready to take on higher risk abroad, the more limited international involvement at home may be appropriate. In other words, be bold but not too bold.

EXHIBIT 9.7 IMPLICATIONS FOR ACTION

- Push for institutions that facilitate entrepreneurship development, both formal and informal.
- When internationalizing, be bold but not *too* bold.

EMERGING MARKETS
The Rise of Alibaba

Founded in 1999 by a former English teacher Jack Ma, Alibaba has risen to become the largest e-commerce firm not only in China, but also in the world—the value of goods sold on its platforms ($170 billion in 2013) is more than Amazon and eBay *combined*. Alibaba started as a business-to-business (B2B) portal connecting overseas buyers and small Chinese manufacturers. Inspired by eBay, Alibaba next launched Taobao, a consumer-to-consumer (C2C) portal that now features nearly a billion products and is one of the 20 most-visited websites worldwide. Finally, with Tmall, Alibaba offers an Amazon-like business-to-consumer (B2C) portal that assists global brands such as Levi's and Disney to reach the middle class in China.

The rise of Alibaba has been breathtaking. As China becomes the largest e-commerce market (already bigger than the United States), Alibaba controls four-fifths of all e-commerce in China. In 2013, on Single's Day (November 11, a marketing invention created to encourage singles to "be nice" to themselves) alone, Alibaba sold more than $5.7 billion. Preparing to initiate an initial public offering (IPO) in New York, Alibaba was predicted by the *Economist* to have the potential "to be among the world's most valuable companies." On September 19, 2014, Alibaba's IPO on the New York Stock Exchange was indeed the world's largest, raising $25 billion.

GIL C/SHUTTERSTOCK.COM

Behind the rise of Alibaba is a story of focus and innovation. "eBay may be a shark in the ocean," Ma once said, "but I am a crocodile in the Yangtze. If we fight in the ocean, I lose; but if we fight in the river, I win." The Crocodile of Yangtze, as Ma became known, has largely focused on China to avoid head-on competition with eBays of the world elsewhere. In China, eBay has been forced to retreat. In a low-trust society such as China where people generally shy away from buying from strangers online and where people hesitate to use credit cards, Alibaba has pioneered an Alipay system. This is a novel online-payments system that relies on escrow (releasing money to sellers only once their buyers are happy with the goods received). This not only facilitates transactions for Alibaba as well as its buyers and sellers, but also helps build trust at the societal level. Alifinance, Alibaba's financing arm, has become a big microlender to small firms, which are typically underserved by China's state-owned banks. Alifinance now plans to lend to individuals as well. Alibaba is also delivering insurance online. Perhaps its biggest treasure lies in its vast amount of data about the creditworthiness of millions of China's middle class and of thousands of firms that do business via Alibaba—clearly a Big Data gold mine.

From an institution-based standpoint, the fact that Alibaba as a privately owned firm can grow to such an enormous size is remarkable about the Chinese government's tolerance of e-commerce. Ironically the US government placed Alibaba on the list of "notorious markets," because counterfeits could be bought and sold on its websites. Alibaba has endeavored to remove fakes from its websites, and its recent removal from the US government's list of "notorious markets" is indicative of its hard work. However, Western managers of genuine items on Tmall continue to complain that cheap fakes can still be found on Taobao. Evidently the fight is still on.

Formidable as Alibaba is, it is not without challenges. Its business model grows on PC-based e-commerce. Recently as China becomes the world's largest market for smartphones, it is fast moving to mobile commerce—at a speed faster than any other major economy. The upshot? According to Alibaba's own prospectus, "we face a number of challenges to successfully monetizing our mobile user traffic." In other words, Alibaba is but one of several contenders. Until fairly recently, Alibaba and two other Internet giants in China largely minded their own business as the "three kingdoms," referring to an historical era during which China was divided three ways. While Alibaba dominated e-commerce, Baidu was king of search engines and Tencent made a killing on online games. The truce among the "three kingdoms" seems to have ended with the arrival of mobile commerce, as all three rush to establish dominance in this new market frontier. Famous for elbowing out Google, Baidu is listed on NASDAQ and is Microsoft's partner in China. In addition to online games, Tencent is more famous for its WeChat social messaging app, which is widely popular. There is no guarantee Alibaba will win in this contest.

In addition to fighting it out in China, the Crocodile of the Yangtze has also been eyeing the wider global ocean. Some 12% of Alibaba's sales are already overseas. Its most attractive overseas markets are likely to be low-trust, underbanked emerging economies in Asia, Africa, and Latin America. But sharks such as eBay and Amazon will not be easy to fight with. Looking forward, whether Alibaba deserves to be one of the world's most valuable companies will depend on how it can defend its e-commerce dominance at home in the mobile era and how it can grow its business abroad.

Case Discussion Questions

1. What are the characteristics of Alibaba's growth, innovation, and financing strategies that are typical of successful entrepreneurial firms? What is unusual about Alibaba?
2. Why has Alibaba become globally famous by focusing on its domestic market?
3. Sometimes the IPO of widely successful firms flops—Facebook's disappointing IPO comes to mind. Does Alibaba deserve to be one of the world's most valued firms?

Sources: "Alibaba plays defense against Tencent," *Bloomberg Businessweek*, 26 August 2013, 38–40; "Tencent's worth," *Economist*, 21 September 2013, 66–68; "The Alibaba phenomenon," *Economist*, 23 March 2013, 15; "The world's greatest bazaar," *Economist*, 23 March 2013, 27–30; "From bazaar to bonanza," *Economist*, 10 May 2014, 63–65; " After the float," *Economist*, 6 September 2014, 66–67; "Alibaba expected to be approved for IPO," *South China Morning Post*, 12 July 2014, B4.

STUDY TOOLS 9

LOCATED AT THE BACK OF YOUR BOOK:

☐ Rip out and study the Chapter Review Card at the end of the book

LOG IN TO WWW.CENGAGEBRAIN.COM TO:

☐ Review key term flashcards

☐ Complete a practice quiz to test your knowledge of key concepts

☐ Take and complete the chapter crossword puzzle

☐ Complete interactive content, watch chapter videos, and take a graded quiz

☐ Track your knowledge of key concepts in Global Business

☐ Read and discuss additional case study content

10 Entering Foreign Markets

RAVEENDRAN/AFP/GETTY IMAGES

LEARNING OBJECTIVES

After studying this chapter, you should be able to . . .

10-1 Identify ways in which institutions and resources affect the liability of foreignness.

10-2 Match the quest for location-specific advantages with strategic goals.

10-3 Compare and contrast first-mover and late-mover advantages.

10-4 List the steps in the comprehensive model of foreign market entries.

10-5 Explain what you should do to make your firm's entry into a foreign market successful.

After you finish this chapter, go to **PAGE 163** for **STUDY TOOLS**

EMERGING MARKETS

Indian Firms Spread Their Wings in Africa

Indian billionaire Ravi Ruia has flown to Africa at least once a month for the past year and a half. He is interested in coal mines in Mozambique, an oil refinery in Kenya, and a call center in South Africa. Soon, he may also have a power plant in Nigeria. "Africa looks remarkably similar to what India was 15 years ago," says Firdhose Coovadia, director of African operations at Essar Group, the $15 billion conglomerate headed by Ruia and his brother, Shashi. "We can't lose this opportunity."

Faced with increasing competition and a welter of bureaucratic obstacles at home, Indian companies are looking to Africa for growth. Since 2005, they have spent $16 billion on the continent versus at least $31 billion spent by the Chinese, according to data compiled by Bloomberg and the Heritage Foundation, respectively. In June 2010, Bharti Airtel, India's largest mobile-phone provider, paid $9 billion for the African cellular operations of Kuwait's Zain. In 2008, India's Videocon Industries paid $330 million for two coal mines in Mozambique, and India's state-run fertilizer maker bought an idled Senegalese phosphorus producer for $721 million.

Beyond these big deals are dozens of smaller acquisitions and investments by Indian companies. "Compared to India, valuations in Africa are quite attractive," says Anuj Chande, who heads the South Asia Group at accounting firm Grant Thornton in London. "We're expecting to see a lot of midsize deals across a variety of sectors."

The Indians view Africa as a place where they can replicate the low-cost, high-efficiency business model they have honed at home. Like India, Africa has hundreds of millions of underserved consumers eager to buy products tailored to their needs. Consumer spending in Africa may double to as much as $1.8 trillion, by 2020. McKinsey & Co. predicts an increase that would be the equivalent of adding a consumer market the size of Brazil. As a pioneer in sales of single-use sachets of soap and shampoo (along with Unilever and Procter & Gamble) for lower-income Indians, Mumbai-based Godrej Consumer Products understands "low-cost, value-for-money products," Chairman Adi Godrej said in an interview. In June 2010, his company acquired Nigerian cosmetics maker Tura, and in 2008, it bought South African hair-care company Kinky. "We want growth. Whether it's from inside or outside India, we are agnostic," Godrej said.

Indian companies also see Africa as a hedge against a possible slowdown at home. "If tomorrow the Indian economy was to take a U-turn, then at least you have other markets which are growing," says Neeraj Kanwar, managing director of Apollo Tyres, India's No. 2 tiremaker. His company bought South Africa's Dunlop Tyres for $62 million in 2006, giving Apollo two manufacturing plants on the continent and brand rights in 32 African countries. Apollo aims to triple sales to $6 billion by 2015, with 60% of revenue from abroad, versus 38% today. "Africa is going to give me growth," says Kanwar.

Essar has endured endless squabbles with Indian landowners who refuse to make way for steel mills. Like other Indian companies tired of regulatory headaches at home, it moved into Africa and now has 2,000 employees there. Bangalore-based Karuturi Global, the world's largest rose producer, couldn't get enough land in India to compete with European and African rivals. Many times flowers wilted on the tarmac as cargo flights were delayed or canceled, including a big Valentine's Day shipment. So in 2004, Karuturi bought a small plot in Ethiopia, and sales have since grown elevenfold, to $113 million in the year ended March 31, 2010. Karuturi now leases 1,200 square miles of land in Ethiopia—larger than the (US) state of Rhode Island—and sells more than half a billion roses a year. "Africa offered us a scale we could never reach in India," says Managing Director Sai Ramakrishna Karuturi. "I'd love to do more in India, but getting even 1,000 acres near Bangalore took years."

Source: "Corporate India finds greener pastures—in Africa," *Bloomberg Businessweek*, 8 November 2010, 61–62.

How do numerous Indian firms enter Africa? Why do they enter certain countries but not others? How do they overcome their liability of foreignness? Why do some of them succeed and others fail? These are some of the key questions driving this chapter. Entering foreign markets is one of the most important topics in international business (IB). This chapter first draws on the institution-based and resource-based views to discuss ways to overcome the liability of foreignness.[1] Then we focus on three crucial dimensions: *where*, *when*, and *how*—known as the 2W1H dimensions. Our discussion culminates in a comprehensive model, followed by a debate.

10-1 OVERCOMING THE LIABILITY OF FOREIGNNESS

It is not easy to succeed in an unfamiliar environment. Recall from Chapter 1 that foreign firms have to overcome a liability of foreignness, which is the inherent disadvantage that foreign firms experience in host countries because of their nonnative status. Such a liability is manifested in at least two ways. First, numerous differences in formal and informal institutions govern the rules of the game in different countries. While local firms are already well versed in these rules, foreign firms have to invest significant resources to learn such rules. Some of the rules are in favor of local firms. For example, after working for years to familiarize itself with US defense procurement rules, European Aeronautic Defence and Space (EADS), the maker of Airbus, in 2008 won a major $35 billion contract to supply the US Air Force with next-generation refueling tankers. Then EADS (along with its US partner, Northrop Grumman) was disappointed to find out that Boeing was able to twist the arms of politicians and change the rules. In 2010, Boeing emerged as the winner of this rich prize and EADS (which more recently changed its name to the Airbus Group) had to drop out.

MARTIN TANNER/GETTY IMAGES

Second, although customers in this age of globalization supposedly no longer discriminate against foreign firms, the reality is that foreign firms are often still discriminated against, sometimes formally and other times informally. For example, activists in India accused both Coca-Cola and PepsiCo that their products contained higher than permitted levels of pesticides but did not test any Indian-branded soft drinks, even though pesticide residues are present in virtually all groundwater in India. Although both Coca-Cola and PepsiCo denied these charges, their sales suffered.

Against such significant odds, how do foreign firms crack new markets? The answer boils down to our two core perspectives introduced earlier (see Exhibit 10.1). The institution-based view suggests that firms need to undertake actions deemed legitimate and appropriate by the various formal and informal institutions governing market entries. Differences in formal institutions may lead to regulatory risks due to differences in political, economic, and legal systems (see Chapter 2). There may be numerous trade and investment barriers on a national or regional basis (see Chapters 5, 6, and 8). In addition, the existence of multiple currencies—and currency risks as a result—may be another formal barrier (see Chapter 7). Informally, numerous differences in cultures, norms, and values create another major source of liability of foreignness (see Chapter 3).

The resource-based view argues that foreign firms need to deploy *overwhelming* resources and capabilities that after offsetting the liability of foreignness, there is still significant competitive advantage left.[2] Applying the VRIO framework introduced in Chapter 4 to our Opening Case, we can suggest that some Indian firms possess some overwhelmingly valuable and rare capabilities in successfully penetrating African markets. The winners from India excel in their low-cost, high-efficiency business model. Their value-for-money products (such as single-use sachets of soap and shampoo) and their abilities to profit from such high-volume, low-price products make it very hard for rivals in Africa to imitate. Entering foreign markets, financing cross-border acquisitions, and hiring local workers require an enormous amount of organizational capabilities. Honed at home, many Indian firms' organizational capabilities have proven to be a tremendous asset in their African forays.

Overall, our two core perspectives shed a lot of light on firms' internationalization. In Focus illustrates the liability of foreignness in the express delivery industry. The institution-based view helps explain how FedEx and UPS experienced tremendous institution-based barriers when competing in China, and the resource-based view points out that DHL's lack of overwhelming resources and capabilities torpedoed its ambition to expand in the United States. Next, we investigate the 2W1H dimensions associated with foreign market entries.

EXHIBIT 10.1 INSTITUTIONS, RESOURCES, AND FOREIGN MARKET ENTRIES

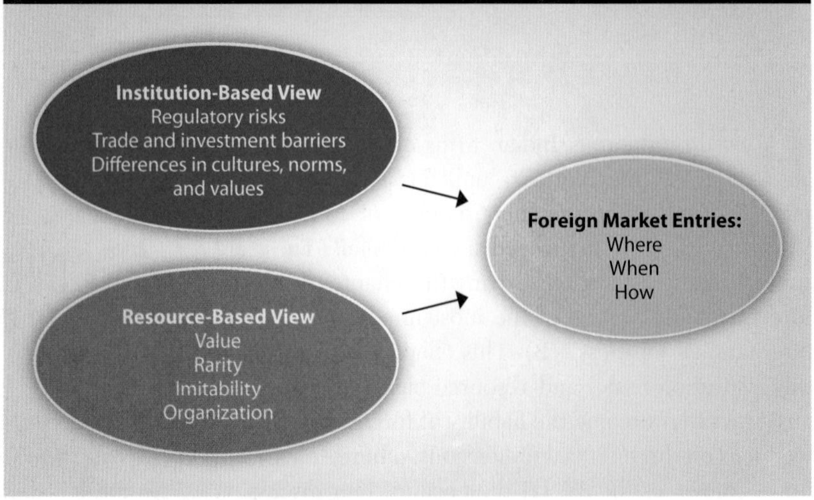

InFocus: Ethical Dilemma/Emerging Markets

Liability of Foreignness in Express Delivery

As Chinese customers increasingly bought online (spending $300 billion in 2013), the express delivery industry in China rose to become the second largest in the world—behind only the United States. Having entered China in 1984 and 1988, respectively, United Parcel Service (UPS) and FedEx were ready to benefit from such growth. But here was a catch. Since 2009, the State Post Bureau—a regulator—implemented a new law requiring that all carriers, foreign and local, needed new licenses. Instead of obtaining a license for operations in the entire country, each of UPS' 33 branches and FedEx's 58 branches required one license. The slow and arduous processes of getting licenses clipped the wings of UPS and FedEx. Domestic carriers such as Suning Commerce and S.F. Express seemed to be able to get licenses faster, thus rocketing ahead of the global giants. UPS and FedEx thus face the dilemma of whether to protest loudly or keep their heads low and wait for the situation to improve.

Back home in the United States, UPS and FedEx had to put up with a new entrant, DHL, which was a subsidiary of Deutsche Post. In 2003, DHL acquired the US-based Airborne Express. However, after losing $10 billion over five years, DHL conceded in November 2008 that it would exit the US express delivery market. Although DHL was a world market leader, its liability of foreignness in the world's largest market was simply too overwhelming. Facing steep sales declines because of the economic crisis, DHL laid off some 10,000 US workers and closed all 18 of its hubs. It would still make international deliveries to and from the United States. Its rivals immediately hustled to grab its customers.

Sources: "For FedEx in China: It's hurry up and wait," *Bloomberg Businessweek*, 10 March 2014, 16–17; "DHL fails to deliver," *BusinessWeek*, 24 November 2008; "Multinationals in China," *Economist*, 24 August 2013, 59.

ROBERTO SCHMIDT/AFP/GETTY IMAGES

10-2 WHERE TO ENTER?

Similar to real estate, the motto for IB is "location, location, location." In fact, such a *spatial* perspective (that is, doing business outside of one's home country) is one of the defining features of IB.[3] Two sets of considerations drive the location of foreign entries: (1) strategic goals and (2) cultural and institutional distances.

10-2a Location-Specific Advantages and Strategic Goals

Favorable locations in certain countries may give firms operating there what are called location-specific advantages. **Location-specific advantages** are the benefits a firm reaps from features specific to a particular place. Certain locations simply possess geographical features that are difficult for others to match. Leading seaports and airports (see PengAtlas Map 14) naturally attract a lot of foreign entrants. For example, Miami, the self-styled "Gateway of the Americas," is an ideal location both for North American firms looking south and Latin American firms coming north. Vienna is an attractive site as multinational regional headquarters for Central and Eastern Europe. Dubai is an ideal stopping point for air traffic

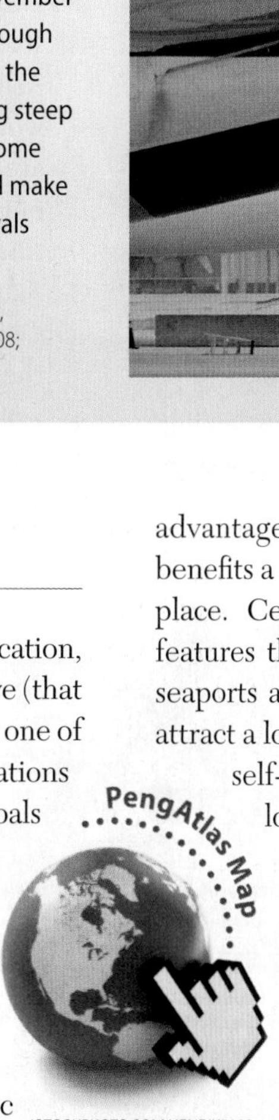

ISTOCKPHOTO.COM HENRIK5000

Location-specific advantage The benefit a firm reaps from the features specific to a place.

between Europe and Asia and between Africa and Asia. Two billion people live within four hours of flying time from Dubai, and four billion can be reached within seven hours. Dubai's airport is already the third busiest international airport in terms of passengers behind only London Heathrow and Hong Kong airports.[4] Similarly, Rotterdam, the Netherlands, is the main hub for sea-bound transportation into and out of Europe. More than 500 liner services connect Rotterdam with over 1,000 ports worldwide. Overall, we may regard the continuous expansion of global business as an unending saga in search of location-specific advantages.

We learned in Chapter 6 about agglomeration—location-specific advantages that arise from the clustering of economic activities in certain locations. The basic idea dates back at least to Alfred Marshall, a British economist who first published it in 1890. Recall that location-specific advantages stem from (1) knowledge spillovers among closely located firms that attempt to hire individuals from competitors, (2) industry demand that creates a skilled labor force whose members may work for different firms without having to move out of the region, and (3) industry demand that facilitates a pool of specialized suppliers and buyers to also locate in the region. For example, due to agglomeration, Dallas has the world's heaviest concentration of telecom companies. US firms such as AT&T, HP, Raytheon, Texas Instruments (TI), and Verizon cluster there. Moreover, numerous leading foreign telecom firms such as Alcatel-Lucent, Ericsson, Fujitsu, Huawei, Siemens, STMicroelectronics, and ZTE have also converged in this region.

EXHIBIT 10.2 MATCHING STRATEGIC GOALS WITH LOCATIONS

Strategic goals	Location-specific advantages	Examples in the text
Natural resource seeking	Possession of natural resources and related transport and communication infrastructure	Oil in the Middle East, Russia, and Venezuela
Market seeking	Abundance of strong market demand and customers willing to pay	Automakers and business jet makers in China
Efficiency seeking	Economies of scale and abundance of low-cost factors	Manufacturing in China
Innovation seeking	Abundance of innovative individuals, firms, and universities	IT in Silicon Valley and Bangalore; telecom in Dallas; perfumes in Paris

Given that different locations offer different benefits, it is imperative that a firm match its strategic goals with potential locations. The four strategic goals are shown in Exhibit 10.2.

- Firms seeking *natural resources* have to go to particular foreign locations where those resources are found. For example, the Middle East, Russia, and Venezuela are all rich in oil. Even when the Venezuelan government became more hostile, Western oil firms had to put up with it.
- *Market-seeking* firms go to countries that have a strong demand for their products and services. As China becomes the largest car market in the world, practically all the automakers in the world are now elbowing into it. General Motors (GM) has emerged as the leader. In 2010, GM for the first time sold more cars in China than in the United States.[5] As demand for business aviation takes off in China, business jet makers are now intensely eyeing the new market (see the Closing Case).
- *Efficiency-seeking* firms often single out the most efficient locations featuring a combination of scale economies and low-cost factors. It is the search for efficiency that induced numerous multinational

Dallas skyline

ISTOCKPHOTO.COM/BEN BLANKENBURG

enterprises (MNEs) to enter China. China now manufactures two-thirds of the world's photocopiers, shoes, toys, and microwave ovens; one-half of the DVD players, digital cameras, and textiles; one-third of the desktop computers; and one-quarter of the mobile phones, television sets, and steel. Shanghai alone reportedly has a cluster of over 400 of the *Fortune* Global 500 firms. It is important to note that China does not present the absolutely lowest labor costs in the world, and Shanghai is the *highest* cost city in China. However, its attractiveness lies in its ability to enhance efficiency for foreign entrants by lowering *total* costs.

- *Innovation-seeking* firms target countries and regions renowned for generating world-class innovations, such as Silicon Valley and Bangalore (in IT), Dallas (in telecom), and Paris (in perfumes). Such entries can be viewed as "an option to maintain access to innovations resident in the host country, thus generating information spillovers that may lead to opportunities for future organizational learning and growth."[6] (See Chapter 12 for details.)

It is important to note that location-specific advantages may grow, change, and/or decline, prompting a firm to relocate. If policy makers fail to maintain the institutional attractiveness (for example, by raising taxes) and if companies overcrowd and bid up factor costs such as land and talents, some firms may move out of certain locations previously considered advantageous. For example, the Chinese government has raised minimum wages and tightened environmental regulations. Also, thanks to the "one child" policy that was first implemented in the 1980s, the number of low-skill youth entering the labor market has declined. These changes have eroded the location-specific advantages of coastal China centered on low costs. As a result, many labor-intensive, cost-conscious firms have either moved to inland China (where labor cost has remained relatively low) or Southeast Asian countries such as Indonesia, Malaysia, Thailand, and Vietnam (where labor cost is now lower than that of coastal China).

10-2b Cultural/Institutional Distances and Foreign Entry Locations

In addition to strategic goals, another set of considerations centers on cultural/institutional distances (see also Chapters 2 and 3). **Cultural distance** is the difference between two cultures along identifiable dimensions such as individualism. Considering culture as an informal

part of institutional frameworks governing a particular country, **institutional distance** is "the extent of similarity or dissimilarity between the regulatory, normative, and cognitive institutions of two countries."[7] Broadly speaking, cultural distance is a *subset* of institutional distance. For example, many Western cosmetics products firms, such as L'Oreal and Victoria's Secret, have shied away from Saudi Arabia, citing its stricter rules of personal behavior. In essence, Saudi Arabia's cultural and institutional distance from Western cultures is too large.

Two schools of thought have emerged in overcoming these distances. The first is associated with the stage model. According to the stage model first introduced in Chapter 9, firms will enter culturally similar countries during their first stage of internationalization and will then gain more confidence to enter culturally distant countries in later stages. This idea is intuitively appealing: It makes sense for Belgian firms to enter France first and for Mexican firms to enter Texas first to take advantage of common cultural and language traditions. On average, business between countries that share a language is three times greater than between countries without a common language. Firms from common-law countries (English-speaking countries and Britain's former colonies) are more likely to be interested in other common-law countries. Colony-colonizer links (such as Britain's ties with the Commonwealth and Spain's with Latin America) boost trade significantly. Overall, certain performance benefits seem to exist when competing in culturally and institutionally adjacent countries.

Citing numerous counter-examples, a second school of thought argues that it is more important to consider strategic goals such as market and efficiency rather than culture and institutions. For example, despite the often hostile Congress and the typically unfriendly US media, many Chinese firms are eager to do business in the United States.[8] Because the United States is the largest market, cultural and institutional distances

Cultural distance The difference between two cultures along identifiable dimensions such as individualism.

Institutional distance The extent of similarity or dissimilarity between the regulatory, normative, and cognitive institutions of two countries.

between China and the United States do not seem to matter. Overall, in the complex calculus underpinning entry decisions, location represents only one of several important considerations. As shown next, entry timing and modes are also crucial.

AP IMAGES/STOCKTREK IMAGES

10-3 WHEN TO ENTER?

Entry timing refers to whether there are compelling reasons to be an early or late entrant in a particular country. Some firms look for **first-mover advantages**, defined as the benefits that accrue to firms that enter the market first and that later entrants do not enjoy.[9] Speaking of the power of first-mover advantages, "Xerox," "FedEx," and "Google" have now become *verbs* such as "Google it." In many African countries, "Colgate" is the generic term for toothpaste. Unilever, a late mover, is disappointed to find out that some of its African customers call its own toothpaste "the red Colgate." However, first movers may also encounter significant disadvantages which, in turn, become **late-mover advantages**. Exhibit 10.3 shows a number of first-mover advantages.

- First movers may gain advantage through proprietary technology. Think about Apple's iPod, iPad, and iPhone.
- First movers may also make preemptive investments. A number of Japanese MNEs have cherry picked leading local suppliers and distributors in Southeast Asia as new members of the expanded *keiretsu* networks (alliances of Japanese businesses with interlocking business relationships and shareholdings), and have blocked access to the suppliers and istributors by late entrants from the West.[10]
- First movers may erect significant entry barriers for late entrants, such as high switching costs due to brand loyalty. Buyers of expensive equipment are likely to stick with the same producers for components, training, and other services for a long time. That is why American, British, French, German, and Russian aerospace firms competed intensely for Poland's first post-Cold War order of fighters—America's F-16 eventually won.
- Intense domestic competition may drive some non-dominant firms abroad to avoid clashing with dominant firms head-on in their home market. Matsushita, Toyota, and NEC were the market leaders in Japan, but Sony, Honda, and Epson all entered the United States in their respective industries ahead of the leading firms.
- First movers may build precious relationships with key stakeholders such as customers and governments. For example, Citigroup, JP Morgan Chase, and Metallurgical Corporation of China have entered Afghanistan, earning a good deal of goodwill from the Afghan government that is interested in wooing more foreign direct investment (FDI).[11]

First-mover advantage Benefit that accrues to firms that enter the market first and that later entrants do not enjoy.

Late-mover advantage Benefit that accrues to firms that enter the market later and that early entrants do not enjoy.

EXHIBIT 10.3 FIRST-MOVER ADVANTAGES AND LATE-MOVER ADVANTAGES

First-mover advantages	Examples in the text
Proprietary, technological leadership	Apple's iPod, iPad, and iPhone
Preemption of scarce resources	Japanese MNEs in Southeast Asia
Establishment of entry barriers for late entrants	Poland's F-16 fighter jet contract
Avoidance of clash with dominant firms at home	Sony, Honda, and Epson went to the US market ahead of their Japanese rivals
Relationships with key stakeholders such as governments	Citigroup, JP Morgan Chase, and Metallurgical Corporation of China entered Afghanistan
Late-mover advantages	**Examples in the text**
Opportunity to free ride on first mover investments	Ericsson won big contracts in Saudi Arabia, free riding on Cisco's efforts
Resolution of technological and market uncertainties	BMW, GM, and Toyota have patience to wait until the Nissan Leaf resolves uncertainties about the electric car
First mover's difficulty to adapt to market changes	Greyhound is stuck with the bus depots, whereas Megabus simply uses curbside stops

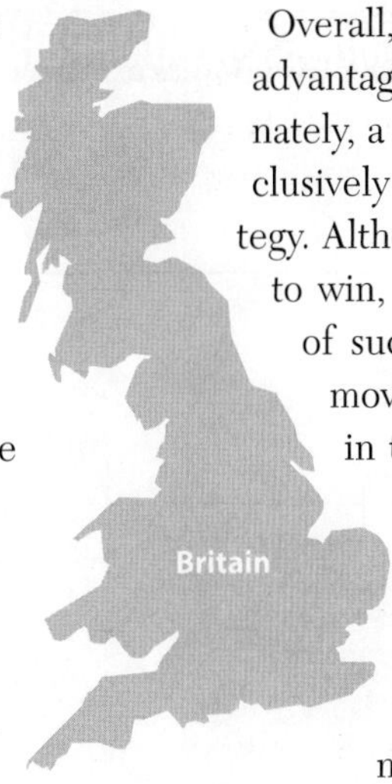

The potential advantages of first movers may be counter-balanced by various disadvantages, which are also listed in Exhibit 10.3. Numerous first-mover firms—such as EMI in CT scanners and Netscape in Internet browsers—have lost market dominance in the long run. It is such late-mover firms as General Electric and Microsoft (Explorer), respectively, that win. Specifically, late-mover advantages are manifested in three ways:

- Late movers may be able to free ride on the huge pioneering investments of first movers. In Saudi Arabia, Cisco invested millions of dollars to rub shoulders of dignitaries, including the king, in order to help officials grasp the promise of the Internet in fueling economic development, only to lose out to late movers such as Ericsson that offered lower cost solutions. For instance, the brand new King Abdullah Economic City awarded an $84 million citywide telecom project to Ericsson whose bid was more than 20% lower than Cisco's—in part because Ericsson did not have to offer a lot of basic education and did not have to entertain that much. "We're very proud to have won against a company that did as much advance work as Cisco did," an elated Ericsson executive noted.[12]
- First movers face greater technological and market uncertainties. Nissan, for example, has launched the world's first all-electric car, the Leaf, which can run without a single drop of gasoline. However, there are tremendous uncertainties. After some of these uncertainties are removed, late movers such as BMW, GM, and Toyota have joined the game with their own electric cars.
- As incumbents, first movers may be locked into a given set of fixed assets or are reluctant to cannibalize existing product lines in favor of new ones. Late movers may be able to take advantage of the inflexibility of first movers by leapfrogging them. Although Greyhound, the incumbent in intercity bus service in the United States, is financially struggling, it cannot get rid of the expensive bus depots in inner cities that are often ill-maintained and dreadful. Megabus, the new entrant from Britain, simply has not bothered to build and maintain a single bus depot. Instead, Megabus uses curbside stops (like regular city bus stops), which have made travel by bus more appealing to a large number of passengers.

Overall, evidence points out both first-mover advantages and late-mover advantages. Unfortunately, a mountain of research is still unable to conclusively recommend a particular entry timing strategy. Although first movers may have an *opportunity* to win, their pioneering status is not a guarantee of success. For example, among the three first movers into the Chinese automobile industry in the 1980s, Volkswagen captured significant advantages, Chrysler had very moderate success, and Peugeot failed and had to exit. Although many of the late movers that entered in the 1990s struggled, GM, Honda, and Hyundai gained significant market shares. It is obvious that entry timing cannot be viewed in isolation and entry timing *per se* is not the sole determinant of success and failure of foreign entries. It is through *interaction* with other strategic variables that entry timing has an impact on performance.

10-4 HOW TO ENTER?

In this section, we will first consider on what scale—large or small—a firm should enter foreign markets. Then we will look at a comprehensive model for entering foreign markets. The first step is to determine whether to pursue an equity or non-equity mode of entry. As we will see, this crucial decision differentiates MNEs (involving equity modes) from non-MNEs (relying on non-equity modes). Finally, we outline the pros and cons of various equity and non-equity modes.

10-4a Scale of Entry: Commitment and Experience

One key dimension in foreign entry decisions is the **scale of entry**, which refers to the amount of resources committed to entering a foreign market. Large-scale entries demonstrate a strategic commitment to certain markets. This helps assure local customers and suppliers ("We are here for the long haul!") while detering potential entrants. The drawbacks of such a hard-to-reverse strategic commitment are (1) limited strategic flexibility elsewhere and (2) huge losses if these large-scale bets turn out to be wrong.

Scale of entry The amount of resources committed to entering a foreign market.

EXHIBIT 10.4 THE CHOICE OF ENTRY MODES: A COMPREHENSIVE MODEL

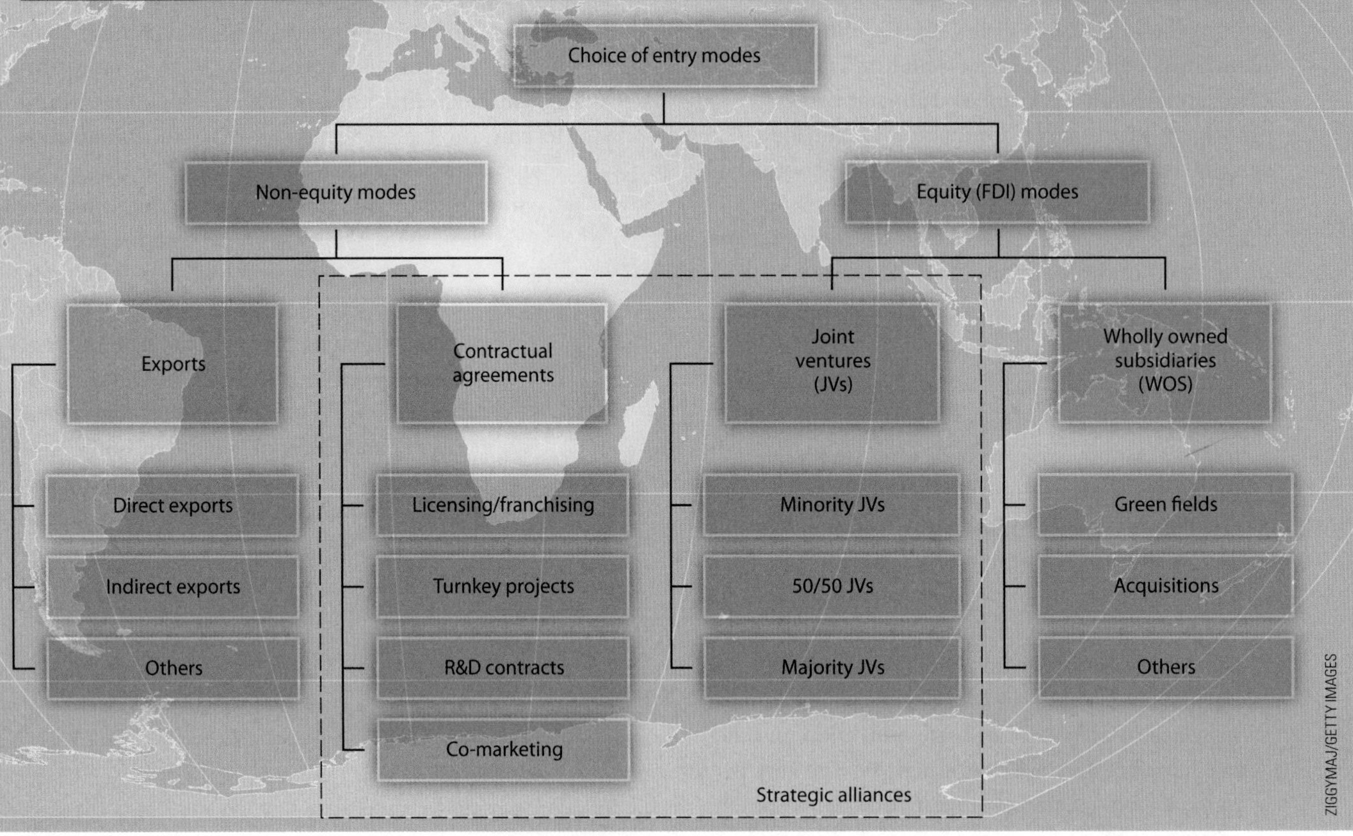

Source: Adapted from Y. Pan and D. Tse, "The hierarchical model of market entry modes," *Journal of International Business Studies* 31 (2000): 535–554. The dotted area labeled "strategic alliances," including both non-equity modes (contractual agreements) and equity modes (JVs), was added by the present author. See Chapter 11 for more details on strategic alliances.

Small-scale entries are less costly. They focus on organizational learning by getting a firm's feet wet—learning by doing—while limiting the downside risk.[13] For example, to enter the market of Islamic finance whereby no interest can be charged (according to the Koran), Citibank set up a subsidiary Citibank Islamic Bank. On a small scale, it was designed to experiment with different interpretations of the Koran on how to make money while not committing religious sins. Overall, the longer foreign firms stay in host countries, the less liability of foreignness they experience. The drawback of small-scale entries is a lack of strong commitment, which may lead to difficulties in building market share and capturing first-mover advantages.

Mode of entry Method used to enter a foreign market.

Non-equity mode A mode of entering foreign markets through exports and/or contractual agreements that tends to reflect relatively smaller commitments to overseas markets.

Equity mode A mode of entering foreign markets through joint ventures and/or wholly owned subsidiaries that indicates a relatively larger, harder-to-reverse commitment.

10-4b Modes of Entry: The First Step on Equity Versus Non-Equity Modes

Managers are unlikely to consider the numerous **modes of entry**—methods used to enter a foreign market—at the same time. Given the complexity of entry decisions, it is imperative that managers *prioritize* and consider only a few key variables first and then consider other variables later. The comprehensive model shown in Exhibits 10.4 and 10.5 is helpful.

In the first step, considerations for small-scale versus large-scale entries usually boil down to the equity (ownership) issue. **Non-equity modes** include exports and contractual agreements and tend to reflect relatively smaller commitments to overseas markets. **Equity modes**, on the other hand, are indicative of relatively larger, harder-to-reverse commitments. Equity modes call for the establishment of independent organizations overseas (partially or wholly controlled). Non-equity modes do not require such independent establishments. Overall, these modes differ significantly in terms of cost, commitment, risk, return, and control.

EXHIBIT 10.5 MODES OF ENTRY: ADVANTAGES AND DISADVANTAGES

Entry modes (examples in the text)	Advantages	Disadvantages
1. Non-equity modes: Exports		
Direct exports (*Pearl River exports pianos to over 80 countries*)	▶ Economies of scale in production concentrated in home country ▶ Better control over distribution	▶ High transportation costs for bulky products ▶ Marketing distance from customers ▶ Trade barriers and protectionism
Indirect exports (*Commodities trade in textiles and meats*)	▶ Concentration of resources on production ▶ No need to directly handle export processes	▶ Less control over distribution (relative to direct exports) ▶ Inability to learn how to compete overseas
2. Non-equity modes: Contractual agreements		
Licensing/franchising (*Pizza Hut in Thailand*)	▶ Low development costs ▶ Low risk in overseas expansion	▶ Little control over technology and marketing ▶ May create competitors ▶ Inability to engage in global coordination
Turnkey projects (*Safi Energy in Morocco*)	▶ Ability to earn returns from process technology in countries where FDI is restricted	▶ May create efficient competitors ▶ Lack of long-term presence
Research and development (R&D) contracts (*IT work in India*)	▶ Ability to tap into the best locations for certain innovations at low costs	▶ Difficult to negotiate and enforce contracts ▶ May nurture innovative competitors ▶ May lose core innovation capabilities
Co-marketing (*McDonald's campaigns with movie studios and toy makers; airline alliances*)	▶ Ability to reach more customers	▶ Limited coordination
3. Equity modes: Partially owned subsidiaries		
Joint ventures (*Shanghai Volkswagen*)	▶ Sharing costs, risks, and profits ▶ Access to partners' knowledge and assets ▶ Politically acceptable	▶ Divergent goals and interests of partners ▶ Limited equity and operational control ▶ Difficult to coordinate globally
4. Equity modes: Wholly owned subsidiaries		
Greenfield projects (*Microsoft's R&D center in China; TI in Japan; Japanese auto transplants in the United States*)	▶ Complete equity and operational control ▶ Protection of know-how ▶ Ability to coordinate globally	▶ Potential political problems and risks ▶ High development costs ▶ Add new capacity to industry ▶ Slow entry speed (relative to acquisitions)
Acquisitions (*Indian firms in Africa*)	▶ Same as greenfield (above) ▶ Do not add new capacity ▶ Fast entry speed	▶ Same as greenfield (above), except adding new capacity and slow speed ▶ Post-acquisition integration problems

The distinction between equity and non-equity modes is not trivial. In fact, it is what defines an MNE: An MNE enters foreign markets via equity modes through FDI. A firm that merely exports/imports with no FDI is usually not regarded as an MNE. As discussed at length in Chapter 6, an MNE, relative to a non-MNE, enjoys the three-pronged advantages of ownership, location, and internalization—collectively known as the OLI advantages. Overall, the first step in entry mode considerations is crucial. A strategic decision has to be made in terms of whether or not to undertake FDI and to become an MNE.

10-4c Modes of Entry: The Second Step on Making Actual Selections

During the second step, managers consider variables within *each* group of non-equity and equity modes. If the decision is to export, then the next consideration is direct exports or indirect exports (see Chapter 9). Direct exports are the most basic mode of entry, capitalizing on economies of scale in production concentrated in the home country and providing better control over distribution. The world's largest piano maker, Pearl River, exports its pianos from China to over 80 countries. This strategy essentially treats foreign demand as an extension of domestic demand, and the firm is geared toward designing and producing first and foremost for the domestic market. While direct exports may work if the export volume is small, it is not optimal when the firm has many foreign buyers. Marketing 101 suggests that the firm needs to be closer, both physically and psychologically, to its customers, prompting the firm to consider more intimate overseas involvement such as FDI. Direct exports may also provoke protectionism, triggering antidumping actions (see the Debate feature).

As you will recall from Chapter 9, another export strategy is indirect exports—namely, exporting through domestically based export intermediaries. This strategy not only enjoys the economies of scale in domestic production (similar to direct exports), but is also relatively worry free. A significant amount of export trade in commodities such as textiles, woods, and meats, which compete primarily on price, is indirect through intermediaries.[14] Indirect exports have some drawbacks. For example, third parties such as export trading companies may not share the same agendas and objectives as exporters. Exporters choose intermediaries primarily because of information asymmetries concerning risks and uncertainties associated with foreign markets.[15] Intermediaries with international contacts and knowledge essentially make a living by taking advantage of such information asymmetries. They may have a vested interest in making sure that such asymmetries are not reduced. Intermediaries, for example, may repackage the products under their own brand and insist on monopolizing the communication with overseas customers. If the exporter is interested in knowing more about how its products perform overseas, indirect exports would not provide such knowledge.

Turnkey project A project in which clients pay contractors to design and construct new facilities and train personnel.

Build-operate-transfer (BOT) agreement A non-equity mode of entry used to build a longer-term presence by building and then operating a facility for a period of time before transferring operations to a domestic agency or firm.

Research and development (R&D) contract Outsourcing agreement in R&D between firms.

Dumping Exporting products at prices that are below what it costs to manufacture them, with the intent to raise prices after eliminating local rivals.

The next group of non-equity entry modes involves the following types of contractual agreement: (1) licensing or franchising, (2) turnkey projects, (3) research and development contracts, and (4) co-marketing. Recall from Chapter 9 that in licensing/franchising agreements, the licensor/franchisor sells the rights to intellectual property such as patents and know-how to the licensee/franchisee for a royalty fee. The licensor/franchisor, thus, does not have to bear the full costs and risks associated with foreign expansion. On the other hand, the licensor/franchisor does not have tight control over production and marketing. Pizza Hut, for example, was disappointed when its franchise in Thailand discontinued the relationship and launched a competing pizza restaurant to eat Pizza Hut's lunch.

In **turnkey projects**, clients pay contractors to design and construct new facilities and train personnel. At project completion, contractors hand clients the proverbial key to facilities ready for operations—hence the term "turnkey." This mode allows firms to earn returns from process technology (such as power generation) in countries where FDI is restricted. The drawbacks, however, are twofold. First, if foreign clients are competitors, selling them state-of-the-art technology through turnkey projects may boost their competitiveness. Second, turnkey projects do not allow for a long-term presence after the key is handed to clients. To obtain a longer-term presence, build-operate-transfer agreements are now often used, instead of the traditional build-transfer type of turnkey projects. A **build-operate-transfer (BOT) agreement** is a non-equity mode of entry used to build a longer-term presence by building and then operating a facility for a period of time before transferring operations to a domestic agency or firm. For example, Safi Energy, a consortium among GDF Suez (France), Mitsui (Japan), and Nareva Holdings (Morocco), has been awarded a BOT power-generation project in Morocco.[16]

Research and development (R&D) contracts refer to outsourcing agreements in R&D between firms. Firm A agrees to perform certain R&D work for Firm B. Firms thereby tap into the best locations for certain innovations

Debate: Ethical Dilemma/Emerging Markets

Dumping and Antidumping

Dumping is defined as an exporter (1) selling abroad below cost and (2) planning to raise prices after eliminating local rivals. Consider the following two scenarios. First, a steel producer in Indiana enters a new market, Texas. In Texas, it offers prices lower than those in Indiana, resulting in a 10% market share in Texas. Texas firms have two choices. The first one is to initiate a lawsuit against the Indiana firm for predatory pricing. However, it is difficult to prove (1) that the Indiana firm is selling below cost and (2) that its pricing is an attempt to monopolize. Under US antitrust laws, a predation case like this will have no chance of succeeding. Thus, Texas firms are most likely to opt for their second option: to retaliate in kind by offering lower prices to customers in Indiana, leading to lower prices in both Texas and Indiana, which benefit consumers.

AMERICAN SPIRIT/SHUTTERSTOCK.COM

Now, in the second scenario, the invading firm is not from Indiana but *India*. Holding everything else constant, Texas steel firms can argue that the Indian firm is dumping. Under US antidumping laws, Texas steel producers, according to an expert, "would almost certainly obtain legal relief on the very same facts that would not support an antitrust claim, let alone antitrust relief." Note that imposing antidumping duties on Indian steel imports reduces the incentive for Texas firms to counterattack by entering India, resulting in higher prices in both Texas and India, where consumers are hurt.

These two scenarios are hypothetical but also highly realistic. An Organization for Economic Co-operation and Development (OECD) study in Australia, Canada, the European Union, and the United States reports that 90% of the practices classified as unfair dumping in these countries would have never been questioned under their own antitrust laws if used by a domestic firm in making a domestic sale. Simply filing an antidumping petition (regardless of the outcome), one study finds, may result in a 1% increase of the stock price for US-listed firms (on average, a cool $46 million increase in market value). Evidently, Wall Street knows that Uncle Sam is on your side. In a nutshell, foreign firms are discriminated against by the formal rules of the game.

From an ethical standpoint, Joseph Stiglitz, a Nobel laureate in economics, writes that antidumping duties "are simply naked protectionism" and that one country's "fair trade laws" are often known elsewhere as "unfair trade laws." A classic response is: What if, through unfair dumping, foreign rivals drive out local firms and then jack up prices? Given the competitive nature of most industries, it is often difficult (if not impossible) to eliminate all rivals and then recoup losses by charging higher monopoly prices. The fear of foreign monopoly is often exaggerated by special interest groups. One solution is to phase out antidumping laws and use the same standards as used in domestic predatory pricing. Such a waiver of antidumping charges has been in place between Australia and New Zealand, between Canada and the United States, and within the European Union. Thus, a Canadian firm, essentially treated as a US firm, can still be accused of predatory pricing but cannot be accused of dumping in the United States. However, domestically, a predation case is very difficult to make. In such a way, competition can be fostered, aggressiveness rewarded, and dumping legalized.

Sources: R. Lipstein, "Using antitrust principles to reform antidumping law," in E. Graham and D. Richardson (eds.), *Global Competition Policy* (Washington: Institute for International Economics, 1997) 405–438; S. Marsh, "Creating barriers for foreign competitors," *Strategic Management Journal* 19 (1998): 25–37; OECD, *Trade and Competition* (Paris: OECD, 1996); J. Stiglitz, *Globalization and Its Discontent* (New York: Norton, 2002) 20.

at relatively low costs. However, three drawbacks may emerge. First, given the uncertain and multidimensional nature of R&D, these contracts are often difficult to negotiate and enforce. While delivery time and costs are relatively easy to negotiate, quality is often difficult to assess. Second, such contracts may cultivate competitors. A number of Indian IT firms, nurtured by such work, are now on a global offensive to take on their Western rivals. Finally, firms that rely on outsiders to perform a lot of R&D may lose some of their core R&D capabilities in the long run.

Co-marketing refers to efforts among a number of firms to jointly market their products and services. Toy makers and movie studios often collaborate in co-marketing campaigns with fast-food chains such as McDonald's to

Co-marketing Efforts among a number of firms to jointly market their products and services.

package toys based on movie characters in kids' meals. Airline alliances such as One World, Sky Team, and Star Alliance engage in extensive co-marketing through code sharing. The advantages are the ability to reach more customers. The drawbacks center on limited control and coordination.

Next are equity modes, all of which entail some FDI and transform the firm to become an MNE. A **joint venture (JV)** is a corporate child, a new entity jointly created and owned by two or more parent companies. It has three principal forms: Minority JV (less than 50% equity), 50/50 JV (equal equity), and majority JV (more than 50% equity). JVs, such as Shanghai Volkswagen, have three advantages. First, an MNE shares costs, risks, and profits with a local partner, so the firm possesses a certain degree of control but limits risk exposure. Second, the MNE gains access to knowledge about the host country; the local firm, in turn, benefits from the MNE's technology, capital, and management. Third, JVs may be politically more acceptable in host countries.

In terms of disadvantages, JVs often involve partners from different backgrounds and with different goals, so conflicts are natural. Furthermore, effective equity and operational control may be difficult to achieve since everything has to be negotiated—in some cases, fought over. Finally, the nature of the JV does not give an MNE the tight control over a foreign subsidiary that it may need for global coordination. Overall, all sorts of non-equity-based contractual agreements and equity-based JVs can be broadly considered as strategic alliances (within the *dotted area* in Exhibit 10.4). Chapter 11 will discuss them in detail.

The last entry mode is to establish a **wholly owned subsidiary (WOS)**, defined as a subsidiary located in a foreign country that is entirely owned by the parent multinational. There are two primary means to set up a WOS. One is to establish **greenfield operations**, building new factories and offices from scratch (on a proverbial piece of "green field" formerly used for agricultural purposes). For example, Microsoft established a wholly owned greenfield R&D center in Beijing. There are three advantages. First, a greenfield WOS gives an MNE complete equity and management control, thus eliminating the headaches associated with JVs. Second, this undivided control leads to better protection of proprietary technology. Third, a WOS allows for centrally coordinated global actions. Sometimes, a subsidiary will be ordered to launch actions that by design will *lose* money. In the semiconductor market, TI faced competition from Japanese rivals such as NEC and Toshiba that maintained low prices outside of Japan by charging high prices in Japan and using domestic profits to cross-subsidize overseas expansion. By entering Japan via a WOS and slashing prices there, TI incurred a loss but forced the Japanese firms to defend their home market. This was because Japanese rivals had a much larger market share in Japan. When the price level in Japan collapsed thanks to the aggressive price cutting unleashed by TI's WOS in the country, NEC and Toshiba would suffer much more significant losses. Consequently, Japanese rivals had to reduce the ferocity of their price wars outside of Japan. Local licensees/franchisees or JV partners are unlikely to accept such a subservient role as being ordered to lose money (!).

Joint venture (JV) A new corporate entity jointly created and owned by two or more parent companies.

Wholly owned subsidiary (WOS) A subsidiary located in a foreign country that is entirely owned by the parent multinational.

Greenfield operation Building factories and offices from scratch (on a proverbial piece of "green field" formerly used for agricultural purposes).

In terms of drawbacks, a greenfield WOS tends to be expensive and risky, not only financially but also politically. Its conspicuous foreignness may become a target for nationalistic sentiments. Another drawback is that greenfield operations add new capacity to an industry, which will make a competitive industry more crowded. For example, think of all the Japanese automobile plants built in the United States, which have severely squeezed the market share of US automakers and forced Chrysler and GM into bankruptcy. Finally, greenfield operations suffer from a slow entry speed of at least one to several years (relative to acquisitions).

The other way to establish a WOS is through an acquisition. Indian firms' acquisitions in Africa are cases in point (see the Opening Case). Although this is the last mode we discuss here, it represents approximately 70% of worldwide FDI. Acquisition shares all the benefits of greenfield WOS but enjoys two additional advantages: (1) adding no new capacity and (2) faster entry speed. In terms of drawbacks, acquisition shares all of the disadvantages of greenfield WOS except adding new capacity and slow entry speed. But acquisition has a unique and potentially devastating disadvantage: post-acquisition integration problems. (See Chapter 11.)

Overall, while we have focused on one entry mode at a time, firms in practice are not limited by any single entry mode. For example, IKEA stores in China are JVs, and its stores in Hong Kong and Taiwan are separate franchises. In addition, entry modes may change over time. Starbucks, for instance, first used franchising. It then switched to JVs and, more recently, to acquisitions.

10-5 MANAGEMENT SAVVY

Foreign market entries represent a *foundation* for overseas actions. Without these crucial first steps, firms will remain domestic players. The challenges associated with internationalization are daunting, the complexities enormous, and the stakes high. Returning to our fundamental question, we ask: What determines the success and failure in foreign market entries? The answer boils down to the two core perspectives: institution-based and resource-based views. Shown in Exhibit 10.6, three implications for action emerge from these perspectives. First, from an institution-based view, managers need to understand the rules of the game, both formal and informal, governing competition in foreign markets. Failure to understand these rules can be costly. Why do Chinese MNEs' high-profile acquisition attempts in the United States (such as CNOOC's bid for Unocal) and Australia (such as Chinalco's bid for Rio Tinto) often fail? Why do Arabic MNEs' similar attempts (such as DP World's bid for US ports) often fail too? While there are many reasons, one key reason is these foreign entrants' failure in understanding the informal, unwritten rules of the game that often have protectionist (or even racist) undertones in developed economies. Knowing these rules of the game does not mean these emerging multinationals need to be discouraged. They just need to do better homework, keep their heads low, and work on *low-profile* acquisitions, which are routinely approved in developed economies.

EXHIBIT 10.6 IMPLICATIONS FOR ACTION

- Understand the rules of game—both formal and informal—governing competition in foreign markets.
- Develop overwhelming resources and capabilities to offset the liability of foreignness.
- Match efforts in market entry with strategic goals.

Second, from a resource-based view, managers need to develop *overwhelming* capabilities to offset the liability of foreignness. The key word is *overwhelming*. Merely outstanding, but not overwhelming, capabilities cannot ensure success in the face of strong incumbents—a painful lesson that DHL learned when it withdrew from the United States (see In Focus). In short, being good enough is not good enough.

Finally, managers need to match entries with strategic goals. If the goal is to deter rivals in their home markets through price slashing as TI did in Japan, then be prepared to fight a nasty price war and lose money. If the goal is to generate decent returns, then withdrawing from some tough nuts to crack may be necessary—as evidenced by Walmart's withdrawal from Germany, India, and South Korea.

EMERGING MARKETS

Business Jet Makers Eye China

"The Chinese economy slows down" is one of the leading themes in recent global business news. Foreign firms interested in the legendary "one billion customers" in China are advised to adjust their high-flying expectations down to earth. Defying this trend, business jet makers continue to have sky-high expectations for China—for a good reason. Arriving in China as recently as in 2003, this industry is literally just "taking off." Business jets (also known as corporate jets or private jets) are ideal for China, which has a vast territory (the third largest in the world behind Russia and Canada) good for flying. China has also amassed the world's second largest number of billionaires (behind the United States) and is rapidly churning out new ones who can afford to buy jets. Yet, only fewer than 400 business jets currently fly in China, a number that is not only smaller than the number in Brazil and Mexico, but also smaller than what can be found in a single airport—Orange County airport outside Los Angeles—in the United States.

The rise of China for business aviation also coincides with the aftermath of the 2008 global financial crisis, during which many buyers canceled their orders. Not surprisingly, anybody who is somebody in business aviation is eager to elbow its way into essentially the virgin skies of China. But here is an institution-based catch. The skies in China are formally controlled by the military, and flight plans have to be submitted via a cumbersome process. Beijing's airport only gives two take-off slots an hour to business jets. Buyers importing jets are hit by onerous duties and taxes, and officials have talked about slapping a new luxury tax on top of those. Further, an anti-corruption (and anti-conspicuous consumption) campaign unleashed by President Xi Jinping has scared away a lot of large state-owned enterprises (SOEs), which used to make up approximately 15% of the business jet market in China—now down to about 5%.

While institution-based barriers persist, the government has offered a glimmer of hope. It seems to have realized the value of business aviation. The latest five-year plan explicitly calls for the development of *non*-airline aviation, and the military is instructed to give up some chunks of air space to leave room for business jets. The industry of course has been marketing and lobbying intensely, claiming that business aviation is not merely a luxury, but also a productivity booster that can propel firms' (and China's) growth to new heights.

Leveraging resources and capabilities, each business jet maker is endeavoring to outshine each other. Beech Hawker, Cessna, and Gulfstream of the United States, Dassault Falcon of France, and Learjet of Canada (owned by Bombardier) are the traditional competitors. Each carrying 8–12 passengers, they offer privacy, luxury, and often very long range. Salivating the growth potential, the top three larger jet makers—Boeing, Airbus, and Embraer (of Brazil)—have also entered the fray.

TOMOHIRO OHSUMI/BLOOMBERG/GETTY IMAGES

Boeing adapted its 737 to offer the Boeing Business Jet (up to 60 passengers). Airbus modified its A320 to launch the Airbus Corporate Jet (up to 40 passengers). Embraer turned its ERJ 190 regional jet into Lineage 1000 (up to 20 passengers). These ultra-large business jets offer more spacious interiors, better circulated air (due to their larger cabin), and longer range—at price ranges competitive to those of the traditional business jets.

In China, the current market leader is Gulfstream, which has sold over 100 jets and holds the biggest market share. Gulfstream does whatever it takes to win orders, including changing the model number instead of offending potential buyers with an unintended meaning. Specifically, in July 2011, Gulfstream renamed its G250 introduced in 2008 to G280. Its website explained: "As demand for Gulfstream business jets grows around the world, the move was prompted by the company's sensitivity to the varied cultures of its international customer base." While it never explained exactly why, it was because "250" means "stupid" or "useless" in some parts of China. One senior executive explained to the press that "we determined that G280 is a more amenable number sequence in certain cultures." Such market-oriented efforts have been handsomely rewarded by eager Chinese customers. In April 2014 at the Asian Business Aviation Conference and Exhibition (ABACE) in Shanghai—a major industry gathering—Gulfstream signed a 60-plane deal with Minsheng Financial Leasing, the aviation-finance arm of a major private bank in China. This is not only one of the largest deals for Gulfstream, but also one of the largest worldwide.

As the industry takes off, rising signs of sophistication emerge. A decade ago, the first Chinese buyers tended to pay cash and rarely flew—only to impress friends. Today's buyers often take advantage of financing or leasing (as evidenced by the Gulfstream-Minsheng deal). They fly more and endeavor to get more bang out of their bucks (or yuans). Some of them cannot wait for 1–2 years, so they have done something *unthinkable* for the super rich: buying *used* jets. Experts estimate that in the next 20 years, demand in China will be the third largest in the world, resulting in 1,500 business jets—behind 9,500 in the United States and 4,000 in Europe.

Case Discussion Questions

1. Why are corporate jet makers so eager to enter China?
2. From an institution-based view, what needs to be done to enhance the prospects of this industry in China?
3. From a resource-based view, what does it take to soar in China?

Sources: "Business jet player plans to spreads its wings in China," *Airport Journal*, June 2013, 17–49; "Business aviation: Fasten seat belts," *Economist*, 19 April 2014, www.economist.com; "Bargain hunting takes flight," *South China Morning Post*, 10 July 2012, A4; www.abace.aero; www.gulfstreamnews.com.

STUDY TOOLS 10

LOCATED AT THE BACK OF YOUR BOOK:

- ☐ Rip out and study the Chapter Review Card at the end of the book

LOG IN TO WWW.CENGAGEBRAIN.COM TO:

- ☐ Review key term flashcards
- ☐ Complete a practice quiz to test your knowledge of key concepts
- ☐ Take and complete the chapter crossword puzzle
- ☐ Complete interactive content, watch chapter videos, and take a graded quiz
- ☐ Track your knowledge of key concepts in Global Business
- ☐ Read and discuss additional case study content

11 Making Alliances & Acquisitions Work

ZRYZNER/SHUTTERSTOCK.COM

LEARNING OBJECTIVES

After studying this chapter, you should be able to . . .

- 11-1 Define alliances and acquisitions.
- 11-2 Articulate how institutions and resources influence alliances and acquisitions.
- 11-3 Describe how alliances are formed.
- 11-4 Outline how alliances are dissolved.
- 11-5 Discuss how alliances perform.
- 11-6 Explain why firms make acquisitions.
- 11-7 Describe what performance problems firms tend to encounter with acquisitions.
- 11-8 Articulate what you can do to make global alliances and acquisitions successful.

After you finish this chapter, go to **PAGE 179** for **STUDY TOOLS**

Fiat Chrysler: From Alliance to Acquisition

The year 2009 was one of the most tragic and unforgettable years in the history of the US automobile industry: two of the Big Three automakers, GM and Chrysler, went bankrupt in April. However, there was one glimmer of hope: Fiat was the "white knight" who came to Chrysler's rescue. Chrysler had recently gone through a traumatic divorce with Daimler in 2007. By 2009, nobody wanted Chrysler, which was pulled down by deteriorating products, hopeless finances, and the Great Recession. Its desperate call asking GM, Honda, Nissan-Renault, Toyota, and Volkswagen to help went nowhere. Only Fiat answered the call with $5 billion. As the "new Chrysler"—Chrysler Group LLC, which is different from the pre-bankruptcy "old Chrysler," formerly called Chrysler LLC—emerged out of bankruptcy in June 2009, the US government (which spent $8 billion to bail out Chrysler) had 10% of equity. The Canadian government had 2%. The United Auto Workers (union) had 68%. Although Fiat only had 20%, clearly as the senior partner in this new alliance it was calling all the shots.

While Chrysler got itself another European partner, Fiat itself was a weak automaker. Would the relationship work? The DaimlerChrysler marriage consisted of a luxury automaker and a working-class truck and SUV maker, which had a hard time working together. The Fiat-Chrysler alliance at least consisted of two similar mass-market operations. Both offered each other a set of complementary skills and capabilities. In addition to cash, Chrysler needed attractive small cars. Fiat supplied Chrysler with its award-winning Alfa Romeo Giulietta small car and its excellent small-engine technology that would comply with the increasingly strict fuel-economy standards in the United States. In 2013, while Chrysler's US factories were running at nearly full capacity, only 40% of the capacity of Fiat's Italian factories was being utilized. Thanks to Italian politics, Fiat could not close any major factories. Therefore, Fiat needed novel models from Chrysler and made them in Italy. Fiat recently assigned Chrysler's brand-new Jeep Renegade SUV to be built in Italy. In third-country markets, while each of these relatively smaller players was weak, their odds would be better by working together. In Brazil, which is Fiat's number-one market (where Fiat sold more cars than in Italy), Fiat faced major challenges from GM and Renault. Assistance from Chrysler in the form of newer models and technologies would certainly be valuable. In Asia (especially China), neither of them was very strong, although Chrysler's Jeep models did better. Combining forces allowed them to scale new heights in the tough but important Asian markets.

After several years of experimentation, both sides seemed satisfied with the alliance. Sergio Marchionne, who served as chairman and CEO for both Fiat and Chrysler, was instrumental in making sure both sides worked together. Many American managers at Chrysler used to resent European dominance, thanks to their bad experience with Daimler. This time as Chrysler owed its existence to Marchionne, its managers tended to give him the benefit of the doubt as he turned Chrysler around. Instead of the more centralized German style, Marchionne practiced a more decentralized management style. He also hired third-country (non-US and non-Italian) executives to help reduce the binational cultural barriers. By 2011, Chrysler repaid $7.6 billion loans to the US and Canadian governments and bought out the shares both governments held. Overall, Fiat gradually increased its Chrysler shares, reaching 59% by 2013. In 2014, Fiat acquired the remaining shares and owned 100% of Chrysler.

Set up in 2014, the combined entity is called Fiat Chrysler Automobiles (FCA), which interestingly is headquartered neither in Turin, Italy (Fiat's home), nor Auburn Hills (a Detroit suburb), Michigan (Chrysler's base). Instead, it is registered in the Netherlands, which has emerged as "Europe's Delaware." Many famous firms that you normally would not think of as "Dutch," such as Airbus Group and IKEA, are in fact registered there. But FCA's CEO and the top management team will be based in London—its operational headquarters. Cross-listed in both Borasa Italiana and New York Stock Exchange, FCA is the world's seventh largest automaker. With combined annual output of 4.5 million cars, FCA would be behind Toyota, GM, Volkswagen, Hyundai, Ford, and Nissan-Renault, but ahead of Honda and Peugeot. This is not bad for the 11th-ranked Chrysler (2.4 million vehicles per year prior to the full merger) and the 13th-ranked Fiat (2.1 million vehicles). FCA has a broad portfolio of brands, such as Alfa Romeo, Chrysler, Dodge, Ferrari, Fiat, Jeep, Maserati, and Ram Trucks. Whether tighter integration would enable FCA to challenge the global heavyweights remains to be seen.

Sources: "This 'baby Jeep' has an Italian accent," *Bloomberg Businessweek*, 7 March 2014, 23–24; "Hoping it will hold together," *Economist*, 24 August 2013, 57; "Here, there, and everywhere," *Economist*, 22 February 2014, 56–57; www.fcagroup.com.

Why did Fiat and Chrysler enter into an alliance relationship? How did they use the alliance to help each other in challenging markets? Why then did Fiat decide to completely acquire Chrsyler? These are some of the key questions driving this chapter. Alliances and acquisitions are two major strategies for growth used by firms around the world, thus necessitating our attention.[1] This chapter first defines alliances and acquisitions, followed by a discussion of how institution-based and resource-based views shed light on these topics. We then discuss the formation, evolution, and performance of alliances and acquisitions.

11-1 DEFINING ALLIANCES AND ACQUISITIONS

Strategic alliances are voluntary agreements of cooperation between firms. Remember that the dotted area in Exhibit 10.4 in Chapter 10 consists of non-equity-based contractual agreements and equity-based joint ventures (JVs). These can all be broadly considered as strategic alliances. Exhibit 11.1 illustrates this further, depicting alliances as degrees of *compromise* between pure market transactions and acquisitions. **Contractual (non-equity-based) alliances** are associations between firms that are based on contracts and do not involve the sharing of ownership. They include co-marketing, research and development (R&D) contracts, turnkey projects, strategic suppliers, strategic distributors, and licensing/franchising. **Equity-based alliances**, on the other hand, are based on ownership or financial interest between the firms. They include **strategic investment** (one partner invests in another—see the Opening Case) and **cross-shareholding** (each partner invests in the other). Equity-based alliances also include JVs, which involve the establishment of a new legally independent entity (in other words, a new firm) whose equity is provided by two or more partners.

Although JVs are often used as examples of alliances, *not* all alliances are JVs. A JV is a corporate child produced by two or more parent firms, as is the case with Sony Ericsson. A non-JV, equity-based alliance can be regarded as two firms getting married but not having children. For example, Renault is a strategic investor in Nissan, but both automakers still operate independently. They have *not* given birth to a new car company.

An **acquisition** is a transfer of the control of operations and management from one firm (target) to another (acquirer), the former becoming a unit of the latter. For example, Volvo is now a unit of China's Geely. A **merger** is the combination of operations and management of two firms to establish a new legal entity. For instance, the merger between Fiat and Chrysler resulted in Fiat Chrysler Automobiles (see the Opening Case).

Although the phrase "mergers and acquisitions" (M&As) is often used, in reality acquisitions dominate the scene. Only 3% of M&As are mergers. For practical purposes, "M&As" basically mean "acquisitions." Consequently, we will use the two terms "M&As" and "acquisitions" interchangeably. Specifically, we focus on cross-border (international) M&As (Exhibit 11.2). This is not only because of our global interest, but also because of (1) the high percentage (about 30%) of international deals among all M&As and (2) the high percentage (about 70%) of M&As among foreign direct investment (FDI) flows.

SOPOTNICKI/SHUTTERSTOCK.COM

Strategic alliance Voluntary agreement of cooperation between firms.

Contractual (non-equity-based) alliance An association between firms that is based on a contract and does not involve the sharing of ownership.

Equity-based alliance An association between firms that is based on shared ownership or financial interest.

Strategic investment A business strategy in which one firm invests in another.

Cross-shareholding A business strategy in which each partner in an alliance holds stock in the other firm.

Acquisition The transfer of the control of operations and management from one firm (target) to another (acquirer), the former becoming a unit of the latter.

Merger The combination of operations and management of two firms to establish a new legal entity.

EXHIBIT 11.1 THE VARIETY OF STRATEGIC ALLIANCES

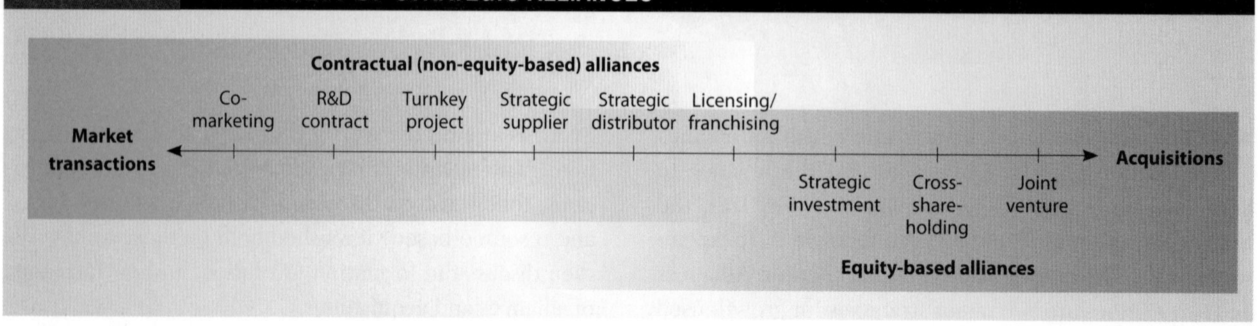

EXHIBIT 11.2 THE VARIETY OF CROSS-BORDER MERGERS AND ACQUISITIONS

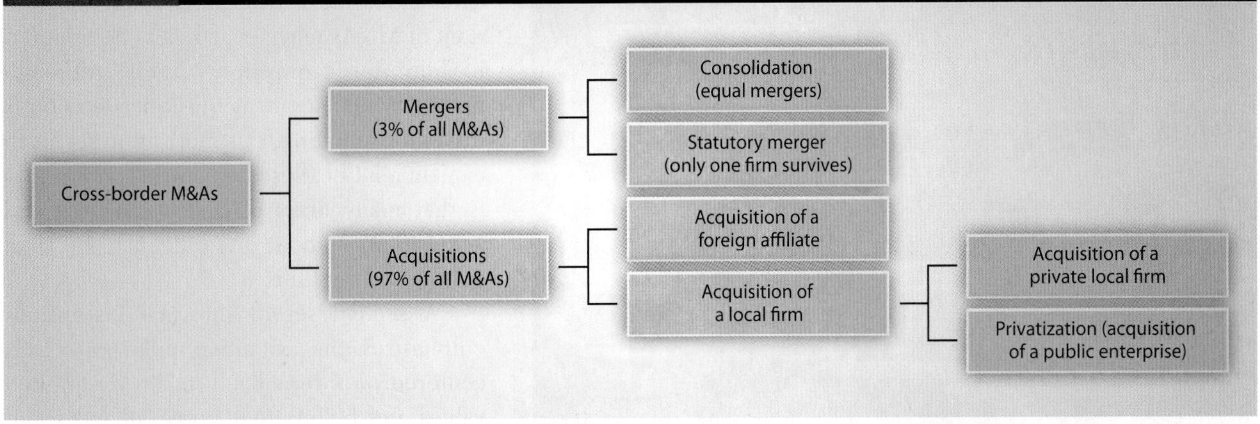

Source: United Nations *World Investment Report 2000* (New York: UNCTAD, 2000) 100.

11-2 HOW INSTITUTIONS AND RESOURCES AFFECT ALLIANCES AND ACQUISITIONS

What drives alliances? What drives acquisitions? The institution-based and resource-based views can shed considerable light on these important questions. The institution-based view suggests that as rules of the game, institutions influence how a firm chooses between alliances and acquisitions in terms of its strategy.[2] However, rules are not made just for one firm. The resource-based view argues that although a number of firms may be governed by the same set of rules, some excel more than others because of the differences in firm-specific capabilities that make alliances and acquisitions work (see Exhibit 11.3).

11-2a Institutions, Alliances, and Acquisitions

Alliances and acquisitions function within a set of formal legal and regulatory frameworks.[3] The impact of these formal institutions on alliances and acquisitions can be found along two dimensions: (1) antitrust concerns and (2) entry mode requirements. First, many firms establish alliances with competitors. For example, Siemens and Bosch compete in automotive components and collaborate in household appliances. Antitrust authorities suspect at least some tacit collusion when competitors cooperate. However, because integration within alliances is usually not as tight as acquisitions (which would eliminate one competitor), antitrust authorities are more likely to approve alliances as opposed to acquisitions. A proposed merger of American Airlines and British Airways was blocked by both US and UK antitrust authorities. But the two airlines were allowed to form an alliance that has eventually grown to become the multipartner One World. In another example, the proposed merger between AT&T and T-Mobile (a wholly owned subsidiary [WOS] of Deutsche Telekom in the United States) was torpedoed by US antitrust authorities. But the US government *blessed* AT&T and T-Mobile's collaboration in roaming and mobile payments.

Another way formal institutions affect alliances and acquisitions is

EXHIBIT 11.3 INSTITUTIONS, RESOURCES, ALLIANCES, AND ACQUISITIONS

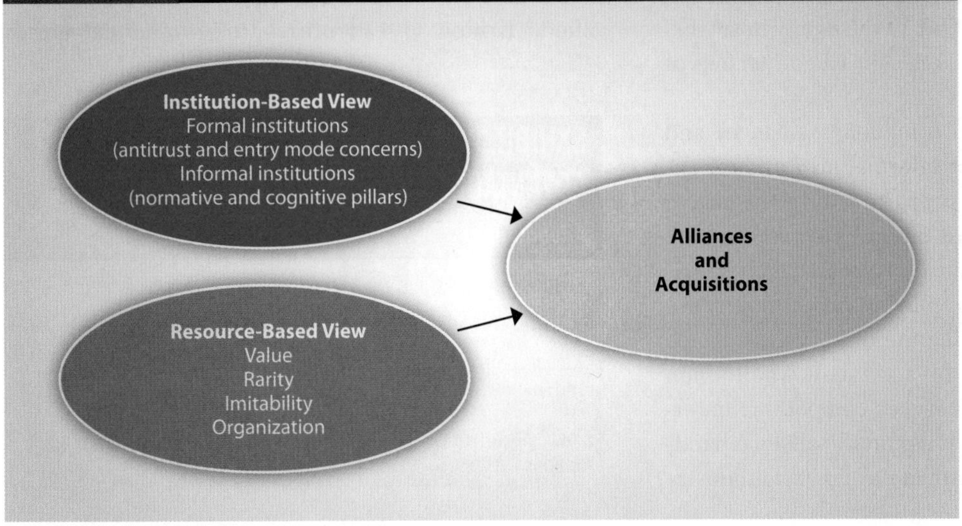

LEON NEAL/GETTY IMAGES

through formal requirements on market entry modes. In many countries, governments discourage or simply ban acquisitions to establish WOSs, thereby leaving alliances with local firms as the only choice for FDI. For example, before NAFTA went into effect in 1994, the Mexican government not only limited multinationals' entries to JVs, but also dictated a maximum equity position of 49%.

Recently, two trends have emerged in the entry mode requirements dictated by formal government policies. The first is a general trend toward more liberal policies. Many governments that historically approved only JVs as an entry mode (such as those in Mexico and South Korea) now allow WOSs. As a result, JVs have declined and acquisitions have increased in emerging economies.[4]

Despite the general movement toward more liberal policies, a second noticeable trend is that many governments still impose considerable requirements, especially when foreign firms acquire domestic assets. The strategically important Chinese automobile assembly industry and the Russian oil industry permit only JVs, thus eliminating acquisitions as a choice. US regulations limit foreign carriers to a maximum 25% of the equity in any US airline, and EU regulations limit non-EU ownership of EU-based airlines to 49%.

Informal institutions also influence alliances and acquisitions. The first set of informal institutions centers on collective norms, supported by a normative pillar. A core idea of the institution-based view is that because firms want to enhance or protect their legitimacy, copying what other reputable organizations are doing—even without knowing the direct performance benefits of doing so—may be a low-cost way to gain legitimacy. Thus, when a firm sees competitors entering alliances, that firm may jump on the alliance bandwagon just to be safe rather than risk ignoring industry trends. When M&As appear to be the trend, even managers with doubts about the wisdom of M&As may nevertheless be tempted to hunt for acquisition targets. Although not every alliance or acquisition decision is driven by imitation, this motivation seems to explain a lot of these activities. The flip side is that many firms rush into alliances and acquisitions without due diligence and then get burned big time.

A second set of informal institutions emphasizes the cognitive pillar, which is centered on internalized, taken-for-granted values and beliefs that guide alliances and acquisitions. For example, BAE Systems (formerly British Aerospace) has announced that *all* of its future aircraft development programs would involve alliances. Likewise, in the area of acquisitions, Spain's Santander is a firm believer. It has undertaken a total of $70 billion of acquisitions throughout Europe, Latin America, and now North America.[5] Clearly, managers at BAE Systems and Santander believe that such alliances and acquisitions, respectively, are the right (and sometimes the only) thing to do, which have become part of their informal norms and beliefs.

11-2b Resources and Alliances

How does the VRIO framework that characterizes the resource-based view influence alliances?

VALUE Alliances must create value. The three global airline alliance networks—One World, Sky Team, and Star Alliance—create value by reducing ticket costs by 18% to 28% on two-stage flights compared with separate flights on the same route if the airlines were not allied.[6] Exhibit 11.4 identifies three broad categories

EXHIBIT 11.4 STRATEGIC ALLIANCES: ADVANTAGES AND DISADVANTAGES

Advantages	Disadvantages
Reduce costs, risks, and uncertainties	Choosing wrong partners
Access complementary assets and learning opportunities	Potential partner opportunism
Possibility to use alliances as real options	Risk of helping nurture competitors (learning race)

InFocus: Emerging Markets

Etihad Airways' Alliance Network

JORDAN TAN/SHUTTERSTOCK.COM

Founded in 2003 and based in Abu Dhabi, Etihad Airways is both inspired by Emirates Airlines and a direct competitor of Emirates, which is based in Dubai, a fellow emirate in the United Arab Emirates (UAE). Etihad, which means "union" in Arabic, quickly became the fastest growing airline in the history of commercial aviation. Now with 101 aircraft, Etihad serves 11 million passengers to nearly 100 destinations around the world. Now the fourth largest airline in the world, Emirates is a mammoth that has 220 aircraft and carries 40 million passengers to over 140 cities.

Etihad imitates the highly successful Emirates by (1) equipping itself with modern long-haul jets (such as Airbus A380 and Boeing 777 Extended Range [ER]) and (2) leveraging the enviable location of the Abu Dhabi International Airport, which is only an hour away by car from Dubai's storied airport. Given the small local population (three million in Abu Dhabi vis-à-vis four million in Dubai), Etihad—like Emirates—can only grow by being a "super-connector" airline. In other words, most of the passengers neither travel from nor to Abu Dhabi. Blessed by its Middle East location, Abu Dhabi, just like Dubai, is an ideal stopping point for air traffic between Europe and Australasia and between Asia and Africa.

One area that Etihad has decisively deviated from its role model Emirates is an interest in weaving an alliance network. Other than a single alliance with Qantas, Emirates either has been very shy or does not care about collaboration. In an industry with three major multipartner networks—One World, Sky Team, and Star Alliance—airlines are no strangers to alliances. But Etihad's alliances are not what you think. Its talks to join these three mega networks did not go anywhere, because none of them was interested in admitting an ambitious new member determined to eat their lunch. Instead, Etihad has built its own alliance network consisting of eight smaller airlines. In 2011, Etihad took a 29% equity in Air Berlin, Europe's sixth largest airline. Since then, through a series of equity-based strategic investments, Etihad acquired stakes in Dublin, Ireland-based Aer Lingus (4% equity); Rome, Italy-based Alitalia (49%)—the largest airline in Italy; Belgrade, Serbia-based Air Serbia (49%)—the largest airline in Serbia, formerly known as Jat Airways; Mahe, Seychelles-based Air Seychelles (40%); Lugano, Switzerland-based Darwin Airline (34%)—recently rebranded as Etihad Regional; Mumbai, India-based Jet Airways (24%); and Brisbane, Australia-based Virgin Australia (20%).

Etihad CEO James Hogan, who is an Australian, is viewed as a "white knight" who bailed out a bunch of money-losing or cash-poor airlines, including the struggling flag carriers of Ireland, Italy, Serbia, and Seychelles. Hogan has argued that his multi-billion dollar investments in airlines that serve smaller markets made economic sense by increasing Etihad's passenger tally and securing economies of scale when competing with Emirates. But can Etihad turn such an alliance network profitable? The most challenging member is Alitalia, which lost €1.1 billion ($1.5 billion) in five years, and Etihad spent €560 million to breathe some new life into it.

Always known for using nasty language, Michael O'Leary, CEO of Ireland's and Europe's largest airline Ryanair, bluntly told journalists that Etihad "bought a lot of rubbish, and increasing their stake in Aer Lingus is consistent with that." Indeed, no other airline in the world is doing what Etihad is doing at this scale. Does Etihad, despite its deep pockets, have what it takes to turn around a whole bunch of also-rans? Stay tuned. . .

Sources: "Will Etihad's flock of also-rans fly?" *Bloomberg Businessweek*, 24 April 2014, 22–24; "Airline alliances: New world order," *CEO Middle East*, June 2013, 36–42.

of value creation in terms of how advantages outweigh disadvantages. First, alliances may reduce costs, risks, and uncertainties. As Emirates Airlines from Dubai rises to preeminence, Etihad Airways from Abu Dhabi, a fellow emirate in the United Arab Emirates, has set up a number of alliances with smaller airlines around the world in an effort to eat some of Emirates' lunch (see In Focus). Second, alliances allow firms such as Fiat and Chrysler to tap into complementary assets of partners and facilitate learning (see the Opening Case).

Finally, an important advantage of alliances lies in their value as real options. Conceptually, an option is the right (but not obligation) to take some action in the future. Technically, a financial option is an investment instrument permitting its holder, having paid for a small fraction of an asset, the right to increase investment by eventually acquiring the asset if necessary.

A **real option** is an investment in real operations as opposed to financial capital.[7] A real options view suggests two propositions:

- In the first phase, an investor makes a small, initial investment to buy an option, which leads to the right to future investment but is not an obligation to do so.
- The investor then holds the option until a decision point arrives in the second phase and then decides between exercising the option or abandoning it.

For firms interested in eventually acquiring other companies but uncertain about such moves, working together in alliances affords an insider view to the capabilities of these partners. This is similar to trying on new shoes to see if they fit before buying them. Since acquisitions are not only costly but also very likely to fail, alliances permit firms to *sequentially* increase their investment should they decide to pursue acquisitions (see the Opening Case). If after working together as partners a firm finds that an acquisition is not a good idea, there is no obligation to pursue it. Overall, alliances have emerged as great instruments of real options because of their flexibility to sequentially scale *up* or scale *down* the investment.

On the other hand, alliances have a number of nontrivial drawbacks. First, there is always a possibility of being stuck with the wrong partner. Firms are advised to choose a prospective partner with caution, preferably a known entity. Yet, the partner should also be sufficiently differentiated to provide some complementary (nonoverlapping) capabilities. Many firms find it difficult to evaluate the true intentions and capabilities of their prospective partners until it is too late.

A second disadvantage is potential partner opportunism. While opportunism is likely in any kind of economic relationship, the alliance setting may provide especially strong incentives for some (but not necessarily all) partners to be opportunistic. A cooperative relationship always entails some elements of trust that may be easily abused.

Real option An investment in real operations as opposed to financial capital.

Relational (collaborative) capability The ability to successfully manage interfirm relationships.

RARITY The ability to successfully manage interfirm relationships—often called **relational (or collaborative) capabilities**—tends to be rare. Managers involved in alliances require relationship skills rarely covered in the traditional business school curriculum, which typically emphasizes competition rather than collaboration. To truly derive benefits from alliances, managers need to foster trust with partners yet be on guard against opportunism.[8]

As much as alliances represent a strategic and economic arrangement, they also constitute a social, psychological, and emotional phenomenon. Words such as "courtship," "marriage," and "divorce" are often used when discussing alliances. Given that the interests of partner firms do not fully overlap and are often in conflict, managers involved in alliances live a precarious existence, trying to represent the interests of their respective firms while attempting to make the complex relationship work. Not surprisingly, sound relational capabilities necessary to successfully manage alliances are in short supply.[9]

IMITABILITY Imitability occurs at two levels in alliances: (1) firm level and (2) alliance level. First, as noted earlier, one firm's resources and capabilities may be imitated by partners. Another imitability issue refers to the trust and understanding among partners in successful alliances. Firms without such "chemistry" may have a hard time imitating such activities. CFM International, a JV set up by GE and Snecma to produce jet engines in France, has successfully operated for over 40 years. Rivals stuck in a bad relationship would have a hard time imitating such a successful relationship.

ORGANIZATION Some successful alliance relationships are organized in a way that is difficult to replicate. Tolstoy makes the observation in the opening sentence of *Anna Karenina*: "All happy families are alike; each unhappy family is unhappy in its own way." Much the same can be said for business alliances. Each failed alliance has its own mistakes and problems, and firms in unsuccessful alliances (for whatever reason) often find it exceedingly challenging, if not impossible, to organize and manage their interfirm relationships better.

11-2c Resources and Acquisitions

VALUE Do acquisitions create *value*?[10] Overall, their performance record is sobering. As many as 70% of acquisitions reportedly fail. On average, the performance of acquiring firms does not improve after acquisitions. Target firms, after being acquired and becoming internal units, often perform worse than when they were independent, stand-alone firms. The only identifiable group of winners is the shareholders of target firms, who may experience on average a 25% increase in their stock value.[11] This is due to **acquisition premium**, which is the difference between the acquisition price and the market value of target firms.

Acquirers of US firms pay, on average, a 20% to 30% premium, and acquirers of EU firms pay a slightly lower premium (about 18%).[12] Shareholders of acquiring firms experience a 4% loss in their stock value during the same period. The combined wealth of shareholders of both acquiring and target firms is only marginally positive, less than 2%.[13] Unfortunately, many M&As destroy value.

RARITY For acquisitions to add value, one or all of the firms involved must have rare and unique skills that enhance the overall strategy. Although acquirers from emerging economies generally have a hard time delivering value from their acquisitions, Lenovo, according to *Bloomberg Businessweek*, was able to "find treasure in the PC industry's trash" by turning around the former IBM PC division and using it to propel itself to become the biggest PC maker in the world (see the Closing Case).[14] Such skills are not only rare among emerging acquirers, but also rare among established acquirers—think of DaimlerChrysler.

IMITABILITY While many firms undertake acquisitions, a much smaller number of them have mastered the art of post-acquisition integration. Consequently, firms that excel in integration possess *hard-to-imitate* capabilities that are advantages in acquisitions. For example, each of Northrop Grumman's acquisitions must conform to a carefully orchestrated plan of nearly 400 items, from how to issue press releases to which accounting software to use. Unlike its bigger defense rivals, such as Boeing and Raytheon, Northrop Grumman thus far has not stumbled with any of its acquisitions.

ORGANIZATION Fundamentally, whether acquisitions add value boils down to how merged firms are organized to take advantage of the benefits while minimizing the costs. Pre-acquisition analysis often focuses on **strategic fit**, which is the effective matching of complementary strategic capabilities. Yet, many firms do not pay adequate attention to **organizational fit**, which is the similarity in cultures, systems, and structures. On paper, Nomura and Lehman Brothers' Asia and Europe operations seemed to have a great deal of strategic fit: Nomura was strong in Asia and weak in Europe. Lehman was strong in Europe and weak in Asia. (Lehman was also strong in its home region, North America, but its North American assets were sold to another firm and thus were not relevant to Nomura.) Why was the integration between the two such a mess? Mostly because of the almost total lack of organizational fit.

11-3 FORMATION OF ALLIANCES

The next few sections discuss in some detail the formation, evolution, and performance of alliances and acquisitions. First: How are alliances formed? A three-stage model in Exhibit 11.5 addresses this process.

In Stage One, a firm must decide if growth can be achieved through market transactions, acquisitions, or alliances. To grow by pure market transactions, the firm has to confront competitive challenges independently. This is highly demanding, even for resource-rich multinationals. As noted earlier in the chapter, acquisitions have some unique drawbacks, leading many managers to conclude that alliances are the way to go. For example, Dallas-based Sabre Travel Network have used alliances to enter Australia, Bahrain, India, Israel, Japan, and Singapore.

In Stage Two, a firm must decide whether to take a contract or an equity approach. As noted in Chapters 6 and 10, the choice between contract and equity is crucial. The first driving force is shared capabilities. The more tacit (that is, hard to describe and codify) the capabilities, the greater the preference for equity involvement. The most effective way to learn *complex* processes is through learning by doing. A good example of this is learning to cook by actually cooking and not by simply reading cookbooks. Many business processes are the same way. A firm that wants to produce cars will find that the codified knowledge found in books, reports, and operating manuals is not enough. Much tacit knowledge can only be acquired via learning by doing, preferably with experts as alliance partners (see the Opening Case).

A second driving force is the importance of direct monitoring and control. Equity relationships allow firms to have some direct control over joint activities on a continuing basis, whereas contractual relationships usually do not. In general, firms that fear their

Acquisition premium The difference between the acquisition price and the market value of target firms.

Strategic fit The effective matching of complementary strategic capabilities.

Organizational fit The similarity in cultures, systems, and structures between two or more firms.

EXHIBIT 11.5 ALLIANCE FORMATION

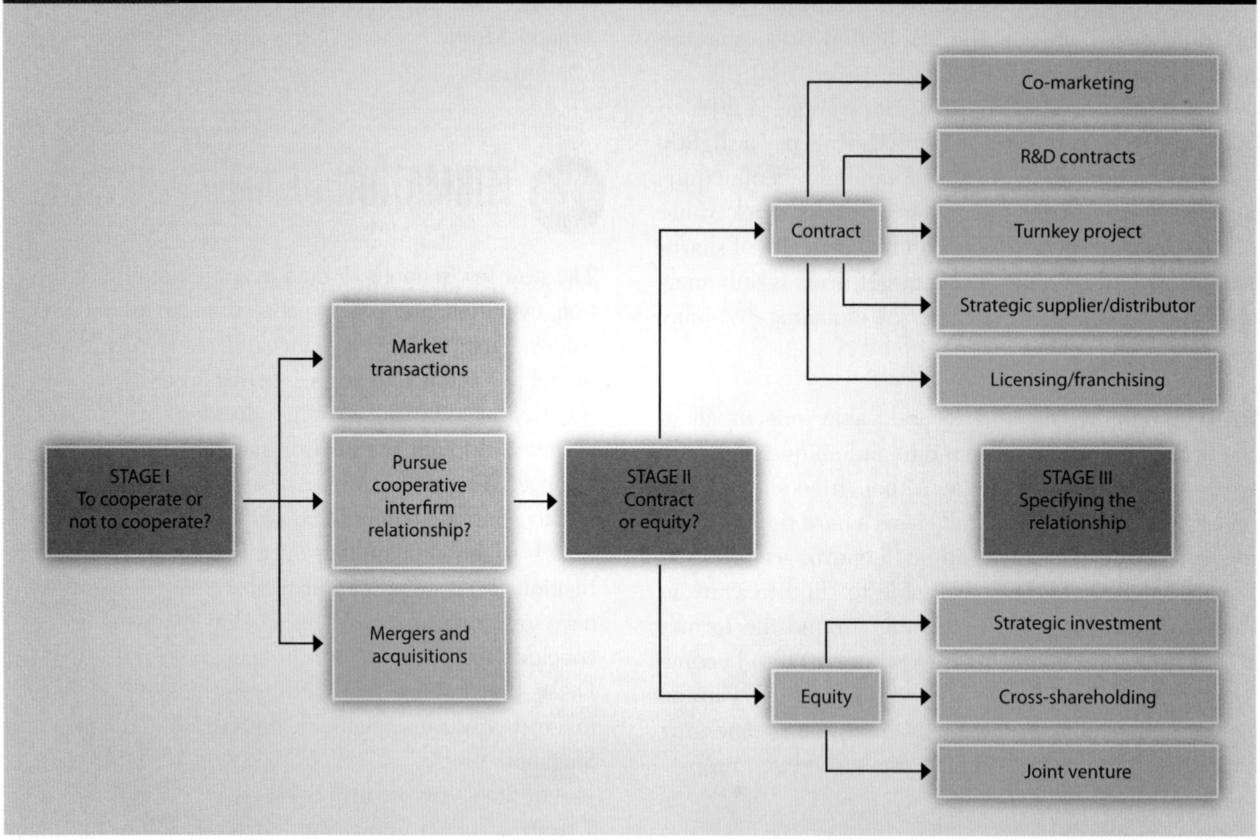

Source: S. Tallman and O. Shenkar, "A managerial decision model of international cooperative venture formation," *Journal of International Business Studies* 25 (1994): 101.

intellectual property may be expropriated prefer equity alliances (and a higher level of equity).

Eventually, firms need to specify a specific format that is either equity based or contractual (non-equity based), depending on the choice made in Stage Two. Exhibit 11.5 lists the different format options. Since Chapter 10 has already covered this topic as part of the discussion on entry modes, we will not repeat it here.

11-4 DISSOLUTION OF ALLIANCES

Alliances are often described as corporate marriages and, when terminated, as corporate divorces.[15] Exhibit 11.6 portrays an alliance dissolution model. To apply the metaphor of divorce, we focus on the two-partner alliance such as the Danone-Wahaha case (and ignore multipartner alliances such as One World). Following the convention in research on human divorce, the party who begins the process of ending the alliance is labeled the "initiator," while the other party is termed the "partner"—for lack of a better word.

The first phase is initiation. The process begins when the initiator starts feeling uncomfortable with the alliance (for whatever reason). Wavering begins as a quiet, unilateral process by the initiator, which was Danone in this case. After repeated demands to modify Wahaha's behavior failed, Danone began to sense that the alliance was probably unsalvageable. At this point, the display of discontent became bolder. Initially, Wahaha, the partner, may simply not "get it." The initiator's "sudden" dissatisfaction may confuse the partner. As a result, initiation tends to escalate.

The second phase is going public. The party that breaks the news first has a first-mover advantage. By presenting a socially acceptable reason in favor of its cause, this party is able to win sympathy from key stakeholders, such as parent company executives, investors, and journalists. Not surprisingly, the initiator is likely to go public first. Alternatively, the partner may preempt by blaming the initiator and establishing the righteousness of its position—this was exactly what Wahaha did. Eventually, both Danone and Wahaha were eager to publicly air their grievances.

The third phase is uncoupling. Like human divorce, alliance dissolution can be friendly or hostile. In

EXHIBIT 11.6 ALLIANCE DISSOLUTION

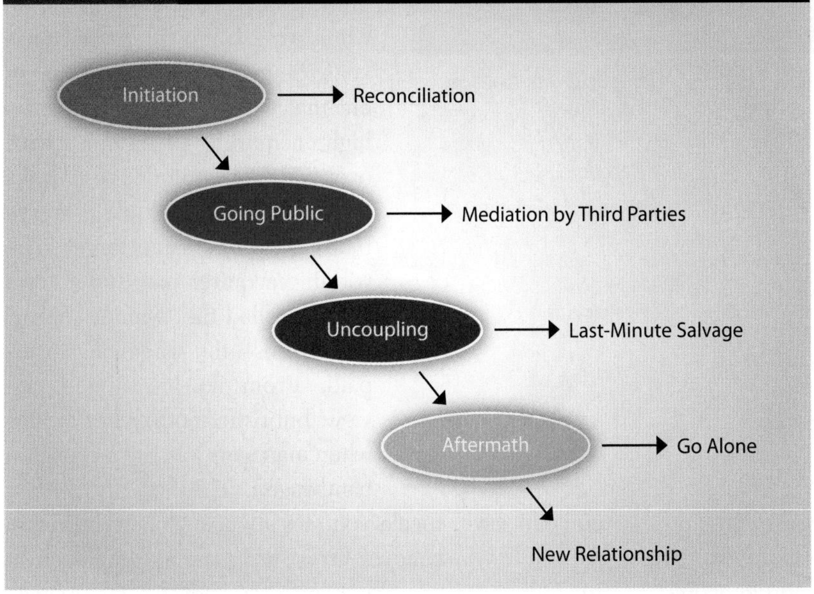

Source: M. W. Peng and O. Shenkar, "Joint venture dissolution as corporate divorce," *Academy of Management Executive* 16, no. 2 (2002): 95.

uncontested divorces, both sides attribute the separation more on, say, a change in circumstances. For example, Eli Lilly and Ranbaxy phased out their JV in India and remained friendly with each other. In contrast, contested divorces involve a party that accuses another. The worst scenario is "death by a thousand cuts" inflicted by one party at every turn. A case in point is the numerous lawsuits and arbitrations filed in many countries by Danone and Wahaha accusing each other of wrongdoing.

The last phase is aftermath. Like most divorced individuals, most (but not all) "divorced" firms are likely to search for new partners. Understandably, the new alliance is often negotiated more extensively. However, excessive formalization may signal a lack of trust—in the same way that pre-nuptials may scare away some prospective human marriage partners.

11-5 PERFORMANCE OF ALLIANCES

Although managers naturally focus on alliance performance, opinions vary on how to measure it. A combination of objective measures (such as profit and market share) and subjective measures (such as managerial satisfaction) can be used. Four factors may influence alliance performance: (1) equity, (2) learning and experience, (3) nationality, and (4) relational capabilities.

- The level of equity may be crucial in how an alliance performs. A greater equity stake may mean that a firm is more committed, which is likely to result in higher performance.
- Whether firms have successfully learned from partners is important when assessing alliance performance. Since learning is abstract, experience is often used as a proxy because it is relatively easy to measure. While experience certainly helps, its impact on performance is not linear. There is a limit beyond which further increase in experience may not enhance performance.
- Nationality may affect performance. For the same reason that marriages where both parties have similar backgrounds are more stable, dissimilarities in national culture may create strains in alliances. Not surprisingly, international alliances tend to have more problems than domestic ones.
- Alliance performance may fundamentally boil down to soft, hard-to-measure relational capabilities. The art of relational capabilities, which are firm specific and difficult to codify and transfer, may make or break alliances.

Overall, none of these four factors has an unambiguous, direct impact on performance. What has been found is that they may have some *correlations* with performance. It would be naïve to think that any of these four single factors would guarantee success. It is their *combination* that jointly increases the odds for the success of strategic alliances.

11-6 MOTIVES FOR ACQUISITIONS

What drives acquisitions? Exhibit 11.7 shows three potential motives for acquisition: (1) synergistic, (2) hubristic, and (3) managerial. All three can be explained by the institution-based and resource-based views. From an institution-based view, synergistic motives for acquisitions

ISTOCKPHOTO.COM/NO LIMIT PICTURES

EXHIBIT 11.7 MOTIVES FOR ACQUISITIONS

	Institution-Based Issues	Resource-Based Issues
Synergistic motives	▶ Respond to formal institutional constraints and transitions	▶ Leverage superior managerial capabilities ▶ Enhance market power and scale economies ▶ Access to complementary resources
Hubristic motives	▶ Herd behavior—following norms and chasing fads of M&As	▶ Managers' overconfidence in their capabilities
Managerial motives	▶ Self-interested actions such as empire building guided by informal norms and cognitions	

are often a response to formal institutional constraints and transitions that affect a company's search for synergy. It is not a coincidence that the number of cross-border acquisitions has skyrocketed in the last two decades. This is the same period during which trade and investment barriers have gone down and FDI has risen.

From a resource-based standpoint, the most important synergistic rationale is to leverage superior resources. Indian firms' cross-border acquisitions have primarily targeted high-tech and computer services in order to leverage their superior resources in these industries (see the Closing Case). Another motive is to access complementary resources, as evidenced by Fiat's interest in Chrysler's Jeep brand (see the Opening Case).

While all the synergistic motives, in theory, add value, hubristic and managerial motives reduce value. **Hubris** refers to overconfidence in one's capabilities. Managers of acquiring firms make two strong statements. The first is: "We can manage *your* assets better than you [target firm managers] can!" The second statement is even bolder. Given that purchasing a publicly listed firm requires paying an acquisition premium, managers of an acquiring firm essentially say, "We are smarter than the market!" Acquiring firm managers can quantitatively state exactly how much smarter they are relative to the market—as evidenced by the specific acquisition premium they are willing to pay. In other words, a 20% acquisition premium, by definition, is the acquiring firm's announcement: "We are 20% smarter than the market."

Hubris Exaggerated pride or overconfidence.

Managerial motive Managers' desire for power, prestige, and money, which may lead to decisions that do not benefit the firm overall in the long run.

To the extent that the capital market is efficient and that the market price of target firms reflects their intrinsic value, there is simply no hope to profit from such acquisitions. Even when we assume the capital market to be inefficient, it is still apparent that when the premium is too high, acquiring firms must have overpaid. This attitude is especially dangerous when multiple firms are bidding for the same target. The winning acquirer may suffer from what is called the "winner's curse" in auctions—the winner has overpaid. From an institution-based view, hubristic motives are at play when managers join the acquisition bandwagon. The fact that M&As come in waves speaks volumes about such herd behavior. After a few first-mover firms start making some deals in the industry, waves of late movers, eager to catch up, may rush in, prompted by a "Wow! Get it!" mentality. Not surprisingly, many of those deals turn out to be busts.

While the hubristic motives suggest that some managers may *unknowingly* overpay for targets, some managers may *knowingly* overpay for targets. Such self-interested actions are fueled by **managerial motives**, defined as managers' desire for power, prestige, and money, which may lead to decisions that do not benefit the firm overall in the long run. As a result, some managers may deliberately grow their firms through M&As for such personal gains. These are known as agency problems.

Overall, synergistic motives add value, and hubristic and managerial motives destroy value. They may *simultaneously* coexist. The Closing Case uses emerging multinationals as a new breed of cross-border acquirers to illustrate these dynamics. Next, we discuss the performance of M&As.

11-7 PERFORMANCE OF ACQUISITIONS

Why do as many as 70% of acquisitions reportedly fail?[16] Problems can be identified in both pre-acquisition and post-acquisition phases (Exhibit 11.8). During the pre-acquisition phase, because of executive hubris and/or managerial motives, acquiring firms may overpay targets—in other words, they fall into a "synergy trap." For example, in 1998, when Chrysler was profitable, Daimler-Benz paid $40 billion, a 40% premium over its market value, to acquire it. Given that Chrysler's expected performance was already built into its existing share price, at a *zero* premium, Daimler-Benz's

EXHIBIT 11.8 SYMPTOMS OF ACQUISITION FAILURES

	Problems for all M&As	Particular problems for cross-border M&As
Pre-acquisition: Overpayment for targets	▸ Managers over-estimate their ability to create value ▸ Inadequate pre-acquisition screening ▸ Poor strategic fit	▸ Lack of familiarity with foreign cultures, institutions, and business systems ▸ Nationalistic concerns against foreign takeovers (political and media levels)
Post-acquisition: Failure in integration	▸ Poor organizational fit ▸ Failure to address multiple stakeholder groups' concerns	▸ Clashes of organizational cultures compounded by clashes of national cultures ▸ Nationalistic concerns against foreign takeovers (firm and employee levels)

willingness to pay for such a high premium was indicative of (1) strong managerial capabilities to derive synergy, (2) high levels of hubris, (3) significant managerial self-interests, or (4) *all of the above*. As it turned out, by the time Chrysler was sold in 2007, it only fetched $7.4 billion, destroying four-fifths of the value. In another case, in 2010, Microsoft paid $8.5 billion to buy Skype, which was 400 times greater than Skype's income. Although many readers of this book use Skype, Skype has remained an underachieving Internet icon—how many people have paid money to Skype each other? Not surprisingly, this acquisition, Microsoft's biggest, raised a lot of eyebrows.

Another primary pre-acquisition problem is inadequate screening and failure to achieve strategic fit. In September 2008, Bank of America, in a hurry to make a deal, spent only 48 hours before agreeing to acquire Merrill Lynch for $50 billion. Not surprisingly, failure to do adequate homework (technically, due diligence) led to numerous problems centered on the lack of strategic fit. Consequently, this acquisition was labeled by the *Wall Street Journal* as "a deal from hell."[17]

Acquiring international assets can be even more problematic, because institutional and cultural distances can be large and nationalistic concerns over foreign acquisitions may erupt (see the Closing Case). When Japanese firms acquired Rockefeller Center and movie studios in the 1980s and the 1990s, the US media reacted with indignation. In the 2000s, when DP World of the United Arab Emirates and CNOOC of China attempted to acquire US assets, they had to back off due to political backlash.

Numerous integration problems may surface during the post-acquisition phase (see Exhibit 11.9). Although "mergers of equals" sound nice, their integration tends to be awful. Organizational fit is just as important as strategic fit. Many acquiring firms (such as Nomura) do *not* analyze organizational fit with targets (such as Lehman Brothers' assets in Asia and Europe). The result is a mess. Firms often fail to address the concerns of multiple stakeholders, including job losses and diminished power. Most firms focus on task issues such as standardizing reporting, and pay inadequate attention to people issues, which typically results in low morale and high turnover.

EXHIBIT 11.9 A CHALLENGE IN POST-ACQUISITION INTEGRATION

"As you know, some details of the new merger have yet to be resolved."

In cross-border M&As, integration difficulties may be much worse because clashes of organizational cultures are compounded by clashes of national cultures. Due to cultural differences, Chinese acquirers such as Geely often have a hard time integrating Western firms such as Volvo (see the Closing Case). But even when both sides are from the West, cultural conflicts may still erupt. When Four Seasons acquired a hotel in Paris, the simple American request that employees *smile* at customers was resisted by French employees and laughed at by the local media as *"la culture Mickey Mouse."* After Alcatel acquired Lucent, the situation became "almost comically dysfunctional."[18] At an all-hands gathering at an Alcatel-Lucent European facility, employees threw fruits and vegetables at executives announcing another round of restructuring.

Although acquisitions are often the largest capital expenditures most firms ever make, they frequently are the worst planned and executed activities of all. Unfortunately, while merging firms are sorting out the mess, rivals are likely to launch aggressive attacks. When Daimler-Benz struggled first with the chaos associated with its marriage with Chrysler and then was engulfed in its divorce with Chrsyler, BMW rocketed ahead of Mercedes-Benz to become the world's number-one luxury carmaker. Adding all of the above together, it is hardly surprising that most M&As fail.

11-8 MANAGEMENT SAVVY

What determines the success and failure in alliances and acquisitions? Our two core perspectives shed light on this big question. The institution-based view argues that alliances and acquisitions depend on a thorough understanding and skillful manipulation of the rules of the game. The resource-based view calls for the development of firm-specific capabilities to make a difference in enhancing alliance and acquisition performance. As two alternatives, neither alliances nor acquisitions should be preordained, and careful analysis of the pros and cons of each should be undertaken before going forward with either one (see Debate).

Consequently, three clear implications for action emerge (see Exhibit 11.10). First, managers need to

EXHIBIT 11.10 IMPLICATIONS FOR ACTION

- Understand and master the rules of the game governing alliances and acquisitions around the world.
- When managing alliances, pay attention to the soft relationship aspects.
- When managing acquisitions, do not overpay, focus on both strategic and organizational fit, and thoroughly address integration concerns.

Debate

Acquisitions Versus Alliances

Although alliances and acquisitions are alternatives, many firms seem to plunge straight into "merger mania." Between 2005 and 2010, Microsoft, IBM, and HP swallowed 79, 60, and 34 firms, respectively. In many firms, an M&A group reports to the CFO, while a separate unit, headed by the VP or director for business development, deal with alliances. M&As and alliances are thus often undertaken in isolation. A smaller number of firms, such as Eli Lilly, have a separate "office of alliance management." Few firms have established a combined "mergers, acquisitions, *and* alliance" function. In practice, it may be advisable to explicitly compare acquisitions vis-à-vis alliances.

Compared with acquisitions, alliances cost less and allow for opportunities to learn from working with each other before engaging in full-blown acquisitions. While alliances do not preclude acquisitions and may lead to acquisitions, acquisitions are often one-off deals swallowing both the excellent capabilities and mediocre units of target firms, leading to "indigestion" problems. Many acquisitions (such as DaimlerChrysler) probably would have been better off had firms pursued alliances first. In comparison, Fiat Chrysler Automobiles (FCA) as a combined entity may have better odds for success, because both Fiat and Chrysler had worked together as alliance partners before getting "married" to each other (see the Opening Case).

Sources: J. Dyer, P. Kale, and H. Singh, "When to ally and when to acquire," *Harvard Business Review*, July–August (2004): 109–115; H. Yang, S. Sun, Z. Lin, and M. W. Peng, "Behind M&As in China and the United States," *Asia Pacific Journal of Management* 28 (2011): 239–255; H. Yang, Z. Lin, and M. W. Peng, "Behind acquisitions of alliance partners," *Academy of Management Journal* 54 (2011): 1069–1080; X. Yin and M. Shanley, "Industry determinants of the "merger versus alliance" decision, *Academy of Management Review* 33 (2008): 473–491.

understand and master the rules of the game—both formal and informal—governing alliances and acquisitions around the world. When negotiating its acquisition of IBM's PC assets, Lenovo clearly understood and tapped into the Chinese government's support for home-grown multinationals. IBM likewise understood the necessity for the new Lenovo to maintain an American image when it persuaded Lenovo to set up a second headquarters in the United States. This highly symbolic action made it easier to win approval from the US government. In contrast, GE and Honeywell proposed to merge and cleared US antitrust scrutiny, but failed to anticipate the EU antitrust authorities' incentive to kill the deal. In the end, the EU torpedoed the deal. The upshot is that, in addition to the economics of alliances and acquisitions, managers need to pay attention to the politics behind such high-stakes strategic moves.

Second, when managing alliances, managers need to pay attention to the soft relational capabilities that often make or break relationships. To the extent that business schools usually provide a good training on hard number-crunching skills, it is time for all of us to beef up on soft but equally important (perhaps even more important) relational capabilities.

Finally, when managing acquisitions, managers are advised not to overpay for targets and to focus on both strategic and organizational fit. Refusing to let the bidding war go out of hand and admitting failure in proposed deals by walking away are painful but courageous. Around the world between 10% and 20% of the proposed deals collapse.[19] Despite the media hoopla about the "power" of emerging multinationals from China, in reality more than half of their announced deals end in tears. Indian multinationals do better, but still one-third of their deals cannot close (see the Closing Case). This is not a problem that only affects emerging acquirers. Experienced acquirers such as AT&T, News Corporation, and Pfizer recently withdrew from their multi-billion dollar deals to acquire, respectively, T-Mobile, Time Warner, and AstraZeneca. Given that 70% of acquisitions fail and that integration challenges loom large down the road even if deals close, acquisitions that fail to close may sometimes be a blessing in disguise.

ETHICAL DILEMMA/EMERGING MARKETS

Emerging Acquirers from China and India

Multinational enterprises (MNEs) from emerging economies, especially China and India, have emerged as a new breed of acquirers around the world. Causing "oohs" and "ahhs," they have grabbed media headlines and caused controversies. Anecdotes aside, are the patterns of these new global acquirers similar? How do they differ? Only recently has rigorous academic research been conducted to allow for systematic comparison (Exhibit 11.11).

Overall, China's stock of outward foreign direct investment (OFDI) (1.7% of the worldwide total) is about three times India's (0.5%). One visible similarity is that both Chinese and Indian MNEs seem to use M&As as their primary mode of OFDI. Throughout the 2000s, Chinese firms spent $130 billion to engage in M&As overseas, whereas Indian firms made M&A deals worth $60 billion.

MNEs from China and India target industries to support and strengthen their own most competitive industries at home. Given China's prowess in manufacturing, Chinese firms' overseas M&As primarily target energy, minerals, and mining—crucial supply industries that feed their manufacturing operations at home. Indian MNEs' world-class position in high-tech and software

EXHIBIT 11.11 COMPARING CROSS-BORDER M&AS UNDERTAKEN BY CHINESE AND INDIAN MNEs

	Chinese MNEs	Indian MNEs
Top target industries	Energy, minerals, and mining	High-tech and software services
Top target economies	Hong Kong	United Kingdom
Top target regions	Asia	Europe
Top acquiring companies involved	State-owned enterprises	Private business groups
Percent of successfully closed deals	47%	67%

Source: Extracted from S. Sun, M. W. Peng, B. Ren, and D. Yan, "A comparative ownership advantage framework for cross-border M&As," *Journal of World Business* 47 (2012): 4–16.

JOHNBRAID/SHUTTERSTOCK.COM

services is reflected in their interest in acquiring firms in these industries.

The geographic spread of these MNEs is indicative of the level of their capabilities. Chinese firms have undertaken most of their deals in Asia, with Hong Kong being their most favorable location. In other words, the geographic distribution of Chinese M&As is not global; rather, it is quite regional. This reflects a relative lack of capabilities to engage in managerial challenges in regions distant from China, especially in more developed economies. Indian MNEs have primarily made deals in Europe, with the UK as their leading target country. For example, acquisitions made by Tata Motors (Jaguar Land Rover [JLR]) and Tata Steel (Corus Group) propelled Tata Group to become the number-one private-sector employer in the UK. Overall, Indian firms display a more global spread in their M&As, and demonstrate a higher level of confidence and sophistication in making deals in developed economies.

From an institution-based view, the contrasts between Chinese and Indian acquirers are significant. The primary M&A players from China are state-owned enterprises (SOEs), which have their own advantages (such as strong support from the Chinese government) and trappings (such as resentment and suspicion from host-country governments). The movers and shakers of cross-border M&As from India are private business groups, which generally are not viewed with strong suspicion. The limited evidence suggests that M&As by Indian firms tend to create value for their shareholders. On the other hand, M&As by Chinese firms tend to destroy shareholder value—indicative of potential hubristic and managerial motives evidenced by empire building and agency problems.

Announcing high-profile deals is one thing, but completing them is another matter. Chinese MNEs have a particularly poor record in completing the overseas acquisition deals they announce. Fewer than half (47%) of their announced acquisitions were completed, which compares unfavorably to Indian MNEs' 67% completion rate and to a global average of 80%–90% completion rate. Chinese MNEs' lack of ability and experience in due diligence and financing is one reason, but another reason is the political backlash and resistance they encounter, especially in developed economies. The 2005 failure of CNOOC's bid for Unocal in the United States and the 2009 failure of Chinalco's bid for Rio Tinto's assets in Australia are but two high-profile examples.

Even assuming successful completion, integration is a leading challenge during the post-acquisition phase. Acquirers from China and India have often taken the "high road" to acquisitions, in which acquirers deliberately allow acquired target companies to retain autonomy, keep the top management intact, and then gradually encourage interaction between the two sides. In contrast, the "low road" to acquisitions would be for acquirers to act quickly to impose their systems and rules on acquired target companies. Although the "high road" sounds noble, this is a reflection of these acquirers' lack of international management experience and capabilities.

From a resource-based view, examples of emerging acquirers that can do a good job in integration and deliver value are far and few. According to the *Economist*, Tata "worked wonders" at JLR by increasing 30% sales and keeping the factory at full capacity. This took place during a recession when European automakers were suffering. Fiat, for example, could only utilize 40% of its factory capacity in Italy (see the Opening Case). According to *Bloomberg Businessweek*, Lenovo was able to "find treasure in the PC industry's trash" by turning around the former IBM PC division and using it to propel itself to become the biggest PC maker in the world. In ten years it grew from a $3 billion company to a $40 billion one. However, Lenovo knew that worldwide PC sales were going down, thanks to the rise of mobile devices. In response, Lenovo recently bought "the mobile phone industry's trash"—Motorola Mobility division—from Google and endeavored to leverage the Motorola brand to become a top player in the smartphone world. This deal quickly made Lenovo the world's third best-selling smartphone maker after Samsung and Apple.

AP IMAGES/PICTURE-ALLIANCE/ULI DECK

Case Discussion Questions

1. Why have M&As emerged as the primary mode of foreign market entry for Chinese and Indian MNEs?
2. Drawing on the institution-based and resource-based views, outline the similarities and differences between Chinese and Indian multinational acquirers.
3. ***ON ETHICS***: As CEO of a firm from either China or India engaging in a high-profile acquisition overseas, shareholders at home are criticizing you for "squandering" their money, and target firm management and unions—as well as host country government and the media—are resisting. Should you proceed with the acquisition or consider abandoning the deal? If you are considering abandoning the deal, under what conditions would you abandon it?

Sources: "Lenovo completes Motorola takeover after Google sale," BBC News, 30 October 2014: www.bbc.co.uk; "Jackpot! How Lenovo found treasure in the PC industry's trash," *Bloomberg Businessweek*, 12 May 2014, 46–51; Y. Chen and M. Young, "Cross-border M&As by Chinese listed companies," *Asia Pacific Journal of Management* 27 (2010): 523–539; "The cat returns," *Economist*, 29 September 2012, 63; O. Hope, W. Thomas, and D. Vyas, "The cost of pride," *Journal of International Business Studies*, 42 (2011): 128–151; S. Lebedev, M. W. Peng, E. Xie, and C. Stevens, "Mergers and acquisitions in and out of emerging economies," *Journal of World Business* (2015, in press); S. Sun, M. W. Peng, B. Ren, and D. Yan, "A comparative ownership advantage framework for cross-border M&As," *Journal of World Business* 47 (2012): 4–16; Y. Yang, "I came back because the company needed me," *Harvard Business Review* (July 2014): 104–108.

STUDY TOOLS 11

LOCATED AT THE BACK OF YOUR BOOK:

- ☐ Rip out and study the Chapter Review Card at the end of the book

LOG IN TO WWW.CENGAGEBRAIN.COM TO:

- ☐ Review key term flashcards
- ☐ Complete a practice quiz to test your knowledge of key concepts
- ☐ Take and complete the chapter crossword puzzle
- ☐ Complete interactive content, watch chapter videos, and take a graded quiz
- ☐ Track your knowledge of key concepts in Global Business
- ☐ Read and discuss additional case study content

12 Strategizing, Structuring, & Learning Around the World

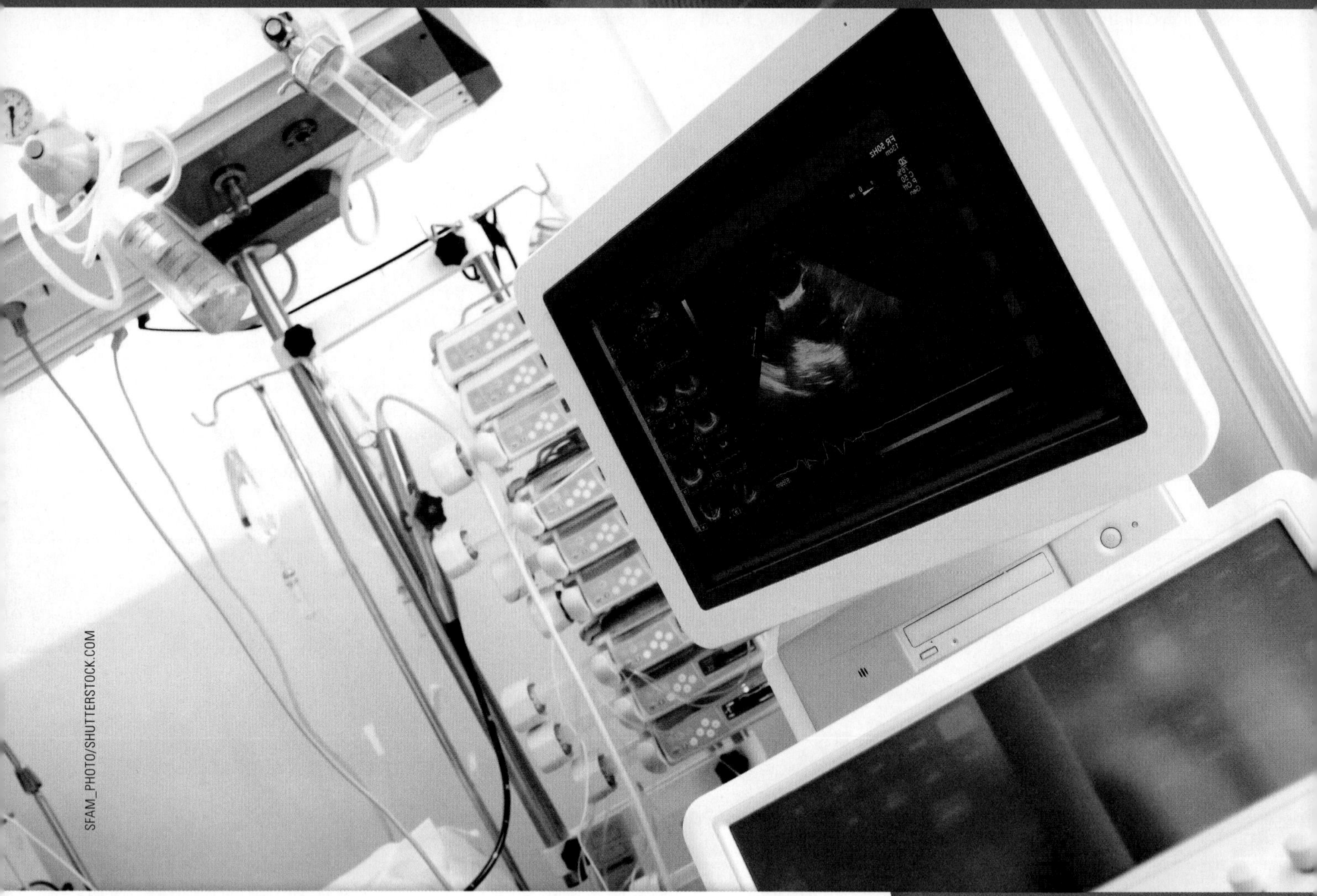

SFAM_PHOTO/SHUTTERSTOCK.COM

LEARNING OBJECTIVES

After studying this chapter, you will be able to . . .

12-1 Describe the relationship between multinational strategy and structure.

12-2 Explain how institutions and resources affect multinational strategy, structure, and learning.

12-3 Outline the challenges associated with learning, innovation, and knowledge management.

12-4 List three things you can do to make a multinational firm successful.

After you finish this chapter, go to **PAGE 195** for **STUDY TOOLS**

EMERGING MARKETS

GE Innovates from the Base of the Pyramid

Multinationals such as General Electric (GE) historically innovate new products in developed economies, and then localize these products by tweaking them for customers in emerging economies. Unfortunately, a lot of these expensive products, with well-off customers at the top of the global economic pyramid in mind, flop at the base of the pyramid (BoP). This is not only because of their price tag, but also because of their lack of consideration for the needs and wants of local customers. Being the exact opposite, reverse innovation, which is from BoP markets, turns innovative products created for emerging economies into low-cost offerings for developed economies.

Take a look at GE's conventional ultrasound machines, originally developed in the United States and Japan and sold for $100,000 and up (up to $350,000). In China, these expensive, bulky devices sold poorly because not every sophisticated hospital imaging center could afford them. GE's team in China realized that more than 70% of China's population relies on rural hospitals or clinics that are poorly funded. Conventional ultrasound machines are simply out of reach for these facilities. Patients thus have to travel to urban hospitals to access ultrasound. However, transportation to urban hospitals, especially for the sick and the pregnant, is challenging. Since most Chinese patients could not come to the ultrasound machines, the machines, thus, have to go to the patients. Scaling down its existing bulky, expensive, and complex ultrasound machines was not going to serve that demand. GM realized that it needed a revolutionary product—a compact, portable ultrasound machine. In 2002, GE in China launched its first compact ultrasound, which combined a regular laptop computer with sophisticated software. The machine sold for only $30,000. In 2008, GE introduced a new model that sold for $15,000, less than 15% of the price tag of its high-end conventional ultrasound models. While portable ultrasounds have naturally become a hit in China, especially in rural clinics, they have also generated dramatic growth throughout the world, including developed economies. These machines combine a new dimension previously unavailable to ultrasound machines—portability—with an unbeatable price in developed economies where containing health care cost is increasingly paramount.

GE's experience in developing portable ultrasound machines in China is not alone. For rural India, it has pioneered a $1,000 hand-held electrocardiogram (ECG) device that brings down the cost by a margin of 60% to 80%. In the Czech Republic, GE has developed an aircraft engine for small planes that slashes its cost by half. This allows GE to challenge Pratt & Whitney's dominance of the small turboprop market in developed economies.

Such outstanding performance in and out of emerging economies, in combination with GE's dismal recent experience in developed economies thanks to the Great Recession (2008–2009), has rapidly transformed GE's mental map of the world (Exhibit 12.1). In 2000, it focused on the Triad and paid relatively minor attention to the "rest of the world." Now strategic attention is on emerging economies and other resource-rich regions, and the Triad becomes the "rest of the world." In an October 2009 *Harvard Business Review* article, Immelt wrote:

> *To be honest, the company is also embracing reverse innovation for defensive reasons. If GE doesn't come up with innovations in poor countries and take them global, new competitors from the developing world—like Mindray, Suzlon, Goldwind, and Haier—will . . . GE has tremendous respect for traditional rivals like Siemens, Philips, and Rolls-Royce. But it knows how to compete with them; they will never destroy GE. By introducing products that create a new price-performance paradigm, however, the emerging giants very well could. Reverse innovation isn't optional; it's oxygen.*

Sources: "GE: Losing its magic touch," *Economist*, 21 March 2009, 73–75; "Frugal healing," *Economist*, 22 January 2011, 73–74; "Life should be cheap," *Economist*, 22 January 2011, 16; J. Immelt, V. Govindarajan, and C. Trimble, "How GE is disrupting itself," *Harvard Business Review* (October 2009): 56–65; C. K. Prahalad and R. Mashelkar, "Innovation's holy grail," *Harvard Business Review* (July 2010): 132–141.

EXHIBIT 12.1 GE'S MENTAL MAP OF THE WORLD

2000	2010
United States	People-rich regions, such as China and India
Europe	Resource-rich regions, such as the Middle East, Australia, Brazil, Canada, and Russia
Japan	Rest of the world, such as the United States, Europe, and Japan
Rest of the world	

Source: Extracted from text in J. Immelt, V. Govindarajan, and C. Trimble, "How GE is disrupting itself" *Harvard Business Review* (October 2009): 59.

How can multinational enterprises (MNEs) such as GE strategically manage growth around the world so that they can be successful both locally and internationally? How can they learn country tastes and global trends? How can they improve the odds for better innovation? These are some of the key questions we address in this chapter, which focuses on relatively large MNEs. We start by discussing the crucial relationship between four strategies and four structures. Next, we consider how the institution-based and resource-based views shed light on these issues. Then, we discuss worldwide learning, innovation, and knowledge management and look at a debate over whether control should be centralized or decentralized. Managerial implications follow.

EXHIBIT 12.2 MULTINATIONAL STRATEGIES AND STRUCTURES: THE INTEGRATION-RESPONSIVE FRAMEWORK

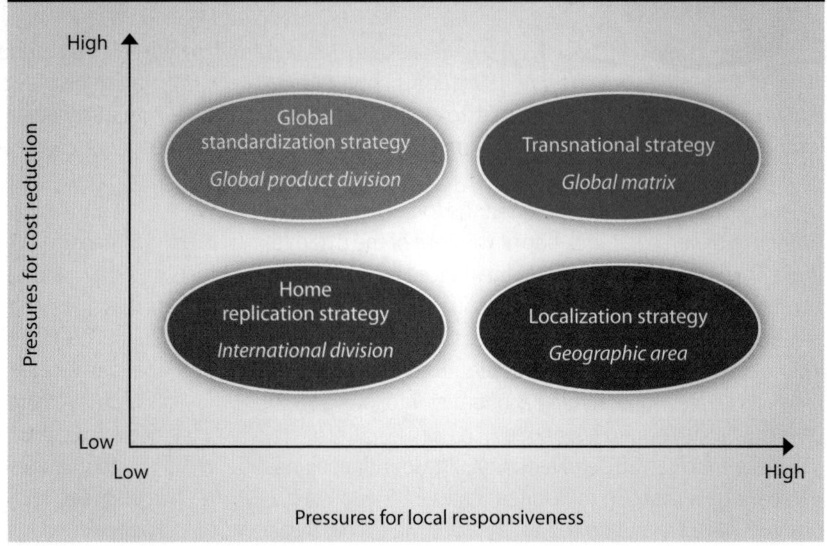

Note: In some textbooks, "home replication" may be referred to as "international" or "export" strategy, "localization" as "multidomestic" strategy, and "global standardization" as "global" strategy. Some of these labels are confusing because one can argue that all four strategies here are "international" or "global," thus resulting in some confusion if we label one of these strategies as "international" and another as "global." The present set of labels is more descriptive and less confusing.

12-1 MULTINATIONAL STRATEGIES AND STRUCTURES

This section first introduces an integration-responsiveness framework centered on the pressures for cost reduction and local responsiveness. We then outline the four strategic choices and the four corresponding organizational structures that MNEs typically adopt.

12-1a Pressures for Cost Reduction and Local Responsiveness

MNEs confront primarily two sets of pressures: cost reduction and local responsiveness. These two sets of pressures are dealt with in the **integration-responsiveness framework**, which allows managers to deal with the pressures for both global integration and local responsiveness. Cost pressures often call for global integration, while local responsiveness pushes MNEs to adapt locally. In both domestic and international competition, pressures to reduce costs are almost universal. What is unique in international competition is the pressures for **local responsiveness**, which means reacting to different consumer preferences and host-country demands. Consumer preferences vary tremendously around the world. For example, McDonald's beef-based hamburgers would obviously find few customers in India, a land where cows are held sacred by the Hindu majority. Thus, changing McDonald's menu is a must in India. Host-country demands and expectations add to the pressures for local responsiveness. Throughout Europe, Bombardier manufactures an Austrian version of rail-cars in Austria, a Belgian version in Belgium, and so on. Bomdardier believes that such local responsiveness, although not required, is essential for making sales to railway operators in Europe, which tend to be state owned.

Taken together, being locally responsive certainly makes local customers and governments happy, but unfortunately increases costs. Given the universal interest in lowering cost, a natural tendency is to downplay or ignore the different needs and wants of various local markets and instead market a global version of products and services. The movement to globalize offerings can be traced to a 1983 article by Theodore Levitt: "The Globalization of Markets."[1] Levitt argued that worldwide consumer tastes are converging. As evidence, Levitt pointed to the worldwide success of Coke Classic, Levi Strauss jeans, and Sony color TV. Levitt predicted that such

Integration-responsiveness framework An MNE management framework for simultaneously dealing with the pressures for both global integration and local responsiveness.

Local responsiveness The need to be responsive to different customer preferences around the world.

Home replication strategy A strategy that emphasizes duplicating home-country-based competencies in foreign countries.

convergence would characterize most product markets in the future.

Levitt's idea has often been the intellectual force propelling many MNEs to globally integrate their products while minimizing local adaptation. Ford experimented with "world car" designs. MTV pushed ahead with the belief that viewers would flock to global (essentially American) programming. Unfortunately, most of these experiments are not successful. Ford found that consumer tastes ranged widely around the globe. MTV eventually realized that there is no "global song." In a nutshell, one size does not fit all. This leads us to look at how MNEs can pay attention to *both* dimensions: cost reduction and local responsiveness.

EXHIBIT 12.3 FOUR STRATEGIC CHOICES FOR MULTINATIONAL ENTERPRISES

		Advantages	Disadvantages
1	Home replication	▸ Leverages home country-based advantages ▸ Relatively easy to implement	▸ Lack of local responsiveness ▸ May alienate foreign customers
2	Localization	▸ Maximizes local responsiveness	▸ High costs due to duplication of efforts in multiple countries ▸ Too much local autonomy
3	Global standardization	▸ Leverages low-cost advantages	▸ Lack of local responsiveness ▸ Too much centralized control
4	Transnational	▸ Cost-efficient while being locally responsive ▸ Engages in global learning and diffusion of innovations	▸ Organizationally complex ▸ Difficult to implement

© ISTOCKPHOTO.COM/BLACKRED

12-1b Four Strategic Choices

Based on the integration-responsiveness framework, Exhibit 12.2 plots the four strategic choices: (1) home replication, (2) localization, (3) global standardization, and (4) transnational. Each strategy has a set of pros and cons outlined in Exhibit 12.3. (Their corresponding structures in Exhibit 12.2 are discussed in the next section.)

Home replication strategy, often known as international (or export) strategy, duplicates home-country-based competencies in foreign countries. Such competencies include production scales, distribution efficiencies, and brand power. In manufacturing, this is usually manifested in an export strategy. In services, this is often done through licensing and franchising. This strategy is relatively easy to implement and usually the first one adopted when firms venture abroad.

On the disadvantage side, home replication strategy often lacks local responsiveness because it focuses on the home country. This strategy makes sense when the majority of a firm's customers are domestic. However, when a firm aspires to broaden its international scope, failing to be mindful of foreign customers' needs and wants may alienate those potential customers. When Walmart entered Brazil, the stores had exactly the same inventory as its US stores, including a large number of *American* footballs. Considering that Brazil is the land of soccer that has won soccer's World Cup five times, more wins than any other country, nobody (except a few homesick American expatriates in their spare time) plays American football there.

Localization strategy is an extension of the home replication strategy. **Localization (multidomestic) strategy** focuses on a number of foreign countries/regions, each of which is regarded as a stand-alone local (domestic) market worthy of significant attention and adaptation. While sacrificing global efficiencies, this strategy is effective when differences among national and regional markets are clear and pressures for cost reductions are low. For example, Disney has attempted to localize some of its offerings in its five theme parks in Anaheim, California; Orlando, Florida; Hong Kong; Paris; and Tokyo. Its newest park in Shanghai will feature traditional Disney rides and those based on Chinese culture. It will drop a standard feature common in Disney parks: Main Street USA.

In terms of disadvantages, the localization strategy has high costs due to duplication of efforts in multiple countries. The costs of producing a variety of programming for MTV are obviously greater than the costs of producing one set of programming. As a result, this strategy is only appropriate in industries where the pressures for cost reductions are not

Localization (multidomestic) strategy A strategy that focuses on a number of foreign countries/regions, each of which is regarded as a stand-alone local (domestic) market worthy of significant attention and adaptation.

360B/SHUTTERSTOCK.COM

significant. Another potential drawback is too much local autonomy, which happens when each subsidiary regards its country as so unique that it is difficult to introduce corporate-wide changes. For example, in the 1980s Unilever had 17 country subsidiaries in Europe and it took four years to persuade all 17 subsidiaries to introduce a single new detergent across Europe.

As the opposite of the localization strategy, **global standardization strategy** is sometimes referred to simply as global strategy. Its hallmark is the development and distribution of standardized products worldwide in order to reap the maximum benefits from low cost advantages. While both the home replication and global standardization strategies minimize local responsiveness, a crucial difference is that an MNE pursuing a global standardization strategy is not limited to its major operations at home. In a number of countries, the MNE may designate **centers of excellence**, defined as subsidiaries explicitly recognized as a source of important capabilities, with the intention that these capabilities be leveraged by and/or disseminated to other subsidiaries. Centers of excellence are often given a **worldwide (or global) mandate**—namely, a charter to be responsible for one MNE function throughout the world. For example, Huawei's Sweden subsidiary has a worldwide mandate in network consulting.

Global standardization strategy A strategy that relies on the development and distribution of standardized products worldwide to reap the maximum benefits from low-cost advantages.

Center of excellence An MNE subsidiary explicitly recognized as a source of important capabilities that can be leveraged by and/or disseminated to other subsidiaries.

Worldwide (global) mandate A charter to be responsible for one MNE function throughout the world.

Transnational strategy A strategy that endeavors to be simultaneously cost efficient, locally responsive, and learning driven around the world.

In terms of disadvantages, a global standardization strategy obviously sacrifices local responsiveness. This strategy makes great sense in industries where pressures for cost reductions are paramount and pressures for local responsiveness are relatively minor (particularly commodity industries such as semiconductors and tires). However, as noted earlier, in industries ranging from automobiles to consumer products, a one-size-fits-all strategy may be inappropriate. Consequently, arguments such as "all industries are becoming global" and "all firms need to pursue a global (standardization) strategy" are potentially misleading.

Transnational strategy aims to capture the best of both worlds by endeavoring to be both cost efficient and locally responsive.[2] In addition to cost efficiency and local responsiveness, a third hallmark of this strategy is global learning and diffusion of innovations. Traditionally, the diffusion of innovations in MNEs is a one-way flow from the home country to various host countries—the label "home replication" says it all (!). Underpinning the traditional one-way flow is the assumption that the home country is the best location for generating innovations. However, given that innovations are inherently risky and uncertain, there is no guarantee that the home country will generate the highest-quality innovations (see the Opening Case).

MNEs that engage in a transnational strategy promote global learning and diffusion of innovations in multiple ways. Innovations not only flow from the home country to host countries (which is the traditional flow), but also flow from host countries to the home country and flow among subsidiaries in multiple host countries (see the Opening Case). Kia Motors, for example, not only operates a design center in Seoul, but also has two other design centers in Los Angeles and Frankfurt, tapping into innovations generated in North America and Europe.

On the disadvantage side, a transnational strategy is organizationally complex and difficult to implement. The large amount of knowledge sharing and coordination may slow down decision making. Trying to achieve cost efficiencies, local responsiveness, and global learning simultaneously places contradictory demands on MNEs (to be discussed in the next section).

Overall, it is important to note that given the various pros and cons, there is no optimal strategy. The new trend in favor of a transnational strategy needs to be qualified with an understanding of its significant organizational challenges. This point leads to our next topic.

EXHIBIT 12.4 INTERNATIONAL DIVISION STRUCTURE AT STARBUCKS

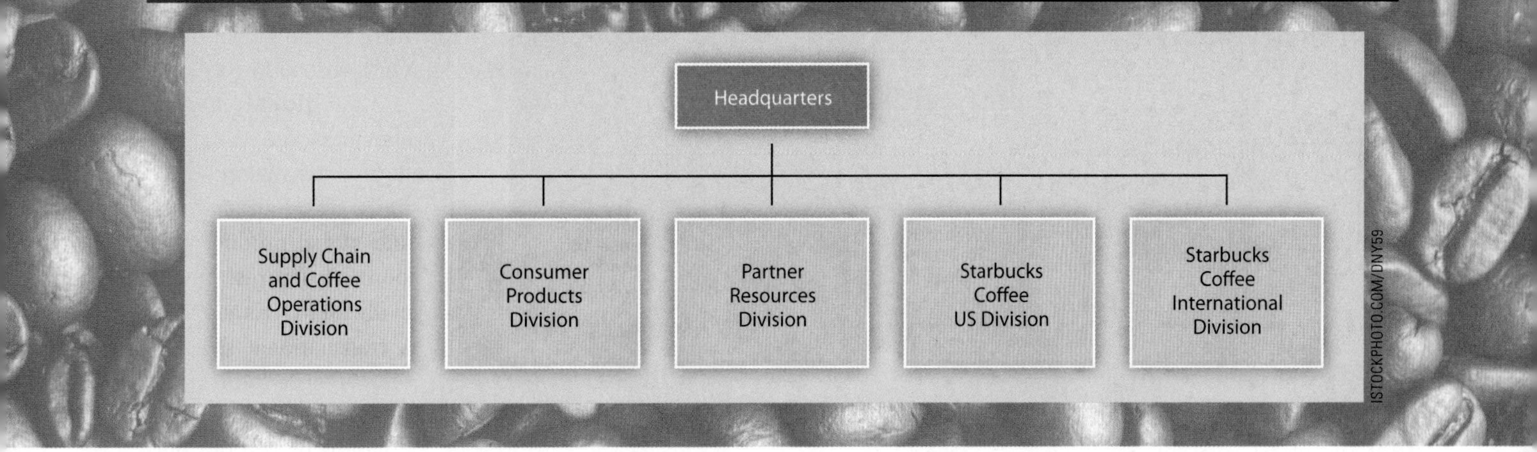

Source: www.cogmap.com http://www.starbucks.com. Headquartered in Seattle, Starbucks is a leading international coffee and coffeehouse company.

12-1c Four Organizational Structures

Exhibit 12.2 also shows four organizational structures that are appropriate for each of the strategic choices: (1) international division, (2) geographic area, (3) global product division, and (4) global matrix.

International division is typically used when firms initially expand abroad, often engaging in a home replication strategy. Exhibit 12.4 shows that Starbucks has an international division, in addition to the four divisions that primarily focus on the United States. Although this structure is intuitively appealing, it often leads to two problems. First, foreign subsidiary managers, whose input is channeled through the international division, are not given sufficient voice relative to the heads of domestic divisions. Second, by design, the international division serves as a silo whose activities are not coordinated with the rest of the firm, which is focusing on domestic activities. Consequently, many firms phase out this structure after their initial stage of overseas expansion.

Geographic area structure organizes the MNE according to different geographic areas (countries and regions). It is the most appropriate structure for a localization strategy. Exhibit 12.5 illustrates such a structure for Avon Products. A geographic area can be a country or a region, led by a **country (or regional) manager**. Each area is largely stand-alone. In contrast to the limited voice of subsidiary managers in the international division structure, country (and regional) managers carry a great deal of weight in a geographic area structure. Interestingly and paradoxically, *both* the strengths and weaknesses of this structure lie in its local responsiveness. While being locally

International division An organizational structure that is typically set up when a firm initially expands abroad, often engaging in a home replication strategy.

Geographic area structure An organizational structure that organizes the MNE according to different countries and regions.

Country (or regional) manager The business leader of a specific country (or a geographic region).

EXHIBIT 12.5 GEOGRAPHIC AREA STRUCTURE AT AVON PRODUCTS

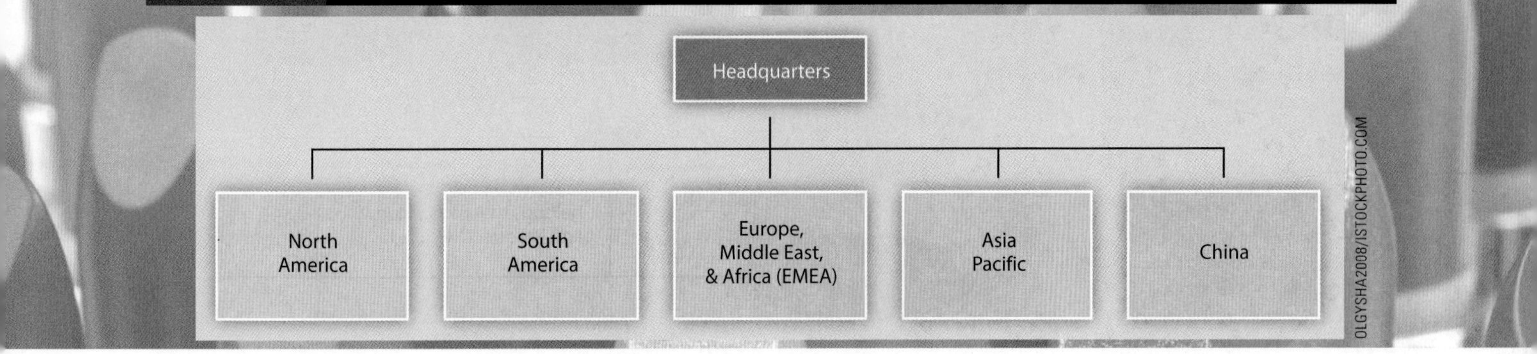

Source: www.avoncompany.com. Headquartered in New York, Avon is a leading global beauty products company.

EXHIBIT 12.6 GLOBAL PRODUCT DIVISION STRUCTURE AT AIRBUS GROUP

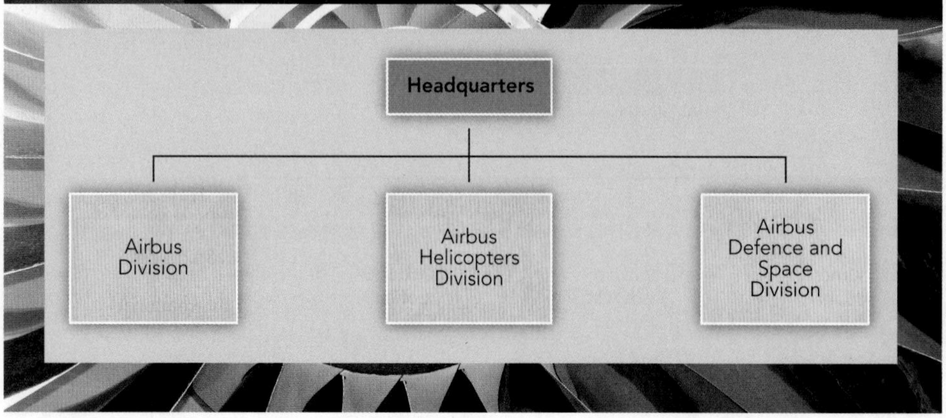

Source: Adapted from www.airbus.com. Headquartered in Toulouse, France, Airbus Group is the largest commercial aircraft maker and the largest defense contractor in Europe. Between 2000 and 2014, it was known as European Aeronautic Defense and Space Company (EADS).

responsive can be a virtue, it also encourages the fragmentation of the MNE into fiefdoms.

Global product division structure, which is the opposite of the geographic area structure, supports the global standardization strategy by assigning global responsibilities to each product division. Exhibit 12.6 shows such an example from Airbus Group. This structure treats each product division as a stand-alone entity with full worldwide responsibilities. This structure is highly responsive to pressures for cost efficiencies, because it allows for consolidation on a worldwide (or at least regional) basis and reduces inefficient duplication in multiple countries. For example, Unilever reduced the number of soap-producing factories in Europe from ten to two after adopting this structure. Recently, because of the popularity of the global standardization strategy (noted earlier), the global product division structure is on the rise. The structure's main drawback is that local responsiveness suffers, as Ford discovered when it phased out the geographic area structure in favor of the global product division structure.

A **global matrix** alleviates the disadvantages associated with both geographic area and global product division structures, especially for MNEs adopting a transnational strategy. Shown in Exhibit 12.7, its hallmark is the coordination of responsibilities between product divisions and geographic areas in order to be both cost efficient and locally responsive. In this hypothetical example, the country manager in charge of Japan—in short, the Japan manager—reports to Product Division 1 and Asia Division, both of which have equal power.

In theory this structure supports the goals of the transnational strategy, but in practice it is often difficult to deliver. The reason is simple: While managers (such as the Japan manager in Exhibit 12.7) usually find dealing with one boss headache enough, they do not appreciate having two bosses who are often in conflict. For example, Product Division 1 may decide that Japan is too tough a nut to crack and that there are more promising markets elsewhere, thus ordering the Japan manager

EXHIBIT 12.7 A HYPOTHETICAL GLOBAL MATRIX STRUCTURE

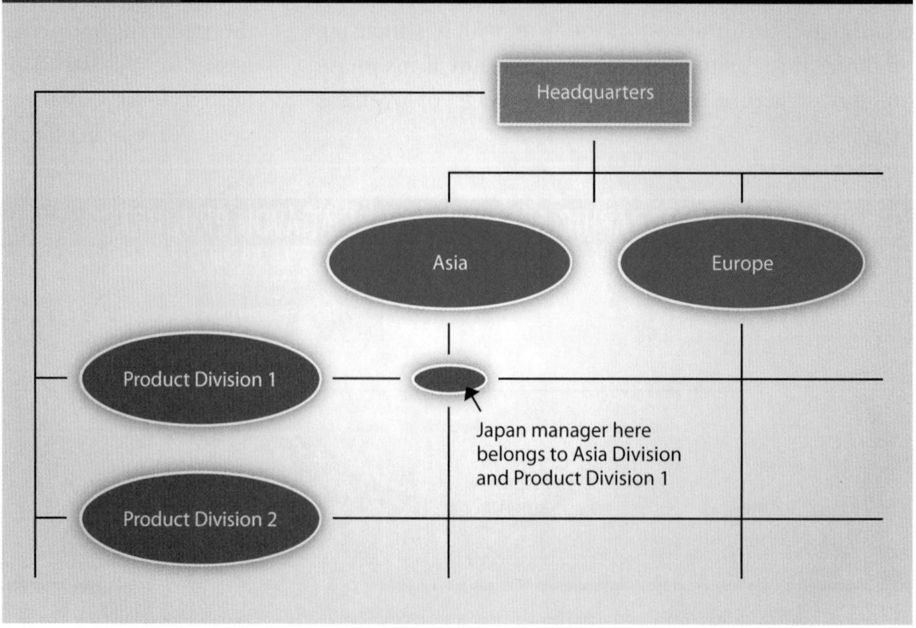

Global product division structure An organizational structure that assigns global responsibilities to each product division.

Global matrix An organizational structure often used to alleviate the disadvantages associated with both geographic area and global product division structures, particularly when adopting a transnational strategy.

to *curtail* his investment and channel resources elsewhere. This makes sense because Product Division 1 cares about its global market position and is not wedded to any particular country. However, Asia Division, which is evaluated by how well it does in Asia, may beg to differ. Asia Division argues that it cannot afford to be a laggard in Japan if it expects to be a leading player in Asia. Therefore, Asia Division demands that the Japan manager *increase* his investment in the country. Facing these conflicting demands, the Japan manager, who prefers to be politically correct, does not want to make any move before consulting corporate headquarters. Eventually, headquarters may provide a resolution. But crucial time may be lost in the process, and important windows of opportunity for competitive actions may be missed.

Despite its merits on paper, the matrix structure may add layers of management, slow down decision speed, and increase costs while not showing significant performance improvement. There is no conclusive evidence for the superiority of the matrix structure. The following quote from the CEO of Dow Chemical, an early adopter of the matrix structure, is sobering:

We were an organization that was matrixed and depended on teamwork, but there was no one in charge. When things went well, we didn't know whom to reward; and when things went poorly, we didn't know whom to blame. So we created a global product division structure, and cut out layers of management. There used to be 11 layers of management between me and the lowest level employees, now there are five.[3]

Overall, the positioning of the four structures in Exhibit 12.2 is not random. They develop from the relatively simple international division through either geographic area or global product division structures and may eventually reach the more complex global matrix stage. It is important to note that not every MNE experiences all of these structural stages, and that the movement is not necessarily in one direction. For example, the matrix structure's poster child, the Swedish-Swiss conglomerate ABB, recently withdrew from this structure.

12-1d The Reciprocal Relationship Between Multinational Strategy and Structure

In one word, the relationship between strategy and structure is *reciprocal*. Three key ideas stand out.

- Strategy usually drives structure. The fit between strategy and structure, as exemplified by the *pairs* in each of the four cells in Exhibit 12.2, is crucial. A misfit, such as combining a global standardization strategy with a geographic area structure, may have grave performance consequences.
- The relationship is not one way. As much as strategy drives structure, structure also drives strategy. The withdrawal from the unworkable matrix structure at MNEs such as ABB has called into question the wisdom of the transnational strategy.
- Neither strategy nor structure is static. It is often necessary to change strategy, structure, or both. In an effort to move toward a global standardization strategy, many MNEs have adopted a global product division structure while de-emphasizing the role of country headquarters. However, unique challenges in certain countries, especially China, have now pushed some MNEs to revive the country headquarters to more effectively coordinate numerous activities within a large, complex, and important host country.[4] Panasonic, for example, set up Panasonic Corporation of China to manage its over 40 operations in China.[5] A further experimentation is to have an emerging economies division, which is not dedicated to any single country but dedicated to pursuing opportunities in a series of emerging economies ranging from Brazil to Saudi Arabia. Cisco pioneered this structure, which has been followed by rivals such as IBM.[6]

12-2 HOW INSTITUTIONS AND RESOURCES AFFECT MULTINATIONAL STRATEGY, STRUCTURE, AND LEARNING

Having outlined the basic strategy/structure configurations, let us now introduce how the institution-based and resource-based views shed light on these issues. This is mapped out in Exhibit 12.8.

12-2a Institution-Based Considerations

MNEs face two sets of rules of the game: formal and informal institutions governing (1) *external* relationships and (2) *internal* relationships. Each is discussed in turn.

Externally, MNEs are subject to the formal institutional frameworks erected by various home-country and

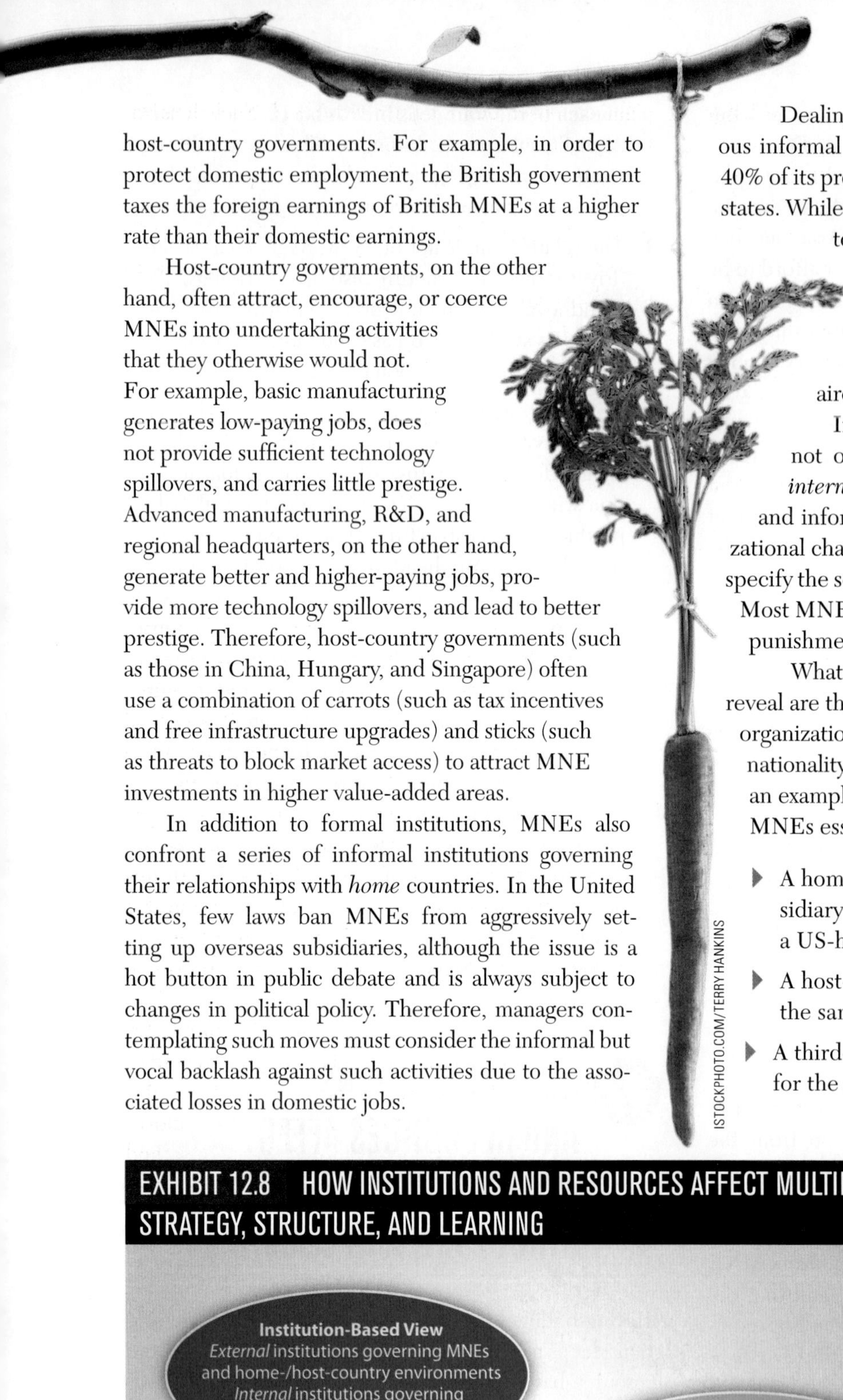

ISTOCKPHOTO.COM/TERRY HANKINS

host-country governments. For example, in order to protect domestic employment, the British government taxes the foreign earnings of British MNEs at a higher rate than their domestic earnings.

Host-country governments, on the other hand, often attract, encourage, or coerce MNEs into undertaking activities that they otherwise would not. For example, basic manufacturing generates low-paying jobs, does not provide sufficient technology spillovers, and carries little prestige. Advanced manufacturing, R&D, and regional headquarters, on the other hand, generate better and higher-paying jobs, provide more technology spillovers, and lead to better prestige. Therefore, host-country governments (such as those in China, Hungary, and Singapore) often use a combination of carrots (such as tax incentives and free infrastructure upgrades) and sticks (such as threats to block market access) to attract MNE investments in higher value-added areas.

In addition to formal institutions, MNEs also confront a series of informal institutions governing their relationships with *home* countries. In the United States, few laws ban MNEs from aggressively setting up overseas subsidiaries, although the issue is a hot button in public debate and is always subject to changes in political policy. Therefore, managers contemplating such moves must consider the informal but vocal backlash against such activities due to the associated losses in domestic jobs.

Dealing with *host* countries also involves numerous informal institutions. For example, Airbus spends 40% of its procurement budget with US suppliers in 40 states. While there is no formal requirement for Airbus to farm out supply contracts, its sourcing is guided by the informal norm of reciprocity: If one country's suppliers are involved with Airbus, airlines based in that country are more likely to buy Airbus aircraft.

Institutional factors affecting MNEs are not only external. How MNEs are governed *internally* is also determined by various formal and informal rules of the game. Formally, organizational charts, such as those in Exhibits 12.4 to 12.7, specify the scope of responsibilities for various parties. Most MNEs have systems of evaluation, reward, and punishment in place based on these formal rules.

What the formal organizational charts do not reveal are the informal rules of the game, such as organizational norms, values, and networks. The nationality of the head of foreign subsidiaries is an example. Given the lack of formal regulations, MNEs essentially have three choices:

- A home-country national as the head of a subsidiary (such as an American for a subsidiary of a US-headquartered MNE in India).
- A host-country national (such as an Indian for the same subsidiary).
- A third-country national (such as an Australian for the same subsidiary above).

MNEs from different countries have different norms when making these appointments. Most Japanese MNEs follow an informal rule: Heads of foreign subsidiaries, at least initially, need to be Japanese nationals. In comparison, European MNEs are more likely to appoint host-country and third-country nationals to lead subsidiaries. As a group, US MNEs are somewhere between Japanese and European practices. These staffing approaches may reflect strategic

EXHIBIT 12.8 HOW INSTITUTIONS AND RESOURCES AFFECT MULTINATIONAL STRATEGY, STRUCTURE, AND LEARNING

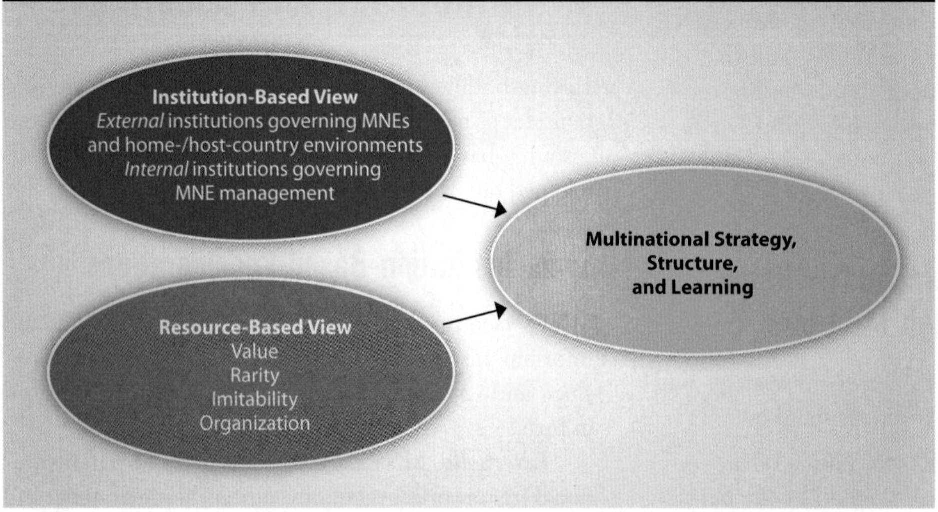

differences. Home-country nationals, especially long-time employees of the same MNE at home, are more likely to have developed a better understanding of the informal workings of the firm and to be better socialized into its dominant norms and values. Consequently, the Japanese propensity to appoint home-country nationals is conducive to their preferred global standardization strategy, which values globally coordinated and controlled actions. Conversely, the European comfort in appointing host-country and third-country nationals is indicative of European MNEs' (traditional) preference for a localization strategy.

Beyond the nationality of subsidiary heads, the nationality of top executives at the highest level (such as chairman, CEO, and board members) seems to follow another informal rule: They are almost always home-country nationals. To the extent that top executives are ambassadors of the firm and that the MNE's country of origin is a source of differentiation (for example, a German MNE is often perceived to be different from an Italian MNE), home-country nationals would seem to be the most natural candidates for top positions.

In the eyes of stakeholders such as employees and governments around the world, however, a top echelon consisting of largely one nationality does not bode well for an MNE aspiring to globalize everything it does. Some critics even argue that this "glass ceiling" reflects "corporate imperialism."[7] Consequently, such leading MNEs as BP, Citigroup, Coca-Cola, Electrolux, GSK, HP, Lenovo, Microsoft, Nissan, Nokia, PepsiCo, P&G, and Sony have appointed foreign-born executives to top posts. Nestlé boasts executive board members from eight countries other than Switzerland. Such foreign-born executives bring substantial diversity to the organization, which may be a plus. However, such diversity puts an enormous burden on these nonnative top executives to clearly articulate the values and exhibit behaviors expected of senior managers of an MNE associated with a particular country. For example, in 2010 HP appointed Léo Apotheker, a native of Germany, to be its CEO. Unfortunately, HP lost $30 billion in market capitalization during his short tenure (over ten months), thanks to his numerous change initiatives. He was quickly fired in 2011. Since then, the old rule is back: HP is again led by an American executive.

12-2b Resource-Based Considerations

Shown in Exhibit 12.8, the resource-based view—exemplified by the value, rarity, imitability, and organization (VRIO) framework—adds a number of insights.[8] First, when looking at structural changes, it is critical to consider whether a new structure (such as a matrix) adds concrete value. The value of innovation must also be considered.[9] A vast majority of innovations simply fail to reach market, and most new products that do reach market end up being financial failures. The difference between an innovator and a *profitable* innovator is that the latter not only has plenty of good ideas, but also lots of complementary assets (such as appropriate organizational structures and marketing muscles) to add value to innovation (see Chapter 4). Philips, for example, is a great innovator. The company invented rotary shavers, video cassettes, and CDs. Still, its ability to profit from these innovations lag behind that of Sony and Matsushita, which have much stronger complementary assets.

A second question is rarity. Certain strategies or structures may be in vogue at a given point in time. For example, when a company's rivals all move toward a global standardization strategy, this strategy cannot be a source of differentiation. To improve global coordination, many MNEs spend millions of dollars to equip themselves with enterprise resource planning (ERP) packages provided by SAP and Oracle. However, such packages are designed to be implemented

MANPREET ROMANA/AFP/GETTY IMAGES

widely and appeal to a broad range of firms, thus providing no firm-specific advantage for the particular adopting firm.

Even when capabilities are valuable and rare, they have to pass a third hurdle—imitability. Formal structures are easier to observe and imitate than informal structures. This is one of the reasons why the informal, flexible matrix is in vogue now. The informal, flexible matrix "is less a structural classification than a broad organizational concept or philosophy, manifested in organizational capability and management mentality."[10] Obviously imitating an intangible mentality is much harder than imitating a tangible structure.

The last hurdle is organization—namely, how MNEs are organized, both formally and informally, around the world (see the Debate). One elusive but important concept is organizational culture. Recall from Chapter 3 that culture is defined by Hofstede as "the collective programming of the mind which distinguishes the members of one group or category of people from another." We can extend this concept to define **organizational culture** as the collective programming of the mind that distinguishes members of one organization from another. China's Huawei, for example, is known to have a distinctive "wolf" culture, which centers on "continuous hunting" and "relentless pursuit" with highly motivated employees who routinely work overtime and sleep in their offices. Although rivals can imitate everything Huawei does technologically, their biggest hurdle lies in their lack of ability to wrap their arms around Huawei's "wolf" culture.

Debate: Ethical Dilemma

Corporate Controls Versus Subsidiary Initiatives

One of the leading debates on how to manage large firms is whether control should be centralized or decentralized. In an MNE setting, the debate boils down to corporate controls versus subsidiary initiatives.

SUBSIDIARY CONTROL

Subsidiaries are not necessarily receptive to headquarters' commands. When headquarters requires that certain practices (such as ethics training) be adopted, some subsidiaries may be in full compliance, others may pay lip service, and still others may simply refuse to adopt the practice, citing local differences. In addition to reacting to headquarters' demands differently, some subsidiaries may actively pursue their own, subsidiary-level strategies and agendas. These activities are known as **subsidiary initiatives**, defined as the proactive and deliberate pursuit of new opportunities by a subsidiary to expand its scope of responsibility. For example, Honeywell Canada requested that it be designated as a global "center for excellence" for certain Honeywell product lines. Advocates argue that such initiatives may inject a much-needed spirit of entrepreneurship throughout the larger, more bureaucratic corporation (see the Closing Case).

CORPORATE CONTROL

From corporate headquarters' perspective, however, it is hard to distinguish between good-faith subsidiary initiative and opportunistic empire building on the part of subsidiary managers. Much is at stake when determining whether subsidiaries should be named "centers of excellence" with worldwide mandates. Subsidiaries that fail to attain this status may see their roles marginalized or, worse, their facilities closed. Subsidiary managers are often host-country nationals (such as the Canadian managers at Honeywell Canada) who would naturally prefer to strengthen their subsidiary, if only to protect local (and their own!) employment and not necessarily to be patriotic. However natural and legitimate these tendencies, they are not necessarily consistent with the MNE's corporate-wide goals. These tendencies, if not checked and controlled, can surely lead to chaos for the MNE as a whole.

The best way, according to the title of an influential article authored by the former chairman and CEO of Intel, Andy Grove, seems to be: "Let chaos reign, then reign in chaos—repeatedly."

Sources: T. Ambos, U. Andersson, and J. Birkinshaw, "What are the consequences of initiative-taking in multinational subsidiaries?" *Journal of International Business Studies* 41 (2010): 1099–1118; R. Burgelman and A. Grove, "Let chaos reign, then reign in chaos—repeatedly," *Strategic Management Journal* 28 (2007): 965–979; F. Ciabuschi, M. Forsgren, and O. Martin, "Rationality versus ignorance," *Journal of International Business Studies* 42 (2011): 958–970; "It's complicated," *Economist*, 23 November 2013, 68; S. Wang, Y. Luo, X. Lu, J. Sun, and V. Maksimov, "Autonomy delegation to foreign subsidiaries," *Journal of International Business Studies* 45 (2014): 111–130.

ISTOCKPHOTO.COM/BILLNOLL

Organizational culture The collective programming of the mind that distinguishes members of one organization from another.

Subsidiary initiative The proactive and deliberate pursuit of new opportunities by a subsidiary to expand its scope of responsibility.

12-3 WORLDWIDE LEARNING, INNOVATION, AND KNOWLEDGE MANAGEMENT

12-3a Knowledge Management

Underpinning the recent emphasis on worldwide learning and innovation is the emerging interest in knowledge management. **Knowledge management** can be defined as the structures, processes, and systems that actively develop, leverage, and transfer knowledge.

Many managers regard knowledge management as simply information management. Taken to an extreme, "such a perspective can result in a profoundly mistaken belief that the installation of sophisticated information technology (IT) infrastructure is the be-all and end-all of knowledge management."[11] Knowledge management depends not only on IT, but also on informal social relationships within the MNE.[12] This is because there are two categories of knowledge: (1) explicit knowledge and (2) tacit knowledge. **Explicit knowledge** is codifiable—that is, it can be written down and transferred with little loss of richness. Virtually all of the knowledge captured, stored, and transmitted by IT is explicit. **Tacit knowledge** is non-codifiable, and its acquisition and transfer require hands-on practice. For example, reading a driver's manual (which contains a ton of explicit knowledge) without any road practice does not make you a good driver. Tacit knowledge is evidently more important and harder to transfer and learn; it can only be acquired through learning by doing (driving in this case). Consequently, from a resource-based view, explicit knowledge captured by IT may be strategically *less* important. What counts is the hard-to-codify and hard-to-transfer tacit knowledge.

12-3b Knowledge Management in Four Types of Multinational Enterprises

Differences in knowledge management among four types of MNEs in Exhibit 12.2 fundamentally stem from the interdependence (1) between the headquarters and foreign subsidiaries and (2) among various subsidiaries, as illustrated in Exhibit 12.9.[13] In MNEs pursuing a home replication strategy, such interdependence is moderate and the role of subsidiaries is largely to adapt and leverage parent-company competencies (see Exhibit 12.10 on Mary Kay around 2005). Thus, knowledge on new products and technologies is mostly developed at the center and flown to subsidiaries, representing the traditional one-way flow. Starbucks, for example, insists on

Knowledge management The structures, processes, and systems that actively develop, leverage, and transfer knowledge.

Explicit knowledge Knowledge that is codifiable (that is, can be written down and transferred with little loss of richness).

Tacit knowledge Knowledge that is non-codifiable, whose acquisition and transfer require hands-on practice.

EXHIBIT 12.9 KNOWLEDGE MANAGEMENT IN FOUR TYPES OF MULTINATIONAL ENTERPRISES

Strategy	Home replication	Localization	Global standardization	Transnational
Examples	Apple, Baidu, Carrefour, Google, Harley Davison, Kraft, P&G, Starbucks, Walmart	Heinz, Johnson & Johnson, KFC, McDonald's, Nestlé, Pfizer, Unilever	Canon, Caterpillar, Haier, HP, Huawei, LVMH, Otis, Texas Instruments, Toyota	GE, Häagen-Dazs, IBM, Kikkoman, Panasonic, Tata, Zara
Interdependence	Moderate	Low	Moderate	High
Role of foreign subsidiaries	Adapting and leveraging parent-company competencies	Sensing and exploiting local opportunities	Implementing parent-company initiatives	Differentiated contributions by subsidiaries to integrate worldwide operations
Development and diffusion of knowledge	Knowledge developed at the center and transferred to subsidiaries	Knowledge developed and retained within each subsidiary	Knowledge mostly developed and retained at the center and key locations	Knowledge developed jointly and shared worldwide
Flow of knowledge	Extensive flow of knowledge and people from headquarters to subsidiaries	Limited flow of knowledge and people to and from the center	Extensive flow of knowledge and people from the center and key locations to subsidiaries	Extensive flow of knowledge and people in multiple directions

Sources: Adapted from C. Bartlett and S. Ghoshal, *Managing Across Borders: The Transnational Solution* (Boston: Harvard Business School Press, 1989) 65; T. Kostova and K. Roth, "Social capital in multinational corporations and a micro-macro model of its formation," *Academy of Management Review* 28 (2003): 299. Examples are added by M. W. Peng.

EXHIBIT 12.10 MARY KAY AROUND 2005

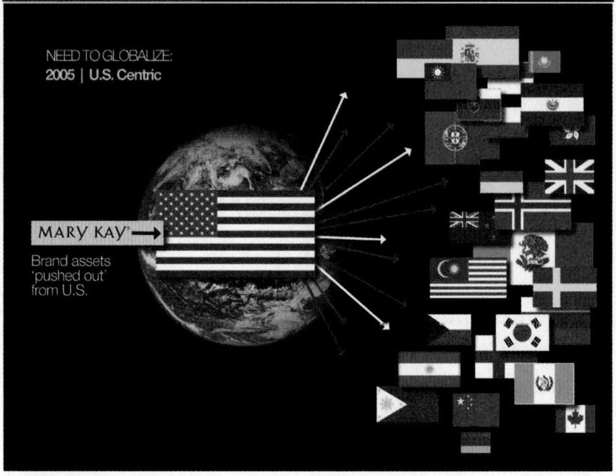

Source: © Mary Kay Inc.

EXHIBIT 12.11 MARY KAY NOW

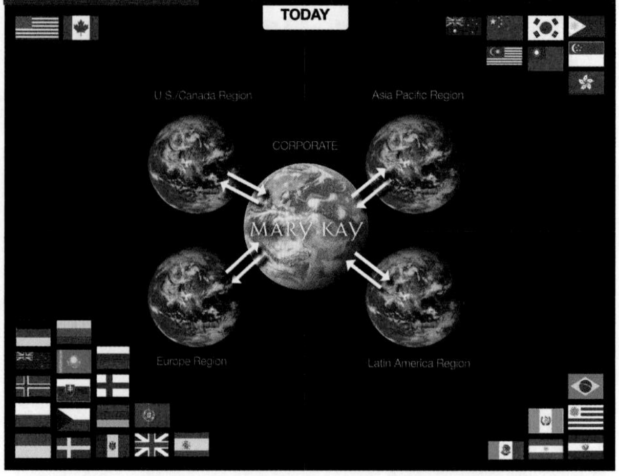

Source: © Mary Kay Inc.

replicating its US coffee shop concept around the world, down to the elusive "atmosphere."

When MNEs adopt a localization strategy, the interdependence is low. Knowledge management centers on developing insights that can best serve local markets. Ford of Europe used to develop cars for Europe, with a limited flow of knowledge to and from headquarters. In MNEs pursuing a global standardization strategy, on the other hand, the interdependence is increased. Knowledge is developed and retained at the headquarters and a few centers of excellence. Consequently, knowledge and people typically flow from headquarters and these centers to other subsidiaries. For example, Yokogawa Hewlett-Packard, HP's subsidiary in Japan, won a coveted Japanese Deming Award for quality. The subsidiary was then charged with transferring such knowledge to the rest of HP, which resulted in a tenfold improvement in *corporate*-wide quality in ten years.

A hallmark of transnational MNEs is a high degree of interdependence and extensive and bi-directional flows of knowledge. For example, Kikkoman first developed teriyaki sauce specifically for the US market as a barbecue glaze. It was then marketed to Japan and the rest of the world. Similarly, Häagen-Dazs developed a popular ice cream in Argentina that was based on a locally popular caramelized milk dessert. The company then sold the flavor as Dulce De Leche throughout the United States and Europe. Within one year, it became the second most popular Häagen-Dazs ice cream, next only to vanilla. Particularly fundamental to transnational MNEs are knowledge flows among dispersed subsidiaries. Instead of a top-down hierarchy, the MNE thus can be conceptualized as an integrated network of subsidiaries. Each subsidiary not only develops locally relevant knowledge but also aspires to contribute knowledge to benefit the MNE as a whole (see Exhibit 12.11 on Mary Kay today).

12-3c Globalizing Research and Development

R&D represents an especially crucial arena for knowledge management. Relative to production and marketing, only more recently has R&D emerged as an important function to be internationalized—often known as innovation-seeking investment (see Chapter 10). For example, Airbus has a significant R&D presence in Wichita, Kansas. Huawei has R&D units in China, India, Sweden, and the United States. Intense competition for innovation drives the globalization of R&D. Such R&D provides access to foreign country's local talents.

From a resource-based standpoint, a fundamental basis for competitive advantage is innovation-based firm heterogeneity (that is, being different). Decentralized R&D work performed by different locations and teams around the world virtually guarantees that there will be persistent heterogeneity in the solutions generated. GSK, for example, began aggressively spinning off R&D units as it became clear that simply adding more researchers in centralized R&D units did not necessarily enhance global learning and innovation.[14] GE's China units have developed low-cost, portable ultrasound machines at a fraction

SEAN LOCKE PHOTOGRAPHY/SHUTTERSTOCK.COM

of the cost of existing machines developed in the United States. GE has not only been selling the developed-in-China machines throughout emerging economies, but has also brought them back to the United States and other developed economies (see the Opening Case).

12-4 MANAGEMENT SAVVY

MNEs are the ultimate large, complex, and geographically dispersed business organizations. What determines the success or failure of multinational strategies, structures, and learning? The answer boils down to the institution-based and resource-based dimensions. The institution-based view calls for thorough understanding and skillful manipulation of the rules of the game, both at home and abroad. The resource-based view focuses on the development and deployment of firm-specific capabilities to enhance the odds for success.

Consequently, three clear implications emerge for savvy managers (see Exhibit 12.12). First, understanding and mastering the external rules of the game governing MNEs and home/host country environments become a must.[15] For example, some MNEs take advantage of the rules that subsidiaries in different countries need to be registered as independent legal entities in these countries, and leverage these subsidiaries to engage in tax avoidance (see In Focus). Other MNEs abandon their original countries of origin and move their headquarters to be governed

In Focus: *Ethical Dilemma*

One Multinational Versus Many National Companies

We often treat each MNE as one firm, regardless of in how many countries it operates. However, from an institution-based standpoint, one can argue that a multinational enterprise may be a total *fiction* that does not exist. This is because, legally, incorporation is only possible under national law, and every so-called MNE is essentially a bunch of national companies (subsidiaries) registered in various countries. A generation ago, such firms were often labeled "multi-national companies" with a hyphen. Although some pundits argue that globalization is undermining the power of national governments, there is little evidence that the modern nation-state system, in existence since the 1648 Treaty of Westphalia, is retreating.

This debate is not just academic hair-splitting fighting over a hyphen. It is very relevant and stakes are high. In 2010, Zhejiang Geely Holding Group (in short, "Geely") of China acquired Volvo Car Corporation (Volvo Personvagnar AB in Swedish—in short, "Volvo Cars" in English) from Ford Motor Company of the United States for $1.8 billion. Volvo Cars thus became a wholly owned subsidiary of Geely. Everybody in the world, including Geely's owner Li Shufu, thought Volvo Cars was "Chinese"—except the Chinese government. Refusing to acknowledge the existence of any "multinational," the Chinese government maintained that Volvo Cars, registered in Sweden and headquartered in Gothenburg, Sweden, was Swedish. When Li sought to produce Volvo vehicles in Chengdu, Daqing, and Zhangjiakou in China, the government advised that he set up a new joint venture (JV) between Volvo Cars (a Swedish firm) and Geely (a Chinese firm). Since Li was chairman of the board for Volvo Cars and chairman of the board for Geely, he ended up signing *both* sides of the JV contract. In other words, *one individual* represented both the Swedish firm and the Chinese firm (!). In 2013, the Chinese government approved this new international JV, in which the Swedish side (Volvo Cars) owned 30% equity.

If Li signing his name twice on a JV contract is funny, a more serious case in point concerns tax avoidance. Legally, Google Ireland

ROBERT GUBBINS/SHUTTERSTOCK.COM

is not a branch of the US-based Google Corporation. Google Ireland is a separate, legally independent corporation registered in Ireland. Although Google Corporation intentionally lets Google Ireland earn a lot of profits, the US Internal Revenue Service (IRS) cannot tax a dime Google Ireland makes unless it sends back (repatriates) the profits to Google Corporation. Google Corporation does not have just one subsidiary. It has lots around the world. Overall, 54% of Google's profits are parked overseas and are not taxable by the IRS. Google is not alone. The list of leading US firms that have left a majority of their profits overseas includes Chevron, Cisco, Citigroup, ExxonMobil, GE, HP, IBM, Johnson & Johnson, Microsoft, P&G, PepsiCo, and Pfizer. These firms claim that they are willing to bring the profits back home to invest and create jobs as long as Congress grants them a tax holiday. Running huge budget deficits, Congress is understandably unhappy.

Sources: "Geely-Volvo JV to push Volvo brand and new energy cars," *21st Century Business Insights*, 1 April 2012, 27; S. Kobrin, "Sovereignty@bay," in A. Rugman (ed.), *The Oxford Handbook of International Business* (New York: Oxford University Press, 2009) 183–204; C. Needham, *Corporate Tax Avoidance by Multinational Firms* (Library of the European Parliament, 2013); "Global tax avoidance: A trillion dollar evil," *Sydney Morning Herald*, 21 February 2014, www.smh.com.au; www.volvocars.com.

EXHIBIT 12.12 IMPLICATIONS FOR ACTION

- Understand and master the external rules of the game governing MNEs and home-country/host-country environments.
- Understand and be prepared to change the internal rules of the game governing MNE management.
- Develop learning and innovation capabilities to leverage multinational presence as an asset—"think global, act local."

by more market-friendly laws and regulations in their new countries of domicile. Despite the Swedish flags in front of its stores, IKEA is now a *Dutch* company, having registered in the Netherlands and enjoyed lower taxes there.

Second, managers need to understand and be prepared to change the internal rules of the game governing MNE management. Different strategies and structures call for different internal rules. Some facilitate and others constrain MNE actions. A firm using a home replication strategy should not appoint a foreigner as its CEO. Yet, as operations become more global, an MNE's managerial outlook needs to be broadened as well.

Finally, managers need to actively develop learning and innovation capabilities to leverage multinational presence. A winning formula is: *Think global, act local*.[16] Failing to do so may be costly. From 1999 until 2000, Ford Explorer SUVs were involved in numerous fatal rollover accidents in the United States. Most of these accidents were blamed on faulty tires made by Japan's Bridgestone and its US subsidiary Firestone. However, before the increase in US accidents, an alarming number of similar accidents had already taken place in warmer-weather countries such as Brazil and Saudi Arabia—tires wear out faster in warmer weather. Local Firestone managers dutifully reported the accidents to headquarters in Japan and the United States. Unfortunately, these reports were dismissed by the higher-up as due to driver error or road conditions. Bridgestone/Firestone thus failed to leverage its multinational presence as an asset. It should have learned from these reports and proactively probed into the potential for similar accidents in cooler-weather countries. In the end, lives were lost unnecessarily, and informed car buyers abandoned the Bridgestone/Firestone brand.

Subsidiary Initiative at LEGO North America

In 1997, Peter Eio, head of LEGO North America, proposed to LEGO Group senior management the idea of licensing *Star Wars* characters for LEGO toys. This would enable LEGO to capitalize on the anticipated release of the new *Star Wars* trilogy starting with *The Phantom Menace* in 1999. From his North America headquarters in Enfield, Connecticut, Eio was convinced that the US toy market had become a license-driven market. Licensed toys such as Disney characters from Disney movies and Buzz Lightyear from *Toy Story* accounted for half of all toys sold in the United States. Despite its success, LEGO's go-it-alone culture had prevented it from messing with any licensed products up to this point.

Encouraged by Lucasfilm executives who were LEGO fans and who wanted to partner with LEGO, Eio thought he had proposed a winning product that would enable LEGO to get into the lucrative world of licensing. Unfortunately, LEGO senior executives' initial reaction, according to Eio himself, "was one of shock and horror. It wasn't the LEGO way." Specifically, LEGO executives felt LEGO did not need to license intellectual property from another player. Further, the specific characters

LEVENT KONUK/SHUTTERSTOCK.COM

centered on war and violence would violate one of LEGO founder Ole Kirk Christiansen's core values: Never let war seem like child's play. According to critics, the very name, *Star Wars*, would violate the essence of the LEGO identity. Heated debate took place. One executive at corporate headquarters even claimed that "Over my dead body will LEGO ever introduce *Star Wars*."

During the next round, Eio and his team surveyed parents in the United States to gauge their opinion on the marriage between LEGO and *Star Wars*. He also convinced his colleague in charge of Germany, which was LEGO's largest and by far its most conservative market, to conduct a similar survey. While US parents strongly supported the idea, German parents were also enthusiastic. Armed with such supportive consumer data, Eio pushed this subsidiary-driven initiative further and continued to meet resistance and push-back from senior executives. Eventually, the founder's grandson and the president and CEO of LEGO Group at that time, Kjeld Kirk Kristiansen, who was a *Star Wars* fan himself, over-ruled his conservative executives and gave the licensing deal his blessing. In 1999, LEGO *Star Wars* products were released on the wings of the blockbuster *The Phantom Menace*, becoming one of the most successful product launches not only for LEGO, but also for the global toy industry. More than one-sixth of LEGO Groups' earnings in the early 2000s came from the *Star Wars* line.

Case Discussion Questions

1. Why was Eio eager to promote the subsidiary initiative of licensing *Star Wars* characters for LEGO toys?
2. Why was there so much resistance from the headquarters initially?
3. If you were a subsidiary manager at a multinational, what are the lessons you can draw from this case that can help you successfully convince the headquarters that your ideas deserve to be supported?

Sources: The author's interviews of LEGO customers and LEGO store personnel; "Unpacking Lego," *Economist*, 8 March 2014, 71; D. C. Robertson, *Brick by Brick: How LEGO Rewrote the Rules of Innovation and Conquered the Global Toy Industry* (New York: Crown Business, 2013).

STUDY TOOLS 12

LOCATED AT THE BACK OF YOUR BOOK:

- ☐ Rip out and study the Chapter Review Card at the end of the book

LOG IN TO WWW.CENGAGEBRAIN.COM TO:

- ☐ Review key term flashcards
- ☐ Complete a practice quiz to test your knowledge of key concepts
- ☐ Take and complete the chapter crossword puzzle
- ☐ Complete interactive content, watch chapter videos, and take a graded quiz
- ☐ Track your knowledge of key concepts in Global Business
- ☐ Read and discuss additional case study content

13 Managing Human Resources Globally

LUCKIES/SHUTTERSTOCK.COM

LEARNING OBJECTIVES

After studying this chapter, you should be able to . . .

- **13-1** Explain staffing decisions, with a focus on expatriates.
- **13-2** Identify training and development needs for expatriates and host-country nationals.
- **13-3** Identify and discuss compensation and performance appraisal issues.
- **13-4** List factors that affect labor relations in both home and host countries.
- **13-5** Discuss how the institution-based and resource-based views shed additional light on human resource management.
- **13-6** Identify the five Cs of human resource management.

After you finish this chapter, go to **PAGE 212** for **STUDY TOOLS**

EMERGING MARKETS

Samsung's Global Strategy Group

Founded in 1938, Samsung Group is South Korea's leading conglomerate. It has 420,000 employees in 510 units in 80 countries, with $327 billion in annual revenues in 2014. The flagship company within Samsung Group is Samsung Electronics Corporation (SEC). With $226 billion revenues in 2014, SEC is the largest electronics firm in the world. In addition to SEC, other major Samsung Group companies include Samsung Life Insurance (the 13th largest life insurer in the world), Samsung C&T Corporation (one of the world's largest developers of skyscrapers and solar/wind power plants), and Samsung Heavy Industries (the world's largest shipbuilder). Samsung's performance has been impressive. Despite the Great Recession of 2008–2009, SEC's profits have been higher than those of its five largest Japanese rivals (Sony, Panasonic, Toshiba, Hitachi, and Sharp) combined.

Clearly, Samsung has done something right. However, it has not been easy. To increasingly compete outside Korea, Samsung needs to attract more non-Korean talents. But given its traditionally rigid hierarchical structure and the language barrier, its efforts to attract and retain non-Korean talents had often been disappointing. In response, Samsung Group headquarters in 1997 set up a unique internal consulting unit, the Global Strategy Group, which reports directly to the CEO. Members of the Global Strategy Group are non-Korean MBA graduates of top Western business schools who have worked for leading multinationals such as Goldman Sachs, Intel, and McKinsey. They are required to spend two years in Seoul and study basic Korean. The group's mission, according to its website, is to "(1) develop a pool of global managers, (2) enhance Samsung's business performance, and (3) globalize Samsung." By 2013, Samsung's global strategists have come from 18 countries, with 19 native languages, six years of average work experience, and an average age of 30 years.

Global Strategy teams work on various internal strategy projects for different Samsung companies. Each team has a project leader, which gives the individual an opportunity to take on a leadership role in a high-level consulting project much earlier than a typical consulting career provides. Each team has one or two global strategists. It also has a project coordinator, who is a senior Korean manager acting as a liaison between the team and the management of the (internal) client company. On average, projects last three months and typically involve some overseas travel. Starting with 20 global strategists in the class of 1997, over 400 projects have been completed. These projects help global strategists form informal ties and expose them to the organizational culture. After two years, global strategists would "graduate" and be assigned to Samsung subsidiaries, many of which are in their home countries.

Despite good-faith efforts by both Korean and non-Korean sides, the success of the Global Strategy Group is anything but assured. Overall, cultural integration is a tough nut to crack. Of the 208 non-Korean MBAs who joined the group since its inception, 135 were still with Samsung as of 2011. The most successful ones are those who have taken the greatest pains to fit into the Korean culture, such as eating kimchi and drinking Korean wine at dinner parties. Before the establishment of the Global Strategy Group, not a single non-Korean MBA lasted more than three years at SEC. With the Global Strategy Group as a cohort group, one-third of the non-Korean MBAs in the first class of 1997 were still with SEC three years later (in 2000). Over the next decade, the retention rate went up to two-thirds. Three experts noted how the non-Korean members of the Global Strategy Group have slowly, but surely, globalized Samsung's corporate DNA:

> *The effects of these employees on the organization have been something like that of a steady trickle of water on stone. As more people from the Global Strategy Group are assigned to SEC, their Korean colleagues have had to change their work styles and mindsets to accommodate Westernized practices, slowly and steadily making the environment more friendly to ideas from abroad. Today, SEC goes out of its way to ask the Global Strategy Group for more newly hired employees.*

Sources: Based on (1) S. Chang, *Sony vs. Samsung* (Singapore: Wiley, 2008); (2) T. Khanna, J. Song, & K. Lee, 2011, The paradox of Samsung's rise, *Harvard Business Review* (July 2011): 142–147; (3) Samsung Global Strategy Group, 2015, gsg.samsung.com.

How can firms such as Samsung select, retain, reward, and motivate the best employees that they can attract? How can they link the management of people from diverse cultural and professional backgrounds with firm performance? These are some of the crucial questions we will address in this chapter. This chapter is devoted to **human resource management (HRM)**—activities that attract, select, and manage employees. As a function, HRM used to be called "personnel" and before that "records management." Few of you are HRM experts, but everyone can appreciate HRM's

Human resource management (HRM) Activities that attract, select, and manage employees.

rising importance just by looking at the evolution of the terminology. The term "HRM" clearly indicates that people are key resources of the firm to be actively managed and developed. From a lowly administrative support function, HRM has now increasingly been recognized as a strategic function that, together with other crucial functions such as finance and marketing, helps accomplish organizational goals and financial performance.[1]

This chapter first reviews the four main areas of HRM: (1) staffing, (2) training and development, (3) compensation and performance appraisal, and (4) labor relations. Then, we use the institution-based and resource-based views to shed light on these issues. We will also consider whether it is better in a crisis to lay off employees or cut pay—a major debate in HRM. To conclude, we will outline the five Cs of HRM.

13-1 STAFFING

Staffing refers to HRM activities associated with hiring employees and filling positions. In multinational enterprises (MNEs), there are two types of employees: **host-country nationals (HCNs**, often known as "locals") and expatriates (expats for short). First introduced in Chapter 1, expatriates are nonnative employees working in a foreign country. Among expatriates, there are two types: (1) **Parent-country nationals (PCNs)** come from the parent country of the MNE and work at its local subsidiary. (2) **Third-country nationals (TCNs)** come from neither the parent country nor the host country.

The majority of an MNE's employees would be HCNs. For example, of Siemens's 400,000 employees worldwide, only a small cadre of 300 executives are expatriates and another 2,000 executives are short-term assignees abroad. Of these 2,300 executives, about 60% are PCNs (Germans) and 40% are TCNs (from countries other than Germany and the host country).

Staffing HRM activities associated with hiring employees and filling positions.

Host-country national (HCN) An individual from the host country who works for an MNE.

Parent-country national (PCN) An employee who comes from the parent (home) country of the MNE and works at its local subsidiary.

Third-country national (TCN) An employee who comes from neither the parent country nor the host country of the MNE.

Ethnocentric approach A staffing approach that emphasizes the norms and practices of the parent company (and the parent country of the MNE) by relying on PCNs.

STEPHEN COBURN/SHUTTERSTOCK.COM

A leading concern is how to staff the *top* positions abroad, such as the subsidiary CEO, country manager, and key functional heads such as CFO and CIO. The three choices for top positions, PCNs, TCNs, and HCNs, all have their pros and cons (see Exhibit 13.1). The staffing choices are not random and are often a reflection of the strategic posture of the MNE—as discussed next.

13-1a Ethnocentric, Polycentric, and Geocentric Approaches in Staffing

There are three primary approaches for making staffing decisions for top positions at subsidiaries. An **ethnocentric approach** emphasizes the norms and practices of the parent company (and the parent country of the MNE) by relying on PCNs. Not only can PCNs ensure and facilitate control and coordination by headquarters, they may also be the best qualified people for the job because of special skills and experience. A perceived lack of talent and skills among HCNs often necessitates an ethnocentric approach. In addition, a cadre of internationally mobile and experienced managers, who are often PCNs, can emerge to spearhead further expansion around the world.

EXHIBIT 13.1 PARENT-COUNTRY, THIRD-COUNTRY, AND HOST-COUNTRY NATIONALS

	Advantages	Disadvantages
Parent-country nationals (PCNs)	▸ Control by headquarters is facilitated ▸ PCNs may be the most qualified people ▸ PCNs gain international experience	▸ Opportunities for HCNs are limited ▸ PCNs' adaptation may take a long time ▸ PCNs are usually very expensive
Third-country nationals (TCNs)	▸ TCNs may bridge the gap between headquarters and the subsidiary (and between PCNs and HCNs) ▸ TCNs may be less expensive than PCNs	▸ Host government and employees may resent TCNs ▸ Similar to disadvantages for PCNs
Host-country nationals (HCNs)	▸ Language and cultural barriers are eliminated ▸ Better continuity of management ▸ Usually cheaper	▸ Control and coordination by headquarters may be impeded ▸ HCNs may have limited career opportunity ▸ International experience for PCNs are limited

Source: Adapted from P. Dowling and D. Welch, *International Human Resource Management*, 4th ed. (Cincinnati: Cengage Learning, 2005) 63.

As the opposite of an ethnocentric approach, a **polycentric approach** focuses on the norms and practices of the host country. In short, "when in Rome, do as the Romans do." Who would make the best managers in Rome? Naturally, Roman (or Italian) managers—technically, HCNs. HCNs have no language or cultural barriers. Unlike PCNs who often pack their bags and move after several years, HCNs stay in their positions longer, thus providing more continuity of management. Further, placing HCNs in top subsidiary positions sends a morale-boosting signal to other HCNs who may feel they can reach the top as well (at least in that subsidiary).

Disregarding nationality, a **geocentric approach** focuses on finding the most suitable managers, who can be PCNs, HCNs, or TCNs. In other words, a geocentric approach is *color-blind*—the color of a manager's passport does not matter. For a geographically dispersed MNE, a geocentric approach can help create a corporate-wide culture and identity. This can reduce the typical us-versus-them feeling in firms that use either ethnocentric or polycentric approaches. On the other hand, molding managers from a variety of nationalities is a lot more complex than integrating individuals from two (parent and host) countries (see the Opening Case).

Overall, there is a systematic link between MNEs' strategic postures (see Chapter 12) and staffing approaches (see Exhibit 13.2). MNEs pursuing a home replication strategy usually use an ethnocentric approach, staffing subsidiaries with PCNs. MNEs interested in a localization strategy are typically polycentric in nature, hiring HCNs to head subsidiaries. Global standardization or transnational strategies often require a geocentric approach, resulting in a mix of HCNs, PCNs, and TCNs. As more firms such as Samsung become more global in their operations, they increasingly have to look beyond the pool of their PCNs to attract and nurture talented HCNs and TCNs (see the Opening Case).

13-1b The Role of Expatriates

Expatriation is leaving one's home country to work in another country. Shown in Exhibit 13.3, expatriates play four important roles.

- Expatriates are *strategists* representing the interests of the MNE's headquarters.[2] Expatriates, especially PCNs who have a long tenure with a particular MNE, may have

Polycentric approach A staffing approach that emphasizes the norms and practices of the host country.

Geocentric approach A staffing approach that focuses on finding the most suitable managers, who can be PCNs, HCNs, or TCNs.

Expatriation Leaving one's home country to work in another country.

EXHIBIT 13.2 MULTINATIONAL STRATEGIES AND STAFFING APPROACHES

MNE strategies	Typical staffing approaches	Typical top managers at local subsidiaries
Home replication	Ethnocentric	Parent-country nationals
Localization	Polycentric	Host-country nationals
Global standardization	Geocentric	A mix of parent-country, host-country, and third-country nationals
Transnational	Geocentric	A mix of parent-country, host-country, and third-country nationals

EXHIBIT 13.3 THE ROLES OF EXPATRIATES

internalized the parent firm's values and norms. They may not only enable headquarters to control subsidiaries, but also facilitate the socialization process to bring subsidiaries into an MNE's global orbit.

- Expatriates are *daily managers* who run operations and build local capabilities where local management talent is lacking.
- Expatriates are *ambassadors*.[3] Representing headquarters' interests, they build relationships with host-country stakeholders such as local managers, employees, suppliers, customers, and government officials. Importantly, expatriates also serve as ambassadors representing the interests of the *subsidiaries* when interacting with headquarters.
- Expatriates are *trainers* for their replacements. Over time, some localization in staffing is inevitable, calling for expatriates to train local employees.[4]

13-1c Expatriate Failure and Selection

Few expatriates can play the challenging multidimensional roles effectively.[5] It is not surprising that expatriate failure rates are high. Expatriate failure can be measured in three ways: (1) premature (earlier-than-expected) return, (2) unmet business objectives, and (3) unfulfilled career development objectives. Using the easiest-to-observe measure of premature return, studies in the 1980s reported that 76% of US MNEs had expatriate failure rates of more than 10%, and that 41% and 24% of European and Japanese MNEs, respectively, had comparable failure rates.[6] More recent studies find that the failure rates may have declined slightly. However, given the much larger number of expatriates now (1.3 million from the United States alone), expatriate failure rates are still high enough to justify attention. Since expatriates typically are the most expensive group of managers, the cost of each failure is tremendous—between a quarter of a million and one million dollars.

Expatriation can fail for a variety of reasons. Surveys of US and European MNEs find that the leading cause is the spouse and family's inability to adjust to life in a foreign country. In the case of Japanese MNEs, the leading cause is the inability to cope with the larger scope of responsibilities overseas. It usually is a *combination* of work-related and family-related problems that leads to expatriate failures.

Given the importance of expatriates and their reported high failure rates, how can firms enhance the odds for expatriate success? Exhibit 13.4 outlines a model for expatriate selection, with six underlying factors grouped along situation and individual dimensions. In terms of situation dimensions, the preferences of both headquarters and the subsidiary are important. The subsidiary may also have specific requests, such as "Send a strong IT person." It is preferable for expatriates to have some command of the local language.

In terms of individual dimensions, both technical ability and cross-cultural adaptability are a must. Desirable attributes include a positive attitude, emotional stability, and previous international experience. Last (but certainly not least), spouse and family preferences must be considered. The accompanying spouse often leaves behind a career and a social network. The spouse has to find meaningful endeavors abroad, but many countries protect local jobs by not permitting the spouse to work. Thus, many families find expatriation frustrating.

Expatriates are expensive and failure rates are high in general, but middle-aged expatriates (forty-somethings) are the most expensive. This age group typically has children still in school, so the employer often

ISTOCKPHOTO.COM/ANTHONYROSENBERG

EXHIBIT 13.4 FACTORS IN EXPATRIATE SELECTION

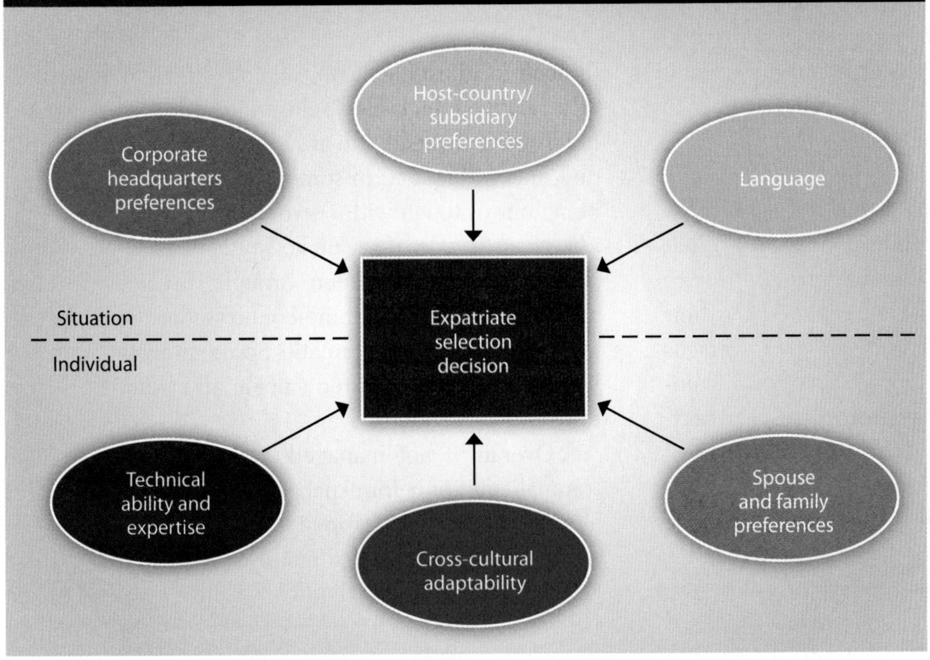

Source: Adapted from P. Dowling and D. Welch, *International Human Resource Management*, 4th ed. (Cincinnati: Cengage Learning, 2005) 98.

has to provide a heavy allowance for the children's education. High-quality schools can be expensive. In places such as Manila, Mexico City, and Moscow, international or American schools cost $15,000 to $35,000 per year. Unfortunately, these expatriates also have the highest percentage of failure rates in part because of their family responsibilities. In response, many MNEs either select expatriates in their fifties, who are less likely to have school-age children, and/or promote younger expatriates in their late twenties and early thirties who may not yet have children. Younger expatriates typically do not need a large home or education allowance. Further, given the importance of international experience, many younger managers are eager to go overseas. This development has strong implications for students studying this book now: Overseas opportunities may come sooner than you expect. Are *you* ready?

13-2 TRAINING AND DEVELOPMENT

Training is specific preparation to do a particular job. **Development** refers to longer-term, broader preparation to improve managerial skills for a better career. Training and development programs focus on two groups: expatriates and HCNs. Each is discussed in turn.

13-2a Training for Expatriates

The importance and cost of expatriates and their reported high failure rates make training necessary. Yet, many MNEs do not provide any pre-departure training for expatriates—other than wishing them "good luck." Even for firms that provide training, many offer short, one-day-type programs that are inadequate. Not surprisingly, many MNEs and expatriates get burned by such underinvestment in preparation for what are arguably some of the most challenging managerial assignments.

Ideally, training length and rigor should correspond to the expatriate's expected length of stay. For a short stay, training can be short and less rigorous. Sometimes survival-level language training—such as how to say "Where is the lady's room?" and "I'd like a beer"—would suffice. However, for a long stay of several years, it is imperative that more in-depth and rigorous training be provided, especially for first-time expatriates. Preparation should involve more extensive language as well as sensitivity training, preferably with an immersion approach (training conducted in a foreign language/culture environment). Enlightened firms concerned about failure rates now often involve the spouse in expatriate training as well.

13-2b Development for Returning Expatriates (Repatriates)

Many expatriate assignments are not one-shot deals; instead, they are viewed as part of a manager's accumulated experience and expertise and enhance a long-term career in the firm (see the Opening Case). Thus, at some point, expatriates may become **repatriates**,

Training Specific preparation to do a particular job.

Development Longer-term, broader preparation to improve managerial skills for a better career.

Repatriate A manager who returns to his or her home country to stay after working abroad for a length of time.

individuals who return to their home countries to stay after working abroad for a length of time. While the idea to develop a repatriate's long-term career sounds good in theory, in practice, many MNEs do a lousy job managing **repatriation**, which is the process of returning to the expatriate's home country after an extended period overseas.

Chief among the problems experienced by repatriates is career anxiety. A leading concern is "What kind of position will I have when I return?" Prior to departure, many expatriates are encouraged by their boss: "You should take (or volunteer for) this overseas assignment. It's a smart move for your career." Theoretically, this is known as a **psychological contract**, an informal understanding of expected delivery of benefits in the future for current services. A psychological contract is easy to violate. Bosses may change their minds. Or they may be replaced by new bosses. Violated psychological contracts naturally lead to disappointments.

Many returning expatriates find readjusting to the domestic workplace to be a painful experience. Ethnocentrism continues to characterize many MNEs. Many employees at headquarters have a bias when it comes to knowledge transfer, which typically moves from headquarters to subsidiaries via expatriates. Consequently, they are not interested in learning from returning expatriates, which would mean knowledge moving from subsidiaries to headquarters. This attitude typically leads repatriates to feel that their international experience is not appreciated. After being "big fish in a small pond" at the subsidiary, repatriates often feel like "small fish in a big pond" at headquarters. Instead of being promoted, many end up taking comparable (or lower-level) positions.

Repatriates may also experience a loss of status. Overseas, they are big shots, rubbing shoulders with local politicians and visiting dignitaries. They often command lavish expatriate premiums, with chauffeured cars and maids. But most of these perks disappear once they return.

Lastly, the spouse and the children may also find it difficult to adjust back home. The feeling of being a part of a relatively high-class, close-knit expatriate community is gone. Instead, life at home may now seem lonely, dull, unexciting, and in some cases, dreadful. Children, being out of touch with current slang, sports, and fashion, may struggle to regain acceptance into peer groups back home. Having been brought up overseas, (re) adjusting back to the home-country educational system may be especially problematic. Some returning Japanese teenagers have committed suicide after failing to make the grade back home.

Overall, if not managed well, repatriation can be traumatic not only for expatriates and their families, but also for the firm. Unhappy returning expatriates do not stay around long. Approximately one in four or one in three repatriates leave the firm within one year. Since a US MNE spends on average approximately $1 million on each expatriate over the duration of a foreign assignment, losing that individual can wipe out any return on investment. Worse yet, the returnee may end up working for a rival firm.

The best way to reduce expatriate turnover is a career development plan. A good plan also comes with a mentor (also known as champion, sponsor, or godfather).[7] The mentor helps alleviate the out-of-sight, out-of-mind feeling by ensuring that the expatriate is not forgotten at headquarters and by helping secure a challenging position for the expatriate upon return. Another way to reduce expatriate turnover is to send more expatriates on short-term or commuter-type assignments, and rely more on local staff.

Overall, despite the numerous horror stories, many expatriates do succeed. Carlos Ghosn, after successfully turning around Nissan as a PCN, went on to become CEO of the parent company, Renault. To reach the top at most MNEs today, international experience is a must. Therefore, despite the drawbacks, aspiring managers should not be deterred from taking overseas assignments. Who said being a manager was easy?

ISTOCKPHOTO.COM/DRRAVE

Repatriation Returning to an expatriate's home country after an extended period overseas.

Psychological contract An informal understanding of expected delivery of benefits in the future for current services.

13-2c Training and Development for Host-Country Nationals

While most international HRM practice and research focus on expatriates, it is important to note that the training and development needs of HCNs deserve significant attention as well. In the ongoing "war for talent" in China, a key factor in retaining or losing top talent is which employer can provide better training and development opportunities.[8] To slow turnover, many MNEs in China now have formal career development plans and processes for HCNs. GE, for example, has endeavored to make promising managers in China stimulated, energized, and recognized. This has resulted in a managerial turnover rate of "only" 7% per year, substantially lower than the nationwide average of 40% for HCNs at the managerial rank working at multinationals in China.

EXHIBIT 13.5 GOING RATE VERSUS BALANCE SHEET APPROACHES TO EXPATRIATE COMPENSATION

	Advantages	Disadvantages
Going rate	▸ Equality among parent-country, third-country, and host-country nationals in the same location ▸ Simplicity ▸ Identification with host country	▸ Variation between assignments in different locations for the same employee ▸ Reentry problem if the going rate in the parent country is less than that in the host country
Balance sheet	▸ Equity between assignments for the same employee ▸ Facilitates expatriate reentry	▸ Costly and complex to administer ▸ Great disparities between expatriates and host-country nationals

13-3 COMPENSATION AND PERFORMANCE APPRAISAL

As part of HRM, **compensation** refers to salary and benefits. **Performance appraisal** is the evaluation of employee performance for the purpose of promotion, retention, or ending employment. Three related issues are: (1) compensation for expatriates, (2) compensation for HCNs, and (3) performance appraisal.

13-3a Compensation for Expatriates

A leading issue in international HRM is how to properly compensate, motivate, and retain expatriates. Exhibit 13.5 shows two primary approaches: going rate and balance sheet. The **going rate approach** pays expatriates the prevailing (going) rate for comparable positions in a host country. When Lenovo acquired IBM's PC division, it sent Chinese expatriates to New York and paid them the going rate for comparable positions for HCNs and other expatriates in New York. The going rate approach fosters equality among PCNs, TCNs, and HCNs within the same subsidiary. It also makes locations where pay is higher than the home country a

Compensation Salary and benefits.

Performance appraisal The evaluation of employee performance for the purposes of promotion, retention, or ending employment.

Going rate approach A compensation approach that pays expatriates the prevailing (going) rate for comparable positions in a host country.

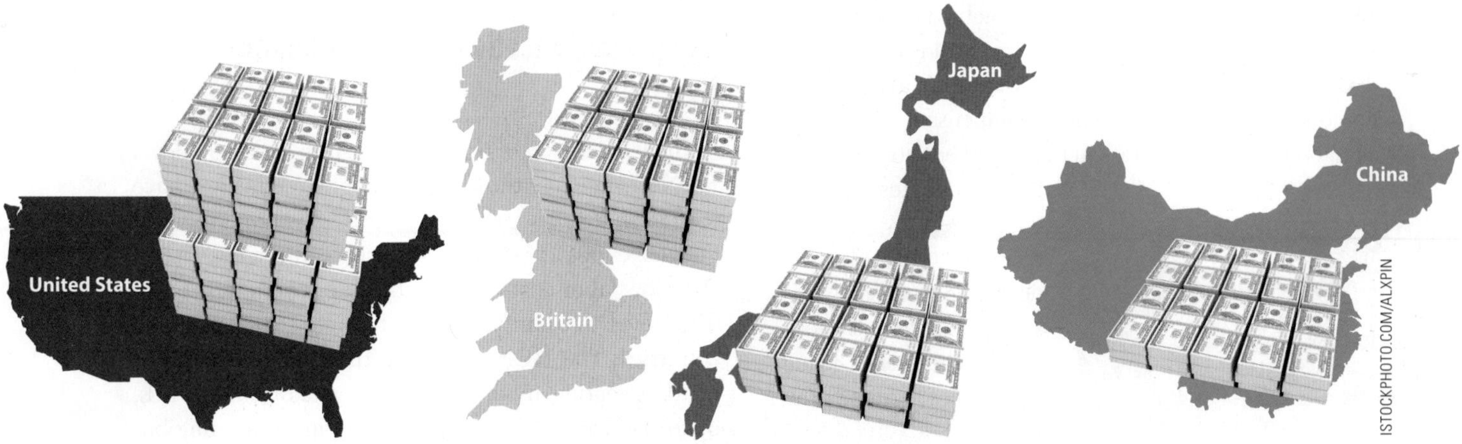

ISTOCKPHOTO.COM/ALXPIN

more attractive place to work for PCNs and TCNs. Overall, this approach excels in its simplicity and fosters strong identification with the host country.

However, the going rate for the same position differs around the world, with the United States leading in managerial compensation. The typical US CEO commands a total compensation package of over $2 million, whereas a British CEO fetches less than $1 million, a Japanese CEO $500,000, and a Chinese CEO $200,000. According to the going rate approach, returning Lenovo expatriates, accustomed to New York-level salaries, will have a hard time accepting relatively lower Beijing-level salaries, thus triggering repatriation problems.

EXHIBIT 13.6 A HYPOTHETICAL ANNUAL EXPATRIATE COMPENSATION PACKAGE USING THE BALANCE SHEET APPROACH

Items for a hypothetical US expatriate	Amount (US$)
Base salary	$150,000
Cost-of-living allowance (25%)	$37,500
Overseas premium (20%)	$30,000
Hardship allowance (20%)	$30,000
Housing deduction (–7%)	–$10,500
TOTAL (pretax)	$237,000

Note: The host country has a cost-of-living index of 150 relative to the United States. Not shown here are (1) the full cost of housing and (2) the cost to pay the difference between a higher income tax in a host country and a lower income tax in the parent country. Adding housing and taxation, the net cost of the MNE can reach $300,000 in this case.

A second approach is the **balance sheet approach**, which balances the cost of living differences relative to parent-country levels and adds a financial inducement to make the package attractive. This method is the most widely used in expatriate compensation. Historically, this approach has been justified on the grounds that a majority of expatriates would come from higher-pay, developed economies and going to lower-pay locations. Under these conditions, the going rate approach would not work because an expatriate from New York probably would not accept the lower going rate in Beijing. The balance sheet approach essentially pays Beijing-bound expatriates "New York Plus." The "Plus" is nontrivial: additional financial inducement (premium), cost of living allowance (for housing and children's education), and a hardship allowance (fewer companies now pay a hardship allowance for Beijing, but many MNEs used to). Exhibit 13.6 shows one hypothetical example. Adding housing and taxation that the MNE pays (not shown in the exhibit), the total cost may reach $300,000 a year.

The balance sheet approach has two advantages (see Exhibit 13.5). First, there is equity between assignments for the same employee, whose compensation is always anchored to the going rate in the parent country. Second, it also facilitates repatriation, because there is relatively little fluctuation between overseas and parent-country pay despite the cost-of-living differences around the world.

Balance sheet approach A compensation approach that balances the cost-of-living differences based on parent-country levels and adds a financial inducement to make the package attractive.

However, there are three disadvantages. The first is cost. Using the example in Exhibit 13.6, the cost can add up to $1 million for a three-year tour of duty. The second disadvantage is the great disparities between expatriates (especially PCNs) and HCNs. Such unequal pay naturally causes resentment by HCNs.

Lastly, the balance sheet approach is organizationally complex to administer. For a US firm operating in South Africa, both the American PCNs and Australian TCNs are typically compensated more than the South African HCNs. The situation becomes more complicated when the US firm recruits South African MBAs before they finish business school training in the United States. Should they be paid as locally hired HCNs in South Africa or as expatriates from the United States? What about TCNs from Kenya and Nigeria who also finish US MBA training and are interested in going to work for the US MNE in South Africa? Ideally, firms pay for a position regardless of passport color. However, the market for expatriate compensation is not quite there yet.

13-3b Compensation for Host-Country Nationals

At the bottom end of the compensation scale, low-level HCNs, especially those in developing countries, have relatively little bargaining power. The very reason that they have jobs at MNE subsidiaries is often because of their low labor cost—that is, they are willing to accept wage levels substantially lower than those in developed countries. The HCNs compare their pay to the farmhands sweating in the fields and making much less, or to the army of unemployed who make nothing but still have a family to feed (see PengAtlas Maps 15 and 16). Despite accusations of exploitation by some activists, MNEs in developing countries typically pay *higher* wages compared to similar positions in the local market.

ISTOCKPHOTO.COM/HENRIK5000

On the other hand, HCNs in management and professional positions increasingly have bargaining power. MNEs are rushing into Brazil, Russia, India, and China (BRIC), where local supply of top talent is limited. Some executives in China reportedly receive calls from headhunters every *day*.[9] It is not surprising that high-caliber HCNs, because of their scarcity, will fetch more pay. The question is: How much more? Most MNEs plan to eventually replace even top-level expatriates with HCNs, in part to save on costs. However, if HCNs occupying the same top-level positions are paid the same as expatriates, then there will be no cost savings. But MNEs unwilling to pay top dollar for local talent may end up losing high-caliber HCNs to competitors who are willing to do so. The war for talent is essentially a bidding war for top HCNs. MNEs may eventually have to pay international rates regardless of nationality.

13-3c Performance Appraisal

While initial compensation is determined upon entering a firm, follow-up compensation usually depends on performance appraisal. Performance appraisal helps managers make decisions about pay and promotion, development, documentation, and subordinate expression. In our case, performance appraisal is based on how expatriates evaluate HCNs and how expatriates themselves are evaluated.

When expatriates evaluate HCNs, cultural differences may create problems. Typically from low power distance countries, Western MNEs typically see performance appraisals as an opportunity for subordinates to express themselves. In high power distance countries such as those in Asia and Latin America, however, such an expression could potentially undermine the power and status of supervisors. Employees themselves do not place a lot of importance on self-expression. Therefore, Western expatriates who push HCNs in these cultures to express themselves in performance appraisal meetings would be viewed as indecisive and lacking integrity.

Expatriates need to be evaluated by their own supervisors. In some cases, however, expatriates are the top manager in a subsidiary (such as country manager), and their supervisors are more senior executives based at headquarters. Some of these off-site managers have no experience as expatriates themselves. They often evaluate expatriates based on hard numbers (such as productivity and market growth), but sometimes these numbers are beyond expatriates' control (such as a currency crisis). This is one of the reasons why many expatriates think they are not evaluated fairly. The solution lies in fostering more visits and communication between on-site expatriates and off-site supervisors.

Always sensitive, compensation and performance evaluation are even more important during tough economic times. Facing grave financial situations, should the firm impose across-the-board pay cut or engage in reduction in force, which is massive layoffs (see the Debate)? If someone has to go, according to what criteria based on performance evaluation should the firm decide who will receive the pink slip first? These are crucial questions that HR managers need to be prepared.

Debate: Ethical Dilemma

Across-the-Board Pay Cut Versus Reduction in Force

Both HR and line managers often have to make tough decisions. One of the most challenging decisions is how to cope with an economic downturn such as the financial market meltdown during 2008 and 2009. Reduction in force (RIF), a euphemism for mass layoffs, is often used in the United States and the United Kingdom. Outside the Anglo-American world, however, mass layoffs are often viewed as unethical. Some critics label mass layoffs as "corporate cannibalism." One alternative is for the entire firm to have an across-the-board pay cut while preserving all current jobs. Which approach is better?

Earlier experiences with an across-the-board pay cut may provide some clue. In 2003, SARS hit Asia. The Portman

Ritz-Carlton in Shanghai, a five-star hotel, implemented an across-the-board pay cut. A majority of Chinese HCNs supported this practice, as evidenced by the 99.9% employee satisfaction in that year. However, when US firms experiment with across-the-board pay cuts, the results tend to be very *negative*. To avoid RIF in its US facilities during the post-2001 downturn, Applied Materials implemented an across-the-board pay cut: Executives took a 10% hit, managers and professionals 5%, and hourly production workers 3%. The pay cut lasted for 18 months. An HR executive at Applied Materials commented:

> *This across-the-board pay cut has a longer lasting and far greater negative impact on morale than an RIF would have. RIFs are very hard on the impacted employees as well as the survivors. However, when managed correctly, impacted employees are able to separate from the company with dignity and in the case of Applied Materials, with a very generous financial package. . . . I don't know of any surviving employees who appreciated having their paycheck impacted every two weeks for 18 months. . . . Ultimately, pay levels were restored. However, employee memories are very long and this particular event was pointed to over and over again throughout multiple employee surveys as an indicator of poor leadership and a major cause of employee dissatisfaction.*

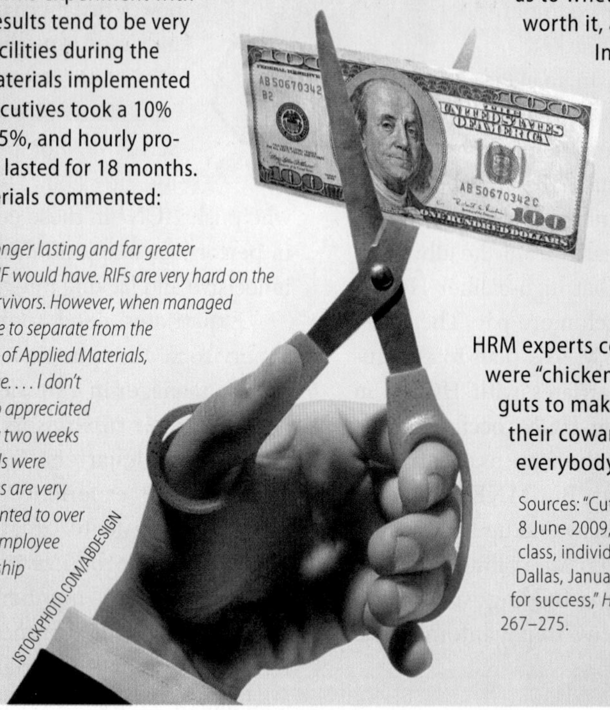
ISTOCKPHOTO.COM/ABDESIGN

Applied Materials and other US firms that implemented across-the-board pay cuts lost numerous star performers who found greener pastures elsewhere. This raises serious concerns as to whether such large-scale sacrifice is worth it, at least in an individualistic culture. In the 2008–2009 recession, a small but increasing number of US firms such as FedEx, HP, and The New York Times Company trimmed base pay for all employees—more for senior executives than for the rank and file. While President Obama praised such practices in his inaugural speech in January 2009, some HRM experts complained that these managers were "chicken managers" who did not have the guts to make tough choices and therefore, in their cowardice, chose to inflict equal pain on everybody.

Sources: "Cutting salaries instead of jobs," *BusinessWeek*, 8 June 2009, 48; S. Parker, EMBA student in the author's class, individual assignment 1, University of Texas at Dallas, January 2007; A. Yeung, "Setting the people up for success," *Human Resource Management* 45 (2006): 267–275.

13-4 LABOR RELATIONS

The term **labor relations** refers to a firm's relations with organized labor (unions) in both home and host countries. Each is discussed in turn.

13-4a Managing Labor Relations at Home

In developed economies, a firm's key concern is to cut costs and enhance competitiveness to fight off low-cost rivals from emerging economies. Labor unions, on the other hand, are organized with the purpose of helping workers earn higher wages and obtain more benefits through collective bargaining. In the United States, unionized employees earn 30% more than nonunionized employees. As a result, disagreements and conflicts between managers and unions are natural.

The bargaining chip of labor unions is their credible threat to strike, slow down, refuse to work overtime, or some other form of disruption. The bargaining chip of managers is the threat to shut down operations and move jobs overseas. It is clear which side is winning. In the United States, union membership dropped from 20% of the workforce in 1983 to 11% now (just 7% in the private sector and 36% in the public sector). Membership of United Auto Workers (UAW), for example, fell from 1.5 million to less than 400,000 at present.[10] The trend is similar in other developed countries exposed to globalization, such as Britain, France, Germany, and Japan.[11]

Labor relation A firm's relation with organized labor (unions) in both home and host countries.

Unlike MNEs, which can move operations around the world, unions are organized on a country-by-country basis. Efforts to establish multinational labor organizations have not been effective. In the 1990s, US MNEs moved aggressively to Mexico to take advantage of NAFTA. The leading US union, the AFL-CIO, contacted the Mexican government and requested permission to recruit members in Mexico. It was flatly rejected.

13-4b Managing Labor Relations Abroad

If given a choice, MNEs prefer to deal with nonunionized workforces. When Japanese and German automakers came

ISTOCKPHOTO.COM/FIREATDUSK

to the United States, they avoided the Midwest, a union stronghold. Instead, these MNEs went to the rural South and set up nonunion plants in small towns in Alabama (Mercedes and Hyundai), Kentucky (Toyota), and South Carolina (BMW). When MNEs have to deal with unions abroad, they often rely on experienced HCNs instead of locally inexperienced PCNs or TCNs.

Throughout many developing countries, governments typically welcome MNEs and simultaneously silence unions. However, things are changing. In 2010, a series of high-profile strikes took place at plants run by Taiwan's Foxconn and Japan's Honda in China. Instead of cracking down, the Chinese government chose to look the other way. Emboldened workers ended up forcing these MNEs to accept 30% to 40% pay increases. The media widely reported that "the days of cheap labor (in China) are gone."[12]

13-5 INSTITUTIONS, RESOURCES, AND HUMAN RESOURCE MANAGEMENT

Having outlined the four basic areas of HRM, let us now turn to the institution-based and resource-based views to see how they shed additional light (see Exhibit 13.7).

13-5a Institutions and Human Resource Management

Formal and informal rules of the game shape HRM significantly, both at home and abroad. Every country has *formal* rules, laws, and regulations governing the do's and don'ts of HRM. Foreign firms ignoring such rules do so at their own peril. For example, in Japan, firms routinely discriminate against women and minorities. However, when Japanese MNEs engage in such usual practices in the United States, they face legal charges.

On the other hand, foreign firms well versed in local regulations may take advantage of them. For example, the legal hurdles for firing full-time workers in France are legendary. When HP announced a plan to lay off 1,200 employees in France, then-president Jacques Chirac called HP directly and complained. However, it is this very difficulty in firing full-time workers that has made France a highly lucrative market for the US-based Manpower. French firms reluctant or unwilling to hire full-time employees value Manpower's expertise in providing part-time workers. France is now Manpower's *largest* market ahead of the United States.

Informal rules of the game, embodied in cultures, norms, and values, also assert powerful influence (see Exhibit 13.8). MNEs from different countries have different norms in staffing. Most Japanese MNEs follow an informal rule: Heads of foreign subsidiaries, at least initially, need to be PCNs. In comparison, European MNEs are more likely to appoint HCNs and TCNs to lead subsidiaries. There is a historical reason for such differences: Most European MNEs expanded globally before low-cost telephones, faxes, e-mails, and Skype were available. Thus, a localization strategy relying on HCNs and TCNs was necessary.

Most Japanese MNEs went abroad in the 1980s, when modern communication technology enabled more centralized control from headquarters. In addition, the Japanese cultural preference for low uncertainty also translated into higher interest in headquarters control. Thus, Japanese MNEs often implemented a home replication strategy that relied on PCNs who constantly communicated with headquarters.

Interestingly, the emerging Chinese MNEs are more likely to appoint HCNs as managers. This may be due to the lack of international talents among their ranks or due to the more open-minded nature of some Chinese MNEs. Regardless of the reason, the upshot is the same: more managerial jobs for locals.[13]

EXHIBIT 13.7 INSTITUTIONS, RESOURCES, AND HUMAN RESOURCE MANAGEMENT

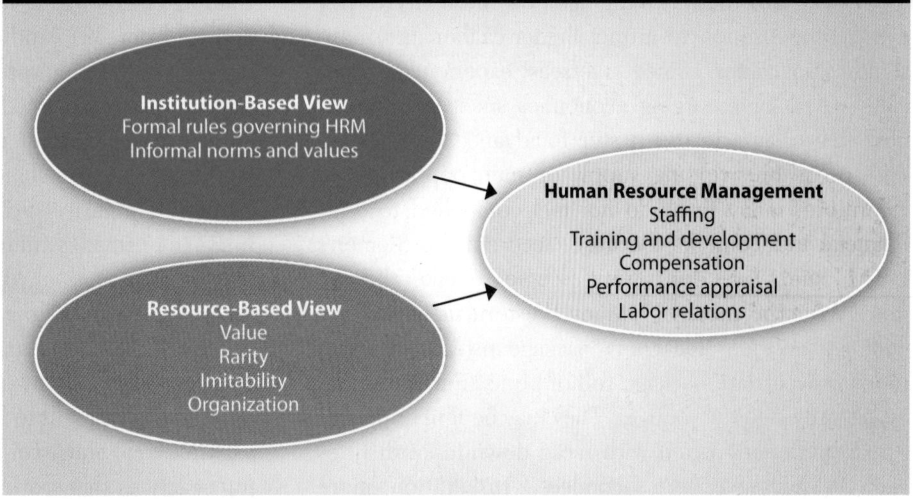

EXHIBIT 13.8 SOME BLUNDERS IN INTERNATIONAL HRM

ISTOCKPHOTO.COM/JUANMONINO

- A Spanish company sent a team of expatriates to Saudi Arabia. The group included a number of young, intelligent women dressed in current Spanish style. Upon arrival, the Saudi immigration official took a look at the women's short skirts and immediately put the entire team on the next flight back to Spain. The expatriate team and the company belatedly learned that despite the heat, women in Saudi Arabia never show their bare legs.
- In Malaysia, an American expatriate was introduced to an important potential client he thought was named "Roger." He proceeded to call this person "Rog." Unfortunately, this person was a "Rajah," which is an important title of nobility. In this case, the American tendency to liberally use another person's first name—and to proactively shorten it—appeared disrespectful and insensitive. The Rajah walked away from the deal.
- A Japanese CEO of a subsidiary in New York held a meeting of his staff, all of whom were Americans, to inform them that the firm had grave financial losses and that headquarters in Japan had requested that everybody redouble their efforts. After the meeting, the staff immediately redoubled their efforts—by sending their resumes out to other employers.

ISTOCKPHOTO.COM/GEOTRAC

Source: Based on D. Ricks, *Blunders in International Business*, 3rd ed. (Oxford, UK: Blackwell, 1999) 95–105.

While informal cultures, norms, and values are important, HR managers need to avoid stereotyping and instead consider changes. In the area of compensation, one study hypothesized that presumably collectivistic Chinese managers would prefer a more egalitarian compensation compared to what their individualistic US counterparts would prefer. The results turn out to be surprising: Chinese managers actually prefer *more* merit-based pay, whereas US managers behave exactly the opposite.[14] In other words, the Chinese seem more "American" than Americans (!). Further digging has revealed that these are not average Chinese—they are HCNs working for some of the most competitive Western MNEs in China. The upshot? Naïve adaptation to presumed local norms and values based on outdated stereotypes may backfire. HR managers must do more homework to better understand their HCNs.

One norm that is changing is the necessity to pay extra compensation to attract higher-caliber and more senior expatriates. Since overseas experience, especially in major emerging economies such as China, is now viewed as a necessary step to advance one's career, demand is outstripping supply of such opportunities. Therefore, many firms do not feel compelled to offer financial inducements, because, according to Siemen's HRM chief, "we don't want people to take the job merely for the money."[15] Many Western managers are willing to accept a "local plus" package instead of the traditional expatriate package full of perks. Further, more expatriates are now younger. They may be sent abroad to gain experience—often with more down-to-earth titles such as "assignees" or "secondees." In addition, more expatriates are now sent on short-term, commuter-type assignments for which they do not need to uproot their family—a major source of stress for the family and a cost item for the firm. Overall, the norms and images associated with the stereotypical expatriate, a more senior executive leading a life of luxury to compensate for hardship overseas, are changing rapidly.

13-5b Resources and Human Resource Management

As HRM becomes more strategic, the VRIO dimensions are increasingly at center stage. To start, managers have to ask: Does a particular HR activity add *value*? Consider two examples. First, labor-intensive chores such as administering payroll, benefits, and basic training may not add value. They can often be outsourced. Second, training is expensive. Does it really add value? Results pooled from 397 studies find that, on average, training adds value by improving individual performance by approximately 20%.[16] Thus, training is often justified.

Next, are particular HR activities *rare*? The relentless drive to learn, share, and adopt best practices may reduce their rarity and thus usefulness. If every MNE in Russia provides training to high-caliber HCNs, such training, which is valuable, will be taken for granted but no longer viewed as rare.

Further, how *imitable* are certain HR activities? It is relatively easy to imitate a single practice, but it is much more difficult to imitate a complex HR *system* (or *architecture*) consisting of multiple, mutually reinforcing practices that work together. Consider the five-star

Portman Ritz-Carlton Hotel in Shanghai. Its expatriate general manager personally interviews *every* new hire. It selects HCNs genuinely interested in helping guests. It cares deeply about employee satisfaction, which has led to superb guest satisfaction. Each single practice here may be imitable, and the Portman Ritz-Carlton, which has been voted the "Best Employer in Asia," has been studied meticulously by rivals (and numerous non-rivals) in China and around the world.[17] Yet, none has been able to successfully imitate its system. On the surface, every firm says, "We care about our people." But the reality at many firms is increasing under-investment by both employers and employees with declining loyalty and commitment. A mutual investment approach is likely to result in excellent performance, as exemplified by Whole Foods (see In Focus).

In Focus:

Human Resource System at Whole Foods

Headquartered in Austin, Texas, Whole Foods is the leading retailer of natural and organic foods and an iconic brand in the United States. It has over 300 locations in the United States, Canada, and Britain with sales of $11 billion. Advocated by its founder John Mackey, its strategy focuses on conscious capitalism, which is a more conscious way of thinking about business and its relationships with various stakeholders. What is the role of HR in all this? Mackey shared his thoughts with *Harvard Business Review*:

> *Management's job at Whole Foods is to make sure that we hire good people, that they are well trained, and that they flourish in the workplace, because we found that when people are really happy in their jobs, they provide much higher degrees of service to the customers. Happy team members result in happy customers. Happy customers do more business with you. They become advocates for your enterprise, which results in happy investors. That is a win, win, win, win strategy. You can expand it to include your suppliers and the communities where you do business, which are tied in to this prosperity circle.*

SUSAN MONTGOMERY/SHUTTERSTOCK.COM

Underpinning this strategy is its HR system. Starting with *staffing*. Each of its 70,000 employees is hired into a particular team. Each store has ten teams. New hires are on a probationary basis for 30–90 days. After that they need to earn two-thirds of votes from team members in order to be accepted as a full member. Employees who do not fit the Whole Foods conscious capitalism culture, even though their performance may be satisfactory, are asked to leave. Teams look for people who are "inclusive" and value diversity. Since teams have a great deal of autonomy in making decisions and are responsible for their performance, being a contributing, productive team member is crucial.

Whole Foods' *performance appraisal* processes are team-oriented. Members are evaluated by their peers on the team. Its *compensation* program is very different from that in other firms. Reflecting the firm's philosophy of egalitarianism, everyone knows what everybody else makes. This transparency enables team members to provide feedback to management on what they deem unfair. The entire team shares one bonus pool. A bonus is divided among team members if above-target performance is achieved. If the team fails to hit performance targets, the bonus is not paid out. Whole Foods also imposes a cap on CEO pay. While in many US publicly listed firms the CEO is paid several hundred times what the average rank-and-file employees are paid, at Whole Foods the ratio of CEO pay vis-à-vis team member pay is only 19 to 1.

Finally, Whole Foods' *training and development* programs are also reflective of the tenets of conscious capitalism. Every team member is cross-trained to ensure everyone can perform multiple tasks. When a manager fails, instead of firing this individual—which is typical of many firms—Whole Foods removes him or her from the current job, but gives the manager six months at full pay to find another position within the firm. In this way, development truly becomes "longer-term, broader preparation to improve managerial skills for a better career" (which is our textbook definition on page 201). Whole Foods is not totally altruistic. It is doing this because each manager represents a significant investment that the firm has made into his or her career. Firing a failed manager would simply wipe out that investment. Keeping the failed manager and encouraging him or her to find a new job that has a better fit is part of the win-win strategy that Mackey has emphasized.

Sources: J. Mackey, "What is it that only I can do?" *Harvard Business Review*, January (2011): 119–123; J. Slocum, D. Lei, and P. Buller, "Executing business strategies through human resource management practices," *Organizational Dynamics* 43 (2014): 73–87; www.wholefoodsmarket.com.

However, it is very difficult to imitate a mutual investment approach that comes together as a system (or architecture).

Finally, do HR practices support *organizational capabilities* to help accomplish performance goals? Consider teamwork and diversity, especially multinational teams that have members from different subsidiaries.[18] While most firms promote some sort of teamwork and diversity, it is challenging to organizationally leverage such teamwork and diversity to enhance performance. Too little or too much diversity may hurt performance. In teamwork, certain disagreements may help promote learning. But obviously too many disagreements may lead to conflict and destroy team effectiveness. However, few managers (and few firms) know where to draw the line to keep team disagreements from getting out of control.

13-6 MANAGEMENT SAVVY

How much does effective HRM impact firm performance? Results from 3,200 firms show that change of one standard deviation in the HR system affects 10% to 20% of a firm's market value.[19] Findings from 92 studies suggest that an increase of one standard deviation in the use of an effective HR system is associated with a 4.6% increase in return on assets (ROA).[20] These recent findings validate a long-held belief among HRM practitioners and scholars: HRM is indeed *strategic*. In other words, HRM has become a direct answer to the fundamental question of our field: What determines the success and failure of firms around the world?

Consequently, we identify implications for actions, listed in Exhibit 13.9, that center on the four Cs developed by Susan Meisinger, president of the Society for Human Resource Management.[21] These insights have important implications for HR managers.

First, savvy HR managers need to be *curious*. They need to be well versed in the numerous formal and informal rules of the game governing HRM worldwide. They must be curious about emerging trends in the world and be prepared to respond to these trends. Second, HR managers must be *competent*. Far from its lowly roots as a lackluster administrative support function, HRM is now acknowledged as a strategic function. Many HR managers may have been trained more narrowly and with a more micro (nonstrategic) focus. Now, HR managers must be able to not only contribute to the strategy conversation, but also to take things off the CEO's desk as full-fledged business partners.

Finally, HR managers must be *courageous* and *caring*. As guardians of talent, HR managers need to nurture and develop employees (see the Opening Case).[22] This often means that as employee advocates, HR managers sometimes need to be courageous enough to disagree with the CEO and other line managers. GE's recently retired head of HR, William Conaty, is such an example. "If you just get closer to the CEO, you're dead," Conaty shared with a reporter, "I need to be independent. I need to be credible." GE's CEO Jeff Immelt called Conaty "the first friend, the guy that could walk in my office and kick my butt when it needed to be"—exactly how a full-fledged business partner should behave.[23]

In addition, there is a fifth "C" for non-HR managers: Proactively manage your *career* in order to develop a global mindset (see the Closing Case). Since international experience is a prerequisite for reaching the top at many firms, managers need to prepare by investing in their own technical expertise, cross-cultural adaptability, and language training. Some of these investments (such as language) are long-term in nature. This point thus has strategic implications for students who are studying this book *now*: Have you learned a foreign language? Have you spent one semester or year abroad? Have you made any friends from abroad, perhaps fellow students who are taking *this* class with you now? Have you put this course on your resume? Arm yourself with the knowledge now, make proper investments, and advance your career. Remember: Your career is in your hands.

EXHIBIT 13.9 IMPLICATIONS FOR ACTION

For HR managers: The four Cs
▸ Be *curious*. Know formal and informal rules of the game governing HRM in all regions of operations.
▸ Be *competent*. Develop organizational capabilities that drive business success.
▸ Be *courageous* and *caring*. As guardians of talent, HR managers need to nurture and develop people.
For non-HR managers: The fifth C
▸ Be proactive in managing your (international) *career*.

EMERGING MARKETS

Dallas Versus Delhi

Prashant Sarkar is director for corporate development for the New Delhi, India, subsidiary of the US-based Dallas Instruments. Sarkar has an engineering degree from the Indian Institute of Technology and an MBA from the University of Texas at Dallas. After obtaining his MBA in 1995, Sarkar worked at a Dallas Instruments facility in Richardson, Texas (a suburb of Dallas in which UT Dallas is located) and picked up a green card (US permanent residency) while maintaining his Indian passport. In 2005, when Dallas Instruments opened its first Indian subsidiary in New Delhi, Sarkar was tapped to be one of the first managers sent from the United States. India of the 21st century is certainly different from the India of the 1990s that Sarkar had left behind. Reform is now in the air, multinationals are coming left and right, and an exhilarating self-confidence permeates the country.

JEREMY WOODHOUSE/GETTY IMAGES

NOWAK LUKASZ/SHUTTERSTOCK.COM

As a manager, Sarkar has shined in his native New Delhi. His wife and two children (born in 2001 and 2003 in Dallas) are also happy. After all, curry in New Delhi is a lot more authentic and fresher than that in Indian grocery stores in Dallas. Grandparents, relatives, and friends are all happy to see the family back. In Dallas, Prashant's wife, Neeli, a teacher by training, taught on a part-time basis, but could not secure a full-time teaching position because she did not have a US degree. Now she is principal of a great school. The two children are enrolled in the elite New Delhi American School, the cost of which is paid for by the company. New Delhi is not perfect, but the Sarkars feel good about coming back.

At the end of 2015, the American CEO of the subsidiary has a conversation with Sarkar:

> *Prashant, I have great news for you! Headquarters wants you to move back to Dallas. You'll be in charge of strategy development for global expansion, working directly under the Group Vice President. Isn't that exciting?! They want someone with proven success. You are my best candidate. I don't know what design they have for you after this assignment, but I suspect it'll be highly promising. Don't quote me, but I'd say you may have a shot to eventually replace me or the next subsidiary CEO here. While I personally enjoy working here, my family sometimes still complains a bit about the curry smell. Or, folks in Dallas may eventually want you to go somewhere else like China or Brazil—frankly, I don't know but I'm just trying to help you speculate. I know it's a big decision. Talk to Neeli and the kids. But they lived in Dallas before, so they should be fine going back. Of course, I'll put you in touch with the folks in Dallas directly so that you can ask them all kinds of questions. Let me know what you think in a week.*

Instead of calling his wife immediately, Sarkar has decided to wait till he gets home in the evening so that he can have a few hours to think about this. Going from Dallas to New Delhi, Sarkar, with his Indian passport, is a host country national (HCN). However, with his green card, he is also considered a US national and thus an expatriate. He wonders whether he would accept the new assignment. He thinks this will be a career move for him, but he is not sure if his family will like it.

Case Discussion Questions

1. What questions should Sarkar ask the people at headquarters in Dallas? Please help him prepare a list.
2. Will Neeli and the children be happy about this move? Why?
3. Should Sarkar accept or decline this opportunity? Why?

Sources: Based on the author's interviews. All individual and corporate names are fictitious.

STUDY TOOLS 13

LOCATED AT THE BACK OF YOUR BOOK:

- ☐ Rip out and study the Chapter Review Card at the end of the book

LOG IN TO WWW.CENGAGEBRAIN.COM TO:

- ☐ Review key term flashcards
- ☐ Complete a practice quiz to test your knowledge of key concepts
- ☐ Take and complete the chapter crossword puzzle
- ☐ Complete interactive content, watch chapter videos, and take a graded quiz
- ☐ Track your knowledge of key concepts in Global Business
- ☐ Read and discuss additional case study content

14 Competing in Marketing & Supply Chain Management

NADEZDA ZAVITAEVA/SHUTTERSTOCK.COM

LEARNING OBJECTIVES

After studying this chapter, you should be able to . . .

14-1 Articulate three of the four Ps in marketing (product, price, and promotion) in a global context.

14-2 Explain how the fourth P in marketing (place) has evolved to be labeled supply chain management.

14-3 Outline the triple As in supply chain management (agility, adaptability, and alignment).

14-4 Discuss how institutions and resources affect marketing and supply chain management.

14-5 Draw three implications for action.

After you finish this chapter, go to **PAGE 227** for **STUDY TOOLS**

Zara Excels in Marketing and Supply Chain Management

Zara is one of the hottest fashion chains. Founded in 1975, Zara's parent, Inditex, has become a leading global apparel retailer. Since its initial public offering (IPO) in 2001, Inditex quadrupled its sales (to $19.1 billion or €13.8 billion) and profits. It doubled the number of its stores of eight brands, of which Zara contributes two-thirds of total sales. In this intensely competitive industry, Zara excels in both marketing and supply chain management. Zara succeeds by first breaking and then rewriting industry rules—also known as industry norms.

Rule number one: The origin of a fashion house usually carries some cachet. However, Zara does not hail from Italy or France—it is from Spain. Even within Spain, Zara is not based in a cosmopolitan city such as Barcelona or Madrid. It is headquartered in Arteixo, a town of only 25,000 people in a remote corner of northwestern Spain that a majority of this book's readers would have never heard of. Yet, Zara is active not only throughout Europe, but also in Asia and North America. Currently, the total number of stores is over 2,000 in 88 countries. Zara stores occupy some of the priciest top locations: Champs-Elysées in Paris, Fifth Avenue in New York, Galleria in Dallas, Ginza in Tokyo, Queen's Road Central in Hong Kong, and Huaihai Road in Shanghai.

Rule number two: Avoid stock-outs (a store running out of items in demand). Zara's answer? Occasional shortages contribute to an urge to buy *now*. With new items arriving at stores *twice* a week, experienced Zara shoppers know that "If you see something and don't buy it, you can forget about coming back for it because it will be gone." The small batch of merchandise during a short window of opportunity for purchasing motivates shoppers to visit Zara stores more frequently. In London, shoppers visit the average store four times a year, but frequent Zara 17 times. There is a good reason to do so: Zara makes about 20,000 items per year, about triple what Gap does. "At Gap, everything is the same," according to a Zara fan, "and buying from Zara, you'll never end up looking like someone else."

Rule number three: Bombarding shoppers with ads is a must. Gap and H&M spend on average 3% to 4% of their sales on ads. Zara begs to differ: It devotes just 0.3% of its sales to ads. The high traffic in the stores alleviates some needs for advertising in the media, most of which only serves as a reminder to visit the stores.

Rule number four: Outsource. Gap and H&M do not own any production facilities. However, outsourcing production (mostly to Asia) requires a long lead time, usually several months. Again, Zara has decisively deviated from the norm. By concentrating (more than half of) its production in-house (in Spain, Portugal, and Morocco), Zara has developed a super-responsive supply chain. It designs, produces, and delivers a new garment to its stores worldwide in a mere 15 *days*, a pace that is unheard of in the industry. The best speed the rivals can achieve is two *months*. Outsourcing may not necessarily be "low cost," because errors in prediction can easily lead to unsold inventory, forcing retailers to offer steep discounts. The industry average is to offer 40% discounts across all merchandise. In contrast, Zara sells more at full price and, when it discounts, it averages only 15%.

Rule number five: Strive for efficiency through large batches. In contrast, Zara intentionally deals with small batches. Because of its flexibility, Zara does not worry about "missing the boat" for a season. When new trends emerge, Zara can react quickly. It runs its supply chain like clockwork with a fast but predictable rhythm: Every store places orders on Tuesday/Wednesday and Friday/Saturday. Trucks and cargo flights run on established schedules—like a bus service. From Spain, shipments reach most European stores in 24 hours, US stores in 48 hours, and Asian stores in 72 hours. Not only do store staff know exactly when shipments will arrive, but regular customers also know that too, thus motivating them to check out the new merchandise more frequently on those days, which are known as "Z days" in some cities.

Zara has no shortage of competitors. Why has no one successfully copied its business model of "fast fashion"? "I would love to organize our business like Inditex [Zara's parent]," noted an executive from Gap, "but I would have to knock my company down and rebuild it from scratch." This does not mean Gap and other rivals are not trying to copy Zara. The question is how long it takes for rivals to out-Zara Zara.

Sources: "Fashion conquistador," *BusinessWeek*, 4 September 2006, 38–39; "Fashion forward," *Economist*, 24 March 2012, 63–64; Inditex, "Presencia internacional," 2014, www.inditex.com; K. Ferdows, M. Lewis, and J. Machuca, "Rapid-fire fulfillment," *Harvard Business Review* (November 2004): 104–110; www.zara.com.

How can firms such as Zara market themselves to attract customers around the world? How can they tailor and adapt their messages to capture the hearts, minds, and wallets of different customers who have different tastes and preferences? Having attracted customers, how can firms ensure a steady supply of products and services? This chapter deals with these and other important questions associated with marketing and supply chain management. **Marketing** refers to efforts to create, develop, and defend markets that satisfy individual and business customers. **Supply chain** is the flow of products, services, finances, and information that passes through a set of entities from a source to the customer. **Supply chain management** refers to activities to plan, organize, lead, and control the supply chain. In this chapter, instead of viewing marketing and supply chain as two stand-alone, separate functions, we view them as one crucial, integrated function.

We first outline major marketing and supply chain activities in global business. Then we discuss how the institution-based and resource-based views enhance our understanding of the drivers behind marketing and supply chain management success. Finally, managerial implications follow.

EXHIBIT 14.1 MARKETING AND FIRM PERFORMANCE

"What's your marketing plan?"

14-1 THREE OF THE FOUR PS IN MARKETING

Shown in Exhibit 14.1, marketing is crucial for firm performance. Exhibit 14.2 shows the four Ps that collectively consist of the **marketing mix**: (1) product, (2) price, (3) promotion, and (4) place. We start with the first three Ps. The last P—place (where the product is sourced, produced, and distributed)—will be discussed in the next section.

Marketing Efforts to create, develop, and defend markets that satisfy the needs and wants of individual and business customers.

Supply chain Flow of products, services, finances, and information that passes through a set of entities from a source to the customer.

Supply chain management Activities to plan, organize, lead, and control the supply chain.

Marketing mix The four underlying components of marketing: (1) product, (2) price, (3) promotion, and (4) place.

Product Offerings that customers purchase.

14-1a Product

Product refers to offerings that customers purchase. Even for a single category (such as women's dress or sports car), product attributes vary tremendously. For multinational enterprises (MNEs) doing business around the world, a leading concern is standardization versus localization. Localization is natural. McDonald's, for example, sells wine in France, beer in Germany, mutton pot pies in Australia, and Maharaja Mac and McCurry Pan in India. In China, Kentucky Fried Chicken (KFC) features menu items that would not be recognizable to its customers in the United States. Alongside the Colonel's "secret recipe" fried chicken, KFC in China also markets congee, a chicken wrap in a Peking duck-type sauce, and spicy

EXHIBIT 14.2 THE FOUR Ps OF MARKETING MIX

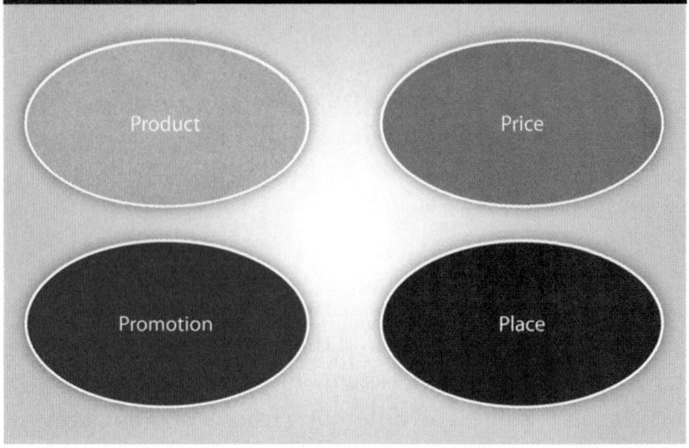

TESTING/SHUTTERSTOCK.COM

tofu chicken rice. In Japan, Wendy's sells a $16 *Foie Gras Rossini* (goose-liver pâté) hamburger.[1]

What is interesting is the rise of standardization, which is often attributed to Theodore Levitt's 1983 article, "The Globalization of Markets."[2] First discussed in Chapter 12, this article advocated globally standardized products and services, as evidenced by Hollywood movies and Coke Classic. However, numerous subsequent experiments such as Ford's "world" car and MTV's "global" (essentially American) programming backfired. Marketers thus face a dilemma: While one size does not fit all, most firms cannot afford to create products and services for just one group of customers when trying to serve many groups around the world.

As first noted in Chapter 12, localization is appealing (in the eyes of local consumers and governments) but expensive. One sensible solution is to have a product that *appears* to be locally adapted while deriving as much synergy (commonality) as possible in ways that customers cannot easily recognize. Consider the two global business weekly magazines, the US-based *Bloomberg Businessweek* and the UK-based *Economist*. In addition to its US edition, *Bloomberg Businessweek* publishes two English (language) editions for Asia and Europe and a Chinese edition for China. While these four editions share certain content, there is a lot of local edition–only material that is expensive to produce. In comparison, each issue of the *Economist* has the following regional sections (in alphabetical order): (1) the Americas (excluding the United States), (2) Asia (excluding China), (3) Britain, (4) China, (5) Europe (excluding Britain), (6) the Middle East and Africa, and (7) the United States. While the content for each issue is identical, the order of appearance of the regional sections is different. For US subscribers, their *Economist* would start with the US section. For Chinese subscribers, their magazine would start with the China section. By doing that, the *Economist* appears to be responsive to readers with different regional interests without incurring the costs of running multiple editions for different regions, as *Bloomberg Businessweek* does. Therefore, how many editions does one issue of the *Economist* have? We can say one—or seven if we count the seven different ways of stapling regional sections together.

One of the major concerns for MNEs is to decide whether to market global brands or local brands in their portfolio.[3] The key is **market segmentation**—identifying segments of consumers who differ from others in purchasing behavior.[4] There are limitless ways of segmenting the market (males versus females, urban dwellers versus rural residents, Africans versus Latin Americans).

For international marketers, the million dollar question is: How does one generalize from a wide variety of market segmentation in different countries to generate products that can cater to a few of these segments *around the world*? One globally useful way of segmentation is to divide consumers in four categories:[5]

- Global citizens (who are in favor of buying global brands that signal prestige and cachet).
- Global dreamers (who may not be able to afford, but nevertheless admire, global brands).
- Antiglobals (who are skeptical about whether global brands deliver higher-quality goods).
- Global agnostics (who are most likely to lead antiglobalization demonstrations smashing McDonald's windows).

The implications are clear. For the first two categories of global citizens and global dreamers, firms are advised to leverage the global brands and their relatively more standardized products and services. "Global brands make us feel like citizens of the world," an Argentine consumer observed. However, MNEs do not necessarily have to write off the antiglobals and global agnostics as lost customers, because they can market localized products and services under local brands. Nestlé, for example, owns 8,000 brands around the world, most of which are local, country-specific (or region-specific) brands not marketed elsewhere.

Market segmentation
Identifying segments of consumers who differ from others in purchasing behavior.

Overall, Levitt may be *both* right and wrong. A large percentage of consumers around the world indeed have converging interests and preferences centered on global brands. However, a substantial percentage of them also resist globally standardized brands, products, and services. Armed with this knowledge, both MNEs and local firms can better craft their products and services.

RADU BERCAN/SHUTTERSTOCK.COM

14-1b Price

Price refers to the expenditures that customers are willing to pay for a product. Most consumers are "price sensitive." The jargon is **price elasticity**—how demand changes when price changes. Basic economic theory of supply and demand suggests that when price drops, consumers will buy more and generate stronger demand. Such strong demand, in turn, motivates firms to expand production to meet this demand. This theory, of course, underpins numerous firms' relentless drive around the world to cut costs and then prices. The question is *how* price sensitive consumers are. Holding the product (such as shampoo) constant, in general the lower income the consumers are, the more price sensitive they are. While American, European, and Japanese consumers buy shampoo by the bottle, in India shampoo is often sold in single-use sachets, each costing about one to ten cents. Many consumers there find the cost for a bottle of shampoo to be prohibitive. Some African telecom operators charge customers by the *second*—a big deal for those making pennies a day.[6]

14-1c Promotion

Promotion refers to all the communications that marketers insert into the marketplace. Promotion includes TV, radio, print, and online advertising, as well as coupons, direct mail, billboards, direct marketing (personal selling), and public relations. Marketers face a strategic choice of whether to standardize or localize promotional efforts. Standardized promotion not only projects a globally consistent message (crucial for global brands), but can also save a lot of money.

Price The expenditures that customers are willing to pay for a product.

Price elasticity How demand changes when price changes.

Promotion Communications that marketers insert into the marketplace.

However, there is a limit to the effectiveness of standardized promotion. In the 1990s, Coca-Cola ran a worldwide campaign featuring a cute polar bear cartoon character. Research later found that viewers in warmer-weather countries had a hard time relating to this ice-bound animal with which they had no direct experience. In response, Coca-Cola switched to more costly, but more effective, country-specific advertisements. For instance, the Indian subsidiary launched a campaign that equated Coke with "thanda," the Hindi word for "cold." The German subsidiary developed commercials that showed a "hidden" kind of eroticism (!). While this is merely one example, it does suggest that even some of the most global brands (such as Coca-Cola) can benefit from localized promotion.

Many firms promote products and services overseas without doing their "homework" and end up with blunders (huge mistakes). GM marketed its Chevrolet Nova in Latin America without realizing that "no va" means "no go" in Spanish. Coors Beer translated its successful slogan "Turn it loose" from English to Spanish as "Drink Coors, get diarrhea." Exhibit 14.3 outlines some blunders that are hilarious to readers but *painful* to marketers, some of whom were fired because of these blunders.

In international marketing, country-of-origin effect refers to the positive or negative perception of firms and products from a certain country (first discussed in Chapter 10). Marketers have to decide whether to enhance or downplay such an effect. This can be very tricky. Disneyland Tokyo became popular in Japan because it played up its American image. But Disneyland Paris received relentless negative press coverage in France, because it insisted on its "wholesome American look." Singapore Airlines projects a "Singapore girl" image around the world. In contrast, Li Ning downplays its Chinese origin by using American NBA players in its commercials. What is the nationality of Häagen-Dazs ice cream? If you thought Häagen-Dazs was a German, Austrian, or Belgium brand and had been happily paying a premium price for "European" ice cream, you were fooled. Häagen-Dazs is a US brand. Sometimes,

EXHIBIT 14.3 SOME BLUNDERS IN INTERNATIONAL MARKETING

- One US toymaker received numerous complaints from American mothers, because a talking doll told their children, "Kill mommy!" Made in Hong Kong, the dolls were shipped around the world. They carried messages in the language of the country of destination. A packing error sent some Spanish-speaking dolls to the United States. The message in Spanish "Quiero mommy!" means "I love mommy!" (This is also a supply chain blunder.)
- AT&T submitted a proposal to sell phone equipment in Thailand. Despite its excellent technology, the proposal was rejected out of hand by telecom authorities, because Thailand required a ten-year warranty but AT&T only offered a five-year warranty—thanks to standardization on warranty imposed by US headquarters.
- Japan's Olympia tried to market a photocopier to Latin America under the name "Roto." Sales were minimal. Why? "Roto" means "broken" in Spanish.
- Chinese exporters have marketed the following products overseas: White Elephant brand batteries, Sea Cucumber brand shirts, and Maxipuke brand poker cards (the two Chinese characters, *pu ke*, means poker, and it should have been translated as Maxi brand poker cards—but its package said "Maxipuke").

Sources: Based on text in (1) T. Dalgic and R. Heijblom, "International marketing blunders revisited—some lessons for managers," *Journal of International Marketing* 4 (1996): 81–91; (2) D. Ricks, *Blunders in International Business*, 3rd ed. (Oxford, UK: Blackwell, 1999).

multiple countries of origin are disclosed. For example, Apple stamped on the back of every iPhone: "Designed in California. Assembled in China." Some Toyota cars' dealer stickers disclose: "Made in USA. Engine made in Japan."

Overall, marketers need to experiment with a variety of configurations of the three Ps (product, price, and promotion) around the world in order to optimize the marketing mix. Next, we discuss the fourth P, place.

14-2 FROM DISTRIBUTION CHANNEL TO SUPPLY CHAIN MANAGEMENT

As the fourth P in the marketing mix, **place** refers to the location where products and services are provided (which now, of course, includes the online marketplace). Technically, place is also often referred to as the **distribution channel**—the set of firms that facilitates the movement of goods from producers to consumers. Until the 1980s, many producers made most goods in-house and one of the key concerns was distribution. Since then, production outsourcing has grown significantly. Many firms (such as Apple) do not physically produce their branded products at all. They rely on contract manufacturers (such as Foxconn) to get the job done. Other firms that still produce in-house (such as Dell and Boeing) rely on their suppliers to provide an increasingly higher percentage of the value-added. Therefore, the new challenge is how to manage the longer distribution channel—more specifically, the distribution from suppliers (and contract manufacturers) all the way to consumers (see Exhibit 14.4).

Consequently, a new term, "supply chain," has been coined, and it has now almost replaced the old-fashioned "distribution channel." To be sure, the focal firm has always dealt with suppliers. Strategy guru Michael Porter labels this function as "inbound logistics" (and the traditional distribution channel as "outbound logistics").[7] In a broad sense, the new term "supply chain" is almost synonymous with "value chain," encompassing both inbound and outbound logistics (see Chapter 4). In the military, logistics is widely acknowledged as a contributor to wartime success. But no army

Place The location where products and services are provided.

Distribution channel The set of firms that facilitates the movement of goods from producers to consumers.

EXHIBIT 14.4 SUPPLY CHAIN MANAGEMENT

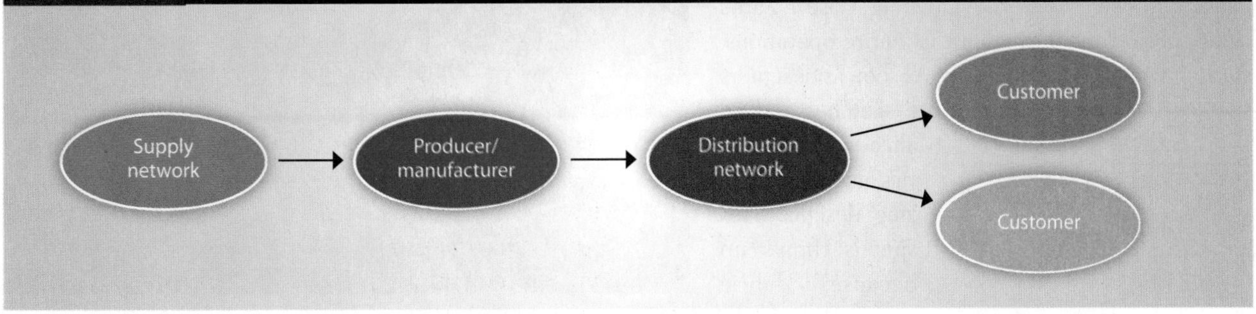

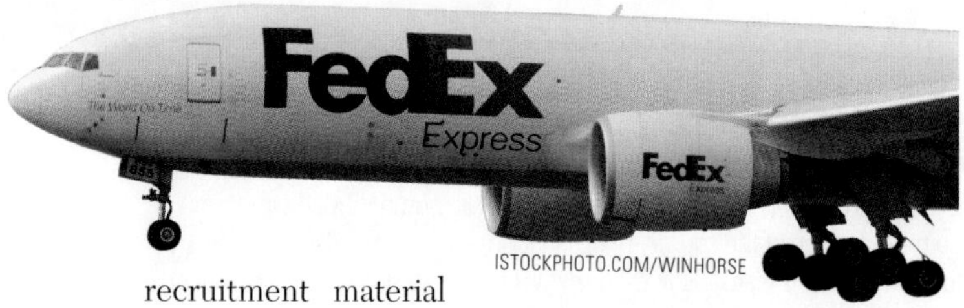

ISTOCKPHOTO.COM/WINHORSE

recruitment material would brag about a glamorous career in logistics in the military to attract new soldiers. Similarly, business logistics tends to be tactical and lacks prestige. However, if supply chain is value chain, then supply chain management essentially handles the *entire* process of value creation, which is the core mission of the firm. Consequently, supply chain management has now taken on new strategic importance and gained tremendous prestige.

One indication that supply chain management has gained traction is that instead of being obscure players, leading supply chain management firms, such as DHL, FedEx, and UPS, have now become household names. On any given day, 2% of the world's GDP can be found in UPS trucks and planes. "FedEx" has become a verb, and even live *whales* have reportedly been "FedExed." Modern supply chains aim to "get the right product to the right place at the right time—all the time."[8] Next, we discuss the triple As underpinning supply chains: (1) agility, (2) adaptability, and (3) alignment.

14-3 TRIPLE AS IN SUPPLY CHAIN MANAGEMENT[9]

14-3a Agility

Agility refers to the ability to quickly react to unexpected shifts in supply and demand. To reduce inventory, many firms now use the trucks, ships, and planes of their suppliers and carriers as their warehouse. In their quest for supply chain speed, cost, and efficiency, many firms fail to realize the cost they have to pay for disregarding agility. Zara thrives in large part because of the agility of its supply chain (see the Opening Case). Zara's agility permeates throughout its entire operations, starting with design processes. As soon as designers spot certain trends, they create sketches and go ahead to order fabrics without finalizing designs. This speeds things up because fabric suppliers require a long lead time. Designs are finalized when stores receive reliable data. Production commences as soon as designs are complete. In addition, Zara's factories only run one shift, easily allowing for overtime production if demand calls for it. Its distribution centers are also highly efficient, allowing it to handle demand fluctuation without creating bottlenecks.

Agility The ability to react quickly to unexpected shifts in supply and demand.

Agility may become more important in the 21st century, because shocks to supply chains are now more frequent. Recently, notable disruptions have included terrorist attacks (such as 9/11), civil wars (such as those in Syria and Ukraine), political unrest (such as Arab Spring, Hong Kong, and Libya), and natural disasters (such as Ebola, H1N1 swine flu, Icelandic volcano eruption, and Japanese earthquake).

Under shocks, an agile supply chain can rise to the challenge, while a static one can pull a firm down.[10] In 2000, Nokia and Ericsson fought in the mobile handset market. Consider how Nokia and Ericsson reacted

VYTAUTAS KIELAITIS/SHUTTERSTOCK.COM

differently to a fire caused by thunderstorm at a New Mexico factory of their handset chip supplier, Philips. The damage was minor, and Philips expected to resume production within a week. However, Nokia took no chances, and it quickly carried out design changes so that two other suppliers, one in Japan and another in the United States, could manufacture similar chips for Nokia. (These were the only two suppliers in the world other than Philips that were capable of delivering similar chips.) Nokia then quickly placed orders from these two suppliers. In contrast, Ericsson's supply chain had no such agility. Set up to function exclusively with the damaged Philips plant in New Mexico, it had no plan B. Unfortunately, Philips later found out that the damage was larger than first reported, and production would be delayed for months. By that time Ericsson scrambled to contact the other two suppliers, only to find out that Nokia had locked up all of their output for the next few months. The upshot? By 2001, Ericsson was driven out of the handset market as an independent player.

14-3b Adaptability

While agility focuses on flexibility that can overcome short-term fluctuation in the supply chain, **adaptability** refers to the ability to change supply chain configurations in response to longer-term changes in the environment and technology. Enhancing adaptability often entails making a series of **make-or-buy decisions**.[11] This requires firms to *continuously* monitor major geopolitical, social, and technological trends, make sense of them, and reconfigure the supply chain accordingly. The damage for failing to do so may not be visible immediately, but across a number of years firms failing to do so may be selected out of market.

Consider Lucent, the American telecommunications equipment giant. In the 1990s, in response to competitive pressures from its rivals Alcatel and Siemens that benefited from low-cost, Asia-based production, Lucent successfully adapted its supply chain by phasing out more production in high-cost developed economies and setting up plants in China and Taiwan. However, Lucent then failed to adapt continuously. It concentrated its production in its own Asia-based plants, whereas rivals outsourced such manufacturing to Asian suppliers that became more capable of taking on more complex work. In other words, Lucent used foreign direct investment (FDI) to "make," whereas rivals adopted outsourcing to "buy." Ultimately, Lucent was stuck with its own relatively higher cost (although Asia-based) plants and was overwhelmed by rivals. By 2006, Lucent lost its independence and was acquired by its archrival Alcatel.

14-3c Alignment

Alignment refers to the alignment of interests of various players in the supply chain. In a broad sense, every supply chain is a strategic alliance involving a variety of players, each of which is a profit-maximizing, standalone firm.[12] As a result, conflicts are natural. However, players associated with one supply chain must effectively coordinate to achieve desirable outcomes. Therefore, this is a crucial dilemma. Supply chains that can better solve this dilemma may outperform other supply chains. For example, for Boeing's 787 Dreamliner, some 70% of the $8 billion development cost is outsourced to suppliers: Mitsubishi makes the wings, Messier-Dowty provides the landing gear, and so forth. Many suppliers are responsible for end-to-end design of whole subsections. Headed by a vice president for global partnerships, Boeing treats its suppliers as partners, has "partner councils" with regular meetings, and fosters long-term collaboration.

Conceptually, there are two key elements to achieve alignment: (1) power and (2) trust.[13] Not all players in a supply chain are equal, and more powerful players such as Boeing naturally exercise greater bargaining power.[14] Having a recognized leader exercising power, such as De Beers in diamonds, facilitates legitimacy and efficiency of the whole supply chain. Otherwise, supply chain members of more or less equal standing may end up engaging in excessive bargaining.

Trust stems from perceived fairness and justice from all supply chain members. While supply chains have become ever more complex, modern practices—such as low (or zero) inventory, frequent just-in-time (JIT) deliveries, and more geographic dispersion of production—have made all parties more vulnerable if the *weakest* link breaks down. This happened during the Japanese earthquake in 2011 (see Debate). Therefore, it is in the best interest of all parties to invest in trust-building mechanisms in order to foster more collaboration.

For instance, Seven-Eleven Japan exercises a

Adaptability The ability to change supply chain configurations in response to longer-term changes in the environment and technology.

Make-or-buy decision The decision on whether to produce in-house ("make") or to outsource ("buy").

Alignment Alignment of interest of various players.

Debate

Just in Time versus Just in Case: Supply Chain Management Lessons from Japan's Earthquake

On March 11, 2011, Japan suffered from a triple disaster—a 9.0 earthquake (its worst in recorded history), followed by a 20-foot tsunami, followed by a nuclear power plant accident that emitted harmful radiation. A lot of non-Japanese firms that relied on made-in-Japan products were ill prepared for such a sudden and major breakdown of their supply chain. Despite the widely noted migration of manufacturing to low-cost countries such as China and Malaysia, Japan has remained an export powerhouse. In 2010, it was the world's fourth largest exporter (after China, Germany, and the United States) with $765 billion exports. For example, Japan produces approximately one-fifth of the world's semiconductors and 40% of electronic components. While low-end products tend to be made overseas, "Japan has higher and higher market share of specialty materials as you go up the value chain," noted one expert. For example, Boeing outsourced 35% of the work on its newest 787 Dreamliner to Japanese manufacturers. Among them, Mitsubishi Heavy Industries built the 787's wings, and no one else in the world could do the job—Boeing had no plan B. On March 17, 2011, General Motors had to close two US-based factories for a week, due to a lack of components arriving from Japan. For planes, cars, and laptops assembled outside of Japan, the made-in-Japan components may represent a relatively small amount, but they tend to be mission critical. "If the Japanese cannot supply," noted another expert, "then no one is going to get their iPad" because no smart factory can build an iPad with only 97% of parts.

Thanks to the "lean manufacturing" movement that also originated from Japan a generation ago, inventory levels at many factories around the world are now days' and even hours' worth. When "just-in-time" delivery fails, the supply chain can easily break down. Surprisingly, only about 10% of firms have detailed contingency plans to deal with severe chain disruptions. From a supply chain management standpoint, one of the most crucial lessons from Japan's earthquake is to always have a plan B. In other words, there is value in "just-in-case" management.

Sources: "Downsides of just-in-time inventory," *Bloomberg Businessweek*, 28 March 2011, 17–18; "Facing up to nuclear risk," *Bloomberg Businessweek*, 21 March 2011, 13–14; "Now, a weak link in the global supply chain," *Bloomberg Businessweek*, 21 March 2011, 18–19; "The cataclysm this time," *Bloomberg Businessweek*, 21 March 2011, 11–13.

great deal of power by dictating that vendors resupply its 9,000 stores at three *specific* times a day. If a truck is late by more than 30 minutes, the vendor has to pay a penalty equal to the gross margin of the products carried to the store. This may seem harsh, but is necessary. This is because Seven-Eleven Japan staff reconfigure store shelves three times a day to cater to different consumers at different *hours*, such as commuters in the morning and school kids in the afternoon—time, literally, means money. However, Seven-Eleven Japan softens the blow by trusting its vendors. It does not verify the contents of deliveries. This allows vendors to save time and money, because after deliveries, truck drivers do not have to wait for verification and can immediately move on to make other trips. The alignment of interest of such a supply chain is legendary. Hours after the earthquake in March 2011, when relief trucks moved at two miles per hour (if they moved at all) on the damaged roads, Seven-Eleven Japan's vendors went the extra mile by deploying helicopters and motorcycles to deliver much-needed food and supplies to the devastated region.

Third-party logistics (3PL) provider
A neutral, third-party intermediary in the supply chain that provides logistics and other support services.

Sometimes, introducing a neutral intermediary (middleman)—more specifically, **third-party logistics (3PL) providers**—may more effectively align the interests in the supply chain. In the case of outsourcing in Asia, buyers (importers) tend to be large Western MNEs such as Gap, Nike, and Marks & Spencer, and suppliers (exporters) are often smaller Asian manufacturers. Despite best intentions, both sides may still distrust each other. MNE buyers are not sure of the quality and timeliness of delivery. Further, MNE buyers are unable to control labor practices in supplier factories, some of which may be dubious (such as running "sweatshops"). In the 1990s, Nike's reputation took a severe hit due to alleged questionable labor practices at its supplier factories. However, suppliers may also be suspicious. Since most contracts for shoes, clothing, toys, and electronics are written several months ahead, suppliers are not confident about MNE buyers' ability to forecast demand correctly. Suppliers thus worry that in case of lower-than-anticipated demand, buyers may reject shipments to reduce excess inventory, by opportunistically citing excuses such as labor practices or quality issues. One solution lies in the involvement of 3PL intermediaries, such as Hong Kong-based Li & Fung. Overall, 3PL firms may add value by aligning the interests of all parties.

14-4 HOW INSITITUTIONS AND RESOURCES AFFECT MARKETING AND SUPPLY CHAIN MANAGEMENT

Having outlined the basic features of marketing and supply chain management, let us now use the institution-based and resource-based views to shed additional light on these topics (Exhibit 14.5).

14-4a Institutions, Marketing, and Supply Chain Management

As an important form of institutions, formal rules of the game obviously have a significant impact. Most countries impose restrictions, ranging from taboos in advertising to constraints on the equity level held by foreign retailers and 3PL providers. Germany bans advertising that portrays another product as inferior. Goodyear Tire exported a successful commercial used in the United States to Germany, by showing that its tire cord could break a steel chain. Because the commercial was viewed as insulting the German steel chain manufacturers, the German government banned it. China forbids foreign retailers from operating wholly owned stores and only approves joint-venture (JV) stores. In China, France's Carrefour is the most aggressive foreign retailer with sales ahead of Walmart. In some cities, Carrefour struck sweetheart deals with officials and operated wholly owned stores, which eventually provoked Beijing's wrath. The upshot? Carrefour was forced to sell a portion of its equity to Chinese partners and convert its wholly owned stores to JV stores to be in compliance with regulations.

Informal rules also place significant constraints on marketing and supply chain management. In marketing, most of the blunders documented in Exhibit 14.3 happen due to firms' failure to appreciate the deep underlying differences in cultures, languages, and norms—all part of the informal institutions. In supply chains, leading firms headquartered in developed economies may be able to diffuse leading-edge practices. In the 1990s, as a new norm, many European firms adopted the ISO 9000 series of quality management systems. They then imposed the standard on their suppliers and partners throughout the world. Over time, these suppliers and partners spread ISO 9000 to other domestic firms. At present, over 560,000 sites in over 150 countries have been ISO 9000 certified. In other words, due to the normative influence, suppliers and partners that export goods and services to a particular country in a supply chain may be simultaneously *importing* that country's norms and practices.

14-4b Resources, Marketing, and Supply Chain Management

Shown in Exhibit 14.5, we can evaluate marketing and supply chain management activities based on the VRIO criteria.

EXHIBIT 14.5 INSTITUTIONS, RESOURCES, MARKETING, AND SUPPLY CHAIN MANAGEMENT

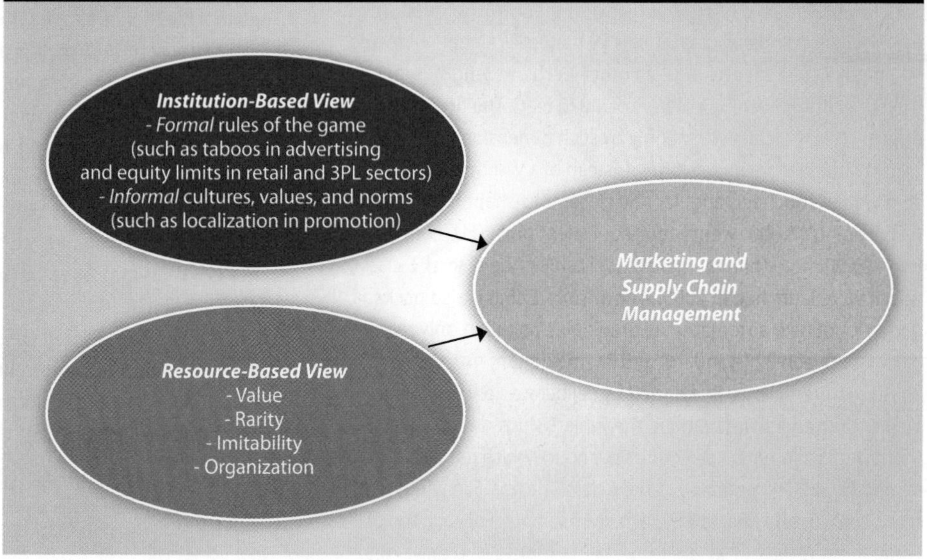

VALUE Do these activities add *value*?[15] Marketers now increasingly scratch their heads, as traditional media are losing viewers, readers, and thus effectiveness. But marketers do not have a good handle on how advertising in the new online media adds value.[16] As the first cohort to grow up Internet savvy, today's teens and twenty-somethings in many countries flock to social networks such as Facebook, Twitter, and their equivalents around the world. These young people "do not buy stuff because they see a magazine ad," according to one expert, "they buy stuff because other kids tell them to online."[17] What is challenging is how marketers can reach such youth.[18] A basic threat to such social networks is the whim of their users, whose interest in certain topics and networks themselves may change or even evaporate overnight.

RARITY Managers need to assess the *rarity* of marketing and supply chain activities. If all rival firms use FedEx to manage logistics (which does add value), these activities, in themselves, are not rare. In supply chain management, first movers in radio frequency identification (RFID) tags may derive benefits, because they are rare. However, as RFID becomes more available, its rarity (novelty value) will drop. In Focus illustrates how the world's largest shipping line Maersk has launched the mightiest ships ever built, the Triple-E class, to enhance the value and rarity of its container shipping services.

In Focus:

Giants of the Sea

GERARD KOUDENBURG/SHUTTERSTOCK.COM

Compared with the high-flying DHL, FedEx, and UPS jets, it is the slow-moving ships that are the backbone of modern supply chains. Everyday container ships carry 90% of the world's traded cargo by value, and such ocean shipping is known as "box trade." Taking off since the 1970s, container shipping has significantly reduced shipping cost so that China's location in the *Far* East does not seem to be too far away from major markets in North America and Europe. Yet, this industry is far from smooth sailing. Just as numerous new ships joined the fleet in the late 2000s, the Great Recession of 2008–2009 reduced trade volume, causing pricing levels to collapse.

As various shipping lines struggle and look for solutions, Maersk Line, the Copenhagen, Denmark-based largest shipping line in the world, has come up with some of the biggest splashes. In 2001, Maersk awarded Daewoo Shipbuilding of South Korea a $3.8 billion contract to build 20 of the world's largest ships: the Maersk Triple-E Class. The maiden journey of the first ship, the *Maersk Mc-Kinney Møller*, sailed in August 2013.

The name "Triple-E" is derived from the class's three design principles: economy, energy, and environment. With a dead weight of 165,000 tons, the colossal ship is 59 meters (194 feet) wide and 400 meters (1,312 feet) long—in other words, its length is longer than the Eiffel Tower (324 meters or 1,070 feet). The first E, economy of scale, is achieved not only by such dimensions, but also by fundamental design changes. Instead of a V-shaped hull, the ship's hull is much rectangular and closer to U-shaped. The upshot? A whopping 18,000 twenty-foot-equivalent unit (TEU) containers—2,500 more than the next biggest ships (the Maersk E class), which were launched in 2006. A new Triple-E ship is also packed with a lot of new automation technologies, so that it only requires a crew between 22 (standard) and 34 (maximum) members.

Energy efficiency is achieved by deliberate slow steaming. Slower than earlier generations, the Triple-E ships' design speed is 19 knots (35 kilometers or 22 miles per hour), which reduces fuel consumption by 20% compared to the E class. The final E, environmental friendliness, is also enabled by such low fuel burn. For each ton of cargo transported one kilometer, a Maersk Triple-E ship only emits three grams of CO_2. This is a far smaller environmental footprint than other modes of transportation: 18 grams of CO_2 for rail, 47 grams for truck, and 560 grams for air freight. The last but nontrivial component of environmental friendliness is that each ship is designed and built for recycling. When the ship is scrapped, all useful materials can be efficiently recycled, tremendously reducing the lifetime (and post-lifetime) environmental footprint of the colossal giant. Winner of the "Sustainable Ship Operator of the Year" award in 2011 (before the launch of the Triple-E class), Maersk believes that environmental friendliness will increasingly be a competitive differentiation factor and that the Triple-E class will help strengthen its edge.

At a cost of $190 million each, the Maersk Triple-E class ships are certainly valuable, rare, hard to imitate, and supported by the strong organizational capabilities of the world's largest shipping line. But they may be too big. No port in the Americas (either North or South) can handle them. Specifically, no crane is wide enough to reach its containers on the far side. With a draft of 14.5 meters (48 feet), they are too deep to cross the Panama Canal anyway. They can transit the Suez Canal when sailing between Europe and Asia. They will be limited to serving routes between Europe and Asia. The Europe-Asia trade represents Maersk's largest market, already with over 100 ships plying the waves. Maersk hopes to strengthen its leading position of the Europe-Asia trade with the addition of the new giants of the sea.

Sources: "An ill-timed bet on the world's largest ship," *Bloomberg Businessweek*, 29 April 2013, 21; "Hedging bets on the high seas," *BusinessWeek*, 27 April 2009, 10; "Container ships," *Economist*, 3 March 2007, 71; "Sea of troubles," *Economist*, 1 August 2009, 55–56; "A slow steaming giant," *Focus Denmark* (Summer–Autumn 2014): 68–71.

INIMITABILITY Having identified valuable and rare capabilities, managers need to assess how likely it is for rivals and partners to *imitate*. While there is no need to waste more ink on the necessity to watch out for rivals, firms also need to be careful about partners in the supply chain. As more Western MNEs outsource production to suppliers (or, using new jargon, contract manufacturers), it is always possible that some of the aggressive contract manufacturers may bite the hand that feeds them by directly imitating and competing with Western MNEs. This is not necessarily "opportunism." It is natural for ambitious contract manufacturers such as Foxconn and Flextronics to flex their muscle. While it is possible to imitate and acquire world-class manufacturing capabilities, marketing prowess and brand power are more intangible and thus harder to imitate. Thus, Western MNEs often cope by (1) being careful about what they outsource and (2) strengthening customer loyalty to their brands (such as Apple) to fend off contract manufacturers.

ORGANIZATION Managers need to ask: Is our firm *organizationally* ready to accomplish our objectives? Oddly, in many firms, Marketing and Sales functions do not get along well—to avoid confusion, here we use the two terms with capital letters, "Marketing" and "Sales," to refer to these functions. When revenues are disappointing, the blame game begins: Marketing blames Sales for failing to execute a brilliant plan, and Sales blames Marketing for setting the price too high and burning too much cash in high-flying but useless commercials. Marketing staff tend to be better educated, more analytical, and more disappointed when certain initiatives fail. Sales people are often "street smart," persuasive, and used to rejections all the time. It is not surprising that Marketing and Sales have a hard time working together.[19] Yet, work together they must. Some leading firms have disbanded Marketing and Sales as separate functions and have created an integrated function—called Channel Enablement at IBM.

14-5 MANAGEMENT SAVVY

What determines the success and failure in marketing and supply chain management? The institution-based view points out the impact of formal and informal rules of the game. In a non-market economy (think of North Korea), marketing would be irrelevant. In a world with high trade and investment barriers, globe-trotting DHL, FedEx, and UPS jets would be unimaginable. The resource-based view argues that holding institutions constant, firms such as Zara (see the Opening Case) and Maersk (see In Focus) that develop the best capabilities in marketing and supply chain management will emerge as winners.[20] The Closing Case illustrates how tour destinations can leverage both the institution-based and resource-based views to better market themselves to Chinese tourists, who are currently the world's largest group of international tourists.

EXHIBIT 14.6 IMPLICATIONS FOR ACTION

- Know the formal and informal rules of the game on marketing and supply chain management inside and out.
- In marketing, focus on product, price, promotion, and place (the four Ps) and do all it takes to avoid blunders.
- In supply chain management, focus on agility, adaptability, and alignment (the triple As).

Consequently, three implications for action emerge (Exhibit 14.6). First, marketers and supply chain managers need to know the rules of the game inside and out in order to craft savvy responses. For instance, given the limitations of formal regulatory frameworks in prosecuting cross-border credit card crimes, many US e-commerce firms refuse to ship to overseas addresses. Legitimate overseas purchasers are, in turn, denied business. As online shopping became a more widespread informal norm, FedEx acquired Kinkos (which was turned into FedEx Office stores), and UPS took over Mail Boxes (which was turned into UPS Stores). E-commerce firms can now ship to the US addresses of FedEx Offices and UPS Stores, and FedEx and UPS can then forward products to the overseas purchasers from these stores. This is but one example of superb problem solving in the face of cumbersome formal rules and changing informal norms.

Second, in marketing, focus on the four Ps. This obviously is a cliché. However, in international marketing, managers need to do all it takes to avoid costly and embarrassing blunders (see Exhibit 14.3). Remember: Despite their magnitude, blunders are *avoidable* mistakes. At the very least, international marketers should try very hard to avoid being written up as blunders in a new edition of this textbook.

Finally, in supply chain management, focus on the triple As. This is not a cliché, as the idea was just published a few years ago. Not aware of the importance of the triple As, many firms would only deliver container loads to minimize the number of deliveries and freight costs. When demand for a particular product suddenly rises, these firms often fail to react quickly—they have to wait until the container (or sometimes even the whole container *ship*) is full. Such a "best" practice typically delays shipment by a week or more, forcing stock-outs in stores that disappoint consumers. When firms eventually ship container loads, they often result in excess inventory, because most buyers do not need a full container load. To get rid of such inventory, as much as a third of the merchandise carried by department stores ends up in sales. Such discounts not only destroy profits for every firm in the supply chain, but also undermine brand equity by upsetting consumers who recently bought the discounted items at full price. In contrast, the triple As urge savvy supply chain managers to focus on agility, adaptability, and alignment of interests of the entire chain.

EMERGING MARKETS

Marketing to Chinese Tourists

Representing one out of every ten international tourists, the Chinese have recently emerged to become the largest group of tourists from any country. Countries ranging from Australia to Zimbabwe are eager to market their destinations to these new tourists, thus necessitating an eagerness to know more about them. Three observations have emerged.

BLUE JEAN IMAGES/ALAMY

Source: "Coming to a beach near you," *Economist*, 19 April 2014, 53.

First, Chinese tourists spend more, and focus more on shopping. In 2013 as a group they spent $129 billion, followed by American tourists who spent $86 billion. In a decade, thanks to the inflow of Chinese tourists, Macau dethroned Las Vegas as the undisputed gambling capital of the world. In 2012, Macau's casino takings were $38 billion vis-à-vis Las Vegas' $6 billion. Per visitor spending is even more striking: $1,354 for Macau (the majority of its gambling visitors are Chinese) versus $156 for Las Vegas. More than 80% of Chinese tourists indicate that shopping is crucial for their travel plans, compared with 56% of Middle Eastern tourists and 48% of Russian tourists. The average Chinese tourist indulges himself or herself with $1,130 tax-free purchases vis-à-vis $494 by the average Russian tourist. Interestingly, the Chinese spend more on luxury goods abroad than at home. Luxury goods purchased abroad have more value—not only the perceived value from made-in-France perfume purchased in France, but also literally the lower cost. Chinese consumption taxes of 20% to 30% on luxury goods mean such goods often end up costing 50% more in China than in Europe, thus motivating tourists to haul home some of these high priced goods as "bargains."

Second, Chinese tourists like to come as groups, often partaking in exhausting group bus tours of "20 cities in ten days." A most unusual format is "6+1," which is a young couple with one (the only!) child and two sets of (grand)parents.

Third, many tourists do not speak English and are outside of China for the first time. They are often uncomfortable with Western food with butter, cheese, and cream—ingredients Chinese never use in their cuisine.

In response, tourist destinations have vigorously competed for a growing share of Chinese tourists. From an institution-based view, removing or minimizing visa hassles will be a booster. In 2014, Chinese citizens could only visit 44 countries visa-free, while Taiwanese could visit 130 countries and Americans and British over 170. A quarter of would-be Chinese tourists had to abandon their plans for visiting Europe, thanks to visa delays. Outside the EU Schengen free-travel area (a visa issued by one Schengen member country can be used to enter all other 25 Schengen member countries—see Chapter 8), Britain requires its own visa. The upshot? Britain only receives one-ninth of the Chinese tourists that France entertains. When the United States no longer requires all Chinese visa applicants to be interviewed, 22% more Chinese visitors showed up the next year. When tiny Maldives waived its visa requirements, 45% more Chinese tourists came, contributing one-third of the 1.1 million total.

From a resource-based view, enhancing the value proposition is a must. For relatively obscure destinations, how to get on the tour itinerary is challenging. Abilities to successfully tap into the group and collectivistic mentality are rare, but—if developed well—can generate a lot of buzz. In 2012, Tourism New Zealand hosted the fairy-tale wedding of Yao Chen, an actress with 66 million followers on Weibo, China's equivalent of Twitter. It generated 7,000 news pieces, 40 million posts on discussion boards, and a significant number of Chinese honeymooners to follow the actress to check out the "100% Pure New Zealand" (Tourism New Zealand's campaign line). To make Chinese tourists feel comfortable, not only are Chinese-speaking tour guides necessary, but Chinese-speaking store personnel can also add value by gently nudging shoppers to commit to big-ticket luxury items in their native tongue. Harrods of London has positioned 100 Union Pay terminals throughout its store to cater to Chinese credit card and ATM card holders. Having store signs and restaurant menus in Chinese helps. In Copenhagen, the sign for its landmark, the Little Mermaid, now sports three languages: Danish, English, and Chinese. Hilton Hotels greet Chinese guests by a Chinese-speaking service member, outfit guest rooms with amenities such as tea kettles and slippers (two items traditionally missing even in high-end Western hotels), and serve such traditional Chinese breakfast items as dim sum, congee, and fried noodles.

While the growing Chinese middle class has already changed the global tourism industry, it is important to know that only about 5% of the population possess passports and that most go to Hong Kong or Macau. Therefore, their impact as well as our learning about them are not likely to stop anytime soon.

Case Discussion Questions

1. For your country's best tourist attraction, how can it attract more Chinese tourists based on the four Ps of marketing?
2. From a VRIO standpoint, identify what the following locations can do to attract more Chinese tourists: (1) Brisbane, Australia; (2) Copenhagen, Denmark; (3) Cozumel, Mexico; (4) Dallas, Texas; and (5) Dunedin, New Zealand.
3. Visit a tourist establishment (such as a hotel, restaurant, souvenir shop, or jewelry shop) frequented by international tourists in (or near) your city. Interview an employee and ask about the similarities and differences between serving Chinese tourists and serving non-Chinese tourists.

Sources: The author's interviews; "Hilton welcomes Chinese travelers at home and abroad," *China Business Review* (January 2012): 16–19; "The rise of the low-rollers," *Economist*, 7 September 2013, 63–64; "Coming to a beach near you," *Economist*, 19 April 2014, 53–54.

STUDY TOOLS 14

LOCATED AT THE BACK OF YOUR BOOK:

- ☐ Rip out and study the Chapter Review Card at the end of the book

LOG IN TO WWW.CENGAGEBRAIN.COM TO:

- ☐ Review key term flashcards
- ☐ Complete a practice quiz to test your knowledge of key concepts
- ☐ Take and complete the chapter crossword puzzle
- ☐ Complete interactive content, watch chapter videos, and take a graded quiz
- ☐ Track your knowledge of key concepts in Global Business
- ☐ Read and discuss additional case study content

15 Managing Corporate Social Responsibility Globally

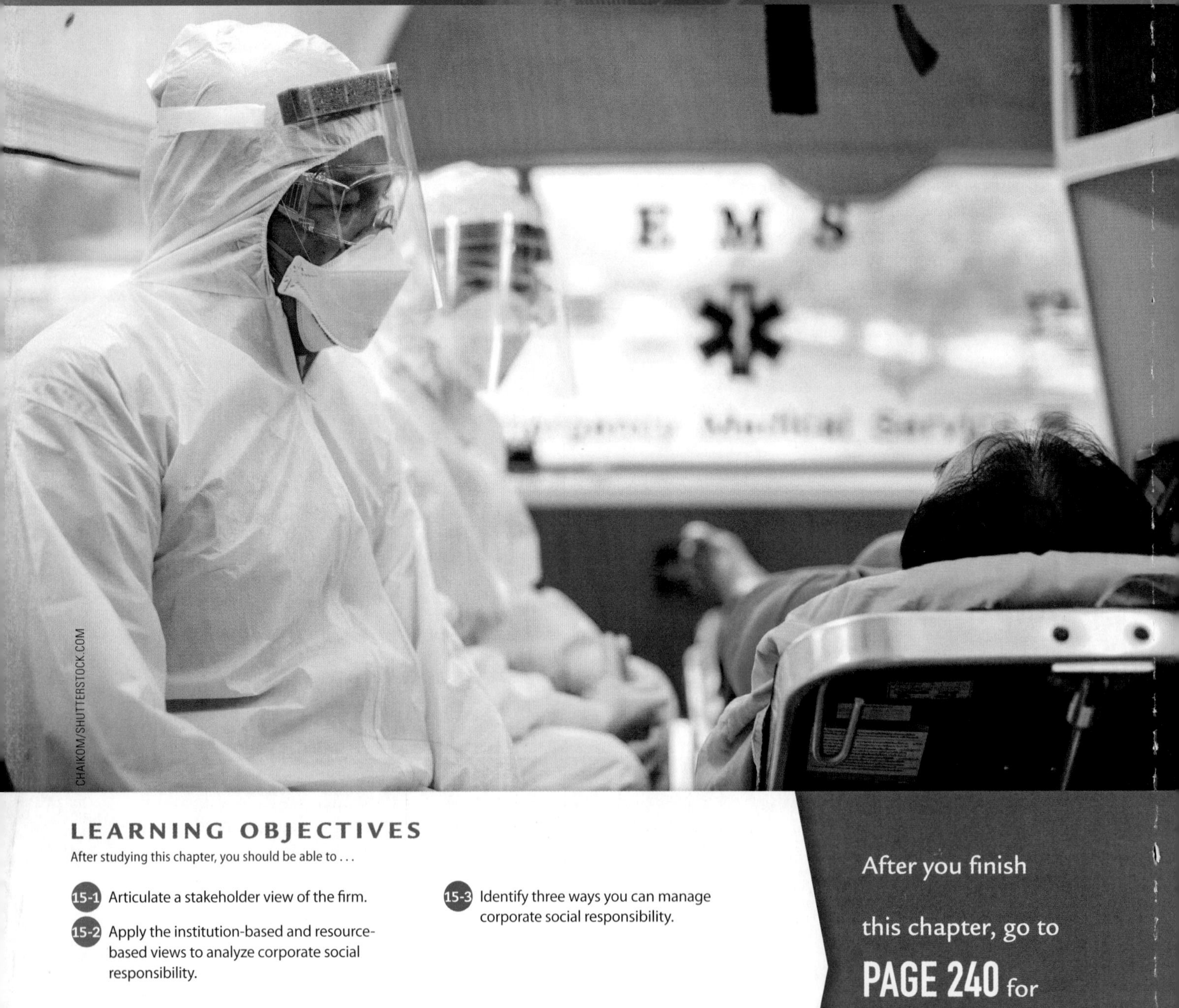

LEARNING OBJECTIVES

After studying this chapter, you should be able to . . .

15-1 Articulate a stakeholder view of the firm.

15-2 Apply the institution-based and resource-based views to analyze corporate social responsibility.

15-3 Identify three ways you can manage corporate social responsibility.

After you finish this chapter, go to **PAGE 240** for **STUDY TOOLS**

ETHICAL DILEMMA/EMERGING MARKETS

The Ebola Challenge

First reported in 1976 in Sudan and Zaire (now called the Democratic Republic of the Congo [DRC]), Ebola has been a known virus for four decades. Yet, there is still no effective vaccine or medicine. Between 1976 and 2013, there were 24 outbreaks in Sub-Saharan Africa with 1,716 cases. What really put Ebola on the center stage of global media—and on the pages of this book—was the 2014 outbreak, which was the most devastating outbreak with 22,000 reported cases and 9,000 deaths. Starting in Guinea, Liberia, and Sierra Leone, the disease quickly diffused to other West African countries such as the DRC, Nigeria, and Senegal. By September 2014, a Liberian man who traveled to Dallas, Texas, was diagnosed to have Ebola. He died there in early October. Two American nurses who treated the patient became the first confirmed cases to be infected by Ebola in the United States, triggering panic and chaos not only in Texas, but also in other parts of the country. State governments in Connecticut, Illinois, New Jersey, and New York demanded that anyone who traveled from affected West African countries be subject to 21 days of quarantine—the longest period the Ebola virus was thought to need to incubate. In October 2014, President Obama appointed a national Ebola response coordinator. All passengers arriving from affected African countries now had to go through screening, and all patients showing up at a US health care establishment had to answer a questionnaire regarding whether they traveled from these countries.

In the absence of effective vaccine or medicine, treatment was indirect. It centered on early supportive care with rehydration and symptomatic treatment. The measures would include management of pain, nausea, fever, and anxiety, as well as rehydration via the oral or by intravenous (IV) route. Blood products such as packed red blood cells or fresh frozen plasma might also be used. Intensive care was often used in the developed world. This might include maintaining blood volume and electrolytes (salts) balance as well as treating any bacterial infections. Thankfully, the two American nurses recovered after several weeks of treatment. So did the other six American health care workers who went to Africa and came home with Ebola. By December 2014, there had been ten Ebola cases in the United States, and only two resulted in death—the second case of death was an African doctor who was contaminated by his patients in an Ebola-infested country.

Throughout the crisis, the initial silence of the pharmaceutical industry was conspicuous. Dr. Margaret Chan, Director-General of the World Health Organization (WHO), criticized the industry for failing to develop a vaccine for Ebola over the four decades during which the virus threatened poor African countries. She complained that "a profit-driven industry does not invest in products for markets that cannot pay." Initially reluctant, some pharmaceutical firms jumped in. In October 2014, British drugmaker GlaxoSmithKline (GSK) announced that it expedited its R&D in search of a vaccine. In 2010, the Canadian government developed an experimental vaccine VSV-EBOV and licensed it to a small, virtually unknown biotech firm NewLink Genetics in Ames, Iowa, for clinical trials. However, progress was slow and funding tight. In November 2014, a US giant Merck paid NewLink $50 million to buy the rights to the vaccine and to expedite R&D. Also in November 2014, a French Big Pharma player Sanofi announced its intention to work with industry partners to combat Ebola. Another experimental drug ZMapp, developed by a small San Diego, California-based biopharmaceutical firm Mapp, showed encouraging results on primates, and had been used on at least seven (human) patients in Africa in 2014. But ZMapp had not received FDA approval. In the absence of the financial, technological, and production capabilities of Big Pharma, ZMapp's stocks quickly ran out. The US government had to provide it with $25 million to scale up production.

The reason that until recently, pharmaceutical firms—especially Big Pharma firms—had been reluctant to apply their significant resources to find a cure for Ebola was simple. Even if successful, these efforts, which would mostly benefit African countries, would not be profitable. In other words, there was "no compelling business case." Now that the disease came to the United States (and a few Western European countries), firms felt compelled to move. Debates continued to rage. One side argued that pharmaceutical firms only focused on markets and products from which they could profit—with "Botox, baldness, and bonus" as their guiding light. Tropical diseases such as malaria and Ebola naturally would receive little (or no) attention. Another side argued that given limited resources, pharmaceutical firms rightly and strategically ignored (relatively) smaller scale diseases such as Ebola. This was because there were other diseases such as HIV/AIDS that impact a lot more people than does Ebola. A number of pharmaceutical firms jumped onto the "Ebola bandwagon" simply to earn kudos for corporate social responsibility, knowing that they would be unlikely to make any profits for their efforts. Or they were simply driven to do so due to public pressure—the series of eager announcements made in October and November 2014 were defensive in nature. Given the long lead time to develop any effective vaccine and the urgency to have a vaccine at hand when confronting an outbreak of Ebola (and other contagious diseases), how pharmaceutical firms proceed remains one of the leading strategic challenges they face.

Sources: C. Campos, C. Cole, and J. Steele, "Ebola and corporate social responsibility," EMBA strategy class term project, Jindal School of Management, University of Texas at Dallas, 2014; "Canada should cancel NewLink Ebola vaccine contract," CBC, 19 November 2014, www.cbc.ca; "Ebola: Predictions with a purpose," *Economist*, 7 February 2015, 58; "Ebola outbreak: Why has 'Big Pharma' failed deadly virus' victims?" *Independent*, 7 September 2014, www.independent.co.uk; "Merck partners with NewLink to speed up work on Ebola vaccine," National Public Radio, 24 November 2014, www.npr.org; "WHO pillories drug industry for failure to develop Ebola vaccine," *Time*, 4 November 2014, www.time.com; World Health Organization, "Ebola virus disease fact sheet," November 2014, www.who.int.

Why until recently had pharmaceutical firms been reluctant to find a cure for Ebola? What motivated them to jump onto the "Ebola bandwagon" lately? Did they really want to solve a major public health problem around the world, or just want to earn some kudos for corporate social responsibility? **Corporate social responsibility (CSR)** refers to "consideration of, and response to, issues beyond the narrow economic, technical, and legal requirements of the firm to accomplish social benefits along with the traditional economic gains which the firm seeks."[1] Historically, CSR issues have been on the back burner for many managers, but these issues are now increasingly being brought to the forefront of corporate agendas.[2] While this chapter is the last in this book, by no means do we suggest that CSR is the least important topic. Instead, we believe that this chapter is one of the best ways to *integrate* all previous chapters concerning international trade, investment, strategy, and human resources. The comprehensive nature of CSR is evident in our Opening Case.

Corporate social responsibility (CSR) Consideration of, and response to, issues beyond the narrow economic, technical, and legal requirements of the firm to accomplish social benefits along with the traditional economic gains that the firm seeks.

Stakeholder Any group or individual who can affect or is affected by a firm's actions.

Global sustainability The ability to meet the needs of the present without compromising the ability of future generations to meet their needs around the world.

At the heart of CSR is the concept of **stakeholder**, which is any group or individual who can affect or is affected by a firm's actions. Shown in Exhibit 15.1, shareholders are important but are not the only group of stakeholders. Other groups include managers, nonmanagerial employees (hereafter "employees"), suppliers, customers, communities, governments, and social and environmental groups. This chapter focuses on *nonshareholder stakeholders*, which we will call "stakeholders" here for simplicity. A leading debate on CSR is whether managers' efforts to promote the interests of these other stakeholders are at odds with their fiduciary duty to safeguard shareholder interests. To the extent that firms are *not* social agencies and that their primary function is to serve as economic enterprises, it is certainly true that firms should not (and are not able to) take on all of the social problems of the world. However, failing to heed certain CSR imperatives may be self-defeating in the long run (see the Opening Case).

The remainder of this chapter first introduces a stakeholder view of the firm. Next, we discuss how the institution-based and resource-based views inform the CSR discussion. Finally, we consider how savvy managers can best manage CSR.

15-1 A STAKEHOLDER VIEW OF THE FIRM

15-1a A Big Picture Perspective

A stakeholder view of the firm represents a big picture. A key goal for CSR is **global sustainability**, which is defined as the ability "to meet the needs of the present

EXHIBIT 15.1 A STAKEHOLDER VIEW OF THE FIRM

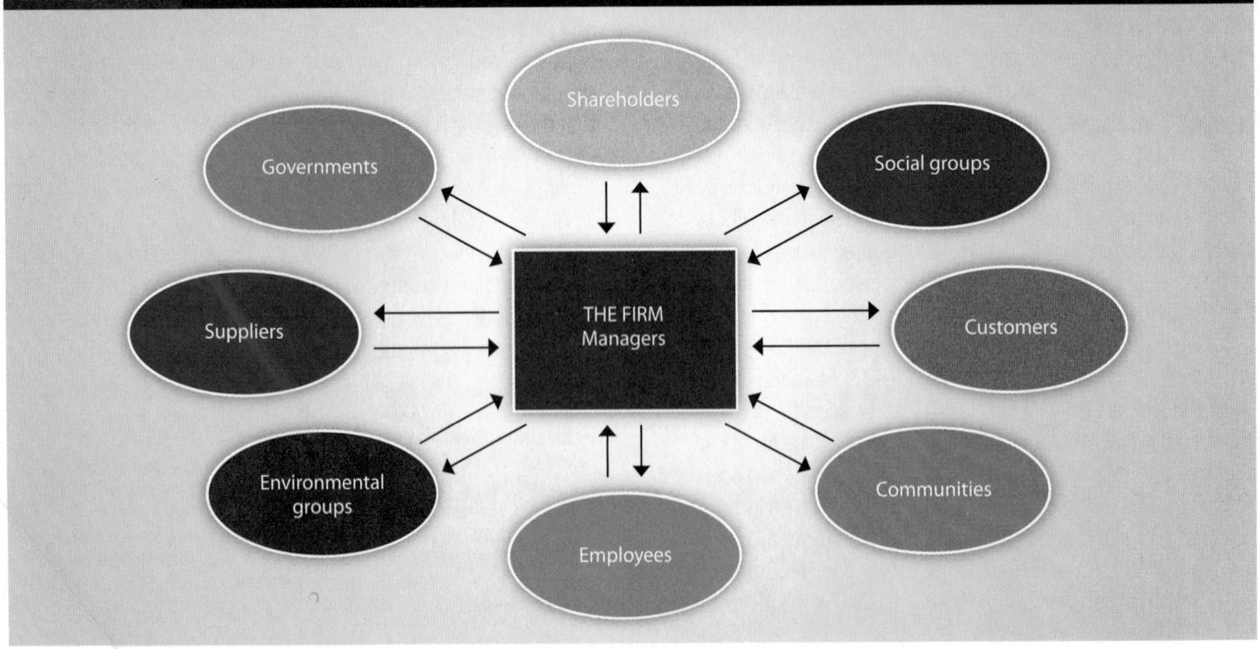

Source: T. Donaldson and L. Preston, "The stakeholder theory of the corporation: Concepts, evidence, and implications," *Academy of Management Review* 20 (1995): 69.

without compromising the ability of future generations to meet their needs." It not only refers to a sustainable social and natural environment, but also sustainable capitalism. Globally, the urgency of sustainability in the 21st century is driven by at least three concerns. First, increasing population, poverty, and inequity require new solutions. The repeated protests, chaos, and terrorist attacks around the world are but the tip of the iceberg of anti-globalization sentiments. Second, the relative power of national governments has eroded in the wake of globalization, but the influence of nongovernmental organizations (NGOs) and other civil society stakeholders has increased. Finally, industrialization has created some irreversible effects on the environment. Global warming, air and water pollution, soil erosion, deforestation, and over-fishing have become problems that demand creative solutions (see In Focus). Because firms contribute to many of these problems, many citizens believe that firms should also take on at least some responsibility for solving them.

In Focus: *Ethical Dilemma/Emerging Markets*

Global Warming and Arctic Boom

BIGROLOIMAGES/SHUTTERSTOCK.COM

Global warming is one of the most dreadful terms in recent times. Hotter summers. Longer droughts. More frequent hurricanes. Rising sea levels that may wash away many island nations and coastal regions. Can anyone like global warming? Can any firms profit from it? It turns out: plenty.

As a stunning illustration of global warming, Arctic sea ice has lost half of its area since record keeping began in 1979. The Intergovernmental Panel on Climate Change (IPCC) predicted that Arctic summers would become ice free beginning in 2070. Other estimates moved the date to around 2035. Instead of being terrified by such warming, many people, firms, and governments in the Arctic region are excited about it.

Two sources of excitements stand out. First, ships sailing between the Pacific Ocean and the Atlantic Ocean can go through the Arctic Ocean. The distance between Shanghai and Rotterdam can be shortened by 15% if ships use the Northwest Passage going through the Canadian Arctic Archipelago and by 22% if ships sail through the Northeast Passage, which the Russians call the Northern Sea Route (NSR), by hugging the northern Siberian coast. An expert noted that "the Arctic stands to become a central passageway for global maritime transportation, just as it already is for aviation." It is likely to become "an emerging epicenter of industry and trade akin to the Mediterranean Sea." While Canada and Russia look forward to profiting from maritime services such as refueling and pilotage, "such cities as Anchorage and Reykjavik could someday become major shipping centers and financial capitals—the high-latitude equivalents of Singapore and Dubai."

Second, the melting north can unearth tremendous oil and mineral wealth in the Arctic region. Canada, Norway, Russia, and the United States have all recently opened more of their Arctic offshore to oil exploration. Although Greenland only has 60,000 people, it is the world's largest island and its area is larger than all of Western Europe. Global warming not only means mining riches, but also Greenland's ultimate freedom: independence.

Colonized by Denmark in the 1700s, Greenland in 2009 gained more autonomy assuming self-government in all affairs except foreign affairs and defense. Denmark provided Greenland an annual grant of 3.6 billion Danish kroner ($660 million), which is roughly a quarter of Greenland's GDP and close to half of the government budget. Both sides agreed to split revenue from oil, gas, and minerals until Greenland could earn enough so that it would not need the subsidy, which meant $12,000 for every Greenlander. Then Greenland can gain its full independence. The Greenlandic government thus has been eager to grant permissions for energy and mining companies to explore the underground and offshore riches. For example, an Australian company called Greenland Minerals and Energy has been developing Greenland's first open pit uranium and rare earth mine. However, some environmentalists and traditionalists are not happy with such development. Overall, how to strike the right balance between exploitation and environmentalism is not only a challenge for Greenland, but also for all the communities, firms, and governments that aspire to take advantage of the coming Arctic boom.

Sources: "Drill sergeant," *Bloomberg Businessweek*, 5 May 2014, 62–67; S. Borgerson, "The coming Arctic boom," *Foreign Affairs*, July 2013, 76–89; "The melting north," *Economist*, 16 June 2012 (special report), 3–5; "Short and sharp," *Economist*, 16 June 2012 (special report), 14–15; "The Arctic: Not so cool," *Economist*, 3 January 2015, 51–52.

Drivers underpinning global sustainability are complex and multidimensional. This bewilderingly complex big picture forces managers to *prioritize*. To be able to do that, primary and secondary stakeholders must be identified (see the Opening Case).

15-1b Primary and Secondary Stakeholder Groups

Primary stakeholder groups are constituents on which the firm relies for its continuous survival and prosperity. Primary stakeholders typically refer to shareholders, managers, employees, suppliers, customers, and governments and communities whose laws and regulations must be obeyed and to whom taxes and other obligations may be due.

Secondary stakeholder groups are groups or individuals who can indirectly affect or are indirectly affected by a firm's actions. Examples include environmental groups (such as Greenpeace) and labor practice groups (such as Fair Labor Association). While firms do not depend on secondary stakeholder groups for survival, such groups may have the potential to cause significant embarrassment and damage. Think of Nike in the 1990s.

A key proposition of the stakeholder view is that firms should not simply pursue the economic bottom line (such as profits and shareholder returns). Instead, firms should pursue a more balanced **triple bottom line**, consisting of *economic, social,* and *environmental* performances that simultaneously satisfy the demands of all stakeholder groups. To the extent that some competing demands obviously exist, it seems evident that the CSR proposition represents a dilemma (see the Opening Case and the Closing Case). In fact, it has provoked a fundamental debate, which is introduced next.

Primary stakeholder group Constituent on which a firm relies for its continuous survival and prosperity.

Secondary stakeholder group Group or individual who can indirectly affect or are indirectly affected by a firm's actions.

Triple bottom line Economic, social, and environmental performance that simultaneously satisfies the demands of all stakeholder groups.

15-1c The Fundamental Debate on CSR

The CSR debate centers on the nature of the firm in society. Why does the firm exist? Most people would intuitively answer: "to make money." Milton Friedman was a former University of Chicago economist and a Nobel laureate who passed away in 2006. In an influential article published in 1970, he eloquently suggested: "The business of business is business."[3] The idea that the firm is an economic enterprise seems to be uncontroversial. At issue is whether the firm is *only* an economic enterprise.

One side of the debate argues that "the social responsibility of business is to increase its profits." In fact, that is the title of Friedman's 1970 article. The free market school of thought goes back to Adam Smith's idea that pursuit of economic self-interest (within legal and ethical bounds) leads to efficient markets. Free market advocates such as Friedman believe that the firm's first and foremost stakeholder group is the shareholders, and managers have a fiduciary duty (required by law) to look after shareholder interests. To the extent that the hallmark of our economic system remains capitalism, the providers of capital—namely, capitalists or shareholders—deserve a commanding height in managerial attention. In fact, since the 1980s, *shareholder capitalism* explicitly places shareholders as the single most important stakeholder group and has become increasingly influential around the world.

Free market advocates argue that if firms attempt to attain social goals such as providing employment and social welfare, managers will lose their focus on profit maximization (and its derivative, shareholder value maximization). Consequently, firms may lose their character as capitalistic enterprises and become *socialist* organizations. The idea of a socialist organization is not a pure argumentative point. It is derived from accurate characterization of numerous state-owned enterprises (SOEs) throughout the pre-reform Soviet Union, Central and Eastern Europe, and China as well as other developing countries in Africa, Asia, and Latin America. Privatization, in essence, removes the social function of SOEs and restores their economic focus through private ownership. Overall, the free market school has provided much of the intellectual underpinning for globalization spearheaded by multinational enterprises (MNEs).

It is against such a formidable and influential school of thought that the CSR movement has emerged. A free market system is, in theory, constrained by rules, contracts, and property rights. But CSR advocates argue that in practice, a free market system that takes the pursuit of self-interest and profit as its guiding light may fail to constrain itself, thus often breeding greed, excesses, and abuses (see the Debate). Firms and managers, if left to their own devices, may choose self-interest over public interest. The financial meltdown in 2008–2009 is often

Debate: Ethical Dilemma/Emerging Markets

Race to the Bottom ("Pollution Haven") Versus Race to the Top

One side of this debate argues that because of heavier environmental regulation in developed economies, multinational enterprises (MNEs) may shift pollution-intensive production to developing countries with lower environmental standards. To attract investment, developing countries may enter a "race to the bottom" by lowering (or at least not tightening) environmental standards and some may become "pollution havens."

The other side argues that globalization does not necessarily have negative effects on the environment in developing countries to the extent suggested by the "pollution haven" hypothesis. This is largely due to many MNEs' *voluntary* adherence to environmental standards higher than those required by host countries. Most MNEs reportedly outperform local firms in environmental management. The underlying motivations behind MNEs' voluntary "green practices" can be attributed to (1) worldwide CSR pressures in general, (2) CSR demands made by customers in developed economies, and (3) requirements of MNE headquarters for worldwide compliance of higher CSR standards (such as ISO 14001). Although it is difficult to suggest that the "race to the bottom" does not exist, MNEs as a group do not necessarily add to the environmental burden in developing countries. Some MNEs, such as Dow, have facilitated the diffusion of better environmental technologies to countries such as China.

GRYNOLD/SHUTTERSTOCK.COM

Sources: P. Christmann and G. Taylor, "Firm self-regulation through international certifiable standards," *Journal of International Business Studies* 37 (2006): 863–878; P. Madsen, "Does corporate investment drive a 'race to the bottom' in environmental protection?" *Academy of Management Journal* 52 (2009): 1297–1318; www.dow.com.

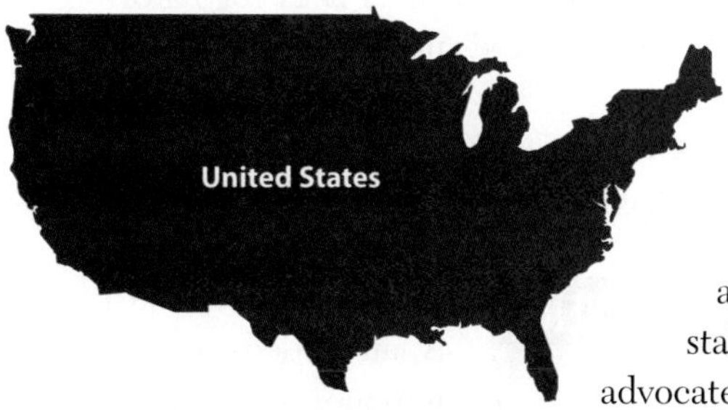

fingered as a case in point. While not denying that shareholders are important stakeholders, CSR advocates argue that all stakeholders have an *equal* right to bargain for a fair deal. Given stakeholders' often conflicting demands, a very thorny issue in the debate is whether all stakeholders indeed have an equal right and how to manage their (sometimes inevitable) conflicts (see the Opening Case and the Closing Case).

Starting in the 1970s as a peripheral voice in an ocean of free market believers, the CSR school of thought has slowly but surely become a more central part of management discussions. There are two driving forces. First, even as free markets spread around the world, the gap between the haves and have-nots has *widened*. While 2% of the world's children who live in America enjoy 50% of the world's toys, one-quarter of the children in Bangladesh and Nigeria are in the workforces of these two countries. Even within developed economies such as the United States, the income gap between the upper and lower echelons of society has widened. In 1980, the average American CEO was paid 40 times more than the average worker. The ratio is now above 400. Although American society accepts greater income inequality than many others do, aggregate data of such widening inequality, which both inform and numb, often serve as a stimulus for reforming a leaner and meaner capitalism. Such sentiments have become especially strong since the Great Recession of 2008–2009. However, the response from free market advocates is that to the extent there is competition, there will always be *both* winners and losers. What CSR critics describe as "greed" is often translated as "incentive" in the vocabulary of free market advocates.

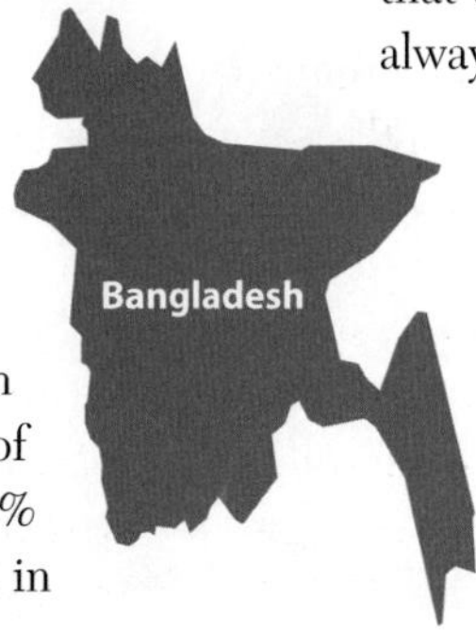

Second, disasters and scandals also drive the CSR movement. In 2001–2002, scandals at Enron, WorldCom, Royal Ahold, and Parmalat rocked the world. In 2008–2009, excessive amounts of Wall Street bonuses distributed by financial services firms receiving government bailout funds were criticized of being socially insensitive and irresponsible. In 2010, BP made a huge mess in the Gulf of Mexico. Not surprisingly, new disasters and scandals often propel CSR to the forefront of public policy and management discussions.

Overall, managers as a stakeholder group are unique in that they are the only group that is positioned at the center of all these relationships. It is important to understand how they make decisions concerning CSR, as illustrated next.

15-2 INSTITUTIONS, RESOURCES, AND CORPORATE SOCIAL RESPONSIBILITY

While some people do not consider CSR an integral part of global business, Exhibit 15.2 shows that the institution-based and resource-based views can inform the CSR discussion with relatively little adaptation. This section articulates why this is the case.

Reactive strategy A strategy that would only respond to CSR causes when required by disasters and outcries.

Defensive strategy A strategy that focuses on regulatory compliance but with little actual commitment to CSR by top management.

15-2a Institutions and Corporate Social Responsibility

The institution-based view sheds considerable light on the gradual diffusion of the CSR movement and the strategic responses of firms. At the most fundamental level, regulatory pressures underpin *formal* institutions, whereas normative and cognitive pressures support *informal* institutions. The strategic response framework consists of (1) reactive, (2) defensive, (3) accommodative, and (4) proactive strategies, as first introduced in Chapter 3 (see Exhibit 3.6). This framework can be extended to explore how firms make CSR decisions, as illustrated in Exhibit 15.3.

A **reactive strategy** is indicated by relatively little or no support by top management for CSR causes. Firms do not feel compelled to act in the absence of disasters and outcries. Even when problems arise, denial is usually the first line of defense. Put another way, the need to accept some CSR is neither internalized through cognitive beliefs, nor does it result in any norms in practice. That leaves only formal regulatory pressures to compel firms to comply. For example, in the United States, food and drug safety standards that we take for granted today were fought by food and drug companies in the first half of the 20th century. The basic idea that food and drugs should be tested before being sold to customers and patients was bitterly contested even as unsafe foods and drugs killed thousands of people. As a result, the Food and Drug Administration (FDA) was progressively granted more powers. This era is not necessarily over. Today, many dietary supplement makers, whose products are beyond the FDA's regulatory reach, continue to sell untested supplements and deny responsibility.

A **defensive strategy** focuses on regulatory compliance. Top management involvement is piecemeal at best, and the general attitude is that CSR is an added cost or nuisance. Firms admit responsibility but often fight it. After the establishment of the Environmental Protection Agency (EPA) in 1970, the US chemical industry resisted the EPA's intrusion (see Exhibit 15.3). The regulatory requirements were at significant odds with the norms and cognitive beliefs held by the industry at that time.

EXHIBIT 15.2 INSTITUTIONS, RESOURCES, AND CORPORATE SOCIAL RESPONSIBILITY

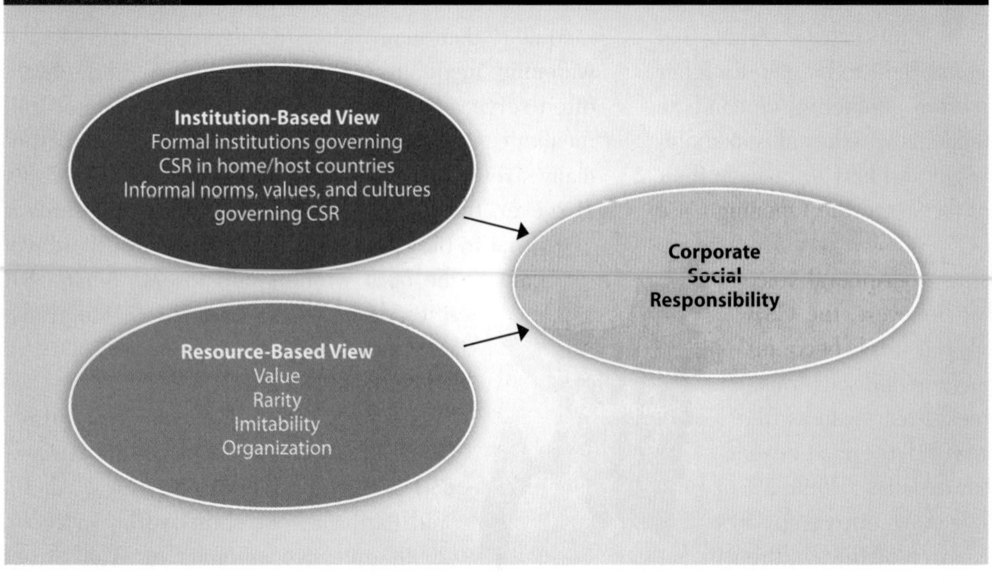

EXHIBIT 15.3 THE US CHEMICAL INDUSTRY RESPONDS TO ENVIRONMENTAL PRESSURES

Phase	Primary strategy	Representative statements from the industry's trade journal, *Chemical Week*
1. 1962–1970	Reactive	Denied the severity of environmental problems and argued that these problems could be solved independently through the industry's technological prowess.
2. 1971–1982	Defensive	"Congress seems determined to add one more regulation to the already 27 health and safety regulations we must answer to. This will make EPA [Environmental Protection Agency] a chemical czar. No agency in a democracy should have that authority." (1975)
3. 1983–1993	Accommodative	"EPA has been criticized for going too slow. . . . Still, we think that it is doing a good job." (1982) "Critics expect overnight fix. EPA deserves credit for its pace and accomplishments." (1982)
4. 1993–present	Proactive	"Green line equals bottom line—The Clean Air Act equals efficiency. Everything you hear about the 'costs' of complying with CAA [Clean Air Act] is probably wrong. . . . Wiser competitors will rush to exploit the Green Revolution." (1990)

Source: A. Homan, "Institutional evolution and change: Environmentalism and the US chemical industry," *Academy of Management Journal* 42 (1999): 351–371 for the phases and statements. Homan's last phase ended in 1993; its extension to the present was done by the present author.

ISTOCKPHOTO.COM/AKURTZ

How do various institutional pressures change firm behavior? In the absence of informal normative and cognitive beliefs, formal regulatory pressures are the only feasible way to push firms ahead. A key insight of the institution-based view—in fact, the very first proposition discussed in Chapter 2—is that individuals and organizations make *rational* choices given the right kind of incentives. For example, one efficient way to control pollution is to make polluters pay some "green" taxes—ranging from gasoline retail taxes to landfill charges. But how demanding these regulatory pressures should be remains controversial. One side of the debate argues that tough environmental regulation may lead to higher costs and reduced competitiveness, especially when competing with foreign rivals not subject to such demanding regulations. Others argue, however, that "green" taxes simply force firms to pay real costs that they otherwise place on others. If a firm pollutes, it is imposing a cost on the surrounding community that must either live with the pollution or pay to clean it up. By imposing a pollution tax that roughly equals the cost to the community, the firm has to account for pollution as a real cost. Economists refer to this as "internalizing an externality."

CSR advocates, endorsed by former vice president and Nobel laureate Al Gore, further argue that stringent environmental regulation may force firms to innovate, however reluctantly, thus benefiting the competitiveness of both the industry and country.[4] For example, a Japanese law set standards to make products easier to disassemble. Although Hitachi initially resisted the law, it responded by redesigning products to simplify disassembly. The company reduced the parts in its washing machines by 16% and in vacuum cleaners by 30%. The products became not only easier to disassemble, but also easier and cheaper to *assemble* in the first place, thus providing Hitachi with a significant cost advantage.

An **accommodative strategy** is characterized by some support from top managers, who may increasingly view CSR as a worthwhile endeavor. Since formal regulations may be in place and informal social and environmental pressures may be increasing, a number of firms themselves may be concerned about CSR, leading to the emergence of some new industry norms. Further, new managers who are passionate about or sympathetic toward CSR causes may join the organization, or some traditional managers may change their outlook, leading to increasingly strong cognitive beliefs that CSR is the right thing to do. In other words, from both normative and cognitive standpoints, it becomes legitimate or a matter of social obligation to accept responsibility and do all that is required. For example, in the US chemical industry, such a transformation probably took place in the early 1980s (see Exhibit 15.3). More recently, Burger King, Kraft, Nestlé, and Unilever were pressured by Greenpeace to be concerned about the deforestation practices undertaken by their major palm oil supplier Sinar Mas in Indonesia. Eventually, the food giants accommodated Greenpeace's demands and dumped Sinar Mas as a supplier, leading to a new industry norm that is more earth-friendly.[5]

Accommodative strategy A strategy characterized by some support from top managers, who may increasingly view CSR as a worthwhile endeavor.

ANTOINE ANTONIOL/BLOOMBERG VIA GETTY IMAGES

Adopting a code of conduct is a tangible indication of a firm's willingness to accept CSR. A code of conduct (sometimes called a code of ethics) is a set of written policies and standards outlining the proper practices for a firm. The global diffusion of codes of conduct is subject to intense debate. First, some argue that firms adopting these codes may not necessarily be sincere. This *negative* view suggests that an apparent interest in CSR may simply be window dressing. Some firms feel compelled to appear sensitive to CSR, following what others are doing, but have not truly and genuinely internalized CSR concerns. For example, in 2009, BP implemented a new safety-oriented operating management system. But after the 2010 oil spill, it became apparent that this system had not been seriously implemented, and the result was a huge catastrophe. Second, an *instrumental* view suggests that CSR activities simply represent a useful instrument to make good profits.[6] Firms are not necessarily becoming more ethical. For example, after the 2010 oil spill, BP reshuffled management and created a new worldwide safety division. The instrumental view would argue that these actions did not really mean that BP became more ethical. Finally, a *positive* view believes that (at least some) firms and managers may be self-motivated to do it right regardless of social pressures.[7] Codes of conduct tangibly express values that organizational members view as central and enduring.

The institution-based view suggests that all three perspectives are probably valid. This is to be expected given how institutional pressures work to instill value. Regardless of actual motive, the fact that firms are practicing CSR is indicative of the rising *legitimacy* of CSR on the management agenda. Even firms that adopt a code of conduct simply as window dressing open doors for more scrutiny by stakeholders. Such pressures are likely to transform the firms internally into more self-motivated, better corporate citizens. It probably is fair to suggest that Nike is a more responsible corporate citizen in 2014 than it was in 1994.

Proactive strategy A strategy that anticipates CSR and endeavors to do more than is required.

From a CSR perspective, the best firms embrace a **proactive strategy**, constantly anticipating responsibility and endeavoring to do more than is required. Top management at a proactive firm not only supports and champions CSR activities, but also views CSR as a source of differentiation that permeates throughout the corporate DNA. Starbucks since 2001 has voluntarily published an annual report on CSR, which embodies its founder, chairman, and CEO Howard Schultz's vision that "we must balance our responsibility to create value for shareholders with a social conscience."[8] Whole Foods' co-founder and co-CEO John Mackey commented:

> *When people are really happy in their jobs, they provide much higher degrees of service to the customers. Happy team members result in happy customers. Happy customers do more business with you. They become advocates for your enterprise, which results in happy investors. That is a win, win, win, win strategy. You can expand it to include your suppliers and the communities where you do business, which are tied in to this prosperity circle.*[9]

Proactive firms often engage in three areas of activity. First, some firms such as Swiss Re and Duke Energy actively participate in regional, national, and international policy and standards discussions. To the extent that policy and standards discussions today may become regulations in the future, it seems better to get involved early and (hopefully) steer the course toward a favorable direction. Otherwise—as the saying goes—if you're not at the table, you're on the menu. For example, Duke Energy operates 20 coal-fired power plants in five states. It is the third largest US emitter of CO_2 and the 12th largest in the world. But its CEO Jim Rogers has proactively worked with green technology producers, activists, and politicians to engage in policy and legislative discussions. These are not merely defensive moves to protect his firm and the power utility industry. Unlike his industry peers, Rogers has been "bitten by the climate bug" and is genuinely interested in reducing greenhouse gas emissions.

Second, proactive firms often build alliances with stakeholder groups. For example, many firms collaborate with NGOs. Because of the historical tension and distrust, these "sleeping-with-the-enemy" alliances are not easy to handle. The key lies in identifying relatively short-term, manageable projects of mutual interests. For instance, Starbucks collaborated with Conservation International to help reduce deforestation practices.

Third, proactive firms often engage in *voluntary* activities that go beyond what is required by regulations. While examples of industry-specific self-regulation abound, an area of intense global interest is the pursuit of the International Standards Organization (ISO) 14001 certification of the environment management system (EMS). Headquartered in Geneva, Switzerland, the ISO is an influential NGO consisting of national standards bodies in 111 countries. Launched in 1996, the ISO 14001 EMS has become the gold standard for CSR-conscious firms. Although not required by law, many MNEs, such as Ford and IBM, have adopted ISO 14001 standards in all their facilities worldwide. Firms such as Toyota, Siemens, and General Motors have demanded that all of their top-tier suppliers be ISO 14001 certified.

From an institutional perspective, these proactive activities are indicative of the normative and cognitive beliefs held by many managers on the importance of doing the right thing. While there is probably a certain element of window dressing and a quest for better profits, it is obvious that these efforts provide some tangible social and environmental benefits.

15-2b Resources and Corporate Social Responsibility

CSR-related resources can include *tangible* technologies and processes as well as *intangible* skills and attitudes. The VRIO framework can shed considerable light on CSR.

VALUE Do CSR-related resources and capabilities add *value*? This is the litmus test for CSR work. Many large firms, especially MNEs, can apply their tremendous financial, technological, and human resources toward a variety of CSR causes. For example, firms can choose to refuse to do business with countries that engage in human rights abuses. Such activities can be categorized as **social issue participation**, which refers to a firm's participation in social causes not directly related to the management of its primary stakeholders. Research suggests that these activities may actually *reduce* shareholder value.[10] Overall, although social issue participation may create some remote social and environmental value, it does not satisfy the economic leg of the triple bottom line, so these abilities do not qualify as value-adding firm resources.

RARITY CSR-related resources are not always *rare*. Remember that even a valuable resource is not likely to provide a significant advantage if competitors also possess it. For example, both Home Depot and Lowe's have NGOs such as the Forest Stewardship Council certify that suppliers in Brazil, Indonesia, and Malaysia use only material from renewable forests. These complex processes require strong management capabilities such as negotiating with local suppliers, undertaking internal verification, coordinating with NGOs for external verification, and disseminating such information to stakeholders. Such capabilities are valuable. But since both competitors possess capabilities to manage these processes, they are common (but not rare) resources.

IMITABILITY Although valuable and rare resources may provide some advantage, the advantage will only be temporary if competitors can *imitate* it. Resources must be not only valuable and rare, but also hard to imitate in order to give firms a sustainable (not merely temporary) competitive advantage. At some firms, CSR-related capabilities are deeply embedded in idiosyncratic managerial and employee skills and attitudes. The socially complex way of channeling their energy and conviction toward CSR at Whole Foods, led by John Mackey, a guru on conscious capitalism whose words are quoted on p. 236, cannot be easily imitated.

ORGANIZATION Does the firm have *organizational* capabilities to do a good job to exploit the full potential of CSR? Numerous components within a firm, such as formal management control systems and informal relationships between managers and employees, may be relevant. These components are often called complementary assets (see Chapter 4), because, by themselves, they typically do not generate advantage. However, complementary assets, when combined with valuable, rare, and hard-to-imitate capabilities, may enable a firm to fully utilize its CSR potential.

Social issue participation Firms' participation in social causes not directly related to the management of primary stakeholders.

THE CSR-ECONOMIC PERFORMANCE PUZZLE The resource-based view helps solve a major puzzle in the CSR debate: the CSR-economic performance puzzle. The puzzle—a source of frustration to CSR advocates—is why there is no conclusive evidence on a direct, positive link between CSR and *economic* performance such as profits and shareholder returns. Some studies do indeed report a *positive* relationship.[11] Others find a *negative* relationship[12] or *no* relationship.[13] Viewed together, "CSR does not hurt [economic] performance, but there is no concrete support to believe that it leads to supranormal [economic] returns."[14]

A resource-based explanation suggests that because of the capability constraints discussed above, many firms are not cut out for a CSR-intensive (differentiation) strategy. Since all studies have some sampling bias (no study is perfect), studies that over-sample firms not yet ready for a high level of CSR activities are likely to report a negative relationship between CSR and economic performance. Likewise, studies that over-sample firms ready for CSR may find a positive relationship. Also, studies with more balanced (more random) samples may fail to find any statistically significant relationship. In summary, since each firm is different (a basic assumption of the resource-based view), not every firm's economic performance is likely to benefit from CSR.

15-3 MANAGEMENT SAVVY

Concerning CSR, the institution-based and resource-based views suggest three clear implications for action (see Exhibit 15.4). First, savvy managers need to understand the formal and informal rules of the game, anticipate changes, and seek to shape such changes. Although the US government refused to ratify the 1997 Kyoto Protocol and only signed the nonbinding 2009 Copenhagen Accord, many US firms such as Chevron, Dow Chemical, DuPont, ExxonMobil, Google, and Microsoft voluntarily participate in CSR activities not (yet) mandated by law (such as being prepared to pay "green" taxes for carbon emissions—known as carbon pricing), in anticipation of more stringent environmental requirements down the road.[15]

EXHIBIT 15.4 IMPLICATIONS FOR ACTION

- Understand the rules of the game, anticipate changes, and seek to shape and influence changes.
- Pick your CSR battles carefully. Don't blindly imitate other firms' CSR activities.
- Integrate CSR as part of the core activities and processes of the firm. Faking it doesn't last very long.

Second, savvy managers need to pick CSR battles carefully. The resource-based view suggests an important lesson, which is captured by Sun Tzu's timeless teaching: "Know yourself, know your opponents." While your opponents may engage in high-profile CSR activities that allow them to earn bragging rights and contribute to their triple bottom line, blindly imitating these practices without knowing enough about yourself as a manager and the firm/unit you lead may result in some disappointment. Instead of always chasing the newest best practices, firms are advised to select CSR practices that fit with their *existing* resources, capabilities, and especially complementary assets.[16]

Third, given the increasingly inescapable responsibility to be good corporate citizens, managers may want to integrate CSR as part of the core activities of the firm instead of faking it and making only cosmetic changes. For example, instead of treating NGOs as threats, Home Depot, Lowe's, and Unilever have their sourcing policies certified by NGOs. Dow Chemical has established community advisory panels in most of its locations worldwide. Many managers traditionally treated CSR as a nuisance, involving regulation, added costs, and liability. Such an attitude may underestimate potential business opportunities associated with CSR.

What determines the success and failure of firms around the world? No doubt, CSR will increasingly become an important part of the answer. The best-performing firms are likely to be those that can integrate CSR activities into their core economic functions while addressing social and environmental concerns (see the Opening and Closing Cases). In the post–Great Recession and post–Occupy Wall Street world, managers, as a unique group of stakeholders, have an important and challenging responsibility. From a CSR standpoint, this means building more humane, more inclusive, and fairer firms that not only generate wealth and develop economies, but also respond to changing societal expectations concerning firms' social and environmental roles around the world.

ETHICAL DILEMMA

Wolf Wars

Wolves are the planet's most widespread land-based large mammals. They used to be humans' most direct competitors for meat. As a result, the Big Bad Wolf occupied a center stage in our psyche as a demon character in many cultures. Humans fought wolves for ages. Relentlessly shot, poisoned, and trapped, wolves were completely defeated in these old wolf wars. In Yellowstone National Park, the last gray wolf was killed in 1926. In the continental United States (except northern Minnesota), the gray wolf was completely exterminated by 1950.

EWAN CHESSER/SHUTTERSTOCK.COM

However, winning the wolf wars made (some) humans feel guilty. In 1995 and 1996, the US Fish and Wildlife Service deliberately reintroduced 66 wolves captured in Canada into the wild by releasing them into Yellowstone National Park and central Idaho's wilderness. By 2009, more than 1,600 wolves populated the northern Rocky Mountain states (primarily Idaho, Montana, and Wyoming), and smaller packs penetrated northeastern Washington (state) and Colorado. "The West is getting wilder by the hour," declared *National Geographic*. Wildlife enthusiasts and tourists were elated. In Yellowstone, thousands of tourists came to watch wolves every year, adding millions of dollars to the local economy. The revival of the gray wolves was viewed one of the most resounding victories of the Endangered Species Act enacted in 1973. In 2008, gray wolves in Wyoming were declared no longer endangered by the Interior Department. In 2009, gray wolves in Montana and Idaho started to enjoy such a status. Finally, in 2011, gray wolves in eight states across the West and upper Great Lakes were delisted.

Will humans and wolves live happily ever after? Not likely! "Packs are back," wrote *National Geographic*, "Westerners are glad, scared, and howling mad." Other than the group who are glad, a lot of people are scared. Small children, cats, and dogs are no longer safe in wolf-infested areas. A pleasant walk in the woods may face unpleasant encounters. But two groups are howling mad. First, hunters complain that too many elk have become wolf food. In a region struggling with economic hardship such as lumber mill closures, wolves are direct competitors for meat to feed the family. In some places, "Howdy?" is replaced by "Get your elk yet?" Some folks openly talk about taking the matter into their own hands by shooting the wolves as their forefathers did. A popular bumper sticker sports a crossed-out wolf with the caption "Smoke a Pack a Day."

The second group that opposes the reappearance of gray wolves is ranchers who raise livestock such as cattle and sheep for a living. Wolves literally *eat* into the thin profits of ranchers and jack up the price of beef, lamb, milk, cheese, yogurt, and ice cream all of us have to pay. A pack of wolves (generally about 3–10) typically kills a (wild) elk or a cattle calf every 2–3 days. In a single night, a pack of three adult wolves and five pups killed 122 sheep on a ranch in Montana, consuming little to no meat—the adults were probably teaching the pups how to kill. Wyoming and Montana compensate ranchers for livestock loss to wolves (for example, about $600 a calf) if ranchers can prove that such losses are due to wolf kills. The problem is that if ranchers do not find and document a carcass right away, scavengers such as grizzly bears may drag off or shred all the evidence. For every wolf kill that is compensated, several more are uncompensated. In addition, surviving cattle harassed by wolves over one season can lose 30–50 pounds each. Further, livestock with injuries scratched by unsuccessful wolf chases or infections from wounds are not marketable, and ranchers have to eat such losses. Finally, stress results in a lot of livestock miscarriages.

Some ranchers are aware of their CSR. One was quoted as saying: "We have to realize that the general US population wants wolves. That population is also our customers for beef. It's not a good idea to tell your customers they don't know what they're doing." But, the other side of the debate argues: Isn't the thinking that the CSR of cattle ranchers is to tolerate their livestock being wolf feed too far?

Frustrated ranchers cannot defend their private property by shooting wolves. Instead, they vote politicians on a pro-wolf platform out of office and fill state legislatures in Idaho, Montana, and Wyoming with candidates who vow to make wolves go away. After gray wolves were delisted from the (federal) engendered species list in Wyoming, the state government immediately labeled them varmints (or pests), allowing virtually unlimited shooting and trapping. A resulting lawsuit filed by environmental and animal protection groups forced the (federal) Interior Department to temporarily put wolves back on the endangered list. Taking the lesson, Montana and Idaho, after wolves were delisted in their states, labeled them game animals and set quotas for the first legal wolf hunts in their history—75 in Montana and 220 in Idaho. In addition, Idaho started shooting wolves from helicopters to kill predators that biologists say are harming elk herds. In response, angry environmentalists went back to court again, arguing that the legislative removal of wolves from federal protection was unconstitutional and that wolves would be annihilated again. Overall, the age-old wolf wars continue to rage. But in this new episode, wolf wars are not waged between wolves and humans—instead they are waged between different groups of humans with opposing views (the rural folks populating the cattle country versus the urban types who vow to protect wild animals at all costs). So stay tuned.

Case Discussion Questions

1. ***ON ETHICS***: Do ranchers have any CSR to help preserve the wolves by tolerating livestock losses? Or does their CSR lie in their efforts to get rid of the wolves from their private property (by doing that, they also generate the social benefits of bringing down the costs on beef, lamb, milk, cheese, yogurt, and ice cream for all of us)?
2. ***ON ETHICS***: If ranchers cannot make a living, they are likely to sell property to developers, who will facilitate more urban sprawl. Urban land almost never goes back to agricultural or ranch use. Should CSR advocates help ranchers make a living or should they push ranchers to accept more losses from wolf predation?
3. ***ON ETHICS***: Compensating ranchers for wolf kills is a solution. However, as state budgets shrink and economic recession bites, should taxpayers (including many who do not hunt and do not make a living by ranching) foot such an escalating bill? (An expanding wolf population will need more food, which will result in more livestock losses.)
4. ***ON ETHICS***: While "wolf wars" take place in the United States, "elephant wars" in Africa (elephants leave protected areas and destroy crops) and "tiger wars" in India (tigers leave protected areas and attack livestock and children) feature similar tensions. Answer Questions 1 to 3 above, using either "elephant wars" or "tiger wars" as your background.

Sources: "Wolf wars: Can man and predator coexist in the West," *Christian Science Monitor*, 3 June 2011; "Three views of the wolf wars," *Missoula News*, 25 August 2009; "Wolf wars," *National Geographic*, March 2010, 34–55.

STUDY TOOLS 15

LOCATED AT THE BACK OF YOUR BOOK:

☐ Rip out and study the Chapter Review Card at the end of the book

LOG IN TO WWW.CENGAGEBRAIN.COM TO:

☐ Review key term flashcards

☐ Complete a practice quiz to test your knowledge of key concepts

☐ Take and complete the chapter crossword puzzle

☐ Complete interactive content, watch chapter videos, and take a graded quiz

☐ Track your knowledge of key concepts in Global Business

☐ Read and discuss additional case study content

NOTES

1

1. J. Dunning, *Multinational Enterprises and the Global Economy* (Reading, MA: Addison-Wesley, 1993) 30.

2. J.-F. Hennart, "Down with MNE-centric models!" *Journal of International Business Studies* 40 (2009): 1432–1454.

3. United Nations, *World Investment Report 2014* (New York and Geneva: United Nations, 2014) ix.

4. "When giants slow down," *Economist*, 27 July 2013, 20.

5. "Emerge, splurge, purge," *Economist*, 8 March 2014, 65–68.

6. T. London, "Making better investments at the base of the pyramid," *Harvard Business Review* (May 2009): 106–113.

7. K. Meyer and M. W. Peng, "Probing theoretically into Central and Eastern Europe," *Journal of International Business Studies* 36 (2005): 600–621.

8. M. W. Peng, "Identifying the big question in international business research," *Journal of International Business Studies* 35 (2004): 99–108.

9. J. Dunning and S. Lundan, "Institutions and the OLI paradigm of the multinational enterprise," *Asia Pacific Journal of Management* 25 (2008): 573–593; M. W. Peng, D. Wang, and Y. Jiang, "An institution-based view of international business strategy," *Journal of International Business Studies* 39 (2008): 920–936.

10. M. W. Peng, "The resource-based view and international business," *Journal of Management* 27 (2001): 803–829.

11. J. Johanson and J. Vahlne, "The Uppsala internationalization process model revisited: From liability of foreignness to liability of outsidership," *Journal of International Business Studies* 40 (2009): 1411–1431.

12. K. Meyer, S. Estrin, S. Bhaumik, and M. W. Peng, "Institutions, resources, and entry strategies in emerging economies," *Strategic Management Journal* 30 (2009): 61–80; D. Zoogah, M. W. Peng, and H. Woldu, "Institutions, resources, and organizational effectiveness in Africa," *Academy of Management Perspectives* 29 (2015): 7–31.

13. J. Stiglitz, *Globalization and Its Discontents* (New York: Norton, 2002) 9.

14. "America the relatively beautiful," *Bloomberg Businessweek*, 2 February 2015, 8–10.

15. P. Ghemawat, "Semiglobalization and international business strategy," *Journal of International Business Studies* 34 (2003): 138–152.

16. The nominal GDP figures are from the World Bank, "GDP (current US$)," World Development Database (Washington: World Bank, 2014). The PPP GDP figures are from the International Monetary Fund (IMF), 2014, "Report for selected countries and subjects (PPP valuation of country GDP)" (Washington: IMF, 2014).

17. "Supersized national champs," *Bloomberg Businessweek*, 8 April 2013, 14.

18. United Nations, *World Investment Report 2010* (New York and Geneva: United Nations, 2010) 10.

19. *Fortune*, "Global 500," 21 July 2014, 53.

20. M. W. Peng, "The global strategy of emerging multinationals from China," *Global Strategy Journal* 2 (2012): 97–107.

2

1. M. W. Peng, "Institutional transitions and strategic choices," *Academy of Management Review* 28 (2003): 275.

2. M. W. Peng, D. Wang, and Y. Jiang, "An institution-based view of international business strategy," *Journal of International Business Studies* 39 (2008): 920–936.

3. D. North, *Institutions, Institutional Change, and Economic Performance* (New York: Norton, 1990) 3.

4. W. R. Scott, *Institutions and Organizations*, 3rd ed. (Thousand Oaks, CA: Sage, 2008).

5. "Looking for someone to blame," *Economist*, 13 August 2011, 25–26.

6. O. Williamson, *The Economic Institutions of Capitalism* (New York: Free Press, 1985) 1–2.

7. P. Collier and J. Gunning, "Explaining African economic performance," *Journal of Economic Literature* 37 (1999): 64–111.

8. "The price is wrong," *Economist*, 28 September 2013 (special report), 5.

9. "NYSE chief Duncan Niederauer on Obama and business," *BusinessWeek*, 8 June 2009, 15.

10. "The overseas tax squeeze," *BusinessWeek*, 18 May 2009, 18–20.

11. "Positively un-American," *Fortune*, 21 July 2014, 30–36.

12. Y. Li, M. W. Peng, and C. Macaulay, "Market-political ambidexterity during institutional transitions," *Strategic Organization* 11 (2013): 205–213.

13. "Wish you were mine," *Economist*, 11 February 2012, 51–52.

14. S. Young, D. Ross, and B. MacKay, "Inward foreign direct investment and constitutional change in Scotland," *Multinational Business Review* 22 (2014): 118–138.

15. "Don't leave us this way," *Economist*, 12 July 2014, 11; "Scottish finance," *Economist*, 6 September 2014, 58.

16. M. Porter and J. Rivkin, "Choosing the United States," *Harvard Business Review* (March 2012): 90.

17. "What's gone wrong with democracy," *Economist*, 1 March 2014, 47–52.

18. R. La Porta, F. Lopez-de-Silanes, A. Shleifer, and R. Vishny, "Law and finance," *Journal of Political Economy* 106 (1998): 1118.

19. H. de Soto, *The Mystery of Capital* (New York: Basic Books, 2000).

20. T. Khoury and M. W. Peng, "Does institutional reform of intellectual property rights lead to more inbound FDI?" *Journal of World Business* 46 (2011): 337–345.

21. P. Hall and D. Soskice, *Varieties of Capitalism* (Oxford, UK: Oxford University Press, 2001).

22. D. North, *Understanding the Process of Economic Change* (Princeton, NJ: Princeton University Press, 2005) 48.

23. D. Acemoglu and J. Robinson, *Why Nations Fail* (New York: Crown, 2012).

24. "Doing business in Africa," *Economist*, 2 July 2005, 61.

25. D. North, *Structure and Change in Economic History* (New York: Norton, 1981) 164.

3

1. G. Hofstede, *Cultures and Organizations* (New York: McGraw-Hill, 1997) xii.

2. Hofstede, *Cultures and Organizations*, 5.

3. K. Leung, R. Bhagat, N. Buchan, M. Erez, and C. Gibson, "Beyond national culture and culture-centricism," *Journal of International Business Studies* 42 (2011): 177–181.

4. R. McCrum, *Globish: How the English Language Became the World's Language* (New York: Norton, 2010).

5. E. Hall and M. Hall, *Hidden Differences* (Garden City, NY: Doubleday, 1987).

6. S. Ronen and O. Shenkar, "Clustering countries on attitudinal dimension," *Academy of Management Review* 10 (1985): 435–454.

7. R. House, P. Hanges, M. Javidan, P. Dorfman, and V. Gupta (eds.), *Culture, Leadership, and Organizations: The GLOBE Study of 62 Societies* (Thousand Oaks, CA: Sage, 2004).

8. S. Huntington, *The Clash of Civilizations and the Remaking of World Order* (New York: Simon & Schuster, 1996) 43.

9. Hofstede, *Cultures and Organizations*, 94.

10. R. Deshpande and A. Raina, "The ordinary heroes of the Taj," *Harvard Business Review* (December 2011): 119–123.

11. This section draws heavily from T. Donaldson, "Values in tension," *Harvard Business Review* (September–October 1996): 4–11.

12. "How to grease a palm," *Economist*, 23 December 2006, 116.

13. S. Lee and D. Weng, "Does bribery in the home country promote or dampen firm exports," *Strategic Management Journal* 34 (2013): 1472–1487.

14. S. Wei, "How taxing is corruption on international investors?" *Review of Economics and Statistics* 82 (2000): 1–11.

15. J. Hellman, G. Jones, and D. Kaufmann, "Far from home: Do foreign investors import higher standards of governance in transition economies," Working paper (2002), World Bank, www.worldbank.org [accessed 21 July 2009].

16. C. Kwok and S. Tadesse, "The MNC as an agent of change for host-country institutions," *Journal of International Business Studies* 37 (2006): 767–785.

4

1. M. W. Peng, "The resource-based view and international business," *Journal of Management* 27 (2001): 803–829.

2. J. Barney, "Is the resource-based view a useful perspective for strategic management research? Yes," *Academy of Management Review* 26 (2001): 54.

3. D. Teece, "Explicating dynamic capabilities," *Strategic Management Journal* 28 (2007): 1319–1350.

4. J. Barney, *Gaining and Sustaining Competitive Advantage*, 2nd ed. (Upper Saddle River, NJ: Prentice Hall, 2002) 157.

5. S. Kotha and K. Srikanth, "Managing a global partnership model," *Global Strategy Journal* 3 (2013): 41–66.

6. D. Levy, "Offshoring in the new global political economy," *Journal of Management Studies* 42 (2005): 685–693.

7. J. Schmidt and T. Keil, "What makes a resource valuable?" *Academy of Management Review* 38 (2013): 206–228.

8. "Can this IBMer keep Big Blue's edge?" *Bloomberg Businessweek,* 31 October 2011, 31–32.

9. "Apple: iThrone," *Economist*, 31 January 2015, 53.

10. Y. Luo, S. Wang, Q. Zheng, and V. Jayaraman, "Task attributes and process integration in business process offshoring," *Journal of International Business Studies* 43 (2012): 498–524.

11. T. Chi and A. Seth, "A dynamic model of the choice of mode for exploiting complementary capabilities," *Journal of International Business Studies* 40 (2009): 365–387; A. Hess and F. Rothaermel, "When are assets complementary?" *Strategic Management Journal* 32 (2011): 895–909.

12. J. Barney, *Gaining and Sustaining Competitive Advantage* (Reading, MA: Addison-Wesley, 1997) 155.

13. Y. Li, M. W. Peng, and C. Macaulay, "Market-political ambidexterity during institutional transitions," *Strategic Organization* 11 (2012): 205–213; M. W. Peng, S. Sun, and L. Markoczy, "Human capital and CEO compensation during institutional transitions," *Journal of Management Studies* 52 (2015): 117–147.

14. A. Chatterji and A. Patro, "Dynamic capabilities and managing human capital," *Academy of Management Perspectives* 28 (2014): 395–408.

15. D. Burrus, *Flash Foresight* (New York: HarperCollins, 2011) 11.

16. "It's not us, it's you: Why customers are breaking up with IBM," *Bloomberg Businessweek*, 26 May 2014, 58–63.

17. The author's paraphrase based on T. Friedman, *The World Is Flat* (New York: Farrar, Straus, & Giroux, 2005) 237.

5

1. C. Arkolakis, S. Demidova, P. Kelnow, and A. Rodriguez-Clare, "Endogenous variety and the gains from trade," *American Economic Review* 98 (2008): 444–450; A. Smith, "Follow me to the innovation frontier?" *Journal of International Business Studies* 45 (2014): 248–274.

2. M. W. Peng and K. Meyer, "Winning the future markets for UK manufacturing output," *Future of Manufacturing Project Evidence Paper* 25 (London: UK Government Office for Science, 2013).

3. I. Colantone and L. Sleuwaegen, "International trade, exit, and entry," *Journal of International Business Studies* 41 (2010): 1240–1257.

4. M. W. Peng, "The resource-based view and international business," *Journal of Management* 27 (2001): 803–829.

5. B. Cassiman and E. Golovko, "Innovation and internationalization through exports," *Journal of International Business Studies* 42 (2011): 56–75; R. Salomon and B. Jin, "Do leading or lagging firms learn more from exporting?" *Strategic Management Journal* 31 (2010): 1088–1113.

6. "Obama: Venture capitalist-in-chief," *Bloomberg Businessweek*, 9 August 2010, 28–31.

7. M. Porter, *Competitive Advantage of Nations* (New York: Free Press, 1990).

8. D. Bernhofen and J. Brown, "An empirical assessment of the comparative advantage gains from trade," *American Economic Review* 95 (2005): 208–225.

9. "Don't go to Rio for a deal on an iPad," *Bloomberg Businessweek,* 13 December 2010, 13–14.

10. Tire Industry Association (TIA), "Tire Industry Association expresses disappointment with President's decision concerning Chinese tire tariff," Bowie, MD: TIA (14 September 2009, www.tireindustry.org).

11. "Japan's micro farms face extinction," *Bloomberg Businessweek*, 6 January 2014, 14–15.

12. "A row over cows," *Economist* , 17 February 2011, www.economist.com.

13. "DHL will pay $9.4M fine to settle shipping dispute," *USA Today*, 7 August 2009, 2A.

14. US-China Business Council, "US exports to China," *China Business Review* (July 2010): 46–49.

6

1. United Nations, *World Investment Report 2014* (New York and Geneva: United Nations, 2014) ix.

2. T. Khoury and M. W. Peng, "Does institutional reform of intellectual property rights lead to more inbound FDI?" *Journal of World Business* 46 (2011): 337–345; S. Sun, M. W. Peng, R. Lee, and W. Tan, "Institutional open access at home and outward internationalization," *Journal of World Business* 50 (2015): 234–246.

3. R. Aggarwal, J. Berrill, E. Hutson, and C. Kearney, "What is a multinational corporation?" *International Business Review* 20 (2011): 557–577.

4. United Nations, *World Investment Report 2009* (New York and Geneva: United Nations, 2009) xxi.

5. J. Dunning, *Multinational Enterprises and the Global Economy* (Reading, MA: Addison-Wesley, 1993).

6. "Vietnam: An Asian-tiger wannabe (again)," *Bloomberg Businessweek,* 21 June 2010, 12–13.

7. R. Tasker, "Pepperoni power," *Far Eastern Economic Review,* 14 November 2002, 59–60.

8. S. Beugelsdijk and R. Mudambi, "MNEs as border-crossing multi-location enterprises," *Journal of International Business Studies* 44 (2013): 413–426.

9. S. Chen, "A general TCE model of international business institutions," *Journal of International Business Studies* 41 (2010): 935–959.

10. K. Meyer and E. Sinani, "When and where does FDI generate positive spillovers," *Journal of International Business Studies* 40 (2009): 1075–1094.

11. United Nations, *World Investment Report 2010* (New York and Geneva: United Nations, 2010) 17.

12. F. Barry and C. Kearney, "MNEs and industrial structure in host countries," *Journal of International Business Studies* 37 (2006): 392–406.

13. M. Zhao, S. Park, and N. Zhou, 2014, "MNC strategy and social adaptation in emerging markets," *Journal of International Business Studies* 45 (2014): 842–861.

7

1. "The Big Mac index: A basket of sliders," *Economist*, 26 July 2014, 61.

2. "McCurrencies," *Economist,* 27 May 2006, 74.

3. M. Kreinin, 2006, *International Economics* (Cincinnati: Cengage Learning, 2006) 183.

4. R. Lyons, *The Microstructure Approach to Exchange Rates* (Cambridge, MA: MIT Press, 2001) 1.

5. "Bretton Woods II," *Guardian*, 14 November 2008, http://www.guardian.co.uk [accessed 24 July 2009].

6. "Life amid the ruins," *Bloomberg Businessweek*, 28 June 2010, 52–60.

7. R. Carbaugh, *International Economics*, 11th ed. (Cincinnati: Cengage Learning, 2007) 360.

8. "Global foreign-exchange turnover," *Economist,* 14 September 2013, 97.

9. S. Lee and M. Makhija, "The effect of domestic uncertainty on the real options value of international investments," *Journal of International Business Studies* 40 (2009): 405–420.

10. "A mixed blessing," *Economist*, 20 May 2010, 68.

11. R. Faff and A. Marshall, "International evidence on the determinants of foreign exchange rate exposure of multinational corporations," *Journal of International Business Studies* 36 (2005): 539–558.

8

1. World Trade Organization (WTO), *10 Benefits of the WTO Trading System* (Geneva: WTO, 2005) 3.

2. "The future of globalization," *Economist*, 29 July 2006, 11.

3. "WTO: No more grand bargains," *Economist*, 9 August 2014, 10.

4. "In the twilight of Doha," *Economist*, 29 July 2006, 63.

5. P. Bustos, "Trade liberalization, exports, and technology upgrading," *American Economic Review* 101 (2011): 304–340.

6. Delegation of the European Commission to the USA, *The European Union: A Guide for Americans* (Washington: Delegation of the European Commission to the USA, 2005) 2.

7. M. Feldstein, "The failure of the euro," *Foreign Affairs*, January 2012, 105–116.

8. N. Berggruen and N. Gardels, "The next Europe," *Foreign Affairs*, July 2013, 134–142.

9. M. Matthijs, "David Cameron's dangerous game," *Foreign Affairs*, September 2013, 10–16.

10. "How Britain could leave Europe," *Economist*, 17 December 2011, 104.

11. "Babelling on," *Economist*, 16 December 2006, 50.

12. "Mexico: Was NAFTA worth it?" *BusinessWeek*, 22 December 2003, www.businessweek.com.

13. Foreign Affairs, Trade, and Development Canada, "January 1 marks 20th anniversary of North American Free Trade Agreement," press release, 1 January 2014, www.international.gc.ca.

14. "The stranger next door," *Bloomberg Businessweek*, 6 May 2013, 8–9.

15. "Deeper, better NAFTA," *Economist*, 4 January 2014, 8.

16. J. Sargent and L. Matthews, "The drivers of evolution/upgrading in Mexico's maquiladoras," *Journal of World Business* 41 (2006): 233–246.

17. "Latin America's great divide," *Bloomberg Businessweek*, 9 June 2014, 18–20.

18. US Trade Representative, *The Case for CAFTA*, February 2005, www.ustr.gov.

19. A. Rugman, *The Regional Multinationals* (Cambridge, UK: Cambridge University Press, 2005) 215.

20. G. Qian, T. Khoury, M. W. Peng, and Z. Qian, "The performance implications of intra- and inter-regional geographic diversification," *Strategic Management Journal* 31 (2010): 1018–1030.

9

1. M. Hitt, R. D. Ireland, S. M. Camp, and D. Sexton, "Strategic entrepreneurship," *Strategic Management Journal* 22 (2001): 480.

2. S. Shane and S. Venkataraman, "The promise of entrepreneurship as a field of research," *Academy of Management Review* 25 (2000): 218.

3. M. W. Peng, S. Lee, and S. Hong, "Entrepreneurs as intermediaries," *Journal of World Business* 49 (2014): 21–31.

4. P. McDougall and B. Oviatt, "International entrepreneurship," *Academy of Management Journal* 43 (2000): 903.

5. S. Lee, M. W. Peng, and S. Song, "Governments, entrepreneurs, and positive externalities," *European Management Journal* 31 (2013): 333–347.

6. D. Kelley, N. Bosma, and J. Amoros, *Global Entrepreneurship Monitor 2010 Global Report* (Wellesley, MA: Babson College/GEM, 2011).

7. M. W. Peng, Y. Yamakawa, and S. Lee, "Bankruptcy laws and entrepreneur-friendliness," *Entrepreneur Theory and Practice* 34 (2010): 517–530; Y. Zhu, X. Wittman, and M. W. Peng, "Institution-based barriers to innovation in SMEs in China," *Asia Pacific Journal of Management* 29 (2012): 1131–1142.

8. "Son also rises," *Economist*, 27 November 2010, 71–72.

9. "In Russia, Facebook is more than a social network," *Bloomberg Businessweek*, 3 January 2011, 32–33.

10. S. Lee, Y. Yamakawa, M. W. Peng, and J. Barney, "How do bankruptcy laws affect entrepreneurship development around the world?" *Journal of Business Venturing* 26 (2011): 505–520.

11. Y. Lu, L. Zhou, G. Bruton, and W. Li, "Capabilities as a mediator linking resources and the international performance of entrepreneurial firms in an emerging economy," *Journal of International Business Studies* 41 (2010): 419–436; Y. Yamakawa, M. W. Peng, and D. Deeds, "Rising from the ashes: Cognitive determinants of venture growth after entrepreneurial failure," *Entrepreneurship Theory and Practice* 39 (2015): 209–236.

12. "The Megabus effect," *Bloomberg Businessweek,* 11 April 2011, 62–67.

13. "The dirtiest job on the Internet," *Bloomberg Businessweek*, 5 December 2011, 95–97.

14. Y. Yamakawa, M. W. Peng, and D. Deeds, "What drives new ventures to internationalize from emerging to developed economies?" *Entrepreneurship Theory and Practice* 32 (2008): 59–82.

15. D. Ahlstrom, G. Bruton, and K. Yeh, "Venture capital in China," *Asia Pacific Journal of Management* 24 (2007): 247–268.

16. Y. Yamakawa, S. Khavul, M. W. Peng, and D. Deeds, "Venturing from emerging economies," *Strategic Entrepreneurship Journal* 7 (2013): 181–196.

17. M. W. Peng and A. York, "Behind intermediary performance in export trade," *Journal of International Business Studies* 32 (2001): 327–346.

10

1. K. Meyer, S. Estrin, S. Bhaumik, and M. W. Peng, "Institutions, resources, and entry strategies in emerging economies," *Strategic Management Journal* 30 (2009): 61–80.

2. M. Guillen and E. Garcia-Canal, "How to conquer new markets with old skills," *Harvard Business Review*, November (2010): 118–122; M. W. Peng, "The resource-based view and international business," *Journal of Management* 27 (2001): 803–829.

3. S. Newman, C. Rickert, and R. Schaap, "Investing in the post-recession world," *Harvard Business Review* (January 2011): 150–155.

4. "Rulers of the new silk world," *Economist*, 5 June 2010, 75–77.

5. "Short takes: Autos," *China Business Review* (January–March 2011): 8.

6. M. W. Peng and D. Wang, "Innovation capability and foreign direct investment," *Management International Review* 40 (2000): 80.

7. D. Xu and O. Shenkar, "Institutional distance and the multinational enterprise," *Academy of Management Review* 27 (2002): 608.

8. M. W. Peng, "The global strategy of emerging multinationals from China," *Global Strategy Journal* 2 (2012): 97–107.

9. J. G. Frynas, K. Mellahi, and G. Pigman, "First mover advantages in international business and firm-specific political resources," *Strategic Management Journal* 27 (2006): 321–345.

10. M. W. Peng, S. Lee, and J. Tan, "The *keiretsu* in Asia," *Journal of International Management* 7 (2001): 253–276.

11. "Land of war and opportunity," *Bloomberg Businessweek*, 10 January 2011, 46–54.

12. "Cisco's brave new world," *BusinessWeek*, 24 November 2008, 56–68.

13. G. Gao and Y. Pan, "The pace of MNEs' sequential entries," *Journal of International Business Studies* 41 (2010): 1572–1580; Y. Luo and M. W. Peng, "Learning to compete in a transition economy," *Journal of International Business Studies* 30 (1999): 269–296.

14. M. W. Peng, Y. Zhou, and A. York, "Behind make or buy decisions in export strategy," *Journal of World Business* 41 (2006): 289–300.

15. A. Chintakananda, A. York, H. O'Neill, and M. W. Peng, "Structuring dyadic relationships between export producers and intermediaries," *European Journal of International Management* 3 (2009): 302–327.

16. United Nations, *World Investment Report 2014* (New York and Geneva: United Nations, 2014) 81.

11

1. J. Reuer, T. Tong, B. Tyler, and A. Arino, "Executive preferences for governance modes and exchange partners," *Strategic Management Journal* 34 (2013): 1104–1122; H. Yang, Z. Lin, and M. W. Peng, "Behind acquisitions of alliance partners," *Academy of Management Journal* 54 (2011): 1069–1080.

2. Z. Lin, M. W. Peng, H. Yang, and S. Sun, "How do networking and learning drive M&As?" *Strategic Management Journal* 30 (2009): 1113–1132.

3. W. Shi, S. Sun, and M. W. Peng, "Sub-national institutional contingencies, network positions, and IJV partner selection," *Journal of Management Studies* 49 (2012): 1221–1245.

4. S. Lebedev, M. W. Peng, E. Xie, and C. Stevens, "Mergers and acquisitions in and out of emerging economies," *Journal of World Business* (2015, in press); M. W. Peng, "Making M&As fly in China," *Harvard Business Review* (March 2006): 26–27.

5. "The surprising strength of Spain's Santander," *Bloomberg Businessweek*, 5 July 2010, 41–42.

6. "Open skies and flights of fancy," *Economist*, 4 October 2003, 67.

7. T. Tong, J. Reuer, and M. W. Peng, "International joint ventures and the value of growth options," *Academy of Management Journal* 51 (2008): 1014–1029.

8. D. Zoogah and M. W. Peng, "What determines the performance of strategic alliance managers?" *Asia Pacific Journal of Management* 28 (2011): 483–508.

9. W. Shi, S. Sun, B. Pinkham, and M. W. Peng, "Domestic alliance network to attract foreign partners," *Journal of International Business Studies* 45 (2014): 338–362.

10. A. Phene, S. Tallman, and P. Almeida, "When do acquisitions facilitate technological exploration and exploitation?" *Journal of Management* 38 (2012): 753–783.

11. "Mergers and acquisitions: The new rules of attraction," *Economist*, 15 November 2014, 67.

12. C. Moschieri and J. Campa, "The European M&A industry," *Academy of Management Perspectives* 23 (2009): 71–87.

13. G. Andrade, M. Mitchell, and E. Stafford, "New evidence and perspectives on mergers," *Journal of Economic Perspectives* 15 (2001): 103–120.

14. "Jackpot! How Lenovo found treasure in the PC industry's trash," *Bloomberg Businessweek*, 12 May 2014, 46–51.

15. M. W. Peng and O. Shenkar, "Joint venture dissolution as corporate divorce," *Academy of Management Executive* 16 (2002): 92–105.

16. D. Siegel and K. Simons, "Assessing the effects of M&As on firm performance," *Strategic Management Journal* 31 (2010): 903–916.

17. "Bank of America-Merrill Lynch: A $50 billion deal from hell," *Wall Street Journal,* 29 January 2009, blogs.wsj.com.

18. "Hi-yah! Alcatel-Lucent chops away at years of failure," *Bloomberg Businessweek*, 2 May 2011, 29.

19. "Coming unstuck," *Economist*, 9 August 2014, 53–54.

12

1. T. Levitt, "The globalization of markets," *Harvard Business Review* (May–June 1983): 92–102.

2. C. Bartlett and S. Ghoshal, *Managing Across Borders* (Boston: Harvard Business School Press, 1989).

3. R. Hodgetts, "Dow Chemical CEO William Stavropoulos on structure," *Academy of Management Executive* 13 (1999): 30.

4. X. Ma and A. Delios, "Home-country headquarters and an MNE's subsequent within-country diversification," *Journal of International Business Studies* 41 (2010): 517–525.

5. T. Wakayama, J. Shintaku, and T. Amano, "What Panasonic learned in China." *Harvard Business Review* (December 2012): 109–113.

6. "Cisco's brave new world," *BusinessWeek*, 24 November 2008, 56–66.

7. C. K. Prahalad and K. Lieberthal, "The end of corporate imperialism," *Harvard Business Review* (August 1998): 68–79.

8. S. Morris, R. Hammond, and S. Snell, "A microfoundations approach to transnational capabilities," *Journal of International Business Studies* 45 (2014): 405–427.

9. "The great innovation debate," *Economist*, 12 January 2013, 11.

10. Bartlett and Ghoshal, *Managing Across Borders*, p. 209.

11. A. Gupta and V. Govindarajan, *Global Strategy and Organization* (New York: Wiley, 2004) 104.

12. P. Gooderham, D. Minbaeva, and T. Pedersen, "Governance mechanisms for the promotion of social capital for knowledge transfer in multinational corporations," *Journal of Management Studies* 48 (2011): 123–150.

13. M. Kotabe, D. Dunlap-Hinkler, R. Parente, and H. Mishra, "Determinants of cross-national knowledge transfer and its effect on firm innovation," *Journal of International Business Studies* 38 (2007): 259–282.

14. A. Witty, "Research and develop," *The World in 2011* (London: The Economist, 2011) 140. Witty is CEO of GSK.

15. K. Meyer, R. Mudambi, and R. Narula, "Multinational enterprises and local contexts," *Journal of Management Studies* 48 (2011): 235–252.

16. P. Ghemawat, "The cosmopolitan corporation," *Harvard Business Review* (May 2011): 92–99.

13

1. P. Cappelli, "HR for neophytes," *Harvard Business Review* (October 2013): 25–27; C. Fey, S. Morgulis-Yukushev, H. Park, and I. Bjorkman, "Opening the black box of the relationship between HRM practices and firm performance," *Journal of International Business Studies* 40 (2009): 690–712.

2. G. Peng and P. Beamish, "MNC subsidiary size and expatriate control," *Journal of World Business* 49 (2014): 51–62.

3. D. Vora and T. Kostova, "A model of dual organizational identification in the context of the multinational enterprise," *Journal of Organizational Behavior* 28 (2007): 327–350.

4. Y. Chang, Y. Gong, and M. W. Peng, "Expatriate knowledge transfer, subsidiary absorptive capacity, and subsidiary performance," *Academy of Management Journal* 55 (2012): 927–948.

5. "A tale of two expats," *Economist*, 31 January 2011, 62–64.

6. R. L. Tung, "Selection and training procedures for US, European, and Japanese multinationals," *California Management Review* 25 (1982): 57–71.

7. S. Carraher, S. Sullivan, and M. Crocitto, "Mentoring across global boundaries," *Journal of International Business Studies* 39 (2009): 1310–1326.

8. F. Cooke, D. Saini, and J. Wang, "Talent management in China and India," *Journal of World Business* 49 (2014): 225–235.

9. C. Schmidt, "The battle for China's talent," *Harvard Business Review* (March 2011): 25–27.

10. "Chattanooga shoo-shoo," *Economist*, 22 February 2014, 57.

11. "Unions, Inc.," *Economist*, 6 April 2013, 68.

12. "A new labor movement is born in China," *Bloomberg Businessweek*, 14 June 2010, 8.

13. M. W. Peng, "The global strategy of emerging multinationals from China," *Global Strategy Journal* 2 (2012): 97–107.

14. C. Chen, "New trends in allocation preferences," *Academy of Management Journal* 38 (1995): 408–428.

15. "Developing your global know-how," *Harvard Business Review* (March 2011): 72.

16. W. Arthur, W. Bennett, P. Edens, and S. Bell, "Effectiveness of training in organizations," *Journal of Applied Psychology* 88 (2003): 234–245.

17. A. Yeung, "Setting the people up for success," *Human Resource Management* 45 (2006): 267–275.

18. D. Zoogah, D. Vora, O. Richard, and M. W. Peng, "Strategic alliance team diversity, coordination, and effectiveness," *International Journal of Human Resource Management* 22 (2011): 510–529.

19. B. Becker and M. Huselid, "Strategic human resource management," *Journal of Management* 32 (2006): 907.

20. J. Combs, D. Ketchen, A. Hall, and Y. Liu, "Do high performance work practices matter?" *Personnel Psychology* 59 (2006): 501–528; K. Jiang, D. Lepak, J. Hu, and J. Baer, "How does human resource management influence organizational outcomes?" *Academy of Management Journal* 55 (2012): 1264–1294.

21. S. Meisinger, "The four Cs of the HR profession," *Human Resource Management* 44 (2005): 189–194.

22. A. Ariss, W. Cascio, and J. Paauwe, "Talent management," *Journal of World Business* 49 (2014): 173–179

23. "Secrets of an HR superstar," *BusinessWeek*, 19 April 2007, 66.

14

1. "Wendy's goes beyond the dollar menu in Japan," *Bloomberg Businessweek*, 9 January 2012, 25–26.

2. T. Levitt, "The globalization of markets," *Harvard Business Review* (May–June 1983): 92–102.

3. D. Alden, J. Kelley, P. Riefler, J. Lee, and G. Soutar, "The effect of global company animosity on global brand attitudes in emerging and developed markets," *Journal of International Marketing* 21 (2013): 17–38.

4. D. Griffith, "Understanding multi-institutional convergence effects on international market segments and global marketing strategy," *Journal of World Business* 45 (2010): 59–67.

5. D. Holt, J. Quelch, and E. Taylor, "How global brands compete," *Harvard Business Review* (September 2004): 68–75.

6. "Africa calling," *Economist*, 7 June 2008, 78.

7. M. Porter, *Competitive Advantage* (New York: Free Press, 1985).

8. R. Slone, "Leading a supply chain turnaround," *Harvard Business Review* (October 2004): 116.

9. The following discussion draws heavily from H. Lee, "The triple-A supply chain," *Harvard Business Review* (October 204): 102–112.

10. C. Bode, S. Wagner, K. Petersen, and L. Ellram, "Understanding responses to supply chain disruptions," *Academy of Management Journal* 54 (2011): 833–856.

11. M. W. Peng, Y. Zhou, and A. York, "Behind make or buy decisions in export strategy," *Journal of World Business* 41 (2006): 289–300.

12. L. Mesquita and T. Brush, "Untangling safeguard and production coordination effects in long-term buyer-supplier relationships," *Academy of Management Journal* 51 (2008): 785–807.

13. Y. Li, E. Xie, H. Teo, and M. W. Peng, "Formal control and social control in domestic and international buyer-supplier relationships," *Journal of Operations Management* 28 (2010): 333–344.

14. E. Katok and V. Pavlov, "Fairness in supply chain contracts," *Journal of Operations Management* 31 (2013): 129–137.

15. P. Skilton, "Value creation, value capture, and supply chain structure," *Journal of Supply Chain Management* 50 (2014): 74–93.

16. C. Schulze and B. Skiera, "Not all fun and games," *Journal of Marketing* 78 (2014): 1–19.

17. "The MySpace generation," *Bloomberg Businessweek*, 12 December 2005, 92.

18. J. Schumann, F. von Wangenheim, and N. Groene, "Targeted online advertising," *Journal of Marketing* 78 (2014): 59–75.

19. P. Kotler, N. Rackham, and S. Krishnaswamy, "Ending the war between sales and marketing," *Harvard Business Review* (July 2006): 68–78.

20. R. Leuschner, D. Rogers, and F. Charvet, "A meta-analysis of supply chain integration and firm performance," *Journal of Supply Chain Management* 49 (2013): 34–57.

15

1. K. Davis, "The case for and against business assumption of social responsibilities," *Academy of Management Journal* 16 (1973): 312.

2. T. Devinney, A. McGahan, and M. Zollo, "A research agenda for global stakeholder strategy," *Global Strategy Journal* 3 (2013): 325–337 .

3. M. Friedman, "The social responsibility of business is to increase its profits," *New York Times Magazine*, 13 September 1970, 32–33.

4. A. Gore, *An Inconvenient Truth* (Emmaus, PA: Rodale Press, 2006).

5. "The other oil spill," *Economist*, 26 June 2010, 71–73.

6. D. Siegel, "Green management matters only if it yields more green," *Academy of Management Perspectives* 23 (2009): 5–16.

7. A. Marcus and A. Fremeth, "Green management matters regardless," *Academy of Management Perspectives* 23 (2009): 17–26.

8. "Message from Howard Schultz," *Starbucks Global Responsibility Report 2010* (Seattle: Starbucks, 2011, www.starbucks.com).

9. J. Mackey, "What is it that only I can do?" *Harvard Business Review* (January 2011): 119–123. Mackey is a co-founder of Whole Foods.

10. A. Hillman and G. Keim, "Shareholder value, stakeholder management, and social issues," *Strategic Management Journal* 22 (2001): 125–139.

11. B. Lev, C. Petrovits, and S. Radhakrishnan, "Is doing good good for you?" *Strategic Management Journal* 31 (2010): 182–200.

12. T. Wang and P. Bansal, "Social responsibility in new ventures," *Strategic Management Journal* 33 (2012): 1135–1153.

13. J. Surroca, J. Tribo, and S. Waddock, "Corporate responsibility and financial performance," *Strategic Management Journal* 31 (2010): 463–490.

14. T. Devinney, "Is the socially responsible corporation a myth?" *Academy of Management Perspectives* 23 (2009): 53.

15. "If it's good enough for Big Oil ..." *Bloomberg Businessweek*, 17 November 2014, 10–11.

16. W. Su, M. W. Peng, W. Tan, and Y. Cheung, "The signaling effect of corporate social responsibility in emerging economies," *Journal of Business Ethics* (2015, in press).

INDEX

A

B

C

D

E

G

H

I

J

K

N

O

P

Q

R

S

T

U

V

W

Y

Z

CHAPTER REVIEW 1
Globalizing Business

CHAPTER SUMMARY

1-1 Explain the concepts of international business and global business.

- International business (IB) is typically defined as (1) a business (firm) that engages in international (cross-border) economic activities, or (2) the action of doing business abroad.
- Multinational enterprises (MNEs) are firms that engage in foreign direct investment (FDI).
- Global business is defined in this book as business around the globe.
- Emerging economies contribute about 50% of global gross domestic product (measured by purchasing power parity, PPP).
- Viewed as a pyramid, the global economy has one billion people at the top and another billion in the second tier. The majority of humanity, approximately five billion people, makes up the base of the pyramid.

1-2 Give three reasons why it is important to study global business.

- To better advance your employability and career in the global economy.
- To better prepare for possible expatriate assignments abroad.
- Expatriate managers generally command an international premium for taking overseas positions.
- To enhance your competence in interacting with foreign suppliers, partners, and competitors, and in working for foreign-owned employers in your country.

1-3 Articulate the fundamental question that the study of global business seeks to answer and two perspectives from which to answer it.

- Our most fundamental question is: What determines the success and failure of firms around the globe?
- The two core perspectives are (1) the institution-based view and (2) the resource-based view.
- The institution-based view suggests that the success and failure of firms are enabled and constrained by different rules of the game.
- The resource-based view says that successful firms have certain valuable and unique firm-specific resources and capabilities that are not shared by competitors in the same environments.
- We develop a unified framework by organizing materials in every chapter according to the two perspectives guided by the fundamental question.

1-4 Identify three ways of understanding what globalization is.

- The three views of globalization are (1) that it is a recent phenomenon, (2) that it is a one-directional evolution since the dawn of human history, and (3) that it is a process similar to the swing of a pendulum.
- Advocates of globalization say that it increases economic growth, standards of living, technology sharing, and cultural integration.
- Critics argue that globalization undermines wages in rich countries, exploits workers in poor countries, gives MNEs too much power, destroys the environment, and promotes inequality.

KEY TERMS AND DEFINITIONS

International business (IB) (1) A business (firm) that engages in international (cross-border) economic activities or (2) the action of doing business abroad.

Multinational enterprise (MNE) A firm that engages in foreign direct investment and operates in multiple countries.

Foreign direct investment (FDI) Investment in, controlling, and managing value-added activities in other countries.

Global business Business around the globe.

Emerging economy (emerging market) A developing country.

Gross domestic product (GDP) The sum of value added by resident firms, households, and governments operating in an economy.

Purchasing power parity (PPP) A conversion that determines the equivalent amount of goods and services different currencies can purchase. This conversion is usually used to capture the differences in cost of living in different countries.

BRIC An acronym for the emerging economies of Brazil, Russia, India, and China.

BRICS An acronym for the emerging economies of Brazil, Russia, India, China, and South Africa.

Triad Three regions of developed economies (North America, Western Europe, and Japan).

Base of the pyramid (BoP) The vast majority of humanity, about five billion people, who make less than $2,000 a year.

Expatriate manager (expat) A manager who works outside his or her native country.

International premium A significant pay raise commanded by expatriates when working overseas.

Institution-based view A leading perspective in global business that suggests that firm performance is, at least in part, determined by the institutional frameworks governing firm behavior around the world.

Institution Formal and informal rules of the game.

Institutional framework Formal and informal institutions that govern individual and firm behavior.

Resource-based view A leading perspective in global business that suggests that firm performance is, at least in part, determined by its internal resources and capabilities.

CHAPTER REVIEW 1

Liability of foreignness The inherent disadvantage that foreign firms experience in host countries because of their nonnative status.

Globalization The close integration of countries and peoples of the world.

Risk management Identification and assessment of risks and the preparation to minimize the impact of high-risk, unfortunate events.

Scenario planning A technique to prepare and plan for multiple scenarios (either high or low risk).

Semiglobalization A perspective that suggests that barriers to market integration at borders are high but not high enough to completely insulate countries from each other.

Nongovernmental organization (NGO) An organization that is not affiliated with governments.

EXHIBIT 1.1 THE GLOBAL ECONOMIC PYRAMID

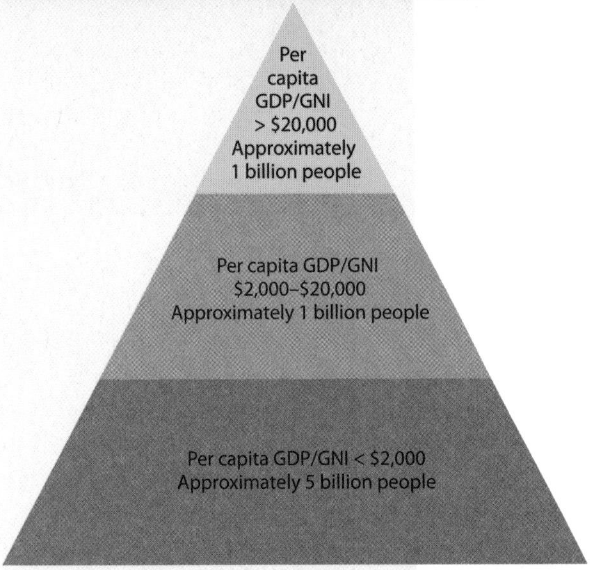

Source: C. K. Prahalad and S. Hart, "The fortune at the bottom of the pyramid," Strategy+Business 26 (2002): 54–67 and S. Hart, Capitalism at the Crossroads (Philadelphia: Wharton School Publishing, 2005) 111.

- Semiglobalization is more complex than extremes of total isolation and total globalization and provides a more accurate picture of the current global economy.

1-5 Appreciate the size of the global economy *and* the strengths of multinationals.

- MNEs, especially large ones from developed economies, are sizeable economic entities.
- Emerging economies have MNEs in the *Fortune* Global 500 as well.
- Current and would-be business leaders need to be aware of their own hidden pro-globalization bias.
- The rapid globalization of the 1990s saw significant backlash around the turn of the century marked by protests and terrorist attacks, largely attributed to a sense of powerlessness in the face of rapid global change.
- Significant opposition to globalization comes from nongovernmental organizations (NGOs) and raises valid points about how MNEs' actions affect various stakeholders around the world.

REVIEW QUESTIONS

1. What is the difference between international business and global business, as defined in this chapter?
2. Why are you studying global business? How does it affect your future?
3. What is the most fundamental question driving global business? Why is it important?
4. How would you describe an institution-based view of global business?
5. How would you describe a resource-based view of global business?
6. After comparing the three views of globalization, which seems the most logical and sensible to you?

CRITICAL DISCUSSION QUESTIONS

1. A classmate says: "Global business is relevant for top executives such as CEOs in large companies. I am just a lowly student who will struggle to gain an entry-level job, probably in a small domestic company. Why should I care about it?" How do you convince her that she should care about it?
2. ***ON ETHICS:*** What are some of the darker sides (in other words, costs) associated with globalization? How can business leaders make sure that the benefits of their various actions (such as outsourcing) outweigh their drawbacks (such as job losses in developed economies)?
3. ***ON ETHICS:*** Some argue that aggressively investing in emerging economies is not only economically beneficial but also highly ethical, because it may potentially lift many people out of poverty. However, others caution that in the absence of reasonable hopes of decent profits, rushing to emerging economies is reckless. How would you participate in this debate?

CHAPTER REVIEW
Understanding Politics, Laws, & Economics

2

CHAPTER SUMMARY

2-1 Identify two types of institutions.

- Institutions are commonly defined as "the rules of the game."
- There are two types of institutions: formal and informal. Each has different supportive pillars.

2-2 Explain how institutions reduce uncertainty.

- Institutions' key function is to reduce uncertainty, curtail transaction costs, and combat opportunism. Institutions accomplish these things by reducing the range of acceptable actions.

2-3 Identify the two core propositions underpinning an institution-based view of global business.

- Proposition 1: Managers and firms *rationally* pursue their interests and make choices within formal and informal institutional constraints in a given institutional framework.
- Proposition 2: When formal constraints are unclear or fail, informal constraints will play a *larger* role.

2-4 List the differences between democracy and totalitarianism.

- Democracy is a political system in which citizens elect representatives to govern the country.
- Freedom of expression is a fundamental aspect of democracy.
- Totalitarianism is a political system in which one person or party exercises absolute political control.
- Totalitarian systems can be communist, right-wing, theocratic, or tribal.
- Totalitarian systems generally carry a greater degree of political risk than democracies do.

2-5 List the differences among civil law, common law, and theocratic law.

- Civil law uses comprehensive statutes and codes as a primary means to form legal judgments and as such is less confrontational.
- Common law is shaped by precedents and traditions from previous judicial decisions and is more confrontational as plaintiffs and defendants argue the relevance of precedent to specific cases.
- Theocratic law is a legal system based on religious teachings, such as Islamic law.

2-6 Articulate the importance of property rights and intellectual property rights.

- Protection of property rights by a functioning legal system is fundamental to economic development.
- Patents, copyrights, and trademarks are the three primary ways that intellectual property is recognized and protected.
- The intangible nature of intellectual property rights makes enforcement difficult, and weak enforcement makes counterfeiting a rational choice for certain firms.

2-7 List the differences among market economy, command economy, and mixed economy.

- A pure market economy is characterized by *laissez faire* and total control by market forces.

KEY TERMS AND DEFINITIONS

Institutional transition Fundamental and comprehensive changes introduced to the formal and informal rules of the game that affect organizations as players.

Regulatory pillar The coercive power of governments exercised through laws, regulations, and rules.

Normative pillar The mechanisms through which norms influence individual and firm behavior.

Cognitive pillar The internalized taken-for-granted values and beliefs that guide individual and firm behavior.

Transaction cost Cost associated with economic transactions or, more broadly, the costs of doing business.

Opportunism The act of seeking self-interest with guile.

Political system The rules of the game on how a country is governed politically.

Democracy A political system in which citizens elect representatives to govern the country on their behalf.

Totalitarianism (dictatorship) A political system in which one person or party exercises absolute political control over the population.

Political risk Risk associated with political changes that may negatively impact domestic and foreign firms.

Legal system The rules of the game on how a country's laws are enacted and enforced.

Civil law A legal tradition that uses comprehensive statutes and codes as a primary means to form legal judgments.

Common law A legal tradition that is shaped by precedents from previous judicial decisions.

Theocratic law A legal system based on religious teachings.

Property right Legal right to use an economic property (resource) and to derive income and benefits from it.

Intellectual property (IP) Intangible property that results from intellectual activity (such as the content of books, videos, and websites).

Intellectual property right (IPR) Legal right associated with the ownership of intellectual property.

Patent Exclusive legal right of inventors to derive income from their inventions through activities such as manufacturing, licensing, or selling.

CHAPTER REVIEW 2

Copyright Exclusive legal right of authors and publishers to publish and disseminate their work.

Trademark Exclusive legal right of firms to use specific names, brands, and designs to differentiate their products from others.

Piracy The unauthorized use of intellectual property rights.

Economic system The rules of the game on how a country is governed economically.

Market economy An economy that is characterized by the "invisible hand" of market forces.

Command economy An economy in which theoretically all factors of production are state-owned and state-controlled, and all supply, demand, and pricing are planned by the government.

Mixed economy An economy that has elements of both a market economy and a command economy.

Washington Consensus A view centered on the unquestioned belief in the superiority of private ownership over state ownership in economic policy making, which is often spearheaded by the US government and the two Washington-based international organizations: the International Monetary Fund and the World Bank.

Moral hazard Recklessness when people and organizations (including firms and governments) do not have to face the full consequences of their actions.

Beijing Consensus A view that questions Washington Consensus' belief in the superiority of private ownership over state ownership, which is often associated with the position held by the Chinese government.

- A pure command economy is defined by government ownership and control of all means of production, distribution, and pricing.
- Most countries operate mixed economies, with a different emphasis on market versus command forces.

2-8 Explain why it is important to understand the different institutions when doing business abroad.

- Have a thorough understanding of the formal institutions before entering a country.
- Recognize when informal relationships must be developed before business can be conducted due to generally weak formal institutions.

REVIEW QUESTIONS

1. Name the one pillar that supports formal institutions and the two additional pillars that support informal institutions.
2. Explain the two core propositions underpinning the institution-based view of global business.
3. How does political risk affect global business?
4. Describe the differences among the three types of legal systems.
5. Name and describe the three economic systems. Which economic system is the most common?
6. Generally, what is the result of strong, effective, market-supporting formal institutions?

CRITICAL DISCUSSION QUESTIONS

1. Without looking at any references, please identify the top three countries with the most significant change in political risk in the last five years. Why do you think so?
2. ***ON ETHICS:*** As a manager, you discover that your multinational firm's products are counterfeited by small family firms that employ child labor in rural Bangladesh. You are aware of the corporate plan to phase out the products soon. You also realize that once you report to the authorities, these firms will be shut down, employees will be out of work, and families and children will be starving. How do you proceed?
3. ***ON ETHICS:*** Your multinational is the largest foreign investor and enjoys good profits in (1) Sudan, where government forces are reportedly cracking down on rebels and killing civilians; and (2) Vietnam, where religious leaders are reportedly being persecuted. As a country manager, you understand that your firm is pressured by activists to exit these countries. The alleged government actions, which you personally find distasteful, are not directly related to your operations. How would you proceed?

EXHIBIT 2.2 INSTITUTIONS, FIRMS, AND FIRM BEHAVIORS

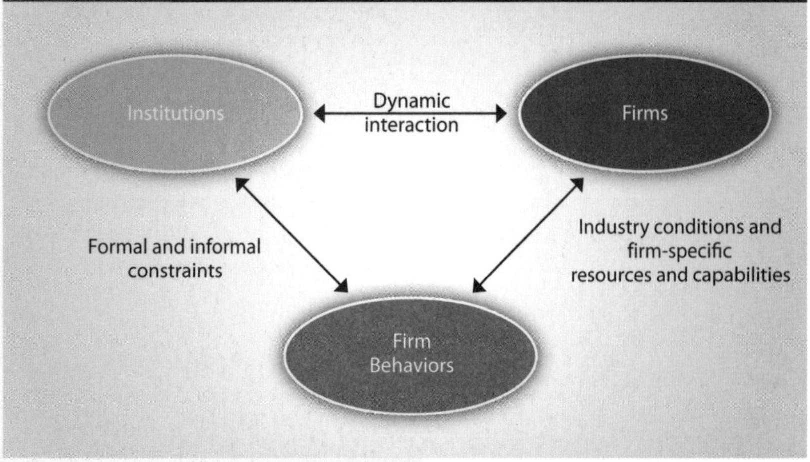

CHAPTER REVIEW 3
Emphasizing Cultures, Ethics, & Norms

CHAPTER SUMMARY

3-1 Explain where informal institutions come from.

- Informal institutions are a pervasive feature of every economy.
- Societies tend to perceive their own culture, ethics, and norms as "natural, rational, and morally right"—a self-centered mentality is known as ethnocentrism.

3-2 Define culture and articulate its two main manifestations.

- Culture is the collective programming of the mind that distinguishes one group from another.
- Managers and firms ignorant of foreign languages and religious traditions may end up with embarrassments and, worse, disasters when doing business around the globe.
- English is the *lingua franca* because of the need in a global market for a common language.
- The four leading religions in the world are Christianity, Islam, Hinduism, and Buddhism.

3-3 Articulate three ways to understand cultural differences.

- The context approach differentiates cultures based on the high- versus low-context dimension.
- The cluster approach groups similar cultures together as clusters and civilizations.
- Hofstede and colleagues have identified five cultural dimensions: (1) power distance, (2) individualism/collectivism, (3) masculinity/femininity, (4) uncertainty avoidance, and (5) long-term orientation.

3-4 Explain why understanding cultural differences is crucial for global business.

- A great deal of global business activity is consistent with the context, cluster, and dimension approaches to cultural differences.

3-5 Explain why ethics is important.

- Ethics refers to the principles, standards, and norms of conduct governing individual and firm behavior.
- When managing ethics overseas, two schools of thought are ethical relativism and ethical imperialism.

3-6 Identify ways to combat corruption.

- The fight against corruption around the world is a long-term, global battle.
- Corruption distorts the basis for competition.
- High levels of corruption and low levels of economic development are strongly correlated.
- Legislation criminalizing corruption must not only be institutionalized, but also must be enforced to be effective.

3-7 Identify norms associated with strategic responses when firms deal with ethical challenges.

- When confronting ethical challenges, individual firms have four strategic choices: (1) reactive, (2) defensive, (3) accommodative, and (4) proactive strategies.
- Using a reactive strategy, a firm is passive and does not feel compelled to act even when problems arise.
- Using a defensive strategy, a firm fights informal pressure and is only concerned with required regulatory compliance.
- Using an accommodative strategy, a firm accepts responsibility and will act beyond what is simply required.

KEY TERMS AND DEFINITIONS

Ethnocentrism A self-centered mentality held by a group of people who perceive their own culture, ethics, and norms as natural, rational, and morally right.

Culture The collective programming of the mind which distinguishes the members of one group or category of people from another.

Lingua franca A global business language.

Context The background against which interaction takes place.

Low-context culture A culture in which communication is usually taken at face value without much reliance on unspoken conditions or assumptions.

High-context culture A culture in which communication relies heavily on the underlying unspoken conditions or assumptions, which are as important as the words used.

Cluster A group of countries that have similar cultures.

Civilization The highest cultural grouping of people and the broadest level of cultural identity people have.

Power distance The extent to which less powerful members within a culture expect and accept that power is distributed unequally.

Individualism The idea that the identity of an individual is fundamentally his or her own.

Collectivism The idea that an individual's identity is fundamentally tied to the identity of his or her collective group.

Masculinity A relatively strong form of societal-level sex-role differentiation whereby men tend to have occupations that reward assertiveness and women tend to work in caring professions.

Femininity A relatively weak form of societal-level sex-role differentiation whereby more women occupy positions that reward assertiveness and more men work in caring professions.

Uncertainty avoidance The extent to which members of a culture accept or avoid ambiguous situations and uncertainty.

Long-term orientation A perspective that emphasizes perseverance and savings for future betterment.

Ethics The principles, standards, and norms of conduct that govern individual and firm behavior.

Code of conduct A set of guidelines for making ethical decisions.

CHAPTER REVIEW 3

Ethical relativism A perspective that suggests that all ethical standards are relative.

Ethical imperialism The absolute belief that "there is only one set of Ethics (with a capital E), and we have it."

Corruption The abuse of public power for private benefits, usually in the form of bribery.

Norm The prevailing practices of relevant players that affect the focal individuals and firms.

Reactive strategy A response to an ethical challenge that often involves denial and belated action to correct problems.

Defensive strategy A response to an ethical challenge that focuses on regulatory compliance.

Accommodative strategy A response to an ethical challenge that involves accepting responsibility.

Proactive strategy A strategy that anticipates ethical challenges and addresses them before they happen.

Cultural intelligence An individual's ability to understand and adjust to new cultures.

- Using a proactive strategy, a firm anticipates institutional changes and does more than required by current regulations.

3-8 Explain how you can acquire cross-cultural literacy.

- It is important to enhance cultural intelligence, leading to cross-cultural literacy.
- Acquisition of cultural intelligence passes through three phases: (1) awareness, (2) knowledge, and (3) skills.
- The most effective way to acquire cultural intelligence is through total immersion in a foreign culture.
- It is crucial to understand and adapt to the changing norms globally.

REVIEW QUESTIONS

1. Where do informal institutions come from?
2. What is the difference between a low-context culture and a high-context culture?
3. Describe the three systems for classifying cultures by clusters.
4. Describe the differences among the five dimensions of Hofstede's framework.
5. What is the difference between ethical relativism and ethical imperialism?
6. How would you define corruption in a business setting?

CRITICAL DISCUSSION QUESTIONS

1. Suppose that you are on a plane and the passenger sitting next to you tries to have a conversation with you. You would like to be nice but don't want to give too much information about yourself (such as your name). He or she asks: "What do you do?" How would you answer the question?
2. ***ON ETHICS:*** Assume that you work for a New Zealand company exporting a container of kiwis to Azerbaijan or Haiti. The customs official informs you that there is a delay in clearing your container through customs, and it may last a month. However, if you are willing to pay an "expediting fee" of US$200, he will try to make it happen in one day. What would you do?
3. ***ON ETHICS:*** Most developed economies have some illegal immigrants. The United States has the largest number with between 10 and 11 million. Without legal US identification (ID) documents, they cannot open bank accounts or buy houses. Many US firms have targeted this population, accepting the ID issued by their native countries and selling them products and services. Some Americans are furious with these business practices. Other Americans suggest that illegal immigrants represent a growth engine in an economy with relatively little growth elsewhere. How would you participate in this debate?

EXHIBIT 3.1 HIGH-CONTEXT VERSUS LOW-CONTEXT CULTURES

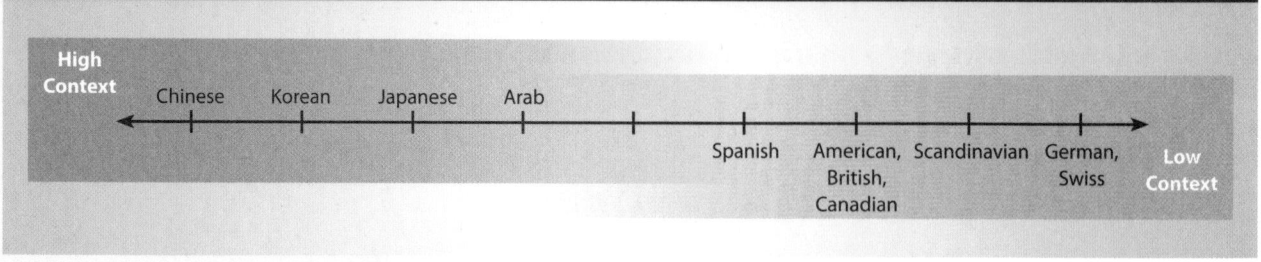

CHAPTER REVIEW 4
Leveraging Resources & Capabilities

CHAPTER SUMMARY

4-1 Define resources and capabilities.

- Resources and capabilities are tangible and intangible assets a firm uses to choose and implement its strategies.
- Although scholars define resources and capabilities differently, in practice the distinctions become blurred.
- Tangible resources and capabilities can be financial, physical, technological, and organizational.
- Intangible resources and capabilities can be human, innovation, and reputational.

4-2 Explain how value is created from a firm's resources and capabilities.

- A value chain consists of a stream of activities from upstream to downstream that add value.
- A SWOT analysis engages managers to ascertain a firm's strengths and weaknesses on an activity-by-activity basis relative to rivals, a process known as benchmarking.
- If a firm's particular activity is unsatisfactory, the manager uses a two-stage decision model to remedy the situation.

4-3 Articulate the difference between keeping an activity in-house and outsourcing it.

- Outsourcing is defined as turning over all or part of an organizational activity to an outside supplier.
- An activity with a high degree of industry commonality and a high degree of commoditization can be outsourced.
- An industry-specific and firm-specific (proprietary) activity is better performed in-house.
- On any given activity, the four choices for managers in terms of modes and locations are (1) offshoring, (2) inshoring, (3) captive sourcing/FDI, and (4) domestic in-house activity.

4-4 Explain how to use a VRIO framework to understand a firm's resources and capabilities.

- A VRIO framework suggests that only resources and capabilities that are valuable, rare, inimitable, and organizationally embedded will generate sustainable competitive advantage.
- Non-value-adding resources and capabilities may become weaknesses instead of strengths.
- Valuable but common resources and capabilities will lead to competitive parity but no advantage.
- Valuable and rare resources and capabilities can be a source of competitive advantage only if they are difficult for competitors to imitate.
- Causal ambiguity refers to the difficulty of identifying the actual cause of a firm's successful performance.
- Only valuable, rare, and hard-to-imitate resources and capabilities that are organizationally embedded and exploited can possibly lead to persistently above average performance.

KEY TERMS AND DEFINITIONS

SWOT analysis An analytical tool for determining a firm's strengths (S), weaknesses (W), opportunities (O), and threats (T).

Resource (capability) The tangible and intangible assets a firm uses to choose and implement its strategies.

Tangible resources and capabilities Assets that are observable and easily quantified.

Intangible resources and capabilities Assets that are hard to observe and difficult (if not impossible) to quantify.

Value chain A series of activities used in the production of goods and services that make a product or service more valuable.

Benchmarking Examining whether a firm has the resources and capabilities to perform a particular activity in a manner superior to competitors.

Commoditization A process of market competition through which unique products that command high prices and high margins gradually lose their ability to do so, thus becoming commodities.

Outsourcing Turning over an activity to an outside supplier that will perform it on behalf of the focal firm.

Offshoring Outsourcing to an international or foreign firm.

Onshoring Outsourcing to a domestic firm.

Captive sourcing Setting up subsidiaries abroad so that the work done is in-house but the location is foreign. Also known as foreign direct investment (FDI).

Business process outsourcing (BPO) The outsourcing of business processes such as loan origination, credit card processing, and call center operations.

Reshoring Moving formerly offshored activities back to the home country of the focal firm.

VRIO framework The resource-based framework that focuses on the value (V), rarity (R), imitability (I), and organizational (O) aspects of resources and capabilities.

Causal ambiguity The difficulty of identifying the actual cause of a firm's successful performance.

Complementary asset The combination of numerous resources and assets that enable a firm to gain a competitive advantage.

CHAPTER REVIEW 4

Ambidexterity Ability to use one's both hands equally well. In management jargon, this term has been used to describe capabilities to simultaneously deal with paradoxes (such as exploration versus exploitation).

Social complexity The socially intricate and interdependent ways that firms are typically organized.

4-5 Identify three things you need to do (and one thing you should avoid) as part of a successful career and business strategy.

- Managers need to distinguish resources and capabilities that are valuable, rare, hard-to-imitate, and organizationally embedded from those that do not share these attributes.
- Relentless imitation or benchmarking, while important, is not likely to be a successful strategy.
- A sustainable competitive advantage does not imply that it will last forever.
- Managers need to build up resources and capabilities for future competition.
- Students are advised to make themselves into "untouchables" whose jobs cannot be outsourced, by nurturing valuable, rare, and hard-to-imitate capabilities indispensable to an organization.

REVIEW QUESTIONS

1. Describe two types of tangible resources and capabilities, and describe two types of intangible resources and capabilities.
2. What is commoditization?
3. What are the components of VRIO?
4. Why is imitation difficult?
5. How do complementary assets and social complexity influence a firm's organization?
6. Outline the two positions in the debate on offshoring versus non-offshoring.

CRITICAL DISCUSSION QUESTIONS

1. Pick any pair of rivals (such as Samsung/Sony, Nokia/Motorola, and Boeing/Airbus) and explain why one outperforms the other.
2. Conduct a VRIO analysis of your business school relative to the top three rival schools in terms of (1) perceived reputation (such as rankings), (2) faculty strength, (3) student quality, (4) administrative efficiency, (5) IT, and (6) building maintenance. If you were the dean and had a limited budget, where would you invest precious financial resources to make your school number one among rivals? Why?
3. ***ON ETHICS:*** Ethical dilemmas associated with offshoring are plenty. Pick one of these dilemmas and make a case either defending your firm's offshoring activities or arguing against such activities. (Assume that you are employed at a firm headquartered in a developed economy.)

EXHIBIT 4.2 THE VALUE CHAIN

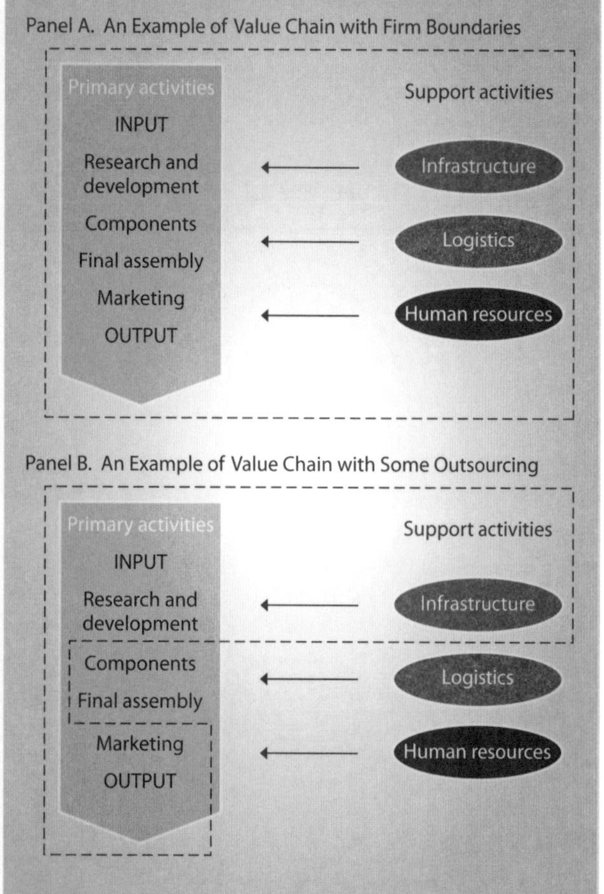

Note: Dashed lines represent firm boundaries.

CHAPTER REVIEW 5
Trading Internationally

CHAPTER SUMMARY

5-1 Use the resource-based and institution-based views to explain why nations trade.

- The resource-based view suggests that nations trade because firms in one nation generate valuable, unique, and hard-to-imitate exports that firms in other nations find it beneficial to import.
- The institution-based view argues that as "rules of the game," different laws and regulations governing international trade determine how the gains from trade are shared or not shared.

5-2 Identify and define the classical and modern theories of international trade.

- Classical theories include (1) mercantilism, (2) absolute advantage, and (3) comparative advantage.
- Mercantilism was widely practiced during the 17th and 18th centuries. It viewed international trade as a zero-sum game, and is the forerunner of modern protectionism.
- The theory of absolute advantage was proposed by Adam Smith in 1776 and advocates specialization and trade as a win-win game for all.
- David Ricardo developed the theory of comparative advantage in 1817 as an explanation for how countries can benefit from trade even when one of them does not have an absolute advantage.
- Modern theories include (1) product life cycles, (2) strategic trade, and (3) national competitive advantage of industries or "diamond."
- The product life cycle theory was developed in 1966 by Raymond Verson to explain the changes in trade patterns over time.
- The strategic trade theory was developed in the 1970s to address the question of whether government intervention can actually add value.
- Developed by Michael Porter in 1990, the theory of national competitive advantage of industries is presented in a diamond-shaped diagram to show why nations are competitive internationally in some industries but not in others.

5-3 Explain the importance of political realities governing international trade.

- The net impact of various tariffs and nontariff barriers is that the nation as a whole is worse off while certain special interest groups (such as specific industries, firms, and regions) benefit.
- Economic arguments against free trade center on (1) protectionism and (2) infant industries.
- Political arguments against free trade focus on (1) national security, (2) consumer protection, (3) foreign policy, and (4) environmental and social responsibility.

5-4 Identify factors that should be considered when your firm participates in international trade.

- Be aware of the comparative advantage of certain locations, and leverage their potential.

KEY TERMS AND DEFINITIONS

Export To sell abroad.

Import To buy from abroad.

Merchandise trade Tangible products being bought and sold.

Service trade Intangible services being bought and sold.

Trade deficit An economic condition in which a nation imports more than it exports.

Trade surplus An economic condition in which a nation exports more than it imports.

Balance of trade The country-level trade surplus or deficit.

Mercantilism A theory that holds that the wealth of the world (measured in gold and silver) is fixed and that a nation that exports more than it imports will enjoy the net inflows of gold and silver and become richer.

Protectionism The idea that governments should actively protect domestic industries from imports and vigorously promote exports.

Free trade The idea that free market forces should determine the buying and selling of goods and services with little or no government intervention.

Theory of absolute advantage A theory that suggests that under free trade, each nation gains by specializing in economic activities in which it is the most efficient producer.

Absolute advantage The economic advantage one nation enjoys because it can produce a good or service more efficiently than anyone else.

Theory of comparative advantage A theory that suggests that a nation gains by specializing in production of one good in which it has comparative advantage.

Comparative advantage The relative (not absolute) advantage in one economic activity that one nation enjoys in comparison with other nations.

Opportunity cost The cost of pursuing one activity at the expense of another activity.

Factor endowment The extent to which different countries possess various factors of production such as labor, land, and technology.

Factor endowment theory (Heckscher–Ohlin theory) A theory that suggests that nations will develop comparative advantages based on their locally abundant factors.

CHAPTER REVIEW 5

Product life cycle theory A theory that suggests that patterns of trade change over time as production shifts and as the product moves from new to maturing to standardized stages.

Strategic trade theory A theory that suggests that strategic intervention by governments in certain industries can enhance their odds for international success.

First-mover advantage Advantage that first entrants enjoy and do not share with late entrants.

Strategic trade policy Economic policy that provides companies a strategic advantage through government subsidies.

Theory of national competitive advantage of industries (or diamond theory) A theory that suggests that the competitive advantage of certain industries in different nations depends on four aspects that form a "diamond" shape when diagrammed.

Resource mobility The assumption that a resource used in producing a product in one industry can be shifted and put to use in another industry.

Tariff barrier A means of discouraging imports by placing a tariff (tax) on imported goods.

Import tariff A tax imposed on imports.

Deadweight cost Net losses that occur in an economy as the result of tariffs.

Nontariff barrier (NTB) A means of discouraging imports using means other than taxes on imported goods.

Subsidy A government payment to domestic firms.

Import quota A restriction on the quantity of goods brought into a country.

Voluntary export restraint (VER) An international agreement that shows that an exporting country voluntarily agrees to restrict its exports.

Local content requirement A rule that stipulates that a certain proportion of the value of a good must originate from the domestic market.

Administrative policy A bureaucratic rule that makes it harder to import foreign goods.

Antidumping duty A cost levied on imports that have been "dumped," or sold below cost, to unfairly drive domestic firms out of business.

Trade embargo Politically motivated trade sanctions against foreign countries to signal displeasure.

- Monitor and nurture the current comparative advantage, and take advantage of new locations.
- Be politically active to demonstrate, safeguard, and advance the gains from international trade.

REVIEW QUESTIONS

1. Why do nations trade? Why do some people argue that this question may be a bit misleading?
2. Summarize the three classical theories of international trade.
3. Compare and contrast the three modern theories of international trade.
4. What are the major political and economic arguments against free trade?
5. Are theories of international trade still valid given the new realities of world trade?

CRITICAL DISCUSSION QUESTIONS

1. Is the government of your country practicing free trade, protectionism, or something else? Why?
2. ***ON ETHICS:*** As a foreign policy tool, trade embargoes are meant to discourage foreign governments. Examples include US embargoes against Cuba, Iraq (until 2003), and North Korea. But embargoes also cause a great deal of misery among the population of the affected countries (such as shortages of medicine and food). Are embargoes ethical?
3. ***ON ETHICS:*** While the nation as a whole may gain from free trade, there is no doubt that certain regions, industries, firms, and individuals may lose their jobs and livelihood due to foreign competition. How can the rest of the nation help the unfortunate ones cope with the impact of international trade?

EXHIBIT 5.8 NATIONAL COMPETITIVE ADVANTAGE OF INDUSTRIES: THE PORTER DIAMOND

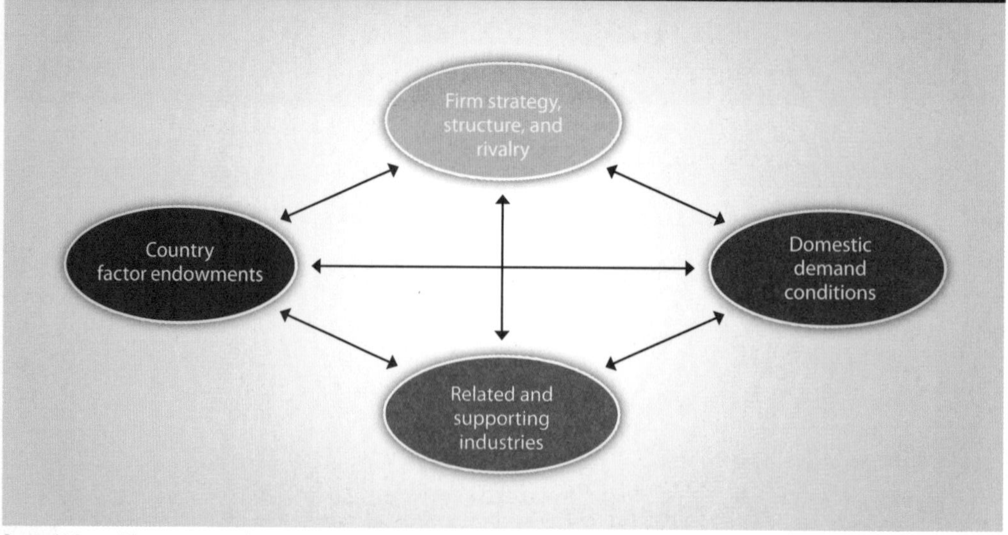

Source: M. Porter, "The competitive advantage of nations," *Harvard Business Review* (March-April 1990): 77.

For more great resources, interactive maps, quizzing, and chapter videos, log in to 4LTR Online through **www.cengagebrain.com**

CHAPTER REVIEW 6
Investing Abroad Directly

CHAPTER SUMMARY

6-1 Identify and define the key terms associated with foreign direct investment (FDI).

- The resource-based view suggests that *direct* is the key word in FDI, which reflects firms' interest in directly managing, developing, and leveraging their firm-specific resources and capabilities abroad.
- The institution-based view argues that recent expansion of FDI is indicative of generally more friendly formal policies and informal norms and values associated with FDI (despite some setbacks).

6-2 Use the resource-based and institution-based views to answer why FDI takes place.

- FDI takes place due to the quest for ownership, location, and internalization (OLI) advantages.

6-3 Explain how FDI results in ownership advantages.

- MNEs generally prefer ownership over licensing because ownership reduces dissemination risks, provides greater control over foreign operations, and makes firm-specific know-how easier to implement.

6-4 Identify the ways you can acquire and neutralize location advantages.

- Location advantages refer to certain advantages that can help MNEs attain strategic goals, whether it is access to labor, natural resources, or markets.

6-5 List the benefits of internalization.

- Internalization refers to the replacement of a cross-border market relationship with a single firm (the MNE) with locations in two or more countries.
- Internalization helps combat market imperfections and failures.

6-6 Identify different political views on FDI and understand its benefits and costs to host and home countries.

- The radical view, with its roots in Marxism, is hostile to FDI, and the free market view calls for minimum intervention in FDI.
- Since the 1980s, many countries, including Brazil, China, Hungary, India, Ireland, and Russia, have moved from radical to more FDI-friendly policies.
- Most countries practice pragmatic nationalism, weighing the costs and benefits of FDI.
- FDI brings a different (and often opposing) set of benefits and costs to host and home countries.
- Host-country benefits include capital inflow, technology spillover, advanced management know-how, and job creation. Costs include loss of sovereignty, adverse competition, and capital outflow.
- Home-country benefits include repatriated earnings, increased exports of components and services, and knowledge gains from operations abroad. Costs include capital outflow and job losses.

KEY TERMS AND DEFINITIONS

Foreign portfolio investment (FPI) Holding securities, such as stocks and bonds, of firms in other countries but without a controlling interest.

Management control right The right to appoint key managers and establish control mechanisms.

Horizontal FDI A type of FDI in which a firm produces the same products or offers the same services in a host country as at home.

Vertical FDI A type of FDI in which a firm moves upstream or downstream in different value chain stages in a host country.

Upstream vertical FDI A type of vertical FDI in which a firm engages in an upstream stage of the value chain.

Downstream vertical FDI A type of vertical FDI in which a firm engages in a downstream stage of the value chain.

FDI flow The amount of FDI moving in a given period (usually a year) in a certain direction.

FDI inflow FDI moving into a country in a year.

FDI outflow FDI moving out of a country in a year.

FDI stock The total accumulation of inbound FDI in a country or outbound FDI from a country across a given period of time (usually several years).

OLI advantages The advantages of ownership (O), location (L), and internalization (I) that come from engaging in FDI.

Ownership Possessing and leveraging of certain valuable, rare, hard-to-imitate, and organizationally embedded (VRIO) assets overseas in the context of FDI.

Location Advantages enjoyed by a firm that derive from the places in which it operates.

Internalization The replacement of cross-border markets (such as exporting and importing) with one firm (the MNE) located in two or more countries.

Licensing Buying and selling technology and intellectual property rights.

Market imperfection (market failure) The imperfect rules governing international market transactions.

Dissemination risk The possibility of unauthorized diffusion of firm-specific know-how.

Agglomeration The clustering of economic activities in certain locations.

CHAPTER REVIEW 6

Intrafirm trade International trade between two subsidiaries in two countries controlled by the same MNE.

Radical view on FDI A political view that sees FDI as an instrument of imperialism and a vehicle for foreign exploitation.

Free market view on FDI A political view that holds that FDI, unrestricted by government intervention, will enable countries to tap into their absolute or comparative advantages by specializing in the production of certain goods and services.

Pragmatic nationalism view on FDI A political view that approves FDI only when its benefits outweigh its costs.

Technology spillover The domestic diffusion of foreign technical knowledge and processes.

Demonstration effect (contagion or imitation effect) The effect that occurs when local rivals recognize the feasibility of foreign technology and imitate it.

Sovereign wealth fund A state-owned investment fund composed of financial assets such as stocks, bonds, real estate, or other financial instruments funded by foreign exchange assets.

6-7 List three things you need to do as your firm considers FDI.

- Carefully assess whether FDI is justified, in light of other options such as outsourcing and licensing.
- Pay careful attention to the location advantages in combination with the firm's strategic goals.
- Be aware of the institutional constraints governing FDI, and enhance legitimacy in host countries.

REVIEW QUESTIONS

1. Explain the differences between horizontal and vertical FDI.
2. What distinguishes an MNE from a non-MNE?
3. Can you summarize each of the OLI advantages?
4. How can FDI be used to overcome high transaction cost and prevent market failure?
5. Compare and contrast the three political views on FDI.
6. What are the costs and benefits of inbound FDI to host countries and of outbound FDI to home countries?

CRITICAL DISCUSSION QUESTIONS

1. Identify the top five (or ten) *source* countries of FDI into your country. Then identify the top ten (or 20) foreign MNEs that have undertaken inbound FDI in your country. Why do these countries and companies provide the bulk of FDI into your country?
2. Worldwide, which ten countries were the largest recipient and source countries of FDI *last year*? Why? Will this situation change in five years? How about 20 years down the road? Why?
3. ***ON ETHICS:*** Undertaking FDI, by definition, means not investing in the MNE's home country (see the Closing Case). What are the ethical dilemmas here? What are your recommendations as (1) MNE executives, (2) labor union leaders of your domestic (home-country) labor forces, (3) host-country officials, and (4) home-country officials?

EXHIBIT 6.5 AN INTERNATIONAL MARKET TRANSACTION

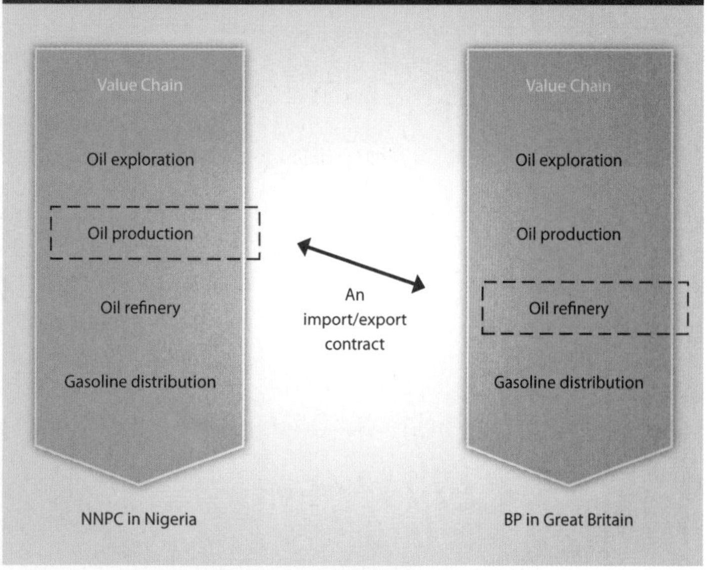

CHAPTER REVIEW 7
Dealing with Foreign Exchange

CHAPTER SUMMARY

7-1 List the factors that determine foreign exchange rates.

- Currency is a commodity, and its price is fundamentally determined by supply and demand.
- A foreign exchange rate is the price of one currency expressed in terms of another.
- Basic determinants of foreign exchange rates include (1) relative price differences and purchasing power parity (PPP), (2) interest rates, (3) productivity and balance of payments, (4) exchange rate policies, and (5) investor psychology.
- The theory of PPP, the "law of one price," suggests that in the absence of trade barriers (such as tariffs), the price for identical products sold in different countries must be the same.
- Variations in interest rates have a powerful effect in the short run, with a high domestic interest rate increasing the demand for a country's currency and a low interest rate decreasing demand.
- A country's rate of inflation, relative to that in other countries, affects its ability to attract foreign funds and thereby its exchange rate. Thus, exchange rates are highly sensitive to changes in monetary policy.
- A rise in a country's productivity, relative to other countries, will improve its competitive position. In turn, more foreign direct investment will be attracted to the country, fueling demand for its home currency and affecting its balance of payments.
- Most countries practice a dirty (or managed) float, with selective government interventions.
- Short-run movements in the exchange rate are largely determined by investor psychology and are thus difficult to predict.

7-2 Articulate and explain the steps in the evolution of the international monetary system.

- The gold standard (1870–1914) pegged the value of each country's currency to gold, providing a predictable and stable system but forcing countries to maintain gold reserves.
- The Bretton Woods system (1944–1973) emerged after World War II and pegged all currencies to the US dollar, which in turn was convertible to gold at a fixed $35 per ounce.
- The current post–Bretton Woods system (1973–present) has various floating and fixed rates, making it a flexible and diverse exchange system. However, the current system is also turbulent and uncertain.
- The International Monetary Fund (IMF) serves as a lender of last resort to help member countries correct balance-of-payments problems.

7-3 Identify strategic responses firms can take to deal with foreign exchange movements.

- The three foreign exchange transactions are (1) spot transactions, (2) forward transactions, and (3) swaps.
- Firms' strategic responses to the risk of losses from fluctuations in the foreign exchange market include (1) currency hedging, (2) strategic hedging, or (3) invoicing in their own currencies.

KEY TERMS AND DEFINITIONS

Foreign exchange rate The price of one currency in terms of another.

Appreciation An increase in the value of the currency.

Depreciation A loss in the value of the currency.

Balance of payments (BOP) A country's international transaction statement, which includes merchandise trade, service trade, and capital movement.

Floating (flexible) exchange rate policy A government policy to let demand and supply conditions determine exchange rates.

Clean (free) float A pure market solution to determine exchange rates.

Dirty (managed) float Using selective government intervention to determine exchange rates.

Target exchange rate (crawling band) Specified upper or lower bounds within which an exchange rate is allowed to fluctuate.

Fixed exchange rate policy A government policy to set the exchange rate of a currency relative to other currencies.

Bandwagon effect The effect of investors moving in the same direction at the same time, like a herd.

Capital flight A phenomenon in which a large number of individuals and companies exchange domestic currencies for a foreign currency.

Gold standard A system in which the value of most major currencies was maintained by fixing their prices in terms of gold.

Common denominator A currency or commodity to which the value of all currencies are pegged.

Bretton Woods system A system in which all currencies were pegged at a fixed rate to the US dollar.

Post–Bretton Woods system A system of flexible exchange rate regimes with no official common denominator.

International Monetary Fund (IMF) An international organization that was established to promote international monetary cooperation, exchange stability, and orderly exchange arrangements.

Quota The weight a member country carries within the IMF, which determines the amount of its financial contribution (technically known as its "subscription"), its capacity to borrow from the IMF, and its voting power.

CHAPTER REVIEW 7

Foreign exchange market The market where individuals, firms, governments, and banks buy and sell currencies of other countries.

Spot transaction The classic single-shot exchange of one currency for another.

Forward transaction A foreign exchange transaction in which participants buy and sell currencies now for future delivery.

Currency hedging A transaction that protects traders and investors from exposure to the fluctuations of the spot rate.

Forward discount A condition under which the forward rate of one currency relative to another currency is higher than the spot rate.

Forward premium A condition under which the forward rate of one currency relative to another currency is lower than the spot rate.

Currency swap A foreign exchange transaction between two firms in which one currency is converted into another at Time 1, with an agreement to revert it back to the original currency at a specified Time 2 in the future.

Offer rate The price at which a bank is willing to sell a currency.

Bid rate The price at which a bank is willing to buy a currency.

Spread The difference between the offer price and the bid price.

Currency risk The potential for loss associated with fluctuations in the foreign exchange market.

Strategic hedging Spreading out activities in a number of countries in different currency zones to offset any currency losses in one region through gains in other regions.

7-4 Identify three things you need to know about currency when doing business internationally.

- Fostering foreign exchange literacy is a must.
- Risk analysis of any country must include an analysis of its currency risks.
- A currency risk management strategy is necessary, be it via currency hedging, strategic hedging, or invoicing in one's own currency.

REVIEW QUESTIONS

1. What are the five major factors that influence foreign exchange rates?
2. What are the differences between a floating exchange rate policy and a fixed exchange rate policy?
3. Describe the IMF's roles, responsibilities, and challenges.
4. Describe the three primary types of foreign exchange transactions made by financial companies.
5. Why is the strength of the US dollar important to the rest of the world?

CRITICAL DISCUSSION QUESTIONS

1. Suppose that US$1 equals €0.7778 in New York and US$1 equals €0.7775 in Paris. How can foreign exchange traders in New York and Paris profit from these exchange rates?
2. Should China revalue the yuan against the dollar? If so, what impact might this have on (1) US balance of payments, (2) Chinese balance of payments, (3) relative competitiveness of Mexico and Thailand, (4) firms such as Walmart, and (5) US and Chinese retail consumers?
3. ***ON ETHICS:*** You are an IMF official going to a country whose export earnings are not able to pay for imports. The government has requested a loan from the IMF. In which areas would you recommend the government make cuts: (1) education, (2) salaries for officials, (3) food subsidies, and/or (4) tax rebates for exporters?

EXHIBIT 7.1 EXAMPLES OF KEY CURRENCY EXCHANGE RATES

	US dollar (US$)	Euro (€)	UK pound (£)	Swiss franc (SFr)	Mexican peso (Mex$)	Japanese yen (¥)	Canadian dollar (C$)
Canadian dollar (C$)	1.10	1.41	1.79	1.16	0.08	0.010	—
Japanese yen (¥)	109.05	139.90	177.61	115.89	8.25	—	99.49
Mexican peso (Mex$)	13.21	16.95	21.52	14.04	—	0.121	12.05
Swiss franc (SFr)	0.94	1.21	1.53	—	0.07	0.009	0.859
UK pound (£)	0.61	0.79	—	0.65	0.05	0.006	0.56
Euro (€)	0.78	—	1.27	0.83	0.06	0.007	0.71
US dollar (US$)	—	1.28	1.63	1.06	0.08	0.009	0.91

Source: Adapted from "Key currency cross rates," *Wall Street Journal*, 19 September 2014 (online.wsj.com). Reading *vertically*, the first column means US$1 ⊠ C$1.10 ⊠ ¥109.05 ⊠ Mex$13.21 ⊠ SFr0.94 ⊠ £0.61 ⊠ €0.78. Reading *horizontally*, the last row means €1 ⊠ US$1.28; £1 ⊠ US$1.63; SFr1 ⊠ US$1.06; Mex$1 ⊠ US$0.08; ¥1 ⊠ US$0.009; C$1 ⊠ US$0.91. The official code for Mexican peso is MXN. The official code for Swiss franc is CHF.

CHAPTER REVIEW 8
Capitalizing on Global & Regional Integration

CHAPTER SUMMARY

8-1 Make the case for global economic integration.

- There are both political and economic benefits for global economic integration.
- The biggest expected political benefit is peace.
- The three economic benefits of global integration are constructive dispute settlement, streamlined trade policies, and increased worldwide income through job creation and economic growth.

8-2 Explain the evolution of the GATT and the WTO, including current challenges.

- The GATT (1948–1994) significantly reduced tariff rates on merchandise trade.
- The WTO (1995–present) was set up not only to incorporate the GATT but also to cover trade in services and intellectual property, settle trade disputes, and provide a peer review of trade policy.
- The Doha Round was intended to promote more trade and development but has so far failed to accomplish its goals.

8-3 Make the case for regional economic integration.

- Political and economic benefits for regional integration are similar to those for global integration.
- Regional integration may undermine global integration and lead to some loss of countries' sovereignty.
- The five levels of regional economic integration are (1) free trade area, (2) customs union, (3) common market, (4) economic union, and (5) political union.

8-4 List the accomplishments, benefits, and costs of the European Union.

- The EU has delivered more than half a century of peace and prosperity, launched a single currency, and constructed a single market.
- The EU's challenges include internal divisions and enlargement concerns.

8-5 Identify the five organizations that promote regional trade in the Americas and describe their benefits and costs.

- Despite initial misgivings, NAFTA has significantly boosted trade and investment among members.
- The two South American customs unions, the Andean Community and Mercosur, have not been effective, because only a relatively small part of any member's trade is within the union and the region's largest trading partner, the United States, is outside the union.

8-6 Identify the four organizations that promote regional trade in the Asia Pacific and describe their benefits and costs.

- Regional integration in Asia Pacific centers on CER, ASEAN, APEC, and TPP.
- APEC is the largest regional integration by both geographic area and GDP.
- TPP is a multilateral free trade agreement that is currently being negotiated.

KEY TERMS AND DEFINITIONS

North American Free Trade Agreement (NAFTA) A free trade agreement among Canada, Mexico, and the United States.

Regional economic integration Efforts to reduce trade and investment barriers within one region.

Global economic integration Efforts to reduce trade and investment barriers around the globe.

General Agreement on Tariffs and Trade (GATT) A multilateral agreement governing the international trade of goods (merchandise).

World Trade Organization (WTO) The official title of the multilateral trading system and the organization underpinning this system since 1995.

European Union (EU) The official title of European economic integration since 1993.

Multilateral trading system The global system that governs international trade among countries—otherwise known as the GATT/WTO system.

Non-discrimination A principle that a country cannot make distinctions in trade among its trading partners.

General Agreement on Trade in Services (GATS) A WTO agreement governing the international trade of services.

Trade-Related Aspects of Intellectual Property Rights (TRIPS) A WTO agreement governing intellectual property rights.

Doha Round A round of WTO negotiations to reduce agricultural subsidies, slash tariffs, and strengthen intellectual property protection that started in Doha, Qatar, in 2001. Officially known as the "Doha Development Agenda," it was suspended in 2006 due to disagreements.

Free trade area (FTA) A group of countries that remove trade barriers among themselves.

Customs union One step beyond a free trade area (FTA), a customs union imposes common external policies on non-participating countries.

Common market Combining everything a customs union has, a common market additionally permits the free movement of goods and people.

Economic union Having all the features of a common market, members also coordinate and harmonize economic policies (in areas such as monetary, fiscal, and taxation) to blend their economies into a single economic entity.

CHAPTER REVIEW 8

Monetary union A group of countries that use a common currency.

Political union The integration of political and economic affairs of a region.

Schengen A passport-free travel zone within the EU.

Euro The currency currently used in 18 EU countries.

Euro zone The 18 EU countries that currently use the euro as the official currency.

Andean Community A customs union in South America that was launched in 1969.

Mercosur A customs union in South America that was launched in 1991.

Union of South American Nations (USAN/UNASUR) A regional integration mechanism integrating two existing customs unions (Andean Community and Mercosur) in South America.

United States–Dominican Republic–Central America Free Trade Agreement (CAFTA) A free trade agreement between the United States and five Central American countries and the Dominican Republic.

Australia–New Zealand Closer Economic Relations Trade Agreement (ANZCERTA or CER) A free trade agreement between Australia and New Zealand.

Association of Southeast Asian Nations (ASEAN) The organization underpinning regional economic integration in Southeast Asia.

Asia-Pacific Economic Cooperation (APEC) The official title for regional economic integration involving 21 member economies around the Pacific.

Trans-Pacific Partnership (TPP) A multilateral free trade agreement being negotiated by 12 Asia Pacific countries.

8-7 Articulate how regional trade should influence your thinking about global business.

- Think regional, downplay global.
- Understand the rules of the game and their transitions at both global and regional levels.

REVIEW QUESTIONS

1. What are some of the political and economic benefits of global economic integration?
2. What happened to the Doha Development Agenda at the WTO?
3. Should the EU remain an economic union, or should it move to become a political union?
4. What achievements do NAFTA supporters point to as evidence of NAFTA's success?
5. What are the leading examples of regional integration in South America and the Asia Pacific?

CRITICAL DISCUSSION QUESTIONS

1. The Doha Round collapsed because many countries believed that no deal was better than a bad deal. Do you agree or disagree with this approach? Why?
2. ***ON ETHICS:*** Critics argue that the WTO single-mindedly promotes trade at the expense of the environment. Therefore, trade—or, more broadly, globalization—needs to slow down. What is your view on the relationship between trade and the environment?
3. ***ON ETHICS:*** Critics argue that thanks to NAFTA, a flood of subsidized US food imports wiped out Mexico's small farmers. Some 1.3 million farm jobs disappeared. Consequently, the number of illegal immigrants in the United States skyrocketed. What is your view on NAFTA and CAFTA?

EXHIBIT 8.1 BENEFITS OF GLOBAL ECONOMIC INTEGRATION

Political benefits
▶ Promotes peace by promoting trade and investment
▶ Builds confidence in a multilateral trading system
Economic benefits
▶ Disputes are handled constructively
▶ Rules make life easier and discrimination impossible for all participating countries
▶ Free trade and investment raise incomes and stimulate economic growth

CHAPTER REVIEW 9
Growing & Internationalizing the Entrepreneurial Firm

CHAPTER SUMMARY

9-1 Define entrepreneurship, entrepreneurs, and entrepreneurial firms.

- Entrepreneurship is the identification and exploitation of previously unexplored opportunities.
- Entrepreneurs may be founders and owners of new businesses or managers of existing firms.
- Entrepreneurial firms in this chapter are defined as small- and medium-sized (SMEs) that employ less than 500 people.

9-2 Identify the institutions and resources that affect entrepreneurship.

- Institutions—both formal and informal—enable and constrain entrepreneurship around the world.
- The more entrepreneur-friendly the formal institutional requirements are, the more flourishing entrepreneurship is and the more developed the economies become.
- Resources and capabilities largely determine entrepreneurial success and failure.

9-3 Identify three characteristics of a growing entrepreneurial firm.

- Growth of an entrepreneurial firm is an attempt to more fully utilize currently under-utilized resources and capabilities, particularly entrepreneurial vision, drive, and leadership.
- Innovation is at the heart of entrepreneurship and allows for a more sustainable basis for competitive advantage.
- The primary sources of entrepreneurial financing are founders, family, friends, and strategic investors.
- The extent to which entrepreneurs draw on resources from outside investors versus family and friends varies from country to country.
- Microfinance has emerged in response to the lack of financing for entrepreneurial opportunities in many developing countries.

9-4 Describe how international strategies for entering foreign markets are different from those for staying in domestic markets.

- Compared with domestic transaction costs (the costs of doing business), international transaction costs are qualitatively higher, so entrepreneurial opportunities exist where innovation can lower transaction costs and bring distant groups of people, firms, and countries together.
- Entrepreneurial firms can internationalize by entering foreign markets through entry modes such as (1) direct exports, (2) licensing and franchising, and (3) foreign direct investment.
- Direct exports are attractive because entrepreneurial firms are able to reach foreign customers directly, but SMEs may not have enough resources to turn overseas opportunities into profits.
- With licensing and franchising, the SME can expand abroad while risking relatively little of its own capital, but may suffer a loss of control over how its technology and brand names are used.
- Foreign direct investment gives a firm better control over how its proprietary technology and brand name are used, but requires both a nontrivial sum of capital and a significant managerial commitment.

KEY TERMS AND DEFINITIONS

Small and medium-sized enterprise SME A firm with fewer than 500 employees in the United States or with fewer than 250 employees in the European Union.

Entrepreneurship The identification and exploitation of previously unexplored opportunities.

Entrepreneur Founders and owners of new businesses or managers of existing firms who identify and exploit new opportunities.

International entrepreneurship A combination of innovative, proactive, and risk-seeking behavior that crosses national borders and is intended to create wealth in organizations.

Microfinance Lending small sums ($50–$300) used to start small businesses with the intention of ultimately lifting the entrepreneurs out of poverty.

Born global firm (International new venture) A start-up company that attempts to do business abroad from inception.

Direct export The sale of products made by firms in their home country to customers in other countries.

Sporadic (passive) exporting The sale of products prompted by unsolicited inquiries from abroad.

Letter of credit (L/C) A financial contract that states that the importer's bank will pay a specific sum of money to the exporter upon delivery of the merchandise.

Licensing Firm A's agreement to give Firm B the rights to use A's proprietary technology (such as a patent) or trademark (such as a corporate logo) for a royalty fee paid to A by B. This is typically done in manufacturing industries.

Franchising Firm A's agreement to give Firm B the rights to use A's proprietary assets for a royalty fee paid to A by B. This is typically done in service industries.

Stage model Model of internationalization that involves a slow step-by-step (stage-by-stage) process a firm must go through to internationalize its business.

Indirect export A way for SMEs to reach overseas customers by exporting through domestic-based export intermediaries.

Export intermediary A firm that acts as a middleman by linking domestic sellers and foreign buyers that otherwise would not have been connected.

CHAPTER REVIEW 9

- Entrepreneurial firms can also internationalize without venturing abroad by (1) exporting indirectly, (2) supplying foreign firms, (3) becoming licensees/franchisees of foreign firms, (4) joining foreign entrants as alliance partners, and (5) harvesting and exiting through sell-offs to foreign entrants.

9-5 Articulate what you should do to strengthen your entrepreneurial ability on an international level.

- Push for both formal and informal institutions that facilitate entrepreneurship development.
- When internationalizing, be bold but not too bold.

REVIEW QUESTIONS

1. How do you define entrepreneurship?
2. From an institution-based view, to what extent do government regulations affect the start up of new firms in developed countries as opposed to developing countries?
3. From a resource-based view, how important are entrepreneurial resources and capabilities in determining the performance of SMEs?
4. Summarize the three modes that SMEs can use to enter foreign markets.
5. Name the five ways that SMEs can internationalize without leaving their home countries.
6. We know it is possible for SMEs to rapidly internationalize. Do you think this is wise?

CRITICAL DISCUSSION QUESTIONS

1. Given that most entrepreneurial start-ups fail, why do entrepreneurs found so many new firms? Why are (most) governments interested in promoting more start-ups?
2. Some suggest that foreign markets are graveyards where entrepreneurial firms over-extend themselves. Others argue that foreign markets represent the future for SMEs. If you were the owner of a small, reasonably profitable domestic firm, would you consider expanding overseas? Why?
3. ***ON ETHICS:*** Your former high school buddy invites you to join an entrepreneurial start-up that specializes in cracking the codes of protection software, which protect CDs, VCDs, and DVDs from being copied. He has developed the pioneering technology and lined up financing. The worldwide demand for this technology appears to be enormous. He offers you the job of CEO and 10% of the equity of the firm. How would you respond to his proposition?

EXHIBIT 9.5 INTERNATIONALIZATION STRATEGIES FOR ENTREPRENEURIAL FIRMS

Entering foreign markets	Staying in domestic markets
▶ Direct exports	▶ Indirect exports (through export intermediaries)
▶ Franchising/licensing	▶ Supplier of foreign firms
▶ Foreign direct investment (strategic alliances, greenfield wholly owned subsidiaries, and/or foreign acquisitions)	▶ Franchisee or licensee of foreign brands
	▶ Alliance partner of foreign direct investors
	▶ Harvest and exit (through sell-off to and acquisition by foreign entrants)

PengAtlas Map

For more great resources, interactive maps, quizzing, and chapter videos, log in to 4LTR Online through **www.cengagebrain.com**

CHAPTER REVIEW 10
Entering Foreign Markets

CHAPTER SUMMARY

10-1 Identify ways in which institutions and resources affect the liability of foreignness.

- When entering foreign markets, firms confront a liability of foreignness.
- The institution-based view suggests that firms need to undertake actions deemed legitimate and appropriate by the various formal and informal institutions governing market entries.
- The resource-based view advises foreign firms to deploy *overwhelming* resources and capabilities to offset the liability of foreignness in order to achieve competitive advantage.

10-2 Match the quest for location-specific advantages with strategic goals.

- Where to enter depends on the location-specific advantages of certain foreign countries and the strategic goals of firms involved.
- Firms seeking natural resources have to go to particular foreign locations where those resources are found.
- Market-seeking firms go to countries that have a strong demand for their products and services.
- Efficiency-seeking firms often single out the most efficient locations featuring a combination of scale economies and low cost factors.
- Innovation-seeking firms target countries and regions renowned for generating world-class innovations.
- Firms must also consider cultural and institutional distance when considering foreign locations.

10-3 Compare and contrast first-mover and late-mover advantages.

- First movers may gain advantages through proprietary technology, preemptive investments, erecting barriers to entry, and building relationships with key stakeholders.
- First movers may be disadvantaged when late movers free rider on their investments as well as by technological and market uncertainties and being locked into fixed assets or existing product lines.
- Late-mover advantages may include free riding on the investments of first movers, resolution of technological and market uncertainties, and leapfrogging the first mover's fixed assets or existing products.
- Late movers could be disadvantaged by lack of access to proprietary technology, barriers to entry, and difficulty in building relationships with key stakeholders who are already loyal to the first mover.
- Each has pros and cons, and there is no conclusive evidence pointing to one direction.

10-4 List the steps in the comprehensive model of foreign market entries.

- How to enter depends on the scale of entry, whether large scale or small scale.
- A comprehensive model of foreign market entries first focuses on the equity (ownership) issue.

KEY TERMS AND DEFINITIONS

Location-specific advantage The benefit a firm reaps from the features specific to a place.

Cultural distance The difference between two cultures along identifiable dimensions such as individualism.

Institutional distance The extent of similarity or dissimilarity between the regulatory, normative, and cognitive institutions of two countries.

First-mover advantage Benefit that accrues to firms that enter the market first and that later entrants do not enjoy.

Late-mover advantage Benefit that accrues to firms that enter the market later and that early entrants do not enjoy.

Scale of entry The amount of resources committed to entering a foreign market.

Mode of entry Method used to enter a foreign market.

Non-equity mode A mode of entering foreign markets through exports and/or contractual agreements that tends to reflect relatively smaller commitments to overseas markets.

Equity mode A mode of entering foreign markets through joint ventures and/or wholly owned subsidiaries that indicates a relatively larger, harder-to-reverse commitment.

Turnkey project A project in which clients pay contractors to design and construct new facilities and train personnel.

Build-operate-transfer (BOT) agreement A non-equity mode of entry used to build a longer-term presence by building and then operating a facility for a period of time before transferring operations to a domestic agency or firm.

Research and development (R&D) contract Outsourcing agreements in R&D between firms.

Dumping Exporting products at prices that are below what it costs to manufacture them, with the intent to raise prices after eliminating local rivals.

Co-marketing Efforts among a number of firms to jointly market their products and services.

Joint venture (JV) A new corporate entity jointly created and owned by two or more parent companies.

Wholly owned subsidiary (WOS) A subsidiary located in a foreign country that is entirely owned by the parent multinational.

CHAPTER REVIEW 10

Greenfield operation Building factories and offices from scratch (on a proverbial piece of "green field" formerly used for agricultural purposes).

- The second step focuses on making the actual selection within that mode, be it exports, contractual agreements, joint ventures, or wholly owned subsidiaries.

10-5 Explain what you should do to make your firm's entry into a foreign market successful.

- Understand the rules of game—both formal and informal—governing competition in foreign markets.
- Develop overwhelming resources and capabilities to offset the liability of foreignness.
- Match efforts in market entry with strategic goals.

REVIEW QUESTIONS

1. What does the institution-based view indicate about how a firm should deal with the liability of foreignness? What does the resource-based view suggest?
2. What are some of the location-specific advantages found in agglomeration?
3. What are the advantages and disadvantages for first movers? What are the advantages and disadvantages for late movers?
4. Summarize the pros and cons for each of the non-equity and equity modes of entry.
5. What is the heart of the debate on geographic diversification?

CRITICAL DISCUSSION QUESTIONS

1. During the 1990s, many North American, European, and Asian MNEs set up operations in Mexico, tapping into its location-specific advantages such as (1) proximity to the world's largest economy (the United States); (2) market-opening policies associated with NAFTA membership; and (3) abundant, low-cost, and high-quality labor. None of these has changed much. Yet, by the 15th anniversary of NAFTA (2009), a significant number of MNEs were starting to curtail operations in Mexico and move to China (see Chapter 8). Use institution-based and resource-based views to explain why this is the case.
2. From institution-based and resource-based views, identify the obstacles confronting MNEs from emerging economies interested in expanding overseas. How can such firms overcome the obstacles?
3. ***ON ETHICS:*** Entering foreign markets, by definition, means not investing in a firm's home country. For example, since 2000, GN Netcom shut down some operations in its home country of Denmark while adding head counts in China. Nissan closed factories in Japan and added a new factory in the United States. What are the ethical dilemmas here? What are your recommendations?

EXHIBIT 10.2 MATCHING STRATEGIC GOALS WITH LOCATIONS

Strategic goals	Location-specific advantages	Examples in the text
Natural resource seeking	Possession of natural resources and related transport and communication infrastructure	Oil in the Middle East, Russia, and Venezuela
Market seeking	Abundance of strong market demand and customers willing to pay	Automakers and business jet makers in China
Efficiency seeking	Economies of scale and abundance of low-cost factors	Manufacturing in China
Innovation seeking	Abundance of innovative individuals, firms, and universities	IT in Silicon Valley and Bangalore; telecom in Dallas; perfumes in Paris

CHAPTER REVIEW 11
Making Alliances & Acquisitions Work

CHAPTER SUMMARY

11-1 Define alliances and acquisitions.

- Strategic alliance is a voluntary agreement of cooperation between firms.
- Acquisition is a transfer of the control of operations and management from one firm (target) to another (acquirer).

11-2 Articulate how institutions and resources influence alliances and acquisitions.

- Formal institutions influence alliances and acquisitions through antitrust and entry mode concerns.
- Informal institutions affect alliances and acquisitions through normative and cognitive pillars.
- The impact of resources on alliances and acquisitions is illustrated by the VRIO framework.
- Alliances and acquisitions must create value.
- The abilities to successfully manage interfirm relationships may be rare.
- Imitability can occur at the firm level or at the alliance level.
- The organization of a successful alliance relationship or an acquisition may be difficult to replicate.

11-3 Describe how alliances are formed.

- Managers typically go through a three-stage decision process when considering alliances.
- Stage one is the decision to cooperate with another firm or to grow purely by market transactions (not cooperate).
- Stage two is the decision whether to use a contract or equity mode.
- Stage three is specifying which specific type of relationship to pursue.

11-4 Outline how alliances are dissolved.

- The phases of dissolution are initiation, going public, uncoupling, and aftermath.
- Managers need to combat opportunism and, if necessary, manage the dissolution process.

11-5 Discuss how alliances perform.

- Alliance performance may be affected by (1) equity, (2) learning and experience, (3) nationality, and (4) relational capabilities.

11-6 Explain why firms make acquisitions.

- Acquisitions are often driven by synergistic, hubristic, and/or managerial motives.

11-7 Describe what performance problems firms tend to encounter with acquisitions.

- Many acquisitions fail because managers fail to address pre- and post-acquisition problems.
- Pre-acquisition problems include managers over-estimating their ability to create value; inadequate pre-acquisition screening; poor strategic fit; a lack of familiarity with foreign cultures, institutions, and business systems; or nationalistic concerns.
- Post-acquisition problems include poor organizational fit, failure to address multiple stakeholder groups' concerns, clashes of organizational cultures and/or national cultures, and nationalistic concerns.

KEY TERMS AND DEFINITIONS

Strategic alliance Voluntary agreement of cooperation between firms.

Contractual (non-equity-based) alliance An association between firms that is based on a contract and does not involve the sharing of ownership.

Equity-based alliance An association between firms that is based on shared ownership or financial interest.

Strategic investment A business strategy in which one firm invests in another.

Cross-shareholding A business strategy in which each partner in an alliance holds stock in the other firm.

Acquisition The transfer of the control of operations and management from one firm (target) to another (acquirer), the former becoming a unit of the latter.

Merger The combination of operations and management of two firms to establish a new legal entity.

Real option An investment in real operations as opposed to financial capital.

Relational (collaborative) capability The ability to successfully manage interfirm relationships.

Acquisition premium The difference between the acquisition price and the market value of target firms.

Strategic fit The effective matching of complementary strategic capabilities.

Organizational fit The similarity in cultures, systems, and structures between two or more firms.

Hubris Exaggerated pride or overconfidence.

Managerial motive Managers' desire for power, prestige, and money, which may lead to decisions that do not benefit the firm overall in the long run.

11-8 Articulate what you can do to make global alliances and acquisitions successful.

- Understand and master the rules of the game governing alliances and acquisitions around the world.
- When managing alliances, pay attention to the soft relationship aspects.
- When managing acquisitions, do not overpay. Focus on both strategic and organizational fit.

REVIEW QUESTIONS

1. What are the two broad categories of strategic alliances?
2. Which is more common, mergers or acquisitions? Why?
3. Outline the three stages of alliance formation.
4. Outline the process of alliance dissolution.
5. What are three of the most common motives for acquisition?
6. How does a manager avoid pre-acquisition and post-acquisition problems?

CRITICAL DISCUSSION QUESTIONS

1. ***ON ETHICS:*** As a CEO leading an acquisition of a foreign firm (think of Anheuser-Busch or Cadbury), you are interviewed by a reporter from the host country. The reporter asks: "A lot of people in our country are mad about this foreign takeover of our iconic company. How would you alleviate their concerns?"
2. ***ON ETHICS:*** During the alliance courtship and negotiation stages, managers often emphasize equal partnerships and do not reveal (or they try to hide) their true intentions. What are the ethical dilemmas here?
3. ***ON ETHICS:*** As a CEO, you are trying to acquire a foreign firm. The size of your firm will double, and it will become the largest in your industry. On the one hand, you are excited about the opportunity to be a leading captain of industry and the associated power, prestige, and income. (You expect your salary, bonus, and stock option to double next year.) On the other hand, you have just read this chapter and are troubled by the findings that 70% of mergers and acquisitions reportedly fail. How would you proceed?

EXHIBIT 11.3 INSTITUTIONS, RESOURCES, ALLIANCES, AND ACQUISITIONS

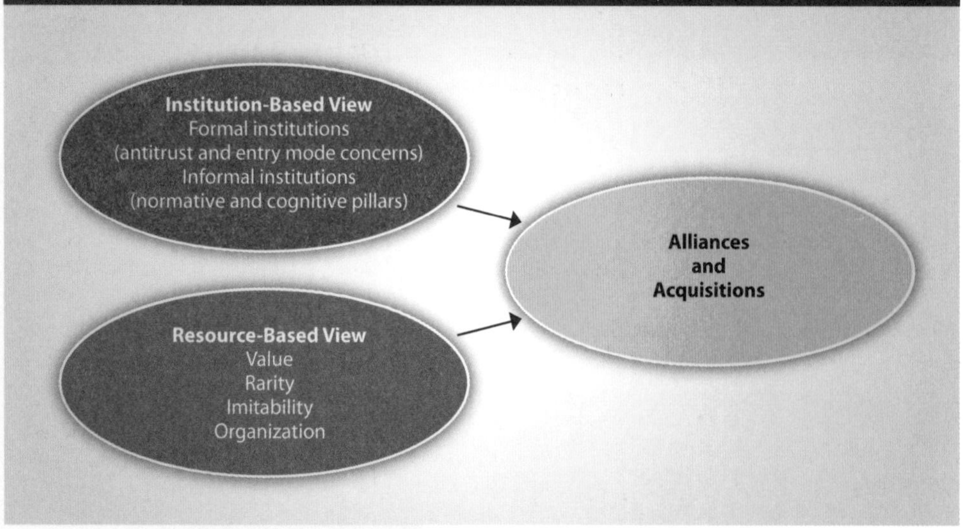

CHAPTER REVIEW 12
Strategizing, Structuring, & Learning Around the World

CHAPTER SUMMARY

12-1 Describe the relationship between multinational strategy and structure.

- An integration-responsiveness framework governs multinational strategy and structure.
- Strategy and structure work in four pairs.
- Home replication strategy duplicates home country strengths in foreign countries and adds an international division to the existing company structure.
- Localization strategy focuses on a number of foreign countries, each of which is regarded as a stand-alone local market supported by a geographic area structure.
- Global standardization strategy relies on the development and distribution of standardized products worldwide in order to reap the maximum benefits from low cost advantages by organizing each product division as a stand-alone entity with full worldwide responsibilities.
- Transnational strategy, which is often supported by a global matrix structure, seeks to be simultaneously cost efficient, locally responsive, and learning driven around the world.

12-2 Explain how institutions and resources affect multinational strategy, structure, and learning.

- "Rules of the game" for multinational enterprises (MNEs) are set by both formal and informal institutions governing (1) external relationships and (2) internal relationships.
- According to the resource-based view, management of MNE structure, learning, and innovation must be handled within the VRIO framework.

12-3 Outline the challenges associated with learning, innovation, and knowledge management.

- Knowledge management should primarily focus on tacit knowledge, which is more important than explicit knowledge but also harder to transfer and learn.
- Differences in knowledge management among four types of MNEs fundamentally stem from the interdependence (1) between the headquarters and foreign subsidiaries and (2) among various subsidiaries.
- Globalization of research and development (R&D) calls for capabilities to combat a number of problems associated with knowledge creation, retention, outflow, transmission, and inflow.

12-4 List three things you can do to make a multinational firm successful.

- Understand and master the external rules of the game from host/home country environments.
- Understand and be prepared to change the internal rules of the game governing MNE management.
- Develop learning and innovation capabilities around the world: "Think global, act local."

KEY TERMS AND DEFINITIONS

Integration-responsiveness framework An MNE management framework for simultaneously dealing with the pressures for both global integration and local responsiveness.

Local responsiveness The need to be responsive to different customer preferences around the world.

Home replication strategy A strategy that emphasizes duplicating home-country-based competencies in foreign countries.

Localization (multidomestic) strategy A strategy that focuses on a number of foreign countries/regions, each of which is regarded as a stand-alone local (domestic) market worthy of significant attention and adaptation.

Global standardization strategy A strategy that relies on the development and distribution of standardized products worldwide to reap the maximum benefits from low-cost advantages.

Center of excellence An MNE subsidiary explicitly recognized as a source of important capabilities that can be leveraged by and/or disseminated to other subsidiaries.

Worldwide (or global) mandate A charter to be responsible for one MNE function throughout the world.

Transnational strategy A strategy that endeavors to be simultaneously cost efficient, locally responsive, and learning driven around the world.

International division An organizational structure that is typically set up when a firm initially expands abroad, often engaging in a home replication strategy.

Geographic area structure An organizational structure that organizes the MNE according to different countries and regions.

Country (or regional) manager The business leader of a specific country (or a geographic region).

Global product division structure An organizational structure that assigns global responsibilities to each product division.

Global matrix An organizational structure often used to alleviate the disadvantages associated with both geographic area and global product division structures, particularly when adopting a transnational strategy.

CHAPTER REVIEW 12

Organizational culture The collective programming of the mind that distinguishes members of one organization from another.

Subsidiary initiative The proactive and deliberate pursuit of new opportunities by a subsidiary to expand its scope of responsibility.

Knowledge management The structures, processes, and systems that actively develop, leverage, and transfer knowledge.

Explicit knowledge Knowledge that is codifiable (that is, can be written down and transferred with little loss of richness).

Tacit knowledge Knowledge that is non-codifiable, whose acquisition and transfer require hands-on practice.

REVIEW QUESTIONS

1. What are the four strategic choices in the integration-responsiveness framework?
2. What are the four corresponding organizational structures?
3. Why is the relationship between strategy and structure reciprocal?
4. What are some of the informal rules of the game governing the selection of subsidiary managers in MNEs headquartered in different countries?
5. Summarize how knowledge is developed and disseminated in each of the four types of MNEs.

CRITICAL DISCUSSION QUESTIONS

1. In this age of globalization, some gurus argue that all industries are becoming global and that all firms need to adopt a global standardization strategy. Do you agree? Why or why not?
2. ***ON ETHICS:*** You are the manager of the best-performing subsidiary in an MNE. Because bonuses are tied to subsidiary performance, your bonus is the highest of all subsidiary managers. Now headquarters is organizing managers from other subsidiaries to visit and learn from your subsidiary. You worry that if performance at other subsidiaries catches up, your subsidiary will no longer be the star unit and your bonus will go down. What are you going to do?
3. ***ON ETHICS:*** If you were a CEO or a business unit head, under what conditions would you consider moving your headquarters overseas? What are the ethical dilemmas here?

EXHIBIT 12.3 FOUR STRATEGIC CHOICES FOR MULTINATIONAL ENTERPRISES

		Advantages	Disadvantages
1	Home replication	▶ Leverages home country-based advantages ▶ Relatively easy to implement	▶ Lack of local responsiveness ▶ May alienate foreign customers
2	Localization	▶ Maximizes local responsiveness	▶ High costs due to duplication of efforts in multiple countries ▶ Too much local autonomy
3	Global standardization	▶ Leverages low-cost advantages	▶ Lack of local responsiveness ▶ Too much centralized control
4	Transnational	▶ Cost-efficient while being locally responsive ▶ Engages in global learning and diffusion of innovations	▶ Organizationally complex ▶ Difficult to implement

CHAPTER REVIEW 13
Managing Human Resources Globally

CHAPTER SUMMARY

13-1 Explain staffing decisions, with a focus on expatriates.

- International staffing primarily uses one of three approaches: ethnocentric, polycentric, or geocentric.
- Expatriates (primarily parent-county nationals [PCNs] and to a lesser extent third-country nationals [TCNs]) play multiple challenging roles and often have high failure rates, defined by (1) premature return, (2) unmet business objectives, and (3) unfulfilled career development objectives.
- Expatriates need to be carefully selected, taking into account a variety of factors in terms of both the individual and the situation.

13-2 Identify training and development needs for expatriates and host-country nationals.

- Training length and rigor should correspond to the expatriates' expected length of stay.
- Expatriates need to be properly trained and be cared for during repatriation.
- Training and development of host-country nationals (HCNs) is now an area of differentiation among many multinational enterprises (MNEs).

13-3 Identify and discuss compensation and performance appraisal issues.

- Expatriates are compensated using the going rate and balance sheet approaches.
- The going rate approach fosters equality among PCNs, TCNs, and HCNs within the same subsidiary, but the going rate for the same position differs around the world, making it potentially problematic to attract or possibly repatriate talent.
- The balance sheet approach balances the cost-of-living differences relative to parent-country levels and adds a financial inducement to make the package attractive. But this approach can be expensive, create disparities between expatriates and HCNs, and is organizationally complex to administer.
- Top talent HCNs now increasingly command higher compensation.
- Performance appraisal needs to be carefully provided to achieve its intended purposes.

13-4 List factors that affect labor relations in both home and host countries.

- Despite revival efforts, unions have been declining in developed countries.
- MNEs prefer to deal with nonunionized workforces, but the power of unions in developing countries deserves some attention.

13-5 Discuss how the institution-based and resource-based views shed additional light on human resource management.

- Formal and informal rules of the game shape human resource management (HRM) significantly, both at home and abroad.
- While informal cultures, norms, and values are important, HR managers need to avoid stereotyping and instead consider changes.
- As HRM becomes more strategic, VRIO dimensions are now more important.

KEY TERMS AND DEFINITIONS

Human resource management (HRM) Activities that attract, select, and manage employees.

Staffing HRM activities associated with hiring employees and filling positions.

Host-country national (HCN) An individual from the host country who works for an MNE.

Parent-country national (PCN) An employee who comes from the parent (home) country of the MNE and works at its local subsidiary.

Third-country national (TCN) An employee who comes from neither the parent country nor the host country of the MNE.

Ethnocentric approach A staffing approach that emphasizes the norms and practices of the parent company (and the parent country of the MNE) by relying on PCNs.

Polycentric approach A staffing approach that emphasizes the norms and practices of the host country.

Geocentric approach A staffing approach that focuses on finding the most suitable managers, who can be PCNs, HCNs, or TCNs.

Expatriation Leaving one's home country to work in another country.

Training Specific preparation to do a particular job.

Development Longer-term, broader preparation to improve managerial skills for a better career.

Repatriate A manager who returns to his or her home country to stay after working abroad for a length of time.

Repatriation Returning to an expatriate's home country after an extended period overseas.

Psychological contract An informal understanding of expected delivery of benefits in the future for current services.

Compensation Salary and benefits.

Performance appraisal The evaluation of employee performance for the purposes of promotion, retention, or ending employment.

Going rate approach A compensation approach that pays expatriates the prevailing (going) rate for comparable positions in a host country.

Balance sheet approach A compensation approach that balances the cost-of-living differences based on parent-country levels and adds a financial inducement to make the package attractive.

CHAPTER REVIEW 13

Labor relation A firm's relation with organized labor (unions) in both home and host countries.

13-6 Identify the five Cs of human resource management.

- HR managers need to be *curious*, *competent*, *courageous*, and *caring* about people.
- Non-HR managers need to proactively develop their *careers*.

REVIEW QUESTIONS

1. What are the three main approaches to staffing?
2. What are the four key roles that expatriates typically play?
3. Why do a high percentage of expatriates fail abroad?
4. In expatriate compensation, what are the differences between the going rate approach and the balance sheet approach?
5. Why have efforts to establish multinational labor organizations been unsuccessful?
6. How do HR managers benefit from the four Cs? What is the fifth C for non-HR managers?

CRITICAL DISCUSSION QUESTIONS

1. You have been offered a reasonably lucrative expatriate assignment for the next three years, and your boss will have a meeting about the assignment with you next week. How would you discuss the assignment with your boss?
2. ***ON ETHICS:*** If you were an HCN, do you think pay should be equal between HCNs and expatriates in equivalent positions? Suppose that you were president of a subsidiary in a host country, and as a PCN your pay was five times higher than that for the highest-paid HCN (your vice president). What do you think?
3. ***ON ETHICS:*** As HR director for an oil company, you are responsible for selecting 15 expatriates to go to work in Iraq. However, you are personally concerned about their safety. How do you proceed?

EXHIBIT 13.7 INSTITUTIONS, RESOURCES, AND HUMAN RESOURCE MANAGEMENT

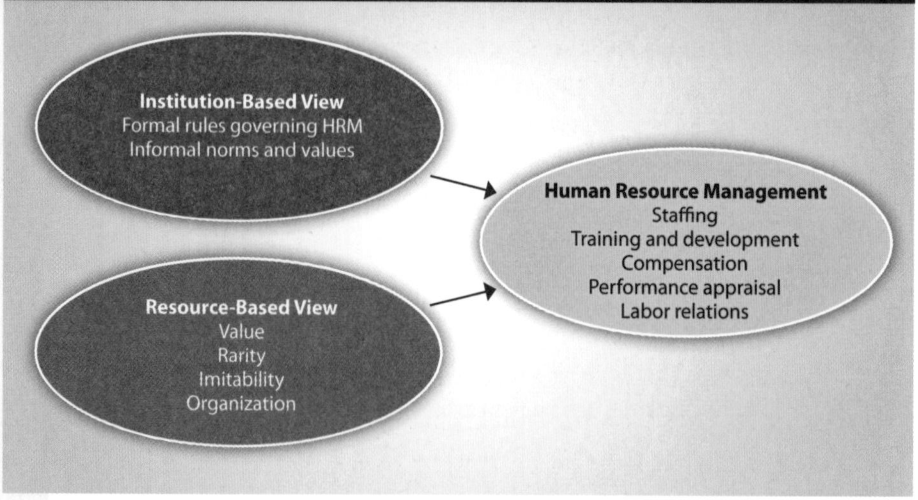

CHAPTER REVIEW 14
Competing in Marketing & Supply Chain Management

CHAPTER SUMMARY

14-1 Articulate three of the four Ps in marketing (product, price, and promotion) in a global context.

- Product refers to offerings that customers purchase.
- There are limitless ways of segmenting the market—males vs. females; urban dwellers vs. rural residents; Africans vs. Latin Americans.
- Price refers to the expenditures that customers are willing to pay for a product.
- Promotion refers to all the communications that marketers insert into the marketplace.

14-2 Explain how the fourth P in marketing (place) has evolved to be labeled supply chain management.

- The fourth P in the marketing mix refers to "place." Place is often referred to as distribution channel.
- The new challenge facing companies is how to manage the longer distribution channel—the distribution from suppliers all the way to consumers.

14-3 Outline the triple As in supply chain management (agility, adaptability, and alignment).

- Agility refers to the ability to quickly react to unexpected shifts in supply and demand.
- To reduce inventory, many firms/companies now use trucks, ships, and planes of their suppliers and carriers as their warehouse.
- Adaptability refers to the ability to change supply chain configurations in response to longer-term changes in the environment and technology.
- Alignment refers to the alignment of interests of various players in the supply chain.
- Trust along the supply chain stems from perceived fairness and justice from all members of the chain.

14-4 Discuss how institutions and resources affect marketing and supply chain management.

- Most countries impose restrictions, ranging from taboos in advertising to constraints on the equity level held by foreign retailers and 3PL providers.
- Informal rules also place significant constraints on marketing and supply chain management.
- Marketing and supply chain activities can be evaluated using VRIO—value, rarity, inimitability, and organization.

14-5 Draw three implications for action.

- Marketers and supply chain managers need to know the rules of the game inside and out in order to craft savvy responses to process changes.
- There must focus on the four Ps in marketing—product, price, promotion, and place.
- They also must focus on the triple As in supply chain management—agility, adaptability, and alignment.

KEY TERMS AND DEFINITIONS

Marketing Efforts to create, develop, and defend markets that satisfy the needs and wants of individual and business customers.

Supply chain Flow of products, services, finances, and information that passes through a set of entities from a source to the customer.

Supply chain management Activities to plan, organize, lead, and control the supply chain.

Marketing mix The four underlying components of marketing: (1) product, (2) price, (3) promotion, and (4) place.

Product Offerings that customers purchase.

Market segmentation Identifying segments of consumers who differ from others in purchasing behavior.

Price The expenditures that customers are willing to pay for a product.

Price elasticity How demand changes when price changes.

Promotion Communications that marketers insert into the marketplace.

Place The location where products and services are provided.

Distribution channel The set of firms that facilitates the movement of goods from producers to consumers.

Agility The ability to react quickly to unexpected shifts in supply and demand.

Adaptability The ability to change supply chain configurations in response to longer-term changes in the environment and technology.

Make-or-buy decision The decision on whether to produce in-house ("make") or to outsource ("buy").

Alignment Alignment of interest of various players.

Third-party logistics (3PL) provider A neutral, third-party intermediary in the supply chain that provides logistics and other support services.

CHAPTER REVIEW 14

REVIEW QUESTIONS

1. Name three ways in which the market can be segmented.
2. Name the four Ps of the marketing mix.
3. What are the triple As in supply chain management?
4. What does VRIO stand for when discussing resources that affect marketing and supply chain management?
5. Do all marketing or supply chain activities add value? Why or why not?
6. Why do marketers and supply chain managers need to thoroughly understand the "rules of the game"?

CRITICAL DISCUSSION QUESTIONS

1. Luxury athletics and yoga apparel retailer Lululemon Athletica has had great success in its less than 20 years of operations. With more than 200 retail locations, the company netted a 51.4% growth in revenue from fiscal year 2010 to 2011 and projected a more than 10% growth in the first quarter of fiscal year 2012. While the company has made its name on high-quality, high-cost apparel for fitness enthusiasts—a pair of yoga pants can cost $100—a recent manufacturing error shook consumer confidence and gave rise to quality control problems in its supply chain. How might Lululemon address this problem going forward and instill confidence with its customers?
2. You have 50 potential products that you will be launching in the upcoming year. In the process of launching those products, you will need to be cognizant of the four Ps of the marketing mix and the triple As of supply chain management. Make a table that has six columns: new-to-the-world products, new product line, addition to existing product line, improvement/revision of existing product line, repositioned product, and lower-priced product. Once the table is created, place each product in one of the six categories. All of the products should be evaluated under the VRIO criteria of marketing and supply chain management. Please be ready to discuss your reasoning.
3. Pick a product with which you are very familiar or that you anticipate being able to research easily. Map the supply chain of your product as far back as is feasible. Identify the mode of transportation used between each stage in the channel. Identify by name and location the component parts of the product, if any.

EXHIBIT 14.3 SOME BLUNDERS IN INTERNATIONAL MARKETING

- One US toymaker received numerous complaints from American mothers, because a talking doll told their children, "Kill mommy!" Made in Hong Kong, the dolls were shipped around the world. They carried messages in the language of the country of destination. A packing error sent some Spanish-speaking dolls to the United States. The message in Spanish "Quiero mommy!" means "I love mommy!" (This is also a supply chain blunder.)
- AT&T submitted a proposal to sell phone equipment in Thailand. Despite its excellent technology, the proposal was rejected out of hand by telecom authorities. This was because Thailand required a ten-year warranty but AT&T only offered a five-year warranty—thanks to standardization on warranty imposed by US headquarters.
- Japan's Olympia tried to market a photocopier to Latin America under the name "Roto." Sales were minimal. Why? "Roto" means "broken" in Spanish.
- Chinese exporters have marketed the following products overseas: White Elephant brand batteries, Sea Cucumber brand shirts, and Maxipuke brand poker cards (the two Chinese characters, *pu ke*, means poker, and it should have been translated as Maxi brand poker cards—but its package said "Maxipuke").

Sources: Based on text in (1) T. Dalgic and R. Heijblom, "International marketing blunders revisited—some lessons for managers," *Journal of International Marketing* 4 (1996): 81–91; (2) D. Ricks, *Blunders in International Business*, 3rd ed. (Oxford, UK: Blackwell, 1999).

CHAPTER REVIEW 15
Managing Corporate Social Responsibility Globally

CHAPTER SUMMARY

15-1 Articulate a stakeholder view of the firm.

- A stakeholder view of the firm urges companies to pursue a balanced triple bottom line consisting of economic, social, and environmental performance.
- Despite the fierce defense of the free market school, especially the shareholder capitalism variant, the corporate social responsibility (CSR) movement has now become a more central part of management discussions.
- The CSR debate centers on the nature of the firm in society.
- Free market advocates argue that the social responsibility of business is to increase its profits, and, if firms attempt to attain social goals, such as providing employment and social welfare, managers will lose their focus on profit maximization.
- CSR advocates argue that a free market system that takes the pursuit of self-interest and profit as its guiding light—although in theory constrained by rules, contracts, and property rights—may in practice fail to constrain itself, thus often breeding greed, excesses, and abuses.

15-2 Apply the institution-based and resource-based views to analyze corporate social responsibility.

- The institution-based view suggests that when confronting CSR pressures, firms may employ (1) reactive, (2) defensive, (3) accommodative, or (4) proactive strategies.
- A code of conduct (sometimes called a code of ethics) is a tangible indication of a firm's willingness to accept CSR.
- CSR-related resources can include *tangible* technologies and processes as well as *intangible* skills and attitudes.
- The resource-based view argues that not all CSRs satisfy the VRIO requirements.
- The resource-based view suggests that because of capability constraints, many firms are not cut out for a CSR-intensive (differentiation) strategy.

15-3 Identify three ways you can manage corporate social responsibility.

- Understand the rules of the game, anticipate changes, and seek to influence such changes.
- Pick your CSR battles carefully. Don't blindly imitate other firms' CSR activities.
- Integrate CSR as part of the core activities and processes of the firm.

REVIEW QUESTIONS

1. How do the concerns for primary stakeholders differ from those for secondary stakeholders?
2. What does triple bottom line mean?
3. What are the four types of strategies underpinning CSR decisions?
4. Using a resource-based view, explain why some firms improve their economic performance by adopting a CSR-intensive strategy, whereas others achieve no or damaging results.
5. Do you think "green" practices should be voluntary or mandatory for businesses? Why?

KEY TERMS AND DEFINITIONS

Corporate social responsibility (CSR) Consideration of, and response to, issues beyond the narrow economic, technical, and legal requirements of the firm to accomplish social benefits along with the traditional economic gains that the firm seeks.

Stakeholder Any group or individual who can affect or is affected by a firm's actions.

Global sustainability The ability to meet the needs of the present without compromising the ability of future generations to meet their needs around the world.

Primary stakeholder group Constituent on which a firm relies for its continuous survival and prosperity.

Secondary stakeholder group Group or individual who can indirectly affect or are indirectly affected by a firm's actions.

Triple bottom line Economic, social, and environmental performance that simultaneously satisfies the demands of all stakeholder groups.

Reactive strategy A strategy that would only respond to CSR causes when required by disasters and outcries.

Defensive strategy A strategy that focuses on regulatory compliance but with little actual commitment to CSR by top management.

Accommodative strategy A strategy characterized by some support from top managers, who may increasingly view CSR as a worthwhile endeavor.

Proactive strategy A strategy that anticipates CSR and endeavors to do more than is required.

Social issue participation Firms' participation in social causes not directly related to the management of primary stakeholders.

CHAPTER REVIEW 15

CRITICAL DISCUSSION QUESTIONS

1. In the landmark *Dodge v. Ford* case in 1919, the Michigan State Supreme Court decided whether or not Henry Ford could withhold dividends from the Dodge brothers (and other shareholders of the Ford Motor Company) to engage in what today would be called CSR activities. Returning a resounding "No," the court opined that "a business organization is organized and carried on primarily for the profits of the stockholders." If the court in your country were to decide on this case this year (or in 2019), what do you think would be the likely outcome?
2. ***ON ETHICS:*** Some argue that investing in emerging economies greatly increases the economic development and standard of living at the base of the global economic pyramid. Others contend that moving jobs to low-cost countries not only abandons CSR for domestic employees and communities in developed economies, but also exploits the poor in emerging economies and destroys the environment. If you were (1) CEO of a multinational enterprise (MNE) headquartered in a developed economy moving production to a low-cost country or (2) the leader of a labor union in the home country of the same MNE and about to lose lots of jobs, how would you participate in this debate?
3. ***ON ETHICS:*** Hypothetically, your MNE is the largest foreign investor in (1) Vietnam, where religious leaders are reportedly being persecuted, or (2) Estonia, where ethnic Russian citizens are being discriminated against by law. As the country manager there, you understand that the MNE is being pressured by nongovernmental organizations (NGOs) of all stripes to help the oppressed groups in these countries. But you also understand that the host government could be upset if your firm is found to engage in local political activities deemed inappropriate. These alleged activities, which you personally find distasteful, are not directly related to your operations. How would you proceed?

EXHIBIT 15.1 A STAKEHOLDER VIEW OF THE FIRM

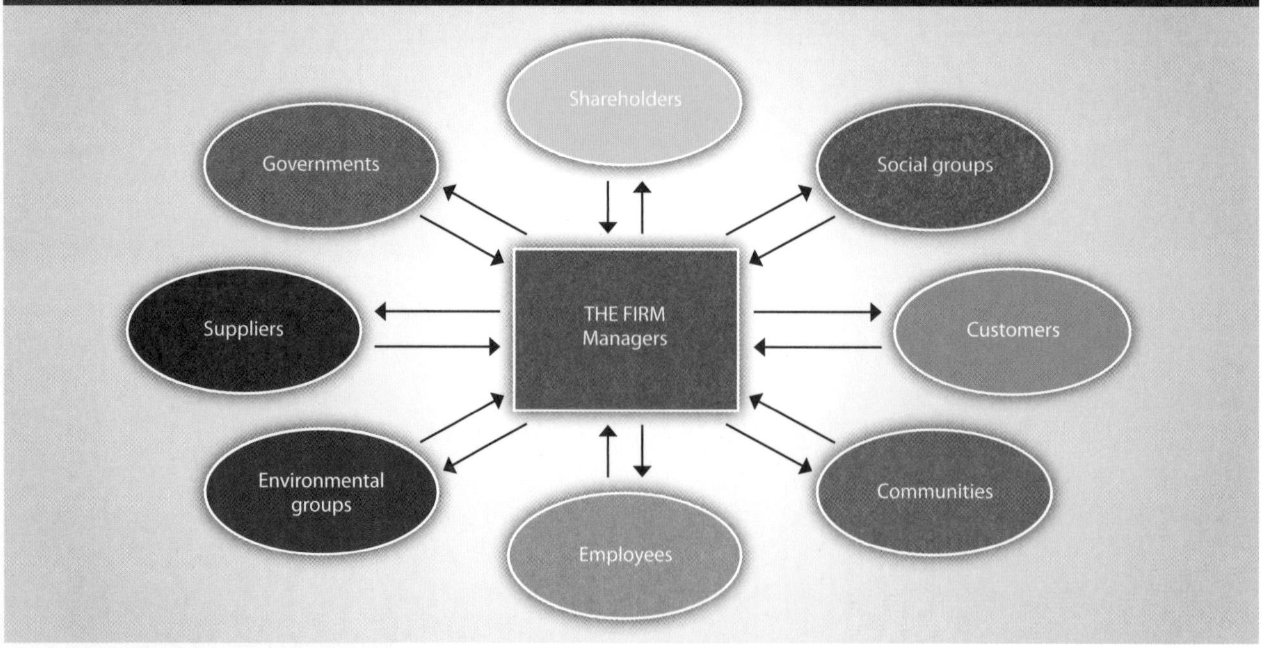

Source: T. Donaldson and L. Preston, "The stakeholder theory of the corporation: Concepts, evidence, and implications," *Academy of Management Review* 20 (1995): 69.

MAP 1 Developed Economies and Emerging Economies

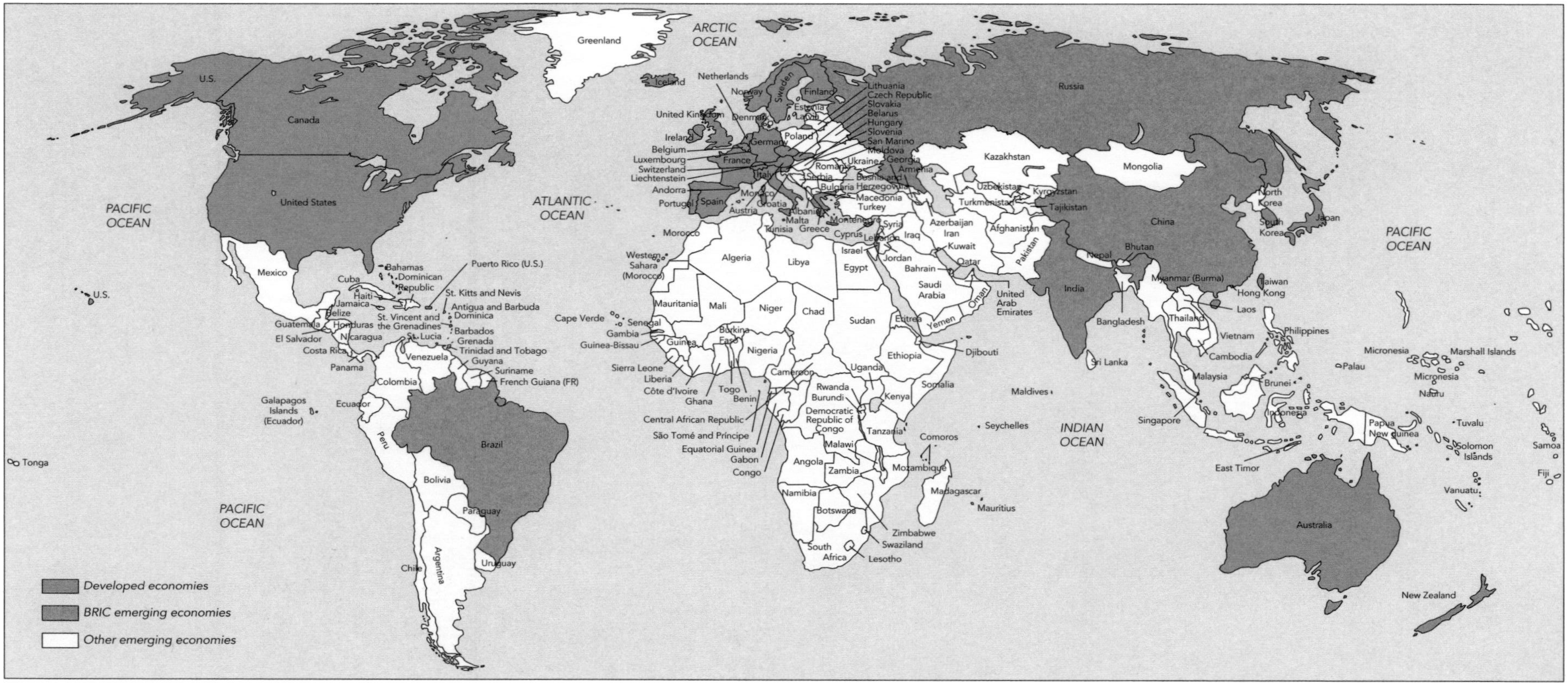

Source: International Monetary Fund (IMF), available online at http://www.imf.org (accessed 16 October 2009). The IMF recognizes 184 countries and economies. It labels developed economies "advanced economies," and labels emerging economies "emerging and developing economies."

MAP 2 The Group of 20 (G-20)

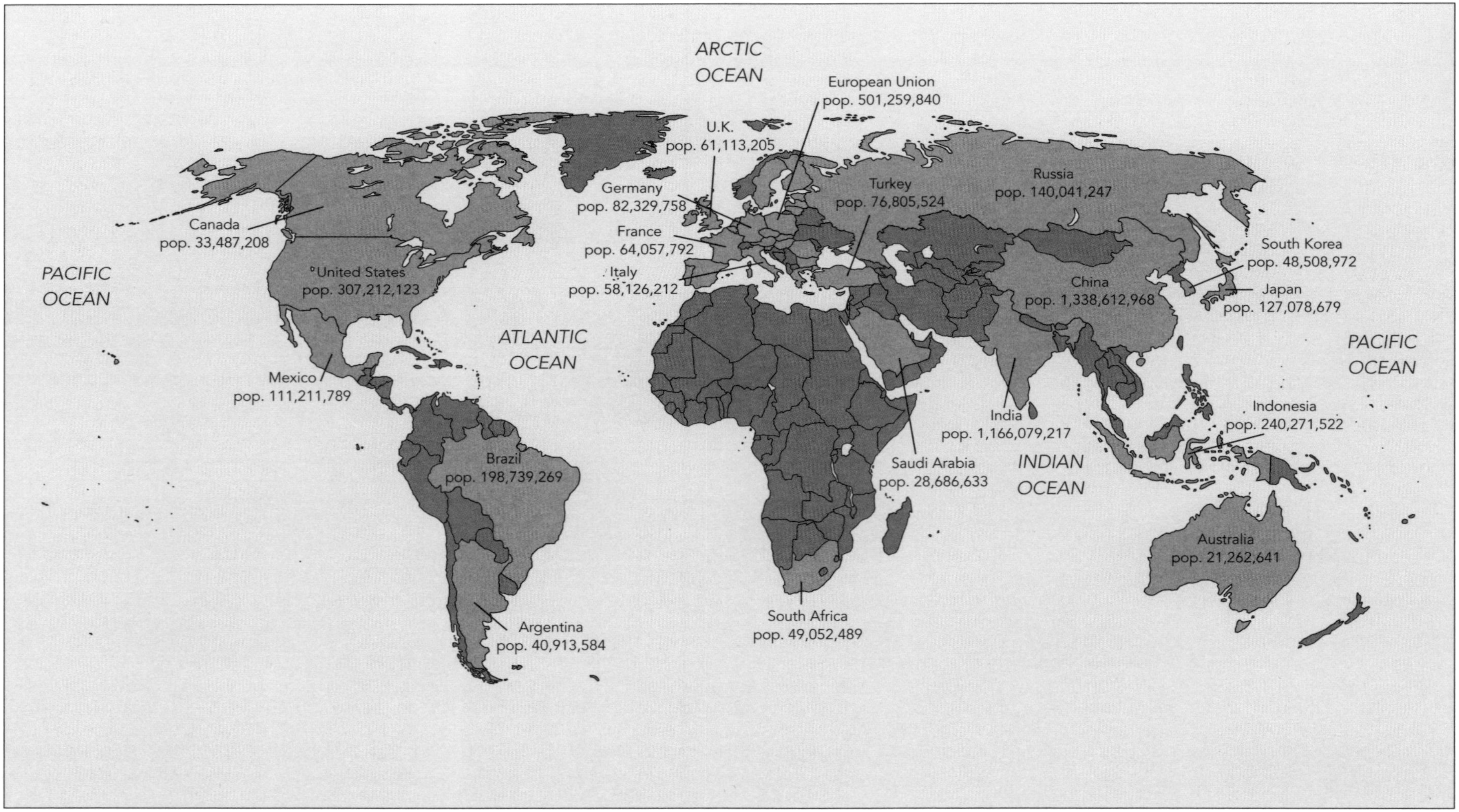

Source: US Census Bureau, International Database; Central Intelligence Agency, 2009, *The World Factbook 2009*. See PengAtlas Map 9 for a map of EU member countries.

MAP 3 Political Freedom Around the World

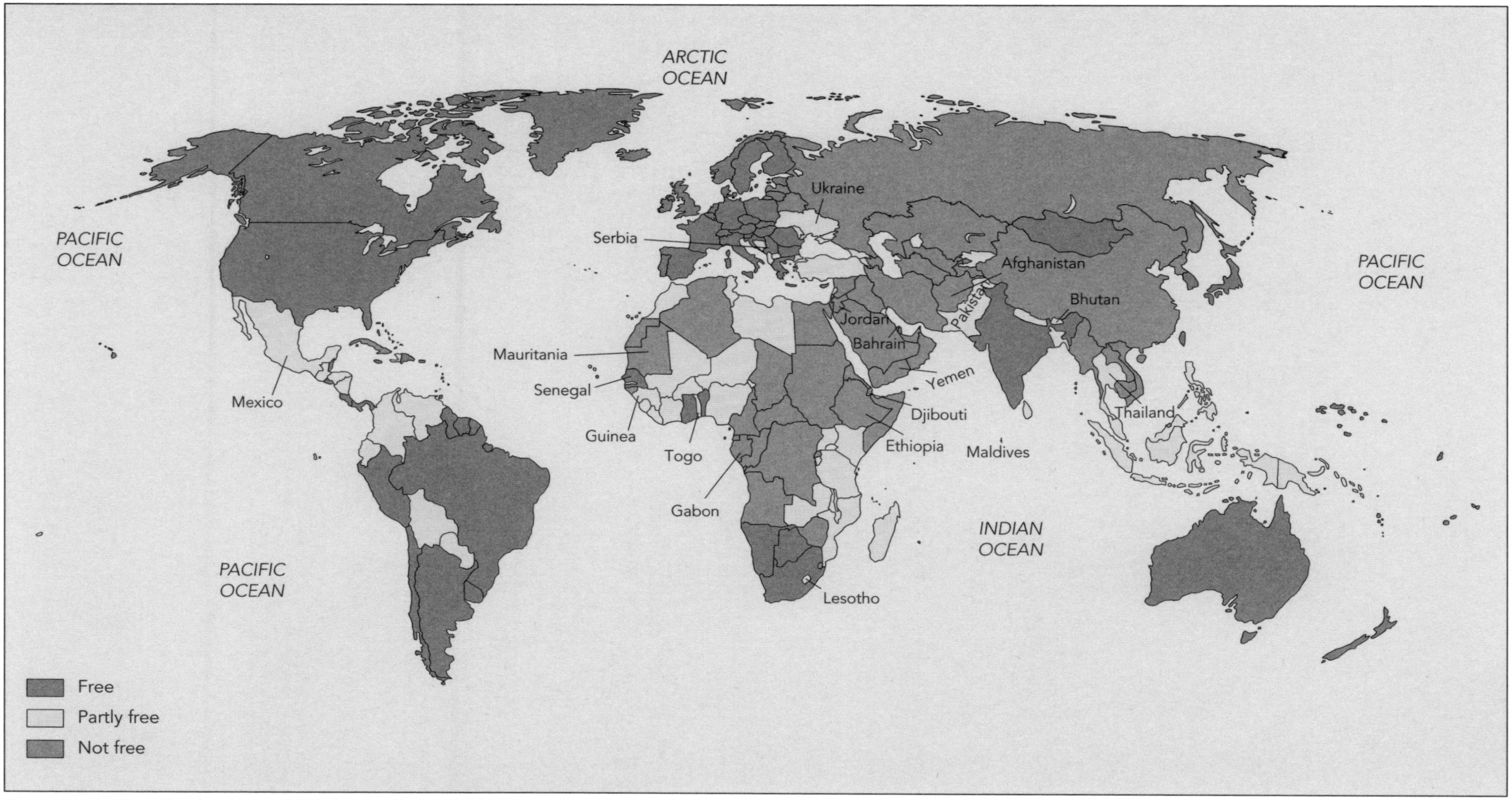

Source: Adapted from Freedom House, 2015, *Freedom in the World 2015*, www.freedomhouse.org.

MAP 4 Top Ten and Bottom Ten Countries by Per Capita Income

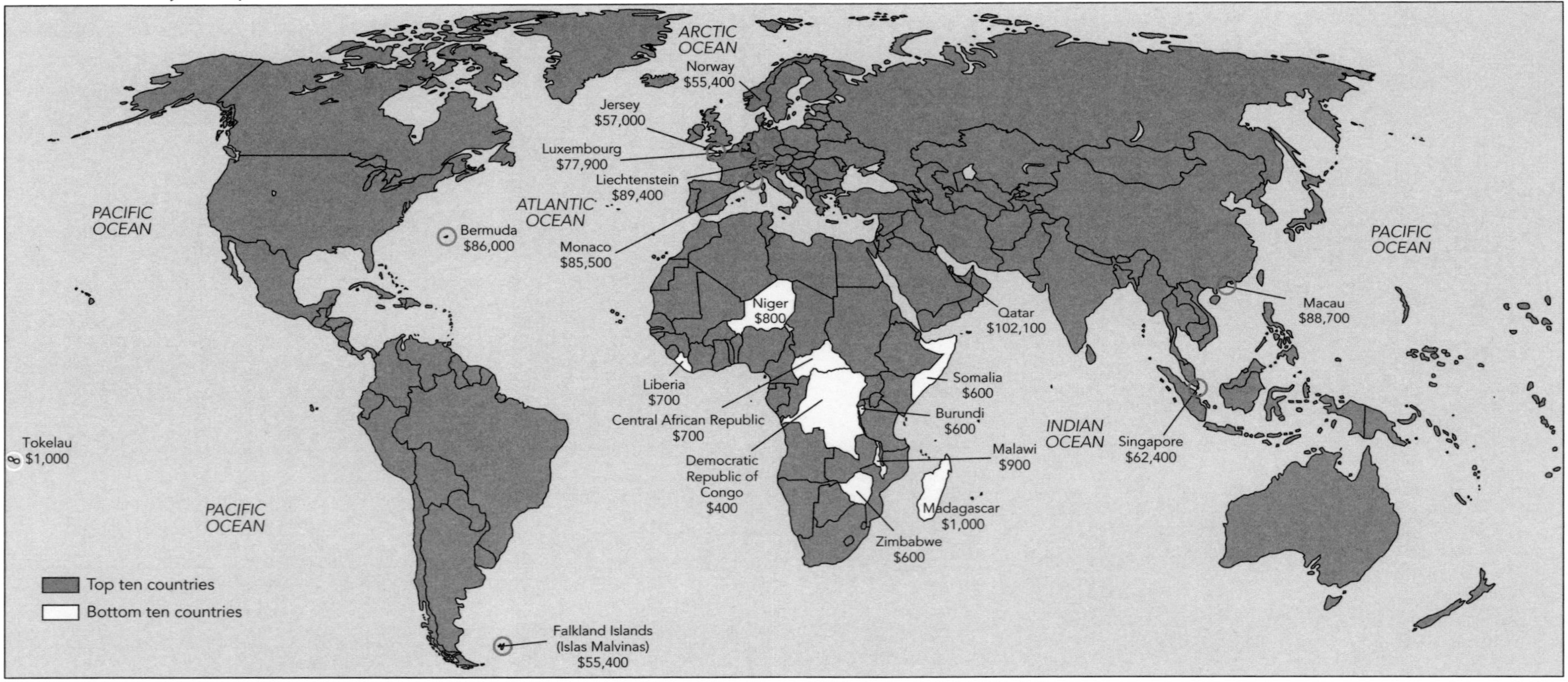

Source: Adapted from Central Intelligence Agency, 2013, *The World Factbook 2013*. Amounts in US dollars.

MAP 5 Religious Heritage Around the World

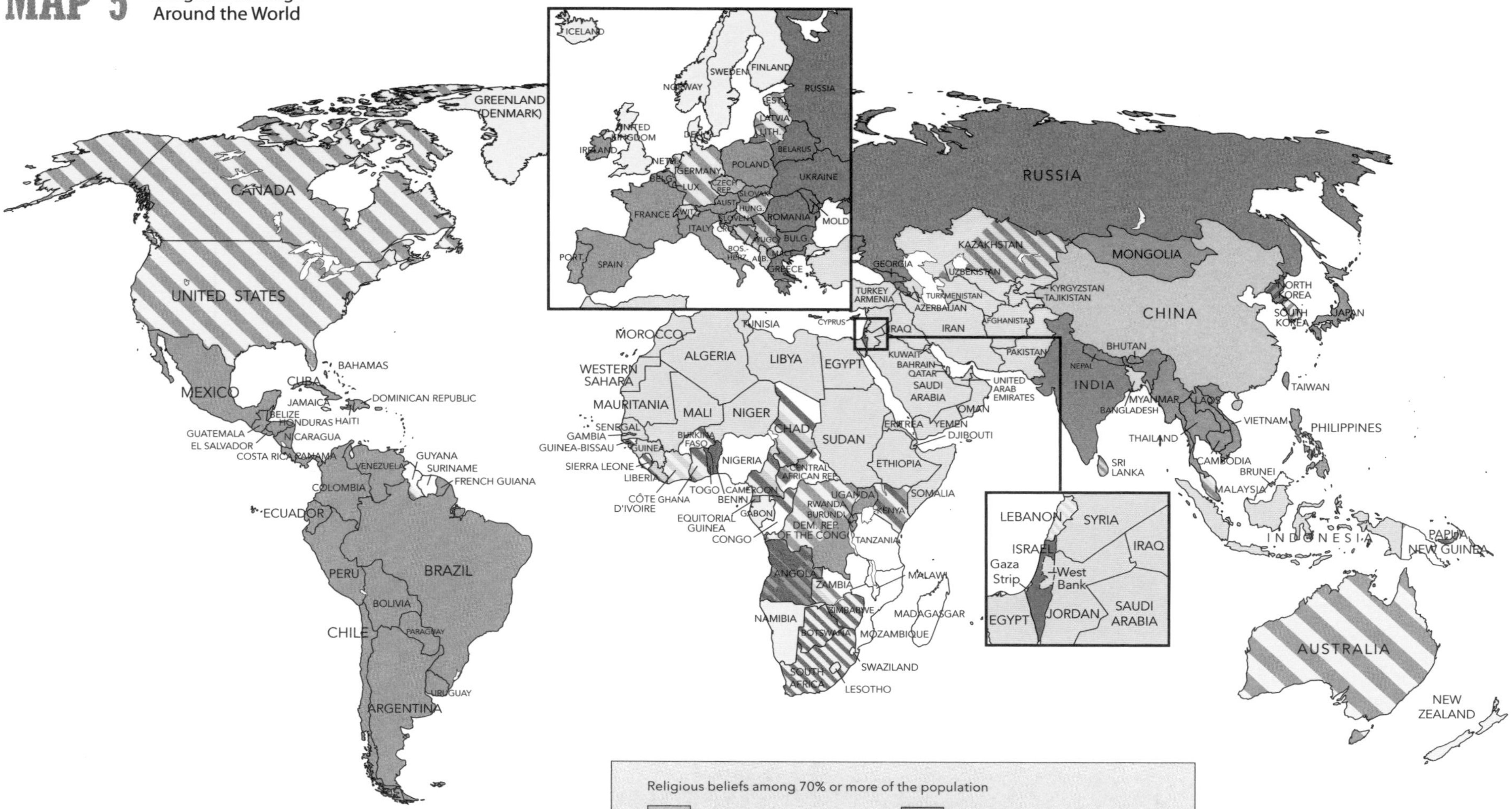

Religious beliefs among 70% or more of the population

- Atheist
- Buddhism
- Confucian
- Christian, other
- Christian, Roman Catholic
- Hindu
- Indigenous
- Judaism
- Muslim
- Orthodox, no major sects

Source: *World Factbook*, 2000. Note that Confucianism, strictly speaking, is not a religion but a set of moral codes guiding interpersonal relationships.

MAP 5

MAP 6

MAP 6 Top Merchandise Importers and Exporters

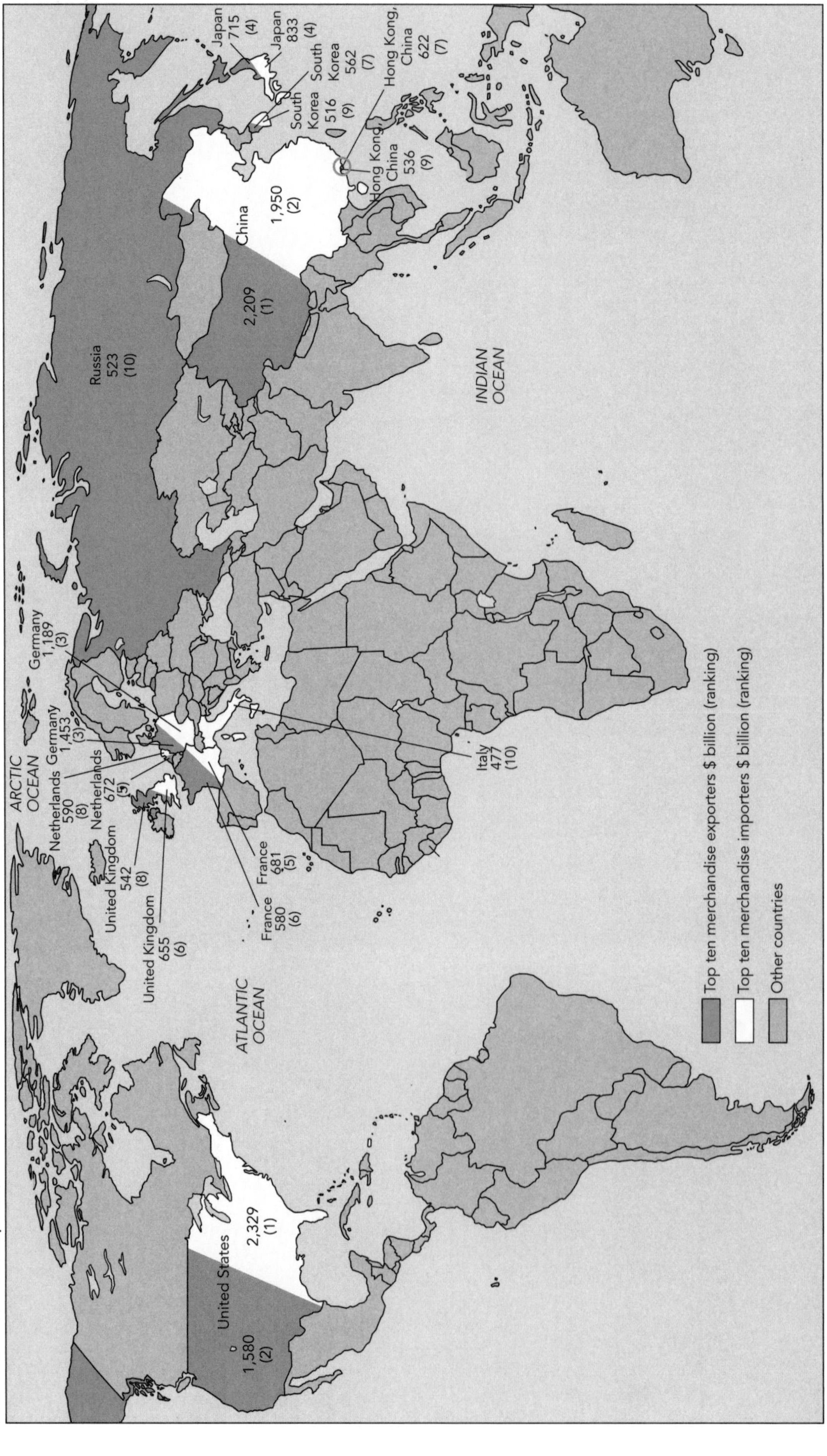

Source: Adapted from World Trade Organization, 2014, *Word Trade Report 2014*, Appendix Tables 3 and 5, Geneva: WTO (www.wto.org). All data are for 2013.

MAP 7 Top Service Importers and Exporters

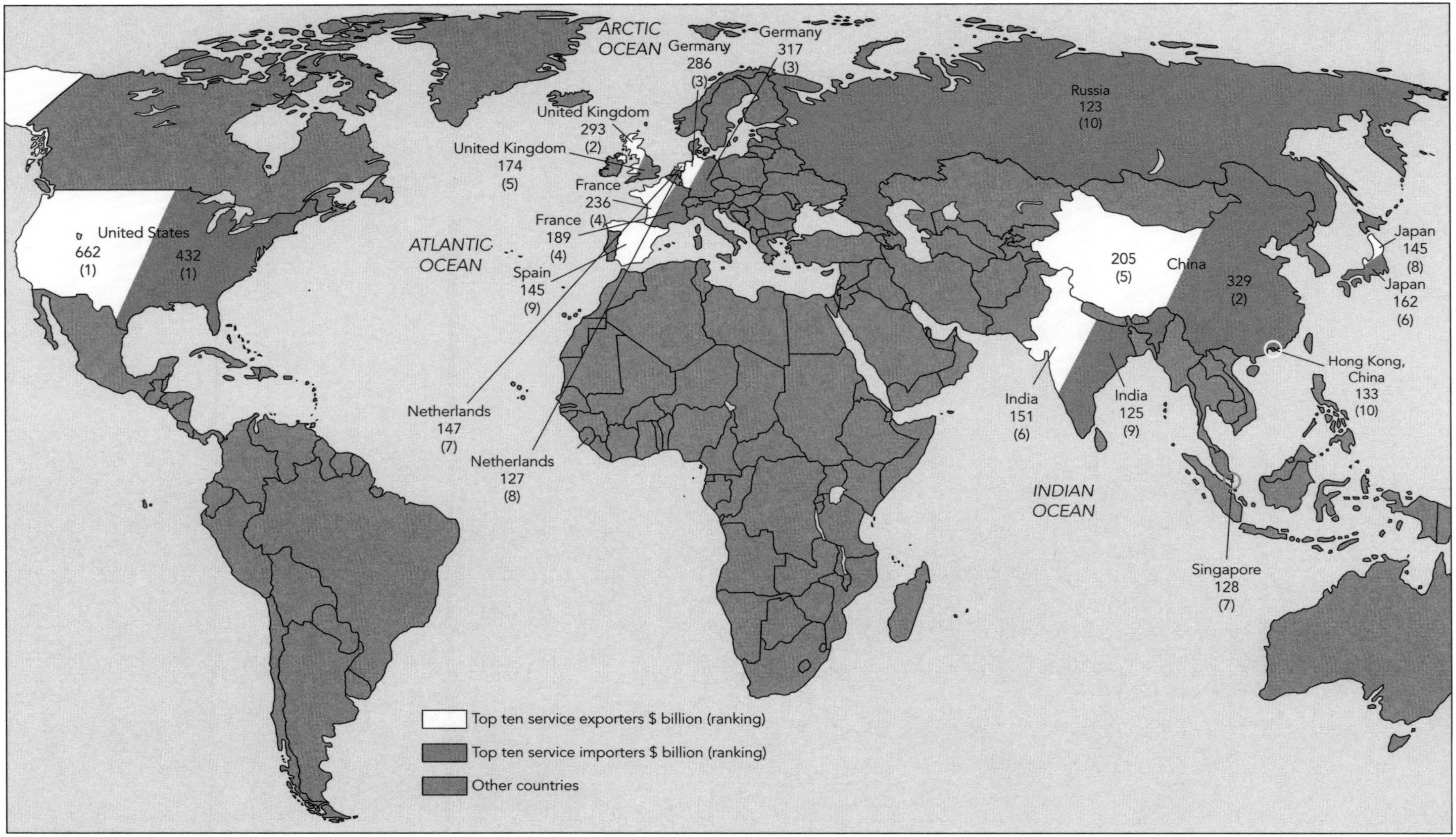

Source: Adapted from World Trade Organization, 2014, *Word Trade Report 2014*, Appendix Tables 3 and 5, Geneva: WTO (www.wto.org). All data are for 2013.

MAP 7

PengAtlas

MAP 8 FDI Inflows and Outflows

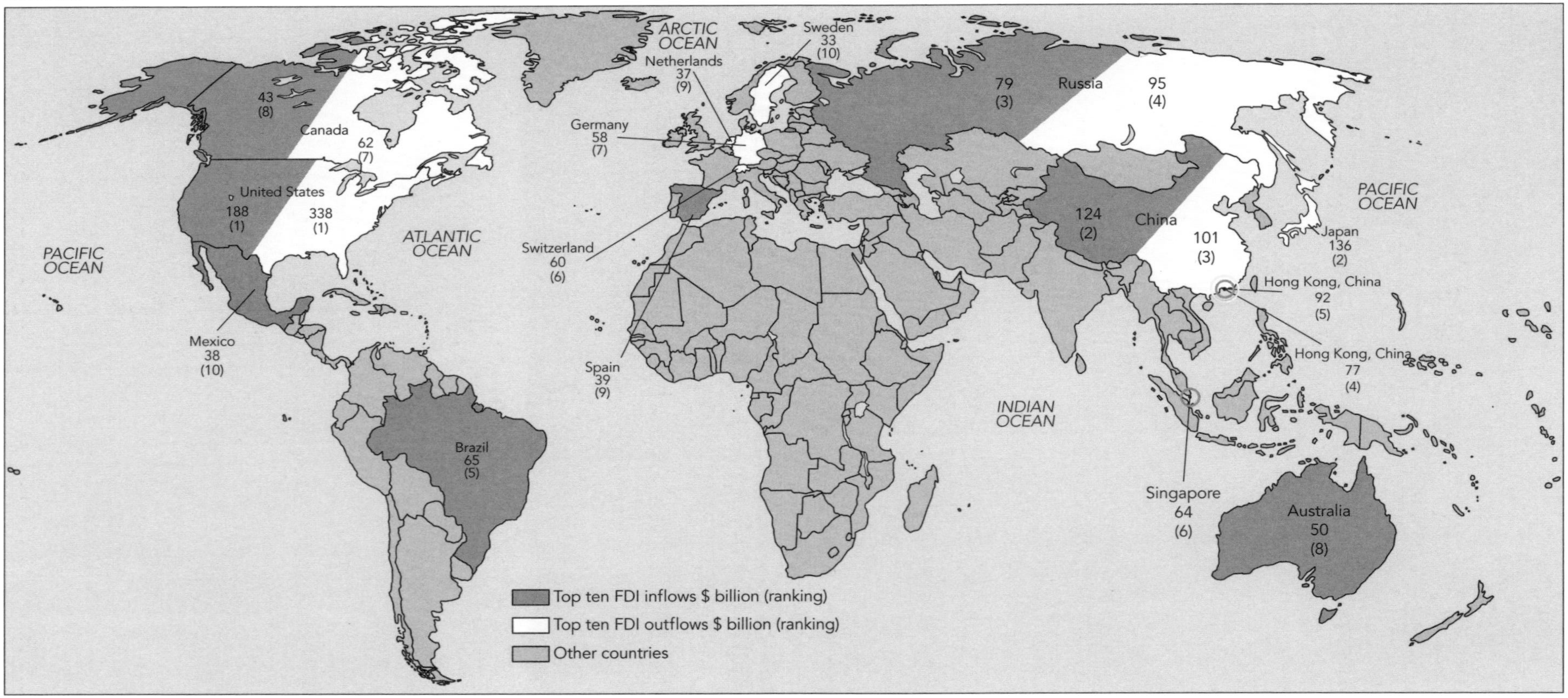

Source: Adapted from United Nations, 2014, *World Investment Report 2014* (p. xv), New York and Geneva: UN. Data refer to 2013.

MAP 9 The European Union

As of February 2015, candidate countries are Albania, Iceland, Macedonia, Montenegro, Serbia, Turkey, and potential candidate countries of Bosnia and Herzegovina, and Kosovo.

Source: Adapted from http://europa.eueuropa.eu

MAP 9

MAP 10

MAP 10 Regional Integration in South America

In May 2008, Andean Community and Mercosur agreed to merge to form the Union of South American Nations (USAN, more commonly known by its Spanish acronym, UNASUR, which refers to Unión de Naciones Suramericanas).

MAP 11 Regional Integration in the Asia Pacific

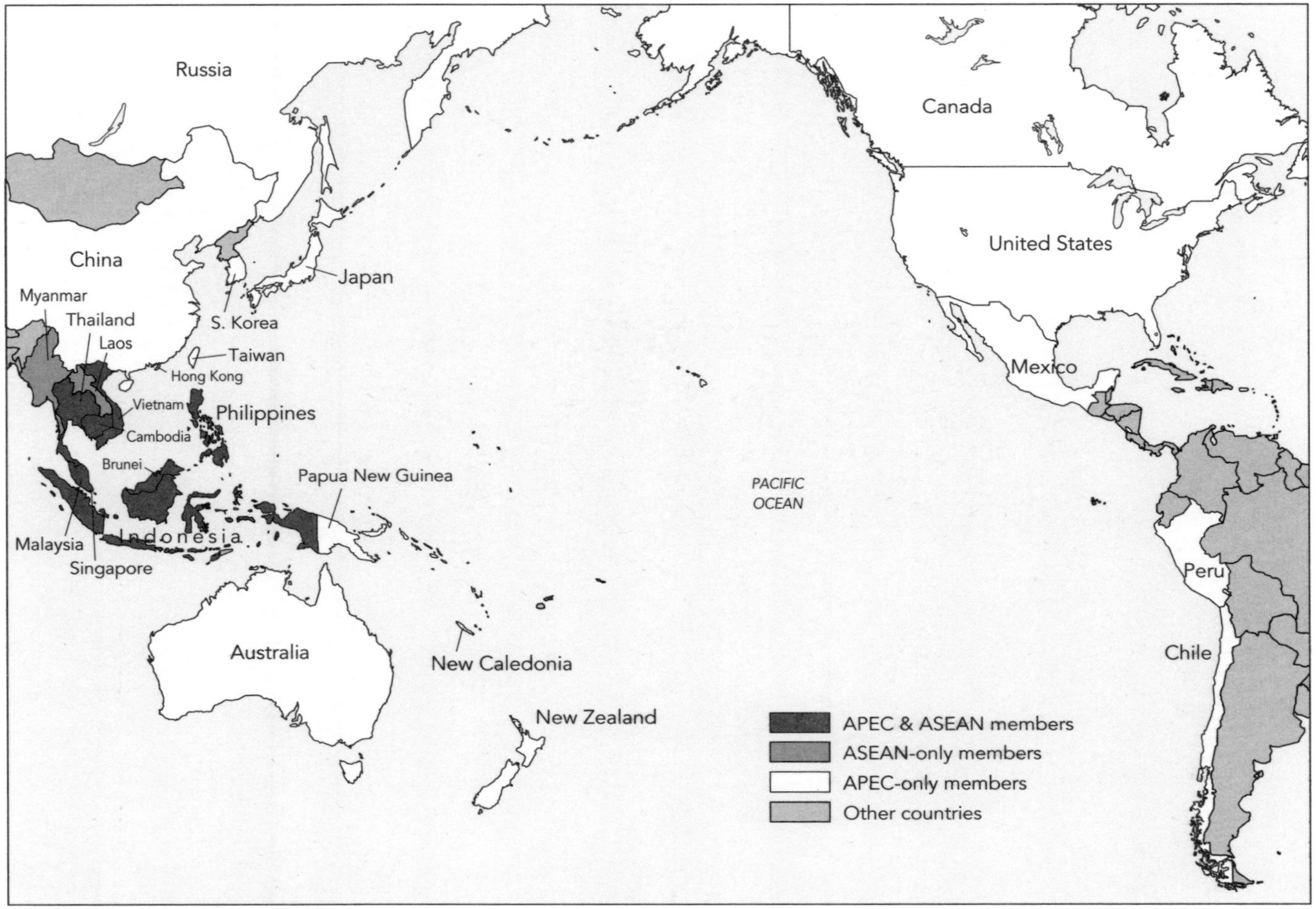

In 2005, four APEC members—Brunei, Chile, New Zealand, and Singapore—established Trans-Pacific Partnership (TPP). As of this writing, eight additional APEC members—Australia, Canada, Malaysia, Mexico, Peru, Japan, the United States, and Vietnam—are negotiating to join TPP.

MAP 12 Ease of Doing Business

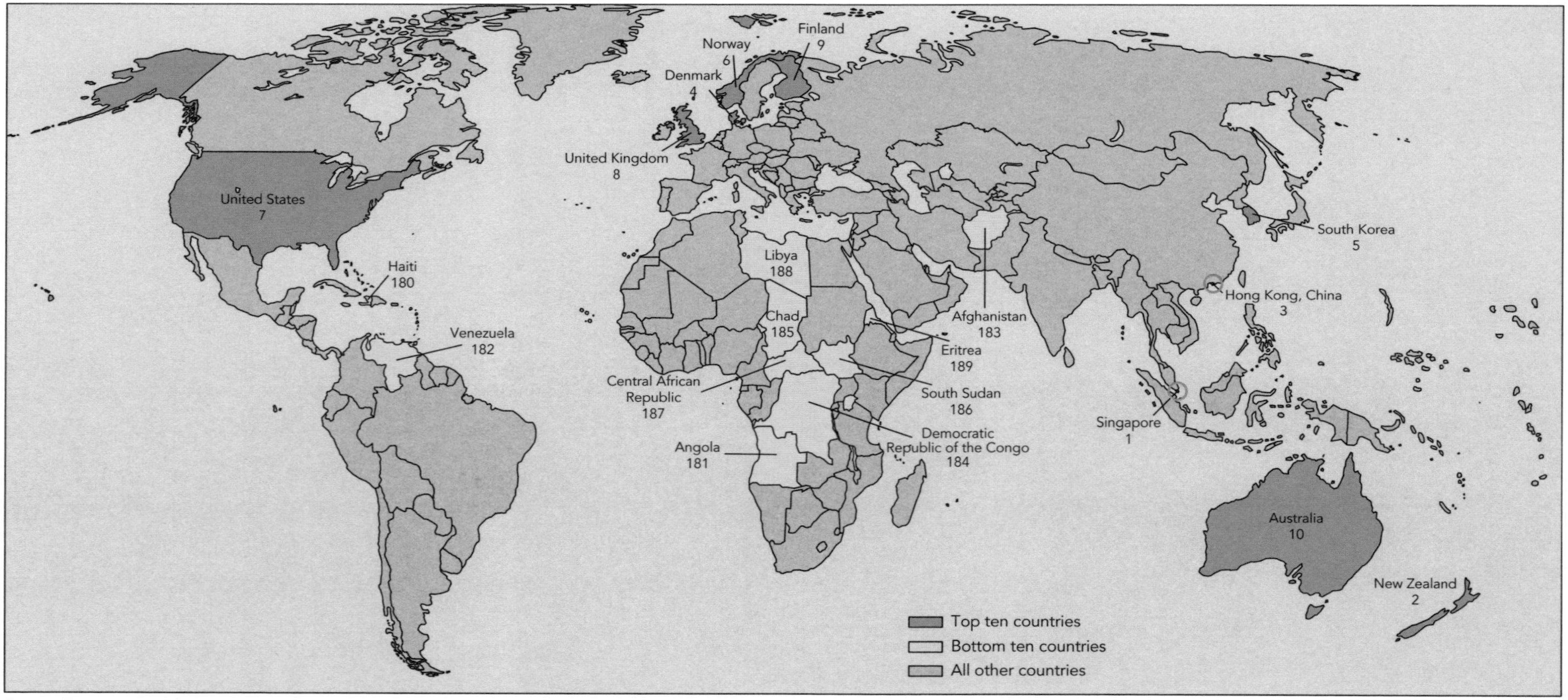

Source: Data extracted from www.doingbusiness.org/rankings. *Doing Business* 2014.

MAP 13 Top Reformers in Doing Business

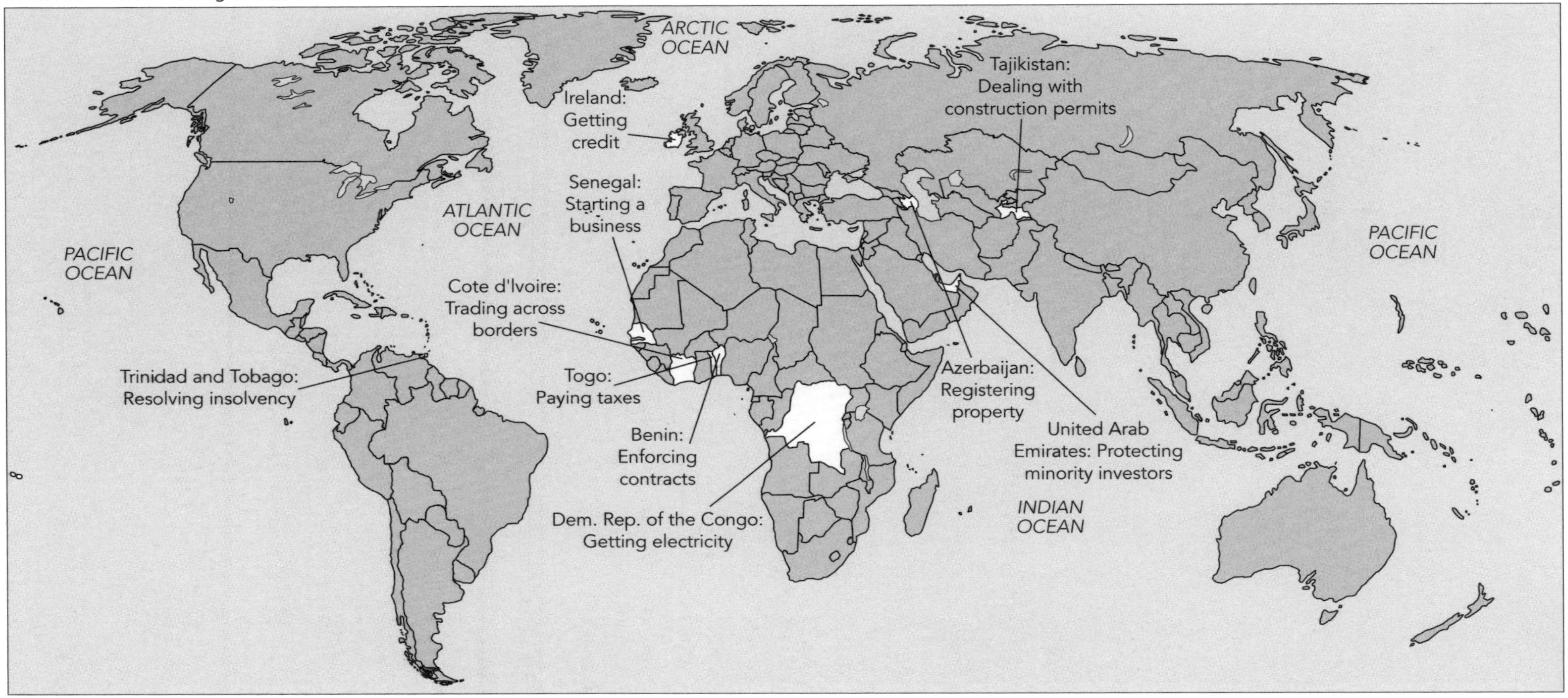

Source: Data extracted from http://www.doingbusiness.org/reforms/top-reformers-2015.

MAP 14 World's Busiest Airports

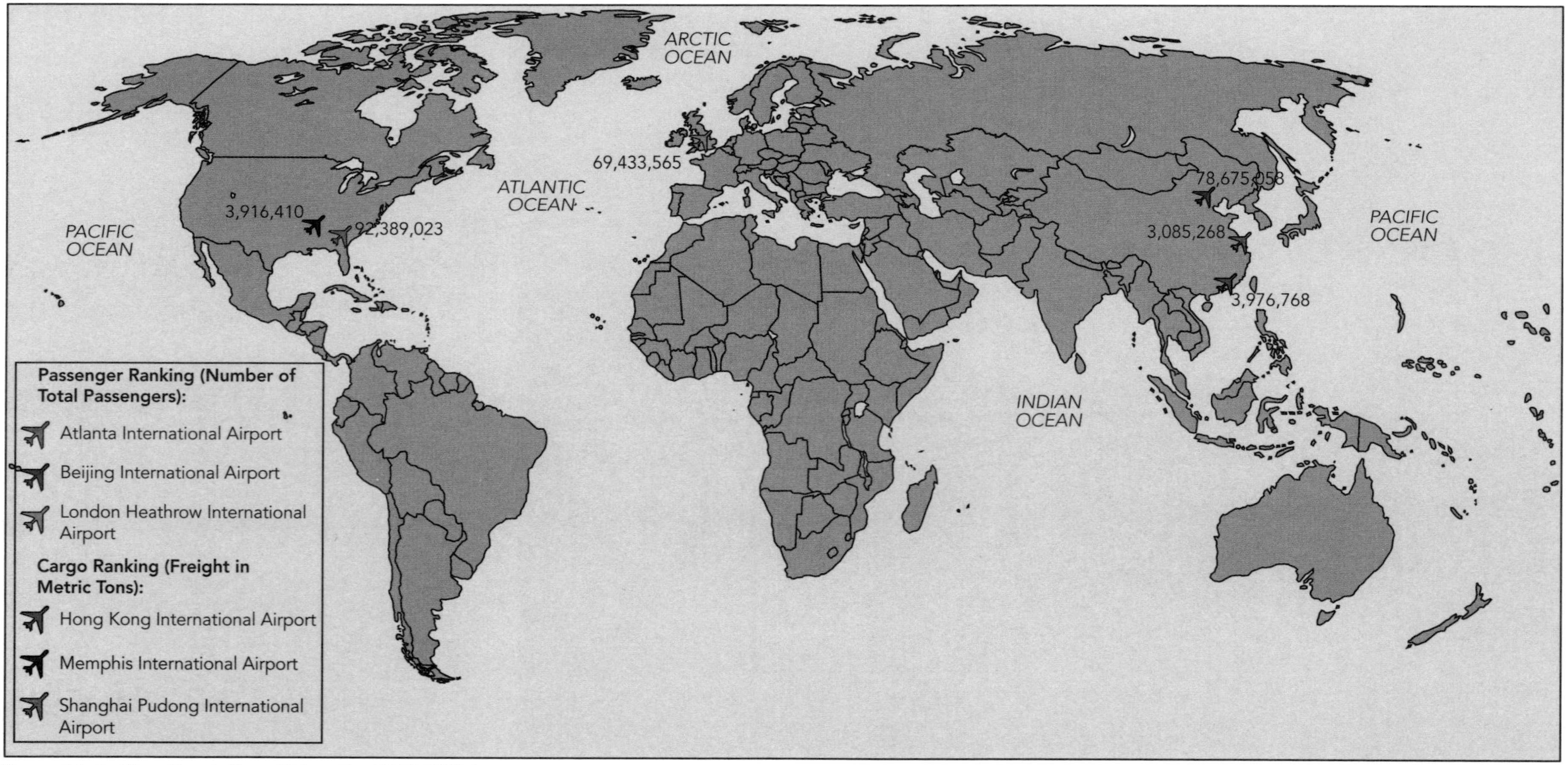

Source: Adapted from Airports Council International (ACI), 2013 data.

MAP 15 Countries with the Largest Labor Forces

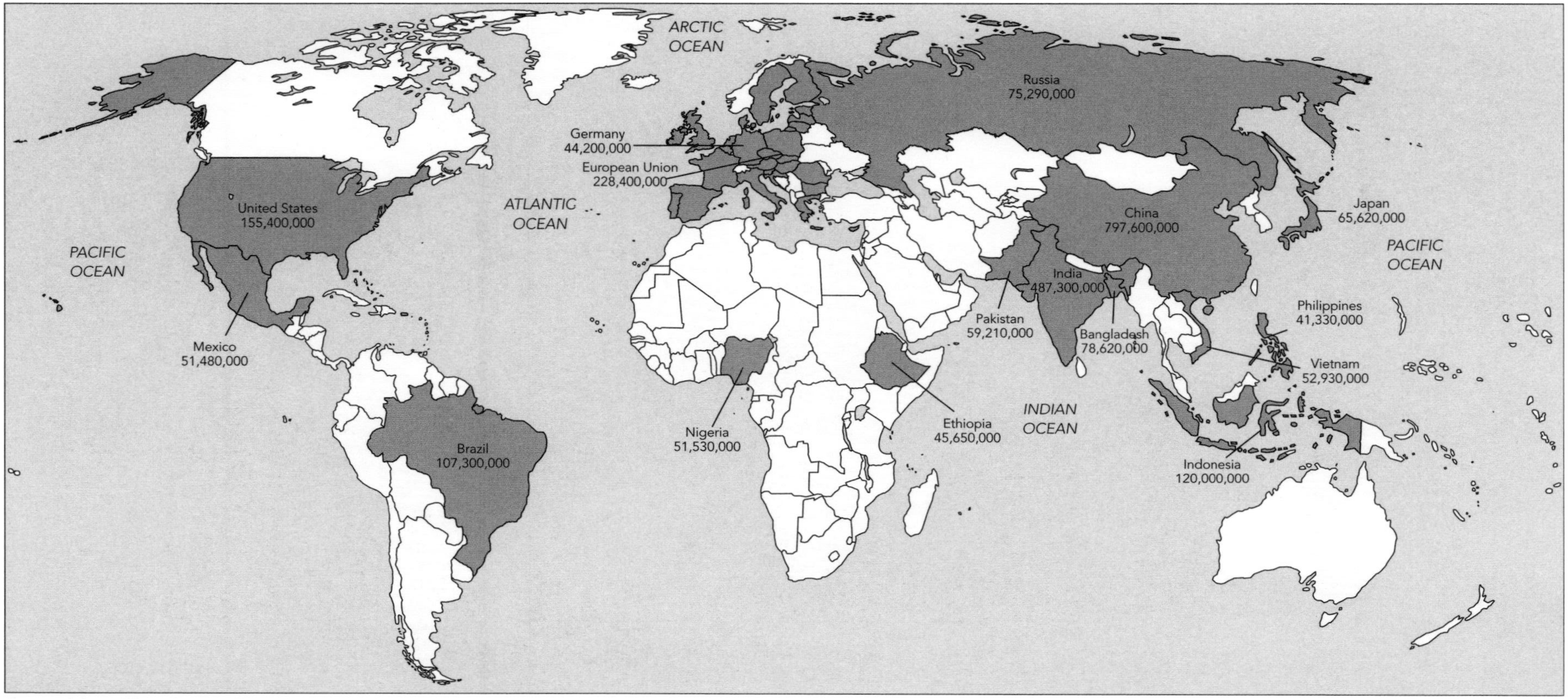

Source: Adapted from Country Comparison: Labor Force, *World Factbook*, 2013.

MAP 16

PengAtlas Map

MAP 16 Unemployment Rates in Select Countries

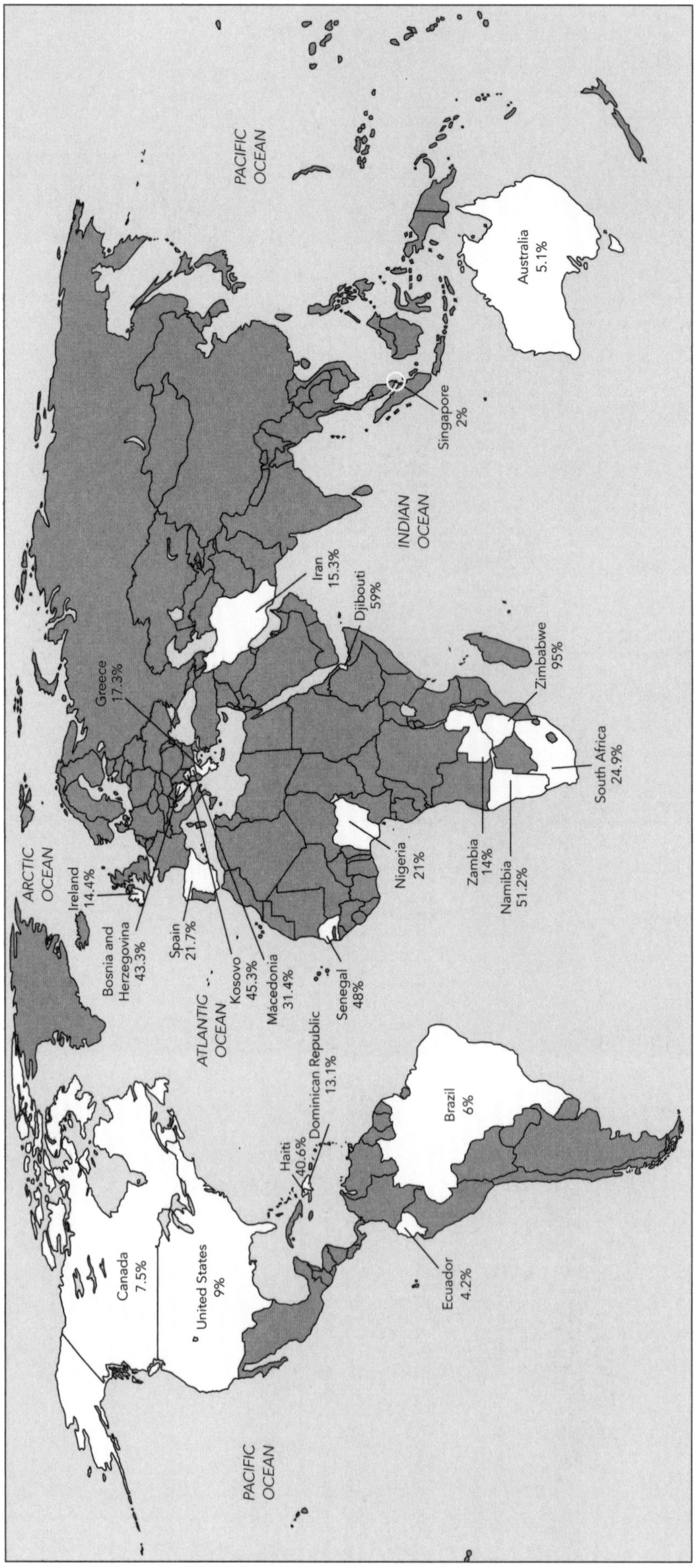

Sources: IndexMundi: http://www.indexmundi.com/g/r.aspx?v=74'; Central Intelligence Agency, 2014, *The World Factbook 2014*, https://www.cia.gov/library/publications/the-world-factbook/

MAP 17 Top CO_2 Emissions in Metric Tons Per Person

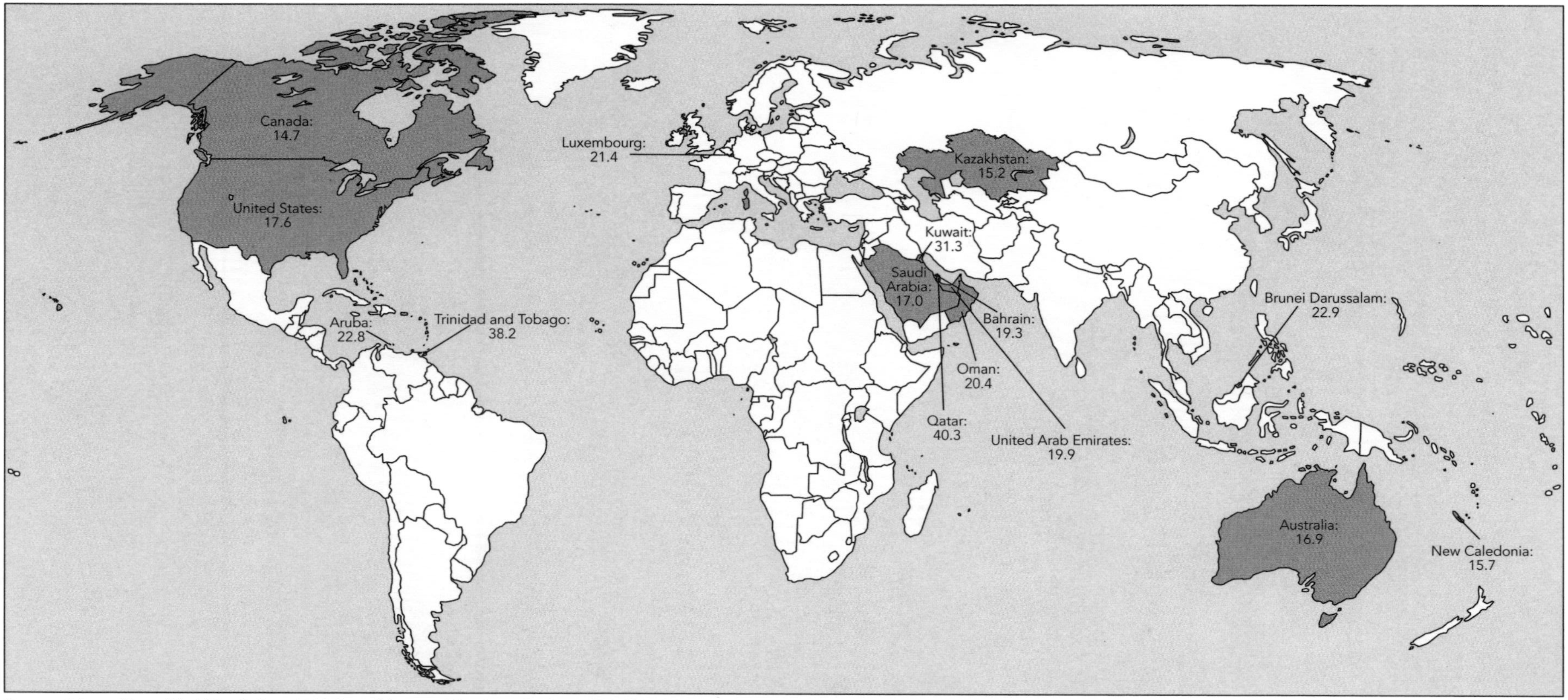

Source: Adapted from World Bank data, 2014, http://data.worldbank.org/indicator/EN.ATM.CO2E.PC?order=wbapi_data_value_2010+wbapi_data_value+wbapi_data_value-first&sort=desc